WORD BIBLICAL COMMENTARY

General Editors
Bruce M. Metzger
David A. Hubbard †
Glenn W. Barker †

Old Testament Editor
John D. W. Watts

New Testament Editor
Ralph P. Martin

Associate Editors
James W. Watts, *Old Testament*
Lynn Allan Losie, *New Testament*

WORD BIBLICAL COMMENTARY

Volume 23B

Song of Songs
DUANE GARRETT

Lamentations
PAUL R. HOUSE

THOMAS NELSON PUBLISHERS
Nashville

*With much love and gratitude,
to the college and young-adult congregation of
St. John's Korean United Methodist Church
of Lexington, Massachusetts*

—D. G.

*To
Molly Elizabeth House
Deuteronomy 32:47*

—P. R. H.

Word Biblical Commentary
Song of Songs, Lamentations
Copyright © 2004 by Thomas Nelson, Inc.

All rights reserved. No portion of this book may be reproduced in any form without the written permission of the publisher.

Library of Congress Cataloging-in-Publication Data
Main entry under title:

Word biblical commentary.

   Includes bibliographies.
   1. Bible—Commentaries—Collected works.
BS491.2.W67   220.7′7   81-71768
ISBN 0-8499-0825-6 (v. 23B) AACR2

Printed in Colombia

By permission of Michael V. Fox, his translation of the Nakhtsobek Songs in *The Song of Songs and the Ancient Egyptian Love Songs* (Madison: Univ. of Wisconsin Press, 1985) is reproduced in the Introduction to Song of Songs. Scripture quotations in the body of the commentary, unless otherwise indicated, are provided by the authors. The authors' own translations of the Scripture texts appear under the head *Translation.*

The Graeca, Hebraica, and TranslitLS fonts used to print this work are available from Linguist's Software, Inc., P.O. Box 580, Edmonds, WA 98020-0580 USA; tel. (206) 775-1130.

1 2 3 4 5 6 7 8 9 10 QWB 08 07 06 05 04

Contents

Editorial Preface	viii
Abbreviations	ix
SONG OF SONGS	1
Author's Preface	3
MAIN BIBLIOGRAPHY	5
Commentary Bibliography	5
General Bibliography	7
INTRODUCTION	13
Song of Songs as Scripture	14
Canonization	14
The Text of Song of Songs	15
Date of Composition	16
Authorship	22
The Structure and Unity of Song of Songs	25
A Plurality of Songs in Song of Songs	26
The Unity of the Song	27
A Redacted Collection by Multiple Poets?	29
A Unified Anthology but without Structure?	30
A Chiastic Structure for Song of Songs	30
The Poetic Devices of the Song	35
Speech-Acts and Motifs	36
Metaphors of Song of Songs	37
Excursus: Hebrew Poetry	40
Comparative Texts: Ancient Near Eastern Love Poetry	47
Mesopotamian Parallels	47
Egyptian Parallels	49
Comparison of One Egyptian Text with Song of Songs	54
Analogies for Song of Songs	57
Interpretations of the Song	59
The Allegorical Interpretations	59
Jewish Allegorizing	60
Early Christian and Roman Catholic Allegorizing	64
Protestant Allegorizing	72
Problems with Allegorizing Interpretations	74
The Dramatic Interpretations	76
The Three-Character Interpretations	77
The Two-Character Interpretations	79
Problems with Dramatic Interpretations	80
The Cultic Interpretations	81
The Wedding Interpretation	83

The Funerary Interpretation	83
Feminist Readings of the Song	84
Song of Songs as Subversive to the Prophets	86
The Song as Love Poetry	90
Excursus: Finding an Approach to Lyric Poetry	91
Song of Songs and Christian Theology	97
Overview of the Problem	97
Lessons about Love and Sexuality	100
The Song as a Rejection of the Ascetic Ideal	100
Romantic Love	102
Sexual Morality	102
Tenderness and the Nurturing of a Relationship	104
Fleeting Joys under the Sun	104
A Sense of Yearning	105
Prospective for a Theology: The Transformation of the Soul	107
A Model for Transformation	107
The Use of *Myth* in Relation to Song of Songs	110
Song of Songs as a Heroic Quest and Transformation	111
Theological Reflection	115
Implications of the Theology of Song of Songs	117

TEXT AND COMMENTARY

Superscript (1:1)	123
I. Chorus and Soprano: The Entrance (1:2–4)	125
II. Soprano: The Virgin's Education I (1:5–6)	131
III. Soprano and Chorus: Finding the Beloved (1:7–8)	135
IV. Tenor, Chorus, and Soprano: The First Song of Mutual Love (1:9–2:7)	140
V. Soprano and Tenor: The Invitation to Depart (2:8–17)	156
Excursus: Virginity in the Ancient World	164
VI. Three Wedding-Night Songs (3:1–4:15)	169
A. Soprano: The Bride's Anxiety (3:1–5)	169
B. Chorus: The Bride Comes to the Groom (3:6–11)	175
C. Tenor: The Flawless Bride I (4:1–15)	184
VII. Soprano, Tenor, and Chorus: The Consummation (4:16–5:1)	200
VIII. Three Wedding-Night Songs (5:2–6:10)	203
A. Soprano, Tenor, and Chorus: Pain and Transformation (5:2–8)	203
B. Chorus and Soprano: The Bride Recovers the Groom (5:9–6:3)	218
C. Tenor and Chorus: The Flawless Bride II (6:4–10)	225
IX. Soprano, Chorus, and Tenor: Leaving Girlhood Behind (6:11–7:1 [6:13])	231
X. Tenor and Soprano: The Second Song of Mutual Love (7:2 [1]–8:4)	235
XI. Chorus and Soprano: Claiming the Beloved (8:5–7)	251
XII. Chorus and Soprano: The Virgin's Education II (8:8–12)	258
XIII. Tenor, Chorus, and Soprano: The Farewell (8:13–14)	264

LAMENTATIONS
Author's Preface   269

MAIN BIBLIOGRAPHY
   Commentary Bibliography   271
   General Bibliography   274

INTRODUCTION   278
Considering Lamentations   278
Text   281
Authorship and Date   283
   Introductions to the Old Testament   284
   Commentaries, Monographs, and Articles   287
   Conclusion   301
Liturgical Uses   303
Place in the Canon   305
Poetic Form and Meter   305
   Acrostic Format   306
   Poetic Meter   308
Lamentations and Ancient Near Eastern Parallels   310
Genre: Lament and Acrostic   314
Theological Purposes in Lamentations   316
   God, the People of God, and Their Suffering   323
   God and Jerusalem/Zion   325
   God and the Nations   326
   God and Prayer   327
   Conclusion   329

TEXT AND COMMENTARY
How She Dwells Alone! (1:1–22)   331
How the Lord Has Clouded the Daughter of Zion! (2:1–22)   367
I Am the Man (3:1–66)   399
How the Gold Has Tarnished! (4:1–22)   431
Remember, O LORD (5:1–22)   453

Indexes

Editorial Preface

The launching of the Word Biblical Commentary brings to fulfillment an enterprise of several years' planning. The publishers and the members of the editorial board met in 1977 to explore the possibility of a new commentary on the books of the Bible that would incorporate several distinctive features. Prospective readers of these volumes are entitled to know what such features were intended to be; whether the aims of the commentary have been fully achieved time alone will tell.

First, we have tried to cast a wide net to include as contributors a number of scholars from around the world who not only share our aims but are in the main engaged in the ministry of teaching in university, college, and seminary. They represent a rich diversity of denominational allegiance. The broad stance of our contributors can rightly be called evangelical, and this term is to be understood in its positive, historic sense of a commitment to Scripture as divine revelation and to the truth and power of the Christian gospel.

Then, the commentaries in our series are all commissioned and written for the purpose of inclusion in the Word Biblical Commentary. Unlike several of our distinguished counterparts in the field of commentary writing, there are no translated works, originally written in a non-English language. Also, our commentators were asked to prepare their own rendering of the original biblical text from the original languages and to use those languages as the basis of their own comments and exegesis. What may be claimed as distinctive with this series is that it is based on the biblical languages, yet it seeks to make the technical and scholarly approach to the theological understanding of Scripture understandable by—and useful to—the fledgling student, the working minister, and colleagues in the guild of professional scholars and teachers as well.

Finally, a word must be said about the format of the series. The layout, in clearly defined sections, has been consciously devised to assist readers at different levels. Those wishing to learn about the textual witnesses on which the translation is offered are invited to consult the section headed *Notes*. If the readers' concern is with the state of modern scholarship on any given portion of Scripture, they should turn to the sections on *Bibliography* and *Form/Structure/Setting*. For a clear exposition of the passage's meaning and its relevance to the ongoing biblical revelation, the *Comment* and concluding *Explanation* are designed expressly to meet that need. There is therefore something for everyone who may pick up and use these volumes.

If these aims come anywhere near realization, the intention of the editors will have been met, and the labor of our team of contributors rewarded.

General Editors: *Bruce M. Metzger*
David A. Hubbard†
Glenn W. Barker†
Old Testament: *John D. W. Watts*
New Testament: *Ralph P. Martin*

Abbreviations

PERIODICALS, SERIALS, AND REFERENCE WORKS

AB	Anchor Bible
ABD	*Anchor Bible Dictionary*. Ed. D. N. Freedman. 6 vols. New York, 1992.
AbrN	*Abr-Nahrain*
AJSL	*American Journal of Semitic Languages and Literature*
AJT	*Asia Journal of Theology*
ALUOS	*Annual of Leeds University Oriental Society*
ANEP	*The Ancient Near East in Pictures Relating to the Old Testament*. Ed. J. B. Pritchard. Princeton, 1969.
ANET	*Ancient Near Eastern Texts Relating to the Old Testament*. Ed. J. B. Pritchard. Princeton, 1969.
AnOr	Analecta orientalia
AOAT	Alter Orient und Altes Testament
ATD	Das Alte Testament Deutsch
AThR	*Anglican Theological Review*
AUSS	*Andrews University Seminary Studies*
BASOR	*Bulletin of the American Schools of Oriental Research*
BDB	Brown, F., S. R. Driver, and C. A. Briggs. *A Hebrew and English Lexicon of the Old Testament*. 1907. Reprint, Peabody, MA, 1999.
BEATAJ	Beiträge zur Erforschung des alten Testaments und des antiken Judentum
BeO	*Bibbia e oriente*
BETL	Bibliotheca ephemeridum theologicarum lovaniensium
BHK	*Biblia Hebraica*. Ed. R. Kittel. Stuttgart, 1905–1906, 1973.[16]
BHS	*Biblia Hebraica Stuttgartensia*. Ed. K. Elliger and W. Rudolph. Stuttgart, 1983.
Bib	*Biblica*
BibInt	*Biblical Interpretation*
BJRL	*Bulletin of the John Rylands University Library of Manchester*
BKAT	Biblischer Kommentar, Altes Testament. Ed. M. Noth and H. W. Wolff.
BRev	*Bible Review*
BSac	*Bibliotheca sacra*
BT	*The Bible Translator*
BTB	*Biblical Theology Bulletin*
BZ	*Biblische Zeitschrift*
BZAW	Beihefte zur Zeitschrift für die alttestamentliche Wissenschaft
CahRB	Cahiers de la Revue biblique
CANE	*Civilizations of the Ancient Near East*. Ed. J. Sasson. New York, 1995.
CBC	Cambridge Bible Commentary
CBQ	*Catholic Biblical Quarterly*
CCSL	Corpus Christianorum: Series latina. Turnhout, 1977–.
CS	*The Context of Scripture*. Ed. W. W. Hallo. Leiden, 1997.
CurTM	*Currents in Theology and Mission*

DAB	Dichter des Alten Bundes
DBI	*Dictionary of Biblical Interpretation.* 2 vols. Ed. J. H. Hayes. Nashville, 1999.
DJD	Discoveries in the Judaean Desert
EncJud	*Encyclopaedia Judaica.* 16 vols. Jerusalem, 1972.
EstBib	*Estudios bíblicos*
EvJ	*Evangelical Journal*
ExpTim	*Expository Times*
FCB	Feminist Companion to the Bible
FOTL	Forms of the Old Testament Literature
GKC	*Gesenius' Hebrew Grammar.* Ed. E. Kautzsch. Trans. E. A. Cowley. 2d ed. London, 1910.
GSAT	Geistliche Schriftlesung Alten Testament
GTJ	*Grace Theological Journal*
HAL	Koehler, L., W. Baumgartner, and J. J. Stamm. *Hebräisches und aramäisches Lexikon zum alten Testament.* Fascicles 1–5, 1967–95 (KBL3). ET: *HALOT.*
HALOT	Koehler, L., W. Baumgartner, and J. J. Stamm. *The Hebrew and Aramaic Lexicon of the Old Testament.* Trans. and ed. under supervision of M. E. J. Richardson. 4 vols. Leiden, 1994–99.
HAR	*Hebrew Annual Review*
HAT	Handbuch zum Alten Testament
HBT	*Horizons in Biblical Theology*
HCOT	Historical Commentary on the Old Testament
HKAT	Handkommentar zum Alten Testament
HTR	*Harvard Theological Review*
HUCA	*Hebrew Union College Annual*
IB	*Interpreter's Bible.* Ed. G. A. Buttrick et al. 12 vols. New York, 1951–1957.
IBC	Interpretation: A Bible Commentary for Teaching and Preaching
IBHS	*An Introduction to Biblical Hebrew Syntax.* B. K. Waltke and M. O'Connor. Winona Lake, IN, 1990.
ICC	International Critical Commentary
Imm	*Immanuel*
Int	*Interpretation*
ISBE	*International Standard Bible Encyclopedia.* Ed. G. W. Bromiley. 4 vols. Grand Rapids, MI, 1979–88.
ITC	International Theological Commentary
JAAR	*Journal of the American Academy of Religion*
JANESCU	*Journal of the Ancient Near Eastern Society of Columbia University*
JAOS	*Journal of the American Oriental Society*
JBL	*Journal of Biblical Literature*
JBQ	*Jewish Bible Quarterly*
JCS	*Journal of Cuneiform Studies*
JEA	*Journal of Egyptian Archaeology*
JETS	*Journal of the Evangelical Theological Society*
JJS	*Journal of Jewish Studies*
JNSL	*Journal of Northwest Semitic Languages*
JOTT	*Journal of Translation and Textlinguistics*
Joüon	Joüon, P. *A Grammar of Biblical Hebrew.* Trans. and rev. T. Muraoka. 2 vols. Subsidia biblica 14.1–2. Rome, 1991.

JQR	*Jewish Quarterly Review*
JR	*Journal of Religion*
JSJ	*Journal for the Study of Judaism in the Persian, Hellenistic and Roman Periods*
JSOT	*Journal for the Study of the Old Testament*
JSOTSup	Journal for the Study of the Old Testament: Supplement Series
JSS	*Journal of Semitic Studies*
JTS	*Journal of Theological Studies*
KAT	Kommentar zu Alten Testament
KHC	Kurzer Hand-Commentar zum Alten Testament
LQ	*Lutheran Quarterly*
LSJ	Liddell, H. G., R. Scott, and H. S. Jones. *A Greek-English Lexicon*. 9th ed. with rev. supplement. Oxford, 1996.
LW	*Luther's Works*. Ed. J. Pelikan. St. Louis, 1972.
NAC	New American Commentary
NCB	New Century Bible
NEchtBib	Neue Echter Bibel
NIB	*The New Interpreter's Bible*
NICOT	New International Commentary on the Old Testament
NIDOTTE	*New International Dictionary of Old Testament Theology and Exegesis*. Ed. W. A. VanGemeren. 5 vols. Grand Rapids, MI, 1997.
NPNF[1]	*Nicene and Post-Nicene Fathers,* Series 1
NPNF[2]	*Nicene and Post-Nicene Fathers,* Series 2
NV	*Nova et vetera*
OBO	Orbis biblicus et orientalis
OCD	*The Oxford Classical Dictionary*. Ed. S. Hornblower and A. Spawforth. 3d ed. Oxford, 1996.
OTE	*Old Testament Essays*
OTL	Old Testament Library
Parab	*Parabola*
Per	*Perspectives*
Proof	*Prooftexts: A Journal of Jewish Literary History*
PTR	*Princeton Theological Review*
RA	*Revue d'assyriologie et d'archéologie orientale*
RB	*Revue biblique*
RHR	*Revue de l'histoire des religions*
RTR	*Reformed Theological Review*
SBL	Society of Biblical Literature
SLBDS	SBL Dissertation Series
SBLMS	SBL Monograph Series
SBLSymS	SBL Symposium Series
SBS	Stuttgarter Bibelstudien
SBT	Studies in Biblical Theology
Scr	*Scripture*
SJOT	*Scandinavian Journal of the Old Testament*
SK	*Skrif en kerk*
Sound	*Soundings*
SR	*Studies in Religion*
SSN	Studia Semitica Neerlandica

SwJT	*Southwestern Journal of Theology*
TBC	Torch Bible Commentaries
TLOT	*Theological Lexicon of the Old Testament.* Ed. E. Jenni, with C. Westermann. Trans. M. E. Biddle. 3 vols. Peabody, MA, 1997.
TLZ	*Theologische Literaturzeitung*
TOTC	Tyndale Old Testament Commentaries
TRev	*Theologische Revue*
TTKi	*Tidsskrift for Teologi og Kirke*
TynBul	*Tyndale Bulletin*
UF	*Ugarit-Forschungen*
UT	*Ugaritic Textbook.* C. H. Gordon. AnOr 38. Rome, 1965.
VT	*Vetus Testamentum*
VTSup	Supplements to Vetus Testamentum
WBC	Word Biblical Commentary
ZAW	*Zeitschrift für die alttestamentliche Wissenschaft*

Texts, Versions, and Ancient Works

Aram.	Aramaic	NIV	New International Version
DSS	Dead Sea Scrolls		
Eng.	English	NJB	New Jerusalem Bible
ESV	English Standard Version	NRSV	New Revised Standard Version
Gk.	Greek		
Heb.	Hebrew	OL	Old Latin
K	Kethib	Q	Qere
KJV	King James Version	REB	Revised English Bible
LXX	Septuagint	RSV	Revised Standard Version
MT	Masoretic Text	Syr.	Syriac
NASB	New American Standard Bible	Tg.	Targum/Targumim
		Vg.	Vulgate
NEB	New English Bible	α´	Aquila
		σ´	Symmachus

Hebrew Grammar

abs.	absolute	impv.	imperative
acc.	accusative	indic.	indicative
act.	active	inf.	infinite
adj.	adjective, adjectival	int.	interrogative
adv.	adverb, adverbial	juss.	jussive
c.	common	masc., m.	masculine
conj.	conjunction, conjunctive	pass.	passive
	consec. consecutive	pf.	perfect
const.	construct	pl.	plural
def. art.	definite article	prep.	preposition
fem., f.	feminine	ptc.	participle
fut.	future	sg.	singular
impf.	imperfect	suf.	suffix(es)

BIBLICAL AND APOCRYPHAL BOOKS

OLD TESTAMENT

Gen	Genesis	Song	Song of Songs, Canticles
Exod	Exodus	Isa	Isaiah
Lev	Leviticus	Jer	Jeremiah
Num	Numbers	Lam	Lamentations
Deut	Deuteronomy	Ezek	Ezekiel
Josh	Joshua	Dan	Daniel
Judg	Judges	Hos	Hosea
Ruth	Ruth	Joel	Joel
1–2 Sam	1–2 Samuel	Amos	Amos
1–2 Kgs	1–2 Kings	Obad	Obadiah
1–2 Chr	1–2 Chronicles	Jonah	Jonah
Ezra	Ezra	Mic	Micah
Neh	Nehemiah	Nah	Nahum
Esth	Esther	Hab	Habakkuk
Job	Job	Zeph	Zephaniah
Ps(s)	Psalm(s)	Hag	Haggai
Prov	Proverbs	Zech	Zechariah
Eccl	Ecclesiastes	Mal	Malachi

APOCRYPHA

1–4 Kgdms	1–4 Kingdoms	Bar	Baruch
1–2 Esdr	1–2 Esdras	Ep Jer	Epistle of Jeremiah
Tob	Tobit	S Th Ch	Song of the Three Children (or Young Men)
Jdt	Judith		
Add Esth	Additions to Esther	Sus	Susanna
4 Ezra	4 Ezra	Bel	Bel and the Dragon
Wis	Wisdom of Solomon	Pr Azar	Prayer of Azariah
Sir	Ecclesiasticus (Wisdom of Jesus the son of Sirach)	1–4 Macc	1–4 Maccabees

NEW TESTAMENT

Matt	Matthew	1–2 Thess	1–2 Thessalonians
Mark	Mark	1–2 Tim	1–2 Timothy
Luke	Luke	Titus	Titus
John	John	Philem	Philemon
Acts	Acts	Heb	Hebrews
Rom	Romans	Jas	James
1–2 Cor	1–2 Corinthians	1–2 Pet	1–2 Peter
Gal	Galatians	1–2–3 John	1–2–3 John
Eph	Ephesians	Jude	Jude
Phil	Philippians	Rev	Revelation
Col	Colossians		

MISCELLANEOUS

B.C.E.	Before the Common Era	n.	note
BM	British Museum	n.d.	no date
ca.	circa	n.s.	new series
C.E.	Common Era	NT	New Testament
chap(s).	chapter(s)	OT	Old Testament
ed(s).	edition; edited by; editor(s)	p(p).	page(s)
esp.	especially	Sup	Supplement
ET	English translation	trans.	translated by; translator
FS	*Festschrift*	Univ.	University
l(l).	line(s)	UP	University Press
lit.	literally	v(v)	verse(s)
MS(S)	manuscript(s)	§	section/paragraph

Song of Songs

Author's Preface

Writing a commentary on Song of Songs is somewhat embarrassing on two counts. First, there are already such great and erudite commentaries on the Song! One is hesitant to submit another interpretation when we already have the works of Marvin Pope, Othmar Keel, Michael Fox, and, above all, Roland Murphy. I trust that the reader will understand that when I criticize a position taken by one of these scholars, it is never meant as a disparagement. To the contrary, I speak as one who regards them with the highest respect and who deeply admires their learning and judgment.

And then there is that other embarrassing issue: the Song of Songs is so thoroughly sexual! Never, when I chose to go into biblical studies, did I imagine that I would spend so many hours digging through erotic texts from the ancient Near East, to say nothing of all the time spent trying to understand the sexual imagery of the Bible itself. I sometimes seem to detect in commentaries and articles on the Song two attitudes that I find unhelpful. One attitude is to minimize and obfuscate the sensuality of the Song wherever possible. The other attitude is to revel in the sexuality of the Song and always to seek the most erotic explanation possible. Now to be sure, there is an enormous amount of sexuality in the Song of Songs. But I hope the reader will understand that my task in this has been to interpret the text as honestly as I knew how, with all sobriety and only a touch of well-intended humor. Having just taught a series on the Song to a group of young-adult women and men, and doing it with all the unflinching directness I could muster, I can attest that no harm was done. On the other hand, I have been doing a number of weddings for members of that group lately.

I certainly owe a lot of people my thanks. First of all, I would like to express my sincere thanks to John Watts for inviting me to write on Song of Songs for the Word Biblical Commentary series; I especially extend gratitude to him for his patience. Many thanks to Jim Watts for his careful review of the manuscript. I would also like to thank Melanie McQuere, copyeditor for the WBC, for her help in the production of this commentary. I am very grateful to the trustees and administration of Gordon-Conwell Theological Seminary for their granting of a sabbatical to me in order that I might complete this project. I also would like to thank my former student assistant, Mr. Wei-Hua Hu, for his help in research. Above everything else, especial thanks go to my family and especially to my wife, Patty, for their patience with a father and husband who spent too many hours plowing through research on the Song of Songs and Hebrew poetry. To Patty in particular I say, "Behold, you are fair, my companion; your eyes are doves."

I have written much of this commentary from my home in Ipswich, Massachusetts. Students of poetry will know that this was the home of one of the first and greatest of American poets, Anne Bradstreet. The original Ipswich, in the United Kingdom, is associated with the great Geoffrey Chaucer. He owned property there and visited it frequently. A central topic for both Christian poets was the love of man and woman, and both poets are cited in this commentary. I can only hope that this coincidence of my residence is matched by my having some small ability to interpret the poetry of love, for it is certain that I do not have their poetic genius.

יהיו לרצון אמרי־פי
והגיון לבי לפניך
יהוה צורי וגאלי

DUANE A. GARRETT

Gordon-Conwell Theological Seminary
May 2002

Commentary Bibliography

In the text of the commentary, references to commentaries on Song of Songs are by author's name only.

Abraham ben Isaac ha-Levi Tamakh. *Commentary on the Song of Songs.* Introduction, variants and comments by L. Feldman. SSN 9. Assen: Van Gorcum, 1970. **Adeney, W. F.** *The Song of Songs and the Lamentations of Jeremiah.* In *The Expositor's Bible,* ed. W. R. Nicoll. London: Hodder and Stoughton, 1895. **Alshich, M.** *Shir Hashirim: Love Song of a Nation.* Trans. R. Shahar. Jerusalem: Feldheim, 1993. **Bergant, D.** *The Song of Songs.* Collegeville, MN: Liturgical, 2001. **Bloch, A. A.,** and **C. Bloch.** *The Song of Songs.* New York: Random House, 1995. **Bunn, J. T.** "Song of Solomon." In *The Broadman Bible Commentary.* Nashville: Broadman, 1971. 5:128–48. **Burrowes, G.** *The Song of Solomon.* 1860. Reprint, London: Banner of Truth Trust, 1958. **Carr, G. L.** *The Song of Solomon: An Introduction and Commentary.* Downers Grove: InterVarsity Press, 1984. **Delitzsch, F.** *Commentary on the Song of Songs and Ecclesiastes.* Trans. M. G. Easton. Edinburgh: T&T Clark, 1877. **Dommershausen, W.,** and **G. Krinetski.** *Ester. Hoheslied.* NEchtBib 2. Würzburg: Echter, 1985. **Durham, J.** *An Exposition of the Song of Solomon.* 1840. Reprint, Carlisle, PA: Banner of Truth Trust, 1982. **Ezra ben Solomon of Gerona.** *Commentary on the Song of Songs.* Selected, edited, and translated by S. Brody. Kalamazoo, MI: Medieval Institute Publications, 1999. **Fuerst, W. J.** *The Books of Ruth, Esther, Ecclesiastes, The Song of Songs, Lamentations: The Five Scrolls.* Cambridge: Cambridge UP, 1975. **Garrett, D. A.** *Proverbs, Ecclesiastes, Song of Songs.* NAC. Nashville: Broadman, 1993. **Gerleman, G.** *Ruth, Das Hohelied.* Neukirchen-Vluyn: Neukirchener, 1965. **Giles of Rome.** *Commentary on the Song of Songs and Other Writings.* Ed. J. Rotelle. Villanova, PA: Augustinian Press, 1998. **Gill, J.** *An Exposition of the Song of Solomon.* 1724. Reprint, Marshallton, DE: National Foundation for Christian Education, 1969. **Ginsburg, C. D.** *The Song of Songs.* 1857. Reprint, New York: Ktav, 1970. **Gordis, R.** *The Song of Songs and Lamentations: A Study, Modern Translation, and Commentary.* New York: Jewish Theological Seminary of America, 1954. **Guillaume de Saint-Thierry.** *Exposé sur le Cantique des Cantiques.* Trans. M. Dumontier. Paris: Cerf: 1998. **Guyon, Madame** (Jeanne Marie Vouvier de la Mothe Guyon). *Song of Songs.* Reprint, Augusta, ME: Christian Books, n.d. **Hontheim, J.** *Da Hohelied: Übersetzt und erklärt.* Biblische Studien. Freiburg 13.4. Freiburg: Herder, 1908. **Joüon, P.** *Le Cantique des cantiques: Commentaire philologique et exégétique.* 2d ed. Paris: Beauchesne, 1909. **Keel, O.** *Das Hohelied.* Zurcher Bibelkommentare AT 18. Zürich: Theologie Verlag, 1986. ———. *The Song of Songs.* Trans. F. J. Gaiser. Minneapolis: Fortress, 1994. **Knight, G. A. F.** *Esther, Song of Songs, Lamentations.* London: SCM Press, 1955. **Levi ben Gershom (Gersonides).** *Commentary on the Song of Songs.* Trans. Menachem Kellner. New Haven: Yale UP, 1998. **Littledale, R. F.** *A Commentary on the Song of Songs: From Ancient and Mediaeval Sources.* London: Masters, 1869. **Longman, T. III.** *Song of Songs.* NICOT. Grand Rapids: Eerdmans, 2001. **Murphy, R. E.** *The Song of Songs: A Commentary on the Book of Canticles or the Song of Songs.* Minneapolis: Fortress, 1990. **Neighbor, R. E.** *The Song of Songs Which Is Solomon's.* Cleveland: Union Gospel Press, 1927. **Origen.** *The Song of Songs: Commentary and Homilies.* Trans. R. P. Lawson. Westminster, MD: Newman, 1957. **Pope, M.** *Song of Songs: A New Translation with Introduction and Commentary.* AB 7C. Garden City, NY: Doubleday, 1977. **Provan, I.** *The NIV Application Commentary: Ecclesiastes, Song of Songs.* Grand Rapids: Zondervan, 2001. **Renan, E.** *The Song of Songs.* Trans. W. M. Thomson. London: Thomson, 1860. **Robert, A.,** and **R. Tournay,** with **A. Feuillet.** *Le Cantique des cantiques: Traduction et commentaire.* Paris: Librairie Lecoffre, 1963. **Rudolph, W.** *Das Buch Ruth, das Hohe Lied, die Klagelieder.*

KAT 17.1–3. Gütersloh: Mohn, 1962. **Stadelmann, L. I. J.** *Love and Politics: A New Commentary on the Song of Songs.* New York: Paulist Press, 1992. **Waterman, L.** *The Song of Songs.* Ann Arbor: Univ. of Michigan Press, 1948. **Weems, R. J.** "The Song of Songs." In *NIB.* Nashville: Abingdon, 1997. 5:363–434. **Zlotowitz, M.** *Shir haShirim.* New York: Messorah, 1977.

General Bibliography

Albrektson, B. "Singing or Pruning?" *BT* 47 (1996) 109–14. **Alden, R. L.** "רדיד." *NIDOTTE* §8100. **Alexander, P. S.** "Tradition and Originality in the Targum of the Song of Songs." In *The Aramaic Bible*. Ed. D. Beattie and M. McNamara. Sheffield: Sheffield Academic Press, 1994. 318–39. **Alexeev, A. A.** "The Song of Songs in the Slavonic Bible Tradition." *BT* 47 (1996) 119–25. **Alter, R.** "The Poetic and Wisdom Books." In *The Cambridge Companion to Biblical Interpretation*. Ed. J. Barton. Cambridge: Cambridge UP, 1998. ———. *The Art of Biblical Poetry*. New York: Basic Books, 1985. **Anderson, A. A.** *2 Samuel*. WBC 11. Dallas: Word, 1989. **Anderson, R. D.** "Music and Dance in Pharaonic Egypt." In *CANE* 4:2555–68. **Archer, G.** *A Survey of Old Testament Introduction*. Chicago: Moody, 1974. **Auder, J.-P.** "Love and Marriage in the Old Testament." Trans. F. Burke. *Scr* 10 (1958) 65–83. **Baars, W.** "Peshitta Text of Song of Songs in Barhebraeus' Ausar Raze." *VT* 18 (1968) 281–89. **Bakon, S.** "Song of Songs." *JBQ* 22 (1994) 211–20. **Bar Ilan, M.** "Text Criticism, Erotica and Magic in the Song of Songs." *Shnaton* 9 (1985) 31–53; xvi–xvii. **Barker, A. D.** "Music." *OCD*. 1003–12. **Barr, J. J.** "Luis de León and the Song of Songs." In *Language, Theology, and the Bible*. Ed. S. Balentine and J. Barton. Oxford: Clarendon, 1994. 311–24. **Bascom, R. A.** "Hebrew Poetry and the Text of the Song of Songs." In *Discourse Perspectives on Hebrew Poetry in the Scriptures*. Ed. E. Wendland. New York: United Bible Societies, 1994. 95–110. **Beare, F. W.** *The Gospel according to Matthew*. San Francisco: Harper and Row, 1981. **Bekkenkamp, J.** "Into Another Scene of Choices: The Theological Value of the Song of Songs." In *The Song of Songs: A Feminist Companion to the Bible*. FCB 2d ser. 6. Ed. A. Brenner and C. R. Fontaine. Sheffield: Sheffield Academic Press, 2000. 55–89. **Bekkenkamp, J., and F. van Dijk.** "The Canon of the Old Testament and Women's Cultural Traditions." In *A Feminist Companion to the Song of Songs*. FCB 1. Ed. A. Brenner. Sheffield: Sheffield Academic Press, 1993. 67–85. **Bergant, D.** "'My Beloved Is Mine and I Am His' (Song 2:16): The Song of Songs and Honor and Shame." *Semeia* 68 (1994) 23–40. **Bernard of Clairvaux.** *Saint Bernard on the Song of Songs; Sermones in Cantica canticorum*. Trans. and ed. a religious of C.S.M.V. London: Mowbray, 1952. **Black, F. C.** "What Is My Beloved? On Erotic Reading and the Song of Songs." In *The Labour of Reading: Desire, Alienation, and Biblical Interpretation*. Ed. F. C. Black, R. Boer, and E. Runions. Atlanta: Society of Biblical Literature, 1999. **Black, F. C., and J. C. Exum.** "Semiotics in Stained Glass: Edward Burne-Jones's Song of Songs." In *Biblical Studies/Cultural Studies: The Third Colloquium*. Ed. J. Exum and S. D. Moore. Sheffield: Sheffield Academic Press, 1998. 315–42. **Bloch, A. A., and C. Bloch.** "From *In the Garden of Delights*." *Judaism* 44 (1995) 36–63. **Bloom, H.,** ed. *The Song of Songs*. New York: Chelsea House, 1988. **Boyarin, D.** "The Song of Songs: Lock or Key? Intertextuality, Allegory and Midrash." In *The Book and the Text*. Ed. R. Schwartz. Oxford: Blackwell, 1990. 214–30. **Brenner, A.** "'My' Song of Songs." In *The Song of Songs*. FCB 2d ser. 6. Ed. C. R. Fontaine and A. Brenner. Sheffield: Sheffield Academic Press, 2000. 154–68. ———. "A Note on *bat-rabbîm* (Song of Songs VII 5)." *VT* 42 (1992) 113–15. ———. "On Reading the Hebrew Bible as a Feminist Woman: Introduction to the Series." In *A Feminist Companion to the Song of Songs*. FCB 1. Ed. A. Brenner. Sheffield: Sheffield Academic Press, 1993. 11–27. ———. *The Song of Songs*. Sheffield: JSOT Press, 1989. ———, ed. *Feminist Companion to the Song of Songs*. FCB 1. Sheffield: Sheffield Academic Press, 1993. **Bright, J.** *Jeremiah*. AB 21. Garden City, NY: Doubleday, 1965. **Broadribb, D.** "Thoughts on the Song of Solomon." *AbrN* 3 (1961–62) 11–36. **Brock, S. P.** "Mingana Syr 628: A Folio from a Revision of the Peshitta Song of Songs." *JSS* 40 (1995) 39–56. **Brooke, G.** "חבר." *NIDOTTE* §2489. **Budde, K.** "Das hebraische Klagelied."

ZAW 2 (1882) 1–52. **Buss, M. J.** "Hosea as a Canonical Problem: With Attention to the Song of Songs." In: *Prophets and Paradigms.* FS G. M. Tucker, ed. S. B. Reid. Sheffield: Sheffield Academic Press, 1996. 79–93. **Cainion, I. J.** "An Analogy of the Song of Songs and Genesis Chapters Two and Three." *SJOT* 14 (2000) 219–59. **Campbell, J.** *The Hero with a Thousand Faces.* 2d ed. Princeton, NJ: Princeton UP, 1968. **Carr, D. M.** "Rethinking Sex and Spirituality: The Song of Songs and Its Readings." *Sound* 81 (1998) 413–35. **Carr, G. L.** "Is the Song of Songs a 'Sacred Marriage' Drama?" *JETS* 22 (1979) 103–14. ———. "The Love Poetry Genre in the Old Testament and the Ancient Near East: Another Look at Inspiration." *JETS* 25 (1982) 489–98. ———. "The Old Testament Love Songs and Their Use in the New Testament." *JETS* 24 (1981) 97–105. **Childs, B.** *Introduction to the Old Testament as Scripture.* Philadelphia: Fortress, 1979. **Christensen, D. L.** "The Masoretic Accentual System and Repeated Metrical Refrains in Nahum, Song of Songs, and Deuteronomy." In *VIII International Congress of the International Organization for Masoretic Studies.* Ed. E. J. Revell. Atlanta: Scholars Press, 1990. 31–36. **Collins, A. Y.** "The Song of Songs in Comparative Perspective." In *Hebrew Bible or Old Testament? Studying the Bible in Judaism and Christianity.* Ed. R. Brook, and J. J. Collins. Notre Dame, IN: Univ. of Notre Dame Press, 1990. 217–19. **Corney, R. W.** "What Does 'Literal Meaning' Mean? Some Commentaries on the Song of Songs." *AThR* 80 (1998) 494–516. **Cotton, J.** *A Brief Exposition with Practical Observations upon the Whole Book of Canticles.* 1655. Reprint, New York: Arno, 1972. **Craigie, P. C.** "Biblical and Tamil Poetry: Some Further Reflections." *SR* 8 (1979) 169–75. ———. *The Book of Deuteronomy.* NICOT. Grand Rapids: Eerdmans, 1976. ———. *Psalms 1–50.* WBC 19. Dallas: Word, 1983. **Crim, K. R.** " Your Neck Is Like the Tower of David (The Meaning of a Simile in the Song of Solomon 4:4)." *BT* 22 (1971) 70–74. **Cross, F. M., Jr.**, and **D. N. Freedman.** *Studies in Ancient Yahwistic Poetry.* 1950. Reprint, Missoula, MT: Scholars Press, 1975. **Davies, W. B.**, and **D. C. Allison.** *The Gospel according to Saint Matthew.* ICC. Edinburgh: T&T Clark, 1997. **Dahood, M.** *Ugaritic-Hebrew Philology: Marginal Notes on Recent Publications.* Rome: Pontifical Biblical Institute, 1965. **Dale, A. M.,** ed. *Euripedes: Alcestis.* Oxford: Oxford UP, 1954. **Davis, V. L.** "Remarks on Michael V. Fox's 'The Cairo Love Songs.'" *JAOS* 100 (1980) 111–14. **Dijk-Hemmes, F. van.** "The Imagination of Power and the Power of Imagination: An Intertextual Analysis of Two Biblical Love Songs." *JSOT* 44 (1989) 75–88. **Dodds, E. R.** *Bacchae: Edited with Introduction and Commentary.* 2d ed. London: Oxford UP, 1960. **Dorsey, D. A.** "Can These Bones Live? Investigating Literary Structure in the Bible." *EvJ* 9 (1991) 11–25. **Driver, G. R.** "Supposed Arabisms in the Old Testament." *JBL* 55 (1936) 101–20. **Driver, S. R.** *Notes on the Hebrew Text and Topography of the Books of Samuel.* 2d ed. London: Oxford UP, 1913. **Dryburgh, B.** *Lessons for Lovers in the Song of Songs.* New Canaan, CT: Keats, 1975. **Edmée, Sister.** "The Song of Songs and the Cutting of Roots." *AThR* 80 (1998) 547–61. **Elegre Heitzmann, A.** "El Cantar de los Cantares: Poesia y Ritual de la Pascua." *EstBib* 43 (1985) 321–30. **Elliot, M. T.** *The Literary Unity of the Canticle.* Frankfurt am Main: Lang, 1989. **Emerton, J. A.** "Lice or a Veil in the Song of Songs 1:7?" In *Understanding Poets and Prophets.* FS G. W. Anderson, ed. A. Auld. Sheffield: JSOT Press, 1993. 127–40. ———. "Printed Editions of the Song of Songs in the Peshitta Version." *VT* 17 (1967) 417–29. **Epstein, I.** *Hebrew-English Edition of the Babylonian Talmud: Seder Nashim.* Trans. B. D. Klein. London: Soncino, 1985. **Exum, J. C.** "In the Eye of the Beholder: Wishing, Dreaming, and Double Entendre in the Song of Songs." In *The Labour of Reading: Desire, Alienation, and Biblical Interpretation.* Ed. F. C. Black, R. Boer, and E. Runions. Atlanta: Society of Biblical Literature, 1999. 71–86. ———. "A Literary and Structural Analysis of the Song of Songs." *ZAW* 85 (1973) 47–79. ———, ed. "Abuse, Desire and the Body: Ezekiel and the Song of Songs." *BibInt* 8 (2000) 205–323. **Falk, M.** *The Song of Songs: A New Translation.* San Francisco: Harper San Francisco, 1993. **Fange, E. A. von.** "Budde Hypothesis." *ABD* 1:783–84. ———. "A Poetic Study of the Song of Songs." *Concordia Historical Institute Quarterly* 66 (1993) 137–43. **Feuillet, A.** "La drame d'amour du Cantique des Cantiques remis en son contexte prophetique: 2e partie." *NV* 63 (1988) 81–136. **Fields, W. W.** "Early and Medieval Jewish Interpretation of the Song of Songs." *GTJ* 2 (1980) 221–31. **Flavel, J.** *The Works of John Flavel.* Edinburgh: The Banner of Truth Trust, 1982. **Fohrer, G.** *Introduction to the Old Testament.* Initiated by E. Sellin. Trans. D. E. Green. Nashville: Abingdon, 1968. **Fox, M. V.** "'Love' in the Love Songs." *JEA* 67 (1981) 181–82. ———. "Scholia to Canticles (I 4b, ii 4, i4bA, iv 3, v 8, vi 12)." *VT* 33 (1983) 199–206. ———. *The Song of Songs and the Ancient Egyptian Love Songs.* Madison: Univ. of Wisconsin Press, 1985. **Garrett, D. A.** *Hosea, Joel.* NAC 19A. Nashville: Broadman and Holman, 1997. ———. *A Modern Grammar for Classical Hebrew.* Nashville: Broadman, 2002. **Geraty, L. T.** "Heshbon." *ABD* 3:181–84. **Gibson, J. C. L.** *Textbook of Syrian Semitic Inscriptions.* London: Oxford UP, 1973. **Glazer, H.** "The Song of Songs: Judaism's Document of Revelation." *Conservative Judaism* 43 (1990–91) 55–60. **Gledhill, T.** *The Message of the Song of Songs.* Downers Grove, IL: InterVarsity Press, 1994. **Gollwitzer, H.** *Song of Love: A Biblical Understanding of Sex.* Trans. K. Crim. Philadelphia: Fortress, 1979. **Goodwin, W. W.,** and **C. B. Goolick.** *Greek Grammar.* Waltham, MA: Blaisdell, 1982. **Gordis, R.** "Root *dgl* in the Song of Songs." *JBL* 88 (1969) 203–4. **Goulder, M. D.** *The Song of Fourteen Songs.* Sheffield: JSOT Press, 1986. **Graves, R.** *The Song of Songs.* London: Collins, 1973. **Gundry, R. H.** *Matthew: A Commentary on His Handbook for a Mixed Church under Persecution.* 2d ed. Grand Rapids: Eerdmans, 1994. **Haag, H.** "Da heutige Verständnis des Hohenliedes in der katholischen Exegese." In *Melanges biblique et orientaux en l'honneur de Matthias Delcor.* Ed. A. Caquot. AOAT 215. Kevelaer; Neukirchen-Vluyn: Butzon und Bercker, 1985. 209–20. **Haïk-Vantoura, S.** *Cantique des Cantique* [sound recording]: *de Salomon dans sa melodie d'origine.* Paris: Fondation Roi David, 1986; Alienor, 1992. **Hamilton, V.** "שור." *NIDOTTE* §6424. **Harman, A. M.** "Modern Discussion on the Song of Solomon." *RTR* 37 (1978) 65–72. **Harrison, R. K.** *Introduction to the Old Testament.* Grand Rapids: Eerdmans, 1969. **Häusl, M.,** and U. **Silber.** "'You Are Beautiful My Love': The Song of Songs of Women." In *The Song of Songs.* FCB 2d ser. 6. Ed. C. R. Fontaine and A. Brenner. Sheffield: Sheffield Academic Press, 2000. 187–95. **Hein, R.** *Christian Mythmakers.* Chicago: Cornerstone, 1998. **Hess, R.** "רסס." *NIDOTTE* §8272. **Hill, A. E.** "תָּרְשִׁישׁ." *NIDOTTE* §9577. **Holdsworth, C.** "Two Commentators on the Song of Songs: John of Forde and Alexander Nequam." In *A Gathering of Friends: The Learning and Spirituality of John of Forde.* Ed. H. Costello and C. Holdsworth. Kalamazoo, MI: Cistercian, 1996. 153–74. **Holladay, W. L.** *Jeremiah 2.* Ed. P. D. Hanson. Hermeneia. Minneapolis: Fortress, 1989. **Howard, D. M., Jr.** "Recent Trends in Psalm Studies." In *The Face of Old Testament Studies.* Ed. D. W. Baker and B. T. Arnold. Grand Rapids: Baker, 1999. 329–68. **Hrushovski, B.** "Prosody, Hebrew." In *EncJud* 13:1200–1202. **Jacob, I.,** and **W. Jacob.** "Flora." *ABD* 2:803–17. **Jacobsen, T.** *The Harp That Once . . . : Sumerian Poetry in Translation.* New Haven: Yale UP, 1987. **Jakobson, R.** "Linguistics and Poetics." In *Roman Jakobson: Selected Writings III.* Ed. S. Rudy. The Hague: Mouton, 1981. 18–51. **Jeremias, J.** *The Parables of Jesus.* 2d ed. New York: Charles Scribner's Sons, 1972. **Jerusalmi, I.,** ed. *The Song of Songs in the Targumic Tradition: Vocalized Aramaic Text with Facing English Translation and Laōdino Versions.* Cincinnati: Laōdino, 1993. **Joffe, A., J. P. Dessel,** and **R. Hallote.** "The 'Gilat Woman.'" *Near Eastern Archaeology* 64.1–2 (March-June 2001) 8–23. **Kallas, E.** "Martin Luther as Expositor of the Song of Songs." *LQ* 2 (1988) 323–41. **Kannengiesser, C.** "Divine Love Poetry: The Song of Songs." In *Hebrew Bible or Old Testament? Studying the Bible in Judaism and Christianity.* Ed. R. Brooks and J. J. Collins. Notre Dame, IN: Univ. of Notre Dame Press, 1990. 211–15. **Kellner, M. M.** "Introduction to the Commentary on Song of Songs Composed by the Sage Levi Ben Gershom: An Annotated Translation." In *From Ancient Israel to Modern Judaism.* Vol. 2, *Judaism in the Middle Ages.* FS M. Fox, ed. J. Neusner, E. S. Frerichs, and N. M. Sarna. Atlanta: Scholars Press, 1989. 187–205. **Kerney, P. J.** "Marriage and Spirituality in the Song of Songs." *BT* 25 (1987) 144–49. **Kessler, R.** *Some Poetical and Structural Features of the Song of Songs.* Leeds: Leeds UP, 1957. **King, P.,** and **L. Stager.** *Life in Biblical Israel.*

Louisville: Westminster John Knox, 2001. **Kinlaw, D. F.** "Charles Williams' Concept of Imaging Applied to the Song of Songs." *Wesleyan Theological Journal* 16 (1981) 85–92. **Konkel, A.** "נקדה." *NIDOTTE* §5925. **Kramer, S. N.** *The Sacred Marriage Rite*. Bloomington: Indiana UP, 1969. **Kurtz, D. C.**, and **J. Boardman.** *Greek Burial Customs*. Ithaca: Cornell UP, 1971. **Kutscher, E. Y.** *A History of the Hebrew Language*. Ed. R. Kutscher. Leiden: Brill, 1982. **Landy, F.** "Beauty and the Enigma: An Inquiry into Some Interrelated Episodes of the Song of Songs." *JSOT* 17 (1980) 55–106. ———. *Paradoxes of Paradise: Identity and Difference in the Song of Songs*. Sheffield: Almond, 1983. ———. "The Song of Songs and the Garden of Eden." *JBL* 98 (1979) 513–28. ———. "Towards a Commentary on the Song of Songs." *CBQ* 39 (1977) 482–96. **LaSor, W. S., D. A. Hubbard**, and **F. W. Bush.** *Old Testament Survey*. 1st ed. Grand Rapids: Eerdmans, 1982. **Lehrman, S. M.** "The Song of Songs: Introduction and Commentary." In *The Five Megilloth*. Ed. A. Cohen. Hindhead, Surrey: The Soncino Press, 1946. **Lemaire, A.** "*Zāmīr* dans la Tablette de Gezer et le Cantique des Cantiques." *VT* 25 (1975) 15–26. **Lévi-Strauss, C.** *Structural Anthropology*. Trans. C. Jacobson and B. G. Schoepf. New York: Basic, 1963. **Lewis, C. S.** *An Experiment in Criticism*. Cambridge: Cambridge UP, 1961. ———. *The Pilgrim's Regress*. London: Bles, 1933. ———. *Studies in Words*. 2d ed. Cambridge: Cambridge UP, 1967. ———. *The Weight of Glory and Other Addresses*. New York: Macmillan, 1949. **Loder, J.** *The Transforming Moment*. 2d ed. Colorado Springs: Helmers and Howard, 1989. **Lyke, L. L.** "The Song of Songs, Proverbs, and the Theology of Love." In *Theological Exegesis*. Ed. C. Seitz and K. Greene-McCreight. Grand Rapids: Eerdmans, 1999. 208–23. **Maranda, E. K.**, and **P. Maranda.** *Structural Models in Folklore and Transformational Essays*. The Hague: Mouton, 1971. **Marks, E.** "The Economy of God in Song of Songs." *Affirmation and Critique* 4 (1999) 24–35. **Martínez, F. G.** *The Dead Sea Scrolls in English*. 2d ed. Grand Rapids: Eerdmans, 1996. **Matter, E. A.** *The Voice of My Beloved*. Philadelphia: Univ. of Pennsylvania Press, 1990. **Matthews, V.**, and **D. Benjamin.** *Social World of Ancient Israel*. Peabody, MA: Hendrickson, 1993. **Mazar, A.** *Archaeology of the Land of the Bible*. New York: Doubleday, 1992. **Mazor, Y.** "The Song of Songs or the Story of Stories? 'The Song of Songs': Between Genre and Unity." *SJOT* 1 (1990) 1–29. **McGinn, B.** "With 'the Kisses of the Mouth': Recent Works on the Song of Songs." *JR* 72 (1992) 269–75. **Meer, W. van der**, and **J. C. de Moor**, eds. *The Structural Analysis of Biblical and Canaanite Poetry*. JSOTSup 74. Sheffield: Sheffield Academic Press, 1988. **Miller, P. C.** "Pleasure of the Text, Text of Pleasure: Eros and Language in Origen's Commentary on the Song of Songs." *JAAR* 54 (1986) 241–53. **Moor, J. C de.** "The Love of God in the Targum to the Prophets." *JSJ* 24 (1993) 257–65. **Mott, S. C.** "The Goodness of Sexual Love in the Song of Songs." *Christian Social Action* 8 (1995) 16. **Moye, J.** "Song of Songs—Back to Allegory? Some Hermeneutical Considerations." *AJT* 4 (1990) 120–25. **Muilenberg, J.** "Poetry, Hebrew." In *EncJud* 13:671–81. **Munk, L.** "Giving Umbrage: The Song of Songs Which Is Whitman's [*Leaves of Grass* against allegorical interpretation of Song of Songs]." *Literature and Theology* 7 (1993) 50–65. **Munro, J.** *Spikenard and Saffron: The Imagery of the Song of Songs*. JSOTSup 203. Sheffield: Sheffield Academic Press, 1995. **Murphy, R. E.** "Form-critical Studies in the Song of Songs." *Int* 27 (1973). 413–22. ———. "History of Exegesis as a Hermeneutical Tool: The Song of Songs." *BTB* 16 (1986) 87–91. ———. "Interpreting the Song of Songs." *BTB* 9 (1979) 99–105. ———. "Patristic and Medieval Exegesis: Help or Hindrance?" *CBQ* 43 (1981) 505–16. ———. "Recent Literature on the Canticle of Canticles." *CBQ* 16 (1954) 1–11. ———. "The Structure of Canticle of Canticles." *CBQ* 11 (1949) 381–91. **Nicol, G. G.** "Of Love and Death: Song of Songs and Ecclesiastes." *ExpTim* 102 (1991) 340–41. **Nielsen, K.** "Other Writings: Ruth, Song of Songs, Esther, Daniel." In *The Hebrew Bible Today*. Ed. S. McKenzie and M. P. Graham. Louisville, KY: Westminster John Knox Press, 1988.173–99. **Nowell, I.** "A Celebration of Love." *BT* 25 (1987) 140–43. **O'Connor, D.** "Eros in Egypt." In *Archaeology Odyssey* 4.5 (Sept./Oct. 2001) 42–51. **Ogden, G. S.** "Some Translational Issues in the Song of Songs." *BT* 41 (1990) 222–27. **Page, D.** *Aeschyli septem quae* *supersunt tragoedias.* Oxford: Oxford UP, 1972. **Parsons, G. W.** "Guidelines for Understanding and Utilizing the Song of Songs." *BSac* 156 (1999) 399–422. **Patterson, P.** *Song of Solomon.* Chicago: Moody, 1986. **Paul, S. M.** "An Unrecognized Medical Idiom in Canticles 6,12 and Job 9,21." *Bib* 59 (1978) 545–47. **Petersen, D. L.,** and **K. H. Richards.** *Interpreting Hebrew Poetry.* Minneapolis: Fortress, 1992. **Pfeiffer, R. H.** *Introduction to the Old Testament.* New York: Harper and Brothers, 1941. **Phipps, W. E.** *Recovering Bible Sensuousness.* Philadelphia: Westminster, 1975. **Pleijel, A.** "Author and Translator: The Stylist's Work with the Song of Songs." *BT* 47 (1996) 114–18. **Pope, M. H.** "A Divine Banquet of Ugarit." In *The Use of the Old Testament in the New and Other Essays.* FS W. F. Stinesping, ed J. M. Efird. Durham: Duke UP, 1972. 170–203. ———. "Metastases in Canonical Shapes of the Super Song." In *Canon, Theology, and Old Testament Interpretation.* Ed. G. M. Tucker, D. L. Petersen, and R. R. Wilson. Philadelphia: Fortress, 1988. 312–28. ———. "Response to Sasson on the Sublime Song." *Maarav* 2 (1980) 207–14. **Pope, M. H.,** and **J. H. Tigay.** "A Description of Baal." *UF* 3 (1971) 117–30. **Reese, J.** *The Book of Wisdom, Song of Songs.* Wilmington, DE: Glazier, 1983. **Reisman, D.** "Iddin-Dagan's Sacred Marriage Hymn." *JCS* 25 (1973) 185–202. **Revell, E. J.** "Masoretic Accents." *ABD* 4:594–96. **Reynolds, W. J.** "Imagery in Christian Song." *SwJT* 37 (1995) 25–30. **Richardson, J. P.** "Preaching from the Song of Songs: Allegory Revisited." *Evangelical Review of Theology* 21 (1997) 250–57. **Roth, N.** "'My Beloved Is Like a Gazelle': Imagery of the Beloved Boy in Religious Hebrew Poetry." *HAR* 8 (1984) 143–66. **Sabar, Y.** *"Tafsir sir hassirim:* An Old Neo-Aramaic Version of the Targum on Canticles." *Maarav* 8 (1992) 303–17. **Sasson, J. M.** "Unlocking the Poetry of Love in the Song of Songs." *BRev* 1 (1985) 10–19. **Schiffman, L. H.,** and **J. C. VanderKam.** *Encyclopedia of the Dead Sea Scrolls.* Oxford: Oxford UP, 2000. **Schmidt, N.** "Is Canticles an Adonis Liturgy?" *JAOS* 46 (1926) 154–64. **Schmidt, W. H.** *Introduction to the Old Testament.* Trans. M. J. O'Connell. London: SCM Press, 1979. **Schoff, W. H.,** ed. *The Song of Songs: A Symposium.* Philadelphia: Commercial Museum, 1924. **Schoville, K. N.** "The Impact of the Ras Shamra Texts on the Study of the Song of Songs." Ph.D. diss., University of Wisconsin, 1969. **Schweizer, E.** *The Good News according to Matthew.* Trans. D. E. Green. London: SPCK, 1976. **Segal, B. J.** "Four Repetitions in the Song of Songs." *Dor le Dor* 16 (1987–88) 249–55. **Segal, M. H.** "The Song of Songs." *VT* 12 (1962) 470–90. **Shippey, T.** *J. R. R. Tolkien: Author of the Century.* Boston: Houghton Mifflin, 2000. **Shults, F. L.** "One Spirit with the Lord." *PTR* 7.3 (Summer 2000) 17–26. **Soden, W. von.** *The Ancient Orient.* Trans. D. G. Schley. Grand Rapids: Eerdmans, 1994. **Stanford, W. B.,** ed. *The Odyssey of Homer.* 2d ed. London: Macmillan, 1959. **Stern, E.** *Archaeology of the Land of the Bible.* 4 vols. New York: Doubleday, 2001. **Strand, M.,** and **E. Boland.** *The Making of a Poem.* New York: Norton, 2000. **Suares, C.** *The Song of Songs: The Canonical Song of Solomon Deciphered according to the Original Code of the Qabala.* Berkeley: Shambala, 1972. **Sviri, S.** "The Song of Songs: Eros and the Mystical Quest." In *Jewish Explorations of Sexuality.* Ed. J. Magonet. Providence: Berghahn Books, 1995. 41–50. **Tanner, J. P.** "The History of Interpretation of the Song of Songs." *BSac* 154 (1997) 23–46. ———. "The Message of the Song of Songs." *BSac* 154 (1997) 142–61. **Thomas, D. W.** *"Kelebh* 'Dog': Its Origin and Some Usages of It in the Old Testament." *VT* 10 (1960) 410–27. **Thompson, H. O.** "Carmel, Mount." *ABD* 1:874–75. **Tolkien, J. R. R.** "Beowulf: The Monsters and the Critics." In *An Anthology of Beowulf Criticism.* Ed. L. E. Nicholson. Notre Dame, IN: University of Notre Dame Press, 1963. 51–103. **Tournay, J. R.** "The Song of Songs and Its Concluding Section." *Imm* 10 (1980) 5–14. **Toynbee, J. M. C.** *Death and Burial in the Roman World.* Ithaca, NY: Cornell UP, 1971. **Treat, J. C.** "A Fiery Dove: The Song of Songs in Codex Venetus 1." In *A Multiform Heritage: Studies on Early Judaism and Christianity.* FS R. A. Kraft, ed. B. G. Wright III. Atlanta: Scholars Press, 1999. 275–301. **Tromp, N. J.** "Wisdom and the Canticle. Ct 8, 6c-7b: Text, Character, Message and Import." In *La Sagesse de l'Ancien Testament.* Ed. M. Gilbert. Gembloux: Duculot, 1979. 88–95. **Tucker, G. M., D. L. Petersen,** and **R. R. Wilson,** eds. *Canon, Theology, and Old Testament Interpretation.* Philadelphia: Fortress, 1988. **Turner, D.** *Eros and Allegory.* Kalamazoo, MI: Cistercian, 1995. **Tyloch, W.** "Ugaritic Poems and Song of Songs." In *Sulmu IV.* Ed. J. Zablocka and S. Zawadzki. Poznan: UAM, 1993. 295–301. **Vendler, H.** *The Art of Shakespeare's Sonnets.* Cambridge, MA: Harvard UP, 1999 [first paperback edition]. **Waldman, N. M.** "A Note on Canticles 4,9." *JBL* 89 (1970) 215–17. **Walker, L. L.** "Notes on Higher Criticism and the Dating of Biblical Hebrew." In *A Tribute to Gleason Archer.* Chicago: Moody Press, 1986. ———. "תַּפּוּחַ." *NIDOTTE* §9515. **Walsh, C. E.** *Exquisite Desire: Religion, the Erotic, and the Song of Songs.* Minneapolis: Fortress Press, 2000. **Walton, J.** "עֲלוּמִים." *NIDOTTE* §6596. **Watson, W. G. E.** "Love and Death Once More (Song of Songs VIII 6)." *VT* 47 (1997) 385–87. ———. *Traditional Techniques in Classical Hebrew Verse.* JSOTSup 170. Sheffield: Sheffield Academic Press, 1994. **Webster, E. C.** "Pattern in the Song of Songs." *JSOT* 22 (1982) 73–93. **Wendland, E. R.** "Seeking the Path through a Forest of Symbols: A Figurative and Structural Survey of the Song of Songs." *JOTT* 7 (1995) 13–59. **Wenham, G.** "*B^etulah:* A Girl of Marriageable Age." *VT* 22 (1972) 326–48. **White, J. B.** *A Study of the Language of Love in the Song of Songs and Ancient Egyptian Literature.* Missoula: Scholars Press, 1978. **Whitesell, C. J.** "Behold, Thou Art Fair, My Beloved." *Parab* 20 (1995) 92–99. **Wright, F. A.,** ed. and trans. *Select Letters of St. Jerome.* Loeb Classical Library. Cambridge, MA: Harvard UP, 1933. **Wright, J.** "Sexuality within the Old Testament." *St Mark's Review* 106 (1981) 3–12. **Würthwein, E.** "Das Hohelied." In *Die fünf Megilloth.* Ed. E. Würthwein, K. Galling, and O. Plöger. Tübingen: Mohr, 1969. 25–71. **Wyk, W. C. van.** "The Peshitta of the Song of Songs (Song of Solomon)." In *Aspects of the Exegetical Process.* Ed. W. C. van Wyk. Hercules, South Africa: N. H. W. Press, 1981. 181–89. **Young, E. J.** *An Introduction to the Old Testament.* Grand Rapids: Eerdmans, 1960. **Zogbo, L.** "Commentaries on the Song of Songs." *BT* 45 (1994) 343–48.

Introduction

Song of Songs is a small book (eight chapters) in the Bible. It is placed as the last of the poetic books of Wisdom after Job, Psalms, Proverbs, Ecclesiastes, and Lamentations. In the Hebrew Bible, at least from the tenth century C.E. on, it was placed among the Wisdom books in the Writings as one of five festal scrolls with Ruth, Ecclesiastes, Lamentations, and Esther. It held a fixed position in Jewish sacred tradition, as the presence of several copies among the Dead Sea Scrolls (first century B.C.E.) shows. It was known to the writers of the Mishnah and the Targums as well as the Talmud. Manuscripts of it exist today in Hebrew from the Masoretes of the tenth century C.E., in Greek from the fifth century C.E., and in other versions from this early period.

The Song of Songs is unique in the Hebrew Scriptures; one is even tempted to say that it is unique in world literature. The latter statement, however, would be an exaggeration. Song of Songs is lyric poetry (see *Excursus: Finding an Approach to Lyric Poetry*). It has roots in Egyptian love poetry and parallels in lyric poetry from all times and places, especially from the ancient world. Nothing is fully "like" the Song of Songs, but there are in other texts important analogies to its use of language, its root concepts, and even its structure. Probably no piece of poetry has been subjected to such a diversity of interpretations as has the Song. This is to a large degree because many have been unwilling to read it according to the normal "rules" of poetry. Its status as a canonical book has meant that readers through the ages have subjected it to hermeneutical reclamation and renovation projects, determined to make it into something that it is not.

Song of Songs *is* canonical Scripture. In the Hebrew Bible, it is one of the five Megilloth, books that are read on various holy days as prescribed in the Mishnah. The other books and their associated holidays are Ruth (Pentecost), Ecclesiastes (Tabernacles), Lamentations (the Ninth of Ab, the traditional anniversary of the destruction of the first and second temples), and Esther (Purim). The Song of Songs is read on the Sabbath of Passover week. However, evidence for the use of the Song as a Passover scroll dates only to the eighth century C.E. Some scholars suggest an earlier usage in village culture where the harvest festivals were the occasions for weddings. The same would apply to the use of Ruth at the Festival of Weeks (Pentecost). Its original purpose is not clear (Fohrer, *Introduction*, 300). In Hebrew Scripture the Song is grouped with the other Megilloth in the third division of the canon, the Writings. In Christian Scriptures, following the Septuagint order, it is grouped with the poetic books of Psalms, Proverbs, and Ecclesiastes.

Jews and Christians use the Song as part of their regular cycles of lectionary readings, and the Song adds a new dimension to the regular reading of the Bible. But that it is canonical does not mean that it should be forced into a role for which it is not suited or given a meaning that it does not have. Its canonical status means that one must take it seriously as poetry that focuses on the love of a man and a woman and then determine how it fits within the message of Scripture.

In his classic 1936 lecture on *Beowulf*, J. R. R. Tolkien wrote, "I have, of course, read *The Beowulf*, as have most (but not all) of those who have criticized it. But I fear that . . . I have not been a man so diligent in my special walk as duly to read all that has been printed on, or touching on, this poem. But I have read enough, I think, to venture the opinion that Beowulfiana is, while rich in many departments, specially poor in one. It is poor in criticism, criticism that is directed to the understanding of a poem as a poem. . . . *Beowulf* has been used as a quarry of fact and fancy far more assiduously than it has been studied as a work of art" ("Beowulf," 51–52). Much the same is true of the study of the Song. It is a quarry for stones ready to be transformed into theological gold by the alchemy of allegorization, for gems that indulge fascination with erotica, for raw metals that can be forged and fitted together as an elaborate dramatic production, for rocks to be used as ammunition in the gender wars waged by feminists, and for verbal ore ready to be melted down in the fires of deconstruction. The commentary that follows is an attempt to understand the Song for what it is: a canonical work of lyric poetry.

Song of Songs as Scripture

Bibliography

Brenner, A. "Aromatics and Perfumes in the Song of Songs." *JSOT* 25 (1983) 75–81. **Broyde, M. J.** "Defilement of the Hands, Canonization of the Bible, and the Special Status of Esther, Ecclesiastes, and Song of Songs." *Judaism* 44 (1995) 65–79. **Dever, W.** *What Did the Biblical Writers Know and When Did They Know It?* Grand Rapids: Eerdmans, 2001. **Fox, M. V.** "The Cairo Love Songs." *JAOS* 100 (1980) 101–9. **Fredericks, D. C.** *Qoheleth's Language.* Lewiston, NY: Mellen, 1988. **LaCocque, A.** *Romance, She Wrote.* Harrisburg, PA: Trinity Press International, 1998. **Rabin, C.** "The Song of Songs and Tamil Poetry." *SR* 3 (1973) 205–19. **Saebø, M.** "On the Canonicity of the Song of Songs." In *Texts, Temples, and Traditions.* FS M. Haran, ed. M. Fox. Winona Lake, IN: Eisenbrauns, 1996. 267–77. **Sasson, V.** "King Solomon and the Dark Lady in the Song of Songs." *VT* 39 (1989) 407–14. **Segal, M. H.** "The Song of Songs." *VT* 12 (1962) 470–90. **Tov, E.** *Qumran Cave 4: XI. Psalms to Chronicles.* DJD 16. Oxford: Clarendon, 2000. 197, 208–9. **Treat, J. C.** "Aquila, Field, and the Song of Songs." In *Origen's Hexapla and Fragments: Papers Presented at the Rich Seminar on the Hexapla, Oxford Center for Hebrew and Jewish Studies.* Ed. A. Salvesen. Tübingen: Mohr (Siebeck), 1998. 135–37. ———. "A Fiery Dove: The Song of Songs in Codex Venetus 1." In *A Multiform Heritage: Studies on Early Judaism and Christianity.* FS R. A. Kraft, ed. B. G. Wright III. Atlanta: Scholars Press, 1999. 275–301. **Young, I.** *Diversity in Pre-Exilic Hebrew.* Tübingen: Mohr (Siebeck), 1993.

Canonization

There is no certain information about the date of the admission of the Song into the canon. However, two common statements made about this matter are wrong. The first is that the Song was not admitted into the canon until very late, possibly as late as the first century C.E. Scholars are abandoning the idea that the canon was established or closed at the so-called Council of Jamnia (cf. M. Saebø, "On the Canonicity," 268). It is true that the Song's status was discussed and debated by rabbis at this time (Gordis, 9). This, however, is no proof that the Song was not already long regarded as canonical. By analogy, John Calvin disputed with Sebastian Castellio over the canonical status of the Song in Geneva during the sixteenth century; surely no one would argue that this dispute shows that the Song up until this time had not yet been placed in the canon. The reason that the canonical status of the Song was debated and occasionally continues to be debated is that it is not what one would expect to find in Holy Writ. One cannot use rabbinical disputes to determine the time it came to be regarded as Scripture.

Scholars may have misunderstood rabbinical terminology in regard to the concept of canon. Many have suggested that Second Temple Judaism did not regard Song of Songs, Ecclesiastes, and Esther as canonical on the grounds of Talmudic statements to the effect that these books do not "defile the hands." To "defile the hands" was taken by scholars to be code for "sacred" and thus "canonical." The term may have nothing to do with canonicity. As M. Broyde (*Judaism* 44 [1995] 65–79) suggests, the injunction that a book "defiles the hands" may mean that one cannot handle the book and then handle food, or store the book near food. The book can render food unclean and thus unfit for eating, and a book that "defiles the hands" must be kept separate from food. The rationale behind this is that these books must not be subject to soiling and to destruction by rodents and must be given special care. Books that "defile the hands" do have a sacred status, but it is not their being canonical that gives them this status; it is the fact that these books contain the divine name יהוה (Yahweh). Texts that contain the divine name must be given special attention to protect them from rot, spoilage, and destruction. Song of Songs, Ecclesiastes, and Esther, however, do not contain יהוה. It is this fact, and not their canonical status or lack thereof, that exempts them from the "defiling the hands" status.

There is a second error regarding the Song's canonicity. This is that the Song was given canonical status because of or under the cover of an allegorical interpretation. Allegorizing the Song (that is, treating it as a parable of the history of Israel's relationship to God) did not pave the way for canonization; that it was in the canon prompted the allegorizing of the Song. It is difficult to imagine why anyone would create the far-fetched and unlikely interpretations of the allegorists except for the fact that they felt theologically compelled to do so. For the allegorizers, the logic of the situation was quite simple: (1) the Song of Songs is in the canon; (2) canonical books are holy; (3) therefore, the Song of Songs is holy; (4) but the Song of Songs appears to be carnal; (5) therefore, we must find an interpretation for the Song that saves it from its apparent carnality and shows it to be spiritual. If the Song were not already Scripture, it is hard to imagine why anyone would allegorize it in the first place.

The Text of Song of Songs

The Hebrew of Song of Songs is some of the most difficult in the OT, but that difficulty appears to be a result of the language itself and not because of textual corruptions. The text contains an enormous number of *hapax legomena*, and occasionally the style is so terse that the sense is difficult to obtain. But by all appearances, the Song has come down in good condition. It is generally supported by Qumran and the ancient versions.

The Qumran fragments of the Song are particularly interesting. There are three manuscripts of the Song from Cave 4: these are 4QCanticles[a] (parts of Song 3:7–11; 4:1–7; 6:11?–12; 7:1–7 [early Herodian period]), 4QCanticles[b] (parts of Song 2:9–17; 3:1–2, 5, 9–10; 4:1–3, 8–11, 14–16; 5:1 [end of first century B.C.E.]), and 4QCanticles[c] (a tiny fragment of Song 3:7–8 [end of first century B.C.E.]). A fragment from Cave 6, 6QCanticles, dates to 50 C.E. and contains Song 1:1–7. A curiosity of the Cave 4 fragments is that they are selective; that is, they deliberately skip sections of the Song. This does not appear to reflect a different *Vorlage*, "text being copied," and is not significant for critical purposes; it may be that the selections had a liturgical purpose. Variants against the MT are minor and probably not significant. For example, at Song 3:11, where MT has "daughters of Zion," 4QCant[a] has "daughters of Jerusalem." These Qumran fragments would be a doubtful basis for emending the MT. The scribe of 4QCant[b], in the words of its editor E. Tov, "made many mistakes and he was much influenced by the Aramaic language" (DJD 16:197, 208–9). This manuscript also contains peculiar scribal markings, possibly Paleo-Hebrew script (DJD 16:205).

Murphy (7–11) has a good survey of the characteristics of the ancient versions. J. Treat ("A Fiery Dove") provides the interpreter with a fascinating look at an Old Greek version of Song of Songs (Codex Venetus 1 or "V"), complete with its original preface and demarcation of singers' parts, in his critical edition of this codex.

There are very few instances where the versions appear to have a superior reading to the MT or where emendation of the MT is advisable. One example is at Song 4:8, where the MT has אִתִּי, "with me." The LXX δεῦρο and the Vg. *veni*, "come!" make more sense in context. Emending to אֲתִי, "come!" is thus preferable to the MT. Also at Song 4:8, one should emend מֵהַרְרֵי, "from the mountains of," to מֵחֹרֵי, "from the lairs of," opposite מִמְּעֹנוֹת, "from the dens of." At Song 7:10 (ET 7:9), it is a bit of a stretch to make good sense of the MT שִׂפְתֵי יְשֵׁנִים, "lips of sleepers." An emendation to שְׂפָתַי וְשִׁנָּי, "my lips and my teeth," with LXX, Syr., and Vg. is preferable. By and large, however, the MT is a reliable witness, and it is the basis for this commentary, notwithstanding the few emendations occasionally suggested.

DATE OF COMPOSITION

Many scholars date Song of Songs to the Persian period. Linguistic arguments have been the chief justification put forward for maintaining a late date for the Song. M. Fox (*Song of Songs*, 186–91) is typical of such a viewpoint: "Linguistic criteria are all we can go on in determining the general period of the Song's composition. The language of the Song resembles mishnaic Hebrew in many ways" (187). Fox goes on to list "characteristically mishnaic words and constructions" that demand a late date for the Song.

Linguistic arguments have been seriously undermined by more recent analyses, especially that of I. Young (*Diversity*). One can add to this the work of D. Fredericks (*Qoheleth's Language*), which, although focused on Ecclesiastes, deals with many of the same issues. Previous arguments for dating books on the basis of language have consisted of lists of words or grammatical structures thought to be Mishnaisms or Aramaisms and thus proof that the work was late. Most of them used a simple, linear model for the history of the language of biblical Hebrew.

Young argues that the origin of Hebrew is found in the continuation of a prior Canaanite literary "prestige language," just as Aramaic was an official language of the larger powers. The Deir Alla inscriptions indicate that there could be a considerable admixture of Canaanite and Aramaic elements in a local language, especially when the two prestige cultures were clashing with each other, as in the eighth century. Even archaic biblical Hebrew demonstrates an Aramaizing tendency. In standard biblical Hebrew, the use of an Aramaic-like style was considered "bad form," although this rule did not apply to Wisdom texts. Young states that "we cannot say with confidence that a word is an 'Aramaism,' that is, a loan from Aramaic into Hebrew" (*Diversity*, 63).

For our purposes, a most important aspect of Young's study is his analysis of the distinctions between standard biblical Hebrew and Mishnaic Hebrew (*Diversity*, 73–96). Scholars have generally assumed that Mishnaic Hebrew is the lineal descendant of biblical Hebrew, but Young suggests a more convincing model. Building on prior research, he argues that a case can be made for diglossia in ancient Israel. *Diglossia* describes two varieties or dialects of a single language coexisting in a single place and time, each with its own role to play. Classic Hebrew coexisted side by side with a colloquial Hebrew that often used Aramaisms. Preexilic Hebrew was already very diverse and included many Aramaic elements. It is impossible to claim that a linear progression from preexilic standard biblical Hebrew, to late biblical Hebrew (moderately Aramaized), then to Mishnaic Hebrew (heavily Aramaized) fairly represents the history of the Hebrew language to that point.

The presence of Aramaisms, as we have seen, is not sufficient grounds for ascribing a book to a late date. They may represent a northern dialect or simply a style that is not concerned to maintain the pure Hebrew of literary prose. D. C. Fredericks (*Qoheleth's Language*, 208–9), citing G. R. Driver, points out that poetry in particular is more likely to contain Aramaisms; like Young, Fredericks also notes that Aramaisms are likely to occur in Wisdom texts regardless of their date of writing.

The numerous *hapax legomena* in the Song hardly suggest a late date. They may reflect a dialect, or they may suggest that "the author was a genius with an exceptionally large vocabulary" (Young, *Diversity*, 164). The high number of unusual words is characteristic of lyric poetry.

The use of the relative pronoun שׁ in the Song is not indicative of a late date, notwithstanding its usage in Mishnaic Hebrew. Young (*Diversity*, 163) notes that it appears to represent some northern Israelite dialect. It occurs twice in the Song of Deborah (Judg 5:7), which Young suggests has characteristics of both archaic and northern Hebrew. It also occurs in the account of the Manassite Gideon (Judg 6:17; 7:12; 8:26) and in a citation of a king of Syria in an account that concerns the northern kingdom (2 Kgs 6:11). I would also observe that שׁ represents a colloquial or more terse form of speech. In Jonah 1:7, the sailors speak to each other very directly and use the expression בשׁלמי for "on whose account." In speaking to Jonah, however, they use a more formal style of speech and replace בשׁלמי with באשׁר למי (Jonah 1:8). Pope (33) rejects taking שׁ as an indicator of late date; he compares it to the Akkadian *ša*, Ugaritic *d* and *ḏ*, Canaanite *z*, Aramaic *d*, and Arabic *ḏū*. See also Fredericks, *Qoheleth's Language*, 147–48.

The two most frequently cited so-called loan words for Song of Songs are פַּרְדֵּס, "park, orchard, paradise," at 4:13 and אַפִּרְיוֹן, "palanquin," at 3:9. פַּרְדֵּס is sometimes thought to be a Persian loan word. Young (*Diversity*, 161–62) shows that the origin of the word is unknown, that it may be of Sanskrit origin, and that there are reasons to think that Indo-Aryans were present in Canaan in pre-conquest times (see also *Diversity*, 7). The situation is similar for אַפִּרְיוֹן, "palaquin." Often said to be of Greek origin, it, too, is an obscure word, possibly of Sanskrit origin (Young, *Diversity*, 162). See Fredericks, *Qoheleth's Language*, 245. A. Brenner (*JSOT* 25 [1983] 75–81) argues for a Persian origin for כַּרְכֹּם, "saffron," and נֵרְדְּ, "spikenard," but nothing is known of how or when these words entered the language.

Another point often raised is that the Song contains only two *wayyiqtol* forms, and both are in Song 6:9. A lack of *wayyiqtol*s is also a characteristic of Mishnaic Hebrew. Yet one would no more expect to see the *wayyiqtol* in the short pieces of lyric poetry that we have in the Song than one would expect to see it in Ps 23, another piece of lyric poetry. As linguistic evidence for the date of the book, this datum is completely worthless.

Taken together, Young's work suggests that none of the linguistic features of the Song need to be assigned to a late date. Rather, perhaps because of its genre, the Song does not have a number of the linguistic features of the standard literary prose of biblical Hebrew. His conclusion to his analysis of the Song (*Diversity*, 165) is worth citing:

> The Song of Songs shares the most significant isoglosses with the Song of Deborah which by content stems from the Northern tribes. The Song of Songs does not exhibit the clustering of archaic elements which places Deborah with Archaic Biblical Hebrew. The distinction is not necessarily one of date, since in the early period which seems to be evidenced for the Song of Songs, the Archaic Biblical Hebrew style was still being composed, and the Standard Style was still in its infancy. The Song of Songs seems to be an early work which is neither in the Archaic nor Standard Biblical styles. It shares specific dialectal features with the Northern Song of Deborah. Yet it seems to have been composed in Jerusalem.

Recent biblical scholarship has distanced itself from dating the Song on the basis of language. Murphy (4) says that such arguments "bristle with difficulties." See also Longman (4–5) and Pope (30–34).

Apart from linguistic issues, there are several lines of evidence that indicate an earlier date for the Song. First, the Song reflects a geographic consciousness one would expect during the Israelite empire of Solomon. Northern locales mentioned in the Song include Sharon, Lebanon, Hermon, and Carmel. Some scholars have been so impressed by the preponderance of northern locations in the Song that they have suggested a northern provenance for the work on that basis (e.g., LaSor et al., *Old Testament Survey*, 602–3). This is not likely; the common term for the woman's female companions in the Song is "daughters of Jerusalem" (1:5; 2:7; 3:5, 10; 5:8; 5:16; 8:4), indicating that the community of the Song is Jerusalem. That is, all other references to places are allusions that function as similes or metaphors, but the people of the Song are actually said to be from Jerusalem. Southern locations (e.g., Engedi) and places in the

Transjordan (Heshbon, Gilead) also appear in the Song. It is of course possible that a poet from any era could have alluded to various locations in the Levant, but the tone of the Song might well be described as pan-Israelite. The idealized heroine of the Song, whose head is like Carmel, who dwells in the remote mountains of Lebanon, who is both the "rose of Sharon" and a vineyard in Engedi, draws upon every region of greater Israel for her self-description. The poem was written at a time when these locales were not alien places but were regarded as the possessions of, or within the sphere of influence of, the Israelite state. M. Segal (*VT* 12 [1962] 483) points out "Such an extended horizon for a Jerusalem poet suits best the age of Solomon, whose rule extended far beyond the confines of the land of Israel." This evidence, although not conclusive, is at least congruent with the implication of the superscript.

The high literary style of the Song suggests that it was written at a time when Israel had the means and the motivation for literary pursuits. By analogy, the great flourishing of Latin literature came in the Augustan age, and the flowering of classical Greek literature came in the Athenian Empire. The Bible indicates that Solomon's reign was such a time. The nation had wealth, international discourse, and a monarch who was interested in literary matters. Of course, it is always possible that Israel was exceptional in this regard and that this book was written by an obscure fifth-century figure, but that would not be the obvious conclusion to reach.

There are other circumstantial indications that the book comes from the Solomonic empire. C. Rabin (*SR* 3 [1973] 205–19) argues that the exotic spices and perfumes mentioned in the Song suggest a time of great wealth and commercial relations with the east, particularly India. One need not accept his thesis that the Song was influenced by Tamil poetry to appreciate the validity of this point, nor need one argue that this was absolutely the only time that spices from the east would have made their way to the Levant. The fact is simply that the Song reflects a time of great wealth and of exotic tastes, and the Solomonic monarchy, according to the Bible, was the foremost example of this in Israelite history (e.g., 1 Kgs 10:25). M. Segal (*VT* 12 [1962] 470–90) notes that the frequent references to gold, alabaster, sapphires, and jewelry in the Song suggest a provenance of great wealth. He suggests that the shields of David's tower (Song 4:4) may be the golden shields taken by Shishak (1 Kgs 10:16–17; 14:26).

I have argued elsewhere (Garrett, 352) that although it is true that a poet can allude to things that he has little experience of, such allusions often tend to be clichés. A poet who had only rarely seen snow might say "white as snow," but a poet who lived in a wintry climate would make much more nuanced references to snow, ice, frost, and so forth. The allusions to alabaster pillars in sockets of gold (Song 5:15) or to the ornately decorated horses of the pharaoh (Song 1:9–11) suggest that the poet had actually seen things like this. The garden metaphors in the Song are equally extravagant: "Your growth is a paradise: / pomegranates with choice fruit, / henna with spikenard, / nard and saffron, / calamus and cinnamon, / with every incense tree, / myrrh and aloes" (Song 4:13–14). People with no genuine acquaintance with gardens of such astoundingly exotic variety would be more likely to use generic language. References to items of luxury in the Song are anything but clichés. The poet spoke from direct experience.

Then there is the reference to Tirzah in Song 6:4: "You are beautiful, my companion, like Tirzah, / Lovely, like Jerusalem." The pairing of the two cities suggests that they are comparably magnificent; the simile would not work if Tirzah were a backwater. Tirzah was a leading city of the northern part of the nation in the early first millennium. It became the capital of the northern kingdom after the secession and apparently remained so under Jeroboam I and his successors Baasha (1 Kgs 15:21, 33), Elah (1 Kgs 16:8), Zimri (1 Kgs 16:15), and Omri (1 Kgs 16:23–24) until Omri (reigned ca. 885–874 B.C.E.) built Samaria.

The location of Tirzah has been the matter of some dispute, but the consensus is that it was at Tell el-Farʿah, north (Dale, "Tirzah," *ABD* 6:573–77; see especially de Vaux's comments on the identification of the site in Stern, *Archaeology*, 2:433). The history of the site reaches from the Neolithic period to Iron II, but it enjoyed a major flourishing in Iron I in the period of the united monarchy. For a full discussion of the history of the site, see the discussion by A. Chambon in Stern, *Archaeology*, 2:433–40. Concerning the level of occupation corresponding to the united monarchy period, Mazar (*Archaeology*, 389) writes: "Tirzah (Tell el-Farʿah [north]) is an exceptional example of a developed town—well planned and densely occupied—in this period. It is characterized by orthogonal planning (almost non-existent in later Israelite towns) and the repeated appearance of a typical 'four-room house.'" This phase of Tirzah's history ended in the ninth century, apparently when Omri moved the capital. In the next major phase, the demoted city continued to prosper, but this phase ended with the destruction of the city, apparently in the Assyrian campaign of 723. The city was briefly occupied after that but was permanently abandoned by 600 B.C.E. Dever states that Level VIIa would have been the city of Solomon's time. He describes it as follows: "This stratum, securely dated to the 10th century by its pottery, incorporated an offset-inset city wall; a two-entryway city gate; a large public place near the gate with a shrine; and several contiguous blocks of four-room courtyard houses, so well laid out that they reflect a measure of urban planning. Thus Tirzah may well have been the administrative capital of Solomon's northern district of Ephraim" (*What Did the Biblical Writers Know?* 142).

The poet of the Song therefore considered Tirzah and Jerusalem to be near equals, and although the city of the early divided monarchy might meet this standard, the earlier phase is a better candidate. Common sense suggests that the comparison would have been made prior to secession of the northern tribes, after which the two cities were bitter enemies. Ascribing this pairing of Jerusalem with Tirzah to a postexilic poet is out of the question. The city did not exist at that time, and there is no reason to think that the memory of the city's glory days survived. There is certainly no reason to think that *Tirzah* was proverbial as a metaphor for glory. A. LaCocque (*Romance*, 28) argues that just as the expression "Pyrrhic victory" does not mean that we are dealing with a third-century B.C.E. text, so this reference to Tirzah has no bearing on the date of the Song. The analogy is absurd; "Pyrrhic victory" is a cliché repeated through the centuries, but Song 6:4 has nothing of the cliché about it, and the comparison of Tirzah to Jerusalem is nowhere else employed. We thus have no reason to suppose that the reference to Tirzah is some kind of retrospective glance at northern Israel's glory days, the significance of which a postexilic audience would supposedly have recognized. This evidence cannot be easily dismissed and is of much greater significance than the more or less circumstantial arguments mentioned above. In the Persian period, Tirzah was a deserted tell.

Murphy (4) rejects dating the book on the basis of Song 6:4 on the grounds that Tirzah may have been chosen by the poet because the name sounds similar to רצה, "to be pleasing." This argument is contrived; the root רצה does not figure anywhere in this text, and allusion to the meaning of the root of a proper name is not a device employed in the Song. Such etymological allusions in Hebrew poetry inevitably involve some kind of paronomasia (as in Mic 1:10), and none is found here.

The similarity of Song of Songs to the Egyptian love poetry is also important for dating the Song. The affinities between the two are too numerous and too close to be accidental. The evidence indicates that the Song of Songs has borrowed much from the Egyptian material, albeit taking the genre in a new direction. If the Hebrew and Egyptian texts are not directly related, one must say that it is peculiar that so many scholars give so much attention to analyzing correspondence between the two. Yet these very scholars will date the Song almost a millennium after the Egyptian texts. That is, instead of dating the Song near the time that the Egyptian love poetry of this kind flourished and to a time when, according to the Bible, Egyptian influence was strong in Jerusalem, these scholars date the Song to a time many hundreds of years after the passing of the Egyptian love songs and to a time when the Jewish community was a tiny department of the Persian Empire. Landy uses the Egyptian material as a model for interpreting the Song (*Paradoxes*, 21–24) but says that the Song comes from a "very late date" (*Paradoxes*, 18). He even concedes that parallels to the Song in Hellenistic poetry are superficial and few in number (*Paradoxes*, 26). J. B. White spends part of a dissertation demonstrating parallels between the Song of Songs and the Egyptian poetry but adds, "It would be unwarranted due to problems of chronology and cultural interchange to propose that the Song of Songs is *literally dependent* on the ancient Egyptian love lyrics" (*Study of the Language*, 153, emphasis original). Are we to assume, then, that the parallels he catalogs are coincidental?

Fox (*Song of Songs*, 186–93) dates the Song to the postexilic period on the basis of lexical data. He does not demonstrate that the Song and the Egyptian material are of different genres. To the contrary, his work, like White's, shows how much the two have in common. The Egyptian love poetry, he suggests, entered Palestine during the Rameside Empire (eighteenth to twentieth dynasties, or early fifteenth through late twelfth centuries), but he says that the Song was composed some time after the exile. How could the Song of Songs have been written in essentially the same genre after a hiatus of nearly a thousand years? Fox argues that the survival of the sonnet in Western poetry is analogous. He also argues that the presence of an Egyptian female singer in the court of Byblos, as reported in the "Report of Wenamun" at the beginning of the eleventh century, attests to the persistence of the Egyptian court music (*Song of Songs*, 186–93). The Megiddo Ivories (ca. 1350–1150 B.C.E.) also refer to a "singer of Ptah."

Fox's argument does not work. The suggestion that Egyptian love poetry entered the Levant in the Rameside period is unlikely. Israel at this time (the Judges period) was a cultural backwater, and it is not credible that the Israelites of this chaotic period were importing samples of aristocratic music from Egypt. One could argue that the Canaanites imported the genre and passed it on to the Israelites, but this is piling hypothesis on hypothesis. The Bible indicates that the Davidic-Solomonic Empire was the period of great musical and literary flourishing in Israel, and it also suggests that this was a time when Egyptian cultural influence was pronounced (in that Solomon's marriage to an Egyptian princess involved bringing much that was Egyptian into Israel; 1 Kgs 3:1; 7:8; 9:24). We do not know when Egyptian love poetry became popular in Israel. It probably occurred nearer to the time that it flourished in Egypt, at a time when Egyptian culture was being directly imported into the kingdom and interest in all things Egyptian would have been high. While no one need doubt that there were some Egyptian singers in Canaan in the late second millennium, this hardly justifies the idea that the genre of Egyptian love song persisted in the Levant until the late first millennium.

Contrary to Fox, the history of the sonnet, as briefly outlined below, is entirely unlike the history of the Egyptian love poetry. The sonnet is a poem of fourteen lines with a fixed meter and rhyme scheme. Developed in Italy around the thirteenth century, it found expression in great masters such as Petrarch and Dante. It became popular in England in the sixteenth century; most modern readers recognize the sonnet as a poetic form of Shakespeare. Its usage declined in seventeenth- and eighteenth-century English poetry (but it by no means disappeared; Milton composed sonnets in the mid-seventeenth century, and other practitioners include Ben Jonson [ca. 1572–1637], John Donne [ca. 1572–1631], and Thomas Edwards [1699–1757]). The sonnet flourished in the German romantic movement in the work of Goethe (1749–1832) and others. In English poetry, the sonnet had a revival in the nineteenth and early twentieth centuries. Examples from the many sonneteers from this period include Edgar Allen Poe (1809–1849), Henry Wadsworth Longfellow (1807–1882), and especially Edna St. Vincent Millay (1892–1950). Unlike the sonnet, there is no evidence that Egyptian love poetry "persisted" as a poetic form. The similarity to the genre suggests that the Song is a late-second-millennium or early-first-millennium work.

In summary, the Hebrew of the Song of Songs in no way demands a Persian or Hellenistic provenance for the text. The imagery used in the Song suggests a pan-Israelite viewpoint and composition by a poet who had direct experience with wealth and exotic luxuries, and this fits well with a provenance in the Solomonic empire. The reference to Tirzah in Song 6:4 suggests that the Song was written during the united monarchy, although on this evidence alone a date in the early divided monarchy is conceivable (but a date in the postexilic period is out of the question). The evidence that the Song draws upon the Egyptian love poetry of the late second millennium demands a date relatively close to that period and suggests a time when Israelite high culture was open to Egyptian influence. Thus, the evidence converges on this conclusion: the book was written during the united monarchy.

Authorship

The superscript tells us that this is the Song of Songs "belonging to" or "written by" or perhaps "for" or "dedicated to" Solomon. The prepositional phrase

לשלמה (lit. "to Solomon") is ambiguous (see *Comment* on 1:1 for further discussion of this). One could interpret the superscript to mean either that the book is anonymous but sponsored by Solomon or that it claims Solomonic authorship for the Song. In either case it indicates that the book came from the Solomonic period. It was written either by or for him. (The idea that a book would be dedicated to a long-dead monarch is without analogy in the ancient or modern world and can be dismissed.) Traditionally, the title has always been taken to mean that Solomon wrote the Song of Songs. Or one could hold that it means that the book belongs to a collection catalogued under Solomon's name. Few contemporary scholars take the superscript of Song of Songs to be evidence of a date in the united monarchy. Readers familiar with recent debates over the historicity of the early monarchy and over the chronology of sites such as Gezer and Hazor will know that the historicity of the Davidic-Solomonic Empire is a hotly debated topic. I believe that the biblical picture of the early tenth through early ninth centuries (2 Samuel–1 Kgs 11; 1 Chr 11–2 Chr 9) as a cultural and political high water mark in Israel's history should be accepted as accurate.

W. Dever (*What Did the Biblical Writers Know?* 131–57) has described a sampling of evidence from archaeology that corroborates this perspective (Dever, as he is at pains to tell us, has no theological commitment to the reliability of the Bible). According to 1 Kgs 9:15–17, an unnamed pharaoh captured Gezer from the Canaanites, burned it down, and gave it to Solomon as a dowry; Solomon then used the corvée to rebuild Hazor, Megiddo, and Gezer. In the reign of Solomon's successor, Rehoboam, Pharaoh Shishak (or Sheshonk) invaded Judah and took away a significant payment of tribute (2 Chr 2:1–9; 1 Kgs 14:25). Shishak destroyed a number of fortress cities in his campaign (2 Chr 2:4), although the Bible does not specify which cities he sacked. He also campaigned through the Negev to the south and Israel to the north. A commemorative relief and text of Shishak on the walls of the temple of Amun at Karnak lists over 150 cities that Shishak claimed to have destroyed.

Excavation of Hazor, Megiddo, and Gezer corroborates the biblical story and sheds additional light on this period. Y. Yadin noticed the similarity of the gates and casemate walls of these three sites and concluded that all were constructed by a corps of engineers under Solomon's administration. The casemate wall of Gezer significant for our purposes was built above a destruction layer and dated by pottery to the mid-tenth century. The fourth entryway gate to the city was "exceptionally well engineered and beautifully preserved" (Dever, *What Did the Biblical Writers Know?* 132). This level, Gezer Stratum VIII, was itself destroyed prior to the ninth century (date determined again by pottery). Dever was thus able to date this as the city that was rebuilt by Solomon but soon afterward destroyed by Shishak and locate it within the dates of ca. 970 to 925. A. Mazar comes to similar conclusions (*Archaeology*, 380–98). Dever adds: "I would stress again that the city defenses and all the rest are part of a dramatic, large-scale process of organization and centralization that utterly transformed the landscape of most of Palestine in the period from the early 10th to early 9th century" (*What Did the Biblical Writers Know?* 137).

Dever also summarizes evidence indicating that the temple of Solomon, as described in 1 Kings and 1 Chronicles, accurately reflects temple architecture from this period. He states, "we now have direct Bronze and Iron Age parallels for *every single feature* of the 'Solomonic Temple' as described in the Hebrew Bible; and the parallels come from, and only from, the Canaanite-Phoenician world of the 15th–9th centuries" (*What Did the Biblical Writers Know?* 145, emphasis original). Specific examples of such parallels include the tripartite plan of the temple, the use of ashlar (masonry of square-hewn stones) and reinforcing wood beams, the use of two bronze columns to flank the entryway, and the use of carved "cherubs" (this is only a partial list). The important point is that the biblical picture of the Solomonic era as Israel's day of glory is not fiction. Solomon and his achievements were real. This does not prove that the man himself wrote Song of Songs, but the idea cannot be dismissed as a postexilic fantasy—or as the dogged fundamentalism of a few conservatives.

Some scholars reject Solomonic authorship of the Song for internal reasons. Murphy (3) states, "this traditional claim of Solomonic authorship finds little support in the work itself. Solomon is nowhere designated among the speakers, who are rather anonymous individuals." This argument implies that a poet should always give himself a prominent role as a speaker in his poems, and even explicitly name himself in such a role. Note that the name of Solomon does appear five other times in the book (Song 1:5; 3:7, 11; 8:11, 12).

Longman (5–7) repeats Murphy's argument and adds two others: that Solomon was morally unfit to have written Song of Songs (after all, Solomon had an enormous number of women, and many of these were foreign women who enticed the king and his kingdom into apostasy) and that the superscript to the Song is like the one attached to Proverbs (Prov 1:1), a book that explicitly has various subdivisions and multiple authors (e.g., Prov 30:1; 31:1).

Against the notion of moral unfitness, one should realize that an enormous amount of great literature on love and even on virtue, including both poetry and philosophical or theological texts, was written by people whose personal lives did not fully reflect the high ideals that their words expressed. Virtuous lives and virtuous words do not always go hand in hand. Solomon was, by the biblical account, a complex man. Like his father, he was said to be wise and pious, but also prone to lechery. He was devoted to Israel, but he was also a major figure in the international discourse of his age and was willing to indulge the religious desires of his foreign wives (see 1 Kgs 4:29–34; 8:1–66; 10:1–10; 11:1–8). Beyond that, we are told virtually nothing of Solomon the man. We are in no position to describe his inner ruminations, reflections, or regrets, and we have no basis for describing his mental state or attitudes at various stages of his life (that is, unless Ecclesiastes is admitted as evidence in this regard). We cannot say that "a man like Solomon" could not have written Song of Songs because we do not know what Solomon was like. We are told in the Bible that he was very fond of writing songs (1 Kgs 4:32). The argument from the superscript is that since Proverbs is ascribed to Solomon but is in fact a diverse work, so also the heading to Song of Songs does not necessarily mean that it is a unified work of Solomon alone. One can grant that a superscript is not certain proof of unity and of authorship by a single writer. At the same time, Song of Songs and Proverbs are two entirely different books. Proverbs tells us that it has a long "redaction history" (e.g., Prov 25:1); it also has marked divisions and subdivisions (e.g., Prov 22:17–19, 20–21) and texts stated to have been written by other people (Prov 30; 31). Song of Songs is a single block of text. The Song has no dividers like Prov 25:1 at all, and certainly no internal indications of multiple authorship. We can only speak of it as having multiple authors if there is specific evidence to that effect. Song 1:1 is more like Prov 30:1 or Ps 8:1 than it is like Prov 1:1–7, a complex heading to a complex book. In summary, the only internal indication we have concerning the provenance of Song of Songs is at 1:1, which states that it is "of Solomon." If we can prove that in reality the Song has a complex redaction history and that it includes individual songs written by different poets, well and good, but we cannot claim that the superscript somehow suggests this conclusion.

Thus, the evidence tells us that Song of Songs was written in Solomon's time and at his court. Whether it was written "by Solomon" or "for Solomon" by a court poet, we can never know, and any attempt to discern the circumstances surrounding the composition of the Song is of necessity speculative. V. Sasson (*VT* 39 [1989] 407–14) suggests that the woman of the Song is Pharaoh's daughter, whom Solomon married (1 Kgs 3:1), but this is mere guesswork. On linguistic grounds, Young's suggestion that the Song was by a northern poet residing in Solomon's court could be correct.

The Structure and Unity of Song of Songs

Bibliography

Dorsey, D. A. "Literary Structuring in the Song of Songs." *JSOT* 46 (1990) 81–96. **Elliot, M. T.** *Literary Unity of the Canticle.* **Exum, J. C.** "A Literary and Structural Analysis of the Song of Songs." *ZAW* 85 (1973) 47–79. **Fox, M. V.** *Song of Songs and the Ancient Egyptian Love Songs.* **Grober, S. F.** "The Hospital Lotus: A Cluster of Metaphors. An Inquiry into the Problem of Textual Unity in the Song of Songs." *Semitics* 9 (1984) 86–112. **Murphy, R. E.** "Cant 2:8–17—A Unified Poem?" In *Mélanges bibliques et orientaux en l'honneur de M. Mathias Delcor.* Ed. A. Caquot. Neukirchen-Vluyn: Neukirchener Verlag, 1985. 305–10. ———. "The Unity of the Song of Songs." *VT* 29 (1979) 436–43. **Shea, W. H.** "The Chiastic Structure of the Song of Songs." *ZAW* 92 (1980) 378–96. **Webster, E. C.** "Pattern in the Song of Songs." *JSOT* 22 (1982) 73–93.

The Song of Songs, on a surface reading, is a chaos of non sequiturs and unrelated poems juxtaposed in the space of eight chapters. The chapter divisions are meaningless. The *sethuma* (ס as a paragraph marker) appears at various points in the Song (and there is one *petucha* [פ] at Song 8:10), usually at obvious breaks in the text, but this is no help in determining any guiding plan for the book. Every introduction to the Song says something about the structure of the book, even if it is only that the Song is a random collection of love poems and has no discernible structure (Keel, *Song of Songs*, 17; Pope, 40–54). Most scholars provide an outline that describes how they believe the structure of the Song works, but a large number of these have little justification or evidence to support them and appear to be no more than impressionistic analyses. Even among those who believe that the text is just an anthology of love songs, there is no agreement about how many songs there are. On Keel's analysis (*Song of Songs*, 18), there are forty-two individual poems in the Song. Murphy (65–67) has nine divisions in the Song. Longman (viii) says that there are twenty-three poems, and Goulder (*Song of Fourteen Songs*) says that there are fourteen poems. The placement of the paragraph markers in the MT suggests that there are nineteen poems. Pope refuses to divide the work into individual poems at all and simply comments on each verse in sequence. The average reader has no reason to prefer one analysis above another.

In the discussion that follows, I will endeavor to establish three points, although not necessarily in the following order. First, although a collection of songs, the Song of Songs is a single piece with a unified structure based on an arrangement of thirteen poems. Second, there are analogies for this kind of opus that may help us to appreciate the nature of Song of Songs. Third, the Song is the work of a single poet.

A Plurality of Songs in Song of Songs

The diversity of the material of Song of Songs suggests that it is exactly what its name implies: a song of many songs. The name may be a kind of double entendre: it is the finest of Solomon's songs (in the superlative sense of "song of songs"), and it is also a single musical work composed of many songs. The Song of Songs is a composition of many individual songs that have been fashioned to work together as a unified opus that is the finest of songs.

Individual songs may be recognized in a preliminary fashion by unity of subject matter as well as by structural unity. For example, Song 1:5–6 has the following song:

> I am dark yet lovely,
> O daughters of Jerusalem,
> like the tents of Kedar, like the curtains of Solomon.
> Do not stare at me, that I am swarthy
> and that the sun has gazed upon me.
> It was my mother's sons! They burned with anger toward me.
> They forced me to be a keeper of the vineyards,
> while my vineyard—the one that was mine—I could not keep.

Nothing before or after this song concerns the woman's skin color or her relationship with her brothers. It is a self-contained unit in the Song and is made up of two strophes making a total of eight lines (see *Form/Structure/Setting* for Song 1:5–6). This does not mean that any macrostructural function for this text is impossible, but it does mean that it, in some sense, can stand alone.

If the Song of Songs is composed of individual poems, then it is either an anthology of love songs or a series of individual songs that are set within the structure of a unified book. The former suggests that Song of Songs is simply a collection of various songs by one or several poets and that it has no controlling structure, theme, or coherence beyond the general topic of male-female love. The latter requires a single poet or editor and suggests that all the songs are woven into a single opus.

Thus, there are actually three issues one must reckon with here. First, is the Song simply a disparate collection of love poetry, or does it have some kind of literary unity and coherence? Second, if it is a unity, does it have a governing macrostructure? Third, is Song of Songs by one poet or many poets? Although one could regard the issue of authorship and the issue of structure to be unrelated, the question of how many poets are behind the Song inevitably comes up in discussions of its unity or lack thereof.

Trying to answer these three questions, one can easily mix and match options. The Song could have no unity whatsoever and be a loose collection of works by various poets (Gordis, 16–18; White, *Study of the Language*, 163). Or, it could be an anthology of poems with thematic unity and some interrelated texts but minimal structure. Murphy (64–67) sees a loose arrangement of the Song into sequential sections based on the concept of dialogue but leaves the question of authorship open; Gledhill (*Message of the Song*, 37–39) argues that it has a meandering style but is arranged in six "cycles"; Longman (55) says there are "centripetal and centrifugal" forces in the Song but no macrostructure. On this view, the book is more or less an anthology that deals with the single theme of sexual love between a man and a woman. For many scholars, this suggests that it is by a multitude of poets but that some order and thematic unity have been imposed on it by a redactor (Longman, 55 n. 161; Keel, *Song of Songs*, 17). One could suggest that it is from one poet but is an anthology having basic thematic unity but lacking structure. Or, Song of Songs could be a collection by a single poet with thematic unity and governed by a larger structure. Someone might argue that it has both unity and structure but that the unified structure is redactional; this, I shall argue below, is most unlikely.

THE UNITY OF THE SONG

The Song of Songs has unity of style. Murphy does not insist that it is the work of a single poet, but he does stress that marks of unity are evident (see Murphy, *VT* 29 [1979] 436–43, and also his "Cant 2:8–17—A Unified Poem?" 310, where he urges that the Song cannot seriously be called "a mere anthology, a collection of disparate poems"). Fox (*Song of Songs*, 202–22) has demonstrated that the Song contains strong signs of unity. Various arguments against the unity of the Song (for example, that it has a variety of life-settings and geographical references, that it contains doublets, that the Egyptian songs support the anthology view) all fail (Fox, *Song of Songs*, 203–4). Regarding the geographical diversity of the Song, for example, Fox comments, "By the same argument we might say that the book of Jonah was written partly in Nineveh, partly in Jaffa, and partly at sea" (203). Fox further observes that the repetends, associative sequences, character portrayal, and narrative frame all suggest that the poem is a unity (209–18).

An associative sequence occurs when words or motifs appear in the same order even though context does not demand this order. A good example of this is Song 8:2–5 compared to 2:6–7 and 3:4b–6a. The common sequence found in all three texts indicates strong stylistic unity. A good example of narrative frame is 8:6–7, where the Song is by all appearances coming to a conclusion. These verses do not fit well anywhere else in the Song. The character portrayal of the Song is certainly unified. Most interpreters today agree that the Song has three identifiable singing parts—a male solo, a female solo, and a female chorus. Each part is consistent through all of Song of Songs. One never gets the sense that the female solo in one song and the female solo in another song are two different people. Even commentaries that take the anthology view routinely speak of "the woman" of the Song as a single character who appears throughout the collection.

M. T. Elliot (*Literary Unity*) argues that the following markers indicate the unity of the Song. (This is a sample of the evidence she has amassed in order to illustrate the points she makes; I add a few comments of my own after page citations.)

1. The setting of the Song, throughout the book, is springtime. One can compare Song 2:10–13 to 7:12–14 (ET 7:11–13) to see this perspective at either end of the book (*Literary Unity*, 237).
2. The focus of the Song is on the woman throughout (*Literary Unity*, 237–38). This is not always the case in ancient Near Eastern love poetry.
3. The theme of the Song is love (אהבה) throughout (*Literary Unity*, 240). This may seem a trite observation, but the fact that it is obvious does not make it unimportant. If one amasses all the Egyptian "love" poetry, one discovers a variety of themes. The Nakhtsobek Songs are really about a moral fall and an obsession, not love in the sense that the term is used in the Song.
4. Dialogue is a stylistic device. Throughout all of the Song, the words come from the individuals within the Song and not from an external, third-person narrator-poet (*Literary Unity*, 240).
5. Similar images and motifs occur throughout the Song. For example, there are the kiss (Song 1:2; 4:10; 8:1), fragrance (Song 1:3, 12–14; 2:13; 3:6; 4:6; 4:10–5:1), and the lily or lotus (Song 2:1–2, 16; 4:5; 5:13; 7:3). When the distribution of all the images is charted out (as Elliot has done), a compelling case for the unity of the text emerges (*Literary Unity*, 241–46).
6. A "mirroring dynamic" is employed throughout the Song, in which some quality is attributed first to one lover and then to the other (*Literary Unity*, 246–51). For example, eyes are like doves in Song 1:15 (of woman) and 5:12 (of man), and love is better than wine or fragrances in Song 1:2 (of man) and 4:10 (of woman).
7. Language about the woman frequently employs an enclosure technique when viewed across the whole Song. For example, in Song 1:4 the woman is taken to the chamber (חדר) of her beloved and in 2:4 she is taken to the house (בית) of wine, but in 3:4 and 8:2 she wants to take her beloved to the חדר and בית of her mother (*Literary Unity*, 251–52).
8. Characterization is consistent throughout the Song (*Literary Unity*, 252–53).
9. The same epithets are used by and for the lovers throughout the Song. Examples are דודי, "my love," as a sobriquet for the man and רעיתי, "my companion," as a sobriquet for the woman. See *Literary Unity*, 253–56, for a complete survey of the usage and distribution of these epithets.
10. Like Fox, Elliot sees associative sequences in the Song. Examples are seen in comparing Song 1:15 to 4:1 and 2:16–17 to 4:5–6 (*Literary Unity*, 256–58).
11. Finally, Elliot suggests that the repeated lines at Song 2:6 and 8:3 and at 2:7; 3:5; and 8:4 have a macrostructural function (*Literary Unity*, 258–60).

Although one might differ at this or that point, the evidence Elliot presents is massive and objectively verifiable to prove her conclusion: "A poetic analysis of the text of the Canticle disclosed eleven major elements of style which pervade the work, unify it, and strongly argue in favor of a single poet" (*Literary Unity*, 260).

S. Grober (*Semitics* 9 [1984] 86–112), moreover, has shown that the metaphor of the lotus/lily (שושנה) functions coherently through the Song. His analysis, like

Fox's and Elliot's, suggests that images and metaphors in the Song are consistent, that the text has a circular modality, and that there are "confluences of images . . . in which the same elements re-appear," leading to the conclusion that this is "a unified text, the work of a single poet" (*Semitics* 9 [1984] 108).

The notion that these are poems by different poets randomly brought together with no thematic unity whatsoever can be substantiated only if one can point out significant stylistic incompatibilities in the Song. Fox (*Song of Songs*, 205) gives a list of signs of disunity one might expect to find in such a text. Tested by these standards, the Song of Songs is a unified piece.

A REDACTED COLLECTION BY MULTIPLE POETS?

Biblical scholars speak of multiple authors and of redactors even where there is no reason at all to think that a work is the product of more than one mind. The idea that poems of disparate poets have been redacted into a loosely unified work is especially arbitrary for Song of Songs. Poets write in a distinctive idiom. It is gratuitous to suggest that the Song of Songs has many poets behind it who all happened to write the same kind of material using the same language and metaphors. A redactor is equally unlikely. Why would the redactor take many different poems and rewrite them in the same style? Would that not make him a poet who borrowed ideas from earlier poets? The Song is not a massive work; it is not inconceivable that one person could have written it all. No one has demonstrated that any single poem has a style or vocabulary that sets it apart from the rest of the book. Keel (*Song of Songs*, 17) suggests that repetition in the Psalter and in Proverbs shows that poets could borrow from each other. That point is a given for the ancient world, but the analogy is misleading. Proverbs is a collection of individual sayings, and some repetition among the sayings is to be expected. But it does not follow that the repetition itself is an indicator of plurality of authors; otherwise, a single author could never repeat himself! The Psalter is a collection of individual songs that are by different poets composing songs in diverse periods of their lives and in different eras in the history of Israel. Some psalms are very similar, and some are very dissimilar. But the Song of Songs is a unified book. Neither style nor content gives reason to posit multiple authorship. In comparison to the Psalms, where repetition is a matter of stock metaphors and formulaic expressions (or full-scale borrowing), the repetends and associative sequences in the Song are different. In the Song, the repetends are refrains; this is not the case in the Psalter. The Psalter is a *collection* of songs and not a unified *Song* of Songs.

Fox (*Song of Songs*, 222–24) suggests that the Song underwent *Zersingen* prior to entering the canon in its present form. This is a process whereby an original poet composes a piece and subsequent generations of poets or troubadours repeat the work through the years, modifying its order, wording, and so forth. Fox admits that we cannot know if this happened in the case of Song of Songs; the versions closely follow the MT and do not attest to such a process. The theory is not like conventional redaction theories; it presupposes an original author but also suggests that what we now have is the version of some other single poet or singer. As such, this approach is purely hypothetical and has no heuristic value.

A Unified Anthology but without Structure?

Some scholars argue that the Song of Songs has some kind of literary unity but little or no structure (e.g., Longman, 55–56). Arguments against a macrostructure for the Song are naturally negative in nature: they assert that no argument in favor of a macrostructure works and that the various proposed macrostructures do not agree with each other and therefore cancel each other out. Saying that there is no macrostructure is a bit like cutting the Gordian knot; it does not solve anything but only claims that the search for structure in the Song is futile. One is left with a book with some thematic cohesion and linguistic unity but no structure.

But this view does have problems of its own. Scholars who call the Song an anthology generally do so without bothering to compare the Song to real anthologies, which are not at all like Song of Songs. The Greek Anthology was created by Meleager (first century B.C.E.), who collected the epigrams of some fifty poets into his *Stephanos*, or garland of flowers. An anthology is thus also called a *florilegium*, or flower collection. Poetic anthologies have remained popular through the centuries. In classical texts, we have collections of odes (Pindar, Ovid). We also have sonnet collections (such as Shakespeare's sonnets). More recently, we have many publications of anthologies by one or many poets. Most anthologies are random collections with neither unity nor structure, although there are collections of poems by a single poet that are formally the same (Shakespeare's sonnets) or follow a common theme (*Spoon River Anthology* by Edgar Lee Masters). Even when the poems in an anthology are of the same genre, such as a collection of nineteenth-century African-American spirituals or the poetry of the "beat" generation, one sees a much wider variety of styles, of types of metaphor, of subject matter, and of themes than one sees in the Song of Songs.

Papyrus Harris 500 is a true anthology of Egyptian love songs; the three groups of songs do not relate to one another in any way except that they are all in the same genre. Taken together, they have neither unity nor structure but do have a common subject matter and a common poetic trope (that either the male or the female sings of his or her love for the other). There is no reason to suppose, for example, that all these songs concern one couple (cf. Fox, *Song of Songs*, 16). These songs have no closure, unity of character, or associative sequence. By contrast, the Song has strong unity of character portrayal, closure, coherence, and associative sequences. In short, if one actually compares Song of Songs to real anthologies, the differences between the Song and the anthologies are obvious and significant.

This commentary will argue that there is a macrostructure. I contend that Song of Songs is a chiasmus and that the Song has 4:16–5:1 as its center or pivot point. At that text, the consummation of the wedding of the man and woman, their first sexual union, occurs.

A Chiastic Structure for Song of Songs

Several scholars have suggested that the Song is chiastic. Exum (*ZAW* 85 [1973] 47–79) argued for a chiastic structure that many reviewers appreciated but that few fully accepted. Less successful were the chiastic structures suggested by Shea (*ZAW* 92 [1980] 378–96) and Webster (*JSOT* 22 [1982] 73–93). Both scholars discovered chiastic elements, but both attempts broke down on careful examination. I published a chiastic analysis of the Song suggested by the late R. Alden (Garrett, 376). Alden's analysis does a good job of showing that many words and phrases are distributed in the Song in a chiastic manner, but he does not demonstrate a full chiastic structure for the book. There are a number of gaps in his analysis, and he focuses on individual words rather than on poems or stanzas. D. Dorsey (*JSOT* 46 [1990] 81–96) suggests that numerous elements in the Song are chiastically arranged, although a weak point in his presentation is that he has the five verses of Song 3:1–5 set in parallel to all of 5:2–7:11 (ET 7:10), with the bulk of the latter section having no parallel in the former section. Proposed chiastic structures have so far contradicted each other and break down at some point or other.

But on one point they agree. In Exum's analysis, Song 4:12–5:1, the garden metaphor, is the climax of the whole poem. This is hardly surprising since it is here that the man and woman consummate their relationship. Exum begins by suggesting that 2:7–3:5 parallels 5:2–6:3. In addition, she suggests that 3:6–5:1 parallels 6:4–8:3. Shea and Alden were even more explicit about this point, structuring their entire chiastic outlines around 4:16–5:1. Shea suggests that the chiastic units are 1:2–2:2 with 8:6–14; 2:3–17 with 7:11 (ET 7:10)–8:5; and 3:1–4:16 with 5:1–7:10. Alden's chiastic analysis is not built around complete texts but is based on repeated words and phrases. For example, Song 1:1–4a has "take me away," and 8:14 has "come away"; 1:5–7 and 8:10–12 both have "my own vineyard"; 3:1–5 and 5:2–9 both have "the watchmen found me." At the center of his chiasmus is "into his garden" at 4:16 and "into my garden" at 5:1a (Garrett, 376). Dorsey (*JSOT* 46 [1990] 94) also describes 4:16–5:1 as the "dramatic climax" of the Song. By my line count, there are four hundred lines of poetry in the Song, and 4:16 begins at line 200. Thus, although no proposed chiasmus "works" perfectly, it is worth noting that near the center of the poem a dramatic sexual union occurs between the man and the woman and that numerous elements are repeated on either side of the event in chiastic sequence.

Biblical scholars often have an overly mathematical notion of how a literary chiasmus works; that is, they demand perfect symmetry. Chiastic perfection is rare unless the text is quite small. Perhaps those who see chiastic structures are guilty of trying to make them perfect, with the result that they force the data. Reviewers, likewise, suggest that an entire proposal has been invalidated when something is shown to be asymmetrical. This is misguided. For example, I suggest that Jonah 2 is an asymmetrical chiastic poem (Garrett, *Modern Grammar,* 306–7). The asymmetry is present because the poet devotes extra lines to describing the drowning experience; this makes for a more dramatic poem, but the chiasmus is still functional. In the Song, evidence at many levels suggests that 4:16–5:1 is the center of the work. The Song repeats or loosely echoes many words, images, and lines, and much of this, though not all, is chiastically centered on 4:16–5:1. This asymmetry is not an imperfection; it points out the complexity and sophistication of the work. A poetic opus in which everything, from the individual poems, to the stanzas, to the images and individual words, functioned as part of one perfectly symmetrical chiasmus might be impressive to biblical scholars, but it would be poor poetry.

I suggest that the Song of Songs is a unified work with chiastic structure and is composed of thirteen individual songs, or *cantos,* for presentation by a male and a female soloist with a chorus. When referring to the parts of the Song, I speak of a "soprano" for the woman's part, a "tenor" for the man's part, and a "chorus" for the girls of Jerusalem. I find this more pleasing than "man" and "woman," but it also makes the point that these are parts in a song, not parts in a drama. Each canto is marked with roman numerals and has one or more *stanzas,* these being the major divisions of each canto. Thus, canto I (1:2–4) has three stanzas. I also divide each canto into *strophes.* The term *strophe* here is basically synonymous with the traditional term *verse,* but my strophes are not always the same length as the numbered verses of the MT. Thus, in the MT, Song 1:2–4 has three biblical *verses,* but on my reckoning it has seven *strophes.* Strophes are numbered consecutively with arabic numerals. Each strophe is also broken down into individual lines marked with uppercase roman letters; thus, "6B" in canto I is strophe 6, line B. Chapters and verses are designated in the traditional manner (e.g., 3:2). If I attempt to demonstrate some structural pattern in a strophe or stanza, in order to avoid confusion with other symbols I use Greek letters to demarcate the structure (see the discussion of Song 1:2–3, for an example). See figure 1 for a diagram of the chiastic structure of the thirteen cantos. This analysis shows repetition, allusion to prior texts, and sometimes contrast with prior texts in the paired songs.

```
        Superscript (1:1)
  A     I.    Chorus and soprano: the entrance (1:2–4)
  B       II.   Soprano: the virgin's education I (1:5–6)
  C         III.  Soprano and chorus: finding the beloved (1:7–8)
  D           IV.   Tenor, chorus, and soprano: the first song of mutual love (1:9–2:7)
  E             V.    Soprano and tenor: the invitation to depart (2:8–17)
  F               VI.   Three wedding-night songs (3:1–5; 3:6–11; 4:1–15)
  Fa                a. Soprano: the bride's anxiety (3:1–5)
  Fb                b. Chorus: the bride comes to the groom (3:6–11)
  Fc                c. Tenor: the flawless bride I (4:1–15)
  G                 VII.  Soprano, tenor, and chorus: the consummation (4:16–5:1)
  F´              VIII. Three wedding-night songs (5:2–16; 6:1–3; 6:4–10)
  Fa´               a. Soprano, tenor, and chorus: the bride's pain (5:2–8)
  Fb´               b. Chorus and soprano: the bride recovers the groom (5:9–6:3)
  Fc´               c. Tenor and chorus: the flawless bride II (6:4–10)
  E´            IX.   Soprano, chorus, and tenor: leaving girlhood behind (6:11–
                       7:1 [ET 6:13])
  D´          X.    Tenor and soprano: the second song of mutual love
                     (7:2 [ET 7:1]–8:4)
  C´        XI.   Chorus and soprano: claiming the beloved (8:5–7)
  B´      XII.  Chorus and soprano: the virgin's education II (8:8–12)
  A´    XIII. Tenor, chorus, and soprano: the farewell (8:13–14)
```
Fig. 1. Chiastic structure of Song of Songs

Canto I (1:2–4) focuses on and glorifies the man, while canto XIII (8:13–14) lauds the "lady who inhabits the garden." Canto I compares the man's love to wine and perfumes, while canto XIII compares the woman's breasts to "mountains of balsam." In Song 1:4, the woman sings, "Take me with you! Let us run!" and in 8:14 she says, "Hasten away, my lover!"

Both canto II (1:5–6) and canto XII (8:8–12) concern the question of the treatment of the "little sister" in the family. In canto II, the woman protests that she is dark because her brothers made her work under the sun, and in canto XII the chorus sings, "We have a sister, a little girl / (she has no breasts). / What shall we do for our sister / on the day that she is engaged?" In addition, in Song 1:6 she complains that she was forced to tend vineyards that were not hers, while in 8:12 she celebrates that although Solomon has his thousand, her own vineyard is hers to keep and tend.

Canto III (1:7–8) begins with the woman asking a series of questions and wanting to know where her lover is ("Where do you graze your flocks? / Where do you rest them at noon?"); the chorus answers her (see *Form/Structure/Setting* for 1:7–8), and they suggest that she must go out among the shepherds and find him. Canto XI (8:5–7) begins with the chorus asking about the woman, "Who is this / coming up from the wilderness, / leaning on her lover?" That is, their question in canto XI contrasts with hers in canto III, and the two songs together indicate that she has gone out and found her lover in the "wilderness" (8:5), "in the tracks of the flocks" (1:8). Also, at Song 1:7 the woman expresses concern about being around other men; she is ill at ease if not frightened about being around them. At Song 8:6 she sees herself as bound to her man: "Set me like a seal upon your heart, / like a seal upon your arm. / For love is strong, like death. / Jealousy is severe, like the grave." In both songs, the concern of the woman is that she and her lover exclusively belong to each other, but in canto III she is seeking him and uncomfortable around men, whereas in canto XI she is leaning on him and claims his exclusive devotion.

Canto IV (1:9–2:7) and canto X (7:2 [ET 7:1]–8:4) both have the man and woman fulsomely expressing their love and desire for each other. Canto IV begins with a declaration that the woman is a stunning beauty in all her jewelry (see *Form/Structure/Setting* for 1:9–2:7); Song 1:10 even adds that they (the chorus) will make more jewelry for her. Canto X begins with praise for the woman's apparently naked body, but it opens by stating, "The curves of your hips are like rings, / the work of an artist!" Thus, her "jewelry" in canto X is her body itself. The two songs conclude with two nearly identical strophes. First, the woman asserts that the man holds her in his arms: "His left hand is under my head / and his right hand embraces me" (2:6; 8:3). Second, the woman adjures the girls, "I call on you to swear, daughters of Jerusalem, / that you will not arouse or awaken / the passions of love until they are ready" (8:4; the adjuration in 2:7 is slightly longer). Between these similar introductions and conclusions, both songs have the man and woman exchanging words of love. For example, in Song 2:3 the woman sings, "Like an apple tree among the trees of the woods, / so is my lover among the young men. / In his shade I take pleasure and sit, / and his fruit is sweet in my mouth." In Song 7:8–9 (ET 7:7–8), the man sings, "This is what your full physique is like: a palm tree. / And your breasts are its clusters. / I said, 'I will climb the palm tree, / I will hold its panicles of dates, / that your breasts may be like the clusters of grapes / and the fragrance of your nipple like apples.'" The two songs do not use the same metaphors throughout, and there are differences between them, but both essentially focus on mutual love.

Canto V (2:8–17) and canto IX (6:11–7:1 [ET 6:13]) both have as their central theme the departure of the woman from the life of the single girl at home. Canto V begins with the woman proclaiming the arrival of her man, who is like a gazelle bounding across the hills. The man then calls on her to come away with him from her domestic world; his invitation focuses on the arrival of spring

(2:12–13): "The flowers appear in the land, / the time of pruning arrives, / the sound of the dove is heard in our land! / The fig tree ripens its figs, / and the vines from blossoms give their fragrance." Canto IX opens with the woman singing (6:11–12), "I came down to the nut grove / to see the young plants by the river, / to see if the vines were budding, / the pomegranates blooming." The heart of canto V is Song 2:13b: "Arise! Come, my companion, my beautiful one! / Come along!" The dramatic outcry of canto IX is Song 7:1 (ET 6:13): "Come back, come back, O Shulammite! / Come back, come back, that we may gaze on you!" In addition, the difficult Hebrew of Song 6:12 also seems to allude to the departure of the woman. I have rendered it, "I do not know my own soul, / It has set me among the chariots of Ammi-nadiv!" (see *Comment* on 6:12). Thus, in canto V the man calls her to come away with him, and in canto IX the girls wish she would come back.

Canto VIa (3:1–5) and canto VIIIa (5:2–8) are the most obviously related pieces in Song of Songs. Both describe surreal accounts of the woman seeking her beloved in the streets. Song 3:2b–3 reads, "'I will seek whom my soul loves.' / I seek him and do not find him. / The guards find me, / those who go about in the city. / 'Have you seen whom my soul loves?'" Song 5:7 reads, "The guards that go about the city find me. / They beat me, they wound me, / they take my veil from me, / the guardians of the walls." Canto VIa, this commentary suggests, concerns the bride's anxiety about her wedding night; canto VIIIa describes her actual suffering on her wedding night.

Canto VIb (3:6–11) and canto VIIIb (5:9–6:3) relate to one another in a way that is not obvious on a superficial reading. Canto VIb begins with a question from the chorus ("Who is this / coming up from the wilderness?" [3:6]); canto VIIIb is in two parts, but each beginning with a question from the chorus ("What makes your lover better than other lovers, / most beautiful of women?" [5:9] and "Where has your lover gone, / most beautiful of women?" [6:1]). Canto VIb is a wedding procession; the bride is brought to the groom in his palanquin with his honor guard. The palanquin is described in luxuriant but awesome terms. Among other things, it is surrounded by sixty warriors (3:7); it is made of "the wood of Lebanon" (3:9); it has "pillars of silver," and "its canopy" is a "framework of gold" (3:10). It is important to realize that although the bride is being brought in the palanquin (see *Explanation* for 3:6–11), the palanquin itself is a projection of the power and glory of the man—it is the palanquin of "Solomon" (3:9). Canto VIIIb describes the man himself (apparently naked), but his body has all the glory of the palanquin, and more. To say nothing of sixty warriors, the man himself is "outstanding among ten thousand" (5:10); his head, arms, and legs are gold (5:11, 14, 15); he is like the cedars of Lebanon (5:15). In their exuberance, the girls had proclaimed the palanquin to be "love" itself (3:10; see *Comment* on v 10). By contrast, the woman proclaims, "Every part of him is desirable! / This is my lover, this is my companion, / O daughters of Jerusalem!" (5:16). In addition, canto VIb sings of the meeting of the bride and groom in the wedding ceremony; canto VIIIb sings of their metaphorical reunification. To understand this, one must recall that canto VIIIa had ended with the woman plaintively singing, "I call upon you to swear, daughters of Jerusalem, / if you find my lover, / what should you say to him? / That I am wounded by love" (5:8). But in VIIIb, the couple is reunited: when the chorus asks where her lover is, she responds, "My lover went down to his garden / to beds of balsam, / to graze in his gardens / and to gather lotuses. / I am my lover's and my lover is mine; / he who grazes among the lotuses" (6:2–3). That is, he is with her. In short, canto VIb describes the ceremonial union of the man and woman whereas VIIIb describes the end of all that separates them.

Canto VIIIc (6:4–10) is an abbreviated version of canto VIc (4:1–15). Each is a *wasf* (from Arabic, a song of admiration or of praise for the beloved), and they have a number of lines in common. Canto VIc begins, "How beautiful you are, my companion, / how beautiful you are!" (4:1), and canto VIIIc begins, "You are beautiful, my companion, like Tirzah, / lovely, like Jerusalem" (6:4). The two songs have several lines that are almost verbatim equivalents: "Your hair is like the flock of goats / skipping from Mount Gilead" (4:1; 6:5), "Your teeth are like a shorn flock / that comes up from washing / in which every one has a twin" (4:2; 6:5), and "Your cheek is like a split pomegranate behind your veil" (4:3; 6:7). Of course, there are differences in the metaphors employed, but the similarity between the two is so great that it needs little demonstration.

Canto VII (4:16–5:1) is the centerpiece of the chiasmus and describes the sexual union of bride and groom on their wedding night. It is an appropriately balanced set of twelve lines, with strophes of four lines, two lines, four again, and two again (see *Form/Structure/Setting* for 4:16–5:1).

This is not to claim that there are no interrelated passages that do not follow this chiasmus. However, many passages revolve around the central pivot at Song 4:16–5:1. For example, at 2:16 (canto V) the woman sings, "My lover is mine and I am his, / he who grazes among the lotuses," and at 6:3 (canto VIIIb) she sings, "I am my lover's and my lover is mine, / he who grazes among the lotuses." In the first occurrence, she is accepting his invitation to come away and accept his love. In the second instance, she is recovering him and his love. The events of their first union (see *Comment* on 6:3) are what lie behind her need to recover him. The fact that these parallels do not fall within the structure I suggest does not invalidate the structure; it only shows that the elements that bind the Song of Songs together are numerous and complex. This commentary argues that the Song develops a dramatic transformation of the bride; many texts throughout the Song, not only those in a chiastic pattern, describe or suggest that transformation.

The Poetic Devices of the Song

Bibliography

Black, F. C. "Unlikely Bedfellows: Allegorical and Feminist Readings of Song of Songs 7.1–8." In *The Song of Songs*. FCB 2d ser. 6. Ed. C. R. Fontaine and A. Brenner. Sheffield: Sheffield Academic Press, 2000. 104–29. **Brenner, A.** "'Come Back, Come Back the Shulammite' (Song of Songs 7:1–10): A Parody of the *wasf* Genre." In *A Feminist Companion to the Song of Songs*. FCB 1. Ed. A. Brenner. Sheffield: Sheffield Academic Press, 1993. 234–57. **Davis, E. F.** "Romance of the Land in the Song of Songs." *AThR* 80 (1998) 533–46. **Falk, M.** "The *Wasf*." In *The Song of Songs*. Ed. H. Bloom. New York: Chelsea House, 1988. 67–78. **Good, E. M.** "Ezekiel's Ship: Some Extended Metaphors in the Old Testament." *Semitics* 1 (1970) 79–103. **Meyers, C.** "Gender Imagery in the Song of Songs." *HAR* 10 (1986) 209–23. **Murphy, R. E.** "Dance and Death in the Song of Songs." In *Love*

& Death in the Ancient Near East. FS M. H. Pope, ed. J. H. Marks and R. M. Good. Guilford, CT: Four Quarters, 1987. 117–19. **Soulen, R. N.** "The *Waṣfs* of the Song of Songs and Hermeneutic." *JBL* 86 (1967) 183–90. **Vendler, H.** *Poems, Poets, Poetry.* Boston: St. Martin's, 1997. **Watson, W. G. E.** "Some Ancient Near Eastern Parallels to the Song of Songs." In *Words Remembered, Texts Renewed.* FS J. F. A. Sawyer, ed. by J. Davies, G. Harvey, and W. G. E. Watson. Sheffield: Sheffield Academic Press, 1995. 253–71.**Whedbee, J. W.** "Paradox and Parody in the Song of Solomon: Towards a Comic Reading of the Most Sublime Song." In *A Feminist Companion to the Song of Songs.* FCB 1. Ed. A. Brenner. Sheffield: Sheffield Academic Press, 1993. 266–78.

Speech-Acts and Motifs

One might rightly regard the term *waṣf* (a song of admiration or of praise for the beloved) as a legitimate formal label for texts such as Song 4:1–15 or 5:10–16, but most so-called forms in the Song are more properly described as "speech-acts." A speech-act is a classification of words in a poetic text according to their manner of expression (Vendler, *Poems,* 108). Examples of such speech-acts are as follows:

Adjuring (2:7; 5:8; 8:4)
Admiration, or *waṣf* (1:2b–3a; 4:1–15; 5:10–16; 6:4–9)
Announcement of arrival (2:8; 3:6; 6:10; 8:5a)
Boast (1:5; 8:12)
Claim (2:1, 16; 6:3)
Command (8:6a)
Conceit (1:9–11, 12–14)
Description (3:7–10)
Exclamation (4:1a)
Exhortation (1:4a; 2:15; 3:11; 7:12–13 [ET 11–12])
First-person narrative (1:6b; 3:1–5; 5:2–7)
Instruction (1:8; 8:6b–7)
Invitation to love (2:14, 17; 8:14)
Plea (2:14b; 5:2; 7:1 [ET 6:13])
Prohibition (1:6b)
Question (1:7; 5:9; 6:1)
Resolution (3:4b; 4:6; 7:9 [ET 7:8])
Yearning (3:1; 8:1–2)

In addition to the speech-acts, there are a number of motifs in Song of Songs. Many of these motifs are found in the Egyptian poetry and in other love poetry of the ancient or modern world. However, the placement, employment, and significance of these motifs in the Song of Songs are sometimes unparalleled. Examples of motifs are as follows:

The male lover is portrayed as king (1:12), shepherd (1:7), brother (8:1), gardener (6:2), prince (6:12), gazelle (2:9), and tree (2:3). The female lover is a vinedresser (1:6), shepherdess (1:8), heroine on a quest (3:1–2), semidivine figure (4:8), flower (2:1), garden (4:12), and city (6:4). By analogy, the girl in the Papyrus Harris group B songs takes on the role of the bird-catcher. One sometimes hears the "human" parts played by the lovers (king, shepherd, vinedresser) called a "travesty," but that term implies a more elaborate, costumed piece of role playing than we have in Song of Songs. One could distinguish the human roles for the characters from the nonhuman images for them by describing the former as personae and the latter as symbolic metaphors (e.g., that the male lover is a gazelle). *All* of these are metaphors, but it is helpful to distinguish the personae the lovers take on from the nonhuman metaphors that the Song uses to bring out different facets of the male and female lovers.

Another motif of the Song is that of being sick or wounded by love (2:5; 5:8). This is a frequent motif in the Egyptian songs, but the lovesickness of the Egyptian songs is the adolescent pining of a boy for a girl or a girl for a boy. The wounding or trauma of the Song concerns the woman's experience, and it is of a much more profound and mysterious nature than is found in the Egyptian texts.

A third motif is that of the man excluded by the door to the woman's house (the *paraklausithyron*). This motif occurs in Song 5:2–8 and, in various forms, in all kinds of treatments of love (Ovid, *Amores* 1.6; Lucretius, *De rerum natura* 4). The most significant parallel to the Song of Songs text is in the Egyptian Papyrus Chester Beatty group C text. The use of a similar motif does not imply similar meaning. In the Egyptian texts, the excluded lover is a man at the house of a prostitute. In Lucretius, the excluded lover illustrates the power of passion in the context of an exposition of Epicurean philosophy and is a condemnation of irrational sexual passion. The use of the motif in the Song is entirely different and is more complex than either of these.

Another motif is that of entrapment, in which one lover complains playfully that the other has captured him or her. In Song 7:6 (ET 7:5), the man says that he is caught in the hair of the woman. Chester Beatty I group C has a similar image, and Papyrus Harris 500 describes a girl as caught by her lover. There are also various minor motifs that often appear in ancient love poetry, such as the fragrance of the beloved, the sweetness of the beloved's lips, and the color of the beloved's skin (see also Watson, "Some Ancient Near Eastern Parallels," 258–63).

A curious motif is the authority figure in the Song in contrast to that in the Egyptian poetry. In the Egyptian poetry, a girl's mother often stands between the two lovers. In the Song, the only authority figure is the brothers, who really have nothing to do with the two lovers but are only represented as having forced the woman to tend the family vineyard (1:6). The governance of the younger sister comes up at Song 8:8–9, but the authority figure is anonymous and a forced separation of lovers is not described. The mother of the woman or occasionally of the man is mentioned several times, but neither mother causes separation between the lovers or does anything at all.

A motif that has no parallel at all in the Song of Songs is the frequent prayer for success in love encountered in the Egyptian and other ancient love poetry. In the Egyptian texts, a boy or girl often asks Hathor (or another god) to cause the object of his or her affection to reciprocate, or to cause the authority figure to yield and allow the two to come together. This never happens in Song of Songs.

METAPHORS OF SONG OF SONGS

Song of Songs contains some seemingly outrageous metaphors and similes. This is how the man praises the woman in Song 4:1–5.

> Your eyes are doves behind your veil.
> Your hair is like the flock of goats
> skipping from Mount Gilead.
> Your teeth are like a shorn flock
> that comes up from washing
> in which every one has a twin:
> not one among them is bereft of its partner.
> Your lips are like scarlet thread,
> and your speech is lovely.
> Your cheek is like a split pomegranate behind your veil.
> Your neck is like the tower of David,
> built in courses.
> A thousand shields hang upon it,
> all of them the armaments of warriors.
> Your breasts are like two fawns,
> twins of a gazelle, that feed among the lotuses.

In Song 7:5 (ET 7:4), he tells her that her nose is like the tower of Lebanon.

What is one to make of this? There are several ways one could understand it. (1) One might suggest that the poetry is ironic or, to use a favorite word of contemporary critics, that the poet is "subverting" the genre of love poetry (thus Whedbee, "Paradox and Parody," 266–78). I see no reason to imagine that this is the case. To the contrary, one never suspects that the poet is winking at the audience or playing a game behind their backs. A. Brenner attempts to read the *waṣfs* as a comic parody ("Come Back," 234–57), but the resultant interpretation is a failure. She argues that Song 7:1–10 (ET 6:13–7:9) describes the dance of the "Shulammite," which in male eyes is seen to be both comical and erotic. The comedy, in her interpretation, includes the fact that the dancing girl is fat (on her reading of 7:3 [ET 7:2]) and that "her breasts move fast, much like two frolicking fawns" (on the basis of 7:4 [ET 7:3]; "Come Back," 248). There is no reason to believe that the woman is dancing. To the contrary, "Why would you gaze on the Shulammite, / as on the Dance of the Two Companies?" suggests that the dancing is a hypothetical comparison. Murphy ("Dance and Death," 117–18) shows that the woman is not dancing in this text. Song 7:3 (ET 7:2) does *not* indicate that the woman is fat, and 7:4 does *not* indicate that her breasts are bouncing about (cf. 4:5). Brenner also cites Shakespeare's Sonnet 130 to illustrate her point, but this, too, does not work. In the Shakespearean sonnet, conventions of love-language are being turned on their head, but in Song 7:1–10 we see no parody of conventional language. Also, although Shakespeare was a master of comedy, Sonnet 130 is manifestly not funny and obviously was not intended to be, and thus it does not exemplify the genre Brenner is proposing. A variation on this is to see the metaphors as grotesque—not praising their subjects at all but deliberately ridiculing them as monstrosities (F. Black, *BibInt* 8 [2000] 302–23; idem, "Unlikely Bedfellows," 104–29). Black argues that the male is ill at ease with the woman's body and her sexuality and so resorts to such language, and that the language generally represents a darker side of love and sexuality. Such a reading is driven by feminist ideology and has little to support it in the text.

(2) This love poetry, in which the woman is described in terms that might be considered "masculine" (e.g., military language, such as when her neck is de-

scribed as a tower in 4:4), demonstrates that in this arena, love, the woman is at least equal if not dominant (Meyers, *HAR* 10 [1986] 209–23; but see also a refutation of Meyers in F. Black, "Unlikely Bedfellows," 121–24). Would an ancient Israelite woman be flattered by being praised in masculine terms? If not, why is it used here? It is precisely at this point that "readings" of the Song as subversive and a feminist text are most obtuse. Such readings are so intent on finding political, social, and sexual criticism in the text that they forget what it actually is: love poetry. When a man tells his beloved of the power she holds over him, he is not deconstructing the social order. No lover (with any sense) praises his woman by suggesting that she is masculine.

(3) These harsh metaphors may have been culturally acceptable ways of describing physical beauty. However garish it seems to us, perhaps the ancient Israelites felt that describing a woman's nose as a tower and her hair as a flock of goats running down a mountain was entirely appropriate. There is some evidence in behalf of this view. In the Egyptian corpus, the woman describes herself as a field and says her boyfriend has scooped out the canal with his hand (Papyrus Harris 500 group C). On the other hand, one finds little material in the Egyptian or other ancient Near Eastern texts that has the kind of sustained extravagance one sees in the Song. (4) Another possibility is that this poetry does in some respects reflect an actual visual similarity between the metaphor and the thing it represents. A woman's nose may give symmetry to her face in the same way that a tower or mountain gives symmetry to a horizon. A cascade of dark hair down a woman's head and shoulders may actually resemble a flock of goats going down a hillside (thus M. Falk on the *wasf* in "The *Wasf*," 67–78; but Falk achieves her objective only via a fairly extreme paraphrase, so that "Your hair is like the flock of goats / skipping from Gilead" becomes "Your hair—as black as goats / winding down the slopes"). (5) Perhaps the speaker is describing his *feelings* more than he is the thing itself (Soulen, *JBL* 86 [1967] 183–90). When he looks at her neck, he is as awestruck as when he looks at the tower of David. (6) It may be that the extravagant metaphors are simply driven by the logic of the descriptive praise form, or *wasf*. As the speaker moves through the list of her body parts (and as she works through his), he is bound by the form to say something about each part. Therefore, the extravagant and peculiar metaphors are simply a function of the form. The descriptive praises in the Egyptian texts are considerably shorter than their biblical counterparts. (7) Finally, the metaphors may tell us that the real subject of the poem is not a woman but the land itself, and that the real message of the Song is God's love for Israel (thus E. Davis, *AThR* 80 [1998] 533–46). This last possibility, apart from leading back down the path of allegorism, is invalidated because many of the metaphors are not geographic and not distinctively Israelite (eyes like doves, arms like gold, a garden with saffron and cinnamon, etc.).

Possibilities 3 through 6 are not mutually exclusive. Each could be and probably is to a degree true. At the same time, there is something peculiar about this mode of description. It suggests that the thing described is larger than life or of great significance. Biblical apocalyptic literature uses language in a similar way. Compare words from Rev 1:13–16 to similes of Song 5:11–15: "In the middle of the lampstands was someone like a son of man. . . . His head and his hair were white like wool or like snow; and his eyes were like a flame of fire. His feet were like burnished bronze, when it glows in a furnace, and his voice was like the sound of many waters. In his right hand he held seven stars, and out of His mouth came a sharp double-edged sword; and his face was like the sun shining in its power" (my translation). And from the Song: "His head is pure gold. / His hair is like the spathe, / black as a raven. / His eyes are like doves / beside streams of water, / washed in milk, / sitting on basins filled with water. / . . . / His arms are rods of gold / set with the golden topaz. / . . . / His thighs are alabaster pillars / set on pedestals of pure gold."

Extravagant or unexpected metaphors also occur in prophetic speech, although they are generally not extended in the manner that we see in the Song (but see E. Good, *Semitics* 1 [1970] 79–103). For example, Jer 46:18 says of Nebuchadnezzar, "He will come like Tabor among the mountains, or like Carmel by the sea" (my translation). One might add to this list, although there are distinct differences, the visions of the world empires in Dan 7 as series of composite beasts, or God's chariot in Ezek 1, which is carried by composite beasts. There are examples of amazing imagery in apocalyptic and prophetic speech. The oversized visions force the reader to stop and reflect on what is being communicated.

The problem with the metaphors and similes of Song of Songs is that we expect to find love poetry of the sort one finds in romantic anthologies and greeting cards. Song of Songs is love poetry, but it is a distinctive kind of love poetry. It is not sentimental, and it is not here to allow us to "put our feelings into words," like Cyrano de Bergerac composing seductive words for Christian to recite to Roxanne. The metaphors of the Song express the affections of the lovers for one another, but they also express the meaning of love for the reader or audience. They draw us into reflection on the qualities of the man, the woman, and their love as an ideal archetype. The lovers in the Song appear to be larger than life because they are larger than life; they are idealizations.

This commentary will argue that Song of Songs is a unified work of individual songs that tell the story of the sexual coming of age and transformation of a young woman. The Song focuses on her marriage as a crucial life event, and it has a concentric structure that centers on her moment of sexual union with her husband. It uses a wide variety of surprising and powerful images that make the reading experience a surprising pleasure. Its language is both extravagant and compact. Appreciating the poetry, we may eventually find truth.

Excursus: Hebrew Poetry

Bibliography

Alter, R. *Art of Biblical Poetry.* **Berlin, A.** *The Dynamics of Biblical Parallelism.* Bloomington: Indiana UP, 1985. **Christensen, D. L.** "Narrative Poetics and the Interpretation of the Book of Jonah." In *Directions in Biblical Hebrew Poetry.* Ed. E. R. Follis. JSOTSup 40. Sheffield: Sheffield Academic Press, 1987. 29–48. **Collins, T.** *Line-Forms in Hebrew Poetry.* Rome: Biblical Institute Press, 1978. **Cross, F. M., Jr.,** and **D. N. Freedman.** *Studies in Ancient Yahwistic Poetry.* **Freedman, D. N.** *Pottery, Poetry, and Prophecy: Studies in Early Hebrew Poetry.* Winona Lake, IN: Eisenbrauns, 1980. **Gray, G. B.** *The Forms of Hebrew Poetry Considered with Special Reference to the Criticism and Interpretation of the Old Testament.* 1915. Reprint, New York: Ktav, 1972. **Haïk-Vantoura, S.** *The Music of the Bible Revealed: The Deciphering of a Thousand Year Old Notation.* Trans. D. Weber. 2d ed., rev.

Paris: Dessain et Tolra, 1987. **Holladay, W. L.** *"Hebrew Verse Structure* Revisited (I): Which Words 'Count'?" *JBL* 118 (1999) 19–32. ———. *"Hebrew Verse Structure* Revisited (II): Conjoint Cola, and Further Suggestions." *JBL* 118 (1999) 401–16. **Hoop, R. de.** "The Colometry of Hebrew Verse and the Masoretic Accents: Evaluation of a Recent Approach, Part I." *JNSL* 26.1 (2000) 47–73. ———. "Part II." *JNSL* 26.2 (2000) 65–100. **Hrushovski, B.** "Prosody, Hebrew." *EncJud* 13:1200–1202. **Jakobson, R.** "Grammatical Parallelism and Its Russian Facet." In *Roman Jakobson: Selected Writings III.* Ed. S. Rudy. The Hague: Mouton, 1981. 98–135. **Korpel, M. C. A.**, and **J. C. de Moor.** "Fundamentals of Ugaritic and Hebrew Poetry." In *The Structural Analysis of Biblical and Canaanite Poetry.* Ed. W. van der Meer and J. C. de Moor. JSOTSup 74. Sheffield: Sheffield Academic Press, 1988. **Kugel, J. L.** *The Idea of Biblical Poetry: Parallelism and Its History.* New Haven: Yale UP, 1981. **Lowth, R.** *Lectures on the Sacred Poetry of the Hebrews.* Trans. G. Gregory. Andover: Crocker & Brewster; New York: Leavitt, 1829. **O'Connor, M.** *The Contours of Biblical Hebrew Verse.* Winona Lake, IN: Eisenbrauns, 1997. ———. *Hebrew Verse Structure.* Winona Lake, IN: Eisenbrauns, 1980. **Pardee, D.** *Ugaritic and Hebrew Poetic Parallelism.* Leiden: Brill, 1988. **Price, J. D.** *The Syntax of Masoretic Accents in the Hebrew Bible.* Lewiston, NY: Mellen, 1990. **Schökel, L. A.** *A Manual of Hebrew Poetics.* Rome: Biblical Institute Press, 1988. **Sendrey, A.** *Music in Ancient Israel.* New York: Philosophical Library, 1969. **Stuart, D. K.** *Studies in Early Hebrew Meter.* Missoula, MT: Scholars Press, 1976. **Vance, D. R.** *The Question of Meter in Biblical Hebrew Poetry.* Lewiston, NY: Mellen, 2001. **Watson, W. G. E.** *Classical Hebrew Poetry.* JSOTSup 26. Sheffield: Sheffield Academic Press, 1984. ———. *Traditional Techniques in Classical Hebrew Verse.* **Williams, J. M.** *Style: Toward Clarity and Grace.* Chicago: Univ. of Chicago Press, 1990.

The easiest way to recognize poetry in the Hebrew Bible is when the text tells the reader it is a poem: "The Song [שִׁיר] of Songs that is Solomon's" (1:1) or "Then David chanted this lament [קִינָה] over Saul and Jonathan his son" (2 Sam 1:17 [my translation]). By implication, every psalm [מִזְמוֹר] is a poem.

Beyond that, it is often difficult to distinguish poetry from prose in the Hebrew Bible. The so-called poetic accents used in Psalms, Job, and Proverbs are of little use since they are not used in texts that clearly are poetic (such as the Song) but are used in texts that, by most people's understanding, are not poetic (Prov 10–29). The editors of the *Biblia Hebraica Stuttgartensia* have distinguished poetry from prose by laying out poetic texts with line breaks, but their conclusions are no more than the opinions of individual scholars and should not be given special consideration.

The study of biblical Hebrew poetry since the enlightenment has been dominated by two concepts: parallelism and meter. Modern awareness of parallelism in Hebrew poetry begins with Bishop Robert Lowth's discussion of it in his *De sacra poesi Hebraeorum* (*Concerning the Sacred Poetry of the Hebrews*) in 1753. For Lowth, parallelism was the "correspondence" of one line with another. He and generations of scholars who followed him essentially argued that the primary unit of the Hebrew poem was the two-line strophe (the bicolon) and that bicola came in three basic varieties: synonymous parallelism, antithetical parallelism, and synthetic parallelism. In synonymous parallelism, the second line more or less repeats the first line, as in Prov 2:11:

Discretion will watch over you;
understanding will guard you. (RSV)

In antithetical parallelism, the second line, using antonyms of certain words that are in the first line, creates a statement that corresponds to the first line as its complement, as in Prov 3:33:

> The LORD's curse is on the house of the wicked,
> but he blesses the abode of the righteous. (RSV)

In synthetic parallelism the correspondence of the two lines is artificial in that there is little or no true parallel present; even so, the bicolon structure mimics the pattern of true parallelism. An example is Prov 4:2:

> For I give you good teaching.
> Do not abandon my instruction! (my translation)

This analysis is overly simple and raises important questions. (E.g., is synonymous parallelism primarily semantic or syntactic?) Even so, it is the foundation of much of the research into Hebrew poetry that has been undertaken to the present day.

The quest to discover the meter of Hebrew poetry has a long and one might say tortured history. Even in antiquity scholars and writers were trying to describe or discover some kind of metrical pattern in Hebrew poetry that corresponded to the meter of Greek and Latin poetry. Since the nineteenth century, however, the quest for the meter of Hebrew poetry has primarily followed an accentual or stress system, in which the meter of a line of poetry is determined by the number of accents, or stresses, it contains. Early advocates of various versions of this system include Ernst Meier (1813–1866), Julius Ley (1822–1901), Karl Budde (1850–1935), and Eduard Sievers (1850–1932). Karl Budde was especially successful in persuading scholars that the Hebrew dirge or lamentation consisted of a 3:2 stress-meter pattern (that is, each bicolon consisted of a line with three stresses followed by a line with two stresses). Scholars who were convinced of the existence of this metrical pattern (called *qinah* meter) naturally drew the conclusion that an accentual metrical system was valid for Hebrew poetry.

The modern analysis of Hebrew poetry is much more complicated than simply looking for parallelism or for stress meter, and many scholars advocate systems that modify or outright reject the two models described above. Some seek to combine the two, and some have entirely different models. The situation is made even more complicated by the fact that scholars do not consistently employ terminology such as line, strophe, or verse when describing the basic elements of a Hebrew poem.

J. Kugel examines the history of the concept of parallelism in the Hebrew Bible, and he makes some provocative statements about its significance. He rejects Lowth's schema in favor of a more careful description of the subtleties and varieties of "seconding." He makes it clear that "seconding" does not mean "synonymous parallelism," stating: "From the beginning our whole presentation has been pitched against the notion that it is actual *paralleling* of any sort that is the point" (*Idea of Biblical Poetry*, 51, italics original). For Kugel, the second line basically adds something that may or may not echo the first line as in: "A is so, and what's more, B." Most significantly, he demonstrates that semantic parallelism occurs frequently in Hebrew prose and that it is by no means confined to poetry. He therefore suggests that the differences between poetry and prose are not sharply drawn. He does not deny the existence of poetry in the Hebrew Bible, but he regards it as significant that there is no word for "poetry" in biblical Hebrew (*Idea of Biblical Poetry*, 69) and states that to some degree the use of the term represents the imposition of an alien concept on the text.

Many scholars have reacted strongly against Kugel's blurring of the lines between poetry and prose and in particular have taken exception to the notion that it is significant that Hebrew lacks a word for poetry. Kugel's model seems to leave us in complete subjectivity with regard to the existence and nature of poetry in the Bible. But some of the reaction against his work is overstated. Kugel's analysis suggests that in Hebrew (as in English) there are degrees of difference from the simplest, most ordinary prose, to high rhetoric, and finally to poetry and song; this is surely correct. One might add that even in poetry there are gradations of how "poetic" a work is; I would suggest that Wisdom poetry (Prov 1–9) tends to be very simple, with an obvious structure and "parallelism," but that other poetry is much more lyrical and subtle (such as Song of Songs or Ps 23). Many poems fall between these two extremes. Still, I believe that scholars are correct to maintain a distinction between prose and poetry.

The term *poetry* as applied to biblical Hebrew is not an anachronism unless by *poetry* one means a nonprose text that is to be spoken and not sung, as is the case with modern English poetry. In the ancient world, by all indications, poetry was not read in a normal speaking voice. It was sung. That is, for the ancients, a poem was a song. Musical instruments are associated with ancient poetry (as is done in many psalm superscripts) precisely for that reason. And biblical Hebrew most certainly does have a word for "song" (שׁיר)! More than that, Hebrew has a great many terms for different kinds of songs (*qinah* ["lament"], *mizmor, maskil*, etc.).

The problem is that both Kugel and his critics share a fundamental assumption about Hebrew poetry; to cite Kugel's starting point again: "the basic feature of biblical songs . . . is the recurrent use of a relatively short sentence-form that consists of two brief clauses." That is, the basic feature of a song is the bicolon. This starting point flies in the face of the evidence: the Song of Songs does not by any means have the bicolon with seconding as its "basic feature." Of course, many psalms and songs do employ the bicolon (and seconding) a great deal. But many do not, and the data indicate that the Hebrews had songs, knew when they were singing songs, and could distinguish songs from prose, but sometimes did, and sometimes did not, stick to the bicolon.

In grouping Hebrew lines into strophes, one should not begin with the assumption that the bicolon is to be preferred. Furthermore, in seeking for some kind of parallelism to link lines together, one should be guided by the principle that in the strophic divisions of a poem, "strong" parallelism wins out over "weak" parallelism. The following example will illustrate these guidelines.

At the very beginning of Song of Songs (1:2–3), according to the MT verse divisions, there are two strophes (verses), which are usually rendered something like the following:

First Strophe (v 2)	a	Let him kiss me with the kisses of his mouth!
	b	For your love is better than wine.
Second Strophe (v 3)	a	Your oils are good for fragrance,
	b	Your name is like perfume poured out;
	c	That is why the girls love you.

It is peculiar that line *a* of strophe 1 (v 2) speaks of the beloved in the third person while line *b* of the same strophe speaks of him in the second person. Both Kugel (*Idea of Biblical Poetry*, 22) and Berlin (*Dynamics of Biblical Parallelism*, 40) point to this verse as proof that parallelism allows for a shift in person, but in fact the parallelism here is minimal, and the verse hardly proves their point. Syntactically the two lines could hardly be more different. The common ground is, first, that line *a* speaks of "kisses" and line *b* speaks of "love" (or, "caresses"), albeit in entirely different constructions, and second, that *in the above translation* line *b* depends on line *a*. One could also argue that both lines have the deep-level meaning "I like his/your lovemaking," although this equivalence depends on translating line *a* with a jussive meaning. As impressive as all this may sound, it makes for extremely weak parallelism; on a casual reading these lines are not parallel at all. On the other hand, the lines of strophe 2 (v 3), like line *b* of the first strophe, speak of the beloved in the second person. In addition, strophe 1 line *b* and strophe 2 lines *a* and *b* all compare the beloved in some way to aromatic liquids (perfumes or wine). This is not done in strophe 1 line *a* or strophe 2 line *c*.

Prima facie, this strophic division of the MT does not make much sense. It appears that v 2 is set forth as a bicolon simply on the assumption either that the bicolon is the norm or that a monocolon is to be avoided. The second strophe (v 3), curiously, is a tricolon, unless this, too, should be regarded as a bicolon in the MT on the grounds that the only line-break is at the *'atnah* (in this case, the verse would be, "Your oils are good for fragrance, your name is like perfume poured out; / that is why the girls love you").

Without attempting to lay out the evidence for an alternative translation at this point (see *Comments* on 1:2 and 1:3), I suggest that a better rendering is:

First Strophe		He will kiss me with the kisses of his mouth.
Second Strophe	a	Indeed your caresses are better than wine,
	b	better than the fragrance of your perfumes.
	c	Your very name is like perfumes poured out.

So understood, Song of Songs begins with a monocolon followed by a tricolon. (The final line of v 3, "That is why the girls love you," probably is a separate monocolon.) There is obvious syntactic and semantic parallelism between line *a* and line *b* in my second strophe; this makes a much stronger case for parallelism than does the traditional versification. But even my second strophe is not a bicolon. It is a tricolon, and the third line relates to the first two but does not have the same kind of parallelism. Line *c* takes "your perfumes" (שמניך) from line *b* and, in a remarkable work of consonance and assonance, breaks it into two parts: "perfume" (שֶׁמֶן) and "your name" (שְׁמֶךָ). Even if one opts for a more traditional translation ("For your love is better than wine / Your oils are good for fragrance / Your name is like perfume poured out"), the strophic division proposed here still makes more sense than the verse division of the MT. But I believe that when one recognizes that v 2b belongs with v 3a, the translation suggested here is fairly obvious.

The above example indicates that Hebrew poems often have two contiguous lines that parallel each other, but these two lines may or may not form a bicolon; very often they will simply be two lines that are part of a larger strophe (verse). Song 2:5 is another illustration of this. With the MT, I take this to be a single strophe of three lines:

a	Lay me on a bed of raisins;
b	stretch me out on a couch of apples,
c	for I am wounded by love.

Lines *a* and *b* are syntactically and semantically parallel, but there is no parallelism (in the traditional sense) linking these two to line *c*; rather, line *c* syntactically depends on lines *a* and *b*. I must insist, moreover, that line *c* is every bit as poetic as the first two lines; it is not merely a supplemental line, with lines *a* and *b* being the real poetry.

In summary, while it is true that the bicolon is very common in Hebrew poetry, it is neither universal nor normative. If what we are looking for in a poem is similarity superimposed on contiguity, then that similarity may appear at any level, and not just on the level of the two-line verse. Indeed, in some cases the similarity may be invisible except at the level of the stanza or indeed of the full poem.

In the second half of the twentieth century came a great upsurge in studies in Hebrew poetry. No longer dependent on Hebrew Scriptures as a source for work, Cross and Freedman devised a method of counting syllables to define the character of the oldest Hebrew verse by ignoring the Masoretic accentuation and drawing on parallels with newly discovered Ugaritic texts. They are followed by their students, Stuart, Christensen, and others. Christensen moved on to a system of counting *morae* following the South African scholar Casper J. Labuschagne. A group of Dutch scholars (the Kampen school led by J. C. de Moor) proposed a more convincing system of counting colons in ancient Hebrew and Ugaritic poetry. Watson evaluated and discounted all the "counting" methods. Some scholars, American and English, drew the discussion of ancient Hebrew poetry into the broader discussion of poetry in current English and other modern languages (Kugel). Others are analyzing ancient Hebrew poetry in comparison with medieval and modern (Israeli) Hebrew poems (Hrushovski and his Tel-Aviv school). No consensus has developed concerning the right approach to Hebrew poetry.

O'Connor's method is the most useful and accurate tool available to summarize the present status of scholarship regarding Hebrew poetry. He argues that a Hebrew poetic line is governed by the following constraints (*Hebrew Verse Structure*, 86–87):

1. A line may have from zero to three "clause predicators." A clause predicator is usually a finite verb, an infinitive absolute functioning as a verb, an infinitive construct functioning verbally (e.g., when it has a pronominal suffix functioning as the subject of the action of the infinitive and has a direct object), or a participle functioning verbally (e.g., not as a substantive). A few other classes of words may be clause predicators, such as יש or אין. Thus, a line need not have a clause predicator, but at most it may have three.
2. A line may have between one and four "constituents." A "constituent" is a word or phrase such as an unbound noun, a construct chain, a noun and attributive adjective, a clause predicator, or a prepositional phrase. A constituent fills a grammatical slot in a line, and it is often indicated with hyphens in translation. For example, the lines of 2 Sam 1:20 have two constituents each:
    a. Tell-it-not in-Gath,
    b. announce-it-not in-the-streets-of-Ashkelon;
    c. lest-they-rejoice the-daughters-of-the-Philistines,
    d. lest-they-exult the-daughters-of-the-uncircumcised.
3. A line may have between two and five "units." A "unit" is a word such as a verb or noun or preposition with a pronominal suffix, but not a particle, such as the negative אל. That is, particles are not normally counted as units.
4. A constituent may have only four units.
5. If a clause contains three clause predicators, it cannot contain a dependent noun or noun phrase (that is, it can contain nothing else). [See my division of Song 5:7, which, in the MT, contains three verbs and a dependent noun phrase.] If a colon has two clause predicators, only one may have a dependent noun or noun phrase.
6. A colon must have syntactical integrity. If it has one or more clause predicators, it cannot have a noun constituent not dependent on one of them.

A significant problem here is determining what constitutes a "unit." Thus, proclitic and enclitic particles are excluded (e.g., a preposition such as על without a pronominal suffix, or נא). On the other hand, some accented particles do not count as units in the O'Connor model, and in O'Connor's model the presence or absence of a *maqqef* is irrelevant. W. Holladay (*JBL* 118 [1999] 23–32) has investigated this problem in detail and provides a great deal of help with this issue. In his analysis, particles that do not count as units include the negatives לא and אל, and most small particles such as כי, אם, גם, and אף. Combinations of particles, such as גם כי, probably do count as a single unit. כל is more difficult; it normally should be counted, but in some cases it makes a line too long and perhaps does not count. Adverbs such as שם, כן, and עוד do count as units; so does the relative אשר. The interrogative מי counts as a unit, but מה is much more difficult. In Holladay's analysis, it counts when it is the object of a direct question or is the subject of a nominal question, yet does not count when it is the subject of a verb and immediately followed by the verb or is the subject of a nominal clause that is an indirect question. As complicated as this sounds, it often appears to involve little more than determining if the מה has an accent or is a proclitic. For example, in Job 34:4, where it is part of a nominal indirect question, it is proclitic and not counted. In Job 7:17, where it is the subject of a nominal direct question and is counted, it is an accented foot.

Even with these constraints in place, determining the colon divisions in a strophe is not an automatic process. Sometimes either a single longer line or two shorter lines will equally fit all the constraints for colometry. In these cases, one may look for other indicators of colon length (e.g., determine which alternative works better with the structure of the strophe). As suggested above, the colometry suggested by the MT may help to resolve a difficult case. But a degree of subjectivity still remains. No system can guarantee a flawless and self-evident method of colometry.

In addition to the constraints of the poetic line, O'Connor has suggested several tropes that function in Hebrew poetry. These are as follows (O'Connor, *Hebrew Verse Structure,* 109–32; my translations of Scripture):

1. Repetition of a word or phrase, as in Ps 106:10, "He saved them from the *power* (יד) of one who hated them / he redeemed them from the *power* (יד) of the enemy." The repetition need not be in contiguous lines.
2. Coloration of a word or phrase, which comes in three varieties:
    a. Binomation, in which two alternative names are used in successive lines, as in Num 22:23, "No one can curse *Jacob,* / no one can hex *Israel.*"
    b. Coordination, which involves frequently paired names of two different entities rather than two names for the same entity, as in Ps 106:16, "They vexed *Moses* in the camp, / (they vexed) *Aaron,* the holy one [or, 'shrine'] of Yahweh."
    c. Combination, in which a phrase is split into two parts and distributed over two lines, as in Ps 106:43, "they were rebellious *in their counsels;* they were brought low *in their iniquity.*" Here, a single phrase, "in their counsels of iniquity," has been split apart and distributed over two lines. The same thing may be occurring in the lines from Ps 106:16 cited in the above paragraph. There, "holy of Yahweh" may be not an epithet of Aaron but a combined phrase that has been split apart: "in the camp of the shrine of Yahweh."
3. Matching of the syntax of two contiguous lines (syntactic parallelism), as in Ps 106:22, "Wonders in the land of Ham, / terrors near the Reed Sea."
4. Gapping, in which a word or phrase in one line is also understood to function in a second line ("double-duty" words), as in Ps 78:47, "*He wiped out* with hail their vines, / their sycamores with frost."
5. Dependency, in which one line syntactically depends on another, as in Ps 106:2, "Whoever can recite the strengths of Yahweh, / let him make known his praise." Here, the nominal phrase in the first line depends on the clause in the second.
6. Mixing, in which two dependent and two independent lines occur in sequence and both dependent lines depend on both independent lines, as in Ps 106:47, "Save us, Yahweh our God, / gather us from the nations, / to praise your holy

name, / to worship in adoration of you!" Here, two independent lines precede two dependent lines.

The line constraints of M. O'Connor are the most reasonable starting point available at this time for the study of Hebrew poetry. Although one may question this or that point, and the matter of what particles "count" as units can be somewhat troublesome, the system itself appears to be valid and fruitful. As a practical matter, this commentary tends to follow the line divisions suggested by the MT as long as they conform to O'Connor's line constraints, unless other concerns persuade me to choose an alternative colometry within the confines of O'Connor's line constraints.

Comparative Texts: Ancient Near Eastern Love Poetry

Bibliography

Black, J. A. "Babylonian Ballads: A New Genre." *JAOS* 103 (1983) 25–34. **Cooper, J. S.** "New Cuneiform Parallels to the Song of Songs." *JBL* 90 (1971) 157–62. **Foster, J. L.** *Ancient Egyptian Literature: An Anthology.* Austin: Univ. of Texas Press, 2001. **Fox, M. V.** "The Cairo Love Songs." *JAOS* 100 (1980) 101–9. ———. "Love, Passion and Perception in Israelite and Egyptian Love Poetry." *JBL* 102 (1983) 219–28. ———. *Song of Songs and the Ancient Egyptian Love Songs.* **Hermann, A.** *Altägyptische Liebesdichtung.* Wiesbaden: Harrassowitz, 1959. **Jacobsen, T.** *The Harp That Once....* **Lichtheim, M.** *Ancient Egyptian Literature.* Vol. 2, *The New Kingdom.* Berkeley: Univ. of California Press, 1976. **O'Connor, D.** "Eros in Egypt." *Archaeology Odyssey* 4.5 (Sept./Oct. 2001) 42–51. **Sasson, J. M.** "A Further Cuneiform Parallel to the Song of Songs?" *ZAW* 85 (1973) 359–60. **Watson, W. G. E.** "Some Ancient Near Eastern Parallels to the Song of Songs." In *Words Remembered, Texts Renewed.* FS J. F. A. Sawyer, ed. J. Davies, G. Harvey, and W. G. E. Watson. Sheffield: Sheffield Academic Press, 1995. 253–71. **Westenholz, J. G.** "Love Lyrics from the Ancient Near East." In *CANE,* 4:2471–84. **White, J. B.** *Study of the Language of Love in the Song of Songs and Ancient Egyptian Literature.*

The discovery of love poetry from ancient Mesopotamia and Egypt has revolutionized the study of Song of Songs. At the very minimum, this poetry has demonstrated once and for all that Song of Songs is not some literary oddity or orphan but is part of a lengthy history of ancient poetry of love. This has numerous repercussions for the study of the Song, the most obvious being that one must take its status as love poetry seriously and not use it as a vehicle for something else. Several scholars have described similarities among amorous texts from Mesopotamia, Egypt, and the Bible (see, for example, Watson, "Some Ancient Near Eastern Parallels").

MESOPOTAMIAN PARALLELS

Ancient Mesopotamian texts have a number of parallels to the Song of Songs, but unlike the Song, Mesopotamian love poetry almost always concerns the love affairs of the gods and tends to be hymnic or liturgical (see Westenholz, "Love Lyrics"). For example, the Akkadian love song of Nabu (Nebo) and Tashmetu (*CS* 1:445) is hymnic in nature. Nabu was the Akkadian god of scribes, and Tashmetu was his consort. Both had some significance in the Akkadian pantheon; the Neo-Babylonian clay cylinder of Nabopolassar invokes these two deities alongside Marduk and other high gods. The poem does have some elements that are more or less similar to the Song of Songs. For example, the Nabu and Tashmetu song refers to the lovers entering a garden together (cf. Song 6:11; 7:13–14 [ET 7:12–13]); it also has descriptive praise in which one of the lovers is said to have thighs like gazelles (cf. Song 7:4 [ET 7:3]). An Akkadian love incantation also bears some resemblance to Song of Songs (J. Sasson, ZAW 85 [1973] 359–60).

Another song with a sexual motif is a Sumerian text that T. Jacobsen calls "The Bridal Sheets" (Jacobsen, *Harp That Once* . . . , 13–15). In this song, the god Utu comes to his sister Inanna to tell her that he has arranged for her to marry Ama-ushumgal-anna. Rather than tell her directly, he begins by telling her that he will bring her green flax. She asks who will ret it for her (i.e., moisten the flax so that the fibers will separate), and he responds that he will bring it already retted. A series of similar questions and answers follow; she asks who will spin it for her, and he says he will bring it already spun, and in like manner he says he will bring it already dyed, woven, and bleached. Finally, she asks him who will lie down with her on it. Utu says that she will lie down with her groom, Ama-ushumgal-anna, and she rejoices because he is the man of her heart.

A series of love songs for Dumuzi and Inanna (Tammuz and Ishtar) has survived in the Sumerian texts of the Third Dynasty of Ur and the Old Babylonian periods. Again, these are essentially hymns, and they were recited as a liturgy. They may have been chanted antiphonally, or accompanied by drums, and they possibly were used in a New Year's festival (*CS* 1:540–43). One can find certain parallels to the Song of Songs. Inanna is sometimes called "sister," her eyes are beautiful, and her mouth is sweet. Dumuzi is described as an apple tree (cf. Song 2:3). Of course, much of this kind of language is so common in love poetry that the value of these parallels is limited (e.g., calling the beloved "sister" is common in the ancient Near East). The third Dumuzi and Inanna song, called "Love by the Light of the Moon" by its translator (Y. Sefati in *CS* 1:542–43), describes the courtship of Inanna by Dumuzi. It opens with the gods described as a pair of young lovers staying out too late in the night; Dumuzi tells Inanna to lie to her mother (the goddess Ningal) and say that she was out dancing with a girlfriend. The ruse was apparently successful; after a break in the tablet, Ningal declares that Dumuzi is worthy of Inanna's "lap"!

Another text with parallels to the Song of Songs is the "Message of Ludingira to His Mother," a Sumerian piece extant in several Old Babylonian and trilingual (Sumerian-Akkadian-Hittite) tablets. This work has material that resembles the type of poem of descriptive praise for the beloved (called the *wasf*, after the Arabic) found in Song of Songs. The peculiarity of the Sumerian piece is that Ludingira uses this elaborate language of praise not for his consort but for his mother. It may be that the "mother" he is referring to is actually the goddess Inanna (see J. Cooper, *JBL* 90 [1971] 162).

A Middle Babylonian text, British Museum 47507, also describes the love of Ishtar/Inanna for Tammuz/Dumuzi. This fragmentary text has some similarities to the Song; for example, Ishtar describes her beloved as a shepherd. Ishtar also refers to a door between her and Tammuz and expresses the wish that it will open of its own accord. J. Black (*JAOS* 103 [1983] 25–34) describes the text and calls it a "ballad," but that is not a well-chosen term for the song.

EGYPTIAN PARALLELS

The love poetry of Egypt is much closer to the Song of Songs in content and form. Following the work of Hermann (*Altägyptische Liebesdichtung*) in German, recent English translations and analyses of this corpus include Lichtheim (*Ancient Egyptian Literature*, 2:181–93), White (*Study of the Language of Love*), Fox (*Song of Songs*), and Foster (*Ancient Egyptian Literature*, 17–31). Students of Song of Songs are especially indebted to Fox for the most complete analysis of the Egyptian material to date. The following summary is based on his translations and to some degree on his comments, although the comparisons to Song of Songs are my own.

The Egyptian love songs come from the nineteenth and twentieth dynasties (respectively, ca. 1305–1200 B.C.E. and ca. 1200–1150 B.C.E.). They are secular in that they are not hymns or liturgies and in that the lovers are not gods but ordinary young people. They do sometimes call on a god for assistance—they especially invoke Hathor, the Egyptian Aphrodite—but the gods play no role in the songs, with the possible exception of an enigmatic figure called Mehi. Otherwise, there is no religious element in the songs at all. The main purpose of the songs is entertainment; they describe young love, infatuation, pining for the beloved, and other recognizable themes. For the most part, they are not especially bawdy in comparison to the Mesopotamian texts, but they are at times enigmatic and probably contained sexual allusions and wordplays that the audience was expected to catch.

The first manuscript is Papyrus Harris 500 and is from the early nineteenth dynasty. It is housed in the British Museum. The text is somewhat damaged, but it seems to contain an anthology of three separate "entertainment songs" (groups A, B, and C in Fox, *Song of Songs*, 7–29). Group A is a fairly straightforward erotic text. Like the Song of Songs, it has parts for a male and a female singer, but—again like the Song—the two are not in true dialogue but are simply singing love songs in an antiphonal fashion. The girl calls on the boy to come back to her and caress her thighs; she urges him to hasten back like a horse dashing to a battlefield; she declares that his lovemaking is like beer to her. The boy in turn says that the girl ("sister") is a lotus and that her breasts are like some kind of fruit or vegetation (Fox, *Song of Songs*, 9, suggests that it is "mandragoras" or mandrakes). The boy also wishes he could be a doorkeeper at the girl's house (the doors being a transparent double entendre). Every element mentioned here has an analogue in the Song of Songs. In the Song, the woman longs to make love to the man and calls him to hasten to her like a young stag (e.g., 8:14); she says that his love is better than wine (1:2); the man calls his beloved "sister" and compares her breasts to clusters of dates (4:9; 7:8 [ET 7:7]); she is a flower (2:1); the doors of the woman's house are also sexual metaphors (5:2–7; see *Comment* on vv 4–5).

Papyrus Harris 500 group B (Fox, *Song of Songs*, 16–25) has fewer parallels in Song of Songs. It is sung exclusively by a girl; she describes how she went out to trap birds but was herself ensnared in her beloved's lovemaking and thus failed to catch any birds—although she does describe catching a bird (referring to her lover) with the fragrance of Punt (the paradise of Egyptian mythology) and claws that are full of balm. Later, she yearns for her lover to come to her but is convinced that he has found another girl, so she runs out after him with her hair only half styled. The use of balm on the bird's claws to signal a sexual metaphor has a parallel in the myrrh on the door-bolt in Song 5:5, and the girl dashing out half-dressed after her lover has an analogy in the woman of the Song roaming the streets in search of her beloved (Song 3:1–5; 5:2–7).

The songs of group C (Fox, *Song of Songs*, 26–29) are again sung by a girl. She declares that her heart has been bound to her lover ever since she lay with him. She says that she is a tree exalted above the other trees (that is, she is his favorite) and that she is a field planted with flowers that has a canal in it, which the man scooped out with his hand (that is, he deflowered her). To her, his voice is like pomegranate wine. The metaphor of the one tree better than all other trees appears in Song 2:3, except that there it is the man who is better than all other trees. The woman is a flower in Song 2:1–2, and she describes his deflowering of her with his "hand" in 5:4 (see *Comment* on 5:4–5). The woman is excited at her lover's voice in Song 2:8.

The second major source for Egyptian love poetry is the Cairo Love Songs. These were "written on a vase of 36.5 cm. high and 43.0 cm. in diameter, inscribed over an effaced copy of the Wisdom of Amenemhet" (Fox, *Song of Songs*, 29). The vase is broken, and some fragments are missing, making for some large lacunae. There are two groups of songs, both probably written by the same poet.

The first group (Fox, *Song of Songs*, 31–37) opens with a female solo. She speaks of how she yearns for her beloved, whose love is like oil, incense, and beer to her (cf. Song 1:2–3). She calls him her god and her lotus and, in a broken fragment, speaks of the north wind (cf. Song 4:16). She desires to bathe before her lover and enigmatically speaks of carrying a red fish. The remainder of the lyrics are sung by a male. He declares that she is on the other side of a river and that a crocodile is between them. Nevertheless, he wades into the water and crosses as if by magic; the crocodile was like a mouse to him. He then speaks of embracing her, kissing her, and entering her bedroom. He is like a man in Punt, and he compares her scent to balm. Song of Songs, too, speaks of the woman as though in an unattainable location (Song 4:8, where she is in a mountain lair surrounded by lions and leopards). But in Song of Songs, the man does not climb up to the woman; rather, he appeals to her to come down.

The second Cairo group consists entirely of songs of a boy who wishes he could be near his beloved; the songs express seven fantasies of intimacy with her. First, he wishes he were her maid, so that he could see her naked in her room. Second, he wishes he were her laundryman, so that he could handle her clothes. Third, he wishes he were her ring, so that he could be with her every day. Fourth, he apparently wishes that he were her mirror (the text is obscure), so that he could see her every morning. Fifth, he wishes that she were about him like a garland of flowers, and he describes her as a lush garden. Sixth, more literally, he wishes that she would come to him, and he promises that he will hold a festival to honor the god who gives her to him; he also declares that he is becoming ill from unfulfilled desire for her. The seventh stanza is broken and obscure, but it seems to continue the sixth. Material such as this is notably absent from Song of Songs, where there are no idle, adolescent fantasies about handling a girl's clothes; nor are there any vows of thank offerings to God in return for giving to a boy the girl of his heart's desire. There are, however, two notable parallels between this Egyptian song group and Song of Songs. The lovesickness of the boy has an echo in Song 2:5, although there it is the woman who is ill, and her condition is of a much more profound nature than that of the Egyptian. In the fifth stanza of the Egyptian song, the girl is described as a profusely lush garden, analogous to the praise of the woman in Song 4:13–14.

The third major collection is the Turin Love Song, found in a twentieth-dynasty papyrus (Fox, *Song of Songs*, 44–51). It is altogether unlike the others. It has three major stanzas, and in each stanza a different tree addresses a young couple. The first tree, on Fox's analysis, is the persea (an evergreen, fruit-bearing tree cultivated in pharaonic Egypt). This tree declares that its pits resemble the woman's teeth and its fruit resembles her breasts, but then it boasts that it is better than all other trees and threatens to reveal what the lovers have been up to. The second stanza is spoken by a "fig-sycamore" tree, and it complains that the couple has failed to give it the honor it is due and also threatens vengeance against them. The third stanza opens with words, apparently coming from the poet, praising the "little sycamore" tree. The tree is said to be colorful, rich in fruit, and abundant in shade. The tree itself then calls on the young couple to celebrate their love and sings happily of their beer drinking and lovemaking beneath its shade; it concludes by promising not to tell what it has seen. Although Song of Songs has nothing in this genre, there are parallels to be found. The notion of lovemaking under the trees appears in the Song also (8:5; see *Comment* on v 5). The woman's body is compared to a date palm tree, with its clusters resembling her breasts (Song 7:8 [ET 7:7]).

The fourth major collection is the Chester Beatty Papyrus I love songs (Fox, *Song of Songs*, 51–77). The papyrus itself is from the twentieth dynasty; it is quite lengthy and contains religious and business texts in addition to the love poetry. The love songs are in three groups.

Chester Beatty I group A (Fox, *Song of Songs*, 52–66; White, *Study of the Language of Love*, 177–81) is a song of seven stanzas in which a boy and a girl sing alternate stanzas, the boy singing first and last. The first stanza opens with the boy declaring that his "sister" is unique and has no equal among other women (cf. Song 6:8–9). He then moves into a description of her skin, eyes, lips, neck, breast, hair, arms, fingers, buttocks, waist, and thighs. He says that her arms surpass gold. The Song of Songs has several similar descriptive songs of the woman's body (e.g., Song 6:4–7). In the second stanza, the Egyptian girl is pining with lovesickness over her mother's determination to keep the two apart. The third stanza is obscure. The boy appears to be going to the home of his girlfriend when he passes by Mehi in his chariot. The identity of this figure is uncertain; Fox (*Song of Songs*, 64-6) suggests he is a cupidlike deity who makes young men confused and lovesick. In the fourth stanza, the girl is distracted with love and desire. She cannot properly dress herself or put on eye makeup, and she is struggling to maintain her composure. In the fifth stanza, the boy prays that Hathor will give him success in love. He says that when he last saw her, all men bowed in awe of her, but it has been five days since he saw her. In the sixth stanza, the girl recalls that she passed by the boy's house; she looked at him and saw that all who know him love him. She also prays to Hathor for success: "If only mother knew my heart— / She would go inside for a while / O Golden One, put that in her heart! / Then I could hurry to (my) brother / and kiss him before his company, / and not be ashamed because of anyone" (Fox, *Song of Songs*, 55). This is strikingly similar to Song 8:1–2, although there are significant differences as well. In the seventh stanza, the boy ruefully says that it has been seven days since he saw the girl and that he now is becoming ill. Priests and physicians will do him no good; he will not revive until he sees her.

Chester Beatty I group B (Fox, *Song of Songs*, 66-68; White, *Study of the Language of Love*, 181–82) expresses three wishes of a young girl. First, she wishes that her lover would hasten to her with the speed of a royal messenger who has fresh horses at the way stations and who will not rest until he is at the house of the "sister." Second, she wishes that her lover would be like a war horse racing to the home of his "sister." Third, she wishes he were like a gazelle, bounding away from the hunter and his dog and taking no rest till he comes to the "cave" of his "sister." In Song of Songs, the man comes bounding like a gazelle over the hills to his beloved (2:8–9).

Chester Beatty I group C (Fox, *Song of Songs*, 68–77; White, *Study of the Language of Love*, 183–85) is quite distinct; it is called the Nakhtsobek Songs after the scribe who copied the words. It has seven stanzas. The first two stanzas are sung not by a young lover but by some person or persons declaring that, if a young man will bring to the "house mistress" an animal for slaughter and an ample supply of wine and ale, he will be able to delight himself in the sexual pleasures of the "sister." It is evident that the "house mistress" is not the girl's mother but the keeper of a brothel. The language of these two stanzas is thoroughly erotic, and it reads like a prostitute's advertisement for the ecstasy that the young man will experience if he is willing to pay the price. A close biblical parallel to this is Prov 7. In the third stanza of the Egyptian song, the boy sings that he has been captured by the girl's hair as by a lasso; he is pulled to her like a bull in a noose and is branded with her seal; the similarity to Prov 7:22 is striking ("he walks right behind her, he goes like a bull to the slaughter"). In the fourth stanza, a girl boldly urges him to embrace her and comes after him with little or nothing on. In the fifth stanza the girl says that the young man has brought the requisite price, an animal for a feast and a supply of beer, and comes to her aroused for sexual union. In the sixth song, the young man complains that the girl is inside her house and will not let him in. This is continued in the seventh stanza, where the boy passes by her house in a daze and knocks on the door, demanding entrance. He declares that he will sacrifice oxen and geese to the door and that he will pay to have the door converted into a door of grass (that is, into a door that cannot exclude him). Then, he says, anytime he comes the door will be open to him and a fine bed and pretty maidservant will be prepared for him. All in all, the Nakhtsobek Songs appear to speak of the entrapment of a young man by a brothel. First, he is enticed to come in with promises of sexual bliss; then he is abruptly seduced by a prostitute and pays the price. But after he becomes addicted to this pleasure, he must bring ever greater gifts and payments if he is to continue to enjoy the entertainment there. As suggested above, Prov 7 may draw on this for its portrayal of the seductive ways of the prostitute. Still, there are echoes of this text in the Song of Songs, albeit in an entirely different context with different significance. Like the young man of stanza 3, the man of Song of Songs says he is captured in the hair of his beloved (7:6 [ET 7:5]). The Song also has the motif of the man excluded and standing outside the door of the woman in 5:2–6. The importance of the Nakhtsobek Songs for Song of Songs is explored more fully below in this Introduction.

There are also a series of small miscellaneous texts in the Egyptian love poetry corpus, but they are fragmentary and of little use here.

What is one to make of a comparison between the Song of Songs and the Egyptian material? The Egyptian corpus has influenced the language and motifs of the Song of Songs. Both have short stanzas sung by a male or female lover, both use a similar set of metaphors (the woman as a tree with her breasts as its fruit, the woman as a garden, the woman entrapping the man with her hair, the man bounding to the woman like a gazelle, and so forth), and both use the same motifs (such as the excluded lover or lovesickness, although these and other motifs are used in different ways in the two bodies of literature). Both draw on a common stock of metaphors, as is apparently the case with the Song of Songs and the Mesopotamian texts. But comparison to the Mesopotamian texts makes the point that what is seen in the Song and the Egyptian corpus was not merely "common stock." The similarities are too close and too numerous to be explained as anything other than the influence of the Egyptian songs on the Israelite poem.

The Egyptian corpus is, apart from the difficulties involved in reconstructing and translating the texts, much simpler love poetry than the biblical material. For the most part, the Egyptian characters are thoroughly adolescent. They are intoxicated with love, react with melodramatic flourish at the thought of separation, are plainly not married, and speak in a manner that is for the most part straightforward. While hidden metaphors may be found, there is little mystery or profound symbolism in them. A girl is upset because her mother disapproves of her boyfriend; a boy is upset because the door to his prostitute is shut. These images are plain and direct. By contrast, the woman in the Song of Songs speaks much more mysteriously of her mother and her mother's house (as in Song 8:1–2). The exclusion at the door in Song 5:2–6 is far more confusing and, I suggest, much more profound than its Egyptian counterparts. It is precisely because of the adolescent, simple quality of the Egyptian poems that these lovers are called "boys" and "girls." The lovers in the much more complex world of Song of Songs are a man and a woman.

Comparison between the two texts indicates that, although they may have the same motif or metaphor, they may not have the same interpretation. Sometimes a metaphor that is used of the man in the Egyptian texts is used of the woman in the Song. Similar motifs and concepts, such as the mother of the girl, can be used in entirely different ways when one moves from the Egyptian material to the Bible. That the boys and girls in the Egyptian texts are not married does not mean that the same is true for the man and woman of the Song.

We should finally note that in addition to written texts, an enormous number of graphical representations of sexuality (bas-relief sculptures, tomb paintings, figurines, and so forth) have come down to us from the ancient Near East. Some of this is restrained, but much is luridly erotic. Much of the erotic material is religious in nature, but some, such as the Turin pornographic papyrus, is apparently secular. The commentaries of Pope and Keel contain many photographs of these images, and sometimes they are helpful in interpreting the imagery of the Song. The Turin pornographic papyrus is described by D. O'Connor (*Archaeology Odyssey* 4.5 [2001] 42–51).

Comparison of One Egyptian Text with Song of Songs

As already indicated, the Egyptian love poetry is closer to the poetic method of Song of Songs than is any other poetry of the ancient world. Analysis of one of these works, the Nakhtsobek Songs (Papyrus Chester Beatty I group C), shows that it is similar to Song of Songs in unexpected ways and helps to clarify issues in the interpretation of the Song. The text, Fox's translation (*Song of Songs*, 68–77), is here presented in full. However, Fox has "poet" as the postulated singer for nos. 41 and 42, and he has "girl" for the singer in nos. 44 and 45; my descriptions of the singers (in brackets) are somewhat different.

41. *Female Singer(s) as Poet(s) [Prostitute(s)]*
(A) When you bring it to the house of (your) sister
       and blow(?) into her cave,
  her gate(?) will be raised up(?)
       that her house-mistress may slaughter it.
(B) Supply her with song and dance
       and wine and ale, which she set aside,
  that you may intoxicate her senses(?),
       and complete her in her night.
(C) And she'll say to you: "Take me in your embrace,
       and when dawn breaks that's how <we> will be."

42. *Female Singer(s) as Poet(s) [Prostitute(s)]*
(A) When you bring it <to> the hall of (your) sister,
       while you are alone, without another,
  you may do your desire in her snare,
       and the halls(?) will blow lightly(?).
(B) The heavens will descend in a breeze,
       (yet) <will not> blow it away.
  It (only) brings you her fragrance:
       an inundating aroma that intoxicates
            those who are present.
(C) The Golden One it is who sends her to you as a gift,
       to make you fulfill your days.

43. *Male Singer as Boy*
(A) How skilled is she—(my) sister—at casting the lasso,
       yet she'll <draw in> no cattle!
(B) With her hair she lassos me,
       with her eye she pulls (me) in,
  with her thighs she binds,
       with her seal she sets the brand.

44. *Female Singer as Girl [Prostitute]*
  While you (yet) argued with your heart—
       "After her! Embrace her!"—
  as Amon lives, it was I who came to you,
       my tunic on my shoulder.

45. *Female Singer as Girl [Prostitute]*
  My brother is at the watercourse,
       his foot planted on the riverbank.
  He prepares a festival altar for spending the day
       with the choicest(?) of the beers.

He "grants (me) the hue" of <his> loins.
   It is longer than broad.
46. *Male Singer as Boy*
   As for what she—(my) sister—did to me,
      should I keep silent to her?
   She left me standing at the door of her house
      while she went inside,
   and did not say to me, "Welcome!"
      but blocked her ears in *my* night.
47. *Male Singer as Boy*
(A)   <I> passed by her house in a daze,
         I knocked, but it was not opened to me.
      A fine night for our doorkeeper!
(B)   Bolt, I will open (you)!
         Door, you are my fate!
      You are my (very) spirit,
         Our ox will be slaughtered inside.
(C)   O Door, exert not your strength,
         so that oxen may be sacrificed to (your) bolt,
            fatlings to (your) threshold,
      a stout goose to (your) jambs,
         and an oriole to (your) lintel(?).
(D)   But every choice piece of our ox
         will be (saved) for the carpenter lad
      that he may fashion us a bolt of reeds,
         a door of grass(?).
(E)   (Then) at any time the brother can come
         and find her house open,
      and find a bed spread with fine linen,
         and a pretty little maidservant too.
(F)   The little maid will say to
         ". . . the mayor."

It is fairly obvious that this set of poems concerns a young man and a house of prostitution. He is told to bring in all manner of food and drink for the privilege of enjoying the ecstasy she has to offer (nos. 41 and 42). In addition, in no. 41A, he is told to bring it to the "house mistress," who is obviously the matron of a brothel. Fox (*Song of Songs*, 69–71) ascribes nos. 41–42 to the "poet," but there does not seem to be any reason to consider these lines anonymous in the songs, much less as the advice that the poet is giving to the boy. They are better taken to be the words of the prostitute herself or perhaps of a chorus of girls representing the women of the brothel. The fact that these poems speak of the "sister" in the third person (no. 41A) is no reason to think that the prostitute could not herself be the speaker. The boy knows that he is being ensnared like a bull in a lasso and that he is about to be branded, but he is able to mount little resistance to the enticements offered him (no. 43). When he does hesitate, the prostitute comes after him and brazenly shows herself to him (no. 44; she is evidently naked or near naked). In no. 45, the prostitute first describes the boy as having come to the watercourse (perhaps the location of the brothel) with the requisite payment: "My brother is at the watercourse, / his foot planted on the riverbank. / He prepares a festival altar for spending the day / with the choicest(?) of the beers."

She then speaks of his private parts: "He 'grants (me) the hue' of <his> loins. / It is longer than broad." White (*Study of the Language of Love*, 184) translates these two lines as "He brought skin to my thighs / He is taller than he is broad." For our purposes, we can accept either translation, but Fox's explanation of these lines is surely wrong: "I surmise that the girl is saying—in a suggestive, 'naughty' fashion—that as her boyfriend bends over while making preparations for their private festivities, she sees his nakedness under his loincloth" (Fox, *Song of Songs*, 74). First of all, he is her client, not her boyfriend. Also, in light of how the selling of sexual pleasure is the theme of this text, it makes little sense for her to slip into a girlish, "naughty" mode, as though she were surprised or embarrassed at the sight. Instead, this text uses a familiar device of graphically taking the audience up to the moment of a crucial event without describing the event itself. By analogy, if a modern poem ends with the words, "He placed the pistol to his head," it need not spell out for us the fact that he committed suicide. Thus, no. 45 ends with the boy taking the sexual favors he was promised. As a literary device, her language is crude but effective. Her words are decidedly not words of playfulness or surprise; the young man is nothing to her but a sexually aroused male. There is no intimacy, passion, or imagery here, only a plain description of the anatomy of the aroused male's penis. Sexuality has been reduced to biology. In contrast to the ardent language of the girls of Papyrus Harris 500, the prostitute has no emotion in her language at all. Whether one follows White's or Fox's translation, her remarks are a blunt description of an aspect of sexual arousal and tell the reader that intercourse takes place.

In the next poems (nos. 46–47), however, the boy is suddenly outside the girl's door and frustrated that she will not let him in. It is evident that this is a subsequent occasion and that this time he has come empty-handed. We are therefore at a new episode. In no. 45 he had a gift in hand, but here he says that he passed by "in a daze." After he recovers from the shock of being excluded, he proclaims that he will bring every manner of meat and drink to gain access to her (that is, he does not have meat and drink at the moment). The situation is not difficult to unravel. The young man, having experienced intimacy with the prostitute, now thinks of her as his lover and goes back to her expecting to be received and given the same favors that he enjoyed before. For her, however, he is just a client, and having no payment, he gets no service.

The boy is at first simply angry and bewildered (no. 46), but then he realizes that he must come with payment in hand (no. 47). The language he uses is the exaggerated bravado of a young man. First, he says that he will glut the doorway with every kind of feast. Fox (*Song of Songs*, 77) cites the Book of the Dead here (spell 125c), where the parts of the Hall of Two Truths refuse to allow passage to the recently deceased until the deceased gives their proper names. This is a false lead. The Nakhtsobek Songs are different in every way; most significantly, the door parts in the love poem do not speak to the young man. Rather, the young man's claim that he will bring a great feast to the door is simply his way of saying that next time he will have more than enough payment for the girl's services. Similarly, his promise to pay a carpenter to put a grass door on her house is merely another boastful assertion that he will bear whatever cost to get regular access to her services.

These songs lampoon the folly of the young man who knowingly lets himself be tied and branded by the prostitute. The similarity of this text to Prov 7 has already been noted. In addition, and despite the different subject matter (going to a prostitute in the Nakhtsobek Songs; marriage in Song of Songs), this material parallels Song of Songs in significant ways beyond the similar imagery (a woman ensnaring a man with her hair, Song 7:6 [ET 7:5]; a man excluded by a door from his lover's house, Song 5:2–6).

Both works are a series of smaller songs that together make up a unified piece. Neither can be called a story, and it would be a mistake to dramatize either or concoct elaborate "stage" instructions. At the same time, both contain the germ of a story, or are built on an implied background story, and the individual songs capture moments in the background story. In both cases, the songs move abruptly from image to image with no transition or explanation. The images in the Nakhtsobek Songs are the general appeal of the prostitute (nos. 41–42), the hesitation of the boy (no. 43), the aggressive enticement of the prostitute (no. 44), the moment of prostitution (no. 45), and the exclusion of the young man, with his boast that next time he will bring more than enough payment (nos. 46–47).

Both works have the sexual union of the man and woman as the crucial turning point (no. 45 in the Egyptian song; I will argue that Song 4:16–5:1 is the central text in Song of Songs). The Nakhtsobek Songs have something of a concentric pattern. In nos. 41–42, the young man is promised sexual ecstasy if he brings the expected payment. He does so, and in nos. 46–47 he claims that he will again bring a payment, and he anticipates sexual ecstasy. This commentary will suggest that Song of Songs has a similar structure.

In addition, the Nakhtsobek Songs describe the sexual transformation of the young man, albeit in very negative terms. He is ensnared, branded, and finally a slave of the brothel, promising to bring to them whatever it takes so that he may have the woman he imagines is his lover, his "sister." This commentary will argue that there is also a transformation in Song of Songs, but that here it is of the woman—and it is a far more positive transformation.

Comparison to the Nakhtsobek Songs shows how Song of Songs takes a model from lyric poetry and reshapes it significantly. It further illustrates that the model used in the commentary, a complex opus composed of many shorter songs arranged into a unified and structured whole, has earlier analogies.

Analogies for Song of Songs

"I acquired singers, male and female, and every human luxury." So saying, Qoheleth tells us a little about music in the ancient Near East (Eccl 1:8). Ancient musicians employed female singers and not boy sopranos, as was common in the medieval era. Egyptian art confirms this with its depictions of female musicians who not only sang but also played instruments and danced. Only the rich and powerful could enjoy professional musical performances, as only they could afford either to hire professional musicians on a regular basis or to acquire slaves who specialized in music.

The Song of Songs appears to be words to music that would have been sung by professionals—individuals who were skilled enough to master a work of this complexity. What strikes the reader most about this material is that it is stunningly intricate. Even though it has repetition, this repetition is not of the mechanically redundant kind one often sees in many ancient songs (witness the Ugaritic epic of Keret). When repetition does occur in the Song, it is often with minor (or major) variations. The Song constantly changes its focus; at one moment the woman is defending her dark skin, and at the next she is seeking her beloved. As a complete opus, it is much longer than the average psalm. Songs of extreme length are made somewhat easier to master if they follow the same pattern throughout, whether it be the acrostics of Lamentations, the dactylic hexameter and repeated epithets of Homer, or the rhyme scheme of a series of sonnets. It is difficult for performers to master such works if they have no memorization aids. Song of Songs is not extremely long, but it offers no obvious aids for mastering the lyrics. Aqiba's complaint about people who sang the Song with a burlesque trill does not contradict this; no doubt many people who were attracted to the Song by its erotic lyrics could sing individual parts of the work. Even assuming that Aqiba is speaking of lay singers, his complaint does not mean that these people mastered the whole Song, or that it is originally folk music.

Song of Songs has three voices: the female lead, the male lead, and the chorus. They participate at many different points throughout the Song, and the vocalists would have to be trained and coordinated. This practically demands what one could call a professional production. Finally, the text says as much; it is "The Song of Songs that belongs to Solomon." In other words, it is court poetry.

Music of more recent vintage composed for court or cathedral may help us understand the Song. Like many of the works of Bach, Handel, and Mendelssohn, the Song is a collection of smaller songs that together form an integrated opus. As in the Western examples, the individual songs could be for male or female voices, for solos, duets, choral groups, or combinations of several of these. Like the oratorio, the Song may have been performed with an instrumental overture, voluntaries, and intermezzi. The psalm superscripts and Egyptian portraiture tell us that ancient music was performed with instrumentation, although the nature of the instruments obviously indicates that the style of music would have been very different from, for example, the overture to *Messiah*.

Like the oratorio, the lyrics of a single song may have been sung many times in the course of the performance of the Song of Songs. One difference between the Song and some oratorio compositions is that the Song does not have any recitative (brief prose narration inserted between songs to explain the setting for a song to the audience). This is important because it reinforces the fact that the Song of Songs does not tell anything like a full story. No narrative is necessary and, for that matter, no changes of scene need be described. By describing the Song as analogous to the *oratorio*, therefore, we must take pains to point out that it is not an *opera*. It celebrates the experience of a man and woman passing through the event of marriage, and it profoundly expresses the emotions and significance of the experience. Once again the analogy of Handel's *Messiah* may help us. Those who know the gospel of Christ perceive the performance of *Messiah* as a worshipful proclamation of the *meaning* of Christ and of the great messianic events of the Christian faith, including his birth, crucifixion, resurrection, ascension, and return. Someone who knew nothing of the gospel, however, would be hard pressed to describe these events if he only had Handel's oratorio. *Messiah* does not *tell* the story of Jesus; it *celebrates the meaning* of the story of Jesus for those who already know the story. The Song of Songs, if one may put it this way, deals with something that is much more of a *non*story than is *Messiah*. While *Messiah* deals specifically with Jesus Christ, the Song only deals with an anonymous, idealized man and woman who anticipate their marriage, consummate their marriage, and begin their married life. It commemorates and idealizes the *marriage event itself*, and not any particular persons.

But just to make the point that the kind of song collection suggested here is not confined to baroque music, we may also think of the Andrew Lloyd Webber musical *Cats*. Based on the poems of T. S. Eliot's *Old Possum's Book of Practical Cats*, this musical celebrates the personalities of "Jellicle cats" by describing them in terms that are at the same time both human and feline. There is a series of individual songs by various singers and groups, but some lines and motifs are repeated throughout the musical. *Cats* is not a story, but its songs are not randomly thrown together. It has a shadow of a story line. Finally, to understand that the notion of a unified collection of songs is not a Western innovation, one should realize that many of the books of the prophets are collections of poems arranged into single, coherent messages (e.g., Hosea, Micah, Amos). To be sure, the poetry of the prophets is not the lyrical poetry of the Song of Songs, but the idea that the Song could be a structurally unified piece composed of individual songs by a single author is not anachronistic. An even closer analogy, however, is in the Nakhtsobek Songs of Papyrus Chester Beatty I discussed above.

Interpretations of the Song

It is almost *de rigueur* for a commentary on Song of Songs to review the history of the interpretation of the Song. There is an important point to this; one's interpretation of the text will be driven from beginning to end by what position one takes with regard to the book's genre (Longman, 21). The history of the interpretation of the Song also raises questions about what constitutes a legitimate hermeneutic. If one regards it as a symbolic portrayal of the love that exists between Christ and the soul and if one accepts the validity of allegorizing a text, then every line will be explored allegorically. The following brief samples from the mass of literature on the Song should enable the reader to get a sense of how various interpreters have handled the Song through the centuries.

THE ALLEGORICAL INTERPRETATIONS

Bibliography

Alexander, P. S. "The Song of Songs as Historical Allegory: Notes on the Development of an Exegetical Tradition." In *Targumic and Cognate Studies*. Ed. K. Cathcart and M. Maher. Sheffield: Sheffield Academic Press, 1996. 14–29. ———. "Textual Criticism and Rabbinic Literature: The Case of the Targum of the Song of Songs." *BJRL* 75 (1993) 159–73. **Alshich, M.** *Shir Hashirim: Love Song of a Nation*. Trans. R. Shahar. Jerusalem: Feldheim, 1993. **Astell, A. W.** *The Song of Songs in the Middle Ages*. Ithaca, NY: Cornell UP, 1990. **Brown, P.** *The Body and Society: Men, Women, and Sexual Renunciation in Early Christianity*. New York: Columbia UP, 1988. **Burrows, M. S.** "Foundations for an Erotic Christology: Bernard of Clairvaux on Jesus as 'Tender Lover.'" *AThR* 80 (1998) 477–93. **Cahill, J. B.** "The Date and Setting of Gregory of Nyssa's Commentary on the Song of Songs."*JTS* 32 (1981) 447–60. **Chaucer, G.** *The Canterbury Tales*. Ed. V. A. Kolve and G. Olson. New York: Norton, 1989. **Dove, M.** "Sex, Allegory and Censorship: A Reconsideration of Medieval Commentaries on the Song of Songs." *Literature and Theology* 10 (1996) 317–28. **Elder, D.** *The Song of Songs: A Metaphysical Interpretation*. Marina del Rey,

CA: DeVorss, 1988. **Goppelt, L.** *Typos: The Typological Interpretation of the Old Testament in the New.* Grand Rapids: Eerdmans, 1982. **Grossfeld, B.** *The Targum to the Five Megilloth.* New York: Hermon, 1973. **John of Ford.** *Sermons on the Final Verses of the Song of Songs.* Trans. W. M. Beckett. Kalamazoo, MI: Cistercian, 1977. **Kellner, M. M.** "Introduction to the Commentary on Song of Songs Composed by the Sage Levi Ben Gershom—An Annotated Translation." In *From Ancient Israel to Modern Judaism.* Vol. 2, *Judaism in the Middle Ages.* FS M. Fox, ed. J. Neusner, E. S. Frerichs, and N. M. Sarna. Atlanta: Scholars Press, 1989. 187–205. **Kimelman, R.** "Rabbi Yohanan and Origen on the Song of Songs: A Third-Century Jewish-Christian Disputation." *HTR* 73 (1980) 567–95. **Lewis, C. S.** *The Allegory of Love.* London: Oxford UP, 1936. ———. *On Stories and Other Essays on Literature.* Ed. W. Hooper. New York: Harcourt Brace and Jovanovich, 1966. **Loewe, R.** "Apologetic Motifs in the Targum to the Song of Songs." In *Biblical Motifs: Origins and Transformations.* Ed. A. Altmann and P. W. Lown. Studies and Texts 3. Waltham, MA: Institute of Advanced Judaic Studies, Brandeis University, 1966. 159–96. **Matter, E. A.** *Voice of My Beloved.* **McCambley, C.** "St Gregory of Nyssa's Commentary on the Song of Songs." *Coptic Church Review* 3 (1982) 145–52. **Miller, P. C.** "Pleasure of the Text, Text of Pleasure: Eros and Language in Origen's Commentary on the Song of Songs." *JAAR* 54 (1986) 241–53. **Newberry, T.** *The Song of Solomon.* Kilmarnock: Ritchie, n.d. **Newton, A. L.** *The Song of Solomon: Compared with Other Parts of Scripture.* New York: Carter & Bros., 1858. **Norris, R. A., Jr.** "The Soul Takes Flight: Gregory of Nyssa and the Song of Songs." *AThR* 80 (1998) 517–32. **Phipps, W. E.** "The Plight of the Song of Songs." *JAAR* 42 (1974) 82–100. **Simon, M.,** trans. *Midrash Rabbah: Song of Songs.* London: Soncino, 1983. **Thomson, R. W.** "Gregory of Narek's Commentary on the Song of Songs." *JTS* 34 (1983) 453–96. **Tournay, J. R.** "Abraham et le Cantique des cantiques." *VT* 25 (1975) 544–52. ———. *Word of God, Song of Love.* Trans. J. E. Crowley. New York: Paulist, 1988. **Turner, D.** *Eros and Allegory.*

Both Christians and Jews have a long history of treating Song of Songs as an allegory. Jews have often taken it to be an allegory either of the history of Israel's redemption or of the love for wisdom. Christians typically regard it as a portrayal of the love between Christ and the church, or Christ and the individual believer's soul. Occasionally other elements, such as the veneration of Mary, are also inserted into Christian interpretations of the Song. The following remarks will sample the views of various allegorizers of the Song in order to enable the reader to appreciate the diversity of viewpoints. Where practical, I will cite various interpretations of the same verse or similar verses in order to illustrate how different interpreters deal with similar texts.

Jewish Allegorizing

The origin of Jewish allegorism is unknown. Rabbi Aqiba is said to have uttered the curse, "He who trills his voice in the chanting of the Song of Songs and treats it as a secular song, has no share in the world to come!" (*t. Sanh.* 12.10, cited in R. K. Harrison, *Introduction to the Old Testament,* 1051, and in virtually every major commentary on the Song). This suggests that in the late first or early second century C.E. there were those who sang it in a bawdy manner as an erotic song. The Targum on the Song (composed after the sixth century but no doubt with material drawn from earlier periods) presents it as an outline of the history of Israel's sin and redemption in five movements: the exodus, Sinai, and conquest (1:2–3:6); the temple of Solomon (3:7–5:1); Israel's apostasy and exile (5:2–6:1); the return and the rebuilding of the temple (6:2–7:11); and the dispersion and messianic era (7:12–8:14). (For a summary of the Targum, see Pope, 95–96; for a translation, B. Grossfeld, *Targum to the Five Megilloth*, 171–252.) The Targum was not simply a recapitulation of the history of Israel; it also extolled the written and oral Torah. R. Loewe ("Apologetic Motifs") argues that elements in the Targum's interpretation are polemic against either Christian allegorization of the Song or Jewish esoteric mysticism.

Pope cites the Targum throughout his commentary; an example will give the reader something of the flavor of targumic exegesis. On Song 2:4 ("He takes me to the house of wine / and his banner toward me is love"), the Targum has, "The assembly of Israel said: YHWH brought me into the Academy of Research on Sinai to learn the Law from the mouth of Moses, the great Scribe, and the regimen of His Commandments I received in love and I said: 'All that YHWH has commanded I will do and I will obey'" (Pope, 377). P. S. Alexander ("Song of Songs as Historical Allegory") gives a full history of the historical-allegorical interpretation of the Song from its beginning in the Targum to its most recent revival among French Catholic interpreters of Robert's school (see discussion below).

The Midrash Rabbah on Song of Songs seems to date from the early midrashic period, ca. 500 C.E. The text illustrates rabbinic interpretations of the Song of Songs, but they never stray far from a historical-allegorical mode. The following excerpt (Simon's translation, *Midrash Rabbah*, 102–3) illustrates this (small caps and italics original).

HE HATH BROUGHT ME TO THE HOUSE OF WINE. R. Meir and R. Judah gave different explanations of this. R. Meir said: The Community of Israel said: 'The Evil Inclination obtained mastery over me like wine, and I said to the calf, *This is thy god, O Israel* (Ex. XXXII, 4). When wine goes into a man it confuses his mind.' Said R. Judah to him: Enough of that, Meir; we do not expound the Song of Songs in a bad sense but only in a good one, since the Song of Songs was composed only for the praise of Israel. What then is meant by HE HATH BROUGHT ME TO THE HOUSE OF WINE? Said the Community of Israel: 'The Holy One, blessed be He, brought me to a great cellar of wine, namely Sinai. There He gave me banners of Torah and precepts and good deeds, and in great love I accepted them.' R. Abba said in the name of R. Isaac: The Community of Israel said: 'The Holy One, blessed be He, brought me to a great cellar of wine, namely Sinai, and from there gave me the Torah which is expounded with forty-nine reasons for declaring clean and forty-nine reasons for declaring unclean, the numerical value of the word *wediglo* (and his banner). And with great love I accepted it, as it says, AND HIS BANNER OVER ME IS LOVE.'

The next significant Jewish interpretation still extant is that of Saadia (ca. 892–942), the spiritual leader of a Jewish community in Babylon. According to Pope (101–2), he also read the Song as an allegorical history of Israel, but his exegesis did not follow the Targum. Rabbi Solomon ben Isaac (ca. 1040–1105), also called Rashi, treated the Song as an allegory of the sin and redemption of Israel more or less along the lines of Hos 1–3. Other medieval Jewish scholars (Rashbam, ibn Ezra) allegorized the Song in various ways.

A more philosophical reading was initiated by Maimonides (1135–1204), who suggested that the Song referred not to the nation of Israel but to the love between God and the individual. Several of his disciples produced commentaries in this mode, including Joseph ben Judah ben Jacob ibn Aknin, Samuel ibn Tibbon, Moses ibn Tibbon, and Joseph ibn Kaspi. These interpreters generally saw the Song as a mystical allegory of the intellect. In the late sixteenth century Don Isaac Abravanel treated the Song as an allegory of Solomon's love for Wisdom, and this interpretation subsequently was developed by a number of Jewish interpreters (Pope, 102–12). A Kabbalistic interpretation, with numerous references to the Shekinah, is found in the commentary of Ezra ben Solomon of Gerona (died ca. 1238). An English version appeared in 1999 (see *Commentary Bibliography*).

Perhaps the greatest interpreter of the Song in the tradition of Maimonides was Levi ben Gershom (Gersonides), who lived from 1288 to 1344. This mode of analysis brought a decisive break from the dominant Jewish tradition. For Gersonides, Song of Songs is essentially a work of epistemology! M. Kellner, in his introduction to Gersonides' commentary (Levi ben Gershom, xviii–xx), says that Gersonides is concerned with the problem of how knowledge is acquired and the impediments to attaining true knowledge. This is a matter of great importance since errors in speculative knowledge actually take the philosopher further from perfection. The Torah, then, gives guidance in the acquisition of true knowledge, and the Song of Songs is an allegory of epistemology. The structure of the Song is as follows: (1) introduction to the purpose of the Song (1:1–8); (2) impediments to knowledge that relate to moral imperfection (1:9–2:7); (3) impediments to knowledge that relate to imagination and opinion (2:8–17); (4) mathematics (3:1–4:7); (5) physics (4:8–8:4); (6) metaphysics (8:5–14). Gersonides' approach is illustrated by his interpretation of Song 4:5, "Your breasts are like two fawns, twins of a gazelle, that graze among the lotuses" (Levi ben Gershom, 56–57; italics original, bracketed items added):

> Since breasts serve to nurse he compared that which emanates to her breasts. He allegorically compared her to *two fawns that are twins of a gazelle* because of their fleetness. He said this because of her diligence to prepare for him what he needs from her in these sciences [mathematics]. His statement *which feed among the lilies* is clear on the basis of what we said in our introduction [that fragrances symbolize the stimulating of the intellect]. This verse accords with the allegory alone.
>
> He began praising her from her head and descended step by step to her breasts since in this science one always proceeds from the prior to the posterior when we judge the existence of one thing because of the existence of another thing. This is clear. On the whole, few things escape this.

At this point, Gersonides moves into an excursus on whether astronomy is an exception to this rule.

It should come as no surprise that this approach to the Song is esoteric and not intended for the Jewish masses. If nothing else, it vividly illustrates the fact that the allegorist can see whatever he wants to see in Song of Songs.

One should not suppose that the rise of philosophical, mystical, and Kabbalistic interpretations of the Song meant the end of Jewish commentaries that focused on Israel's history. The mysterious Rabbi Abraham ben Isaac ha-Levi Tamakh, apparently a thirteenth-century Spanish Jew, wrote a commentary that treats every passage in two parts: its natural meaning and its hidden meaning. In dealing with the natural meaning, Rabbi Abraham is very straightforward in describing it as love poetry, and he does not shy away from its erotic nature. At the same time, he does not explore the significance of the metaphors or symbolism, from a sexual standpoint, in any detail at all. Throughout the Song he sees allusions to the history of Israel. On the two breasts in Song 4:5, he says, "The breasts are the king and high priest. Just as the breasts are a woman's glory and beauty as the source of her influence on her babes, so are the former the people's glory and beauty and the source of the influence upon them of the Urim and Tumim, as stated in the Mishnah" (Abraham ben Isaac ha-Levi Tamakh, 115).

Rabbi Moshe Alshich (ca. 1502–1591) wrote a commentary influenced by mystical theology. Nevertheless, he focused on the love relationship between God and Israel that persists even in Israel's diaspora. His more traditional reading of the Song is illustrated by his interpretation of Song 4:5 (Alshich, 166–67 [emphasis original]):

> Israel was blessed with another merit, *for your two breasts,* Moses and Aaron, who sustained you, enabled you to draw nourishment from the heavenly influence. They were *like two fawns* who run extremely fast, for they hastened the redemption from slavery in Egypt, as the Sages say (Shemoth Rabbah 15:3), that in their merit Israel were [sic] redeemed at that time.
>
> How can we measure the greatness of their piety? They were so closely attached to one another that we were redeemed in their merit. Like *twins of a gazelle,* their souls were bound up with each other to such an extent that one could not exist without the other, and if one were to die, the other would likewise die of a broken heart.
>
> Aaron was originally Israel's leader and prophet. Yet his heart rejoiced when he heard of Moses' rise to greatness. And when Moses was commanded by God to take over the mantle of leadership, he declined at first, saying, *Send by the hand of whom You will send* (Exodus 4:13). For seven days he persisted in his refusal, fearing that he was infringing on his brother's authority, as the Sages comment on the above verse in Exodus (Shemoth Rabbah 3:16): "Send by the hand of the one whom You usually send, and that is Aaron."
>
> Alternatively, the meaning can be explained as follows:
>
> *Twins of a gazelle.* The Talmud (Bava Bathra 16b) reports that a gazelle only gives birth once her womb opens after it is bitten by a snake. Similarly, the birth of Moses and Aaron also came about by the bite of a snake, so to speak. As we have said, the reason for the exile in Egypt was to purge Israel of the moral impurities injected into mankind by the snake because of Adam's sin. This moral cleansing prepared them for the giving of the Torah and entry into the Land of Israel. To help Israel toward this aim, God furnished them with great leaders, Moses and Aaron. Hence the brothers' existence was, in part, due to a snake.

Alshich's interpretation is driven in part by reading הרועים בשושנים not as "that graze among the lotuses" but as "the shepherds of the lotuses/roses." This view is not original to him; Midrash Rabbah and Rashi also identified the two breasts as Moses and Aaron (although Rashi also suggested that the two breasts are the two tables of the Decalogue). The Targum, however, was somewhat more nuanced (cited in Pope, 471):

> Your two commanders who will save you, Messiah Son of David, and Messiah Son of Ephraim, resemble Moses and Aaron, sons of Jochebed, who are likened to two young antelopes, twins of a gazelle. By their merit the people of the House of Israel were fed for forty years in the wilderness on manna and plump fowl, and water of Miriam's well.

As we have seen, however, Gersonides took this text in an altogether different direction.

Allegorism has certainly not perished among the Jews. Alshich's translator, R. Shahar, says, "The Song of Songs has no literal interpretation; the verses are either symbolic or allegorical" (Alshich, 13). A recent Jewish commentary on the Song, M. Zlotowitz (1977), really an anthology of the history of Jewish interpretation, celebrates the mode of interpretation of the Targum, Midrash Rabbah, and Rashi. In the "Overview" to this commentary, N. Scherman says, "There are times when to understand a verse according to the simple translation of the words is not to understand it at all. Song of Songs is surely a song of love, but not of one human's love for another" (Zlotowitz, lx). The song of human love is merely the allegorical vehicle whereby God condescends to reveal himself to us in language we can understand. Why is such an allegory necessary? It helps us to sublimate earthly desires in order to achieve victory over carnal lusts: "But whatever the point of struggle, man must make use of his human desires for heavenly ends" (Scherman, in Zlotowitz, liv). The resemblance to Christian monastic theology is so strong here that one wonders who is borrowing from whom.

Early Christian and Roman Catholic Allegorizing

Early Christian interpreters who allegorized the Song include Hippolytus of Rome (d. 235), Origen, Jerome, Gregory of Nyssa, Gregory the Great, and Augustine. They allegorized the Song in different ways. For Hippolytus, the Song described salvation history: it was Solomon's prophecy of the end of the old covenant and the beginning of the new (Murphy, 15). In the fragments of the commentary of Hippolytus that remain, the two breasts of Song 4:5 are the Old and New Testaments that Christians suck upon (Phipps, *JAAR* 42 [1974] 87). Origen (ca. 185–254) taught that the Song celebrates the love between Christ and the soul, or Christ and the church, and this approach came to dominate Christian exegesis.

Origen's commentary was a massive work of ten volumes produced in 240–245 C.E. Unfortunately, except for excerpts in later writers, the only part to survive was his prologue and exposition of Song 1:1–2:15. Although rightly regarded as the fountainhead of Christian allegorism, he describes the Song as an "epithalamium" (wedding song; see discussion below) in the form of a drama. That is, he could be claimed as father of three different modern schools of interpretation—albeit with tongue in cheek. Origen gives far more attention to the literal meaning of the words than his hermeneutical heirs do. Most allegorizing interpreters simply pass over the "plain sense" of the text without comment, but he always begins there. An example of his work, using the Lawson translation (Origen, 179–85), illustrates his method. On Song 2:3 ("Like an apple tree among the trees of the woods, / so is my lover among the young men. / In his shade I take pleasure and sit, / and his fruit is sweet in my mouth."), he begins by simply asserting that it was fitting for the bride to respond to the groom's words (in Song 2:2) with praise directed toward him. He notes that she compares the man favorably to all other men. As an aside, Origen moves into something of a pastoral concern; he does not want his Latin audience to think that the "apple tree" (*arbor mali*) is an "evil tree" (*arbor mala*), so he says that, after the Greek μῆλον, he will call it the "melum tree" (Origen, 179).

At this point, his search for the deeper sense of the words begins. First, the superiority of the groom to other men suggests Christ's superiority to the heavenly ministers, and he cites Ps 82:6 to clinch the point. Moving on, he says that the taste and smell of the apple suggest that Christ is the bread of life, the word made flesh. He concludes:

> We can, then, take the trees of the wood as meaning those angels who have been the authors and promoters of every heresy; so that in this passage, when the Church compares the sweetness of Christ's teaching with the sourness of heretical dogmas and their barren and unfruitful doctrine, she describes as "apples" the sweet and pleasant doctrines preached in the Church of Christ, but as "trees of the wood" those that are asserted by the various heretics. (Origen, 181)

The "trees of the wood" suggest to him Matt 3:10, that the axe is laid to the root, and every tree that does not yield good fruit will be thrown into the fire. The bride thus sits in his shade; that is, the church or the soul clings to God. But the term "shadow" suggests to him Lam 4:20, "Under his shadow we shall live among the Gentiles," which indicates that the Gospel of Christ should come to the Gentiles. It also suggests Luke 1:35, that the Holy Spirit would "overshadow" Mary. Thus the church desires to dwell in the shadow of God, where there is life; in the shadows of the other trees there is only death (Ps 23:4). Origen finally seems to trip himself up with his ruminations on shadows. He goes on to say,

> And further, in order to make the passage before us plainer still, let us also look into what the Apostle means when he speaks of *the Law having a shadow of the good things to come*, and calls all the things that are written about feast days and Sabbaths and new moons *a shadow of the good things to come*—meaning, of course, things that were done according to the letter; and in what sense he declares that the rites of the ancients were *an example and shadow of heavenly things*. If that is so, certainly it follows that all who were under the Law and had the shadow rather than the substance of the true Law, sat under the shadow of the Law. We, however, are strangers to their shadow; for *we are not under the Law, but under grace*. (Origen, 182–83; italics original, representing biblical quotes)

At this point, it is not clear to us whether the "shadow" is a good thing or a bad thing, and Origen does not seem to know either. He is, as it were, chasing shadows. But he is not yet done. He declares that Christ is the truth, and that if we persevere, we shall see him face to face. Paraphrasing (perhaps) Job 8:9, he then says that a man's whole life is a shadow! He finally pulls it all together, more or less, and says that the Law afforded some protection from the heat of the day, but now Christ is our true shade as we await the end of this age, an age that itself is a shadow of the heavenly reality!

Finally, commenting on the clause "his fruit is sweet in my mouth," he contrasts that with the false teachers, whose "throat is an open grave" (Rom 3:13 RSV). Of the true Gospel, he notes that the Bible says, "Our mouth is open to you, Corinthians" (2 Cor 6:11 RSV).

A few observations on Origen's approach are in order. He does recognize and deal with the "plain sense" of the text, although he seems to see no theological value in it. Allegorizing is only part of his method; often he engages in what is sometimes loosely called the midrash-pesher method of exegesis of being pulled from text to text by catchwords and associations. He is almost rabbinical in this regard. His exegesis is probably a Christian variation on midrashic exegesis; R. Kimelman (*HTR* 73 [1980] 567–95) demonstrates that Rabbi Yoḥanan and Origen almost certainly knew each other's exegetical tendencies and that Yoḥanan was attempting to counter Origen's christological expropriation of the Song. The notion that Origen is simply allegorizing is thus not altogether accurate.

Origen is unconcerned about any logical structure to the connections he makes; he puts together a catena of biblical quotes organized around the following of a word, concordance fashion, through the Bible. The end result is a series of biblical quotes that cover a vast array of topics but have no real coherence in the text at hand. There is often no meaningful tie between the associative chains he forges and the text of the Song he is interpreting—or even with an allegorized interpretation of that text. When he moves into his discussion of the Law as the "shadow" of Christ, he apparently has no concern with the fact that his original text spoke positively of sitting under "his shadow." The text of the Song seems to be little more than the first link in his word-chains. Later allegorists would not be nearly as thorough as Origen, but would more consistently and coherently allegorize. P. Miller (*JAAR* 54 [1986] 241–53) suggests that Origen's handling of the text is rooted in a Platonic linking of Eros and language. That is, the text attracts and incites the reader to contemplation.

For the Christian church, Origen is the *beginning* of allegorism in at least two respects. He does not simply ignore the natural significance of the text in the way that later allegorists will. And his work might be better described as a biblical word-associative process than as full-fledged allegorization. His successors will tend to do simple, straightforward allegorization.

Gregory of Nyssa worked from a similar theological and philosophical foundation; in fact, his homilies on the Song are so heavily indebted to Origen that they could be called a revision of Origen's work (see R. Norris, *AThR* 80 [1998] 517–32; C. McCambley, *Coptic Church Review* 3 [1982] 145–52). His homilies are also anagogical, using the Song of Songs to draw the reader up from the carnal to the spiritual (J. Cahill, *JTS* 32 [1981] 447–60) in a theological construct that is influenced by neoplatonist thinking. In his tenth homily on Song 5:2, he says, "Therefore when the soul only enjoys the contemplation of the divine Being, it will not rise from sleep for that which operates according to the senses' pleasure. It will put to rest all bodily movement, and by a naked and pure thought, this soul will receive insight into God's vision through watchfulness" (McCambley, *Coptic Church Review* 3 [1982] 49). Discussing the "drops of the night" in the same verse, he says that they are drops of truth that come from the words of the saints to the contemplative soul (McCambley, *Coptic Church Review* 3 [1982] 150).

Origen is not solely responsible for the rise of allegorism in the Christian church. In addition to his Alexandrian colleagues, significant theologians of the Western church also advocated the use of allegory. Augustine, in *De utilitate credendi*, suggested four levels of meaning in the biblical text: historical (what was written or done), etiological (the cause for which a thing is done), analogical (showing that the two testaments do not conflict), and allegorical (things to be understood figuratively rather than literally). Eventually the fourfold way of the fifth-century monk John Cassian would dominate exegesis (the four ways are the historical [Jerusalem as a historical city], allegorical [Jerusalem as the church], anagogical [Jerusalem as the celestial city], and tropological [Jerusalem as the human soul]); see E. A. Matter, *Voice of My Beloved*, 53–54.

Jerome illustrates the attraction the church fathers had to the allegorical interpretation of the Song, and he fairly clearly states why they clung to this view. In a letter to his disciple Laeta concerning the education of her daughter Paula, he outlines a curriculum for Paula that focuses on biblical studies. Only after she completed an intense study of almost all of the Old and New Testaments was she to be allowed to read the Song (*NPNF*[2] 6:194): "When she has done all these she may safely read the Song of Songs but not before: for, were she to read it at the beginning, she would fail to perceive that, though it is written in fleshly words, it is a marriage song of a spiritual bride. And not understanding this she would suffer from it."

Like Origen, Jerome was trained in Hebrew by rabbis and also tended to cite the Song in a catena fashion that at times seems to make no sense. For example, in his tract on Ps 80 (CCSL 78:76), he devotes a great deal of time to the superscript, which in the Latin reads "for the winepresses" (*pro torcularibus*). He thus cites numerous texts that relate to wine and winepresses, as follows:

> Winepresses are found nowhere else but where there are vineyards and boundless vintages. *For the winepresses*. Therefore the Lord and Savior says: "I have trodden the winepress alone, and of the Gentiles no man is with me" [Isa 63:3]. Therefore he carried a vineyard from Egypt and planted it. And he says in Jeremiah: "I planted a vineyard of all true and chosen seed. How then are you changed toward me into something bitter, strange vine?" [Jer 2:21]. And Noah drank wine, and became drunk. And it was said by Solomon—it was said in the form of a mystery (*dicitur in mysterio*)— "Drink, friends, and become drunk" [Song 5:1].

Jerome then moves into an extended discussion of the drunkenness of Noah and the feasting of Joseph (Gen 43). For him the Song spoke "in the form of a mystery," and he, too, frequently grouped other biblical texts together with the Song for apparently no more reason than the presence of similar words.

As the Christian church embraced celibacy and sexual renunciation as the spiritual ideal, an allegorizing interpretation of the Song became inevitable. Not everyone who allegorized the Song also exalted the life of celibacy; Jewish rabbis and, much later, Protestant ministers would also allegorize the Song even though they did not regard marriage as contrary to their religious calling. Still, the emerging ideal of the Christian man or woman who not only renounced all sexual activity but also was free of sexual desire made a "plain sense" interpretation of the Song inconceivable. For a thorough history of the rise of the ideal of celibacy in the church, see P. Brown, *Body and Society*, and further remarks below on the theology of the Song.

The affair of the monk Jovinian (died ca. 409) illustrates how the attitude toward sexuality in the church at that time guaranteed the triumph of the allegorizing interpretation. This man stated that a married woman was spiritually equal to a virgin, and he also rejected the notion of the perpetual virginity of Mary. Jerome bitterly opposed him; Jovinian was declared to be a heretic and exiled by Emperor Theodosius. In *Adversus Jovinianum* Jerome relegated marriage to a licit but second-class status in the church, and even pillaged classical history and literature for examples of shrewish and unfaithful wives to better make the point that happiness is best found in celibacy (i.48). This work became the mainstay of the church's arguments in favor of clerical celibacy, and it was widely known in Western Christendom for the next thousand years. Its influence can be measured by Chaucer's inclusion of these lines in the Prologue of the Wife of Bath (lines 669–72, *Canterbury Tales,* 121), in which the Wife of Bath protests against the recorded history of the evils of women. She here describes a habit of one of her previous husbands:

> He hadde a book that gladly, night and day,
> For his desport he wolde rede alway.
> He cleped it Valerie and Theofraste,
> At which book he lough alwey ful faste.
> And eek ther was somtyme a clerk at Rome,
> A cardinal, that highte Seint Jerome,
> That made a book agayn Jovinian;
> In which book eek ther was Tertulan.

In other words, her husband would read and chuckle over learned books by Jerome and others that describe the folly of women and of marrying them.

Jerome's attitude toward sexuality emerged in his translation of Song of Songs. Song 8:5b reads in translation from the Hebrew (see *Comment* on 8:5), "Under the apple tree I aroused you. / That is where your mother conceived you, / that is where she conceived, she gave you birth." Jerome translates it, "Under the apple tree I raised you up; there your mother was corrupted, there she who bore you was violated" (*sub arbore malo suscitavi te ibi corrupta est mater tua ibi violata est genetrix tua*). In his translation, Jerome has exploited two homonyms from חבל; the one means to "ruin" and the other "to conceive" or to "give birth." In reality, there should be no confusion here; context (which also has the verb ילד, "to give birth") implies that procreation and not ruination is in view, and the LXX renders the verb as ὠδίνησέν, "she went into labor/gave birth." But Jerome rendered the verb as a passive of חבל, "ruin," and in one case translated it *corrupta* and in the other *violata*. It is difficult to avoid the suspicion that his own tortured attitude toward sexuality markedly influenced his translation at this point (see Brown, *Body and Society,* 374–76). For him, even the sexual act that led to the conception of the beloved is both a defiling (*corrupta*) and deflowering act, if not a rape (*violata*). There is great opportunity for allegorizing here—the "apple tree" or "evil tree" suggests the cross. Using the Latin text, one could take the speaker to be the virgin-born Christ and the one to whom he speaks, who is born of corruption, to be the woman (i.e., the church, first found by Christ in its natural state of idolatry and wickedness). This is in fact precisely the interpretation that Giles of Rome (ca. 1243–1316) gives it (p. 167). In the Hebrew, however, it is clear from the gender of the pronouns that the *woman* is the speaker. Following Jerome's translation, this would imply that it is the *man* who was born of a corrupt, deflowered mother—a theological catastrophe for a Catholic allegorist.

The tendency both to allegorize and to link unrelated texts on the basis of superficial correspondence caused a good deal of trouble for early exegetes, but it also allowed them to exercise their creativity to the fullest. Augustine, when preaching on the washing of the disciples' feet in John 13 (Tractate 57; *NPNF*[1] 1:303–4), observes that baptism washes away all sin but that Christians still defile themselves and need to seek forgiveness, the washing of their feet. But then he almost inevitably cites Song 5:3, "I have washed my feet, how can I dirty them again?" The problem for Augustine is that in his understanding of the Song, the woman (that is, the church) is here addressing her beloved (that is, Christ) and making an excuse for why she cannot let him inside her home. Augustine can solve this only with a homiletical tour de force. "O lofty mystery!" he shouts. The hidden message is that ministers would prefer to be in heaven, with Christ, but that they must serve Christ here in the defiling world instead (citing Phil 1:23–24).

One can find countless citations of this sort among the Fathers. They are spontaneous, often linked to other passages in what to us seems a tenuous and artificial manner, and built on an approach that regards the validity of allegorizing the Song to be a given. M. Dove (*Literature and Theology* 10 [1996] 319–20) argues that in Augustine's mind the fact that Song of Songs had Christ and the church as its subject matter was not allegorizing at all but was the plain meaning of the text!

The medieval period witnessed strong interest in the Song. Bernard of Clairvaux (1090–1153) famously preached eighty-six sermons on the first two chapters of Song of Songs. One should not assume, however, that this mass of material is in any sense a commentary on the Song. Passages in the Song are starting points for sermons on the love between the Christian soul and God. Still, typical examples of allegorizing are everywhere evident. On Song 1:6, he comments that the mother of the woman is the heavenly Jerusalem and her brothers are the apostles, who fought to tear her (that is, the Gentiles) away from paganism. Bernard's sermons are powerful, clear, and stirring, and his place in Christian history should not be taken away because of his role in the Crusades. At the same time, his use of the Song is arbitrary, and his sermons are not grounded in the text of the Song, except as heavily filtered by a theological model of divine Eros drawing the soul from the love of the carnal to the love of the spiritual (cf. M. S. Burrows, *AThR* 80 [1998] 477–93).

The sermons of John of Ford (late twelfth century) are similar. Based on selected passages from the Song, these sermons, although clearly relying on a long tradition of an allegorical hermeneutic, do not attempt anything like a sustained interpretation of the Song. Verses from the Song are again simply the occasion for various sermons. For example, on Song 5:10, taking his cue from "my beloved is radiant and ruddy," he preaches two sermons (John of Ford, 97–124). The first, based on *radiant*, describes the fourfold nature of whiteness (of milk, lilies, snow, and light, symbolizing the sanctity of children, adults, the penitent, and the resurrected). The second, based on *ruddy*, describes the fourfold nature of redness (of vermilion, the rose, blood, and the ruby, symbolizing the blush of penitents, the chaste, the martyr, and those burning with a love for Christ). These sermons could be considered profound (depending on one's theology), and they were certainly pious, but they can hardly be said to be based in the Song. He could have preached the same two sermons with virtually no changes had he made no reference to Song of Songs at all.

A fairly straightforward piece of allegorizing interpretation comes from the tenth-century Armenian monk Gregory of Narek (died ca. 1010). On Song 1:4, where the bride says she is black and beautiful, Gregory says that she represents Gentile Christians. On Song 2:9, where the man is described as a roe behind a wall and looking through a window and a lattice, he says that the roe is Christ, the wall is the body he took from the virgin, the window is the prophets, and the lattice is the Law. On Song 4:5, he says that the two breasts represent the body and soul of man. For a full summary of Gregory of Narek's commentary, see R. Thomson, *JTS* 34 (1983) 453–96.

Medieval Christian interpreters frequently saw Mary in the Song of Songs. The logic is straightforward: the woman of the Song represents the church; Mary is the embodiment of the pure church; therefore, the Song points us to Mary. Honorius Augustodunensis, a prolific writer of the early twelfth century, says the following about the Song of Songs (E. A. Matter, *Voice of My Beloved*, 59):

> Therefore, this book is read on the feast of Blessed Mary, for it shows the type of the Church, which is virgin and mother. Virgin, because uncorrupted by all heresy; mother, because through grace it always bears spiritual children. And therefore everything which is said about the Church can also be said about the Virgin, understood as both bride and mother of the bridegroom.

Another interpreter in this vein was Rupert of Deutz (born ca. 1075), who produced a sustained mariological exposition of the Song. For Rupert, the Song proclaims Mary as the saving counterpart to Eve. Song 1:11 ("my nard gives off its fragrance"), for example, refers to Eve's "stink of pride" and to Mary's fragrant humility (Matter, *Voice of My Beloved*, 162). A late twelfth-century commentator, Alan of Lille, also used the Song to glorify Mary. On "the beams of our house are of cedar," in Song 1:16, he argued that although the words primarily describe the incorruptible nature of Jesus' physical body, they also suggest that Mary's physical body, too, did not undergo any decay (Matter, *Voice of My Beloved*, 166). More than that, for Alan of Lille, the king's houses represent church buildings, all of which are Mary's homes. Astell (*Song of Songs in the Middle Ages*, 46) explains, "She is the pattern for their construction as the womblike home of Christ ('domus Christi'). Even more, she is the maternal 'informatio,' the guiding idea, the pattern for the Church, the *genetrix* whose features appear in all the children of God, even as they do in Jesus, her firstborn."

The combination of allegorizing, Marian devotion, and the Song of Songs could produce interpretations that we could have done without. For example, Denys the Carthusian (ca. 1402–1471), as he ruminated over various ways to take Song 1:2–3 as it appears in the Vg. (*Osculetur me osculo oris sui quia meliora sunt ubera tua vino*; "let him kiss me with the kisses of his mouth, because your breasts are better than wine" [cf. LXX]), came up with an astounding suggestion. He said that "Let him kiss me" represents Mary's words at the annunciation ("Here am I, the servant of the Lord; may it be with me according to your word" [Luke 1:38]) and that "because your breasts" represents the words of Jesus, as both bridegroom and baby, to Mary. That is, the "kissing" is the baby Jesus sucking at the breasts of Mary: "Again, it may be said of those bodily breasts of the most divine Virgin that they, most blessed as they are, are made almost divine by the continual contact of the adorable, incarnate bridegroom who sucked from them; *they are more fragrant than the finest ointments*, more fragrant, that is to say, than the most delicious virginal milk, which the Lord of all things took and sucked from them against that hunger and thirst which he freely in his providence took upon himself and suffered for our sakes" (italics original, representing Song 1:3a;

Turner, *Eros and Allegory*, 442). In the Hebrew, the word *breasts* is not present, and the gender of the pronouns indicates that the man is not the speaker.

Of course, not every commentary of this time was Marian in exposition. In fact, the whole program of Marian exegesis in the Song seems to be have been regarded as a dubious novelty. Guillaume de Saint-Thierry (William of Saint-Thierry), an early twelfth-century monk and mystic, produced an allegorical commentary on the Song that avoided Marian theology. Marian expositions of the Song continued into the twentieth century.

The Song continued to find allegorical interpreters in the Catholic Church through the centuries. Treating the Song as an allegory of love between Christ and the soul appealed to the ascetic and quietist Madame Guyon (1648–1717), who interpreted Song 7:9 ("I said, 'I will climb the palm tree, / I will hold its panicles of dates, / that your breasts may be like the clusters of grapes / and the fragrance of your nipple like apples'") in a manner that reflected her own experience of seeking spiritual direction in a convent (Guyon, 480–81):

> The young virgins having heard the comparison made by the King of Glory, and transported with a desire to partake of the graces of the Spouse, cry out with one voice, or rather, one, expressing the feelings of the rest, exclaims . . . I will become a pupil of this mistress of perfection, and if one so wise and so rich will condescend to become a mother to me I will be her daughter, that I may experience the effects of the anointing of the Bridegroom, which is in her. The fruit of her words will become to me like a cluster of grapes of an exquisite sweetness, and the purity of her teaching will embalm me in its perfume.

As Pope (179–83) points out, more recent Catholic interpretations have allegorized the Song in a historical manner. Among these is the commentary of the distinguished Hebrew scholar Paul Joüon *(Cantique des cantiques* [1909]*),* which suggests that the Song was composed to encourage Jews to return to their homeland. His analysis is thus in the tradition of the Targum, and he asserts that the Song is primarily for Jews and that application of the Song to the church or to Mary is secondary. This approach was further developed in the work of A. Robert (1883–1955) and his students, A. Feuillet and R. Tournay. For these scholars, signs that the Song refers to Israel's history, land, and religion are everywhere to be seen. Thus, for Tournay (*VT* 25 [1975] 546–47), the double call of the man to the woman to "come" (Song 2:10, 13) recalls the double command of Yahweh to Abraham to "go" (Gen 12:1; 22:2), and the beautiful appearance of the woman of the Song (2:14) recalls the beautiful appearance of Sarah (Gen 12:11). There are many other such examples. Following the Targum, Tournay (*Word of God*, 87) argues that the "mountain of myrrh" and "hill of incense" in Song 4:6 allude to the incense offerings of the temple; the very word for myrrh (מוֹר) brings to mind the name of the temple hill, Mount Moriah. In Song 6:12, the name Amminadiv calls to mind the Abinadab of 1 Sam 7:1, who had the ark of the covenant stationed at his home. This, to Tournay (*Word of God*, 101–2), suggests the whole history of the ark of the covenant and especially the language of 1 Chr 29:5–6!

An analogous interpretation from a recent Roman Catholic expositor is that of L. Stadelmann. He reads the text as an allegory that uses "political prudence so as to cover Jewish nationalism from the eyes of the Persian authorities since they might suspect a burgeoning insurrection against their domination over

Judah" (Stadelmann, 1). The book is a kind of disguised patriotic tract written by postexilic Jews. Song 4:1–7 "deals with the nation, integrating social groups from both the rural and urban area, harmoniously incorporated so as to constitute a political community. . . . The nation is portrayed as a youthful woman, whose figure from the head down to the chest is rendered with elegance and clever simplicity" (Stadelmann, 115). When v 6 speaks of the bridegroom going to the mountain of myrrh and hill of frankincense, it refers to the king coming to the hills around Jerusalem to re-establish a Jewish monarchy (Stadelmann, 114, 116).

Protestant Allegorizing

The position of Luther on allegorizing the Song of Songs is somewhat ambiguous and debated. On the one hand, he distrusted the allegorism of the medieval church and observed that "it takes no effort to invent [allegories]" (*LW* 15:200). At the same time, many individual comments follow typical allegorical models: "kisses" (Song 1:2) are the word of God (*LW* 15:196); "dark skin" (Song 1:5) is the sinfulness of the church (*LW* 15:201–2); "my beloved is like a young stag" (Song 2:9) refers to the word of God leaping from one city to another (*LW* 15:217–18); the "turtledove" (Song 2:12) is godly people learning the word of God (*LW* 15:219); and so forth. Indeed, contrary to E. Kallas (*LQ* 2 [1988] 323–41), the Song is allegorized from beginning to end in Luther, although probably not in any coherent manner. But Luther has a most interesting comment on Song 4:5, a text that I have used as something of a test case for allegorizing interpreters:

> But what is the connection between breasts and twin fawns? Perhaps he is suggesting that they are not breasts like those of whores but chaste and delicate breasts. . . .
> Yet they feed in the woods. But this is part of the same description, that he means delightful and more delicate breasts, namely, such as derive their fullness not from the crude pasture of grass but from roses.
> Here I will issue no warning concerning those impure thoughts which befall youth when they hear such descriptions. For the Holy Spirit is pure and so mentions women's bodily members that He wants them to be regarded as good creatures of God. And indeed, there is nothing in this book that pleases me more than the fact that I see Solomon speaking in such sweet figures about the highest gifts which God has conferred on His people. (*LW* 15:230–31)

Still, he considers this, too, to have allegorical significance. He was aware of the "natural" sense of the words and could not help but comment in that vein from time to time.

The viewpoint of Calvin is also open to some dispute, and in his case we have little evidence to work with. For the vast majority of Protestants, the Song was strictly an allegory of the love between Christ and the church/pious soul. Seventeenth-century divines such as J. Flavel and J. Cotton abandoned taking Scripture in its natural sense when it came to Song of Songs, and this trend dominated Protestant exegesis until the rise of the dramatic interpretations in the nineteenth century. Even then this mode of reading the Song did not die out; Protestant allegorizing continued into the twentieth century.

The Scottish divine J. Durham (1622–1658) is exceedingly thorough in his analysis of Song 4:5 (212). To him, two breasts enhance the "comeliness of the body," are "useful to give suck," and "signify warmness of affection." They symbolize believers' fitness to nurture others as well as their "warmliness and kindliness to Christ" since they have taken him "into their bosom." A mammoth Protestant allegorizing of the Song is that of John Gill (1697–1771), who finds an enormous variety of truths in Song 4:5 (148–50). For him, the two breasts are first ministers of the Gospel, in that they nurture the church. They are like twin roes in that they are loving and pleasant, sharp-eyed in watching out for the truth, and swift to spread the gospel. That there are two of them implies that they are sufficient in number to do the job required of them (as two breasts are enough to feed a baby). They are twins, that is, are in harmony, and they feed among the lilies, meaning that they feed on the Scriptures and work among the saints. In addition, Gill continues, the two breasts are the Old and New Testaments. They are alike in their promises and doctrines. The two breasts are also the two ordinances of baptism and the Lord's Supper. In short, the two breasts are anything in the Christian faith that comes in a pair.

The analysis of Richard F. Littledale (1833–1890) is similar (156–57). He takes the two breasts to be Mother Church nurturing her children with the Old and New Testaments. To A. L. Newton, the two breasts of Song 4:5 suggest the unity of Christ's church, and she cites 1 Cor 1:10 and numerous other NT texts to describe this virtue (A. L. Newton, *Song of Solomon*, 118–19). Another nineteenth-century interpreter, T. Newberry (*Song of Solomon*, 45), takes Song 4:1–5, with its description of the woman's eyes, hair, teeth, temples, neck and breasts, to be a representation of the complete and holy state of the church triumphant at the marriage supper of the Lamb.

The nineteenth-century American Presbyterian George Burrowes also allegorizes the Song. In general, his commentary reflects an admirable education in the classics (it frequently alludes to ancient and European literary works), but is otherwise unimaginative. On the text that we have used as a test case for various interpreters, Song 4:5, he simply says that "the thing to be illustrated is the general beauty of the pious soul in the eyes of Jesus" (285). He seems uncomfortable at the thought that Jesus would look upon the saints as a man looks upon a woman's breasts and is at pains to suggest that the ancient "orientals" really did not regard the female breasts as something to be hidden, and that it would be inappropriate to develop a metaphor of Christ's beloved as a woman and not include the breasts. Referring to various NT passages, he says that Song 4:5 illustrates how Christ has glorified humanity (284–88).

This kind of allegorical interpretation persisted in Protestant Bible studies into the twentieth century. R. E. Neighbor's commentary (107) treats the Song as an allegory of Christ and the soul, and so comments on Song 5:16a ("His thighs are alabaster pillars / set on pedestals of pure gold") with only the faintest reflection on what the text of the Song actually says, but drawing heavily on the NT.

> Here is a picture of stately strength, builded upon a foundation of incalculable worth. How matchless is the power, how marvelous is the strength of our God. The Lord Jesus upholds all things by the word of his power. When he speaks, the lame walk; the sick are healed; the deaf hear; the dead come forth. Our Lord is the omnipotent God, and in His omnipotence, He is all glorious.

Neighbor says nothing about Song 4:5; he skips verses that are conspicuously sexual (e.g., Song 7:8–9 [ET 7:7–8]).

Problems with Allegorizing Interpretations

To read a single allegorical interpretation is to be impressed, and to wonder if the author is on to something profound; to read a hundred allegorical interpretations is to be depressed, and to want to discard the whole. Allegorizing interpretations cannot withstand comparison and analysis. No single interpretation has any more claim to legitimacy or makes any more sense than any other. Allegorical interpretation is forced, subject only to the creative imagination of the interpreter, and extraneous to the Song of Songs. Are the breasts of the woman (Song 4:5) to be understood as Moses and Aaron, or the two tablets of the Decalogue, or mathematical reasoning, or Christian pastors, or the two testaments of the Christian Bible, or the church as a whole, or the two ordinances of Protestant worship, or the beauty of the church in the eyes of Christ? No reading is inherently more reasonable or plausible than another. A recent allegorizing commentary, written from the perspective of the modern eclectic religion broadly called "new age" (Elder, *Song of Songs,* 1988), illustrates the point. This book's meandering thoughts about Christ, Buddha, Krishna, and the "Universal God" are absurdly arbitrary, but as an allegory of the Song they have as much claim to legitimacy as any other.

An allegory, that is, a story that is actually intended to be read as an allegory, generally tells the reader that it is an allegory in a very obvious and deliberate way. C. S. Lewis, describing Tolkien's *Lord of the Rings,* makes the following point (*On Stories,* 85): "What shows that we are reading myth, not allegory, is that there are no pointers to a specifically theological, or political, or psychological application." By contrast, Jotham's allegory of the trees (Judg 9:7–21) could hardly be more conspicuously a political allegory. The Song never suggests that an allegorical meaning is intended. Allegorizing of the sort one sees with the Song has no antecedent in the NT; Paul's use of the verb ἀλληγορέω in Gal 4:24 does not correspond to allegorizing as we see it in the interpretation of the Song; cf. Goppelt, *Typos,* 139–40.

A few obvious trends emerge from a survey of allegorical interpretations. The first and most obvious is that the imagination of the individual interpreter drives the entire process. The second is that interpreters almost always see their own religious traditions in the text. For Jews, two breasts suggest Moses and Aaron, or the two tables of the Law. For Christians, they suggest Mother Church, or the two testaments of the Bible, or pastors (recent Catholic interpreters who read the Song as a Jewish political tract are an exception here). The third trend is that allegorical interpretations are often suggested by simple psychological association. Breasts = nurture, and therefore breasts refer to the great leaders of Israel, or to pastors. The number two suggests things that come in pairs, such as Moses and Aaron or the two testaments of the Bible. The fourth trend is that allegories are often suggested by word associations to other passages in the Bible. Many an allegorizing interpreter appears to believe that his or her interpretation is the last word on the subject—and sometimes will say so!

The origin and underpinnings of allegorizing leave one uneasy with the method. Allegorizing arose among pagans who wanted to find a way to salvage morsels of truth from the stories about the drunkenness, pettiness, violence, homosexuality, and lechery of their gods. Early pagan allegorists, such as Pherecydes of Syros and Theogenes of Rhegium (both sixth century B.C.E.), provided a way for the Greeks to do just that; thus, when Saturn devours his offspring, it turns out to be no more than an allegory of the passing of time. This manner of interpretation began a tradition that extended into the scholarship of Alexandria and on into the Jewish synagogue and Christian church.

Allegorism of the Song is rooted in a neoplatonic worldview that was more gnostic than Christian. This worldview asserts that the body, with its needs, appetites, and excretions, is by nature base, unspiritual, and finally evil. True spirituality is liberation from the powers of the body. It is true that some pagans and gnostics claimed one could attain this liberation through indulging bodily appetites, but the more standard route, and certainly the one that religious monotheists chose, was asceticism. Ascetic or libertine, the philosophical foundation is still the same: the physical is bad and antispiritual. Thus, an allegorizing interpretation of the Song was inevitable. The Song cannot be about sexual love, the reasoning goes, since we know that sexual love is the quintessence of carnality and therefore is by nature evil, even if licit in marriage. And it is not only Christians who fall into this pattern of thinking. N. Scherman, the Jewish allegorist cited above, is positively Augustinian in tone, if not neoplatonic!

The Christian church in late antiquity and the medieval period adopted a hostile attitude toward sexual desire. As C. S. Lewis has described it in *The Allegory of Love* (14–15: italics original):

> The views of medieval churchmen on the sexual act within marriage (there is no question, of course, about the act outside marriage) are all limited by two complementary agreements. On the one hand, nobody ever asserted that the act was intrinsically sinful. On the other hand, all were agreed that some evil element was present in every concrete instance of this act since the Fall. It was in the effort to determine the precise nature of this concomitant evil that learning and ingenuity were expended. Gregory, at the end of the sixth century, was perfectly clear on this question: for him the act is innocent but the desire is morally evil. If we object to the conception of an intrinsically wicked impulse towards an intrinsically innocent action, he replies by the example of a righteous rebuke delivered in anger. What we say may be exactly what we ought to have said; but the emotion which is the efficient cause, remains guilty. But the concrete sexual act, that is, the act *plus* its unavoidable efficient cause, remains guilty. When we come down to the late Middle Ages this view is modified. Hugo of St. Victor agrees with Gregory in thinking the carnal desire an evil. But he does not think that this makes the concrete act guilty, provided it is "excused" by the good ends of marriage, such as offspring.

This attitude is well illustrated in Chaucer's *Canterbury Tales*. In book 2 of the Man of Law's Tale, the story of the virtuous Christian Princess Constance, he all but apologizes for the fact that she had sexual relations with her beloved husband, King Alla, and mentions that this is something that a pious woman must endure as a necessary part of marriage. By contrast, in the Miller's Tale, the adulterous affair of Fly Nicholas and Alison, the carpenter's wife, is, to say the least, robust.

This viewpoint is contrary to the teachings of the Bible, which declares the creation of the physical world, the living creatures, and man as male and female to be "good," and which explicitly celebrates the union of man and woman (Gen 1;

2:18–25). There are two viewpoints that biblical theology equally disavows: fertility paganism, which regards sex as a point of intersection between the physical and the divine, and a gnostic type of asceticism, which regards the physical, and in particular the sexual, as innately evil. While the Bible condemns lust after the other woman as evil, it never describes the sexual desire itself as evil, least of all when expressed toward one's wife. Also, while Paul urges believers to consider whether it is wise to marry and have children in light of the "impending crisis" (1 Cor 7:26), and although he would prefer that more believers were, like himself, free to devote their entire lives to the service of Christ (1 Cor 7:32–35), he never implies that celibacy or virginity is innately a *holier* state than matrimony—and for him, matrimony by definition includes sexual relations (1 Cor 7:1–5).

The language of sexual love is brought into the realm of spiritual devotion to the detriment of both. In Song 7:8–9 (ET 7:7–8), the man declares that the woman is like a palm tree and her breasts are like its clusters of dates. He will climb the tree and seize the clusters! One cringes at using these terms to describe the love of God for his people, or the love of the soul for the truth, or whatever other spiritual sense can be attached to it. This is not appropriate language for worship and spirituality. Spiritualizing the words prevents the hearer from appreciating how they celebrate the joy a young man has in his wife's body.

I do not believe that the allegorization of any text of the Song is of theological or exegetical value. To say that the man in the Song is the redeemer figure just as Christ is the redeemer is true, but this does not validate allegorization as such. Rather, the Song brings out the deep structure of human transformation, and this process of transformation has its quintessential expression in the Christian gospel. Understood in this way, we may yet achieve some reconciliation of Antioch (the natural reading of the text) and Alexandria (the spiritual reading of the text). That is, one can grasp the spiritual meaning of the Song without abandoning the straightforward meaning of the love poetry.

But one must work through the natural, ordinary and in my view self-evident meaning of the Song in order to comprehend this process of transformation. One cannot allegorize it, for when the Song is allegorized, its transformational image is lost. The woman and her loss of virginity become invisible. To put it bluntly, the Song of Songs really is a song about kisses, physical beauty, and sexual union. When Song 4:5 mentions female breasts, it means female breasts and not Moses and Aaron, Mary as spiritual mediatrix, or the nurturing power of the church. But physical sex is not the whole story; transformation is at the heart of the Song. Understood in this way, the Song of Songs and the gospel both speak of the same need for intimacy and transcendence. One can find this message only when one is willing to give the Song an honest reading.

THE DRAMATIC INTERPRETATIONS

Bibliography

Bullock, C. H. *An Introduction to the Old Testament Poetic Books.* Chicago: Moody Press, 1979. **Emmerson, G. I.** "The Song of Songs: Mystification, Ambiguity and Humour." In *Crossing the Boundaries.* FS M. D. Goulder, ed. S. Porter, P. Joyce, and D. E. Orton. Leiden: Brill, 1994. 97–111. **Goulder, M. D.** *Song of Fourteen Songs.* **Waterman, L.** *The Song of Songs.*

Ann Arbor: Univ. of Michigan Press, 1948. **Woods, T. E. P.** *Shulammith.* Grand Rapids: Eerdmans, 1940.

In the last two centuries, it has been fairly popular to interpret the Song as some kind of drama. Two major varieties exist: the three-character drama and the two-character drama.

The Three-Character Interpretations

All three-character interpretations follow the same basic story line. Solomon wants to bed a young Israelite girl and takes her into his harem, but she is in love with another, usually identified as a shepherd, and she resists his ardent pleas for her sexual favors. In the end, she escapes and makes her way to her beloved. The theory, supposedly but probably not actually suggested by ibn Ezra, was developed by J. F. Jacobi, S. Löwisohn, and H. Ewald; see M. Pope (104, 111–12), who considers Löwisohn to be the true founder of this interpretation, and R. K. Harrison (*Introduction*, 1054).

The three-character drama is arbitrary in nature; its advocates tend to see what they want to see in the lyrics. If an interpreter assigns a love song to the "shepherd," the words are ardent and pure; if another interpreter assigns the same text to Solomon, it is lustful and manipulative. Sometimes a single interpreter will take the same words to be both empty flattery and pure love. This is illustrated by Adeney (8), who comments, "Solomon's compliments are frigid and stilted; they describe the object of his affection in the most extravagant terms, but they exhibit no trace of feeling." As an example of Solomon's hollow praise, he singles out Song 1:15, where "Solomon" says that the woman's eyes are like doves (Adeney, 19). Adeney has not noticed that the woman uses the same empty flattery when speaking to her own true love (Song 5:12).

Certainly no one has surpassed T. Woods for an imaginative interpretation of Song of Songs as a three-character play. He introduces the Song with a lengthy and highly creative retelling of the story behind the biblical book, complete with "Shulammith" (the woman of the Song) weeping and pleading to her uncle to save her from the king's advances. An excerpt from this commentary (*Shulammith*, 50–51) will illustrate how this approach forges a full-scale novel out of thin air (words of the Song are in bold, as in Woods's original text):

The door opens and Shulammith comes in. Solomon rises, meets her, and conducts her to the couch already arranged for her. His eyes devour her beauty. Then the king kneels before her, touches her arm gently, as he speaks in low tones charged with passion he cannot control.

Thou art beautiful,
O my love, as Tirzah;
Comely as Jerusalem;
Fair as the moon,
Clear as the sun;
Terrible as an army with banners.

In spite of her resolution, Shulammith is affected by the emotion in his voice. She lifts her eyes and looks at him searchingly. Is there not something of greatness, something generous in this man of high rank, to which she can appeal? She is about to speak, when Solomon, grasping her arm till it hurts, cries out,

Turn thine eyes away from me,
For they quite conquer me.

With a sigh of disappointment, she bows her head and gestures with her free hand to the arm he is holding so tightly. He releases her and struggles for mastery over himself. There is silence in the room.

This novelization of the Song illustrates what can happen in "dramatic" interpretations: the setting, actions, and motivations behind the lines of the Song are created by the interpreter without any warrant from the text. This excerpt also illustrates a problem specific to the three-character model, that some of the most beautiful lines of love of the Song are transformed into the self-indulgent attempts of an oversexed king to seduce one of his female subjects.

L. Waterman develops a redaction history for the Song and uses it to propose a history of Solomon's succession to the throne. Equating "Shunammite" with "Shulammite," he suggests that Solomon tried to woo Abishag the Shunammite (the young woman who kept the dying David warm in 1 Kgs 1:3–4) but that she rejected the king and returned to her lover in the north. His interpretation suggests that Song 4:2 lampoons Solomon for examining the girl as if she were an animal (*Song of Songs*, 41), that 4:4 is meant to make Solomon look ridiculous (*Song of Songs*, 42), and that 6:4 serves to exalt Tirzah, the capital of the northern kingdom (*Song of Songs*, 41). Many three-character interpretations turn the Song into an anti-Solomonic tract.

The three-character drama is more recently represented in a commentary by I. Provan. He argues that the Song begins with the woman in Solomon's harem, that is, already married to Solomon (Provan, 246). From the harem she yearns for her lover on the outside; the two are not married but consider themselves married. Various texts in the Song alternately describe the lovers' passion for one another and her disdain for Solomon.

Every dramatic interpretation of the Song is a tour de force, but Provan's is extraordinarily confused and confusing. His analysis of Song 3:6–11 (Provan, 298–305), for example, asserts that the אפריון, "palanquin, sedan chair," is really Solomon's palace. He argues that the structure cannot be a palanquin because it has עמוד, "pillars," and says that this word "always refers to large pillars of a size and strength sufficient to support a building" (Provan, 300). He makes this claim although he acknowledges that the word is also used of "pillars of smoke" and of tent poles. The word describes something standing upright, be it a column of smoke, a tent pole, a support post, or a pillar, and it does not suggest a massive building. He argues that at the center of this "palace" is a "chariot" (so interpreting מרכב; Song 3:10). But this "chariot" turns out to be not a real chariot at all but Solomon's bed, his place of sexual adventuring. Provan also takes 3:6 to mean that the woman is a sacrificial victim (taking עולה not as "coming up" but as "whole offering"). He thus seems to understand 3:6a to mean, "Who is this? A whole offering from the desert." The text, with its smoke and incense, is thus a kind of parody of a sacrificial rite. In Hebrew, an interrogative followed by a participle is very common, and one would naturally take it to mean "Who is this coming up from the desert?" To Provan the "desert" is not a literal desert but a metaphor for Solomon's bed (that is, a place of barren sex). On the other hand, the "sixty warriors" *are* literal: "Here is the great Solomon driving around in his pretentious chariot-bed. He is the mighty Solomon, but he needs sixty elite warriors to get him safely through the night" (Provan, 303). Song 3:6–11 is "a dark and bitter satire concerning Solomon and his string of female victims" (Provan, 304). One can only assume that the celebratory mood of this text, on Provan's reading, is ironic.

Provan's commentary is deconstructive; it plays games with the language of the text in order to obtain a socially subversive meaning. But it is forced at every point. Determined to turn the Song into an anti-Solomonic diatribe, it misreads even elementary signs of the language of love. Provan states, "There is, by contrast, no true intimacy experienced in the desert, which is the extraordinary royal bedchamber" (305). He seems unaware of texts such as Hos 2:14: "Therefore, I will now allure her, bring her into the desert, and speak tenderly to her" (Yahweh speaking of his love for Israel). Provan similarly argues that Solomon knows no joy and, contrary to the exuberant mood of the text, says that Song 3:11 is only a bitter reminder of former days (Provan, 305). His commentary illustrates how three-character interpretations of the Song turn its sweetest fruit into sour grapes and create havoc with the language.

The Two-Character Interpretations

Two-character interpretations view the Song as a dramatic presentation of the story of Solomon's devotion to his one true love. This approach was supported by the poet John Milton (see Pope, 35). More recently, M. D. Goulder has adopted this position. He asserts that the woman is an Arabian princess and that the Song is a tract against racism (*Song of Fourteen Songs*, 11–14, 75–78). G. Emmerson ("Song of Songs"), although writing in a *Festschrift* in Goulder's honor, unravels his analysis of the Song.

F. Delitzsch (1813–1890) is perhaps the foremost expositor of the two-character dramatic interpretation. Delitzsch was reacting against the violence done to the text in the three-character drama and had no doubts about the validity of his interpretation. Commenting on his initial 1851 monograph on the Song, Delitzsch wrote: "I certainly succeeded in finding the right key to the interpretation of this work" (Delitzsch, 4). His interpretation is careful throughout. He is determined to destroy the three-character drama (or as he and others call it, the "shepherd hypothesis"). On Song 5:7, he observes that the woman seeks her beloved not in the open field, nor in the villages, but in the city. This is "fatal to the shepherd-hypothesis," he claims (Delitzsch, 96). If not fatal, it at least scores a point.

Delitzsch divides the Song into six "acts": (1) the mutual affection of the lovers (1:2–2:7); (2) the mutual seeking and finding of the lovers (2:8–3:5); (3) the marriage (3:6–5:1); (4) love scorned but won again (5:2–6:9); (5) "Shulamith" the fair but humble princess (6:10–8:4); and (6) the ratification of the covenant of love in Shulamith's home (8:5–14; Delitzsch, 9–10). His analysis is in many respects perceptive, but it fails in the attempt to derive some kind of complete, coherent story from the Song. He asserts that Song 5:2–8 describes "love scorned," but the evident absurdities encountered in a literal reading of 5:2–8 force him to retreat into the "dream" interpretation (that is, none of this really happened—it was all a dream; Delitzsch, 97). But why is this love scorned if it was only a dream? In addition, as is common in dramatic interpretations, he reads a massive amount of information into the text. In his comments on Song 8:5, he describes the exact route taken by Solomon and his young princess as they stroll through Israel to her village in the area of Hermon (Delitzsch, 140–41). Implied claims to omniscience on Delitzsch's part do not inspire confidence in his overall treatment of the text; to the contrary, they engender suspicion about the whole enterprise.

As suggested by the title of his book, Goulder divides the Song into fourteen individual songs (1:2–8; 1:9–2:7; 2:8–17; 3:1–5; 3:6–11; 4:1–7; 4:8–5:1; 5:2–9; 5:10–6:3; 6:4–12; 7:1–10; 7:11–8:4; 8:5–10; 8:11–14). He says that the fourteen songs were written together as a single opus in the fourth century B.C.E. He considers the Song to tell the story of Solomon's marriage to an Arabian princess and asserts that the work functions as a tract against racism. In order to create this interpretation he must, as all dramatic interpretations do, read an enormous number of narrative details into the Song. For example, the first song (1:2–8) is said to describe the "arrival" of the Arabian princess while the second song (1:9–2:7) is said to be an account of her first audience with Solomon (*Song of Fourteen Songs*, 10–20). There is nothing in either text to suggest such settings or activities. He argues that the woman is Arabian for no clear reason save that she has dark skin like the tents of Kedar (1:5). In reality, the "tents of Kedar" are merely a simile and say nothing about her origin, and her dark skin is attributed to her having worked in the sun, not to her ethnicity (1:6). In Song 8 (5:2–9), harem guards beat the princess for wandering about in the night (*Song of Fourteen Songs*, 42; one wonders if those guards would still have their heads on their shoulders the next morning). Song 11 (7:1–10), he says, describes how the Arabian princess must contend with competition from another member of Solomon's harem, Abishag the Shunammite of 1 Kgs 2:17; however, the Arabian princess recaptures Solomon's attention by doing an erotic dance for him (*Song of Fourteen Songs*, 54–59). Similar arbitrary readings are found throughout the commentary.

Problems with Dramatic Interpretations

The treatment above shows that there are numerous problems with dramatic interpretations of the Song. The most obvious and the most commonly cited problem is that these interpretations *read into* the text more information than they actually *find*. As it stands, the Song simply does not have enough information to support any of the stories that have been suggested.

Not only must information be added *to the Song*, information present *in the Song* must be subjected to radical transformation in meaning. We saw this in Provan's astonishing analysis of Song 3:6–11. The same is true of the two-character dramas. In his analysis of 3:1–5, Goulder (*Song of Fourteen Songs*, 27) says that the "streets" are actually corridors of a palace, the city "guards" are actually eunuchs who watch over the harem, and the "daughters of Jerusalem" are not the young women of Jerusalem but are other members of the harem. For dramatic interpreters, the text is malleable in every way.

As it stands, Song of Songs has minimal plot, no character development, and no subplot. On the two-character reading, Solomon and his beloved fall in love. On the three-character reading, the woman spurns Solomon for her shepherd. Neither of these really makes for a story. As a drama, Song of Songs is decidedly inferior to the Greek dramas of fifth-century Athens. It will not do to say that the ancient Israelites might have considered such a barren plot an adequate story because we know that in the actual narratives of the Bible (Genesis, Samuel, Esther, etc.) stories are fully developed and often very complex. Interpreters have made up for this deficiency by creating no end of detail, including the invention of new characters and elements of conflict.

There is no indication that the drama existed as an art form in Israel. Nothing in the preexilic period suggests it existed in Israel or anywhere else in the Near East. The Greeks developed the drama in the fifth century B.C.E., but we have no reason to think that it was imported into the postexilic community (and I have already argued that the book cannot be that late). If the Song were a late work and if it did represent a Jewish appropriation of the Greek dramatic model, then one would expect the Song to resemble Greek drama. There is no resemblance at all. In contrast with dramatic interpretations of the Song, where confusion abounds and details must be invented at every turn, the plot, speaking parts, and developments of dramatic tension in Greek dramas are clear. G. L. Carr (34) states that in his experience the Song is "unactable." The Song is not a play.

Two problems beyond these are specific to the three-character interpretations. They tend to spoil a great deal of the beauty of the Song by treating its love poetry as an attempt at seduction by the wicked Solomon. And their dramatic reconstructions often make no sense. Bullock (*Introduction*, 252) has Solomon attempting to seduce the woman at Song 7:10–8:4. The woman responds by declaring her love for her missing shepherd, yet she addresses the shepherd as "you" (e.g., Song 8:1) and says to him, "Let us go out into the country" (Song 7:12 [ET 7:11]), even though he is not there at all. The shepherd, whom she addresses, is absent; Solomon, whom she ignores, is present and speaking words of love to her! One finds the same thing in E. Renan's commentary, where Solomon says to the woman, "Yea, thou art fair, my love," and the woman responds to her absent lover, "Yea, thou art fair, my beloved" (Renan, 129). A play that had stage directions like that would have left the ancient audience as baffled as it does the modern reader.

THE CULTIC INTERPRETATIONS

Bibliography

Albright, W. F. "Archaic Survival in the Text of Canticles." In *Hebrew and Semitic Studies Presented to Godfrey Rolles Driver.* Ed. D. W. Thomas and W. D. McHardy. Oxford: Clarendon, 1963. 1–7. **Carr, G. L.** "Is the Song of Songs a 'Sacred Marriage' Drama?" *JETS* 22 (1979) 103–14. **Fox, M. V.** *Song of Songs and the Ancient Egyptian Love Songs.* **Kramer, S. N.** *Sacred Marriage Rite.* **Meek, T.** "The Song of Songs and the Fertility Cult."

In *The Song of Songs: A Symposium*. Ed. W. H. Schoff. Philadelphia: The Commercial Museum, 1924. 48–79. **Pope, M. H.** "Metastases in Canonical Shapes of the Super Song." In *Canon, Theology, and Old Testament Interpretation*. Ed. G. M. Tucker, D. L. Petersen, and R. R. Wilson. Philadelphia: Fortess, 1988. 312–28. **Rowley, H. H.** "Interpretation of the Song of Songs." In *The Servant of the Lord and Other Essays*. London: Lutterworth, 1952. 187–234. **Schmidt, N.** "Is Canticles an Adonis Liturgy?" *JAOS* 46 (1926) 154–64.

A distinctive contribution of the twentieth century is the "cultic interpretation" of the Song, which essentially regards it as a sanitized mythic poem from the fertility cults. These cults focus on a central god who goes by various names in various myths (Baal, Dumuzi/Tammuz, Osiris, Adonis) and who dies but is raised back through the agency or intercession of his goddess-consort (respectively to the previous list, Anat, Inanna/Ishtar, Isis, Aphrodite). The death of the fertility god is associated with drought or barrenness in the land, and the resurrection of the god is associated with spring, the calving of cattle, the fruitfulness of the land, and human pregnancy. The worship of Baal was the principal rival to orthodox Yahwism in preexilic Israel. In addition, some kind of worship of a mother-goddess fertility figure seems to be very ancient indeed in the Levant.

T. Meek ("Song of Songs") noticed parallels between the Song of Songs and Akkadian hymns and came to the conclusion that the Song was an expurgated version of a fertility hymn. N. Schmidt (*JAOS* 46 [1926] 154–64) responded that there are no exact parallels between the Song and the Akkadian hymns and that the Song in no way suggests a connection to a fertility cult. S. N. Kramer supported Meek's position, except that, unlike Meek, Kramer did not think that the Song celebrated Yahweh and the goddess; rather he said that it concerned a sacred marriage between the Israelite king and a goddess. In addition, he did not try to argue that the Song originally contained dirges for a dying god; he said that the celebratory marriage songs from the Sumerian texts eliminated the need for this motif (Kramer, *Sacred Marriage Rite*, 90–92). Other interpreters suggested ties between the Song and pagan myths. W. F. Albright said of the "mother" mentioned in Song 8:5–7, "The mother of the beloved was a mythical figure, possibly a girl who had escaped to the desert after becoming pregnant by a god ("Archaic Survival," 7). M. Pope (465, 548) argues that the descriptions of the man and woman in the Song imply that they are idols of gods. The male in particular appears to be made of precious metals (Song 5:11–15), but the female also is sometimes described as towerlike (Song 4:4). Pope has also argued that the woman's enormous nose (Song 7:5) suggests she is a goddess ("Metastases in Canonical Shapes," 322–23).

This approach does not have a large following (cf. Murphy, 40), and for good reason. H. H. Rowley ("Interpretation," 213–32) gave the theory a thorough analysis and found it wanting while it was still on the rise among scholars. The Song of Songs has none of the critical elements of a fertility text. There is no dying and rising god, which, Kramer's suggestions notwithstanding, separates the Song from a critical, central element in the fertility cult. There is no hint that the fertility of the world depends upon the sexuality of the couple. There is no suggestion in the Song that it is a religious text or that the sexuality that it celebrates has sacred significance. There is nothing hymnic about the Song at all. Kramer (*Sacred Marriage Rite*, 90) suggests that the epithet "sister" in the Song was parallel to the use of the same term for Inanna/Ishtar, but in fact this is best paralleled by the use of the same term in the Egyptian love songs, which are certainly secular songs (cf. Fox, *Song of Songs*, 234–43). Suggestions that the woman of the Song has a colossal nose and therefore must be a goddess do not enhance one's appreciation for the theory. In reality, the only parallel is that fertility cult texts and the Song of Songs both have lyrics that focus on marriage and sexuality. This does not mean that the Song is an expurgated version of the hymns.

The reverse may in a sense be true. Some of the Sumerian love songs are not particularly hymnic; to the contrary, they seem to be casual love songs that have been brought into the cult by ascribing the love play they describe to the gods Dumuzi and Inanna. Y. Sefati observes that, except for the liturgical annotations, the song of the wooing of Inanna by Dumuzi under the moon appears to be little more than casual entertainment for women, something that they could hum while doing their chores (*CS* 1:542). It may be the case, therefore, that at least some of the "hymns" to these gods are Sumerian love ditties that have been brought into the cult.

The Wedding Interpretation

In 1873 J. G. Wetzstein published an account of what he observed at wedding ceremonies among the Syrians and compared their customs to what the Song of Songs seemed to reflect (*Die syrische Dreschtafel* ["The Syrian Threshing Table"]). His views were subsequently published by F. Delitzsch as an appendix to his commentary on the Song (Delitzsch, 162–76). This approach to the Song suggests that it is an ancient Israelite epithalamium, a series of songs meant to be performed over the course of a wedding celebration. This would have been an elaborate, drawn-out event, perhaps lasting a week. The bride and groom would take on the roles of fictive queen and king, and there would be numerous dances and songs. The *waṣf*, or descriptive song of praise, was thought to play a prominent role in these festivities. As documented by Pope (141–45), this theory was hailed as the key to Song of Songs for about a quarter of a century, but since then support for it all but disappeared.

Obvious problems are that there is an enormous chronological and cultural gap between nineteenth-century Syrian culture and ancient Israelite culture and that, the presence of a few *waṣf* songs notwithstanding, it is hard to see how the Song of Songs could work as an epithalamium. In addition, the Syrian wedding celebration probably has roots that go back to many cultures, not all of them in the Levant, and more recent studies suggest that even in Syria there is no widespread practice of a "king's week" at weddings (see Pope, 144). Fohrer has aptly commented that although there is no doubt that the Song of Songs has some connection to ancient Israelite wedding ceremonies, "the book cannot be interpreted totally from this perspective and called the textbook for an Israelite wedding" (Fohrer, *Introduction to the OT*, 302).

The Funerary Interpretation

If the Song of Songs was not performed for weddings, perhaps it was used for funerals. That, at least, is the thinking of M. Pope (210–29). He claims that "funeral feasts in the ancient Near East were love feasts celebrated with wine, women, and song" (Pope, 228). He is curiously fascinated by what a prominent role dogs have in the orgies of the time and devotes an extraordinary amount of space to the issue (Pope, 211–14). He is also very interested in the appearances of the word *mrzḥ*, "cultic feast," in biblical and Ugaritic sources (Pope, 214–21). Neither study is particularly helpful since there are no dogs in Song of Songs, and the closest thing to a *mrzḥ* is the "house of wine" at Song 2:4. Furthermore, the reference to death in Song 8:4 does not suggest that anyone has actually died or that a funeral is going on. Death is a simile for the power of love. This theory fails in that Pope cannot relate the Song of Songs to its supposed original setting. In his massive commentary on the text, he refers to the theory so rarely that one sometimes wonders if he had forgotten about it.

FEMINIST READINGS OF THE SONG

Bibliography

Arbel, D. V. "'My Vineyard, My Very Own, Is for Myself.'" In *Song of Songs: A Feminist Companion to the Bible*. FCB 2d ser. 6. Ed. A. Brenner and C. R. Fontaine. Sheffield: Sheffield Academic Press, 2000. 90–101. **Black, F. C.** "Unlikely Bedfellows: Allegorical and Feminist Readings of Song of Songs 7.1–8." In *Song of Songs: A Feminist Companion to the Bible*. FCB 2d ser. 6. Ed. A. Brenner and C. R. Fontaine. Sheffield: Sheffield Academic Press, 2000. 104–29. **Brenner, A.** "Women Poets and Authors." In *A Feminist Companion to the Song of Songs*. FCB 1. Ed. A. Brenner. Sheffield: JSOT Press, 1993. 86–97. **Brettler, M. Z.** "Sensual or Sublime: On Teaching the Song of Songs." In *Approaches to Teaching the Hebrew Bible as Literature in Translation*. Ed. B. Olshen and Y. S. Feldman. New York: Modern Language Associaton of America, 1989. 133–35. **Butting, K.** "Go Your Way: Women Rewrite the Scriptures (Song of Songs 2.8–14)." In *Song of Songs: A Feminist Companion to the Bible*. FCB 2d ser. 6. Ed. A. Brenner and C. R. Fontaine. Sheffield: Sheffield Academic Press, 2000. 142–51. **Chave, P.** "Towards a Not Too Rosy Picture of the Song of Songs." *Feminist Theology* 18 (1998) 41–53. **Exum, J. C.** "Developing Strategies of Feminist Criticism/Developing Strategies for Commentating the Song of Songs." In *Auguries: The Jubilee Volume of the Sheffield Department of Biblical Studies*. Ed. D. J. A. Clines and S. D. Moore. Sheffield: Sheffield Academic Press, 1998. 206–49. ———. "Ten Things Every Feminist Should Know about the Song of Songs." In *Song of Songs: A Feminist Companion to the Bible*. FCB 2d ser. 6. Ed. A. Brenner and C. R. Fontaine. Sheffield: Sheffield Academic Press, 2000. 24–35. **Falk, M.** *Song of Songs: A New Translation*. **Fontaine, C. R.** "The Voice of the Turtle: Now It's *MY* Song of Songs." In *Song of Songs: A Feminist Companion to the Bible*. FCB 2d ser. 6. Ed. A. Brenner and C. R. Fontaine. Sheffield: Sheffield Academic Press, 2000. 169–86. **Goitein, S. D.** "The Song of Songs: A Female Composition." In *A Feminist Companion to the Song of Songs*. FCB 1. Ed. A. Brenner. Sheffield: Sheffield Academic Press, 1993. 58–66. **Merkin, D.** "The Women in the Balcony: On Rereading the Song of Songs." In *Out of the Garden*. Ed. C. Büchmann and C. Spiegel. New York: Fawcett Columbine, 1995. 238–51, 342. **Meyers, C.** "Gender Imagery in the Song of Songs." *HAR* 10 (1986) 209–23. **Ostriker, A.** "A Holy of Holies: The Song of Songs as Countertext." In *Song of Songs: A Feminist Companion to the Bible*. FCB 2d ser. 6. Ed. A. Brenner and C. R. Fontaine. Sheffield: Sheffield Academic Press, 2000. 36–54. **Polaski, D. C.** "What Will Ye See in the Shulammite? Women, Power and Panopticism in the Song of Songs." *BibInt* 5 (1997) 64–81. **Trible, P.** "Depatriarchalizing in Biblical Interpretation." *JAAR* 41 (1973) 30–48. **Walsh, C. E.** *Exquisite Desire: Religion, the Erotic, and the Song of Songs*. Minneapolis: Fortress, 2000. ———. "A Startling Voice: Woman's Desire in the Song of Songs." *BTB* 28 (1999) 129–34. **Weems, R. J.** "The Song of Songs." In *NIB*. Nashville: Abingdon Press, 1997. 5:363–434.

There is no single "feminist" interpretation of Song of Songs, and we can only speak of certain tendencies in feminist analyses of the Song. In A. Brenner's view (*Song of Songs*, 88),

> Applied to the SoS [Song of Songs], feminist readings deal with the following specific features: possible female authorship of the book or parts thereof; the lack of sexism (discriminating persons on grounds of their sex, usually used for the social prejudices against women); equality in the love relationship, and predominance of the female figures; elements of matristic practices (power in the hands of women) and matrilineal practices (tracing male kinship and inheritance through the mother's line) as against institutions of patriarchy; gender analysis of female and male discourse, that is, the defining of the emotional and psychological attributes that society expects of its male and female members; comparisons of the SoS with love lyrics of cognate Near Eastern cultures; and investigations into the intertextual connections between the SoS and other treatments of love-themes in the Hebrew Bible.

Exum gives a detailed analysis of current feminist thinking on the Song. She describes and advocates in particular the deconstructive nature of this work. For example, "A promising strategy for getting at women's perspectives in androcentric texts is to look for alternative, competing discourses within the text" ("Developing Strategies," 217).

Many feminist concerns and perspectives appear in recent commentaries on the Song, such as that of R. Weems ("Song of Songs"). A number of scholars have pondered whether the Song might have been written by a woman; that the female singer has more lines than the male is frequently cited to support this possibility. In 1957, S. D. Goitein argued that a woman wrote the Song ("Song of Songs," reprinted in 1993; so also Bekkenkamp and van Dijk, "Canon of the OT," 79). On the basis of supposed female authorship, D. Arbel ("My Vineyard") reads the whole Song as a woman's internal and personal discourse. A. Brenner is less confident that a woman wrote the whole Song but says, "My personal guess is that passages such as 1.2–6, 3.1–4, 5.1–7 and 5.10–16 are so essentially feminine that a male could hardly imitate their tone and texture successfully" ("Women Poets," 91). If any single theme dominates earlier feminist readings of the Song, it is that the Song is a countertext to the patriarchy of the Hebrew Bible (e.g., M. Falk, *Song of Songs*, xv–xvi; C. Meyers, *HAR* 10 [1986] 209–23; A. Ostriker, "Holy of Holies"; see also Brenner, *Song of Songs*, 90–91). P. Trible (*JAAR* 41 [1973] 30–48) and K. Butting ("Go Your Way") read it as a reversal of the patriarchal order that is found in Genesis; Trible in particular makes much of what she sees as gender egalitarianism in the Song. A distinctive feminist interpretation, taken up in the next section, is that the Song subverts the patriarchal order upheld by the prophets.

Feminist readings of the Song labor under a heavy weight of ideological baggage. Brenner ("On Reading the Hebrew Bible," 13) could hardly put it more clearly: "Being a feminist woman, or womanly reader, means that every issue is a feminist issue, and there is a feminist perspective on every subject." Brenner continues in the same article, answering the charge that feminist readers are biased: "A womanly reader can easily be incensed by the injustices of a text and its interpretation which she or he diagnoses. Womanly readership, especially that of a feminist hue, is indeed in that sense biased, for its preliminary stance is self-defined as such. It has been argued above that the bias is more than compensated for by the achievements of the discipline, chief of which is the characteristic comprehensiveness of vision" (21). Although it is debatable whether feminist writers have a particular claim to "comprehensiveness of vision," her claim to reading the text with a particular bias is unassailable. The Song is subjected to a higher law, the political and theological agenda of feminism, and judgments about the Song's value, validity, and usefulness in social criticism are made on the basis of whether the text, or a "reading" of the text, supports that agenda. If not, the Song by default supports the agenda of terrorizing women—the patriarchy. Those seem to be the only two alternatives. Feminist readings, no less than ancient allegorizing interpretations, explicitly and intentionally pass the text through a grid, albeit a postmodern political and philosophical grid rather than a traditional theological grid (cf. from the feminist perspective, F. C. Black 2000 ["Unlikely Bedfellows"], and from my perspective, Garrett, *Hosea, Joel,* 124–33). In such circumstances, the Song is not a poem to be appreciated and interpreted; it is grist for a mill.

Feminist readings of the Song also tend to be unusually self-referential for scholarly publications. A number of feminist musings on the Song are more about the interpreter than they are about the text (e.g., Brenner, "'My' Song of Songs" [Brenner's upbringing as an Israeli woman], and Fontaine, "The Voice of the Turtle: Now It's *MY* Song of Songs," [Fontaine's fundamentalist childhood]; see also D. Merkin, "Women in the Balcony," 246–51, where she describes her childhood as an unbelieving Orthodox Jew and her current feelings on the Song). Even a full-scale commentary, such as that by C. E. Walsh (*Exquisite Desire*), repeatedly returns to the commentator's experiences, social setting, and opinions on extraneous issues. This tendency suggests that the interpreter is in a privileged position over the text and over other interpreters.

There are indications that the feminist attitude toward the Song is becoming more negative. A number of feminists now argue that the notion that the Song is egalitarian or even gynocentric is misguided (D. C. Polaski [*BibInt* 5 (1997) 64–81]; P. Chave [*Feminist Theology* 18 (1998) 41–53]; F. Black ["Unlikely Bedfellows"]; J. C. Exum ["Ten Things Every Feminist Should Know"]). Exum's essay in particular warns feminists that Song of Songs deadens their critical faculties (by arousing romantic sentimentalism), that it is not about real women at all, that it may be a male perspective from a male author, that there is no gender equality in the Song, that it maintains control over female sexuality and displays the female body, and that it is seductive and must be read with care. Exum appears to be saying that the Song of Songs is a subversive text—subversive of feminist ideology.

THE SONG OF SONGS AS SUBVERSIVE OF THE PROPHETS

Bibliography

Butting, K. "Go Your Way: Women Rewrite the Scriptures (Song of Songs 2.8–14)." In *The Song of Songs: A Feminist Companion to the Bible.* FCB 2d ser. 6. Ed. A. Brenner and C. R. Fontaine. Sheffield: Sheffield Academic Press, 2000. 142–51. **Garrett, D. A.** *Hosea, Joel.* **LaCocque, A.** *Romance, She Wrote.* Harrisburg, PA: Trinity Press International, 1998.

In current scholarship, the notion of the "subversive text" has gained such standing that one can hardly proceed without taking this viewpoint into account.

With regard to Song of Songs, the argument is that the Song is a countertext that subverts the prevailing theology and ethos of Israel. This approach is a variety of feminist interpretation, but it is distinctive in its focus on intertextual analysis of the Song. Several scholars could be regarded as advocates of the subversive approach (e.g., K. Butting, "Go Your Way"), but A. LaCocque has given us the most coherent statement of the hermeneutics of this method (*Romance, She Wrote*), and his analysis will serve as the point of interaction for this section.

In LaCocque's view, Song of Songs is fundamentally an intertextual work whereby a female poet took the images and language of Scripture, reversed their significance, and thereby subverted the orthodox and patriarchal worldview of the prophets. A common strategy of the poet was to revive the images that the prophets had used, but also to restore them as signifiers and so deconstruct the prophets' subjection of these images to the orthodox worldview. For example, in the prophets Israel is the wife of Yahweh, but in the Song the reader is pulled back from this sanitized appropriation of the sexual image. The Song celebrates the image, Eros, as the thing itself. This poet thus reveled in the luxury and Eros that the prophets despised (*Romance, She Wrote*, 56). Therefore:

> The composer of the Canticle did not make it her business to praise the chaste love between Israel and her God or between Israel and Wisdom personified. There is not a single word about *hokmâ* in the Song. What the poet is doing here is shedding her societal chains; she is shouting her freedom from gender and stereotypes. She is daringly mocking consecrated definitions and formulas. She is throwing in the faces of the "magistrates" her rejection of Agape devoid of Eros, by which they have castrated religion and mores. She is magnifying romance in terms that parody their theological jargon, terms that deceivingly echo things tamed and familiar, things annexed and made comfortable. The Song of Songs is carnivalesque: kings, bishops, magistrates, are caricatured and made fun of. (*Romance, She Wrote*, 64)

Foundational to LaCocque's approach is a distinction between the midrashic and the allegorizing interpretation (*Romance, She Wrote*, 6–33). A midrashic reading is rooted in the concrete metaphor; an allegorizing interpretation has its locus in the heavenly abstraction and casts aside the metaphor. The midrashic reading delights in the free expression of the power of Eros; the allegorizing reading seeks to maintain the institutional ideals. Above all, the midrashic reading is intertextual, reshaping and subverting the words of the prophets; the allegorizing interpretation subverts Eros itself and forces it into conformity to its own regimented worldview. LaCocque states that in Midrash, "the interpretation is not allegorical, that is, relating signifier to signified, for it relates signifier to signifier (the passage of the Red Sea; the events at Sinai, for example). The signifiers cross-reference with one another; there is no discarding of the signifier as if it were the shell around the signified" (*Romance, She Wrote*, 13–14).

But LaCocque's distinction between midrash and allegory is artificial and only clouds the issue of the interpretation of the Song. The historical reading of the rabbis, and later of the French interpreters Robert, Tournay, and Feuillet, is valuable to him because they link the images of the Song to contexts in the prophets (albeit incorrectly, because they do not see how the Song restores these images and so subverts the prophets). The *bête noire* of Song of Songs interpretation for LaCocque is, not surprisingly, Origen, that despiser of passion, whom he cites, making the assertion that the natural reading of the Song only hurts the reader (*Romance, She Wrote*, 11). But LaCocque demonstrates little acquaintance with Origen's actual exegetical method, which was highly midrashic and intertextual, and it had only gone part way toward becoming a full-fledged allegory. Although he worked from a different theological foundation from that of contemporary rabbis, his methods were not strikingly different. LaCocque's claim that midrash relates signifier to signifier is particularly misleading. The phrases "your eyes are doves" and "your breasts are like two fawns" hardly use language in the same way as does the phrase "the events at Sinai." He often does not really link "signifier to signifier"; he simply scours the Hebrew Bible for expressions that are similar to those found in the Song. The results of the midrashic handling of the Song as codified in the Targum and in the comments of the rabbis are, *mutatis mutandis*, not all that different from the allegories of the Christians.

The "intertextual reading" that LaCocque espouses is especially troubling. The method is of itself fairly simple. First, for any text in the Song he looks for any use of similar language elsewhere in the Hebrew Bible, more or less after the manner of the Targum and of Robert or Tournay. Then, he seeks to show how the Song has reversed or modified the image in order to subvert an oppressive structure. Hosea in particular comes in for scrutiny, and it is there that LaCocque's weaknesses are most apparent. For him, Hosea is the epitome of the upholder of the patriarchy: in Hosea, sin is equated with the eroticism of the woman, God/the male is the victim of evil, and violence against women is fully justified (*Romance, She Wrote*, 34–36). But this completely misconstrues Hosea's message. An honest reading of Hosea shows that the "sinful woman" that Hosea addresses represents none other than the *male leadership* of the nation—the very priests, prophets, and magistrates that Hosea, in LaCocque's analysis, wishes to keep in power. Furthermore, the fundamental image of Hosea is not of the promiscuous *wife* but of the wayward *mother*. Hos 1–2 and 4, for example, focus on the mother (the institutions of Israel) and her children (the people of Israel as misled by the leaders). By defending the woman, LaCocque and similar interpreters are actually defending the oppressive hierarchy! For further discussion of this, see Garrett, *Hosea, Joel*, esp. 124–33. But even if the true significance of Hosea be open to debate, a major issue remains: if it is the Song's intent to subvert Hosea through intertextual appropriation of his language, why does it fail to appropriate the most emotionally charged image of the book, *that of the mother and her children*? This basic image is ignored entirely! It is impossible to believe that a poet who had as her aim the satirizing of Hosea could discard this metaphor if she intended her reader to catch on to her satire.

In actual interpretations of the text, LaCocque is as arbitrary and absurd as the allegorists. For example, he asserts that in Song 2:3, the "shade" of the beloved alludes to Yahweh as the giver of shade for his people (*Romance, She Wrote*, 84). Thus, the beloved and Eros have replaced Yahweh! Hos 3:1 is the "source text" for Song 2:5 (the former describing "lovers of raisin cakes" and the latter describing the woman as sustained by raisins and apples). Comparing this to Hos 5:12–13, where Israel is gangrenous and wounded, we see that the Song, in defiance of Hosea, is exulting in lovesickness and raisin cakes (*Romance, She Wrote*, 85)! In Song 2:14, "Let me see your face" alludes to Moses' desire to see the face of God in Exod 33:18–23. But God remains hidden and terrifying, while the lady of the Song shows herself and is beautiful to see and sweet to hear. "In the ears of religionists, all this no doubt sounded like borderline blasphemy" (*Romance, She Wrote*, 89). The "foxes" of Song 2:15 are drawn from Ezek 13:4 and Lam 5:18, where they are false prophets and those who prowl in Zion. But the Song has transmuted this image into the sour orthodox people "who are frowning at the free love of the couple in the Song" (*Romance, She Wrote*, 89–90).

This approach is nothing but allegorizing from a new perspective. Any allegorizer (or "midrashic interpreter") could take all of the "intertextual links" that LaCocque has created and use them equally well to sustain an orthodox and devotional reading of the Song. The "subversive reading" LaCocque has seized upon is not a function of the texts; it is a function of how the interpreter chooses to manipulate the alleged linkages. A rabbi sees the history of Israel; Origen sees the soul and Christ; LaCocque sees the subversive work of the angry female poet. But each is equally arbitrary. There is also no reason to think that the author of the Song had these linkages in mind or intended what LaCocque claims; exegesis by concordance does not establish literary dependence.

At the core of the Song, in this interpretation, is the angry female poet who recasts the words of Torah and Prophet for subversive ends. Is it reasonable to ascribe the Song to a woman poet, and what may such a move imply? LaCocque argues that the fact that the woman has most of the lyrics in the Song and conspicuously speaks of herself implies that a woman must have written the Song (*Romance, She Wrote*, 41–44). This only tells us that the woman is the protagonist and central figure of the book; it tells us nothing about authorship. The claim that a man simply could not have enough understanding of a woman's viewpoint to write the Song is wrong (and sexist!). Are we to claim that Chaucer could not have written the tale of the Wife of Bath as well?

LaCocque's efforts to make his case leads him to make some dubious assertions. For example, he says that the "funeral song" is in the "women's domain" and cites 1 Sam 1:24 [*sic;* apparently a typo for 2 Sam 1:24]; Jer 9:16–19; Lam 1; 2; 4 (*Romance, She Wrote*, 42). But the fact that women are exhorted to make lamentation over national disasters hardly makes this genre their "domain"; contrast 2 Sam 1:17–27, the lament over Saul composed by David.

The overwhelming majority of poets and authors in the ancient world were men. Although women were perhaps more active in composition in Israel than in the Greek world (where Sappho is the exception that proves the rule), very little of the Hebrew Bible is ascribed to women writers or poets. Where she does exist in the Hebrew Bible, the woman poet is hardly the defiant *provocatrice* of modern scholarly imagination. The most significant female poets of the Bible are Deborah, Hannah, perhaps Miriam, and, in the NT, Mary. But what do we find in their songs? They could hardly be more orthodox! Indeed, Deborah and Miriam are not only orthodox but fervently nationalistic. Deborah's song in particular is conventional. She embraces the ideal that a man should be a warrior and that it is to a man's disgrace that he should be slain by a woman (cf. Judg 4:9). Hannah and Mary exploit in a traditional manner the prophetic theme of Yahweh's concern for the oppressed. To claim that the "male hierarchy" has only let us see what it wants us to see of female poets is itself a hypothetical construct and an *ad hoc* argument. There is no example of a Hebrew female poet using her art for subversive ends. Yet LaCocque not only ascribes the Song to the angry female poet, intent on turning the prophets on their heads, but says that she represents a "counterculture" within Second Temple Judaism (*Romance, She Wrote*, 46). Where is the evidence for this female counterculture? Is this anything other than the anachronistic projection of current ideological trends? This is not to say that a woman *could not* have written the Song; we simply do not know. Building an interpretation of the Song on the hypothesis of the angry woman poet is precarious.

At the opening of his book, LaCocque gives us two pairs of options. Either the Song is "aphoristic and apologetic of an established worldview," or it denounces that worldview as "wrong and deceptive." Either it is a remnant of frivolous court poetry written for the titillation of the pampered aristocrats, or it is a "satirical piece" that was "smuggled into the biblical compendium" (*Romance, She Wrote*, 1). Here, from the very beginning, LaCocque reveals his complete misunderstanding of what the Song is. The Song is none of the things he describes: *it is lyric poetry*. It is not a religious or political tract, and it is neither didactic nor satirical. It is a celebration of love. Song of Songs is neither patriarchal nor subversive.

The Song as Love Poetry

Almost by default, we are driven to the conclusion that the Song is just what it appears to be, poems about love between a man and a woman. This view is not new; Aqiba's complaint about people singing the Song in a bawdy manner presupposes that many people in his day understood the Song in that way. Even in the early church, there were dissenters against allegorizing the Song. Theodore of Mopsuestia, a follower of the Antiochene school of biblical interpretation (which preferred a natural, "plain sense" understanding of the Bible to an allegorical approach), rejected the allegorizing interpretation of the Song. He was posthumously condemned in the Fifth Council of Constantinople (553 C.E.), and his writings on the Song are lost. In more recent times, however, this approach to the Song has come to dominate biblical scholarship.

Saying that the Song of Songs is "love poetry" does not advance interpretation of the Song very far. It does not say if the Song is unified or is a loose anthology, if it has a dominant theme, or if it has any meaningful theology. However, attributing it to this genre is a good beginning.

This approach forces us to seek the significance of the metaphors and symbols in the context of ancient Near Eastern love poetry. The images are not theological, political, ideological, or philosophical ciphers.

Also, this approach frees us from the need to "fill in the gaps" of the story, in the manner of dramatic interpretations. In reality, there are no gaps. The poet has said all that he means to say, although he does expect the audience to be perceptive about the implications of his words. A love song may have an implied story behind it (e.g., "once you loved me, but now you are gone," or, "my life was empty before I met you"), but it is not itself a story (we are here excluding the ballad, which does not exist in ancient Near Eastern poetry—notwithstanding J. A. Black ["Babylonian Ballads: A New Genre," *JAOS* 103 (1983) 25–34]—and at any rate the Song is clearly not a ballad).

Reading the Song as love poetry forces us to deal with the conventions of poetry in the interpretation of the Song. How are the stanzas formed? What constitutes a line of poetry in this book? How do the images convey meaning? These are the questions one must ask of Song of Songs.

Great poetry, particularly great love poetry, is often inspired by some beloved person. Sometimes, the name of the beloved and his or her relationship to the poet is known. For example, the love poems of Anne Bradstreet (1612?–1672) are directed to her husband, Simon Bradstreet. Sometimes the object of affection is hidden behind a pseudonym or is left anonymous. Catullus (c. 84–54 B.C.E.) devotes his love poems to a certain married woman he calls "Lesbia." Shakespeare's latter sonnets speak of love for some woman now known to readers simply as the "dark lady."

It is by no means necessary for the poet to have had an actual love affair with the one who inspired his verse. Dante was passionately in love with Beatrice, and she is prominent in much of his poetry, not least in the *Divine Comedy*. Now identified as Beatrice Portinari, the real Beatrice briefly met Dante when they were both children and only occasionally spoke to him as a young adult. However, by his account he fell in love with her immediately. She married another man but died at the age of twenty-four. Dante was devastated at her death, but she, forever young in his mind, served as a kind of muse for his poetry.

Could such a figure be behind Song of Songs? We will never know. I have already argued that the Song of Songs belongs in the united monarchy period and have suggested that Solomon could have been the author of the piece, although the superscript does not demand this conclusion. It may be that the poet of Song of Songs had someone in mind when he wrote his work. But it is by no means necessary to suppose that the poet actually had any kind of relationship with the object of his affection—in fact, the idealized nature of this poetry suggests the contrary. Also, this is *not* to suggest that there is any kind of a history that one can tease out of Song of Songs in the manner of the dramatic interpretations. But it may be that the explorations of love in the Song are borne of adoration for a woman who was once real but who, in the poet's mind, became progressively idealized—a Beatrice. Surely, something or someone motivated the writing of the poem, since even sacred Scripture arises in a human context.

All of this, of course, is pure guesswork. The poet could have based his work on observations of a loving couple he knew, or the whole thing could be the product of his imagination, the people and situations being composites from the poet's observations. *We have no idea what circumstances led to the writing of this poem.* This bit of idle speculation serves at least to remind us that Song of Songs could be accounted for in various ways and that we should be careful about claiming more knowledge about it than we possess. Further speculations about the background of the poem will take on a life of their own and cloud the issue rather than illuminate it. All we have is an idealized portrait of love, the Song itself, and that is what we will analyze.

Excursus: Finding an Approach to Lyric Poetry

Bibliography

Barthes, R. *The Pleasure of the Text*. Trans. R. Miller. New York: Hill and Wang, 1975.
Brooks, C., and **R. P. Warren**. *Understanding Poetry*. 4th ed. New York: Holt, Reinhart,

& Winston, 1976. **Corney, R. W.** "What Does 'Literal Meaning' Mean? Some Commentaries on the Song of Songs." *AThR* 80 (1998) 494–516. **Cureton, R. D.** "Helen Vendler and the Music of Poetry: A Review of *Poems, Poets, Poetry: An Introduction and Anthology* by Helen Vendler." *Versification* 1.1 (March 1997) [an electronic journal]. **Hall, D.** *The Pleasures of Poetry.* New York: Harper & Row, 1971. **Vendler, H.** *The Art of Shakespeare's Sonnets.* ———. *The Music of What Happens: Poems, Poets, Critics.* Cambridge, MA: Harvard UP, 1988. ———. *Poems, Poets, Poetry: An Introduction and Anthology.* Boston: St. Martin's, 1997.

"The question 'What is lyric poetry?' has never been adequately answered," according to R. Cureton ("Helen Vendler," 1). Our difficulty with the Song of Songs arises at least in part from a lack of guiding principles for dealing with this genre. Caught between reading lyric poetry and reading a canonical text, biblical scholars struggle to find an approach that is true both to its poetic form and to its canonical status. The recognition that it is erotic in nature has not led to a satisfactory interpretation (cf. R. Corney, *AThR* 80 [1998] 494–516).

Perhaps we need to learn afresh how to read lyric poetry. I shall not here attempt anything like a full-scale description of what constitutes lyric poetry or anything like a complete theoretical foundation for the criticism of lyric poetry. But I will try to set forth a few basic observations on the nature of this literary genre, which I hope will be of help to the reader. I have principally drawn on the work of Helen Vendler, who is widely regarded as the premier American critic of lyric poetry of our time. She is not without her detractors, and I am not here endorsing everything she says or even suggesting that my brief survey represents her viewpoint. Her writings have been helpful in working through the problem of what constitutes lyric poetry.

It may be necessary to orient the reader to what is meant by "lyric" poetry. The term is related to the word *lyre*, and thus suggests a poem that may be sung accompanied by a lyre. In classical civilization, the lyric poem is essentially what in Greek is called a μέλος, a "song" intended to be sung by an individual poet. Greek examples of lyric poetry are the poems of Sappho, Alcman, and Pindar; Latin masters included Catullus and Horace. Pindar, for example, celebrated the triumphant victories of Greek athletes in his odes. These short, self-contained poems contrast, for example, with the poetic dialog of Greek tragedy.

At some point, Western civilization separated the poem from the song, and a lyric poetry emerged that was designed to be spoken and not sung. The Renaissance created the sonnet, a poetic form that is arguably the quintessential Western lyric poem. Thus, we have wonderful examples of lyric poetry in the sonnets of Shakespeare. Still, we should not draw too keen a distinction between a song and a lyric poem, since many of the songs of Shakespeare's plays could also be classified as lyric poetry. The nonmusical lyric poem became a major genre of Western literature. The lyric poem was the perfect vehicle for the romantic era, with its profound literary investigations of the human condition. The reflections on art, vitality, and death in the odes of John Keats (e.g., "Ode to a Nightingale") vividly illustrate how well suited the lyric poem is for meditation that does not seek to free itself of emotion. Goethe's poetry also exemplifies the lyric poem; his "An den Schlaf" (To Sleep) captures the emotional desperation of a young man in love (like the young lovers of the Egyptian poetry, he sees his girlfriend's mother as a barrier between himself and bliss!).

Lyric poems are essentially the reflections of a poet on a situation, event, or idea. Thus, they tend to be short. One cannot set a specific maximum length to a lyric poem, but a lyric poem of five hundred lines would be unusual. Lyric poems are often broadly romantic. Although they are not necessarily about love (yet they often are) and although they are not necessarily introspective or sentimental, they do delve into the feelings and reflections that occupy the poet's mind. It is not surprising, therefore, that the romantic era in Western civilization produced an enormous amount of lyric poetry. It is especially important to realize that lyric poems do not *tell* a story but *reflect upon* and *allude to* a story. The story itself may be totally unfamiliar to the reader; the reader, when he begins to read a poem, does not know that the poet's husband has just died and that she is attempting to enunciate and understand her sorrow. Upon entering the poem, the reader is initially at a loss to understand the poet's tone and the allusions she makes. She does not begin with the words "Two days ago my husband died of a massive heart attack while lifting bales of hay, and now I want to tell you what I am thinking." But as he reads her reflections on the event, the reader begins to understand the situation and to pick up details about the incident as she alludes to them. Furthermore, the "story" behind a lyric poem is very simple and one dimensional: a young man is in love, or a parent has lost a child, or a young girl picks flowers. Since lyric poems only allude to stories rather than tell them, the reader would be hopelessly lost if the story behind the poem were complex, having multiple characters or a subplot. It is this allusive feature that especially sets apart the Song of Songs as lyric poetry and not as drama. The poems of the Song do not *tell* a story but are *reflections on* a story. Furthermore, the story behind the Song is exceedingly simple: a man and woman marry.

Lyric poetry may be recognized by comparing it with other kinds of poetry. For example, no one would consider epics such as Gilgamesh, the Ugaritic epic of Kirta, or the Odyssey to be lyric poetry. Similarly, the discourses and diatribes of the prophets and Job, although often in poetic form, are not lyric poems. A ballad should not be classified as lyric poetry, since a ballad is essentially a story in song and verse. Liturgical poetry should not be classed as lyric poetry since its primary function is not to reflect the inner thoughts of the poet but to serve as a vehicle for public worship. Most of the psalms should not be called lyric poetry. But some psalms can be classified as lyric poems; Ps 23 is a wonderful example. Biblical Wisdom poetry (e.g., Ps 1; Prov 2) is not lyrical; Wisdom poetry is essentially didactic and thus tends to be structured and straightforward in meaning, whereas lyric poetry is more concerned with creativity and artful expression. This is not to say that didactic poetry is inferior; it is simply a different kind of poetry. Similarly, in my view, a dirge or lamentation should not be classified as lyric poetry since its primary function is to serve as a text for a public expression of grief. Thus, the book of Lamentations is not lyric poetry. By contrast, an elegy, an inner reflection on a death or a calamity, is lyric poetry. With this admittedly inexact description of lyric poetry, we should be able to enunciate a few guidelines for reading lyric poetry.

Lyric poetry is often enigmatic by nature. This is a matter of degree, and some lyric poems are plain and straightforward in meaning. Still, lyric poetry generally demands that the reader or listener invest mental and even emotional energy to the understanding of the piece. A lyric poem is not an essay, a political speech, a dramatic monologue, or a news article, where the burden of communication lies heavily on the writer or speaker and where condescension to the audience's lack of familiarity with the topic is essential. The principal duty of the lyric poet is to find the *mot juste* and to combine words and phrases into crafted and interrelated lines of poetry. Although a lyric poem communicates, *it is essentially a work of art* that the reader is expected to *investigate* and *appreciate* and not just *comprehend*. There are several other reasons that a lyric poem can be difficult to follow, and we will explore some of these below. The important point is this: reading lyric poetry with comprehension requires some training, patience, and practice. Novices will sometimes shrug their shoulders and walk away from a lyric poem simply because its meaning is not obvious on the first reading. In working with the Song of Songs, students of the Bible should not expect it to be as plain and direct as Deuteronomy or 2 Kings.

Second, however, a lyric poem does have a specific meaning that the poet intended. I reject the idea of the "intentional fallacy" (i.e., that it is wrong to seek an author's intended meaning, or that meaning resides solely in the reader). Critical analysis of a lyric poem frequently begins with a prose paraphrase of the poem. (Although Vendler insists that paraphrase is only the *beginning* of the understanding of a poem, she repeatedly follows this practice herself; e.g., *Art of Shakespeare's Sonnets,* 495, 540.) The common practice of paraphrasing poems in order to explain them implies at least two things. First, poems are often not easy to understand. Second, the poem does have an *essential* meaning that the poet intended the reader to get. That a poem can also have specific significance for a specific reader or that individual readers bring their own perspectives to poems does not invalidate this; readers also bring their personal viewpoints to newspaper articles, but that does not mean that newspaper articles are open-ended in meaning. Some modern poetry and song purposefully strings together words in a nonsensical manner so that the only meaning is that it has no meaning. But this is not true of classical poetry and is certainly not true of Song of Songs.

Third, lyric poetry is highly allusive. A sonnet may allude in passing to an episode in the *Iliad* or to a character from German mythology or a valley in France. If the reader does not recognize the allusion, he or she will miss the point or have to guess at it from context. Because a poem is allusive, it is also elusive. Lyric poetry is in one respect like a scientific or professional journal, in that it expects the reader to come to the text with a basic understanding of its code. No modern reader recognizes Mehi of the Papyrus Harris 500 songs, and thus his identity and significance are matters of conjecture. This is to some degree true of the Song as well; Song 7:5 (ET 7:4) says that the woman's nose is like the tower of Lebanon. This leaves those of us who have never seen the tower of Lebanon (today, that would be everybody) at a disadvantage.

Fourth, lyric poetry is highly compact. Discussing poems that deal with a historical topic, Vendler says, "In thinking about history poems, the main thing to remember is that there is always a tension between the copiousness of history and the brevity of lyric" (*Poems, Poets, Poetry,* 251). The same could be said of other varieties of lyric poetry. Shakespeare frequently packs several perspectives and many diverse particulars into the fourteen lines of a sonnet. Thus, lyric poetry is often quite dense. When the woman of the Song calls on the girls of Jerusalem not to arouse love until it pleases (e.g., 2:7), she is alluding to the standards of sexuality and virginity understood in her society and giving advice to them in a very condensed manner.

Fifth, and somewhat paradoxically in comparison to the fourth point, lyric poetry may explore the significance of an event in great detail, even when the event itself could be described in very few words. Herman Melville's "The March into Virginia" (explored in Vendler, *Poems, Poets, Poetry,* 239–41) essentially says, "Young Union soldiers cheerfully marched off to do battle at Manassas; most died, but those who survived became grim." Melville spends almost the entire poem describing the gleeful atmosphere of their march south and in so doing enables the reader to appreciate the cruel enlightenment of battle. The Song of Songs can basically be described like this: "A young woman in love marries and loses her virginity." It is, however, the significance of the experience that is the real stuff of the Song.

Sixth, as Vendler says, "Poems have their origins in life, especially in the formal or informal ceremonies that occur at crucial moments or phases in a single private life—birth, adolescence, marriage, death—or at public moments when we collectively commemorate a war, a religious feast, a holiday" (*Poems, Poets, Poetry,* 3). She observes (*Poems, Poets, Poetry,* 4, 13) how William Blake draws out the meaning of childbirth in "Infant Sorrow" and how Shakespeare understands the passage of time under different images in Sonnet 60. The Egyptian love poems do much the same thing; some explore the melodramatic emotions of a boy and girl in love, and one group exposes the entrapment of a boy by a prostitute. The Song of Songs investigates and celebrates the emotional journey of a woman into marriage.

Seventh, and again following Vendler, lyric songs not only *explore* the significance of life-events but *arrange* them as well (*Poem, Poets, Poetry,* 25–51). The devices poetry uses to do this have already been mentioned. They include the sounds of the language (rhyme, stress meter, syllabic meter, alliteration, etc.), the arrangement of stanzas, matching syntactical units, and so forth. The chiasmus of thirteen cantos of the Song of Songs described above connotes the marriage of the man and woman as a fulfillment of a purpose in life. It is perhaps significant that the moment of their union, the center of the chiasmus, is the seventh canto from both the beginning and from the end of the opus. Marriage is midway between birth and death, and looked at from either end, it is regarded as the high point.

Eighth, lyric poetry does not *tell* a story but *draws out the meaning* of a story. Vendler notes that a novel has time to spell out in detail its episodes, characters, and circumstances; a poem depends on the reader to catch the implications of the words it uses (Vendler, *Poems, Poets, Poetry,* 150). George Herbert (an Anglican clergyman [1593–1633]) illustrates this principle in his poem "Redemption" (Vendler, *Poems, Poets, Poetry,* 161, also cites this poem).

HAVING been tenant long to a rich Lord,
Not thriving, I resolved to be bold,
And make a suit unto him, to afford
A new small-rented lease, and cancell th' old.

In heaven at his manour I him sought:
They told me there, that he was lately gone
About some land, which he had dearly bought
Long since on earth, to take possession.

I straight return'd, and knowing his great birth,
Sought him accordingly in great resorts;
In cities, theatres, gardens, parks, and courts:
At length I heard a ragged noise and mirth

Of theeves and murderers: there I him espied,
  Who straight, *Your suit is granted,* said, and died.

The gospel of Christ is the story behind this poem. At the same time, it is clear that the poem does not *retell* the story but *explores the importance* of it. Someone who did not already know the Christian faith, in fact, would have great difficulty making sense of the poem. Thus, the essential facts of the gospel (God came down from heaven, became human in the person of Jesus, dwelt among sinners, and died to redeem them) are *givens* that are antecedent to the poem itself. To simply restate those facts, as I have just done, is not to explain the poem at all. But, knowing those facts, the reader of the poem can appreciate how Herbert has opened for us a new perspective on their significance. Herbert does not retell the events of the life of Jesus or recount the Christian theology of redemption. But when one recognizes the story behind the poem, one can comprehend how the larger background story (the Gospel) impacts the individual life. Similarly, the reader of Song of Songs is expected to recognize the life-event behind the Song, a marriage. The Song itself no more tells the story of a particular marriage than Herbert recounts particulars of the Gospel of Matthew.

A point of tension in the reading of the Song already alluded to here is the matter of reading it as a canonical text versus reading it as art. As a work of art, a lyric poem should give pleasure to the reader. (See Hall, *Pleasures of Poetry,* for a useful introduction to the pleasures of poetry.) One need not fall into the peculiar and sexually charged aesthetics of Roland Barthes (*Pleasure of the Text*) to affirm that a primary reason for reading a text, and certainly for reading a poetic text, is that it gives pleasure. After all, if the only point were to communicate data, one could do that much better in plain and simple prose. Paraphrases of poems are easier to comprehend than the poems themselves. But the communication achieved in a poem is not merely in the transfer of information ("the Union soldiers were excited and carefree as they marched off to their first battle, but they were quickly educated about the realities of war"). The very reading of the poem draws the reader into the experience, and the "pleasures" of a poem, be it the intoxicated joy of a love song or the plaintive mourning of an elegy, constitute a major element of the "meaning" of a poem. Full appreciation of a poem involves cognitively grasping its essential message and situation, but it also involves hearing its words and apprehending why these particular words were chosen, enjoying its tropes, empathizing with emotive response, and finally, appreciating the craft of the poet. Understanding a poem thus implies, first and on the simplest level, comprehending what the poem is *about*, then the ability to respond to it with the emotions and the self, and finally an understanding of why the poem works.

Appreciation of the pleasure of the poem, however, forces one to give due attention to the language, images, and sounds of the poem, that is, to its *surface* qualities. How is this understanding of poetry potentially at odds with the reading of a canonical text? Vendler, discussing Roland Barthes in "The Function of Criticism" (Vendler, *Music of What Happens,* 16), puts it like this:

> These two models are radically incompatible. The Barthian model, centering on bliss, refuses to dispense with the signifier; the biblical model, centering on "truth," finds its true repose in the signified. Though the second, hermeneutical, model could not finally avoid form-criticism, it regards attention to the form chiefly as a means to a higher end. It is from the hermeneutical model, with its persistent allegorizing tendency, that the vulgar notion of there being a "hidden meaning" in literature has arisen. The secular critic stays his eye on the surface; the religious critic chooses to pass through the surface in search of divine meaning. Both sorts of critics are always with us, though under different names. The two critical schools will always remain distrustful of each other, each finding the value of the work of art by a method repellent to the other.

Nothing so fully illustrates Vendler's point regarding biblical hermeneutics as the history of the interpretation of Song of Songs, with its persistent and determined allegorizing. But other, nonallegorizing approaches to the Song are no less dedicated to the same method and aims; neither the dramatic modes nor the feminist modes of interpretation escape using the Song as anything other than a quarry for theological or political dogma. Even interpreters who read the poem simply in its "plain sense" as a "love poem" are fundamentally in the business of seeking truth in the poem, although often with inconsistent and meager results. I, too, will seek the truth within the poems of Song of Songs.

On the other hand, although biblical scholarship has always focused on truth and meaning, the biblical writers themselves do not seem to have felt themselves to be on the horns of a dilemma between "bliss" and "truth"—certainly not the poet behind Ps 119, who could write, "Oh, how I love your Law! / All day long it is my meditation!" (v 97). He is not just saying, "I find much truth in your Law," although he repeatedly makes that point as well. The very act of reading and hearing the Law was a source of intense pleasure; to him the very words were like carefully chosen notes in a superb musical score. And the psalmist is here speaking of the *Law*—hardly what the general reader would consider the most aesthetically pleasing of the books of the Bible!

Where does this leave us while in the practical business of interpreting Song of Songs? It suggests that we must begin with the *pleasures* of the Song before progressing to the *truth* of the Song. Its lines and tropes, its sounds and images, and the emotive quality of the words chosen and the feelings evoked must be explored. Sometimes—and I am here as guilty as any biblical interpreter—we focus too much on what a metaphor *signifies* and not enough on what it *evokes*. The search for bliss is not, however, at variance with the search for meaning in the Song. If the Song does contain profound truth, and I am convinced that it does, that truth cannot be found without feeling what the poet felt and expected us to feel. Appreciation for the metaphors of the Song (the gazelles, does, foxes, spikenard, towers, fountains, and so forth) should lead to an appreciation for the love and sensuality of the Song, and finally for an appreciation of the truth of the Song.

Song of Songs and Christian Theology

Bibliography

Ayo, N. *Sacred Marriage.* New York: Continuum, 1997. **Boer, R.** "The Second Coming: Repetition and Insatiable Desire in the Song of Songs." *BibInt* 8 (2000) 276–301. **Blumenthal, D. R.** "Where God Is Not: The Book of Esther and Song of Songs." *Judaism* 44 (1995) 80–92. **Brown, P.** *The Body and Society: Men, Women, and Sexual Renunciation in Early Christianity.* New York: Columbia UP, 1988. **Campbell, J.** *Hero with a Thousand Faces.* **Davidson, R. M.** "Theology of Sexuality in the Song of Songs: Return to Eden." *AUSS* 27 (1989) 1–19. **Dillow, J. C.** *Solomon on Sex.* Nashville: Nelson, 1977. **Elliott, M. W.** "Ethics and Aesthetics in the Song of Songs." *TynBul* 45 (1994) 137–52. **Gledhill, T.** *Message of the Song of Songs.* **Glickman, S. C.** *A Song for Lovers.* Downers Grove: InterVarsity Press, 1978. **Hein, R.** *Christian Mythmakers.* **Jakobson, R.** "Linguistics and Poetics." In *Roman Jakobson: Selected Writings III.* Ed. S. Rudy. The Hague: Mouton, 1981. 18–51. **Kinlaw, D. F.** "Charles Williams' Concept of Imaging Applied to the Song of Songs." *Wesleyan Theological Journal* 16 (1981) 85–92. **Lévi-Strauss, C.** *Structural Anthropology.* **Lewis, C. S.** *The Allegory of Love.* London: Oxford UP, 1936. ———. *Experiment in Criticism.* ———. *Pilgrim's Regress.* ———. *Surprised by Joy.* New York: Harcourt, Brace, 1955. ———. *Weight of Glory and Other Addresses.* **Loder, J.** *Transforming Moment.* **Maranda, E. K., and P. Maranda.** *Structural Models in Folklore and Transformational Essays.* **Murphy, R. E.** "Cant 2:8–17—A Unified Poem?" In *Mélanges bibliques et orientaux en l'honneur de M. Mathias Delcor.* Ed. A. Caquot. Neukirchen-Vluyn: Neukirchener Verlag, 1985. 305–10. ———. "The Song of Songs: Critical Biblical Scholarship vis-à-vis Exegetical Traditions." In *Understanding the Word.* FS B. W. Anderson, ed. J. T. Butler, E. W. Conrad, and B. C. Ollenburger. Sheffield: JSOT Press, 1985. 63–69. **Payne, R.** "The Song of Songs: Song of Woman, Song of Man, Song of God." *ExpTim* 107 (1996) 329–33. **Shippey, T.** *J. R. R. Tolkien: Author of the Century.* **Shults, F. L.** "One Spirit with the Lord." *Princeton Theological Review* 7.3 (2000) 17–26. **Snaith, J. G.** *The Song of Songs.* Grand Rapids: Eerdmans, 1993. **Trible, P.** *God and the Rhetoric of Sexuality.* Philadelphia: Fortress, 1978. **Tolkien, J. R. R.** "Beowulf: The Monsters and the Critics." In *An Anthology of Beowulf Criticism.* Ed. L. E. Nicholson. Notre Dame, IN: Univ. of Notre Dame Press, 1963. **Walsh, C. E.** *Exquisite Desire: Religion, the Erotic, and the Song of Songs.* Minneapolis: Fortress, 2000.

Overview of the Problem

The demise of the allegorical interpretation appears to have left the Song of Songs a theologically impoverished book. Theological ruminations tucked away in the back of modern introductions to the Song (like this one) often chew endlessly over a very meager amount of cud. Their point seems to be this: "Love and sex are good!" (sometimes the message is pared down to, "Sex is good!"). The Song "legitimizes sexual need and fulfillment," the Song "openly celebrates the erotic nature of human love," the Song "declares the primacy of love in human life," and so forth and so on (for a full presentation of a "theology of sexuality" from the Song, see R. M. Davidson, *AUSS* 27 [1989] 1–19). Is a "theology of sexuality" all that the Song has to offer? Does Song of Songs have any real theology? Is it a nontheological love song from which one can get a theological message only by an exegetical tour de force?

The problem of finding a theology in the Song of Songs is complicated by the fact that the name of God (יהוה) and the word for God (אלהים) never appear in the book. It is possible that there is a circumlocution for "God" in Song 2:7 (see *Comment* on v 7), and it is possible that in Song 8:6 the suffix יה is "Yah," from "Yahweh." Neither case is a real use of the name of God, and neither suggests a theology. D. R. Blumenthal (*Judaism* 44 [1995] 80–92) tries to make something of this absence of the divine name along feminist lines, but his suggestion is not persuasive.

Murphy (100–105) wrestles with the problem at length and concludes, "Human sexual fulfillment, fervently sought and consummated in reciprocal love between woman and man: Yes, that is what the Song of Songs is about, in its literal sense and theologically relevant meaning" (103). But Murphy is also more sympathetic with the allegorical interpretation than most modern scholars are, and he almost wistfully looks back to the early allegorists and their rich celebration of the love of God (12–28; see also his "Song of Songs: Critical Biblical Schoarship"). He also cites a few texts that describe the relationship between God and his people under the metaphor of marriage (e.g., Isa 62:4–5) and makes the point that love is a great gift from God (104–5). G. A. F. Knight (64–65) likewise sees the theological significance of the Song in a loose analogy between divine and human love. N. Ayo exploits this analogy to the fullest. In his view, the Song celebrates sexuality but is ultimately spiritual as well since "the sensual and the spiritual are two sides of the same coin" (*Sacred Marriage*, 61). Longman's analysis (58–70) is similar: the Song celebrates sexual love, it portrays sexual love as a kind of redeeming reversal of the effects of Gen 3, and it exalts sexual love as an illustration of the love between God and humanity (citing texts such as Jer 2:1 and Rev 19:6–8).

The problem is that, except for the point that the Song celebrates sexual love, all of these theological insights are drawn from *outside* Song of Songs. Murphy (105 n. 400) has an impressive list of verses making the point that love is a gift from God; no citation from the Song is among them. The point that marital and sexual love *illustrates* the love between God and his people draws exclusively on texts outside the Song. The church is the bride of Christ, but this theological concept is not rooted in the Song (no NT text alludes to the Song), and the Song does not suggest any such theological construct. There is no suggestion in the Song of Songs that human, sexual love illustrates divine love.

Ayo's commentary has well nigh come full circle back to Origen. Working with the premise that Eros and spiritual yearning are fundamentally one and the same, he begins with a "literal" reading of the Song, but then, in catenalike fashion, looks for links that can bring him around to the NT. For example, the mention of the word כרם, "vineyard," in Song 7:13 (ET 7:12) prompts a discussion of Christ as the true vine in John 15:1–11 (*Sacred Marriage*, 230). This is not theological interpretation; this is theological sleight of hand.

Relating the Song to Gen 2–3 is similarly extraneous. P. Trible (*God and the Rhetoric of Sexuality*, 144–65) makes this tie. Clear links between the two are few and far between (e.g., that the word for "desire," תשוקה, appears in Gen 3:16 and Song 7:11 [also in Gen 4:7]). Even these ties are of dubious value; there is little reason to think that they are deliberate allusions to Genesis in the Song. The Song mentions gardens, trees, and a natural setting, but these are no indication that the Song is focused on reversing the story of the fall in Genesis. Pastoral and garden settings, with a general preference for nature over the city, are often found in love poetry, be it pagan or Christian. P. Trible's assertion (*God and the Rhetoric of Sexuality*, 47) that "in many ways, then, Song of Songs is a Midrash on Genesis" is not convincing. One can say that the Song, over against Gen 2–3, represents sexual love as paradise regained, but it is a mistake to say that this is the intrinsic message of the Song. Rather, it is a message that *we* have created by juxtaposing the Song and Gen 2–3. Comparing the Song to Genesis is not illegitimate, but when an interpreter repeatedly turns to Genesis to find the meaning of the Song, it is obvious that the alleged meaning is not germane to the Song at all. R. Payne (*ExpTim* 107 [1996] 331–32) follows similar logic using Gen 1: God created humanity as in his image male and female, and therefore the love between male and female in Song of Songs is a reflection of divine love. It is an observation that is fundamentally rooted in Gen 1, not in the Song, and it provides no clear guidance for interpreting the Song or appropriating the Song theologically.

Other approaches have fared no better. J. G. Snaith (*Song of Songs*, 134) finds no moral theology in the Song other than that it is "a celebration of God-given human love." Keel ([1994] 32–37) focuses on "Love as an Elemental Force" and concludes that the Song almost personifies love—or deifies it as a goddess (34). Pope's contention that the Song of Songs is rooted in a funerary feast (210–29) suggests that in love and sexuality, people cling to life and seek to transcend death. M. W. Elliott (*TynBul* 45 [1994] 137–52) argues that metaphors such as the lover as gazelle (Song 8:14) remind the reader of how our corporeality binds us to the created order and thus calls us to a higher spirituality, symbolized by the leaping of the gazelle. Such an analysis demonstrates how close we come back to allegorizing when we try to find theology in the Song.

Recent attempts to use the Song as the biblical guide to good sex (cf. J. C. Dillow, *Solomon on Sex*) are not to be taken seriously. T. Gledhill (*Message of the Song*) looks for moral lessons throughout the Song; much of what he says is valid, and some is rooted in the text of the Song. Provan imports extraneous material into the supposed moral teaching of the Song and launches an attack on the evils of the OT view of women and in particular of the harem system, using texts drawn from Exod 20, Judg 11, and Esther (Provan, 272–77). Like other dramatic/historical interpretations, Provan moralizes on his reconstructed drama rather than on the Song itself (so also, but with a differently reconstructed story, S. C. Glickman, *Song for Lovers*).

The notion that the love of woman and man is analogous to the love of humanity and God, particularly when a Platonic understanding of Eros is used, can lead in a much darker direction. Eros becomes the vehicle for finding God.

Ultimately, the sexual impulse is so glorified that it becomes the thing itself and eclipses the yearning for God. C. E. Walsh moves in this direction through an extravagant exploration of eroticism and spirituality in her aptly named commentary *Exquisite Desire: Religion, the Erotic, and the Song of Songs*. This is a dangerous path. As Eros is legitimized as an expression of spiritual desire, there is ultimately no difference between reading the Bible and reading pornography.

LESSONS ABOUT LOVE AND SEXUALITY

All this is *not* to say that the point that "love and sex are good" is invalid; to the contrary, it is correct and is *part* of the message of Song of Songs. The Song has more to say than that. There are some moral lessons in the Song, and it is useful to categorize them while reading Song of Songs as a celebration of human, sexual love.

The Song as a Rejection of the Ascetic Ideal

In contrast to the tendency to treat sexuality as intrinsically vile and the antithesis to holiness, the Song of Songs presents sexual love as a thing of great beauty and an activity that enriches human life. The Song teaches that love and sex are good. Paganism hardly needs such a lesson; it already worships sexuality as the bacchanalian point of access to the power and pleasure of the gods (although, I should add, the idealization of the virgin and the celibate also has pagan roots). In some forms of monotheism, however, there is a dark cellar of guilt and suspicion, and sexuality looks up from the bottom of that cellar. This mentality detests the physicality of the human body with all its appetites and excretions, and it desires freedom from the flesh, so that the soul may be spiritual and immune from bodily desires. It takes very seriously the injunction of the Apostle Paul to "mortify therefore your members which are upon the earth" (Col 3:5 KJV). Hair shirts, self-flagellation, and prolonged fasting broken only by the occasional small meal deliberately made unpalatable by the addition of bitter herbs are common strategies in Christian asceticism for freeing oneself from the constraints of the flesh. (Paul had no such practices in mind; for him, mortification referred to abstention from "fornication, impurity, lust, evil desire, and greed, which is idolatry" [Col 3:5], and for him ascetic practices were misleading and useless [Col 2:16–23].)

Peter Brown has thoroughly documented the sexual attitudes of early Christianity in his magisterial *The Body and Society: Men, Women, and Sexual Renunciation in Early Christianity*. Even a sampling of his findings are eye-opening, and it is worthwhile to peruse the teachings of the church fathers. For many early Christians, the idea that the Holy Spirit could come in full power on a person who was sexually active (in marriage) was simply inconceivable (*Body and Society*, 65–82); it should be noted that this attitude owes as much to pagan and platonic tradition as it does to biblical texts. A strong tendency toward perpetual celibacy emerged quite early in the churches of Asia Minor and Syria. The orthodox community resisted such extremism, but even here sex (within marriage, again) was regarded as a fundamental threat to Christian spirituality. Clement of Alexandria, although an exponent of the ideal of the Christian marriage, went so far as to lay down rules for copulation, which he suggested should be entered into with careful attention to deportment, in a stoical manner (Brown, *Body and Society*, 133). Christians were encouraged to avoid intercourse during pregnancy and lactation, making sexual encounters between even married couples rare indeed.

Exuberant praise for the ideal of the virgin notwithstanding, the spiritual bliss promised for celibate men often had to contend with the enormous impediment posed by flesh-and-blood women, be they consecrated virgins or not. At the end of late antiquity, the desert fathers sought refuge in the wilderness from the spiritual snare posed by the female body. "In the fourth and fifth centuries, the ascetic literature of Egypt became a repository of vivid anecdotes concerning sexual seduction and heroic sexual avoidance. In this new monastic folklore, the body leapt into sharp focus. Women were presented as a source of perpetual temptation to which the male body could be expected to respond instantly. For a nun simply to pat the foot of an elderly, sick bishop was considered enough provocation to cause both of them to fall instantly into fornication" (Brown, *Body and Society*, 242). Even complete separation from women did not save them from the powers of sexuality, however, as attested by the detailed injunctions and regulations to guard against homosexuality and pederasty among the monks (*Body and Society*, 246).

It was left to Augustine to establish a *modus vivendi* for dealing with the flesh and with women in the church. This former follower of the Manichaeans—this scholar who, for the sake of his Christian calling, dismissed his faithful concubine (in effect, a common-law wife) and son—would not turn against the ideal of the celibate. On the other hand, he had less stridency and more charity than did Jerome. For Augustine, the fundamental problem of the human race was not that humans were physical beings or even that humans experienced sexual desire; it was that the will itself was warped and ever turning toward strife, envy, and hatred. This was true of all persons, married or celibate. Augustine would honor marriage and the family, and he would not despise sexual union in marriage, even if he did hold to a rather passionless ideal. Still, he had deep admiration for married couples who renounced sexual intercourse but remained together as spiritual companions (Brown, *Body and Society*, 387–407).

For Augustine, then, the higher level of holiness was found in celibacy. The end result, intellectually codified for centuries in the Western church and ultimately institutionalized in the Catholic Church, was a two-tiered spirituality in which marriage is legitimate, to some degree even wondrous, but forever held back in a lower level of spirituality by that most carnal of activities, sex. To be close to God, one had to be continent.

The exuberant delight in sexuality that the Song reflects can hardly proceed from a theology that regards the flesh as innately evil or sexual activity as innately degrading. Similarly, the extravagant praise heaped on the woman's body cannot come from an outlook that regards female sensuality as dangerous and ungodly; the praise that the woman of the Song heaps on the man's body suggests that males, too, are sensual beings. If the presence of the Song in the biblical canon suggests anything, it is this: loving God with one's heart and soul and loving a member of the opposite sex with one's heart and flesh are not opposed to one another. The celibate is not on a straighter path to holiness than is the sexually active husband or wife.

The Song has no place for the ideal of man and woman associating as sexless creatures. In the real world, there are men and there are women; the sexless "human" is an abstraction, and the Song does not deal in abstractions. The fundamental reality of sex, the grim discovery of Jerome and Augustine, does indeed leave women and especially men struggling with lust and infidelity. On this matter, the Song is not silent. "Set me like a seal upon your heart, / like a seal upon your arm. / For love is strong, like death. / Jealousy is severe, like the grave" (Song 8:6). Love is a stern taskmaster and demands absolute fidelity to the beloved. Marriage must be fully monogamous. But the Song is not moralizing and offering up a restatement of the command against adultery. Rather, the passion that *demands* fidelity is also a *shield* to fidelity. To try to live without the passions of love is not merely frustratingly hopeless; it is unwise, unbiblical, and an open doorway to the very lusts it is trying to bar. In the Song, right passion is a protection against wrong passion.

Romantic Love

We have already noted that the medieval church regarded sexual desire as inherently evil. As C. S. Lewis has written (*Allegory of Love*, 14), "But according to the medieval view passionate love itself was wicked, and did not cease to be wicked if the object of it were your wife. If a man had once yielded to this emotion he had no choice between 'guilty' and 'innocent' love before him: he had only the choice, either of repentance, or else of different forms of guilt." Under this conception of sexual desire, a romantic, passionate love for one's own wife is impossible—and it is no surprise that the romantic ideal of courtly love in the medieval period exclusively concerned adulterous and extramarital affairs. There is no place for chronological snobbery here. Modern (or postmodern) culture also has great difficulty in seeing marriage as a promising setting for romance and passion. In current fiction, hot love is invariably in an extramarital setting.

The Song of Songs is filled with passion and desire from beginning to end. That expression of passion was probably of greater concern to the medieval churchman than was any explicit reference to breasts and thighs. The medieval man was told to keep concupiscence under control; the ideal was a man who could have sexual intercourse with his wife without passion and only for the sake of procreation. Passion is what the Song celebrates. References to sexual acts are fairly rare and usually indirect. What is not indirect or veiled is the fervent desire of the couple for each other. I have already noted that I believe that a marriage is at the center of the Song. What the Song therefore establishes is the legitimacy and beauty of a husband and wife experiencing heated desire for each other. The Song achieves something that medieval Christian culture could not fathom and that modern and postmodern culture cannot artfully attain: a man and woman who maintain passionate desire for each other in the context of conventional morality.

Sexual Morality

Song of Songs does not prescribe rules for human sexual life or even explicitly speak of them (with one significant exception), but this does not mean that there is no moral outlook pervading the text. The sexuality of the Song is monogamous and heterosexual. This is not imposing a bourgeois Protestant morality on the Song. In reality, heterosexual monogamy is the foundation for all of the Song's celebration.

The sexuality of the Song is heterosexual; a "gay reading" of the Song is the most violent kind of an imposition of extrinsic values on the Song (cf. the self-described "perverse" reading of R. Boer, *BibInt* 8 [2000] 276–301). Not only are the central lovers in the Song male and female, but it is understood that this is the outlook of the community at large. At the beginning of the Song, when the splendors of the man's love are being praised, the woman responds that the girls "rightly" love the man (Song 1:3–4).

This love is monogamous in nature. The woman is to the man "my sister, my companion, my bride" (e.g., Song 5:1). She is the lotus blossom; all other women are thorns (Song 2:2). Among sixty queens, and eighty concubines, and an endless number of girls, "my dove" is perfect and unique (Song 6:8–9; the figures represent a contrived comparison; the man is not saying that he has other queens, concubines, and girlfriends [see *Comment* on 6:8–9]). To the woman, the man is simply "my lover" and the one "whom my soul loves" (e.g., Song 1:7; 5:10). He is an apple tree; all other men are just trees in the forest (Song 2:3). He is the best among ten thousand men (Song 5:10). Most powerfully, the woman proclaims, "My lover is mine and I am his" (e.g., Song 2:16). To dismiss all this as white lies and empty "sweet talk" (as when a man who has several girlfriends tells one of them, "You're the only girl for me!") is to indulge in the kind of cynicism that the Song of Songs is itself set against. The Song portrays an idealized, perfect love; when these idealized lovers express their absolute devotion to each other, we can assume that they mean it.

Three other texts suggest that this is a monogamous (and married) relationship. First, Song 3:6–11, the arrival of the bride in a palanquin, reflects what is almost certainly an ancient Israelite wedding tradition (see *Comments* on 3:6–11). An ancient audience would have recognized this and understood that this is not a couple engaging in extramarital sex.

In Song 8:6–7, the woman sings what is one of the few didactic passages in the Song: "Set me like a seal upon your heart, / like a seal upon your arm. / For love is strong, like death. / Jealousy is severe, like the grave. / Its spark is a blaze of fire! It is the flame of Yahweh! / Many waters are not able to extinguish love, / and rivers cannot overwhelm it. / If a man were to give all his worldly possessions for love, / his offer would be utterly scorned." She claims ownership over him, in the same manner that a bulla marks ownership over a scroll among the scribes of ancient Israel. She declares that with powerful love comes powerful possessiveness. A woman who loves in this manner cannot share her man with other women. Such love is as strong as death; it utterly consumes the heart of the lover. She claims that such love is a rare, once-in-a-lifetime experience. Many never experience love at all. Like wisdom, it cannot be bought with money, and fidelity to one's bride is here equated with fidelity to Wisdom herself (see *Explanation* for 8:5–7). Such a rare gift as love must be protected; to throw it away for a fling with an outsider would be the utmost folly.

A third exemplary text is Song 2:7 and parallel passages, where the woman calls on the girls to swear that they will not arouse or awaken love until it pleases. The woman means: do not enter into a sexual relationship until the right time. Following the pattern of the Song itself, the "right time" is when a woman has found and wedded the one man she can love all her life. That is, the woman asserts that girls should remain virgins until marriage. This is not bourgeois morality or a Christian manipulation of the text; this is Wisdom, and the ancient audience would have understood it as such (see *Excursus: Virginity in the Ancient World*).

The only grounds for claiming that the couple is not married is in the woman's declarations at various points that she will take the man to "my mother's house" (e.g., Song 3:4). Taken literally, this suggests that the woman still lives at home, is not married, and is having trysts with her lover in her parents' home. Song 5:2–8 is often read in the same way. This commentary will suggest that this literal understanding of the passages completely misreads them. Her "mother's house" is her womb, and she is determined to have sexual relations with the man. But she is not living at home and having sex with a boyfriend under her mother's nose. She is speaking of her husband.

Tenderness and the Nurturing of a Relationship

As described above, many interpreters seek to mine the Song for hints on how to have a good relationship. This can be overdone. It is correct to treat the Song as a portrayal of ideal love and to see that how the two lovers treat one another is in some respects paradigmatic for the marriage relationship. The verbal affection that the couple shares implies that tender expressions of devotion are right and proper if love is to flourish. The love of Song of Songs is not strictly physical activity; often the *words* that praise the beloved's body and affection are the thing itself. Using words to declare intimacy and devotion are necessary and are part of the joy of love.

One can find many other texts that suggest practical ideals about the sexual relationship. Song 1:5 suggests that beauty, as determined by contemporary culture, can be misleading. Comparing Song 1:9–10 to 1 Peter 3:3 may enable the reader to come to a balanced view of the appropriateness of jewelry for women. Peter says that the real adornment of feminine beauty is a godly life, and he discourages fascination with fashion. The Song suggests that jewelry enhances a woman's beauty and that there are times when jewelry is appropriately given to the woman one loves. No doubt both sentiments are true. Song 1:13 suggests that the most wonderful adornment to a woman's beauty is her husband's love.

Fleeting Joys under the Sun

The man and woman of Song of Songs are young. Their bodies are perfect: beautiful eyes, black hair, golden skin, and not a tooth is missing (Song 4:2). The young man leaps on the hills like a gazelle (Song 2:9). The young woman's cheeks have the blush of youth (Song 6:7). They are new to love and to sexuality. It is a glorious, wonderful, and fleeting time—like the springtime that the Song itself describes (Song 2:10–13).

> Arise, my companion, my beautiful one,
> and come along!
> For see, the winter has passed,
> the rain is done,
> it is gone away.
> The flowers appear in the land,

the time of singing and pruning arrives,
the sound of the dove is heard in our land!
The fig tree ripens its figs,
and the vines from blossoms give their fragrance.

One cannot read the Song of Songs without awareness that it is indeed an ephemeral moment. "Rejoice, young man, in your youth, and let your heart give you joy in the days of your prime. Follow the ways of your heart and the visions of your eyes, but know that for all these things God will bring you to judgment. Banish care from your heart and throw away the troubles of your body, for youth and vigor are fleeting" (Eccl 11:9–10). The Song puts flesh on Qoheleth's injunction. Life is short, our days under the sun are few, and the hours in which we have the bloom of youth pass quickly. The young man and woman of the Song have seized their moment of glory under the sun.

More than that, wherever there is the poetry of love, there is also the shadow of death. As in the following lines, it is linked to jealousy.

This sour informer, this bate-breeding spy,
This canker that eats up Love's tender spring,
This carry-tale, dissentious Jealousy,
That sometime true news, sometime false doth bring,
    Knocks at my heart, and whispers in mine ear
    That if I love thee, I thy death should fear.
                            (Shakespeare, *Venus and Adonis,* ll. 655–60)

In the Song, love and death are equal in power: "For love is strong, like death. / Jealousy is severe, like the grave" (Song 8:6). It is jolting and sobering to encounter death at the end of a read through the idyllic love poetry of the Song. Although death and the grave in the Song are fundamentally illustrations of the possessive power of love, they are also reminders that whenever lovers vow eternal fealty to one another, they do so knowing that someday one will bury the other. But this is all the more reason to make the most of this brief but glorious spring: "We will rejoice and celebrate! / We will commemorate your caresses rather than wine!" (Song 1:4).

A Sense of Yearning

The Song of Songs, as argued above, is not an allegory of Christ and the church or of God and Israel. The love relationship between man and woman, however, expresses fundamental needs of the human soul or, to put it another way, is a type for the transformation and redemption of the soul. This is not a new insight. Writers and poets have long sensed this and have tried to describe the experience of how romantic love draws a person out of insular unhappiness and into a transformative experience. This transformation opens the inner self to an intimacy that recreates the inner person without destroying his or her identity. The man (or woman) in love typically declares that for the first time he can give without fear of hurt and betrayal. The woman (or man) in love says that for the first time she knows what the words *happiness, trust,* and *fulfillment* mean. This is of course an ideal portrait, and in a world where people are often selfish, foolish, and evil, the ideal is often not achieved. As a force for great happiness, romantic love is easily perverted into a force for domination, manipulation, and betrayal, making it also a great source of unhappiness, violence, and despair. Nevertheless, there are those whose love approximates the ideal, and the ideal is the subject matter of Song of Songs, so our concern here is with the ideal and not with the perversions and failures.

A major theme in the apologetic of C. S. Lewis is that our desires, inclinations, and emotions indicate who and what we are. In *Weight of Glory* he argued,

> A man's physical hunger does not prove that the man will get any bread; he may die of starvation in a raft in the Atlantic. But surely a man's hunger does prove that he comes of a race which repairs its body by eating and inhabits a world where eatable substances exist. In the same way, though I do not believe (I wish I did) that my desire for Paradise proves that I shall enjoy it, I think it a pretty good indication that such a thing exists and that some men will. A man may love a woman and not win her; but it would be very odd if the phenomenon called falling in love occurred in a sexless world (6).

Lewis had already developed this concept years earlier. It is expressed in a different form, for example, in his preface to *The Pilgrim's Regress* (10).

This idea is related to the notion of the experience of *Sehnsucht,* or yearning, as a momentary realization of something fundamental about ourselves, the world, and God. Lewis typically used the word *joy,* and it was a major theme in his personal experience of conversion, as described in *Surprised by Joy.* The concept was woven through all of Lewis's fiction (see Hein, *Christian Mythmakers,* 201–45). Lewis perhaps best expressed it in these words from *Weight of Glory* (12–13):

> And this brings me to the other sense of glory—glory as brightness, splendour, luminosity. We are to shine as the sun, we are to be given the Morning Star. I think I begin to see what it means. In one way, of course, God has given us the Morning Star already: you can go and enjoy the gift on many fine mornings if you want to get up early enough. What more, you may ask, do we want? Ah, but we want so much more—something the books on aesthetics take little notice of. But the poets and the mythologies know all about it. We do not want merely to see beauty, though, God knows, even that is bounty enough. We want something else which can hardly be put into words—to be united with the beauty we see, to pass into it, to receive it into ourselves, to bathe in it, to become part of it.

Sehnsucht may come during the reading of a line of a poem, or in a sudden glimpse of a sunset, or in the moment a man and a woman discover that they love each other. At that moment, we understand that there is something outside of us that answers the unspoken and perhaps unrecognized needs of the heart. We long for the freedom to open ourselves to the Good in the certainty that it will change us without swallowing us. The transcendental moment of *Sehnsucht* tells us that redemption and transformation are really necessary and really possible, and that life without them is empty. We cannot seize, create, or repeat the moment of *Sehnsucht,* for the moment is not the thing itself but the testimony to the reality in ourselves that seeks the reality outside of ourselves. *Sehnsucht* is not thus merely an analogy for the experience of knowing God; it is a moment of grace. To attempt to repeat or create the moment is to make an idol of the experience, but the actual event is a genuine apprehension of our basic need and of how that need is met.

Related to this is the notion Lewis derived from Charles Williams that although the creature can stand in the eye of its beholder as a *rival* to God (that is, as an idol), it can also serve as a *bridge* to God as a small token of the goodness of God. Because the creature bears the imprint of the creator, it is the type or image that affirms and points to the creator. The creature thus has the power to awaken *Sehnsucht* and provoke a yearning for God. At the same time, the creature remains true to itself. It has not become invisible, in contrast to the allegorical interpretations of the Song where the creature (that is, the human couple and their love) is invisible and has actually ceased to be (cf. D. F. Kinlaw, *Wesleyan Theological Journal* 16 [1981] 85–92).

Prospective for a Theology: The Transformation of the Soul

We have come back to where we began: according to Song of Songs, love and sex are good. For all the beauty and pathos the Song brings to that blunt statement, it falls short of a profound theology. This commentary will suggest that, in fact, that is not all there is. The Song portrays an experience of transformation of great theological significance. A claim to find such a theology in the Song would have to fulfill certain requirements.

1. It needs to come from within the Song itself. This is not to say that one cannot look for hermeneutical keys to bring to the interpretation of the text. However, the message itself should arise from within the Song. To say that the Song celebrates the love Christ has for the church is to build a theology out of Ephesians, not Song of Songs.

2. The theology of the Song of Songs must be exegetically fruitful and allow one to interpret its specific texts in an honest way, without taking refuge in a quasi-allegorical catena of biblical texts.

3. Eroticism as such cannot be called the theology of the Song. While sexuality is a dominant feature of the Song, if the Song's message is to be called a theology, the essential yearning it describes should transcend sexuality and not lead back to sexuality itself. There is an analogy between yearning for God and yearning for another person, but having sex is not a spiritual act, and desire for sex is not a desire for God.

4. An interpretation of the Song should lead to the true allegory of love. This is not the allegorizing of texts but an appreciation of how the love and desire of the Song of Songs are aspects of the fundamental longings of the human heart.

I believe such a theological interpretation of the Song can be found in a theology of transformation. I will suggest that Song of Songs gains perspective when seen as a heroic quest and transformation in the sense that J. Campbell (*Hero with a Thousand Faces*) and C. Levi-Strauss (*Structural Anthropology*) have taught.

A Model for Transformation
F. LeRon Shults (*Princeton Theological Review* 7.3 [2000] 17–26), building on the cultural anthropology of Claude Lévi-Strauss and its application to theology in the work of James Loder (*Transforming Moment*), argues that beneath all transformational myth is a common structure that might be described as the grammar of transformation. Lévi-Strauss (*Structural Anthropology*, 206–31), on the basis of an analysis of the structure of myth, determined that there was an analogy be-

tween myth and linguistics. Specifically, structural linguistics can distinguish *langue* from *parole*. The former, *langue*, is the unchanging deep structure of human linguistics. The latter, *parole*, is the grammar and vocabulary of a given language with its specific, arbitrary symbols. Lévi-Strauss contended that myth uses the structure of *langue* and the specificity of *parole* to produce a new referent of timeless truth. One can understand myth on one level as a specific, diachronic (or, sequential) story. But on another level one can see myth as a declaration of a synchronic (or, timeless) representation of the structure of human existence. He found that a single myth tends to have parallel episodes because the parallels helped to bring out the deep structure of the story.

Lévi-Strauss found that myth tends to relate two pairs of concepts as "A is to B as C is to D." He expressed the structure of myth in a simple formula (Lévi-Strauss, *Structural Anthropology*, 228): There are two "characters" in this structure: the protagonist of the story and the redeemer, the person (or event or thing) that transforms the protagonist. There are also two initial functions or spheres of existence.

The formula, as developed further by a number of scholars, describes the structure of transformation in which the protagonist of the story begins in one sphere of existence but longs to be in another sphere of existence. We may call these two, respectively, the "unhappy situation" and the "desired situation." The protagonist, however, is incapable of achieving this change of sphere of existence. The protagonist needs the redeemer. In order to fill the redeeming or transforming function, it is necessary that the redeemer be simultaneously in both spheres of existence—in both the unhappy situation and the desired situation. The redeemer cannot relate to the protagonist if the redeemer is not also in the unhappy situation. On the other hand, the redeemer cannot help the protagonist if the redeemer is not in the desired situation. The redeemer is an agent who functions simultaneously in both spheres of existence and relates to the protagonist on each side of the equation.

There are three movements that take place in the grammar of transformation as described in this model. First, there is a mediation of opposites, whereby the redeemer simultaneously exists in both spheres of existence. This enables the redeemer to mediate for the protagonist, who longs to move from the unhappy situation to the desired situation or sphere of existence yet also desires to do so without loss of identity or self.

Second, a double negation occurs. This double negation involves, first, the fact that the protagonist is in a negative situation and must accept the fact that he/she is in such a condition. Specifically, the protagonist must acknowledge his/her inability to move from the first sphere of existence (unhappy situation) to the second sphere of existence (desired situation). This negation is itself negated when the protagonist allows the redeemer to mediate transformation. When the protagonist submits to the mediation of the redeemer, the protagonist is able to attain his/her desire, but it is only attained by negation, the protagonist's abandonment of attempts to attain the desired situation by acting as agent.

Third is the emergence of dialectical identity, in which the protagonist goes through a permutation from the unhappy situation to the desired situation. In the first, the protagonist is an agent in that sphere of existence (the unhappy situation). As an agent, the protagonist is free but trapped (e.g., suffers from lack of intimacy, joy, life, or significance). Then the protagonist moves from being agent to being a sphere of existence. That is, after the redemption, the protagonist is no longer agent but is now a sphere of existence in which the real agent of existence, that which gives identity, is the desired condition. The permutation or inversion of the protagonist is this: he/she no longer claims to be the agent of his/her existence but finds "real existence" under the agency of that which was sought as mediated by the redeemer. The protagonist does not become a controlling agent in the desired situation; rather, the protagonist becomes the domain of the desired reality. This reality can be called "real existence."

By "real existence," one means significance, love, intimacy, value, or life. The protagonist sought "real existence" but was unable to attain it while continuing to act as agent, governing and directing his/her existence. The protagonist feared, however, that he/she would be destroyed, swallowed up, or lose identity if he/she simply surrendered to the desired reality and allowed it to make him/her its domain. But the redeemer, functioning at the same time in both spheres of existence, is able to bring the protagonist through the process of transformation. One might say that the redeemer gives the protagonist the means and the courage to undergo this transformation. And the protagonist is not swallowed up at all. In the redeemed condition, he/she is not consumed. Loss of status as "agent" does not entail loss of identity; it means a new identity that is also a dialectical identity. Through a relationship with the redeemer, who exists in both spheres of existence, the protagonist finds both freedom and access to the desired sphere of existence. But the protagonist does not become the exact counterpart to the redeemer, who operates in both spheres. The protagonist accepts the negation of his/her role as controlling agent and becomes the domain in which the desired condition operates. Pierre and Elli Maranda (*Structural Models*) modify Lévi-Strauss and introduce varieties of structure to folklore and transformational models; nevertheless, they still operate with this basic framework.

At this point, several objections to the entire project here described need to be dealt with. Structuralism has been criticized for approaching the analysis of texts and stories with a misleading, pseudo-mathematical precision. One may question whether this model really dominates mythology. Or a reader with a high regard for the canonical authority of the Hebrew Scriptures may wonder whether a structure derived from myth can be rightly applied to the Song of Songs, and whether such an application means that we regard the Song as myth. Finally, even if some validity is granted to the above model, one may ask whether and how it can be convincingly applied to the Song.

Regarding the first question, whether the method of structuralism is pseudomathematical, I think that to some degree it is. While structuralist formulas may be convenient shorthand, it is a peculiar method for doing literary interpretation, and it can be confusing. More than that, the scientific notation certainly does not prove anything. One cannot say that this approach to myth is correct because it has been demonstrated in a formula that resembles a scientific proof. Nevertheless, although structuralism may be overambitious about its claims of scientific objectivity and may use some questionable notations, this does not mean that all of its interpretive insights are invalid. The suggestion that a protagonist goes through a transformation in the midst of a quest to achieve a new sphere of existence is valid in many cases. Also, as Shults notes, "Deconstructivist and post-structuralist scholars would criticize Lévi-Strauss along with anyone who claims to find similarities or common structures among human beings . . . , but it is important to note that their criticisms at this philosophical level are subject to the problems of self-referential incoherence one finds in all radical relativist and nihilist positions" (*Princeton Theological Review* 7.3 [2000] 25 n. 6).The Lévi-Strauss model works well with the Song of Songs, as is argued below.

In answer to the second question, one can say that although this model is not necessarily present in all myths, it or elements of it are surely present in some myths, stories, and songs. Even some modern mythology and fiction to a degree follows this model.

The Use of Myth *in Relation to Song of Songs*

Does the application of this model to the Song of Songs mean that it is to be regarded as myth? I would not describe the Song as myth for several reasons. The term *myth* often connotes a pagan worldview characterized preeminently by a pantheistic and animistic view of nature. This is not present at all in the Song. The Song shares the outlook of the Hebrew Scriptures—and especially the outlook of Wisdom—that this world is created by God but is separate from him. The world is not God's body, and there is no magic. In the Song, sex has no sacral significance and there is no celebration of a fertility cult. Although the world of the Song is idealized, there is nothing fantastic here. There are no gods, no magical creatures, and no elements that do not have correspondents in the real world. Metaphors are simply metaphors; the woman is not really a flower, and she mates with a man and not with a bull or swan or gazelle. The term *myth* is unhelpful for many because in the Bible it can simply connote a story that is false and worthless, as in Paul's disdain for those who "turn away from listening to the truth and wander into myths" (2 Tim 4:4 RSV). As far as genre is concerned, Song of Songs is lyric poetry and not epic mythology.

At the same time, the fact that a structure is discovered behind many myths does not mean that the structure itself is false or perverse, nor does it mean that the structure only exists in myth. Even pagan myths could symbolically present many profound truths about the human situation. And the Song is rich in symbolism.

C. S. Lewis provides a description of myth that is illuminating and can help to further refine the significance present in the Song. In *An Experiment in Criticism* (43–44), Lewis gives six characteristics of myth as a vehicle of timeless truth.

1. Myth is in a sense extraliterary. That is, the story itself, and not the artful telling of the story, is what constitutes myth. The literary pleasure of reading myth is altogether separate from the apprehension of its mythic significance. Lewis illustrates by showing how even a simple, abbreviated telling of the story of Orpheus carries all its mythic power (*Experiment in Criticism*, 40–41).

2. The pleasure and power of myth do not depend on the normal narrative techniques of suspense and surprise. In fact, the narrative element itself is often minimal.

3. Human sympathy with the characters is minimal. "We feel indeed that the pattern of their movements has a profound relevance to our own life, but we do not imaginatively transport ourselves into theirs" (*Experiment in Criticism*, 44).

4. Myth is fantastic, dealing with impossible and preternatural things.
5. Myth may be sad or joyful, but it is always grave. It is never comic.
6. Myth is also awe-inspiring. "We feel it to be numinous. It is as if something of great moment had been communicated to us" (*Experiment in Criticism*, 44).

How does this list stack up against Song of Songs? In contrast to myth, the pleasure of the Song is clearly *not* extraliterary. As high lyric poetry, its literary creativity and its manipulation of language are of supreme importance. Take away the art of the Song and there is nothing left. Using Roman Jakobson's terms ("Linguistics and Poetics," 18–51), in the Song the poetic function dominates the cognitive function.

As in Lewis's use of the term *myth*, the Song's power does not depend on suspense and narrative technique. The Song is not narrative. There is no real sympathy with the characters of the Song. They are idealized and remain outside of the reader. We are observers and listeners. The Song does not deal with magic or impossible things. On the other hand, the language of the Song does transcend normal human experience. The woman, whose head is like a mountain, who dwells with lions in the high lairs of Lebanon, whose breasts are two deer, or who is a living garden or date-palm tree, or who is as glorious as the sun, moon, and stars, is no normal woman. The Song is between two worlds. Its characters are mythic in their literary proportions, and yet they do not inhabit a world of magic, and they are not gods. They are ordinary and yet much larger than ordinary. The Song is grave and never comic. It is often joyful, but its celebrations are serious celebrations and never frivolous. The Song is awe-inspiring. Lewis's words, "We feel it to be numinous. It is as if something of great moment had been communicated to us" (*Experiment in Criticism*, 44), could have been written as a description of the Song. Although Song of Songs is not fully myth or epic, it contains elements that suggest that the interpretive tools one brings to epic or myth may also shed light on the Song.

Can the structure described by Lévi-Strauss be meaningfully applied to the Song? One may try it and see what happens. The reader can decide whether the effort is successful or not, but I think it can be done. The application of this structural analysis to the Song of Songs will both clarify the meaning of the structural analysis and show how the structural analysis functions in Christian theology.

One caveat is necessary, however. Song of Songs is lyric poetry and not epic poetry, and one should not expect numerous or obvious parallels to heroic tales, or force parallels where they do not exist. But if analogies from other literature help to understand the Song more fully, so much the better.

Song of Songs as a Heroic Quest and Transformation

J. Campbell, in *The Hero with a Thousand Faces,* studied common elements in stories of the hero and his quest. One does not need to follow Campbell's understanding of this model fully, nor need one assume that the Song fulfills every aspect of this model, in order to gain some insights from the concept of the heroic quest.

The protagonist of Song of Songs is the woman. This is of itself unusual. The hero of the classical heroic quest is a man, whether Gilgamesh, Jason, Aeneas, or Luke Skywalker. The quest is often a means of initiation. It usually involves an initial hesitation if not an outright refusal to act on the hero's part, a departure from familiar surroundings, and a conflict with a monster or super villain. The hero is often aided in the quest by some wise old man, god, or wizard, and the hero frequently has a group of companions.

The woman of the Song, this commentary suggests, struggles at Song 2:5–7 and 3:1–5 with hesitation and anxiety over proceeding with the marriage and loss of virginity. She does not do battle with the forces of evil, but she does have an encounter with the violence of the "guards" at 5:2–8 in the course of her "quest." She has no wise sage to guide her, but she does repeatedly refer to her mother and her mother's house. She specifically says that her mother "used to teach me" (Song 8:2). The woman does have a group of companions in the girls of Jerusalem.

Beyond those similarities, the woman's "quest" is exceedingly domestic. She is, after all, only getting married. There are some female heroic figures in myth and legend. The most obvious is the goddess Isis (or Anat, or Inanna), who rescues her fallen consort Osiris (or Baal, or Dumuzi). There are also human heroic females, such as Electra. But the experience of the woman of the Song is far removed from these figures, and trying to find parallels in these myths to the Song spreads more confusion than light. The woman of Song of Songs is decidedly not a warrior.

Still, her experience and her person are made to be larger than life. She is the one whose body is described in sometimes titanic terms, whose radiance is like that of the sun, and who dwells in the mountains. The point is *not* that she is a goddess (as in the cultic interpretation). Rather, she is made into an archetype—she is given universal significance—in order to define the meaning of the ordinary feminine experience of marrying, having sexual relations with a man, and ending her virginity. The Song, furthermore, seeks to mediate two pairs of opposites, where virginity is to nonvirginity as autonomy is to love.

Her initial condition or "unhappy situation," as described in this commentary, is that of virgin. Her desired situation, therefore, is "nonvirgin." Virginity in the Song is a condition of isolation and imprisonment. She has no intimate relations with a man and thus is sexually autonomous; she is the locked garden and the sealed well. She is like a walled city with guards on the walls or like a goddess high in a mountain lair, surrounded by wild beasts. Her autonomy is that no man has access to her body. Ironically, however, her autonomy is not freedom but the antithesis of freedom. In the condition of virgin, her only relationship with men is with her brothers, who regard her as an outsider, or even as a servant fit only to work in the vineyards. Working as a slave, she has no opportunity to cultivate her own "vineyard" (Song 1:6). Although sexually *autonomous,* she has no *liberty* to nurture her life, joy, or significance, nor can she give and receive love. Virginity is both a protection and a prison. She longs to be free of it but is terrified to leave her domain. The pain of the loss of virginity is both physical and emotional. She fears that the loss of virginity will mean her death (that is, the destruction of her identity as well as the physical trauma).

She cannot resolve this dilemma by her own agency, that is, through promiscuity. Doing this, she would lose the virginity without gaining the intimacy, joy, or significance she seeks. In terms of the Lévi-Strauss formula, she cannot force her way into the desired situation "nonvirgin" and become an agent controlling that sphere of existence. Were she to try that, she would continue to be autonomous and yet not have freedom (ironically, true freedom in sexuality only exists when one man has exclusive claim to her sexual pleasures and she has exclusive claim to his desire, as in her refrain, "I belong to my beloved and his desire is for me," Song 7:11 [ET 7:10]). In promiscuity, freedom and intimacy would be further from her than ever before. She would emotionally still be behind the walls of virginity while physically not a virgin. She would be in effect not free but a promiscuous virgin, with *virgin* here meaning, "unloved by a man." This is the prostitute's dilemma, that she is sexually active but alone and without love. Thus, the woman of the Song repeatedly tells the girls of Jerusalem not to awaken or arouse sexual desire until the time is right (Song 2:7; 3:5; 8:4). Her message is that virginity is the key to attaining sexual freedom—a freedom understood not simply as the ability to have sex but as the attainment of joy and intimacy in the sexual relationship.

The man of the Song is the mediator or redeemer figure. In terms of the formula, he is at the same time in the unhappy situation and the desired situation: he is both a virgin (sexually inexperienced) and a nonvirgin (a male). The man is in the sphere of existence of being a nonvirgin in that, being a man, he does not have the physical attribute of virginity, the hymen. That is, he can engage in sexual intercourse without the physical trauma of the tearing of the hymen. Perhaps even more significant than the physical matter of virginity is the fact that society does not enclose him within the walls of virginity. This does not mean that Israelite culture necessarily endorsed a double standard regarding the man's freedom to be promiscuous; the book of Proverbs emphatically rejects that option for the man. Nevertheless, the male is not secluded from the world within the title of "virgin." Thus, he at the same time occupies both spheres of existence.

One may immediately ask on what basis can one assert that the man has no prior sexual experience since he never explicitly declares that he has never had sex before (a very odd thing to do in a love song). There are three reasons for drawing this conclusion. The Song stands in the tradition of biblical Wisdom literature. Its title, "the Song of Songs of Solomon," already establishes this link, and its position in the Hebrew canon in the midst of Job, Proverbs, Ruth, and Ecclesiastes further reinforces this classification (an argument can be made for seeing Ruth as woman's Wisdom literature). Wisdom literature is explicit and emphatic in its demand that the young man avoid promiscuity in the person of the prostitute and that he direct all his affection and sexual energy to the "wife of his youth" (e.g., Prov 5 and 7). The archetype for the male lover in Song of Songs can hardly be someone who has dallied with the prostitutes, like the young man of the Nakhtsobek Songs. The very nature of the poem, a celebration of young love, speaks against seeing the man as anything other than new to love. The essence of this poem is the excitement and newness of the sexual experience. Young lovers and first love are what the poem is all about. The man expresses a sense of awe in his stance toward the woman. He is overwhelmed in her presence and feels himself incapable of approaching her. She is a tower, and he is in awe of her. His attitude here is the attitude of the unaffected male—not jaded, but innocent and amazed in the presence of feminine beauty. His words are not the words of a man acquainted with casual sex, incapable of feeling the newness and wonder of the sexual relationship.

As a redeemer, the man and the love he gives mediate the transition of the woman from isolated virgin to the status of being free, loving, loved, and at peace.

The woman begins the Song as an outsider. She has a peasant's dark skin and even within her own family she does peasant's work. She has no freedom to pursue her own interests and in that sense is not her own person (Song 1:5–6). She desires to be with her lover but is fearful of men (1:7). Nevertheless, the love between herself and her lover is strong—they adore one another (1:9–2:7). Her lover comes to her and calls her away to love (2:8–17). It is his passion for her that allows her to confront the power of sex and the loss of her virginity, even though the prospect makes her swoon (2:5). With the prospect of the wedding night looming before her, she has a night of terror. She seeks her lover, the one who will provide intimacy and freedom, but she finds the guardians of the walls—her virginity. Suddenly, the groom appears, and she makes a determined decision to take him to "her mother's house," that is, to end her virginity with him (3:1–5). A marriage ceremony follows (3:6–11). He then woos her with a tender seduction (4:1–15). His passion for her gives her the strength to open up the "locked garden" (4:12) and let her lover into his feast (4:16–5:1).

This does not mean that the loss of virginity is without trauma; as she goes through the experience, she suffers pain and feels alone (Song 5:2–8). Mere loss of virginity is not transformation; as with the promiscuous woman, she could yet become physically loosed from virginity but without intimacy, freedom, and joy. Her transformation is completed in two stages. She reflects on how wonderful her lover is (that is, on how much she loves him) in 5:9–16, and he comes to her again and makes it clear that his desire and admiration of her is unabated (6:1–9). The woman's body has become the domain of love. In terms of the structural formula, the protagonist woman has become the sphere of existence of the desired reality, love. As all can see, she is the garden, the embodiment of love, pleasure, and life (6:9–13). The lover's desire is for her. Love, intimacy, and sexual pleasure have their true place in her person (7:1–10). She has not simply lost her virginity; she has taken her man into herself. This does not mean that she is simply passive, much less that she has lost her personality. To the contrary, she has true sexual freedom. She delights in her lover's body (5:10–16). She is so happy in her role as sexual woman that her only regret is that she cannot be more public about it (8:1–4). She understands the meaning of love, and she has become the true interpreter and guide to love (8:6–7).

Perhaps the apotheosis of the woman occurs at Song 8:10: "I was a wall, and my breasts were like towers; / then I was in his eyes as one who finds peace." Previously she was like a walled city with guards all about and the gates closed. She was prepared for war, ready to defend her virginity. In his eyes, however, peace came. He did not storm the walls and conquer her. Peace between her and the male sex was found "in his eyes," that is, in his love for her. The guards and walls are no longer needed. She attained in intimacy a true end to her virginity. She now has freedom; she can tend her own vineyard at last (8:11–12). Her freedom came not by promiscuity (she did not awaken love before it was ready) or by rejection of the male (perpetual virginity) but by the transformation that made her the domain of love.

Theological Reflection

The distinctively *female* experience of loss of virginity as described in the Song of Songs explores in an ideal form a crucial aspect of the *human* experience and of the *human* soul (it is not uniquely the *feminine* experience of the *feminine* soul). In contrast to the church fathers, for whom virginity was the closest thing in this world to holiness, in the Song of Songs virginity represents isolation and imprisonment. The virgin is the locked-up garden and the walled city. As an emblem of seclusion, the virginity of the woman of the Song speaks to the isolated souls of both men and women.

We humans, male and female, exist behind emotional barriers as lonely, autonomous souls longing for freedom and love. Our yearning or *Sehnsucht* is for release from isolation, rejection, and death. We are autonomous but not free. We nevertheless fear intimacy and its theological counterpart, holiness. If it breaks through to us, it may destroy us. If we fall into a sea of holiness, we may drown. We have eaten from the tree of the knowledge of good and evil, have recognized our nakedness, and have clothed ourselves. We do not want to be found naked, and we know that if intimacy breaks through our barriers, our shame will be made visible. We cannot bear to let go of the false freedom of being an autonomous agent.

Put in more abstract terms, we are aware of our need to transcend our isolation, corruption, and finitude, yet we fear the eternal, infinite, and pure. We are in need of transformation, and the Song celebrates that process of transformation: the virgin marries and becomes the joyful domain of love. The Song tells us that the human need for intimacy is universal and that the condition is not hopeless.

Shults (*Princeton Theological Review* 7.3 [2000] 17–26) argues that the Lévi-Strauss structural analysis of transformation also describes the Christian gospel. He argues that the grammar of permutation functions within the Christian experience of becoming "one spirit" with the Lord (1 Cor 6:17). Comparing the Song to the Christian gospel, we can see that both describe the same process of human transformation. Describing the Christian gospel in terms of the structure of transformation, we can see where the gospel and the Song of Songs meet.

The Eastern church perceives the fundamental human dilemma to be mortality. Christ delivers us through his incarnation, death, and resurrection and the subsequent pouring out of the Spirit. The soteriology of the Eastern church is sometimes described as a kind of divination of humanity. It is not that we literally become gods but that by the deity of Christ and by his resurrection we partake of the divine nature (2 Peter 1:4). Understood in this way, humanity (or the individual person) can be described as the protagonist in the unhappy situation. That is, our sphere of existence is bounded by death. We are mortal, finite, and perishing. We long to escape this dilemma and enter the desired situation: God's sphere of existence, that is, immortality.

Christ, the God-man, is simultaneously mortal and immortal, finite and infinite, and perishing and imperishable. He is the redeemer in the structure of our existence. He is the mediator. As God he shows us our negation, our mortality, but as man he is united to us. In him, the human race undergoes the process of transformation. In his death he negates our negation, and in his resurrection he releases the human race from the bondage of death. In him we have a new identity, a dialectical identity grounded not in our becoming gods but in our becoming domains in which the divine life now exists. Our eternal life is not a matter of our becoming agents that have power over life and death. It is a matter of the divine spirit, or the power of the resurrection, living in us. We have surrendered all attempts to become divine through our own agency or to control the power of life and death. Instead, "the life which I now live in the flesh I live by faith in the Son of God, who loved me, and delivered Himself up for me" (Gal 2:20 NASB).

The Western church perceives humanity's principal problem to be the guilt whereby we merit only divine wrath. Once again, humanity, the protagonist of this story, is in the unhappy situation but longs to be free of it. As before, the protagonist cannot enter the desired domain, righteousness, via his own agency. If he could by his "works" enter the domain of righteousness, then he would be an agent that controls righteousness and, in Paul's words, have something to boast about (Rom 4:2). In fact, however, this is not possible.

Christ enters our dilemma as the one who is without sin and yet is made sin for us (2 Cor 5:21). Once again, he is the redeemer who mediates the two opposites. As the one who is in the desired situation of being without sin, he confronts us in our negation (our guilt), but as the one who is in the unhappy situation, the one who bore our sin, he negates our negation. Our quest for righteousness ends not with our attaining it but with our inversion or permutation. We are not agents who attain righteousness or masters over righteousness; we are the dwelling in which righteousness lives (Rom 6:16–20). The body is now dead because of sin, but the spirit lives because of righteousness (Rom 8:10). In short, we become the sphere of existence where righteousness now rules as controlling agent. Christ himself is now our wisdom, righteousness, sanctification, and redemption (1 Cor 1:30).

We should not forget that there is an ongoing dynamic in the grammar of transformation. The woman in the Song becomes the domain of love, but the man continues to relate to her with awe for her beauty and purity, as though she were perpetually virginal. As Christians, we continue to relate to Christ on both sides of the formula of transformation. On the one hand, we remain mortals who ever look to him as our hope of eternal life, and we remain sinners who continue to seek forgiveness. On the other hand, as transformed beings who are now the domain of the life and righteousness of God, we relate to Christ as the mortal who is the channel of our immortality and as the one in whom we are clothed in righteousness. Our redemption is not static but dynamic and forever bound to the person of our redeemer.

This understanding of redemption allows us to come to a better grasp of the distinctive nature of Christian spirituality. We do not in gnostic fashion climb up the ladder of existence toward the region of pure being and away from the lower regions of matter. We do not seek absorption in the One or the annihilation of personality. In Christian spirituality, individuality and the body are not an illusion from which we seek release.

Christian spirituality focuses on two realities. First, there can be no redemption without a redeemer. Second, Christian spirituality is not so much a matter of "being spiritual" as it is a matter of being the domain of the Spirit. This explains how we can speak of being "dead with Christ" and yet alive, or of being alive in the Spirit yet without the annihilation of personality. We have not ceased to be, but we are now the domain of the Spirit rather than agents that control life and righteousness. We do not speak of being absorbed into the Spirit; rather, the Spirit lives in us. We are free but not autonomous, because as the domain of the Spirit we experience intimacy, love, righteousness, and life. As the woman is united to her husband, so we who are united to the Lord are one Spirit with him. Christian spirituality is this: through the redeemer, we become the domain of the love of God.

The point of what we are saying is this: the gospel and the Song of Songs both describe, on different levels of existence, the most basic need of the human soul. We should make clear that the connection between the Song of Songs and the Christian gospel is not merely a matter of analogy. The point is not that the woman's experience of losing virginity is an *allegory* of Christ and the church or even that our need for God and redemption in Christ is *analogous* to our need for intimacy. Rather, our need for love and significance is a single thing that expresses itself on the different planes of our existence. As creatures who are flesh and blood, created by God to multiply, fill the earth, and build families, our need expresses itself as the desire for heterosexual love and sex. As beings created in the image of God, made to glorify God and honor him forever, it expresses itself as the yearning of the heart for spiritual redemption. But to make a fine point, this does not mean that Eros and the desire for God are one and the same. It means that Eros and the desire for God are both born of a desire for love and significance, but it also means that to function rightly each desire must be fulfilled in its own realm and not in the other.

The woman's experience in the Song of Songs brings out the deep structure of the human soul. The *Sehnsucht* that C. S. Lewis describes is not an *allegory* of our need for love and ultimately for God; it is an *expression* of it. A passing glimpse of glory one may catch when looking at the heavens, or when listening to music, or when reading the words of an epic poem is a breaking out of this deep yearning for that which is good, beautiful, and loving. When people experience love, joy, freedom, or intimacy on any level, they are experiencing something that redeems human nature. Knowing God is therefore the ultimate experience of redemption; every other redemptive experience is real but limited, like a foreshadow.

IMPLICATIONS OF THE THEOLOGY OF SONG OF SONGS

The theology of Song of Songs as described above has significant ramifications. What follows is not strictly the theology of the Song but implications of that theology for the body and society as we also draw on other areas of biblical teaching.

This interpretation of the Song indicates that the solution to the problem of integrating men and women together into the spiritual life of the church is quite different from what many early Christians imagined. To be sure, the Augustinian solution, with its more all-encompassing understanding of the bondage of the will, was better than that of Tatian, Origen, or Jerome, but even Augustine's model is fundamentally marred. A two-tiered spirituality—the holy celibate over against the married Christian—is established, and even the married believers are constantly urged to move toward the ideal of continence. If my reading of the Song is correct, Holy Scripture does something that most of the Fathers of the church would have considered inconceivable and some would have considered horrible: *it celebrates a woman's loss of virginity.*

This is a far more significant issue, from the standpoint of the history of Christian theology, than are the Song's references to breasts and kisses and thighs. Focusing on erotic tidbits of the text, as some feminist readings and other modern commentaries do, is both adolescent and obtuse, missing the point of the Song entirely. Rather, the Song is shocking to the Christian because the ideal exalted in much of Christendom, virginity, is stood on its head in Song of Songs. In a word, celibacy is neither the norm nor the ideal, and it does not confer a spiritual advantage.

This does not forbid celibacy or denigrate the wonderful examples of men and women who have the *charis*, "spiritual gift," of celibacy. But it does imply that celibacy is not itself the path to *charis*. Rather, celibacy is a gift that allows some believers freedom from other responsibilities in order that they may give more of themselves to God's work and to the church (1 Cor. 7:32–35). In a word, what celibacy gives is not more holiness but more time. It is difficult to judge the character of a person across the ages, but if his writings are any indication, it is doubtful that many of us would have found Saint Jerome to be a model of Christian charity. Certainly many Christians of his own time did not care for him. A bitter, conflicted celibate who shouts the spiritual virtues of continence but who has no charity is no more than a clanging cymbal. In the angry celibate, one is reminded of the Prioress's Tale in *The Canterbury Tales*. The prioress speaks adoringly of a small boy who sang the praises of the Virgin Mary, but she portrays the Jewish community as a pack of vicious, unnatural animals, and she revels in the slaughter of the Jews. Surely the irony was not lost on Chaucer's readers. Virginity confers no holiness on a hateful heart.

The Jews, too, went through a period of sexual searching, as witnessed by the sexual continence demanded by the Qumran community. But as the rabbis reconstructed Judaism in the face of the calamity of the fall of Jerusalem, they chose not to elevate celibacy but to make marriage the normative pattern for Judaism. Doing this, they placed the family at the core of Jewish life. R. Aqiba is cited by virtually every commentator for his famous curse on those who trill the Song of Songs in a burlesque manner. What is less well known is that Aqiba is proverbial in Jewish lore for the love he had for his wife, Rachel (see S. Sviri, "Song of Songs," 48). In elevating marriage and the family in their religious life, the Jewish leadership showed more wisdom than did the Christian. It is curious that they did this while allegorizing Song of Songs; this pattern would be repeated in many Protestant theologians, who, like Luther, also turned from celibacy as a spiritual ideal but continued to allegorize the Song.

The theology of the Song of Songs leads to certain ramifications for the life of the church. First, acceptance of the beauty and significance of the sexual union of man and woman of necessity entails acceptance of the full meaning of the doctrine of creation. The world may be fallen, but it is still a creation of God. Procreation is, in the words of Gen 1, "good," and the goodness specifically includes being fruitful and multiplying. Christians did finally reject the creation-despising doctrines of Gnosticism and Manichaeism, but they never could fully bring themselves to believe that the body and its appetites were not, in the final analysis, disgusting and incompatible with life in the Spirit.

By accepting the doctrine of creation, Christians come to terms with what it means to be between the times. On the one hand, we are dead with Christ and living by the power of the Spirit, in which we eagerly await the resurrection of the body. We groan inwardly, hoping to escape the defilements of this world and weakness of mortality. Our citizenship is in heaven, where Christ is seated at the right hand of the Father. At the same time we are mortals, living under the sun, to whom God has given a few short days to enjoy the good things of creation before the silver cord snaps and the golden bowl breaks. The blessings of the hearth and of the field, the blessings of the womb and of the garden, and the blessings of parents, children, family, and friends are ours for but a brief time. No matter how spiritual we are, we still need to eat and to have a place to call home, and most of us need a companion to sleep beside us. No amount of prayer and fasting will change the fact that we are mortal and members of the first creation; we have not transcended the basic facts of our humanity. We are not of this world, but we are creatures who live in this world. Learning how to relate rightly to both domains is a difficult challenge, but the wise will hold on to the one and not let go of the other.

The theology of creation and of the Song thus has bearing on sanctification. Relating to both the heavenly and the earthly realms does not mean that we serve both God and mammon. But it is possible to accept the fact that we are humans, with all that this entails, without being self-indulgent. One is not free either to mentally rape a pretty girl or to demonize her, to say nothing of indulging in promiscuity or pornography. One should seek to be not a spiritual super being but one who finds grace in the brokenness of repentance. One should enjoy the good things God has given and not follow the teachings of those who forbid people to marry and order them to abstain from certain foods, which God created to be received with thanksgiving by those who believe and who know the truth. But victory over lust is often not attained solely by prayer and fasting or even solely by seeking to provoke a passion for God.

When we speak of the quest for purity and the war with the lusts of the flesh, we are speaking of something that is not exclusively but is especially a man's problem. It was this single problem that drove the church to distraction as monks, priests, and theologians heroically sought out an elusive inner peace. If the believing man knows the Song of Songs, deliverance comes also through passion for his wife. Sexual passion is a fire that many waters cannot quench, but if this passion exists in the context of a love that is tender and yet as strong as death, a passion whereby he sets her as a seal upon his heart and upon his arm, then in God's sight it is "good." *Marriage as described in the Song protects the heart, not simply by giving the flesh an outlet for its biological appetite but by giving the heart a passion for the beloved.* Perfect love casts out fear, and there is also a right passion that displaces lust. Lust is, after all, the craving hunger of an empty heart. For those with the true *charis* of celibacy, the love of God alone will still that hunger, but most do not have this gift. The promise of holiness through celibacy is a deceit for all who do not have it; such men are fighting an impossible battle against their very selves. For them, this hunger of the heart and body should be filled in a normal and righteous way, in a passionate love for one's spouse. In this case, "He who finds a wife finds a good thing, and obtains favor from the LORD" (Prov 18:22 RSV). Both the knowledge of God and the good wife are, each in its own way, a pearl of great price. It is something for which a man gives up everything else, including lust. He will find a peace that many continent church fathers, sadly, never knew.

This is not a triumphalist gospel, promising to overcome the basic bondage of the will. The man who loves God and his wife is still subject to strange perversities that Augustine recognized in the human heart. What is suggested here is assuredly not a new variety of the spiritual superman; to the contrary, it works from the assumption that such an ideal is impossible for us. But if some form of peace within oneself is not possible, if there is no life of rejoicing in the heart, in the family, and in God, then the gospel is vain.

Again, the passionate love described in Song of Songs does not seek to displace the passion for God. God does not draw us through Eros. Sexuality, in the Song, is not an act of worship. It has no sacral meaning and plays no role in finding God. It is an activity that belongs solely to this world, since in the kingdom of heaven people neither marry nor are given in marriage (Matt 22:30). God is not named in the Song, and no prayers are voiced in the Song. A keen appreciation for the Song and the doctrine of creation does not confuse heavenly and earthly realms, and it does not seek to fill the heart's need for God with sexuality or even with a passionate love for another person.

There is, however, a separation of the sacred and the profane that is not helpful. The exaltation of the married state in the Song implies that the redemption of the family, and indeed the locus of the church in the family, is something that we have missed. There are many fine synagogues in the world, but because Judaism made the Jewish family the locus of Jewish life, the Hebrew heritage and faith permeated secular life and did not concentrate on magnificent, cathedral-like structures. The splendor of the Passover Seder in the home is no less great than the splendor of reading Torah in the synagogue. Christians, by contrast, sought to make their churches into little theaters of heaven and abandoned entirely the house churches of the early centuries. Christianity borrowed much of its ecclesiastical liturgy from Judaism but neglected entirely to appropriate the liturgy of the home. As a result, it is sadly impoverished in this area. The root problem is that we have not believed that the home, the domain of this world and perpetuated by sexual reproduction, can be the domain of the Spirit.

As the theology of the Song addresses the man's urgent sexual needs, it also meets the woman's need for intimacy and respect. In the ancient world, women were often despised as weak, defective humans. This tendency is sometimes exaggerated in modern scholarship, but it was nevertheless real. In the Song, as described above, the woman is the heroic protagonist. But her heroism is not that of Anat, the warrior-goddess who plays the role of a man. Rather, her heroism is in the quintessentially feminine act of her willingness to take her man into herself. The message here is simple: the trials of everywoman—deflowering, pregnancy, childbirth—are not to be despised. They are acts of courage no less than the man's willingness to stand in battle is an act of courage. Nevertheless, Paul says, she shall be saved through childbirth (1 Tim 2:15).

Rightly appreciated in the manner of the Song, the woman is the domain of love in the believing household. The husband leaves father and mother and clings to his wife. The reality of the woman as domain of love is made a vivid reality by the children that grow within her. She is the glory of the family's love: beautiful as the moon, bright as the sun, and awesome as the panoply of heaven. Her husband and her children will rise up, and they will call her blessed.

Superscript (1:1)

Bibliography

Cotterell, P. "The Greatest Song: Some Linguistic Considerations." *BT* 47 (1996) 101–8.

Translation

¹ *The Song of Songs.*ᵃ *Of Solomon.*

Notes

1.a. MT includes אשר, "which."

Form/Structure/Setting

This is a superscript, similar to the many psalm superscripts that appear in the Psalter (e.g., in Hebrew versification, Pss 3:1; 4:1; 5:1; 6:1; 7:1) and elsewhere (e.g., Hab 3:1; Exod 15:1; Deut 31:30). In contrast to many of the psalm superscripts, however, the Song of Songs lacks both musical directions and reference to any historical incident. Musical directions include notations such as "for the choir director," "on stringed instruments," and "(to the tune of) 'the morning doe'" (see the superscripts to Pss 4, 5, 6, 7, 8, 9, 11, 12, 13, 14, 18, 19, 20, 21, 22, 31, and others). One may best explain the lack of musical directions with the observation that the Song is a lengthy, complex libretto that no doubt required a variety of tunes, instruments, and musical styles. No single annotation would suffice to describe the variety of musical directions required to perform the entire Song of Songs.

The lack of a notation about any historical incident is itself significant, especially with respect to the contention that the Song represents an account of an episode from the life of Solomon (e.g., that this is the story of his failed attempt to win the love of the Shulammite away from the "shepherd lover"). Quite a few of the psalm superscripts refer to historical episodes or persons, even where the psalm itself does not explicitly describe such details. Examples include the superscripts to Pss 3, 7, 18, 34, 51, 52, and 56. The superscript to Ps 56, for example, states that the psalm comes from the time when the Philistines seized David in Gath. It would appear that the framers of the canon included historical notations in the superscripts if they felt they had reliable information regarding their historical provenance. One might suggest, therefore, that they had no information linking the Song to any actual episode or simply did not consider the Song to be a presentation of historical events. This is not, of itself, a decisive argument for abandoning the historical/dramatic interpretation of the Song, but at the least it tells us that one does not find evidence for such an interpretation where one might expect it to be found.

Comment

1 The phrase שיר השירים functions as a superlative and could legitimately be translated, "The finest of the songs that belong to Solomon." At the same time, it can be read more literally as "the song of songs," a single musical production that is a collection of smaller songs, analogous to the oratorio tradition in Western music (see discussion of the structure of the Song in the Introduction).

לשלמה may be rendered "of Solomon" in the sense of "belonging to Solomon's collection." It could also be taken as the *lamed auctoris,* "(written) by Solomon." It could possibly mean "to Solomon" in the sense of dedicated to Solomon or written for Solomon. Finally, it could mean "concerning" after the analogy of Jer 48:1, "concerning Moab" (למואב). Contrary to Longman (3), there are no grounds for translating it "in the Solomonic/wisdom literary tradition." It is most unlikely that it means "concerning Solomon." Although Solomon is mentioned in the Song (1:5; 3:7, 9, 11; 8:11–12), the Song certainly does not concern Solomon in the sense that Jer 48 concerns Moab. To say that the Song of Songs "concerns" Solomon is to say that he is the central topic of the Song, which is self-evidently not the case. The translation "(dedicated) to Solomon" suggests that a poet in Solomon's court composed the Song in his honor. This interpretation has many analogies outside of Israel; Augustus was the patron of Virgil, who composed the Aeneid in his master's honor. Unfortunately, we have no certain grounds for interpreting לשלמה in this manner. The translation "of Solomon" is as ambiguous as the Hebrew; it may mean that Solomon wrote it, or it may mean that someone else wrote it and Solomon, as the sponsor, owned it. We probably cannot get beyond that ambiguity. See the Introduction for further discussion of the authorship of the Song.

Explanation

The superscript tells us three things about Song of Songs. First, it belongs to the Solomonic collection. Second, the superscript tells us that this Song is regarded as the best example of a musical work from Solomon's collection. Finally, it indicates that the song is a collection of shorter works in a single musical production.

I. Chorus and Soprano: The Entrance (1:2–4)

Bibliography

Bloch, A. A., and **C. Bloch.** "From *In the Garden of Delights.*" *Judaism* 44 (1995) 36–63.
Callow, J. "Units and Flow in the Song of Songs 1:2–2:6." In *Biblical Hebrew and Discourse Linguistics.* Ed. R. D. Bergen. Dallas: Summer Institute of Linguistics, 1994. 462–88.
Dahood, M. *Ugaritic-Hebrew Philology.*

Translation

First Stanza

SOPRANO
² *He will kiss*[a] *me with the kisses of his mouth.*   1A
CHORUS
  Indeed your caresses are better than wine,[b]   2A
³ [a]*better than the fragrances of your perfumes.*[a]   2B
  Your very name is like perfumes poured out.[b]   2C
SOPRANO
  That is why the girls love you.   3A

Second Stanza

⁴ *Take me with you! Let us run!*   4A

Third Stanza

  The king brings[a] *me to his chamber.*   5A
CHORUS
  We will rejoice and celebrate!   6A
  We will commemorate your caresses rather than wine!   6B
SOPRANO
  Rightly they love you!   7A

Notes

2.a. Nothing is gained by emending נשק, "kiss," to שקה, "give someone a drink." ישקני is universally read to be juss., "let him kiss me," but morphologically it is a simple impf. A juss. translation is possible but not required. The parallel structure of the two strophes suggests that it is indic., but it is traditionally taken to be juss.

2.b. LXX, followed by OL and Vg., perhaps implies that the man, not the woman, sings v 2b. It reads, "For your breasts [μαστοί] are better than wine," reading the noun דד here. Of course, it is possible that the LXX translators imagined the woman singing these lines, but that would be very strange. There is no reason, however, to adopt the LXX reading here.

3.a-a. LXX reads καὶ ὀσμὴ μύρων σου ὑπὲρ πάντα τὰ ἀρώματα, "your perfume is more fragrant than any perfume."

3.b. If left unemended, one could translate שמן תורק as "oil is poured out" (*hopʻal* impf.), although the use of a fem. verb with the noun שמן is peculiar and the impf. does not fit well here. One may remedy both problems by emending תורק, "poured out," to the ptc. מורק, "pouring out," following Q LXX (ἐκκενωθὲν) αʹ OL Vg. Otherwise, one may take תורק as a proper name and translate it as "oil of Turac."

4.a. The pf. הביאני, "brings me," in a poetic text such as this does not necessarily require a past-tense translation.

Form/Structure/Setting

The Song opens with three stanzas that announce its theme, the celebration of love. The text implies that a soprano and a chorus of young women both sing in these opening verses. The first words, "He will kiss me," indicate that this part of the libretto is for a single female singer. Other pronouns are used here to maintain the gender identification of the singers: they sing of "your" (masculine singular) caresses, perfumes, and name, as well as of the "king," the man whom the girls "rightly love." All of this suggests that these lines are sung by girls.

It is more difficult to determine whether all of this text belongs to a female solo or if at least parts of it belong to a chorus. The text contains several hints, however, that enable us to separate the parts. First, the perspective of the text changes several times in these few lyrics. It begins with a third-person statement ("He will kiss me with the kisses of his mouth") and immediately moves into second person ("Indeed your caresses are better than wine"). This cannot be explained on the grounds that the woman is addressing the man as a superior and thus initially uses formal, deferential language before shifting into the more familiar second person (thus A. A. and C. Bloch, *Judaism* 44 [1995] 51–52). She never addresses the man in so formal a manner, and the characteristic language of formal, third-person address ("my lord" and "your servant") is nowhere used in the Song. Second, a female singer—the "soprano"—declares that the young girls rightly love the man. It is unlikely that she would sing such a line if the chorus had been silent up to this point (otherwise, how would the audience know that they love him at all?). All in all, therefore, it seems fairly clear that the opening verses are made of lyrics sung by both the female soloist and the chorus.

As described above, the opening words, "He will kiss me with the kisses of his mouth," presumably belong to a female solo. Lines 2A–C ("Indeed your caresses are better than wine, / better than the fragrances of your perfumes. / Your very name is like perfumes poured out") change from third person to second person, and one may suggest that this change represents a change of singers; thus, these three lines are sung by a chorus of girls. Lines 2A–C are linked by the repetition of טובים at the beginning of 2A and the end of 2B; also, both 2A and 2B are three-unit verbless clauses in which the second unit ends with the second masculine singular suffix (observe the chiastic matching described above). Line 2C, another three-unit line, continues the metaphorical analogy that the beloved is somehow better than costly and fragrant liquids; only here his name is better than perfume. Also, line 2C is linked to 2B by consonance with the sound of שׁ. The middle word of line 2B is שׁמניך, "your perfume," and line 2C begins with שׁמן, "perfume," and ends with שׁמך, "your name." All of this suggests that strophe 2 is a tightly bound unit and is sung by the chorus. Line 3A ("That is why the girls love you!") is obviously sung by the soprano, and again it makes more sense if it was the female chorus that sang lines 2A–C. The audience does not have to surmise that the girls "love" the young man; they have heard it for themselves.

The second stanza is but a single line. This seems incredible, and there are no other one-line stanzas in the Song of Songs, but there appears to be no convincing way to join it to the lines of another strophe. The one-line stanza can exist; see Ps 15:5c.

Like stanza 1, stanza 3 again opens with a one-line strophe (line 5A, "The king brings me to his chamber") sung by the soprano and expressing the man's lovemaking toward the woman. Like line 1A, this line speaks of the man in the third person. The following two lines (6A–B, "We will rejoice and celebrate! / We will commemorate your caresses rather than wine!"), however, match one another (each is a first plural cohortative of three units; 6A has two verbs followed by a one-unit prepositional phrase, and 6B is one verb followed by a two-unit prepositional phrase). These are best taken as lyrics assigned to the chorus. The "we" suggests that the chorus sings, and the theme of this bicolon, in which the man's love is favorably compared to wine, repeats the theme of strophe 2. Finally, the third stanza ends with a one-line strophe (7A) that belongs to the soprano, in which she again declares that the women "rightly" celebrate the man. It is not clear why the third stanza is one line shorter than the first; it may be that for musical reasons the poet wanted to keep this canto at ten lines.

So interpreted, stanzas 1 and 3 each begin with the soprano singing a line describing the man's acts of affection toward her. The chorus then celebrates the man's love for the woman under metaphorical comparisons to wine and perfumes. The woman closes each of these stanzas with a strophe affirming that the choral assessments of the man are valid. The structure of canto I is illustrated in figure 2.

α Account of the man's lovemaking 1A
   β Choral praise of the man's lovemaking 2A–C
      γ Affirmation of choral praise 3A
         δ Call to depart from woman to man 4A
α' Account of the man's lovemaking 5A
   β' Choral praise of the man's lovemaking 6A–B
      γ' Affirmation of choral praise 7A
Fig. 2. Structure of canto I

The formal function of the introduction is to prepare the audience for the theme of the performance, the joys of love between a woman and a man, and it also indicates that for the most part the interpretation of love comes from the woman's perspective (since women do all the singing here). The words, "We will rejoice and celebrate! / We will commemorate your caresses rather than wine!" tell the audience precisely what is coming: a celebration of love.

This canto is therefore proleptic; that is, it tells the audience where the Song of Songs is going before it gets there. Several themes are suggested in these lines. The opening words focus on kissing and indicate that sexual play is a prominent theme in the Song of Songs. The comparison of the man and his love to perfume and wine suggests that metaphorical images of love taken from nature and from other (nonsexual) pleasures will figure predominantly in Song of Songs. That is, love and the beloved will frequently be described using language drawn from the beautiful and delightful flora, fauna, fragrances, and foods of ancient Israel. There are two indications of marriage in these lines. First, line 4A, "Take me with you! let us run!" suggests that the woman will escape the confines of her present status, seen to be the household of her brothers in Song 1:6. Second, line 5A, "The king brings me to his chamber," suggests a wedding and wedding night. The "king" is a motif of the groom (developed, for example at 3:6–11), and his taking her to his chamber suggests a wedding night. Again, however, this is proleptic; she does not begin the Song in a wedding chamber. The soprano's lines to the effect that the girls "rightly" love the man suggest that Song of Songs celebrates the love of man for woman as something good and glorious.

The position and nature of the second stanza, "Take me with you, let us run," is significant. Standing between what is otherwise two strophes with the same structure, it is to a degree the focal point of this canto. It is filled with exhilaration and sets the tone for the Song of Songs, and tells the audience that the couple desires to escape and be together.

Comment

2 "He will kiss me" involves a wordplay with the use of ישקני, "he will kiss me," from נשק) in that it sounds similar to verbs from the root שקה, "to give a drink" (*hipʿil* stem). This pun leads into the comparison in 1:2b, that his love is better than wine. This does not, however, justify translating the line as something like "Let him make me drunk with his kisses," as was done by A. A. and C. Bloch in *Judaism* 44 (1995) 47.

דודים here refers more to "caresses"—making love—than to the mental state of being loving, although the latter is obviously not excluded. For analogous usage, see Prov 7:18 (נרוה דדים עד־הבקר, "Let us drink in lovemaking until morning"), Ezek 16:8 (והנה עתך עת דדים, "indeed, your time was the time of lovemaking" [i.e., you had attained sexual maturity]), and Ezek 23:17 (למשכב דדים, "to a bed of lovemaking").

3 The ל on לריח continues the force of the מן with מיין at the end of v 2. A full translation of this line could be "As for the fragrance of your perfume, (your love) is better." However, the ל can have the force of מן in Ugaritic (*UT* §10.1), and the same appears to be the case here. The use of ל in a comparative text is described in Dahood *Ugaritic-Hebrew Philology,* 29–30. Or, the ל could be an "emphatic ל" (Gerleman, 94). See also *IBHS* 11.2.10h. The Hebrew forms a chiasmus; see figure 3.

"indeed your caresses are better," כי־טובים דדיך	α	2A
"than wine," מיין	β	
"than the fragrances of your perfumes," לריח שמניך	β′	2B
"(they are) better," טובים	α′	

Fig. 3. Chiasmus of Song 1:3

Line 2A (αβ) begins with טובים, "better," and line 2B (β′α′) ends with טובים, "better." Each line has three units, the first hemistichoi of each line (α and β′) each having two units and the second hemistichoi (β and α′) each having one. דדיך, "your caresses," is the implied subject of טובים, "better," in α′ (gapping); טובים cannot modify לריח, "than the fragrances," because it is plural and ריח is singular. Thus, "the fragrance of your perfumes is good" is not an option here. It is possible that line 2B could be translated "for fragrance, your perfumes are good." However, this interpretation obliterates the syntax of the chiasmus since it requires that the grammar of line 2B be unlike that of 2A. Also, such a translation makes the perfumes, rather than the man and his love, the object of praise. The whole point of the choral lyrics seems to be that he and his love are better than wine and perfume.

As indicated above, the lines 2A and 2B should be read together: "Indeed your caresses are better than wine, / better than the fragrances of your perfumes." This suggests that although the fragrance of his body oils is wonderful, his love is better yet. The third line (2C) builds upon this by asserting that his "name" (his character, his person, or the very thought of him) is better than the finest or most extravagant use of perfumes. The phrase שֶׁמֶן תּוּרַק, if it does not mean "oil poured out" (see *Note* 3.b.), could be the proper name of some specific variety of perfume, the "oil of Turac" (Fox, *Song of Songs,* 98). Thus, the phrase either refers to a prodigious application of fragrant oils or to especially expensive or delightful oils. Either way, this line suggests that the very mention of his name is like an aromatic delight.

4 The line "The king brings me to his chamber" seems odd as usually translated: "The king *has brought* me into his chamber." Two-character dramatic interpretations (see Introduction) may take this to be Solomon with his young bride, and three-character dramatic interpretations see it as Solomon having abducted the shepherdess and holding her there as a captive while he attempts to seduce her. Neither is satisfying. Both interpretations begin with the woman already in the man's bedroom. Short of forcing interpretations and peculiar readings at every turn, it is impossible to make sense of the Song if she is in his chamber at the very outset of the story. (See *Form/Structure/Setting.*)

Explanation

The Song begins by describing the man's affection for the woman in the simplest and most straightforward manner: he will kiss her. The kiss is here the fundamental act of affection, and it is one of the few love acts not veiled under an allegorical description in the Song. The kiss is the beginning of love play, and it is surpassingly intimate in that it brings mouths and faces of two people together. Of course, the man's kisses may reach other parts of the woman's body as well, and the language suggests that Song of Songs will explore their sexual relationship. But the kiss, a direct and simple act, binds the man to the woman and opens the Song of Songs.

The point of "your caresses are better than wine" is twofold: his love is both pleasant and intoxicating. Love leads to a delirium of pleasure. Like perfume, his caresses overwhelm the senses and produce a kind of rapture. Perfumed oils imply health (oils were fundamental to both preventive and healing medicine in the ancient world), pleasure (these are oils perfumed with exotic spices), and value (the perfumes are very expensive).

The woman's praise of the man and of the quality of his love is extreme; he is so wonderful that he is larger than life. By contrast, in the next canto (1:5–6) the woman seems to be little more than a pretty peasant girl. In the course of the Song of Songs, however, the woman will undergo a transformation with the result that all will look upon her as the very embodiment of love. At Song 4:10, the man praises the woman in words that, in a significantly reworked form, recall 1:2b–3: *her* love will be better than wine. The chorus, moreover, will speak of her as the most beautiful of women and ultimately be dazzled by the sight of her (e.g., Song 6:10; 7:1 [ET 6:13]).

The suggestion above that the chorus sings these lines does not imply that the chorus is experienced in making love to the man, as though he had given his affection to every girl in the village. Such an interpretation would be reading the canto as though it were a drama. The chorus, as they will do throughout Song of Songs, is merely acting as a foil and is praising love and the lovers.

The appeal to run away together is a frequent motif of the Song, and it expresses the common desire of young lovers: that they escape the constraints that hold them back and that they be free to explore their love together. In Song of Songs, however, this desire is of particular concern to the woman because she wants to be liberated from the control of her brothers and from the status of being a child—or a slave—in her home.

The words are a programmatic statement of what the audience should expect to hear in the cantos that follow. Song of Songs concerns the movement of a woman into the wedding chamber of her chosen bridegroom, a figure to whom she here gives the wedding designation of "king." It is a canto about her abandonment of the security and isolation of virginity, an event that takes place when she is taken into the chamber of the king. Furthermore, the title "king" suggests that the man as groom plays the archetypal role of powerful savior. This, too, will be explored in the Song of Songs, albeit in a surprising way since the outcome will be the exaltation of the woman.

The woman's twice-repeated refrain, that the girls rightly love the man, establishes her position vis-à-vis the other girls. She has come to a passage in her life that they desire. Thus, there is a touch of rivalry in the lyrics. She has a man whom they all admire with a fervency that drives them to envy her success. She is embarking on a journey they have not yet begun. Their position in the Song of Songs is set from the outset: they are observers who will interact with her as she enters the world of love. They represent the world she is leaving, but, for the most part, they do not seek to hold her back because they, too, desire to experience love someday. She also draws strength to move forward into this relationship because of the encouragement she receives from their admiration. Understood as a proleptic and programmatic text, the first canto tells the audience or reader what is coming. "The king brings me to his chamber" alerts us to the central event of Song of Songs, the wedding night, and "we will rejoice and celebrate" tells us its mood. "Rightly they love him" suggests that the mystery and power of love, marriage, and sexuality are well worth appreciating.

II. Soprano: The Virgin's Education I (1:5–6)

Bibliography

Ogden, G. S. "'Black but Beautiful' (Song of Songs 1.5)." *BT* 47 (1996) 443–45.

Translation

SOPRANO
5 I am dark yet lovely,   1A
  O daughters of Jerusalem,   1B
  like the tents of Kedar, like the curtains of Solomon.   1C
6 Do not stare ᵃ at me, that I am swarthy   1D
  and that the sun has gazed upon me.   1E
  It was my mother's sons! ᵇ They burned with anger toward me.   2A
  They forced me to be a keeper of the vineyards,   2B
  while my vineyard—the one that was mine—I could not keep.   2C

Notes

6.a. Nine MSS read חיראוני, "do not fear me." Read MT.
6.b. The clause-initial position of בני אמי, "the sons of my mother," makes this the focus of the line.

Form/Structure/Setting

A new canto is indicated by the fact that the subject matter of the lyrics has abruptly changed. This canto is eight lines divided into two strophes. Lines 1A–C (v 5) are joined by the syntactical dependence of 1C on 1A (line 1B being a vocative phrase). In addition, 1A is a verbless clause with two predicates, and 1C has two phrases, each beginning with the preposition כ. Lines 1D and 1E are joined by matching (two relative clauses begun with שׁ) and gapping ("Do not stare at me" in 1D governs both lines). The consonance with שׁ linking lines 1D to 1F is pronounced; counting the doubled letters (with *dagesh forte*), שׁ occurs no less than eight times in four consecutive words! In addition, the two predicate adjectives in 1A and the pairing of phrases with the preposition כ in 1C is answered by the two relative clauses in 1D–E with the relative שׁ. This suggests that 1D–E are part of the same strophe as 1A–C (contrary to the MT versification).

The final three lines (2A–C) are coherent in that all concern the brothers' actions. Line 2A ends with "they burned with anger toward me," and 2B begins with "they forced me," with "my mother's sons" serving as subject of both verbs. In addition, the three words נחרו, "they burned with anger," נטרה, "keeper," and נטרתי, "I could [not] keep," link these three lines via consonance.

The female solo sings this entire canto. As a speech-act, it is a self-appraisal set against the standards of her culture. It expresses an underlying fear that she will not attain love because she does not measure up to its standards of feminine beauty.

Comment

5 The woman is embarrassed that the other girls are looking at her and is defensive about her dark skin. Some interpreters take her words to mean, "I am black *and* beautiful" (e.g., Pope, 307–18). Her defensiveness about her dark skin, however, implies that her culture does not regard dark skin as attractive. Thus the conjunction at ונאוה requires the translation "but" rather than "and."

She compares herself to the "tents of Kedar" and the "curtains of Solomon." קדר, "Kedar," refers to an Arab bedouin tribe; Assurbanipal says he defeated the king of *ki-da-ri* in a campaign against the Arabs (*ANET*, 298–99). Some interpreters emend "Solomon" to "Salma," the name of another Arab tribe, but no textual evidence supports this. Furthermore, although the emendation makes for tidy parallelism, it probably misses the main point of the analogy. As the shelters of Arab bedouin, one may surmise, the tents of Kedar were probably made of tanned hides or coarse sackcloth and were dark in color. They also must have been very sturdy since they had to withstand the rigors of the wind, sand, heat, and the occasional storm as the only shelter these travelers would possess. They may have been proverbial as tough, reliable tents. The curtains of Solomon, by contrast, would have been of the finest craftsmanship and would have had exquisite detail. Perhaps the curtains had interwoven colors, beads, or even pearls, as well as lacelike patterns. Therefore, the woman claims that she is dark like the tents of Kedar—and she is equally as sturdy as those tents. But she is also beautiful, like the curtains of Solomon, and worthy to receive the admiration given to princesses. The structure of v 5 also brings out a pattern meaning "dark like the tents of Kedar" and "beautiful like the curtains of Solomon." It has two pairs of parallel concepts divided by a vocative; see figure 4.

"I am dark," שחורה אני	α		1A
"yet lovely," ונאוה	β		
"O daughters of Jerusalem," בנות ירושלם	γ		1B
"like the tents of Kedar," כאהלי קדר	α'		1C
"like the curtains of Solomon," כיריעות שלמה	β'		

Fig. 4. Structure of canto II, stanza 1

שחורה, "dark," relates to כאהלי קדר, "like the tents of Kedar," as ונאוה, "but lovely," relates to כיריעות שלמה, "like the curtains of Solomon." This kind of "redistribution" has long been recognized as a feature of biblical Hebrew poetry.

6 She explains that her skin is dark because her brothers forced her to work out in the vineyards under the glare of the sun. She uses a number of wordplays to describe her situation. She asks the girls not to stare (ראה) at her, but says that the sun has "gazed" (שזף) on her. Her wordplay makes use of the fact that שזף means to "gaze" at but שרף means to "scorch"; it is all the more effective a wordplay because of the common interchange of ד and ז, a phenomenon often observed in Aramaic. She then says that her brothers "burned [חרה] with anger" toward her, using an obvious synonym of שרף.

She does not explain why her brothers were angry at her. It is certainly possible that this a determination by her brothers to keep her chaste, especially in light of the lines about protecting the little sister who has small breasts at the end of the book (Song 8:8–9). It is true that chapter 1 does not state that the brothers set her to work in the vineyard in order to keep her from being involved with a man. On the other hand, the woman's declaration of independence under the image of the vineyard at Song 8:12 suggests that her sexuality is the issue here. At the least, one can say that the brothers represent authority figures who intrude into the lives of young lovers and prevent them from coming together.

Explanation

Some interpreters take the line "I am dark yet lovely" to imply that the woman is a non-Israelite, perhaps of African heritage. For example, Weems (5:384) asserts that "this is not the first time in the Bible when a foreign woman becomes a reminder of how diverse is God's vision of covenant people (e.g., Ruth and Rahab)." This exposition is the basis for construing the woman to be a valiant opponent of racial prejudice who, against the hostility of society, pursues her love for a much lighter-skinned Israelite man. Intriguing as that interpretation may be, it is not the meaning of the text. The woman clearly states the reason her skin is dark: she has been outside working under the sun in the vineyard. She never hints that she is of non-Israelite extraction. The Song nowhere addresses the matter of racial tension or implies that an interracial relationship is at the center of the story.

We may well ask, however, why the Song raises the issue of her sun-darkened skin. Modern Caucasian Europeans and North Americans regard tanned skin as attractive and healthy looking, and readers from this culture are naturally puzzled that she would be defensive about this feature. In agrarian societies, however, dark skin is ordinary and is a sign that one is a member of the peasant class. Tan women in such a society are common and are not the stuff of male fantasy or female aspiration. Indeed, almost every society tends to regard the different as exotic and therefore alluring. The Japanese geisha, the ideal contrast to the farm woman, had astoundingly white skin (or wore white makeup). In an era when even the average European peasant woman would have been fairly tan, lean, and muscular, contemporary artists depicted the sensual woman as pale, soft, and plump (cf. "The Rape of the Daughters of Leucippus" by Rubens and "Cupid a Captive" by Boucher).

These verses, therefore, do not concern racial issues but assert that the joys of love, particularly the appreciation of a woman's body, belong to all social classes and not simply to the elite. More than that, they protest against artificial, culturally imposed standards of beauty that fail to appreciate the comeliness of a woman on the grounds that she is common. The love between a plebeian and his wife is as wondrous as that between two members of the court, and the admiration a peasant girl has from her beloved is as worthy of celebration in song as any love that a princess has inspired. Shakespeare's sonnets to the "dark lady" eloquently testify to this notion of beauty, as in Sonnet 127:

> In the old age black was not counted fair,
> Or if it were it bore not beauty's name;

But now black is beauty's successive heir,
And beauty slandered with a bastard shame."

Also, this description of the woman's appearance is strikingly similar to what we read of the young David's appearance: "he was reddish [deeply tanned?] with beautiful eyes and good looks" (1 Sam 16:12). Even the reason for David's reddened skin is similar: "he is looking after the sheep" (1 Sam 16:11). Perhaps the woman's keeping of the vineyard is to be regarded as the feminine counterpart to David's watching of the sheep. It is difficult to know what to make of this parallel; is it coincidental or deliberate on the part of the Song? If the latter, perhaps the point is to endow the woman with the same youthful vigor and heroic stature that the attentive reader associates with David.

She therefore demands that the girls not look at her with disdain for her dark skin (1D-E). Her concern here is with standards of beauty in her society and with class identification, not with race. Her words are a cultural code for "Do not regard me as a plain, unimportant peasant girl."

The brothers represent a general sense of oppression that the young woman feels in her paternal home. As a sister, destined to marry and leave the household, she receives the harsh treatment that is otherwise reserved for slaves. Regarded as a quasi-outsider who consumes the goods of the household, she is forced by her brothers into menial tasks for the common good of the family and is not free to pursue her own interests. There is, therefore, something of a Cinderella motif here. Marriage to her "king" suggests that he is her Prince Charming. It means more than sensual pleasure; it is her freedom to be herself and be at the center of a new family. In this relationship, the man she loves mediates her transformation from peasant and outsider to queen and insider.

Her complaint that she could not tend her own vineyard explores this further. Her vineyard is her body, her interests, and her very self. She will give her "fruit" to her husband (Song 4:16). More than that, the tending of a vineyard represents the ability to cultivate one's aspirations and see them bear fruit.

The woman's treatment at the hands of her brothers is important, however, as the "education" she received during childhood and adolescence. It was, to say the least, a hard education composed of long hours working in the vineyard. But it has made her strong and mature, and it has given her an appreciation of the benefits of freedom and adulthood. She will enjoy these to the maximum when she can take care of her own vineyard (Song 8:12).

Modern readers need to understand the woman's outlook in her context. In ancient Israel, no young single woman (except perhaps the prostitute or the destitute widow) lived alone. Furthermore, the fact that the daughter was destined to be married away into another family made her to some degree an outsider in her own family (although one should not exaggerate this reality). Thus, for the woman of the Song, marriage meant entering her own family and having the freedom to cultivate her own life. Of course, this picture is to some degree idealized. No doubt some marriages put women into a worse position of oppression than they had experienced in their childhood homes. Still, the ideal she yearns for—love and true freedom in a marriage relationship—is valid in all times and all cultures.

III. Soprano and Chorus: Finding the Beloved (1:7–8)

Bibliography

Brooke, G. "חבר." *NIDOTTE* §2489. **Emerton, J. A.** "Lice or a Veil in the Song of Songs 1:7?" In *Understanding Poets and Prophets*. FS G. W. Anderson, ed. A. Auld. Sheffield: JSOT Press, 1993. 127–40. **Holladay, W. L.** *Jeremiah 2*.

Translation

SOPRANO
7 Tell me,   1A
   you whom my soul loves: 1B
   Where do you graze your flocks?   1C
   Where do you rest them at noon?   1D
   You don't want[a] *me to be like a woman picking at fleas*[b]   1E
   among the flocks of your companions!   1F
CHORUS
8 *Well,*[a] *if you don't know,*   2A
   most beautiful of women,   2B
   get yourself out in the tracks of the flock   2C
   and tend your kids   2D
   at the tents of the shepherds.   2E

Notes

7.a. MT שלמה, lit. "who" [ש] why [למה]?" the idiom is used in a request to imply "This will be the outcome if you do not do what I request; it is an outcome that I am sure you agree is to be avoided." See, e.g., Exod 32:12; Num 27:4.

7.b. The interpretation of עטה is most difficult. LXX has περιβαλλομένη, "wrapped about," which conforms to an attested meaning of עטה. On the other hand, כעטיה is an act. ptc.; one would expect the reflexive or pass. if the meaning were "like a wrapped woman." Tg. Syr. σ´ Vg. all take it to mean "wander about." עטה could be emended to טעה, a by-form of תעה, "to wander" (cf. Ezek 13:10). Inasmuch as this requires an emendation of the text, however, it should not be regarded as probable unless alternative interpretations are for other reasons less likely. A third possibility is that עטה here is to "snatch at" (*HALOT* עטה II) and thus to pick at fleas and lice, or to "delouse."

8.a. The לך, "for yourself," at the end of אם־לא תדעי לך, "if you don't know for yourself," may imply "You ought to know this." See Fox, *Song of Songs*, 103. The closest parallel is in Job 5:27, שמענה ואתה דע־לך, "Hear it and know it for yourself."

Form/Structure/Setting

This canto contains two strophes. It follows the motif of seeking the beloved. The structure of v 7 is: an opening imperative ("tell me"), followed by a vocative phrase ("you whom my soul loves"), a matching pair of lines (1C and 1D), and a complaint couched as a rhetorical question (literally, "Why should I be like a woman picking at fleas among the flocks of your companions!"). There are chiastic elements in lines 1B–E. As already noted, 1C and 1D form a matching pair (each line begins with איכה, "where?" followed by a second masculine singular imperfect). Also, 1B and 1E each begin with the letter, שׁ, "who?" an interrogative proclitic pronoun, and there is assonance with the opening words שאהבה, "you whom my soul loves," and שלמה, "who why?" Line 1F is syntactically dependent on 1E; it could be read as a hemistich of 1E, but cf. Masoretic cantillation.

In v 8, the line "if you do not know" (line 2A) responds to the command "tell me" in v 7 (line 1A). Also, 1A ends with לי, "to me," and 2A ends with לך, "to you." The four lines of v 8 are in chiastic structure, in which "women" is answered by "shepherds" and "get yourself out in the tracks of the flock" is answered by "tend your kids" (see figure 5). Line 2E could be read as a hemistich of 2D rather than as an independent line, but again the cantillation indicates otherwise, and there is nothing that compels us to reject this.

"most beautiful of women,"	היפה בנשים	α
"get yourself out in the tracks of the flock,"	צאי־לך בעקבי הצאן	β
"and tend your kids,"	ורעי את־גדיתיך	β´
"at the tents of the shepherds."	על משכנות הרעים	α´

Fig. 5. Chiastic structure of Song 1:8

The lines of strophe 2 match or answer the lines of strophe 1. The command "tell me" (line 1A) is answered by "well, if you don't know" in line 2A, and the vocative "you whom my soul loves" (line 1B) is answered by the vocative "most beautiful of women" in line 2B. The two matching questions in lines 1C–D ("Where do you graze your flocks? / Where do you rest them at noon?") are answered by the two matching directives in lines 2C–D ("get yourself out in the tracks of the flock / and tend your kids"). Line 1E ("You don't want me to be . . . picking at fleas") has no counterpart, but line 1F ("among the flocks of your companions") has a clear match in line 2E ("at the tents of the shepherds"). Both 1F and 2E are two-unit prepositional phrases beginning with על, "upon" (by itself על does not count as a unit). The imperfect symmetry suggests that the woman's concern about "picking at fleas" is dismissed as unworthy of an answer. In other words, the woman is implicitly told to set that concern aside.

Commentators frequently treat the second strophe (v 8) as the man's line, no doubt because the text refers to the woman as the "most beautiful of women" and especially because she addressed her question to the man. Thus, it may be a tease by him (e.g., Murphy, 134). But there is no reason to think that the chorus could not answer her question or refer to her as beautiful. Exum (ZAW 85 [1973] 72) demonstrates a pattern in vv 5–10 that indicates that the chorus sings in v 8 (see figure 6). So construed, this strophe is the response of the chorus to the woman, notwithstanding the fact that she addressed her question to the man. In addition, elsewhere only the chorus calls her "most beautiful of women" (היפה בנשים, "the most beautiful among women"; the phrase also appears in 5:9 and 6:1, both of which belong to the chorus). The tenor does not employ this sobriquet; he characteristically calls her רעיתי, "my companion"; אחתי, "my sister"; and כלה, "bride." Thus, it is fairly certain that v 8 belongs to the chorus.

α	נאוה	("beautiful"; vv 5–6; woman to daughters)
β	תרעה	("you shepherd"; v 7; woman to man)
β'	ורעי	("and shepherd?"; v 8; daughters to woman)
α'	נאוו	(they are beautiful"; v 10; man to woman)

Fig. 6. Exum's analysis of Song 1:5–10

Comment

7 In this strophe she seeks the man. The phrase "whom my soul loves" is one of the sobriquets the woman uses of the man. It appears here and in Song 3:1, 2, 3, 4. The language is now not regal but pastoral, and her lover is now a shepherd and not a king. Again, these are metaphors for roles the lover takes on in her eyes. We need not try to develop a literal story of a shepherd and his lover.

Commentators who take עטה to mean "wrap" here frequently suggest a parallel with Gen 38:14, in which Tamar veils herself and is taken by the shepherds (particularly Judah) to be a prostitute (e.g., Fox, *Song of Songs,* 103). But the woman in the Song is not threatening to play the prostitute or even to be a flirt. The verb עטה does not appear in Gen 38, and it is not at all clear that being veiled was a sign of a prostitute. As Emerton ("Lice or a Veil," 129) says, "If it was the practice of prostitutes to wear veils, then presumably the woman in Song 1.7 was not wearing a veil. It would be strange to say that she, though unveiled, would be 'like one who is veiled.' Further, it would be self-contradictory to suppose both that prostitutes wore veils as a badge of office and that the woman would be taken for a prostitute when she was not appropriately dressed." Finally, as mentioned in *Note* 7.b., the verb here is not a passive or reflexive participle.

Still, if one should pursue the translation of "wrapped" or "covered" for עטה here, it may be that the woman's desire not to be like a "cloaked woman" has to do with the widow rather than the prostitute. עטה does appear in contexts of mourning or shame. In Lev 13:45, the leper is to go about with his "moustache" (i.e., the lower half of his face) covered. This was a customary sign of grief or shame (see Ezek 24:17, 22; Mic 3:7). The psalmist sometimes speaks of his adversaries as covered (עטה) with shame (e.g., Ps 89:46 [ET 89:45]). To be sure, the root עטה does not always connote shame or grief (e.g., Ps 104:2). If Israelite widows cloaked themselves in a time of mourning in the same way that the widowers did, the woman might be saying that if her lover does not come to her, she will be like a widow among the shepherds. That is, she would seem to have lost him, be bereft and alone. Still, it is quite a stretch to say that "cloaked woman" would have been recognized by an Israelite audience to mean, "defenseless widow woman."

The second alternative translation suggested in *Note* 7.b. above, "Why should I be like a *wandering* woman among your companions?" is certainly intelligible, but it is perhaps too plain and prosaic. It merely suggests that she does not want to wander around lost and lacks any poetic connotation. Also, as mentioned in the notes above, it requires both an emendation and understanding that this is a by-form verb.

One may object to the third alternative, "Why should I be like a woman picking at fleas/lice," on aesthetic grounds: it suggests that the lady of the Song has lice! In reality, however, this is what it suggests is *not* the case. She is not saying that she has fleas or lice and that she will sit around picking her fleas while she waits for her man (contrary to Emerton, "Lice or a Veil," 138; Fuerst, 171). She is saying that if she goes in search of him among shepherds, then she will catch their fleas and lice and start to pick at them.

The strongest case for the meaning "pick at fleas" is at Jer 43:12, "and he [Nebuchadnezzar] will burn them and take them captive. And he will pick off (the leadership of) the land of Egypt as a shepherd picks off (lice from) his garment, and he will depart from there in peace." A number of translations render עטה in Jer 43:12 as "wrap himself," but in this context it makes no sense to imagine Nebuchadnezzar "wrapping himself" in Egypt, nor is it clear why there would be some significance to a shepherd wrapping himself in a cloak. See Emerton, "Lice or a Veil," and Holladay, *Jeremiah 2*, 302. In addition, the LXX renders עטה in Jer 43:12 as φθειρίζω, "to pick lice." This interpretation of עטה makes the most sense; shepherds spend a great deal of time around animals, and they would be more likely than most men to have fleas, ticks, or lice in their garments. By analogy, the leaders of Egypt are as lice or fleas to Nebuchadnezzar. This interpretation works best in Isa 22:17–18 as well, where Yahweh threatens a certain steward named Shebna that he will snatch him up (עטה), roll him in a ball, and cast him away because he is a disgrace in his master's house. Here too, the suggestion is that Shebna is no more than vermin, and that Yahweh will roll him up as one rolls up a flea or tick to kill it (one cannot kill a flea by simply squeezing it). Here in Song 1:7, the connection to shepherds suggests that the meaning is to pick at fleas or lice. See further discussion below. "Companions" translates חבריך, a word from the root חבר, "join," which describes peers (Ps 45:8 [ET 45:7]), allies (Gen 14:3; Isa 1:23), associates (Aramaic of Dan 2:13, 17), or colleagues (Eccl 4:10; see also Ezek 37:16, 19). Here, the term implies men who are her lover's associates and economic peers—that is, other shepherds. The companions are not necessarily good (Dan 2:13) or evil (Isa 1:27); they are simply an association of men, and as such represent a domain in which the woman is uncomfortable and perhaps feels threatened. For her, the "shepherds," here representing the world of men, are a foul, dirty, lice-ridden lot. If she moves among them, she is afraid, she will soon be scratching and picking at herself just as they do!

8 The tone of this text is not a tease but a mild rebuke. The Jerusalem girls answer (rather than allowing the man to answer) because to them the appropriate response is self-evident. Their response, however, is anything but a set of directions to a geographic location.

Explanation

The woman desires to see her beloved but does not want to have to go on a search for him. If she does not know precisely where he is, she contends, she will have to go about looking for him among all the shepherds, a situation with which she is not comfortable. Her words suggest discomfort around men. She is a young woman who is comfortable with other women; her one experience with men, her brothers, has not been good. She may find the culture and bodies of men to be frightening if not repulsive, and the thought of entering among them is not welcome. She loves her man, but she wants him to come to her; she does not want to go into his world. Her words signify that she is caught between two worlds of men—her brothers, to whom she is a virtual outsider and subject to forced labor, and the other shepherds, to whom she is a true outsider.

The answer she receives is assurance that she can become an insider, but to do so will require an act of courage on her part. The Jerusalem girls urge her to forget about her qualms about picking at fleas among the shepherds and simply go out and find him where he is to be found, with the flocks. More than that, they urge her to become a shepherdess herself. Their point is that when she goes out and joins him, she will no longer be an outsider—a woman among the shepherds—but will find her community and family. Her lover's community will be hers, and she need have no fear or discomfort. She will be an insider. The point behind their mild rebuke is that she cannot be one with her lover without entering his world. More specifically, she must allow herself to get close to a man, with all that this involves. Hence, they tell her that she must abandon fear and reserve; she must boldly claim the man she loves. On a deeper level, she must overcome her fear of male culture and the male body.

IV. Tenor, Chorus, and Soprano: The First Song of Mutual Love (1:9–2:7)

Bibliography

Brenner, A. "Aromatics and Perfumes in the Song of Songs." *JSOT* 25 (1983) 75–81. **Chaucer, G.** *The Canterbury Tales.* Ed. V. A. Kolve and G. Olson. New York: Norton, 1989. **Grober, S. F.** "The Hospital Lotus: A Cluster of Metaphors. An Inquiry into the Problem of Textual Unity in the Song of Songs." *Semitics* 9 (1984) 86–112. **Hamilton, V.** "עור." *NIDOTTE* §6424. **Hunt, P. N.** "Sensory Images in Song of Songs 1:12–2:16." In *Dort ziehen Schiffe dahin: Collected Communications to the XIVth Congress of the International Organization for the Study of the Old Testament.* Ed. M. Augustin, and K. Schunck. New York: Lang, 1996. 69–78. **Keel, O.** *Deine Blicke send Tauben: Zur Metaphorik des Hohen Liedes.* SBS 114–15. Stuttgart: Katholisches Bibelwerk, 1984. **Konkel, A.** "נקדה." *NIDOTTE* §5925. **Pope, M. H.** "A Mare in Pharoah's Chariotry." *BASOR* 200 (1970) 56–61. **Saebø, M.** "On the Canonicity of the Song of Songs." In *Texts, Temples, and Traditions.* FS M. Haran, ed. M. Fox. Winona Lake, IN: Eisenbrauns, 1996. 267–77. **Walker, L. L.** "תפוח." *NIDOTTE* §9515.

Translation

First Stanza

TENOR

9 To a mare[a] belonging to the horses with the chariots of Pharaoh   1A
   I liken you,[b] my companion.   1B
10 So[a] attractive are your cheeks with[b] jewelry;   1C
   so attractive is your neck with[b] its necklace!   1D

CHORUS

11 Jewelry of gold we shall make for you   2A
   with the decorations of silver!   2B

Second Stanza

SOPRANO

12 Until[a] the king is at his circle,   3A
   my spikenard[b] gives of its fragrance.   3B
13 Like the bundle of myrrh is my lover to me: 4A
   he will pass the night between my breasts.   4B
14 Like a bunch of henna blossoms is my lover to me   4C
   in the vineyards of Engedi.   4D

Third Stanza

TENOR

15 How beautiful you are, my companion,   5A
   how beautiful you are: 5B
   your eyes are doves!   5C

SOPRANO

16 How beautiful you are, my lover; really delightful!   6A
   Our bed is really verdant!   7A

¹⁷ The beams of our house are cedars!	7B
Our rafters are firs!	7C

Fourth Stanza

2:1 I am a rose of Sharon,	8A
a lotus^a of the valleys.	8B

TENOR

² Like a lotus among thorns,	9A
so is my companion among the other young women.	9B

SOPRANO

³ Like an apple tree among the trees of the woods,	10A
so is my lover among the young men.	10B
In his shade I take pleasure and sit,	10C
and his fruit is sweet in my mouth.	10D

Fifth Stanza

⁴ He takes me to the house of wine,	11A
and his banner^a toward me is love.	11B
⁵ Lay me on a bed of raisins;	12A
stretch me out on a couch of apples,	12B
for I am wounded by love.	12C

Sixth Stanza

⁶ His left hand is under my head,	13A
and his right hand embraces me.	13B
⁷ I call on you to swear, daughters of Jerusalem,	14A
^aby the gazelles or by the does of the field,^a	14B
that you will not arouse or awaken the passions of love^b	14C
until they are ready.	14D

Notes

9.a. The ending ׳ in לסֻסָתִי, "to a mare," is not the pronoun suf. but the *hireq compaginis* (GKC §90, k–n; Joüon §93, l), which emphasizes the connection between two nouns and is related to the const. state. On its significance here, see *Comment* on v 9.

9.b. A. A. and C. Bloch (*Song of Songs*, 143–45) take דמיתי to mean "I dreamed" and so translate it "My love, I dreamed of you as a mare, my very own, among Pharaoh's chariots" (*Song of Songs*, 51). But דמה does not mean "to dream." It means "to compare, to suppose, to ponder, or to consider (something/someone) to be (something/someone)." Here it is simply, "I compare."

10.a. LXX σ´ OL Tg. insert מה, "how," which captures the meaning of the line but is unnecessary. Read MT.

10.b. MT ב, "with." LXX OL Vg. = כ, "like." Read MT.

12.a. The phrase עד־ש in עד־שהמלך means "until," not "while." See Judg 5:7; Ps 123:2; Song 2:7, 17; 3:4, 5; 4:6; 8:4. The same is true of the much more common עד אשר.

12.b. The term נרדי (from נרד) seems to mean "spikenard." The term is well attested in cognate and other ancient languages, such as the Gk. νάρδος. Cf. *HALOT* "נֵרְדְּ." In the Hebrew Bible, it only appears here and at Song 4:13–14.

2:1.a. שושנה is best taken to mean "lotus" rather than simply "lily" (although the lotus is a kind of lily). See *Comment* on 2:1.

4.a. Although דגל can mean "banner" (notwithstanding Murphy, 132), the phrase "his banner toward me is love" strikes many as an odd metaphor in this context, where the terms are not military but are derived from the gardens and vineyards. One might, therefore, follow Gordis (81–82) and Pope (376) in reading this as a cognate to the Akkadian *diglu*, "wish, intention." Gordis (*JBL* 88 [1969] 203–4) also suggests that it means "And his glance upon me is loving." But a good case for "banner" can be made from the use of the root דגל in Song 5:10; 6:4, 10, where it means something like "marked with a banner." There may be deliberate ambiguity here; see *Comment* on v 4.

7.a-a. LXX ἐν ταῖς δυνάμεσιν καὶ ἐν ταῖς ἰσχύσεσιν τοῦ ἀγροῦ, "by the power and might of the field."

7.b. Vg. Syr. have pass. meanings: "being loved."

Form/Structure/Setting

The woman and man dominate this canto; the chorus has but one verse (1:11). One can argue, as many interpreters do, that Song 1:11 also belongs to the man, but the plural verb implies otherwise, and the interpretation of the wider context validates ascribing this verse to the chorus. Specifically, the man begins by declaring that jewelry enhances the woman's beauty (1:9–10), and the chorus follows with an enthusiastic promise to provide more jewelry for the woman (1:11). This does not mean that young women literally want to buy jewels for a bride; they simply provide a foil for the woman's response. They voice the general opinion that if jewelry enhances a woman's beauty, then by all means she should have more of the same. To this, the woman responds that the real enhancement to her beauty is her love for her man (1:12–15).

This canto comprises six stanzas with a total of thirty-eight lines. Stanzas 1 and 2 have six lines each. Stanza 3 has seven lines, stanza 4 has eight, and stanza 5 has five. Stanza 6 has six lines. On my reckoning, the tenor has nine lines, the chorus has two lines, and the soprano has twenty-seven. A stanza need not be sung entirely by one singer. The lines of stanza 3 clearly belong together since the tenor and soprano alternately praise one another's beauty, and just as obviously the parts are sung by different singers.

The first stanza of the canto centers upon the adornments that enhance the woman's beauty. It is composed of two strophes; line 1A is dependent on 1B, and there is gapping in v 10 (lines 1C–D) in that the verb נאוו, "so attractive," in 1C does double duty. One could take these four lines (1A–D) to be two strophes of two lines each, but the significance of 1C–D (v 10) depends on 1A–B (v 9). In v 11, line 2B syntactically depends upon 2A.

The second stanza (vv 12–14) also has two strophes, but here the first has two lines and the second four, thus reversing the pattern of the first stanza. The first strophe (v 12) speaks of her lover as a "king" and declares that her spikenard gives off fragrance while she awaits him; the two lines are bound by syntactic dependence. In the second strophe (vv 13–14), lines 4A–B are matched by lines 4C–D with repetition of דודי לי, "my lover to me." In this strophe, the lover himself is metaphorically the perfumed spices between her breasts.

In the third stanza, the lines are bound together through repetition and matching. Lines 5A–B repeat הנך יפה, "how beautiful you are," twice. This text appears again in Song 4:1, but 4:1 has מבעד לצמתך, "behind your veil," after "your eyes are doves," requiring that we treat "your eyes are doves behind your veil" as a separate line in that text. For that reason, it is probably best to regard "your eyes are doves" as a separate line in 1:15 also. Line 6A picks up הנך יפה from 5A–B in the woman's response: הנך יפה, "how beautiful you are." There is a transition from strophe 6 to strophe 7 through the use of אף, here translated "really," in lines 6A and 7A. Even so, the matching structure in lines 7A–C and change of subject matter suggest that we have two separate strophes in line 6A and lines 7A–C. Lines 7A–C are verbless clauses and are semantically related (dealing with greenery and kinds of wood), and all three lines have the suffix נו, "our," added to the subject. In this stanza, as in the next, the soprano and tenor take turns singing their parts.

The fourth stanza continues the antiphonal singing but changes the focus of the lyrics; here, the woman and man are metaphorically flowers or trees. This stanza is eight lines long. In Song 2:1 (8A–B), the woman compares herself to a flower in a bicolon with gapping (אני, "I," does double duty). The man picks up this metaphor and expands its significance in v 2 (9A–B). He uses syntactic dependence, with "like . . . so . . ." (כ and כן) joining the two lines. The woman responds in 10A–B with precisely the same pattern, and she compares him to an apple tree. But she extends the metaphor of the apple tree for another two lines (10C–D). This gives closure to both the antiphonal singing and the metaphors of flowers or plants. Once again, the lines are tightly bound together and revolve around a single conceptual metaphor (the beloved as a wonderful plant); we might imagine that the singers responded to one another in a rapid-fire fashion.

The soprano continues to sing solo through to the end. The topic abruptly changes at Song 2:4, and, inasmuch as the tenor no longer sings, I would suggest a stanza break. Stanza 5 has a two-line strophe (v 4 [lines 11A–B]) and a three-line strophe (v 5 [lines 12A–C]). These should be regarded as separate strophes; note that v 4 is indicative, having a perfect verb and verbless clause, whereas v 5 is volitive, in that it has two imperative verbs. There is consonance in that 11A begins הביאני, "he takes me," and 11B ends אהבה, "love." The three lines of v 5 are bound first by matching; 12A and 12B each have a suffixed imperative (רפדוני and סמכוני) followed by a prepositional phrase with ב. Line 12C is then bound to 12A–B through dependence (כי).

The sixth stanza has the same pattern as the fifth. Here too the soprano begins with a two-line strophe that describes the man's loving actions toward her (v 6 [lines 13A–B]). She uses the dyad "right hand—left hand" to bind these two lines together. She then moves into another volitive section, here adjuring the girls of Jerusalem not to awaken love before it is time to do so (v 7 [lines 14A–D]).

Thus, the six stanzas of the fourth canto come in pairs. The first two are each of six lines, and each has a four-line and a two-line strophe. Stanzas 3 and 4 are both sung antiphonally with the woman closing each with a part of four lines. Stanzas 5 and 6 are each sung by the woman solo, and in both she begins with a two-line account of the man's loving action and follows that with a longer, volitive strophe.

The six strophes are interrelated. The concepts developed in the six stanzas are as follows:

Stanza 1	Tenor and chorus praise soprano regarding jewelry
Stanza 2	Soprano speaks of tenor as simple necklace reposing between her breasts
Stanza 3	Tenor praises soprano; soprano responds
Stanza 4	Soprano's self-appraisal; tenor praises soprano; soprano responds and speaks of reposing under tenor's "shade" as "apple tree"
Stanza 5	Soprano speaks of tenor's love actions; asks to be laid out on "raisins" and "apples"
Stanza 6	Soprano speaks of tenor's love actions; urges chorus not to arouse love

The linkage between the three pairs of stanzas is fairly obvious. Both stanzas 1 and 2 speak of jewelry for the woman, although in stanza 1 it is jewelry of gold and silver and in stanza 2 it is a simple pouch hanging presumably on a leather thong. Stanzas 3 and 4 both have the man and woman in succession praising one another. Stanzas 5 and 6 both begin by speaking of the man's love actions; also, stanza 5 speaks of the woman stretched out as if on a bed, and stanza 6 advises the girls not to "arouse" or "awaken" love. In addition, there is linkage between stanzas 2 and 4. In stanza 2, the man reposes between the woman's breasts, and in stanza 4 the woman reposes under the man's shade. Also, stanza 4 describes the man as an apple tree, and in stanza 5, the woman asks to be stretched out on apples. Finally, the chorus appears at the beginning and end of the canto. In stanza 1, they enthusiastically promise to secure jewelry for the woman, but in stanza 6, they are addressed with a warning not to awaken love too soon.

Comment

9 To a modern reader, it is somewhat bewildering that the man would compare his beloved to a horse. The point is not that she looks like a horse. Instead, she is likened to a horse among pharaoh's chariots in that she, like the horse, is magnificent to look upon. The only point of actual visual similarity is that both she and the mare attached to pharaoh's chariot are adorned in splendid ornamentation. Egyptian artwork depicts the horses of the royal chariots with headdresses and finery (e.g., the chariots of Tutankhamen, *ANEP*, 60; see also Keel ([1994] 57, fig. 13).

Pope (338–39) suggests that she is like a mare in the midst of the chariots of pharaoh in that she causes great disruption and excitement among the male war horses. He argues that pharaoh's chariots were drawn by stallions and that an estrous mare among them created so much disorder that an enemy might well render pharaoh's chariot corps ineffective in battle by sending a mare into their midst. The idea is that she drives him wild with passion.

If this is the meaning of the metaphor, however, it is odd that the canto does not develop it at all. From the following verses, it appears that the ornamentation and stately appearance of the woman are the real point. The woman is likened to a mare rather than to a stallion for the simple reason that she is female, and the point that in the Egyptian order of battle the chariot corps actually used only stallions, even if true, is irrelevant. The text says nothing about a military setting for this verse, much less about a mare running loose among stallions during a battle. Pharaoh's chariots are not necessarily war chariots going into combat (Keel's extravagant paraphrase [(1994) 56], "a mare among the battle horses of pharaoh's chariots," is completely unfounded). Pope himself cites a text that describes the fondness Amenhotep II had for one of the mares of his stable (339).

The interpreter of this verse should not ignore the *hireq compaginis* of לְסֻסָתִי, "to a mare." Although perhaps archaic, we should not pass over the sufformative as though it were meaningless. The *hireq compaginis* emphasizes the genitival or construct relationship between two nouns. Examples include שֹׁכְנִי סְנֶה, "inhabitant of the bush" (Deut 33:16), and עֹזְבִי הַצֹּאן, "the abandoner of the flock" (Zech

11:17). More interesting yet is Lam 1:1, where the *hireq compaginis* appears three times: Jerusalem was רַבָּתִי עָם, "great of people" (i.e., populous); רַבָּתִי בַגּוֹיִם, "a great one of [the cities] in the nations"; and שָׂרָתִי בַּמְּדִינוֹת, "a princess of [the cities] in the provinces." In the latter two cases, where it appears with the preposition ב, the *hireq compaginis* is not a meaningless archaism or metrical ballast; both times it points to a *nomen rectum* that is *implied* but not *explicit*: "cities." Jerusalem was not a great nation or province, it was a great example *of the cities that are in* the nations and provinces. In the Song, similarly, the man does not compare the woman to a mare "among the chariots of pharaoh" but "to a mare *belonging to [the horses that are with]* the chariots of pharaoh" (לְסֻסָתִי בְּרִכְבֵי פַרְעֹה). Put another way, the mare is *a member of the class of horses* that are with the chariots of pharaoh. As such, the mare cannot be an alien horse released by an enemy among the stallions.

Interpreters who take this to mean a mare creating havoc among pharaoh's chariot corps generally point out that רכב, "chariots," here is plural. This is the only place in the Hebrew Bible where רכב is found in the plural. Normally the singular noun either refers to one single chariot or is used as a collective to refer to the chariot corps of an army. Examples of the latter usage include Exod 14:9 (רכב פרעה, "chariots of Pharaoh") and 14:23 (כל סוס פרעה רכבו ופרשיו, "every horse of Pharaoh, his chariots and his cavalry"). What is significant here is that the Hebrew expression for "pharaoh's chariot corps" is רֶכֶב פַּרְעֹה. Thus, the phrase בְּרִכְבֵי פַרְעֹה probably means, "individual chariots belonging to pharaoh." That is, it does not refer to a *military unit* but describes *individual chariots that are used by pharaoh himself*.

If the real point of comparison is the ornamentation on one of pharaoh's mares, then one should understand that by implication the woman wears equally elaborate adornments. V 10 confirms this. A woman in elaborate jewelry implies a wedding scene (or some other special occasion) since Israelite women did not wear such ornamentation on a day-to-day basis. This does not mean that all the following verses need refer to specific elements of a wedding ceremony.

10 The meaning of תרים is to some degree a matter of conjecture. The term is apparently related to the root חור, "turn," and means something twisted in a decorative fashion. Because of its proximity to the cheeks and neck, it is presumably a kind of jewelry. It is impossible to tell much more about this jewelry than that it is about her head and neck. She seems to wear some kind of beaded jewelry, similar to the necklaces and earrings with multiple rows of beads seen in depictions of goddesses and women from the ancient Near East. This corresponds also with the pictures of the decorations on the heads of royal horses from ancient Egypt. The necklaces that the women wore were virtually collars in that they were worn tightly around the neck. In some erotic artwork, the women are wearing only the collar necklaces, but the woman in this verse seems to have on a more elaborate display of jewelry and ornaments since they hang down over her cheeks. There is no suggestion that she is nude.

11 נקדות, "decorations," are studs or points; נקדות הכסף are probably "decorations of silver" and patterns worked into gold jewelry. A possible cognate is נקד, "speckled," a term that describes Jacob's variegated sheep in Gen 30:32–33, 35, 39; 31:8, 10, 12. The precise meaning of נקדות is a matter of conjecture; see A. Konkel, *NIDOTTE* §5925.

If the chorus sings this verse and if the implied image is of a bride decked out in the elaborate ornamentation her culture prescribes, then this verse expresses the general desire of people—and especially of women—to see a bride dressed as elaborately and as gorgeously as possible. The verse may allude to the young women at a wedding helping to dress up the bride.

12 The woman declares enigmatically that her spikenard gives off its fragrance until "the king" is at his "circle." The term "circle" here (מסב) may be a banquet or a couch or may be related to the enigmatic surrounding of a man by a woman described in Jer 31:22, נקבה תסובב גבר, "a woman shall encircle a man." מסב, "circle" (from סבב), could be taken to be a circle of feasters, a room, a table, or whatever else one may imagine to be somehow rounded. Used adverbially in 1 Kgs 6:29, it means "all about." In 2 Kgs 23:5 it is the "surroundings" of Jerusalem (i.e., the suburbs). Lacking any other clear evidence, most interpreters prefer to go with the LXX ἐν ἀνακλίσει and on the basis of ἀνακλίνω, "to recline," take it to be a couch or bed used for dining or sleeping. See also Pope (347), who observes that in postbiblical Hebrew *měsibbā* means a banqueting party. I prefer to preserve the ambiguity of מסב with the translation "circle."

It is clear, however, that some kind of sexual meaning is present; the sensual intent of the next verse is stated fairly boldly. If the "circle" is a couch or bed, then the intimate implications are obvious. If it is a banquet, on the analogy of *měsibbā*, "banquet party," the idea is possibly that the groom will feast as if at a banquet upon the pleasures the woman provides. This kind of imagery is used so frequently in the Song (e.g., at 2:4–5) that such an interpretation cannot be considered peculiar or forced. If the "circle" functions in a way analogous to the woman's "circling" of a man in Jer 31:22, it probably refers to her embrace, if not to sexual union. On the other hand, this may allude to a literal feast that was held in conjunction with a wedding. It is quite possible that "circle" is left deliberately ambiguous to allow for a blending of metaphors. "King" is here a metaphor for her lover, the bridegroom, who has in her eyes the significance, beauty, and charm worthy of a king. She thus declares that her spikenard gives off its fragrance until he comes to his "circle," that is, to the feast and to her embrace. Translated into simple terms, she is saying that the spikenard gives off its fragrance in expectation of the "king," her groom, coming to her.

13 In contrast to the expensive and somewhat theatrical beauty of necklaces of gold and silver (vv 10–11), the woman mentions a "bundle of myrrh" between her breasts. The bundle is not metallic and cold like the gold, silver, or pearls of her jewelry but is a soft pouch of cloth or leather, probably hung from a simple thong. It is not as expensive but is far more intimate. Unlike gold, it gives off an enticing fragrance. Its position between her breasts is obviously sensual. In equating her lover to this bundle, she does not distinguish between the emotions of her *experience* of love—symbolized by myrrh—and the *object* of her love, the man himself. Her "love" is at the same time her man and her feelings. The bundle of myrrh also serves as a surrogate for the man as she awaits his coming between her breasts. The imperfect ילין should be given a future translation, "he will pass the night between my breasts." This continues the orientation toward the future seen already in the previous verse, where she waits "until" the man comes to his "circle."

14 The woman next compares him to a cluster of henna flowers in the vineyards of Engedi. Henna, a bush that grows to ten feet (three meters) in height, has clusters of white, fragrant flowers that apparently were used for perfumes. This verse places it among the vines of the vineyard, where it adds beauty and fragrance to the vineyard. Engedi, an oasis located west of the Dead Sea, is known to have been the location of carefully tended vineyards from at least the seventh century B.C.E. (Keel [1994] 67). The spikenard of v 12 and the bundle of myrrh of v 13 both adorn the woman's body, and thus one should take the vineyard that the henna adorns to refer at least in part to the woman's body as well. This agrees with frequent references to her "fruit" that the man will eat (e.g., Song 4:12–16) and to the description of her breasts as a cluster of grapes (Song 7:9 [ET 7:8]). Thus, the henna, the man, is a flowering plant that adorns the vineyard, the woman, even as he is also a sachet of myrrh between her breasts. Vv 12–14 must be understood in the context of his praise of her wearing her jewelry and in the context of the desire of the chorus to add to those adornments (vv 9–11).

15 This verse begins a third strophe in which the lovers toss words of adoring praise to one another. The meaning of "your eyes are doves" is not self-evident. Some interpreters have argued that the eyes of the woman look like doves, but this idea is garish if not nonsensical. Some take it to mean that her eyes look like the eyes of a dove, but the text simply states her eyes are doves. At any rate, a dove's eyes are not particularly remarkable. References to doves elsewhere in the Bible are generally of little help (e.g., the dove in the story of the flood, Gen 8; the dove's wings, which allow it to escape trouble, Ps 55:7 [ET 55:6]; the sound of the dove's cooing, Isa 38:14 and 59:11; the dove as a senseless animal, Hos 7:11; the dove as a symbol of the Spirit, Matt 3:16).

On the other hand, Jer 48:28 describes the dove as an animal that seeks refuge high in craggy rocks, a metaphor that has a parallel in Song 2:14. It could be that "your eyes are doves" in 1:15 is an abbreviated form of "your eyes are like doves behind your veil" in 4:1. In this case, the metaphor would imply that her eyes behind her veil remind the man of doves that are high and safe in nests built in the sides of cliffs. By analogy, the woman is equally beautiful but out of reach. It is not certain, however, that 1:15 should be interpreted in the light of Song 2:14 or 4:1. יונה, "dove," is simply a hypocorism for the woman in Song 5:2 and 6:9, and in 5:12 the woman says that the man's eyes are like doves. Thus, the dovelike quality of the eyes does not belong exclusively to the woman, and the metaphor of 1:15 does not necessarily relate to the woman's veil and to the dove hiding in the cliffs.

Keel ([1994] 70–73) argues that iconographic evidence conclusively demonstrates that the dove was a symbol of sexuality across the ancient eastern Mediterranean world. He cites, among other examples: a Syrian cylinder seal from ca. 1750 showing the fertility goddess unveiling herself before her mate as a dove flies overhead; a Mitanni cylinder seal from the thirteenth century in which the goddess holds a staff with a flying dove; also, a scarab from eight- or seventh-century Lachish in which a dove is beneath the sign of the moon, a symbol of the goddess. This evidence seems to be sufficient to demonstrate that ancient peoples associated doves with sexuality, albeit not exclusively with sexuality (as the other biblical texts, cited above, indicate). It is possible that "your eyes are doves" is cultural code for "I find you sexually attractive."

It is possible, of course, that we are trying too hard. The doves may not strictly symbolize anything. The phrase "your eyes are like doves" may be simply an expression of attraction and affection that transcends any logical connection. When one thinks of a dove, one thinks of soft cooing, fluttering wings, gentleness, and in the case of the white dove, brightness of color. Rather than bind the term in a metaphoric equation, we should perhaps simply take pleasure in the connotations.

16 The woman returns the man's praise in kind, declaring him to be יָפֶה, which is simply the masculine form of יָפָה, "beautiful." She then declares that their bed is verdant. The word רַעֲנָן, "verdant," almost always appears in the Bible in conjunction with the word עֵץ, "tree," or with some specific species of tree, such as the olive (Jer 11:16). Although רענן, "verdant," occasionally means "prospering" (Ps 92:15 [ET 92:14]; Dan 4:1 [ET 4:4]), that would not seem to be the sense here. In light of the reference to trees in the next verse (1:17), the greenness of their bed must refer somehow to the greenness of trees. In the rest of the Bible, "every green tree" (כל־עץ רענן) invariably refers to the groves and woodland shrines where the sacred prostitution of the fertility cult flourished (Deut 12:2; 1 Kgs 14:23; 2 Kgs 16:4; 17:10; Isa 57:5; Jer 2:20; 3:6,13; Ezek 6:13; 2 Chr 28:4). In describing their bed as a leafy bower, she is saying that their time of sexual pleasure is about to come.

17 It is possible that this line belongs to the man and so sustains the antiphonal singing. On the other hand, there is no clear indication of a change of part here. In addition, the next stanza is also antiphonal and ends with the soprano singing a part in four lines, and we may suggest that the same is taking place here. Continuing her proclamation that their bed is verdant, she says that the rafters are cedar and fir. That is, they have greenery beneath them and an arbor above them; they are in a secluded grove of trees.

2:1 Scholars interpret this verse according to two extremes. On the one hand, many take the woman's self-description as a חבצלת, "rose of Sharon," to be self-deprecation, as though she were saying, "I am just one of many girls." In this interpretation, the "rose of Sharon" is taken to be some kind of crocus or other small flower and the "lily of the valley" is also assumed to be common. Thus interpreted, she means, "I am nobody special." Apart from whatever other problems this interpretation may entail, it is not likely that she would make such a self-effacing statement in a song where the man and woman are extravagantly praising each other.

On the other hand, Keel ([1994] 78–80) argues that she is claiming herself to be the center of love and life. He argues that שׁוֹשַׁנָּה (masculine form: שׁוֹשָׁן) means not "lily" but "lotus." His strongest argument is that the capitals of Solomon's pillars had the שׁוֹשָׁן design (1 Kgs 7:19, 22), as did the great metal יָם, "sea," the washing basin in the temple complex (1 Kgs 7:26). He observes that the lotus design is common for the capitals of Egyptian columns and cups but that an ordinary lily pattern is never found. Furthermore, Egyptian and Phoenician art regularly portrays the lotus as the flower of the gods and the symbol of life. See also S. Grober (*Semitics* 9 [1984] 88), who argues that שׁוֹשָׁן is an Egyptian loanword that clearly means "lotus." These arguments are compelling; it is best to translate the word as "lotus" rather than as "lily." Even so, one should bear in mind that the lotus is in fact a variety of lily and that the Israelites may not have carefully distinguished the two.

In addition, Keel ([1994] 78) argues that the flower here translated as "rose of Sharon" must also be of great significance because the only other place in the

OT where the word (חבצלת) occurs it represents the dawning of eschatological salvation (Isa 35:1). Here, however, Keel has overreached himself. In Isa 35:1, the main point about the חבצלת is not that it was individually a spectacular flower but that when it was in bloom it was so abundant that it apparently covered an entire valley. This is more in keeping with the interpretation that takes "I am the חבצלת of Sharon" to mean, "I am one among many girls."

It appears that there is truth in both interpretations. On the one hand, she is saying, "I am one among many girls." But she does not mean by this that "I am nobody special." She is a flower, a thing of beauty and life. She emphasizes this when she declares that she is the "lotus of the valleys" and invokes traditional notions of the power of the lotus. She does not claim that she is unique in all the world, but she does claim that her role as woman is beautiful and powerful.

As an afterthought, we should also observe that a number of psalms are set to the tune of "lotuses" (על־ששנים). These include Pss 69 and 80, but the most interesting example for our purposes is Ps 45, the wedding psalm. The superscript not only sets it to the tune על־ששנים but also calls it a "love song" (שיר ידידת). It may be that the tune or musical style called "lotuses" was chosen for Ps 45 because the music was associated with love poetry (Pss 69 and 80 are psalms of lament; we cannot say if there is any significance to these psalms also having this music, although the music may have been in a style appropriate both for tenderness and for mourning).

2 The man responds that in fact she is unique in all the world. He declares that, compared to all other young women, she is a lotus among thorns. In light of this response, it is fairly clear that her claim to being a "rose of Sharon" does describe her as one among many flowers. But for him she is not *one* flower, however good that may be; she *the one and only*, the lotus. It goes without saying that these words imply that he is devoted to her. His declaration also has monogamous implications; she is the only flower and he loves only her.

3 The woman begins by continuing the antiphonal series: the man has said she compares to other women as a lotus compares to brambles, and she responds that he compares to other men as the apple tree to the trees of a forest. The point of comparison is of course that the apple tree bears delicious fruit but that forest trees do not.

A number of scholars argue that the edible apple was unknown in ancient Israel and contend that the תפוח was an apricot (especially Fox, *Song of Songs*, 107, but other suggestions include the orange and even the lemon). The apple was known in ancient Mesopotamia (von Soden, *Ancient Orient*, 102–3). Also, the ancient Greeks and Romans knew and enjoyed the apple. It is certainly conceivable that the ancient Israelites knew the apple as well. The apple tree probably originates from the area between the Caspian and Black Seas; it was brought to the New World by immigrants. L. Walker notes that the apricot was a late import from China but that later use of תפוח associates it with the making of sauce and cider, which also suggests the meaning "apple" (*NIDOTTE* §9515). The word is rendered as "apple" in both LXX (μῆλον) and Vg. (*malum*).

As mentioned above, the apple was quite significant in Greco-Roman literature. It is especially associated with women (or goddesses) and sexuality. According to (Pseudo) Apollodorus, *Library* 2.173, Eris ("strife") offered the prize of an apple in the beauty contest between Hera, Athena, and Aphrodite and so ultimately provoked the Trojan wars. In the tale of Atalanta and Melanion (more commonly known as Hippomenes), the athletic virgin Atalanta issued the challenge that she, wearing full armor, would race any man who desired to marry her. If she won, the man would die on the spot, but if he won, he could marry her. After many had died in the attempt, Melanion succeeded by throwing in front of her the golden apples of the Hesperides that Aphrodite had given him, which she could not resist stooping to pick up (*Library* 1.401). Another myth tells how Earth presented Zeus with the golden apples of the Hesperides after his marriage to Hera. The Hesperides (nymphs) and a dragon guarded these apples at the western end of the world; Herakles' eleventh labor was to fetch them (*Library* 1.221). Pausanias, in his guide to Greece (2.10.5), describes an image to Aphrodite in which the goddess holds an apple in her hand. The figure of the apple also appears on a number of extant vases. For example, an early classical vase from Attica (catalogue London D 6) depicts a girl (or nymph) picking apples from a tree. A red figure vase from Campania, about 450 B.C.E. (Boston 01.8083), depicts three women at a festival of Dionysius, and the central woman holds an apple. Artwork on other vases reflects the fact that the apple had sexual implications.

In short, classical evidence for the association of apples with women and sexuality is fairly strong; the woman's claim that the man is to her like an apple tree is in keeping with this motif. She speaks of taking pleasure in his shade and his fruit and abiding with him. As in the myth of Atalanta and Melanion, she is the virgin who finds the apples to be irresistible.

4 As stated in *Note* 4.a., in this context ודגלו might have the meaning, "his intention." The more common Hebrew meaning of דגל, "banner," cannot be excluded, however. Later in the Song, the woman as virgin is a walled city (6:4) and is surrounded by guards. The man has not conquered the city but has come to her in peace and has been freely admitted (see, e.g., Song 8:10). Understood in light of this metaphor, the line "his banner toward me is love" becomes comprehensible; the man is a "king" who comes as an ally and not an enemy. He has approached her in peace and not to conquer. "His banner toward me is love" is a veiled anticipation of the metaphor of the woman as a walled city that the man takes without combat or violence.

He has brought her to the "house of wine" with the intent to give her his love. Interpreters have understood the phrase בית היין, "house of wine," in a wide range of ways—as a banqueting hall, as a symposium, or as an arbor where one drinks and makes love. If a wedding banquet is in view here, the "house of wine" is on one level the banquet and on another level the anticipated love play. In the Song, wine often connotes or is associated with lovemaking, especially kisses (1:2, 4; 4:10; 5:1; 7:3 [ET 2], 10 [ET 9]; 8:2).

5 The verb סמך in the *qal* means "to rest upon, support, lean against." In Gen 27:37, ודגן ותירש סמכתיו means, "with grain and wine I supported him," and thus many conclude that here the word means to "refresh" or "feed." On the other hand, the phrase וסמכת את־ידך עליו means, "and lay your hand on him" (Num 27:18), indicating that the primary meaning of סמך is that one thing is leaning or resting on another (other examples include Exod 29:10, 15, 19; Lev 1:4; 3:2, 8). It is best to understand Gen 27:37 as a metaphorical use of סמך, analogous to the English word *support* used with the meaning "provide the necessities of life for someone." סמך is also used metaphorically to mean "rely upon" (e.g., 2 Chr

32:8 [*nipʿal*]). But in English one would not use "I supported him" to mean "(in the course of a meal) I served him food," and we may doubt that the Hebrew סמך should be so understood here. It is probable that the *piʿel* of סמך (used only here) means, "make (me) to rest upon" rather than "feed me."

The verb רפד appears three times in the Hebrew Bible. In Job 41:22 (ET 41:30) we have תחתיו חדודי חרש ירפד חרוץ עלי־טיט, "Beneath him are jagged potsherds; he stretches out [like] a sledge over mud," in the description of Leviathan (using *qal* stem of רפד). A *piʿel* form appears in Job 17:13, "If I spread out [רפדתי] my bed in darkness." From these two examples, it appears that the *qal* has the intransitive or middle meaning, "to spread oneself out" or "stretch oneself out," whereas the *piʿel* has the transitive meaning, "to spread something out." The *piʿel* example here (רפדוני) thus could mean, "Spread me out," but it is probably more appropriate to give it the translation, "stretch me out." The word never connotes giving someone food.

The verb חלה means to be hurt or in pain. The source of the hurt may be an illness (1 Sam 19:14; 1 Kgs 14:1, 5; 17:17), weariness (Isa 57:10), or an injury or wound (2 Kgs 1:2; 2 Chr 22:6). It is often used of illness, and one could translate this as "lovesick." However, to the modern reader this implies adolescent pining, and there is more to it than that. In what sense has love wounded the woman or made her ill, and why does she ask that they lay her on raisin cakes and apples? Scholars often take this text to mean simply that she is flushed with excitement over love and that she needs raisin cakes and apples to restore her strength. Also, many interpreters point out that these foods probably were thought to have an aphrodisiac quality.

The image of lying on a bed of raisins and apples has layers of meaning. Lying down implies rest for someone who is weary or ill, and the eating of food gives strength to such persons. On the other hand, lying down has sexual implications, and sweetmeats such as raisins and apples probably connote love play. Lying down in these foods also betokens luxuriant extravagance. Her request is thus an appeal for both strength and for affection, but it suggests a paradise setting. She needs this because she is "wounded by love." The real question, then, concerns the significance of her sickness.

Her lovesickness does reflect her deep desire for her lover, but it is not desire for an absent lover or grief over unrequited love. It is, rather, a conflicted desire. חלה, "wounded," implies real illness or impairment; it is unlikely that the term here means only that she is overly excited or flushed from overstimulation. Similarly, there is more here than adolescent pining; the language implies real suffering that the reader is to empathize with rather than smile at. It is better to take this as mental pain produced by profound anxiety and conflict. The solution to her anxiety, here metaphorically described as lying down in a bed of raisins or apples, is the affection of her beloved. It is his affection that will enable her to overcome her internal conflict. She has already described her lover as an apple tree in Song 2:3; it is hardly an interpretive leap to take "apples" here to refer to his affection.

6 The dyad "right hand" and "left hand" also appears in the Sumerian love poetry, but the usage there is more erotic. In one of the Sumerian songs, the woman asks the man to place his left hand at her head and his right hand at her nakedness, that is, her genitals (*CS* 1:541). Here in the Song, the right-hand–left-hand dyad only implies affection and support, not genital stimulation.

This verse answers the request of the previous verse. The man lets her rest upon his left arm while he caresses her with his right hand. He sustains her with tender affection; his love is the raisins and apples upon which she rests. As described in *Form/Structure/Setting* above, however, it seems to be bound to strophe 6 rather than to strophe 5. The declaration that the girls should not awaken love (Song 2:7) before the right time is closely related to this verse.

7 This is the first of three texts in which the woman demands that the Jerusalem girls forswear "arousing love before it pleases." The other two are at Song 3:5 and 8:4 (the latter lacks the line concerning gazelles and does of the field). We naturally wonder why she asks the girls to swear by gazelles and also what specifically they are supposed to forswear.

Many modern interpreters take בצבאות או באילות השדה, "by gazelles or by the does of the field," to be a circumlocution for "by (Yahweh) Sabaoth [צבאות]" and "by God Shaddai [אלהים שדי]" (cf. *Note* 2:7.a-a. on the LXX). The coincidence is remarkable, and it is easy to see why interpreters have taken this as a circumlocution. But if the similarity is deliberate, it is probably little more than a wordplay, and we still have to deal with the words that are actually present in the text. The words for gazelles and does have not been chosen simply because of their similarity to Sabaoth and El Shaddai; gazelles and deer play an important role in the Song and in love imagery from the ancient Near East. The woman's lover is like a gazelle (Song 2:9, 17), and her breasts are like the twins of a gazelle (Song 4:5; 7:3). Keel ([1994] 91–93) has documented the place of gazelles or deer in the iconography of the Near East that relates to sexuality and the goddess. It is probable that in the wider culture of the ancient Near East as well as in the vocabulary of the Song itself, gazelles and deer represent the joys of love. In charging the women with an oath in the name of the gazelles, she is calling on them to swear by love itself rather than by the name of a deity.

Fox (*Song of Songs*, 110) argues that she is asking the chorus not to disturb the lovers until they are finished. He states that עור never means to arouse sexually but that it only means to "awaken" someone. He thus concludes that waking someone is equivalent to disturbing someone, and thus that she is asking that they not be disturbed. His interpretation, however, is very unnatural; "Do not awaken love until it desires" cannot possibly mean "Do not disturb us until we have finished making love." Arguing that עור does not of itself mean "to arouse sexually" misses the point that this is metaphorical language. She is telling them not to "wake up" love itself. One can readily understand "waking up love" as a metaphor for arousal (or more precisely as a metaphor for becoming sexually active for the first time in one's life) without having to demonstrate that עור alone connotes sexual arousal. Apart from that, Fox's translation is simply wrong. V. Hamilton (*NIDOTTE* §6424, 3:357) summarizes the meaning of עור as follows: "In the simple and passive stems the vb. is used for being aroused or excited to some activity. In the factitive and causative stems the vb. is used for arousing or stirring somebody to action. The activities to which one is aroused are those that require extra effort, such as war, work, or love." The word does not mean "disturb."

Explanation

Symbolically, this text describes the tension between the glory of the *wedding* and the glory of the *marriage*. The glory of the wedding is in ceremony and elaborate costuming. The glory of a marriage is in the love of a man and woman. It remains for the woman of the Song to redirect attention to where it belongs, not on the trappings of the wedding but on its significance as the beginning of a marriage.

"King" is here a metaphor for her lover, the bridegroom, who has in her eyes the significance, beauty, and charm worthy of a king. She thus declares that her spikenard gives off its fragrance until he comes to his "circle," that is, to the feast and to her embrace. Translated into simple terms, she is saying that the spikenard gives off its fragrance in expectation of the "king," her groom, coming to her.

The governing topic is the question, What enhances the woman's beauty? The man and the chorus desire to adorn her with expensive ornaments of gold and silver. This sentiment is not bad, and it is born of love for her, but it substitutes a superficial embellishment for true adornments. She asserts rather that her desirability is enhanced by her fragrances of spikenard, myrrh, and henna and that her beauty is enhanced by the love of her lover. She gives off the fragrance of spikenard as she waits for him to come to her. She will have him, like her myrrh, between her breasts. He is like henna in that he adorns the beauty of her, the vineyard. The fragrance of these perfumes is like love itself; it is invisible but powerful and sweet. Her real adornment, she asserts, is the groom and the love she has for him.

The association between love play and a verdant paradise ("Our bed is really verdant") are universal, and it is not surprising that the fertility cult seized this setting as the locus for sexuality. It is probably safe to assume that the Israelites would have heard "our bed is verdant" to be an indication that it is ready for their love play. At the same time, the image is not of itself evil. God himself seizes the language of the fertility cult when he promises that he will be a lush, life-giving tree or vineyard for Israel (Hos 14:4–8 [ET 14:5–9]). The grove is the domain of sexual love. While the sacred prostitute (or, in a more modern setting, the mistress) might make use of the language of sexual pleasure, such imagery rightly belongs in a setting of a couple committed to one another in love. The question the Song confronts us with is this: Which of these two, the liaison with the prostitute or the unity of a married couple, is the real arena of sexual pleasure?

A very common motif in love poetry is yearning for an absent lover, or distress over an unrequited love, or wasting away in agony in a love that one dare not or cannot declare openly. Egyptian love poetry also makes use of the motif of lovesickness, often because one is longing to see the beloved again. For example, in Papyrus Chester Beatty I group 34, a woman describes how vexed and agitated she is in the absence of her lover; she cannot even put on her scarf or paint her eyes. In group 37 of the same text, a boy declares that he is sick from not having seen his beloved for a full seven days and that medicines do him no good.

A classic expression of this kind of lovesickness in English is in the Knight's Tale in Chaucer's *Canterbury Tales,* and it well illustrates what one frequently sees in love literature. When Arcita is freed from prison in Athens and banished from the city, he is despondent over the thought that he will never see Emily, the object of his undeclared love, again (p. 36, lines 497–508):

> Whan that Arcite to Thebes comen was,
> Ful ofte a day he swelte and seyde "allas,"
> For seen his lady shal he nevermo.
> And shortly to concluden al his wo,
> So muche sorwe had nevere creature
> That is, or shal, whyle that the world may dure.
> His sleep, his mete, his drink is him biraft,
> That lene he wex and drye as is a shaft.
> His eyen holwe, and grisly to biholde;
> His hewe fallow and pale as asshen colde;
> And solitarie he was and evere allone,
> And waillinge al the night, makinge his mone.

The Song of Songs is strikingly different. Here, the soprano does not imply that the man is absent or that she can be cured by seeing him again. To the contrary, v 6 suggests that he is with her. Instead of longing for an absent lover, she asks to lie upon raisin cakes and apples. The Song has taken the motif of lovesickness and, by doing away with the absent-lover device, has transformed a formulaic device and taken it in an entirely new direction.

A desire may be conflicted for a number of reasons: a woman may love a man whom her family rejects (as in *Romeo and Juliet*), or she may love a man but know that loving him is at odds with another duty. This commentary will argue that Song 3:1–5 describes symbolically the conflicted state of the woman's love. She fully confronts the source of her suffering in 5:2–8, where she once again declares herself "wounded by love" (5:8).The Song is distinctive in ancient love poetry in that it refuses to invoke the goddess (or a god) of love. Neither the woman nor the man calls upon Aphrodite (under any of her many titles) to give aid in the quest for happiness in love. But neither is Yahweh explicitly invoked. This is not because the Song is "secular" but because it avoids any suggestion that Yahweh will play the role of Eros or Aphrodite. It does not participate in the superstitions that surrounded love in the ancient world. The Song offers no sanctioned prayer, ritual, or amulet for calling upon Yahweh to make this or that person fall in love. By using words that sound like Sabaoth and El Shaddai, the woman forces the girls of Jerusalem to reckon with the importance of the oath she calls them to take. Nevertheless, she avoids naming God and has them swear by love instead.

Her appeal is that they not awaken the passions of love until those passions are ready. That is, it is a simple moral injunction (cf. M. Saebø, "On the Canonicity," 276). Put another way, she is telling them to avoid sexual experience until the proper time. A modern, Western reader might take this to mean "Do not become involved in sexual activity until you are sure that you are emotionally prepared for it." Such an interpretation would be quite out of character with the moral code of ancient Israel and the message of the Song. In this context, the exhortation can only mean that they should avoid promiscuity and save their virginity for marriage. This is not a matter of imposing Christian or bourgeois ethics on the text. To the contrary, ancient moral codes in this regard are far more conservative than modern Western codes. At the heart of the Song, moreover, is the event of a young woman marrying the man she loves and giving up her virginity. The passion of love and of the powerful emotions of the transition from virgin to sexually active woman are to be experienced with what the OT calls the "husband of your youth." The woman is simply telling the younger girl to wait until she finds and marries the man she loves.

In this light, lines 14C–D (Song 2:7b) make more sense. Because her man tenderly sustains her, she is at peace about "awakening love" with him. A woman who awakens love with a man who is not giving of himself or prepared to sustain her will find herself bitter and desolate.

V. Soprano and Tenor: The Invitation to Depart (2:8–17)

Bibliography

Albrektson, B. "Singing or Pruning?" *BT* 47 (1996) 109–14. **Butting, K.** "Go Your Way: Women Rewrite the Scriptures (Song of Songs 2.8–14)." In *Song of Songs: A Feminist Companion to the Bible.* FCB 2d ser. 6. Ed. A. A. Brenner and C. R. Fontaine. Sheffield: Sheffield Academic Press, 2000. 142–51. **Gibson, J. C. L.** *Textbook of Syrian Semitic Inscriptions.* **Lemaire, A.** "*Zāmīr* dans la Tablette de Gezer et le Cantique des Cantiques." *VT* 25 (1975) 15–26. **Murphy, R. E.** "Cant 2:8–17—A Unified Poem?" In *Mélanges bibliques et orientaux en l'honneur de M. Mathias Delcor.* Ed. A. Caquot. Neukirchen-Vluyn: Neukirchener Verlag, 1985. 305–10. **Weems, R. J.** "The Song of Songs." In *NIB.* Nashville: Abingdon, 1997. 5:363–434.

Translation

First Stanza

SOPRANO

⁸ *The sound of my lover!*   1A
There, he is coming,   1B
leaping on the mountains,   1C
springing on the hills!   1D
⁹ *My lover is similar to a gazelle*   1E
or the stag of the deer.[a]   1F
There, he is standing behind our wall,   2A
gazing through the windows,   2B
peeking[b] *through the lattices!*   2C
¹⁰ *My lover spoke up and said to me,*   2D

Second Stanza

TENOR

Arise, my companion, my beautiful one,[a]   3A
and come along!   3B
¹¹ *For see, the winter*[a] *has passed,*   4A
the rain is done,   4B
it is gone away.   4C
¹² *The flowers appear in the land,*   5A
the time of pruning and singing[a] *arrives,*   5B
the sound of the dove is heard in our land!   5C
¹³ *The fig tree ripens its figs,*   5D
and the vines from blossoms give their fragrance.   5E

Third Stanza

Arise! Come, my companion, my beautiful one!   6A
Come along!   6B
¹⁴ *My dove in the clefts of the rock,*   7A
[a]*in the coverts of the cliff!*[a]   7B

Show me your form!	7C
Let me hear your voice!	7D
For your voice is sweet	7E
and your form is lovely.	7F

Fourth Stanza

CHORUS
¹⁵ *Catch foxes for us,* — 8A
   little foxes ruining vineyards! — 8B
   Our vineyards are in bloom. — 8C

Fifth Stanza

SOPRANO
¹⁶ *My lover is mine and I am his,* — 9A
   he who grazes among the lotuses. — 9B
¹⁷ *Until the day comes to life* — 10A
   and the shadows flee, — 10B
   Take your fill!^a *Make yourself, my lover, like the gazelle* — 10C
   or like the stag of the deer on the cleft mountains!^b — 10D

Notes

9.a. LXX adds ἐπὶ τὰ ὄρη Βαιθηλ, "on Bethel's mountain."

9.b. צוץ (hip'il) normally means to "bloom" (e.g., Isa 27:6), although the concept sometimes is used metaphorically (Ps 72:16). Here alone it means to "peek."

10.a. LXX adds περιστερά μου and Vg. *columba mea*, both meaning "my dove."

11.a. סתו (Q סְתָיו) is known from Jewish Aram. as well as Syr. and Arabic cognates but is a *hapax legomenon* in the OT. It may mean either "winter" or "winter rains." Cf. Lemaire, *VT* 25 (1975) 23.

12.a. Scholars and translators struggle with the question of whether זמר here has its more common meaning "song" (I זמר, "sing"), or if it is from the root II זמר, "to prune" (B. Albrektson, *BT* 47 [1996] 109–14). See *Comment* on vv 10b–13a.

14.a-a. LXX ἐχόμενα τοῦ προτειχίσματος, "clinging to an outer wall."

17.a. Interpreters are divided regarding whether סב, "turn," here means "depart" or "come back" (with LXX Syr. Vg.). Read "eat." See *Comment* on v 17.

17.b. The root בתר means to "split" or "cut in two." The phrase על־הרי בתר thus means "on the cleft mountains" (cf. *BDB* בתר). See further discussion in *Comment* on v 17.

Form/Structure/Setting

At the heart of this unit is an invitation speech-act by the man appealing for the woman to come to him and come away with him (vv 10b–14). The woman sings an introduction to his canto (vv 8–10a) and concludes the unit by answering him with words of encouragement that the two of them belong to each other and that he can love her until morning dawns. The chorus also has a brief part in this unit; at v 15 they encourage the lovers with an enigmatic line about catching foxes (see discussion below concerning the attribution of this verse to the chorus).

The two strophes that make up the first stanza parallel each other. Matching is employed in 2:8–10a to link the two strophes together as illustrated in figure 7. Line αα has בא הנה־זה, "There, he is coming," which corresponds to עומד הנה־זה, "There, behind our wall," in α'. The two lines β and ββ are matched by the two lines β' and ββ' in that both pairs have participles followed by prepositional phrases (and assonance is maintained by using four participles with the מ

preformative). Line γ begins דומה דודי, "my lover is similar," and line γ´ begins ענה דודי, "my lover spoke up," using repetition, before it breaks off for the man's lines.

"The sound of my lover!" קול דודי	α	1A
"There, he is coming," הנה־זה בא	αα	1B
"leaping on the mountains," מדלג על־ההרים	β	1C
"springing on the hills!" מקפץ על־הגבעות	ββ	1D
"My lover is similar to a gazelle," דומה דודי לצבי	γ	1E
"or the stag of the deer." או לעפר האילים	γγ	1F
"There, he is standing behind our wall," הנה־זה עומד אחר כתלנו	α´	2A
"gazing through the windows," משגיח מן־החלנות	β´	2B
"peeking through the lattices!" מציץ מן־החרכים	ββ´	2C
"My lover spoke up and said to me," ענה דודי ואמר לי	γ´	2D

Fig. 7. Matching in Song 2:8–10a

The second and third stanzas parallel each other in that each begins with a call from the man to the woman to come away (lines 3A–B and 6A–B). In the second stanza, this invitation to depart is followed by a series of strophes that describe the advent of spring. Strophe 4 describes the ending of winter, and strophe 5 describes the awakening of the flora and fauna. In the third stanza, after the invitation to depart (lines 6A–B), the man addresses the woman as a dove in the cleft of a rock. This metaphor links this stanza to the previous one, in which the turtledove's voice is heard again with the return of spring (v 12 [line 5C]). In strophe 7 (v 14), however, the image is not the harbingers of spring but the dove as a beautiful but inaccessible creature. Strophe 7 also illustrates again many of the tropes of Hebrew poetry. Line 7A is linked to 7B by matching and gapping (note the "double-duty" use of יונתי, "my dove"). Line 7C is bound to 7A–B by syntactical dependence (in this case, because 7A–B by itself is only a vocative, 7A–B depends on the imperative in 7C). Line 7D matches 7C, and line 7E depends on 7D via the subordinating particle. Line 7F matches line 7E.

The fourth stanza (v 15) has no syntactical relation to either what precedes it or what follows it, and therefore it should be treated as an independent stanza. Still, it fits well within the fifth canto, a celebration of the advent of spring and young life. The significance of this enigmatic verse is explored below.

The soprano sings the fifth stanza, and in it she resumes the metaphor of the groom as a stag on the hills. Like his stanzas, this stanza begins with a two-line strophe, then moves into a longer second strophe. Unlike his stanzas, however, which begin with imperatives and then move into lengthy explanations of the imperatives, she begins with a description of him in strophe 9 and moves into a series of inviting imperatives in strophe 10. The line division of strophe 10 calls for some explanation: lines 10A–B depend on 10C, and 10D matches (with gapping) line 10C.

Comment

8–10a The woman describes her lover as מדלג, "leaping," on the hills. This is obviously a function of the metaphor that follows, the gazelle. Leaping connotes energy and vitality, and the woman expresses her excitement with the words "The sound of my lover! There, he is coming!" The gazelle or deer implies beauty and grace as well as strength without violence (unlike, for example, the lion). Anyone who has seen a deer leaping up a mountain will readily comprehend the image of graceful power that these words evoke. The Chester Beatty Papyrus I also describes the woman's lover as a gazelle, so it was to some extent a stock metaphor. The lover is not to be regarded as a "peeping Tom." It is more likely that the peeking through the window is a function of the metaphor of the deer. The image of a young woman who is excited to see a deer outside her window is merged with the image of a young woman who is excited at the coming of her lover. He is outside כתלנו, "our wall," that is, the wall of her parents and brothers. The lover is thus a beautiful outsider, a gazelle, who comes to take her away from her childhood home. Her domestic environment, the home, is thus contrasted with the wilderness, the domain of the gazelle. The point is that the man is wooing the woman; he wants her to leave her childhood home and run with him in the wilderness—here suggesting the wilds of sexual maturity and the danger of abandoning the security of her childhood home.

10b–13a The man's lines are in two parts, each beginning with "Arise, my companion, my beautiful one, and come along!" at 10a and 13b. רעיתי, "my companion," is his usual name for her, but he calls her יפתי, "my beautiful one," only here and in v 13b. It is interesting that the man does not use the terms אחתי, "my sister," and כלה, "bride," for her at this point; these terms will dominate his words in 4:8–15.

This portion of the man's canto is a beautiful account of the coming of spring. The link between springtime and romance is natural and universal. As mentioned in *Note* 12.a., it is difficult to decide if זמיר (v 12) means "song" or "pruning." Context could incline one in either direction; the flowering of the plants in 12a favors "pruning" while the cooing of the doves in 12c favors "song." Keel ([1994] 101) contends that the pruning of vines takes place between January and March before the sap begins to rise but that the winter rains can last until the end of April. He also argues that the flowering of the plants and the emergence of young figs takes place in April or May, too late for the pruning season. Thus, he contends that זמיר means "song" here. On the other hand, it is difficult to imagine that no pruning at all took place while plants were in flower and beginning to bear fruit. In fact, Isa 18:5 explicitly asserts that the pruning and cutting of vines occurred while they were in flower. The term זמיר also appears in line 6 of the Gezer Calendar (see Gibson, *Textbook of Syrian Semitic Inscriptions*, 1.1–4), and it may be that the two occurrences illuminate one another (Lemaire, *VT* 25 [1975] 15–26). However, the meaning of the Gezer Calendar is unclear here, and it is difficult to correlate the two. The ancient versions unanimously take the word to mean "pruning" (e.g., the LXX: καιρὸς τῆς τομῆς ἔφθακεν). The meaning "pruning" cannot be excluded on horticultural grounds.

At the same time, זמיר routinely means "song" (e.g., Isa 24:16; Ps 95:2; Job 35:10), and the reference to the cooing of doves is suggestive of singing. We probably have here a case of deliberate ambiguity or double meaning. The text demonstrates this with a form of Janus parallelism; it is a time both of pruning (with 12a) and of singing (with 12c). He is continuing to woo her and to appeal to her to come out to him; spring is the time when the earth awakens, and he is seeking to awaken love in her.

13b–14 Once again the man associates his beloved with the dove, a creature that has romantic or sexual implications in the ancient Near East. Here, however, the woman herself, and not her eyes, is called a dove. He portrays her as nesting high in the crags and rocky cliffs, far away from human contact, the main point being that she is out of his reach. The motif of the woman's inaccessibility appears repeatedly in the man's songs. He cannot get to her; for them to come together, she must come out to him, or open the door to him, or descend to him. But he does not attempt to gain her by force or entrapment. His only means of attaining her are his words. He appeals to her, praises her, calls her by many pet names, and speaks fervently of the pleasures that she has the power to give.

15 This verse is often attributed either to the man or to the woman, but the plural forms אחזו־לנו, "catch for us," imply that we here have the chorus addressing the couple. It is of course possible that either the man or the woman is addressing the chorus, but this would be unusual because in the Song the man and the woman are usually the focus of the action. If the chorus is asked to do something, they are generally addressed as the "daughters of Jerusalem" (e.g., Song 5:8). It is hard to imagine, moreover, why the chorus would be asked to catch foxes for the couple. What is unacceptable, however, is to take this as a verse addressed by the man to the woman or as addressed by the woman to the man. This interpretation disregards entirely the plural form of the imperative (אחזו). Clues to the identity of the singers of the parts of the Song of Songs are few enough as it is; nothing is gained by disregarding the indications that are explicit in the text.

In the ancient world, foxes were notorious for their stealing of grapes from vineyards. In Aristophanes' *Knights* 1075–77, Demos and a sausage seller are discussing the interpretation of an oracle concerning the "dog-fox." Demos asks, "Why does the oracle then not say 'dog' instead of 'dog-fox'?" The sausage seller replies, "Because it compares the soldiers to young foxes who, like them, eat the grapes in the fields." Aristotle considered the fox to be "mischievous and crafty" (*History of Animals* 488b.1). Other classical writers also reflect this sentiment, including Pindar (*Pythian Odes* 2.75), Sophocles (*Ajax* 101), and Plato (*Republic* 365c). Images of hunting scenes on classical pottery attest to the fact that young people hunted foxes. Closer to this text, in the Papyrus Harris 500 Egyptian texts, a woman refers to her lover as her fox (on the translation, see Keel [1994] 110 n. 2; he also cites a hymn to Hathor in which wreathed young women and drunkards raise their heads to the goddess of passion and to the foxes).

Biblical texts on foxes do little to illumine the meaning of this passage. Samson caught foxes and used them to get revenge on the Philistines (Judg 15:4–5). Other texts allude to the small size of the fox (Neh 3:35 [ET 4:3]) or to its behavior as a scavenger (Ps 63:11 [ET 63:10]; Ezek 13:4; Lam 5:18). Jesus uses the fox as a metaphor for craftiness (Luke 13:32).

Some interpretations of the text are highly unlikely if not absurd. Some see a royal hunting party here and claim that the king is speaking. Apart from the fact that the use of a royal plural would be odd in the Song, a king on a hunt would not ask others to do the hunting for him, nor would concern for vineyards be his motivation. Also, classical pottery indicates that hunting foxes was the sport of boys, not kings. In the Assyrian bas-reliefs, kings hunt lions. Foxes would be puny game for a king in the ancient Near East! More preposterous yet is the interpretation of Robert Graves that foxes are a metaphor for hallucinogenic mushrooms (cited in Pope, 403). Some say that the foxes are anything that might prevent the love of the young couple from coming into full bloom or anything that might keep the woman from blossoming with all her feminine charm. Weems ("Song of Songs," 394) says they are the cunning stratagems of the lovers to consummate their relationship in secret. None of these interpretations has much to commend it, and none relates meaningfully to the rest of the Song. Gordis (82) asserts that the line should be emended to read "Little foxes have seized us." He argues that the line belongs to the woman and that she is confessing that she has already lost her virginity. But the woman never speaks of herself in the plural, and Gordis's emendation of אֶחֱזוּ (imperative form) to a perfect tense is gratuitous. Another unlikely interpretation is that of Falk (*Song of Songs*, 178), who takes the foxes to be city guards who abuse defenseless women in the streets. A more exotic interpretation is that the foxes represent the wild and untamed nature of sexuality and that this verse is a call to domesticate that power and bring it into the realm of civilized life (Landy, *Paradoxes of Paradise*, 240–41).

Some say that the foxes are boys who would deflower the girls (e.g., Murphy, 141) and that the chorus here calls for protection from such boys. This has something to commend it in that the woman does charge the girls to refrain from sexual activity (e.g., Song 2:7), and girls are represented as flowers (Song 2:1), a fact that could explain the line "Our vineyards are in bloom" in this verse. However, in Song 2:7 the girls are charged to take responsibility upon themselves to maintain their virginity; it is peculiar to see them here asking the lovers to keep boys away from them. Also, foxes go after grapes, not flowers. In short, what one finds in the interpretation of this verse is an enormous amount of guesswork, usually carried out without benefit of inquiry into how the ancients thought about foxes and grapes.

In the metaphor of Song 2:15, the chorus asks the couple to "catch the foxes" because the "vineyards are in bloom." That is, they should catch the foxes now while the vines are in flower and before the grapes begin to emerge. But this language should probably not be taken too seriously, as though it concerned a significant threat to the world of the Song. The foxes are called "little," and they are to be "caught" rather than killed (which would give the verse a more ominous tone). This verse surely reflects upon life in rural Israel. One can well imagine that, when spring arrived and the vineyards were blossoming with the young grapes beginning to form, the young people made a game of trying to catch foxes. As mentioned above, chasing foxes was a task for boys in classical Greece, and no doubt they made a game of it. For them it would have been fun, and it would have helped to insure a larger grape harvest for the farmers, but it would not have been a matter of the life and death of the community, as though the little foxes were the equivalent of a locust plague. In short, the real focus of this verse is not the *threat* posed to the vineyard but the *game* of chasing the "little foxes." The imagery of the language—the flowering of the vineyard and the role of foxes as metaphors for the playful young lovers—gives a sexual flavor to the words. The hunters have been assimilated to the hunted. The couple, like the foxes they chase, are young, excited, and full of life. It is springtime, and young people are out playing. In my view, there is nothing more to be said about the verse than that, and there is no deep symbolism that must be rooted out.

16 This simple sentiment "My lover is mine and I am his" is perhaps the most beautiful line of the Song. This looks back to the decree of Gen 2:24, "For this reason a man will leave his father and his mother and be united to his wife; and they will become one flesh" (NIV), and it looks ahead to 1 Cor 7:4, that the husband has authority over his wife's body and the wife has authority over her husband's body. True love is monogamous. It implies devotion to the other but also implies that one has the right to expect fidelity from the other.

רעה here means not to "lead cattle to pasture" but to "browse"; i.e., it refers to an animal that grazes on plants and not to a shepherd that leads an animal to graze. Its use here is a function of the metaphor of the man as a gazelle or deer. The woman describes her lover as browsing on the lotuses. The metaphor is somewhat mixed since deer were probably not known for routinely grazing among lotuses. However, as Keel ([1994] 111–15) demonstrates, the lotus was associated in Egyptian art with sexuality. Among other items, he cites a painted ivory tile from the tomb of Tutankhamen in which the queen, Ankhesenamen, stands before Tutankhamen. She holds a bouquet of lotus flowers and is wearing a diaphanous gown that is open at the middle, exposing her from the waist down. It is probably an invitation to love and indicates how the Egyptians associated the lotus with lovemaking.

17 עד שיפוח היום is literally "until the day breathes." Since breathing is associated with the force or presence of life in ancient thought (as in the varied meanings for נפש), the idea is probably of the day coming to life (i.e., sunrise). The metaphor catches how the world seems to awaken from death when the light shines, the wind begins to stir, the birds sing, and so forth.

The woman invites her lover to stay with her until morning dawns, that is, through the night. Interpreters are divided over whether ונסו הצללים, "until shadows flee," denotes sunrise or sunset, but taking it to be sunset is most unnatural. One would not normally think of the time that the whole world is engulfed in darkness as the time that shadows "flee." Some contend that the fleeing of shadows means that they are getting longer as the sun goes down, but "fleeing" has the connotation of going away, not getting larger. She is inviting him to love her all night, until the morning dawns. His enjoyment of her body is described under the metaphor of eating, like the grazing of the gazelle in v 16, but she represents the eating in more human terms when she tells him to "recline and eat."

סב has been translated as "turn" or "return," but neither makes sense in this context. It is more likely that the verb here has the same sense that it has in 1 Sam 16:11, to sit or recline at a meal; v 16 speaks of the man as a gazelle that feeds on the lotuses. Of course, gazelles do not literally lie down to eat, but this is not supposed to be a literal portrayal of the natural history of gazelles. The language of this verse melds several images, including the gazelle or deer, the taking of a meal, and making love. Reclining was a normal human way of taking a meal and also of making love. Efforts to identify a possible geographical location for the הרי בתר as the "mountains of Bether" are useless and obtuse, notwithstanding the fact that Aquila and Symmachus related it to Battir, a place conjecturally identified with Khirbet el-Yehud, about eleven kilometers southwest of Jerusalem. "Battir" as a place name appears in the Codex Alexandrinus of Josh 15:59 and 1 Chr 6:44 as $Bαιθηρ$ or $Bαιθθηρ$. The word בֶּתֶר does not appear in the MT of either of these texts, and it is doubtful that it would be written

בֶּתֶר if it were there; בְּיֶתֶר would possibly be the spelling (cf. *HALOT* בֶּתֶר III). The identification of this site with בתר of Song 2:17 should be regarded as unlikely (cf. Murphy, 139).

The root בתר refers to "splitting" something into two parts. It occurs six times in the OT, here and in Gen 15:10 (3x) and Jer 34:18–19. In the latter two texts it describes the covenant ceremony of cutting a sacrificial animal into two halves and walking between the parts. The verb (both *qal* and *pi'el*) means to split into two parts, and the noun בֶּתֶר describes the two parts, unless in Song 2:17 it refers to the fissure itself. The LXX of our text has ὄρη κοιλωμάτων, "mountains of hollow places," evidently seeing the root בתר, "to split," behind the term and referring to cleft places in the mountains. The phrase הרי בתר fairly conspicuously refers to the split between a woman's two breasts. Song 8:14 is identical to this verse except that the woman changes the name of the metaphorical mountains from "cleft mountains" to "the mountains of balsam" (הרי בשׂמים). In both texts these "mountains" describe her breasts, in Song 2:17 represented as two mountains separated or split from one another by a valley and in 8:14 portrayed as mountains fragrant with spices (referring to the woman's perfume). The man, similarly, immediately after comparing his beloved's breasts to two fawns (4:5), declares at Song 4:6 that he will get himself "to Myrrh Mountain" (הר המור) and "to Frankincense Hill" (גבעת הלבונה); using these terms, he evidently names her two "cleft mountains" individually. One need not comb the topography of the Levant for "mountains of Bether," "Frankincense Hill," or "Mountains of Balsam" to find the meaning of these verses.

Explanation

This canto should be read as the man's wooing of the woman and her positive response to him. It shows the place of words in love between a man and woman. For him to gain her affection and devotion, he must touch her soul with language. The Song of Songs is not just about sexuality and the bodies of the man and woman; it is a work of tender, affectionate speech. These motifs—the inaccessibility of the woman and the man's attempt to reach her with tender words—are another indication of how thoroughly the concept of virginity dominates the Song. In the culture of ancient Israel, virginity makes the woman unattainable to the man; he must entice her to open her heart and body to him with words of love. The two motifs dominate the man's canto in Song 3.

The woman calls the man to her breasts as a way of declaring her readiness to give him her love. In light of Prov 5:19 (to say nothing of the many references to breasts in the Song), we can hardly doubt that the Israelites focused on the female breasts as a place of sexual pleasure. In short, she responds to his invitation with an invitation of her own and signals her willingness to have him; the event itself is described in Song 4:16–5:1. In closing the fifth canto with this dramatic invitation, the woman signals her willingness to give him her love and her body. He has aroused and awakened love in her. Note, however, that this is an invitation. The text does not indicate that the couple has already consummated their relationship with sexual intercourse.

Excursus: Virginity in the Bible and the Ancient World

Bibliography

Anderson, A. A. *2 Samuel.* **Bergant, D.** "'My Beloved Is Mine and I Am His' (Song 2:16): The Song of Songs and Honor and Shame." *Semeia* 68 (1994) 23–40. **Dale, A. M.** *Euripedes: Alcestis.* **Driver, S. R.** *Notes on the Hebrew Text and Topography of the Books of Samuel.* **Matthews, V.,** and **D. Benjamin.** *Social World of Ancient Israel.* **Page, D.** *Aeschyli septem quae supersunt tragoedias.* **Roth, M.,** trans. "The Laws of Eshnunna." In *CS* 2.332–35. **Walton, J.** "עלומים." *NIDOTTE* §6596. **Wenham, G.** "B^etulah: A Girl of Marriageable Age." *VT* 22 (1972) 326–48.

This commentary suggests that the Song of Songs focuses on the marriage and sexual relationship between a young couple in love. It shows that much of the Song deals with the loss of a young woman's virginity on her wedding night. The modern reader should understand that this event was far more important and received far more attention in ancient Israel than it does in the modern West. One needs to give special attention to the significance of virginity in the ancient world and in Israel in particular.

בתולה, "virgin," does not appear in the Song. That does not mean that the idea of virginity is absent. The Song uses a wide variety of images to focus on the virginal status of the woman. In 1:6, she is under the care and control of her brothers. In 1:7, she does not want to be around men. In 2:9, she is behind a wall and a lattice. In 2:14, she is a dove out of reach and in the cleft of a rock. In 3:3, she is under the eyes of the watchmen. In 3:7, she is surrounded by a troop of warriors. In 4:4, her neck is like a fortified tower. In 4:8, she is in a lofty mountain lair. In 4:12a, she is a locked garden. In 4:12b, she is a sealed spring. In 5:2–8, she is behind an implied door. After the union of the couple, in 8:8–9, the Song discusses the proper barricading of the "little sister," but the woman of the Song declares herself to be a city at peace (8:10). The virginal status of the young woman is very much in view in Song of Songs.

For the young Israelite woman, the loss of her virginity was one of the most significant milestones of her life. Her own honor and her family's sense of honor were represented in her virginity. She and they protected it with a view toward someday entering marriage in purity, not having "played the harlot." It was the symbol of her belonging to her parents' home. It was also the sign of her independence from any outside man and of her basic goodness. Losing it *even in marriage* would be traumatic. In the texts that follow, the Song explores that sense of trauma.

The Hebrew Scriptures use a number of terms for young women and girls, including בתולה, usually "virgin"; עלמה, "young woman"; נערה, "girl"; and ילדה, "girl." The term נערה appears to mean simply a girl or young woman without any reference to her sexual history. In Judg 19:4, the concubine of the Bethlehem Levite is called a נערה. The word ילדה also seems to have no sexual connotations beyond simply giving the gender of the child. It can be used of a girl who has reached sexual maturity (Gen 34:4) or for a little child (Zech 8:5). The meaning of עלמה has been the subject of much debate in light of the fact that it is used in Isa 7:14: "Behold, a young woman [עלמה] shall conceive and bear a son, and shall call his name Immanuel" (RSV). The best solution to the meaning of the word seems to be that of Walton (*NIDOTTE* §6596): that a woman ceases to be an עלמה not when she first has sexual relations but when she becomes a mother (see Isa 54:4).

The term בתולה has received a good deal more attention since Wenham (*VT* 22 [1972] 326–48) argued that the term does not connote sexual inexperience; it simply describes a woman of marriageable age. His arguments are strongest at four texts (Esth 2:17–19; Joel 1:8; Ezek 23:3; Job 31:1) and seem to gain support from the fact that בתולה is often paired with בחור, "young man," a term that does not appear to have any reference to sexual history. The Esther text states that Esther pleased the king more than any of the other women (אשה) or any of the virgins (בתולה) of the harem. Joel 1:8 calls on the people to wail like a virgin (בתולה) who mourns for the husband of her youth. In Ezek 23:3, 8, "they handled her virgin [דדי בתוליהן] breasts" describes the apostasy of Israel and Judah under the metaphor of the promiscuous sisters. In Job 31:1, the patriarch declares that he has not looked upon a virgin (בתולה).

None of this is a convincing reason to overturn the basic idea that בתולה connotes "virgin." In Esth 2:17–19, the term בתולה is a backward reference to the group of virgins who, according to Ezek 2:2, had been assembled for the purpose of finding Ahasuerus a new queen. Ahasuerus loved Esther more than any other members of the original group of women designated as the "virgins." It does not imply that a woman who had lost her virginity would still normally be called a בתולה. The Joel text (1:8) is best understood as an engaged couple, legally married although they had not yet consummated their marriage; the plight of the young virgin who lost her "husband" before the consummation of the marriage was all the more pathetic and thus useful as an analogy in Joel's rhetoric. Similarly, the graphic language of Ezek 23:3, 8 does not mean that a sexually active girl would be called a בתולה. The point of Ezek 23 is that they *lost their virginity* with their foreign lovers, and the statement that her lovers fondled her "virgin breasts" expresses this idea in a startling but effective manner. In other words, their breasts, which had been virginal and should have remained so, are now being fondled. The Job text (31:1) tells us nothing about the meaning of the בתולה; she is a young woman whom Job asserts he has not lusted after. The choice of the word בתולה implies that he refused to contemplate taking advantage of his position as a man of power, and that he would not take away the virginity of young women.

Deut 22:13–21 has great significance for this discussion. The text concerns a man who marries a woman but who after the consummation of their marriage comes to despise her and begins to tell people that she did not come to the marriage as a virgin: "I came to her but did not find evidence of virginity" (בתולים, v 14). In response, the family of the woman was to produce the evidence of virginity (v 17). The elders of the town were to fine the man a hundred shekels for slandering the girl (v 19). If, however, the woman had in fact "acted like a prostitute" and had lost her virginity prior to her marriage, she was to be stoned to death (v 21).

Wenham (*VT* 22 [1972] 334–36) argues that the issue is that she was accused of being already pregnant by another man at the time of her wedding and that her father was to refute this charge by bringing out clothing that she had stained while menstruating in order to prove that she was not pregnant when she married. For Wenham, therefore, בתולים seems to mean "menstruation." Many scholars are persuaded by this analysis, but it is in reality quite far-fetched. The text says nothing to imply that a pregnancy is involved in the case. It is also difficult to imagine how anyone could regard a piece of a woman's clothing that she had at some time stained with her menstrual blood as proof that she was not pregnant when she got married—and Wenham provides no historical analogies for this peculiar custom he proposes. If the law did concern the kind of situation Wenham imagines, it would only apply to a woman who had become pregnant immediately prior to her marriage. A woman who had become pregnant more than a month or two before her marriage would prove her own guilt by coming to term too soon (and a woman who had been pregnant much longer than that would already be showing at the wedding). It would be highly unusual for such a detailed piece of legislation to be included in the Torah for the sake of such unusually narrow circumstances—the woman who became pregnant by another man days before her wedding.

Furthermore, usage in other texts makes it clear that בתולים means "virginity" and not "menstruation." In Judg 11:37–38, Jephthah's daughter wept over her "virginity" (בתולים) and not for her "menstruation." Lev 21:13 says that a priest must marry a woman who is in her בתולים, her virginity. The word does not mean a woman who is menstruating and is therefore able to bear children for the priest (contra Wenham, *VT* 22 [1972] 337-38). Context indicates that the concern of this text is the woman's sexual history, not her childbearing ability. It is worth reading Lev 21:13-15 in full (NRSV): "He shall marry only a woman who is a virgin. A widow, or a divorced woman, or a woman who has been defiled, a prostitute, these he shall not marry. He shall marry a virgin of his own kin, that he may not profane his offspring among his kin; for I am the LORD; I sanctify him." In context, it makes no sense to take v 13 to mean, "He shall marry only a woman who is menstruating." The "virgin" is here contrasted with "a widow, or a divorced woman, or a woman who has been defiled, a prostitute." Obviously any one of these could still be menstruating and capable of bearing children. Similarly, the point to marrying a בתולה is not that he might *have* offspring but that he might *not defile* his offspring.

The common interpretation of Deut 22:13-21 is undoubtedly correct. After a woman's wedding night, it appears that she deposited with her parents a piece of cloth stained with the blood from the rupture of the hymen. This was to serve as proof of her virginity, and its presentation to the family may have been done in ritual fashion in the presence of witnesses (see Craigie, *Book of Deuteronomy*, 292-93). Similar customs are known in other cultures (Wenham himself notes an analogy to this from Palestinian culture [*VT* 22 (1972) 334]). Of course, the presence of a blood-stained cloth was not an infallible proof that a woman was a virgin on her wedding night (and for that matter, not every woman bleeds when she loses her virginity). The real purpose of the law was not to provide absolute proof but to reinforce the necessity of maintaining the virginity of one's daughters. Note that a woman who had been promiscuous was to be stoned "at the door of her father's house" because she had been immoral while yet "living in her father's house." In short, *it is the responsibility of the paternal household to maintain the virginity of its daughters*. The maintenance of a daughter's chastity was of great significance in a culture dominated by honor and shame (see D. Bergant, *Semeia* 68 [1994] 23-40). The superficial effect of the law was no doubt that young women and their parents were careful to get and preserve the בתולים, the official proof of the girl's virginity. The intended, more significant outcome was that they would be careful to maintain her actual virginity. Also, the fact that the girl's parents preserved official evidence of her virginity deterred her husband from publicly questioning her character without strong evidence.

For our purposes, Deut 22 indicates again the enormous amount of attention that Israelite society gave to the matter of the virginity of young women. The issue can be fairly said to have governed the lives of young women and to have been a primary concern of their parents. The virginity of one of their daughters or lack of the same was their pride or their shame. (This phenomenon is also reflected in the story of the rape of Tamar by Amnon [2 Sam 13].)

The use of בתולה opposite בחור, "young man," usually occurs in a text of lamentation over the destruction of a city. For example, Amos 8:13 asserts that in the day of wrath "virgins and young men" will collapse from thirst (also Deut 32:25; Jer 31:13; Ps 78:63; 2 Chr 36:17). Of itself, the pairing of the two words really tells us nothing about whether בתולה means "virgin," but its use in these pairs is probably deliberate. The fall of a city is all the more tragic when it is viewed as entailing the deaths of young women who have not yet married as well as of the young men who would have become their husbands. The mourning of Jephthah's daughter indicates that the Israelites felt that the death of a young woman was particularly sad if she had never married. The difficulty with the word בתולה probably comes from the fact that one uses the word *virgin* specifically and only with regard to sexual inexperience. Indeed, the modern English word *virgin* has moved so far in the direction of referring *only* to sexual inexperience that one regularly hears of sexually inexperienced *males* described as "virgins," a usage that would have been unthinkable in the ancient world for בתולה, *virgo*, or παρθένος (none of which has a masculine counterpart). Biblical Hebrew uses the word בתולה in contexts where modern English would simply use the word *girl*. The same applies to the Latin *virgo* and the Greek παρθένος, which also appear often in the literature. That these languages used these terms so frequently does not mean that the words do not connote sexual inexperience. Rather, this common usage demonstrates how much the ideal of virginity dominated these societies.

The English word that probably comes closest to semantic equivalence with בתולה is *maiden*. Like בתולה, *maiden* implies that a woman is young (but not a child), single, and without sexual experience. The word does not strictly focus on sexual inexperience (as the contemporary English word *virgin* does), but it would be very peculiar or ironic to construct a sentence such as "That maiden has had sex with several men." That *maiden* has dropped out of ordinary English usage (in contrast to its much more routine usage in English texts from two or three centuries ago) reflects a cultural shift. Virginity no longer dominates our ideal for a young woman, and many people no longer regard it as the expected norm for an unmarried woman. Although the term בתולה probably does not connote clinical precision about a woman's sexual past, biblical evidence indicates that a Hebrew speaker would not refer to a woman known to be sexually experienced as a בתולה.

One should also note that the epexegetical "she had not known a man" after בתולה (e.g., Gen 24:16) does not mean that a Hebrew reader would not have thought virginity already to be implicit in the word בתולה. The epexegesis makes the point more forcefully or directly and arises from the fact that the ancients spoke of "maidens" far more frequently than we do, thus necessitating further comments if one wanted to draw attention to the *specific issue* of sexual inexperience. By contrast, "she had not known a man" is not used with a term such as נערה, "girl," without adding בתולה; otherwise, the phrase would not be epexegetical but would be introducing an entirely new idea.

Sometimes a woman is called a virgin to establish her credentials as a suitable candidate to be the wife of a young man from a good family (Gen 24:16). Levitical legislation requires that the priests take virgins rather than prostitutes, divorced women, or even widows as wives, since to do otherwise would violate the holiness of the priesthood (Lev 21:13–14). The virgin daughters of David were identified by the long-sleeved or embroidered garment that they wore (2 Sam 13:18, referring to the כתנת פסים, the same term used for the garment that Jacob gave to Joseph in Gen 37:3). The garments identified young women *in terms of their marriageability and implied lack of sexual experience*. The gap between ancient and modern Western culture in this area is quite large; there is no garment in modern society that carries the implication "virgin" for the woman who wears it.

Classical literature abounds with references to the importance attached to young women maintaining their virginity. In Aeschylus' *Suppliant Maidens* 1000–1017, Danaus appeals to his daughters (the Danaids) to maintain their virtue in the face of the lustful desires of men. He exhorts, "Honor your chastity more than your life" (τὸ σωφρονεῖν τιμῶσα τοῦ βίου πλέον [D. Page, *Aeschyli septem,* 130, line 1013]). The daughters respond that as far as the "bloom of virginity" is concerned, they will not sway from their path of virtue. In Euripides' *Alcestis* 175–79, the unhappy wife of that name who is about to give up her life for her husband looks on her bed, the place where she gave up her virginity, and laments the fact that now, because of her virtue and fidelity, she is soon to die: "O bed, where I lost my virginal maidenhood by this man for whom I die. Farewell" ('Ω λέκτρον, ἔνθα παρθένει' ἔλυσ' ἐγὼ / κορεύματ' ἐκ τοῦδ' ἀνδρός, οὐ θνῄσκω πέρι, / χαῖρ' [A. M. Dale, *Euripedes: Alcestis,* lines 177–79]). What is remarkable in this scene is that a woman who is about to die focuses her attention on the place where she lost her virginity. In short, the importance attached to a girl's keeping her virginity until marriage held enormous power in the minds of ancient peoples. It was, for Alcestis, her badge of honor and proof that she did not deserve what was to befall her. None of this is to suggest that the Greco-Roman world was particularly puritanical about sexuality—the truth lies in the other direction. Still, even this society held fervently, albeit often hypocritically, to this ideal. More than that, these examples reflect a fixation on virginity that goes far beyond what modern, Western culture practices or readily comprehends.

The world of Josephus included both OT Judaism and Greco-Roman culture. In the *Jewish Antiquities* 1.246, he retells Israelite history for the benefit of his Gentile audience. In his account of the first meeting between Rebekah and the servant whom Abraham had sent to find a wife for Isaac (Gen 24), Josephus has Rebekah introduce herself in this manner: "They call me Rebekah. My father was Bethuel, but he is dead, and Laban is my brother and, together with my mother, he takes care of all our family affairs and is the guardian of my virginity." Josephus has expanded the Genesis account of Rebekah's words, although not entirely without justification (see Gen 24:16). What is remarkable, however, is that Josephus believed that Laban's guardianship of Rebekah entailed two primary duties: he managed the family business affairs and served as guardian of her virginity. Josephus apparently felt that this understanding of Laban's role was in keeping with Jewish culture and was equally comprehensible to members of his Greco-Roman audience.

VI. Three Wedding-Night Songs (3:1–4:15)

A. Soprano: The Bride's Anxiety (3:1–5)

Bibliography

Edmée, Sister. "The Song of Songs and the Cutting of Roots." *AThR* 80 (1998) 547–61.
Lundbom, J. R. "Mary Magdalene and Song of Songs 3:1–4." *Int* 49 (1995) 172–75.

Translation

SOPRANO
1   On my bed night after night   1A
    I seek whom my soul loves;   1B
    I seek him[a] and do not find him.   1C
2   "I will arise and I will go about in the city;   2A
    in the streets and in the plazas   2B
    I will seek whom my soul loves."   2C
    I seek him and do not find him.[a]   2D
    The guards find me,   3A
    those who go about in the city: 3B
    "Have you seen whom my soul loves?"   3C
4   It is just a moment from when I turn from them   3D
    until I find whom my soul loves.   3E
    I hold him and will not let him go   3F
    until I bring him to the house of my mother,   3G
    to the chamber of my conceiver.   3H
5   I call on you to swear, daughters of Jerusalem,   4A
    by the gazelles or by the does of the field,   4B
    that you will not arouse or awaken   4C
    the passions of love until they are ready.   4D

Notes

1.a. LXX OL and some MSS of Syr. add "I called him, but he did not answer."
2.a. LXX[A + MSS] add "I called him, but he did not answer."

Form/Structure/Setting

This canto consists of four strophes. Line 1A is linked to 1B by dependence, and 1B to 1C by matching (both lines begin with בקש, "seek"). Lines 2A and 2B are joined by dependence, and the two lead into 2C and 2D, which are again bound by the repeated pair of verbs from בקש at the beginning of each line.

The third strophe is in eight lines and has several pairs of matched expressions. The verb מצא, "find," appears in 3A and 3E, the expression שאהבה נפשי,

"whom my soul loves," in 3C and 3E, and the pattern עד־שׁ, "until . . . ," with a finite verb in 3E and 3G. There are also cases of syntactical dependency: line 3C depends on 3B, line 3F depends on 3E, and line 3H matches the final phrase of 3G. These eight lines make for a long strophe, but there are a sufficient number of poetic tropes to hold them together.

The fourth strophe (four lines) is simply the adjuration formula found also in Song 2:7 and 8:4. It lacks the lines "His left hand is under my head / and his right hand embraces me" found in the other texts. The full formula is found only in Song 2:7.

The passage is bound together by a number of catchwords, including בקשׁ, "seek" (4x), מצא, "find" (4x), and סבב, "go around" (2x). The woman is the only singer in this canto; it is a solo.

This text is dominated by perfect verbs, and many translations therefore place the whole passage in the past tense. This is probably incorrect. The perfect form does not necessarily denote past action and frequently is not past action in a poetic text. In a narrative text, a sequence of past events (giving the main story line or "foreground" action) employs a chain of *wayyiqtol* forms (*vav*-consecutive imperfects). Even in a poetic text, however, a sequence of past events may be given with a string of *wayyiqtols;* the high number of *wayyiqtols* in the recounting of events in Ps 18 provides a good example of this. Here, however, there are no *wayyiqtol* forms. It is somewhat unusual for a simple recital of past events to use the perfect form exclusively, and since this text is poetic anyway, we have all the more reason to doubt that it should be translated as simple past tense. The perfect forms here focus on the action of the verbs rather than on their time frame. Further indications that this is not a narrative of some specific past event include the fact that she introduces it as an event that occurs "night after night," v 1, and the fact that she uses cohortative forms in v 2 without putting them in a past-tense framework by means of an expression such as "and so I said." The only perfect that is clearly past tense is ראיתם, which appears in a direct question ("have you seen?"), a situation in which the past tense usage of the perfect is more common.

Comment

1 בלילות means not "all night long" but literally "in the nights" or "night after night" or simply "by night." The point is that it is a regular nocturnal occurrence, not that it is an event that took place during the course of one specific night. See Fox, *Song of Songs*, 118; Murphy, 145. She seeks her lover night after night on her bed but does not find him. This indicates nocturnal yearnings for sexual fulfillment and for the companionship of a man. It should not be taken to mean that she actually expected to find her lover in her bed. What she describes, simply enough, is the desire one experiences when sleeping alone. She wants "the one whom [her] soul loves." Her words both reflect desire for the specific man whom she already loves and refer to her loneliness in bed and to her desire for affection and a husband. The *yearning and agitation* of the young woman are the actual focus here.

Today, many would translate this as "whom I love" instead of "whom my soul loves." Notwithstanding the variety of meaning that נפשׁ can have, the term "soul" should not be washed out in the translation of this idiom. Cf. Edmée, *AThR* 80 (1998) 556–61.

2 Here, she overcomes her indolent wishing and takes positive action to find her lover. This decision is comparable to Song 1:7–8 (where she wants to find her lover without having to pick at fleas among the shepherds but finds herself mildly rebuked by the chorus). The women in that text tell her that if she wants her lover, she must go where he can be found. Here, the woman of her own accord makes a move from inaction to action. The cohortative verbs in Song 3:2 (אקומה נא, ואסובבה, and אבקשה, "I will arise," "I will go about," and "I will find") are strongly assertive and connote determination: she has made up her mind to find him. She stops her idle, romantic fantasizing and actually goes after him with all the emotional risks that this action entails (again, this is all metaphorical). Her act of looking for a man in the streets and plazas of the city is comparable to the behavior of both Lady Wisdom and the prostitute in Prov 1:20–21; 7:10–13; 8:1–4. In each case, the "woman" in question is hunting for a man in order to entice him. This is of itself neither good nor evil; the character and purposes of the woman in question give the action its moral quality. The woman of the Song does not seek to instruct the man (as does Lady Wisdom) or to drag him down to Sheol (as does the prostitute); she seeks the true lover and companion for her heart.

Still, we should not take this to mean that she literally wandered the streets of the city (Lady Wisdom, too, does not literally roam the streets). Rather, the words describe a movement from a passive desire to a focused determination to bring her lover to her bed. In fantasy, the pleasures of sex are easy, uncomplicated, and come of themselves to a passive subject. In reality, sexual pleasure and the fulfillment of a relationship require effort, maturity, active participation, and a determination to overcome obstacles. For a woman to comb the streets alone at night would require great determination; as a metaphor, her action is a coming of age.

Many myths describe a *quest* in which the protagonist puts himself at risk by going outside of the security of home or civilization in order to obtain the object of his desire. Often, the quest itself is part of the process of transformation of the protagonist. From the ancient Mesopotamian world, the most famous quest legend involved Gilgamesh who, after the death of his friend Enkidu, sought the plant of eternal youth in the sea (he found it only to lose it again). Greek mythology has many journeys and quests, such as the story of Jason, the hero who with the Argonauts sailed to Colchis to obtain the golden fleece. Another great but failed quest was that of Orpheus, who journeyed to Hades and almost succeeded in bringing his wife, Eurydice, back with him.

The woman of the Song shows herself to be the true protagonist of Song of Songs by metaphorically embarking on a heroic journey. The wandering in the streets of Jerusalem represents the ideal of the quest. Reading these lyrics as actual events misses the deeper point. The woman takes upon herself the responsibility of nurturing her love by courageous determination to take the man to herself. Nevertheless, she does not immediately find him; she must first deal with the guards of the city.

3 The appearance of the guards is altogether unanticipated. מצאוני השמרים, "the guards find me," appears immediately after ולא מצאתיו, "but I do not find him," without even a particle to provide transition. Also, the audience has no prior knowledge of the existence of the guards. The suddenness with which they enter the Song is only one aspect of the enigma they pose for the interpreter, however. All we know about them is that in this verse they find the woman and she asks them where her lover can be found, and that in Song 5:7 they again find her but on that occasion beat her, injure her, and take away her veil. It is also noteworthy that Egyptian love poetry and ancient sexual imagery have no analogy for the guards of the Song.

Clearly Song 3:3 and 5:7 are bound together. Already, here in 3:3, we have reason to suppose that the guards represent the virginity of the woman. An ancient city was a "virgin" (cf. Lam 2:13; Isa 47:1). The woman of the Song, moreover, is characterized as a city (Song 6:4, where she is compared to Tirzah and Jerusalem). For an ancient reader, conditioned to think of a young marriageable woman in terms of her virginity, the notion that the "guards" of the "city" represent the woman's virginity would not be far-fetched at all. In light of Song 5:7, it is fairly certain that the guards represent her virginity. It simply makes no sense to have a love song in which the leading lady is physically assaulted. More than that, no one in the Song finds it surprising that the woman has been beaten; the Song implies no astonishment or outrage at the event. The "guards" themselves are strikingly impersonal. They have no appearance, no emotion, no words, no weapons, no fists, no faces, and no names. In short, they do not appear to be persons at all. If we are expected to understand that the woman literally met guards on two occasions and on one occasion was assaulted, we would expect her to say something more about the perpetrators, if only to make the experience more vivid for the reader and provoke more sympathy for the victim. The account is not coherent unless the suffering she received from the guards itself is symbolic and represents something else. For further discussion, see the *Comment* on 5:7 below.

On the other hand, the difference between how the guards treat her here and how they treat her in 5:7 is also conspicuous. In 5:7, the guards simply assault her; there is no indication of an interview of any kind. Here, she asks them for help in finding her lover. They do not respond, but neither are they hostile. They are simply mute. What can this mean? It is again hopeless to try to resolve this difference on a literal level, as though actual guards in the first encounter stood by dumbly but in the second encounter were suddenly, irrationally hostile. As a symbolic series of events, however, the encounter of 3:3 is laden with meaning. First, the guards abruptly come upon her as she seeks her lover. That is, as she yearns for her lover, the brute fact of her virginity suddenly presents itself before her mind. Second, she asks the guards if they have seen her lover. That is, she looks on her virginity as a key to finding her lover. Without virginity, she will not be able to obtain him, virginity being the *sine qua non* for marriage in ancient Israel (except in the case of widows). Nevertheless, the guards themselves do not show her the way to her lover. They are silent and (at this point) passive.

4 As the third step in the sequence, she turns from the guards and immediately finds her lover. The verbs here are remarkable. The verb rendered "turn from" is עבר, which connotes crossing a barrier or boundary. She then seizes (אחז) her lover and will not loosen (רפה) her grip. The language is dramatic and speaks of determination, decision, and steadfastness. She has in her mind stepped across a border. She has turned away from her virginity and instead clings tightly to her lover. That is, she has chosen him over her virginity.

More than that, she is determined to take him to the house and chamber of her mother, the one who conceived her. The term הורתי, "my conceiver," here is used to match to אִמִּי, "my mother." A similar parallel appears in Hos 2:7 (ET 2:5). These are the only two texts that use the *qal* feminine participle of הרה. This idea is also quite difficult if taken literally. It seems quite clear that her desire is for sexual relations with the man (in that she holds him tightly), but we can scarcely imagine that a decent Israelite maiden would drag the man she wants to her mother's home for a night of sex. Such an understanding of the situation is highly anachronistic. Of course, one could argue that by taking him to her mother's house she only means that she will take him to her mother in the sense of formally declaring her intent to marry the man. If so, this line would only mean that she wants to declare her willingness to marry him. In Song 8:2, however, a text that certainly comes after the consummation of their relationship (Song 4:16–5:1), she again declares that she will take him to her mother's house. There, she is undoubtedly describing her intent to have sexual relationships with her husband (see *Comment* on 8:2), and it is unlikely that the terms in 3:4 have a different meaning. More than that, the focus of Song 3:1–5 is on her passionate desire for the man as she seeks him from her bed; it is not concerned with fulfilling wedding protocol. It is very peculiar at any rate to imagine that she would jump out of bed, find him wandering in the city, and bring him home to her mother for an official wedding announcement.

Therefore, the mother's בית, "house," and the חדר, "room," of the woman who conceived her are again representative terms. They can only be the womb; this is the house and room where all are conceived. She is determined to bring her lover into her maternal chamber, so to speak. More than that, the woman identifies with her mother in the matter of confrontation with the loss of virginity. Her mother, in effect, has become a role model for her and gives her the strength to face this event (see also *Comment* on 8:2).

We should finally note that the character of the man is hardly part of the episode at all. We are given no explanation for why he was lost to the woman in the first place, and when she finds him, he says nothing and he does nothing. This only adds to the sense of unreality in this canto and further indicates that the real "story" takes place in the mind and emotional struggles of the woman.

5 The woman abruptly calls on the Jerusalem girls not to arouse sexual passion until the proper time arrives (see Song 2:7). As part of the sequence of 3:1–5 this is a non sequitur; it makes little sense for her to be in the process of dragging the young man to her mother's house and then abruptly turn and give an admonition on sexual morals to her friends. (Did they suddenly appear out of nowhere, too?) But this problem is irrelevant so long as one does not read this as a literal series of events. The woman is not at this point actually taking her young man for a night of love. Rather, she has in her mind confronted the issue of her virginity and has resolutely decided to take her lover rather than retain her virginity. Understood in this way, the sudden charge to the Jerusalem girls suits the context perfectly. She is in effect saying that this is a very big decision and that her friends should not rush into it. Wait for the right time and right man, she suggests.

Explanation

The motif of this canto is the yearning of the young woman for her lover. The structure is simple: in vv 1–4 she seeks and finds her lover, and in v 5 she repeats her charge to the girls of Jerusalem to avoid sexual activity until the proper time.

The interpretation of this passage is much debated. Dramatic and historical readings of the Song often take it literally. This entails an obvious difficulty that most such commentaries fail to deal with: it implies that she is still living with her mother and thus is unmarried. An unmarried girl who roamed the streets looking for her lover and then dragged him home (apparently for sexual purposes) does not seem like the woman we want for the heroine of the book. The fact that the guards of the city beat her up in the parallel passage (Song 5:2–8) hardly helps things. In a canto where virtually every line is metaphorical, it is odd that readers would even try to defend a literal reading of this bizarre episode.

In addition, several commentators have noted that it is unlikely that an Israelite maiden would be roaming the streets of the city at night. Such a girl would likely be taken as a prostitute (Hos 2:7; Prov 7:10). It is true that Ruth went out at night to the threshing floor to find Boaz (Ruth 3), but this was in a rural village (Bethlehem) and not in the city of Jerusalem. Besides that, Ruth was not wandering around looking for Boaz; she knew precisely where he was. In light of the burden Deut 22:13–21 places on parents with respect to their daughters' virginity, it is unlikely that they would allow them to wander the streets in the middle of the night (much less allow them to bring their lovers home with them!).

This passage is often described as a dream (e.g., Rudolph, 137–38; Gledhill, *Message*, 143–46), primarily because of the self-evident absurdity of the details that the text gives (that the event happened night after night, that she would go out wandering at night, that she would expect the guards to know who her lover was, that she would suddenly find her lover, and so forth). More recent commentators, however, have abandoned the "dream" strategy in dealing with the text because calling this text a dream is really no interpretation at all. It is in effect saying that in a dream anything can happen and dreams often make no sense anyway, and that therefore the reader is under no obligation to try to comprehend the odd goings-on of this text. More significantly, the text never implies that this is a dream.

Cultic interpretations of the Song relate this text to Anat seeking Baal or to Ishtar seeking Tammuz. Supposed parallels include the fact that Ishtar had to parley with the guards of seven gates in her descent to the underworld and that Anat sought the aid of Shapsh, the sun goddess, in her search for Baal (see Pope, 419–22). None of this, however, is sufficient to convert this text into a cultic document. The woman is not a goddess and the man is not a god, and he is neither dead nor in danger.

The only coherent interpretation of this text is that it represents the mental anxiety of the woman as she goes through the process of preparing to become a wife. Alone at night, she yearns for her lover. As she mentally seeks him out and contemplates a physical relationship with him, she confronts her own virginity. She knows she cannot have him without going through the event of losing her virginity. Nevertheless, she resolves to take him to herself. She does not view this decision as a trivial matter, and she closes the canto by admonishing her friends to hold on to their virginity until they are certain that the proper time has come. The parallel event, Song 5:2–8, describes not her anxiety over the loss of her virginity but the event itself. The message of Song 3:1–5 appears to be that the virgin who has not faced the emotions of this issue prior to her wedding night is not prepared for marriage.

B. Chorus: The Bride Comes to the Groom (3:6–11)

Bibliography

Beare, F. W. *Gospel according to Matthew.* **Davies, W. B.,** and **D. C. Allison.** *Gospel according to Saint Matthew.* **Dirksen, P. B.** "Song of Songs 3:6–7." *VT* 39 (1989) 219–25. **Driver, G. R.** "Supposed Arabisms in the Old Testament." *JBL* 55 (1936) 101–20. **Epstein, I.** *Hebrew-English Edition of the Babylonian Talmud: Seder Nashim.* **Garrett, D. A.** *Hosea, Joel.* **Gundry, R. H.** *Matthew.* **Jeremias, J.** *Parables of Jesus.* **Schweizer, E.** *Good News according to Matthew.*

Translation

CHORUS
6 Who is this	1A
coming up from the wilderness	1B
like columns ᵃ of smoke	1C
when there is a fragrant burning ᵇ of myrrh and frankincense,	1D
the best of exotic fragrances?	1E
7 Oh, it is his palanquin! The one that belongs to Solomon!	1F
Sixty warriors are about it,	2A
the elite of the warriors of Israel!	2B
8 All of them are skilled with swords	2C
and trained in warfare.	2D
Each man has his sword at his side	2E
because of the terrors of the night.	2F
9 The king made a sedan chair for himself;	3A
Solomon made it from the wood of Lebanon.	3B
10 He made its pillars of silver	3C
and its canopy framework of gold.	3D
Its seat is purple,	3E
and its interior is fitted together—this is love!	3F
Daughters of Jerusalem, ¹¹ come out!	4A
And look, O daughters of Zion,	4B
at King Solomon with his crown—	4C
the one with which his mother crowned him	4D
on the day of his wedding,	4E
on the day his heart was full of joy.	4F

Notes

6.a. MT כתימרות, "like columns of." α´ reads כתמונה, "like a form of." Syr. reads כעטרת, "like abundance of." Read MT.

6.b. MT מקטרת is a fem. *puʿal* ptc.: "being burned." α´ Vg. Tg. read an act. ptc. with the prep. מן: "from the burning of."

Form/Structure/Setting

The chorus alone sings this canto; there are no parts for the tenor or soprano. This canto is unified and gives no indication of exchanges among two or more singers and thus should not be divided into several parts. Fox (*Song of Songs,* 119–27) argues that v 6 belongs to the chorus but that vv 7–11 is the woman's portrayal of her beloved, but this is not persuasive. Since the woman's arrival is the object of all the attention in this canto, she obviously is not the singer. The tenor also is a poor choice to be the singer of this part; it is unbecoming for a man to be calling excitedly for the girls of the city to come out and have a look at his beloved or at "Solomon." He never does anything like this elsewhere in the Song. One might object to assigning these lines to the chorus on the grounds that in vv 10–11 they summon the girls of Jerusalem to come out, and therefore the singers are thus not themselves the girls of Jerusalem. But this objection is flimsy; the chorus is not all of the Jerusalem girls but a small, representative group. The people who are most likely to call out girls to come see a spectacle are other girls.

This canto has four strophes of six lines each, for twenty-four lines in total. Lines 1A and 1B could be taken to be a single line, but the parallels in Song 6:10 and 8:5 (the other places where מי זאת, "Who is this?" appears) work best with מי זאת taken as a separate line. In both 6:10 and 8:5 the מי זאת is followed by a series of matching lines (with participles). Here, מי זאת is followed by a single participle line, but it seems best to maintain the structural parallel with the other texts. In the first strophe, 1A is answered by 1F, and 1B–E is epexegetical of זאת, "this," describing the entourage of the woman whom they see approaching.

The second strophe has somewhat the same structure as the first. Line 2A focuses the attention on the sixty soldiers, and 2F answers the unstated but obvious question, "Why are the sixty soldiers there?" with the line, "because of the terrors of the night." In between, lines 2B–E are epexegetical of the sixty warriors, giving their characteristics.

The third strophe is also descriptive; it announces in 3A that the king made the palanquin and proceeds to describe in 3B–F its materials and features. But 3F ends with a strange twist, concluding with the word אהבה, "love," standing alone. Following the analogy of the structure of the first two strophes, this would seem to be an answer to the unstated question, "What is the palanquin's name?" Or, "What is its purpose?"

The last strophe is a six-line unit. It is structurally different in that it begins with two lines that employ matching, calling the girls to come out and see a spectacle (4A–B). Lines 4C–D are joined by words with the root עטר, "crown," and a dependence on 4B. Lines 4E–F are held together by repetition, with both lines beginning with ביום, "on the day," and by their dependence on 4D.

This is an arrival song celebrating the appearance of a bride and groom at a wedding. The woman is brought to the man in a sedan chair (vv 6–10), and he, wearing a crown, comes outside of the wedding house to await her arrival (v 11). It is important to note that it is the woman and not the man who rides in the palanquin (contrast Murphy, 151).

Comment

6 The phrase מִי זֹאת means "Who is this (woman)?" Many scholars argue that context indicates that a man is at the center of the sight on the basis of v 11. In reality, however, the text never indicates that the "Solomon" of v 11 is in the palanquin of vv 6–10. The fact that v 7 says that it is Solomon's palanquin, moreover, does not mean that he is inside. It is true that זֹאת can be a neutrum, a feminine pronoun with a vague or undefined reference (*IBHS*, 692), and one might suggest that the word refers to the whole spectacle that is approaching and not to a single person. A problem with this interpretation is that the text does not have מַה־זֹּאת, "What is this?" as in Exod 13:14; it reads מִי זֹאת, "Who is this?" implying that the feminine pronoun is indeed a person. The phrase מִי זֹאת appears elsewhere in the Hebrew Bible only at Song 6:10 and 8:5, and in both of these the object of attention is the woman.

The simplest solution is that the woman is in the palanquin (v 6) and that the man is awaiting her arrival (v 11). See also P. Dirksen, *VT* 39 (1989) 219–25. The chorus exclaims that she is coming up מִן־הַמִּדְבָּר, "from the the wilderness," with what seem to be columns of smoke. For the biblical reader, this language immediately connotes the wanderings in the wilderness with the Shekinah in the form of a "pillar of cloud." The language is not precisely the same. The word for "column" here (תִּימְרָה) is not used of the pillar of cloud in the exodus narrative (עַמּוּד הֶעָנָן; e.g., Exod 13:22). The text is describing not a theophany but the wedding party. Still, the visual image is reminiscent of classic theophany language. We should also note that they arrive specifically from the "wilderness." Against G. L. Carr (108), מִן־הַמִּדְבָּר should here be rendered "the wilderness" and not "the desert." The latter is misleading and misses the significance of the wilderness motif. The historic, literary, and religious connotations of the wilderness are driving this language. The mention of wilderness does not mean that it literally figured significantly either in Solomon's life or the wedding rituals of ancient Israel. From a canonical and literary standpoint, the wilderness is highly significant (see Garrett, *Hosea, Joel*, 88–91). The wilderness is the place of Israel's sojourn with God, and from the wilderness Israel came into Canaan to seize the land of promise. It was there also that Moses resided during his years of formation and there that he had his mystical experience with the burning bush. Wilderness almost connotes images of Eden: Hosea invokes wilderness as the place of divine wooing, where God would win back the heart of the woman Israel (Hos 2:16 [ET 2:14]). Keel ([1994] 126) observes that both Ashtarte and Ishtar were goddesses of the wilderness. This canto speaks of the arrival in these terms in order to endow the event with grandeur and wonderment. Like the armies of Israel or like God himself, the entourage appears from the wilderness with clouds of glory.

The pillar of smoke that the chorus sees may be dust kicked up by the entourage, dust that looks like columns of smoky incense, or it may actually be clouds of incense. The word קטר describes the burning of a sacrifice of an animal or of incense to send it up in smoke. The word could imply that the coming spectacle is heavily perfumed by the burning of various forms of incense. Alternatively, it may mean that the approaching troop is kicking up a column of dust that looks like a cloud of smoke sent up by incense; but even if this is the meaning, the metaphor of incense is still significant for the sense of opulence and pleasure it provokes. Against many modern translations, rendering מקטרת simply as "perfumed" without reference to smoke or burning is misleading since this would seem to imply that the individuals involved had merely splashed on some cologne. קטר implies the burning of a fragrant powder. מקטרת is not in apposition to זאת, "this," although it may be feminine singular by attraction to that pronoun. If it were in apposition to זאת, that would imply that the thing that זאת refers to (whether it be the woman or the whole spectacle) was being burned up as a sacrifice, which is not the case. It is the fragrant resins, myrrh, and frankincense, and not the wedding party, that are being burned up. Myrrh (מור) is a masculine noun and usually is used as a fragrant ointment rather than as an incense for burning. Frankincense (לבונה), however, is feminine and is used for such purposes (e.g., Lev 2:2), and the gender of מקטרת may be determined by לבונה. Burning up myrrh and other exotic powdered resins is a measure of how extravagant and opulent this scene is.

מכל אבקת רוכל is literally "from every powder of a merchant," but it probably refers to fragrances that could not be locally manufactured and for which one had to go to an importer. Thus they were "exotic." The מ in מכל is partitive and implies that only the best incense is being used.

It is obviously unrealistic to suppose that a group of women viewing an approaching entourage from a distance could detect the presence of specific spices and incense. But the actual nature of the cloudy pillars and the literal limits to human sensation are not at issue here. Elsewhere in the Bible burning incense occurs in a context of sacred worship (e.g., Exod 30–31; Lev 2:1–2; Num 7). For an audience living in this culture, incense would connote the mystery, awe, and indeed the pleasure of worship and the holy. Here, by drawing upon the connotations of incense, the Song directs that awe toward human love.

7 The meaning of מטה as "palanquin" or "litter" in conjunction with אפריון, "sedan chair," in v 9 is fairly well established even though the etymology of אפריון is uncertain. G. L. Carr (111) takes the two words to refer to two different objects, but this is improbable. The word מטה basically means "bed," but context demands that it be some kind of royal litter here since, according to v 6, it is coming up from the wilderness. See also Gerleman (138). This plainly could not be a fixed bed. Fox (*Song of Songs*, 125–27) tries to separate v 6 from vv 7–11 and so argue that מטה and אפריון describe a fixed bed rather than a palanquin. Fox's linguistic arguments that אפריון is a fixed bed are unpersuasive. Scholars sometimes relate אפריון to the Sanskrit *paryanka* ("palanquin"; cf. BDB) or to the Greek φορεῖον, "litter." The LXX has φορεῖον, and the Vulgate has *ferculum*, "bier, litter," telling us at least how the ancients understood this term. Even without v 6, moreover, it is hard to see how the אפריון or מטה could here be a bed. If that were the meaning, the girls of Jerusalem would not be invited to come and have a look at it (as though they could invade Solomon's private chambers, v 11). The image of sixty warriors standing around his מטה is equally jolting if we take that to be the bed he sleeps in (with a woman!).

The grammar here is somewhat awkward; thus the translation "Oh, it is his palanquin! The one that belongs to Solomon!" The style befits an excited exclamation and sudden recognition, like that of a modern teenager unexpectedly encountering a celebrity. The sixty warriors are a kind of honor guard. The מן in

מגברי, "of the warriors," is partitive and implies men chosen from the warriors of Israel—i.e., elite troops of an honor guard. Scholars have observed that the number is twice that of David's guard, thirty (2 Sam 23:18–19). If the doubling is intentional, it is probably a hyperbole meant to imply that this spectacle is glorious beyond description. In reality, a bridal procession in a normal wedding probably was accompanied by some friends of the groom, but the royal trappings here add further spectacle to the scene.

8 The phrase אחזי חרב is literally "seized of the sword." Today many scholars take it to mean "skilled with the sword" in parallel to מלמדי מלחמה, "trained in war." The Akkadian cognate *aḫāzu*, "learn," and the Ugaritic *aḥd ḥrṯ*, "skilled in plowing," support this; see Pope (435) for further discussion.

The military prowess and preparedness of the guard again adds to the splendor of the scene, but one wonders if there is more to it than military trappings in light of the odd note that they are armed against the "terrors of the night." Scholars regularly relate this to superstition about a jealous demon who would kill either the bride or the groom on the wedding night (as in Tobit 6:14–18). For a full discussion of this, see Pope (435–40). Such superstition is found nowhere else in the Song, however, and employing soldiers to ward off demons is at any rate rather odd. Certainly no one would want sixty soldiers standing around his bed on his wedding night, as some interpretations seem to suggest. I have theorized that the guards of the city in Song 3:1–5 refer to the woman's virginity. While the warriors of this text are probably not strictly a metaphor for her virginity, the image may connote some of the same ideal. The woman must be delivered pure and safe to the man. The terrors of the night are ambiguous, but it is significant that they are of the "night." This is the time of love, but it is also the time of treachery, stealth, ambush, and rape. The woman is protected so that she may come safely to her night with the groom.

All in all, the text may reflect an actual custom of ancient Israelite weddings, that the bride was escorted by an honor guard of local men (perhaps her brothers, or the friends of the groom). The need for the guard was more symbolic than real, but they had the function of delivering the woman to her wedding safe and sound.

9 At first reading, it seems surprising that the focus of the text is on the sedan chair and the entourage rather than on the bride or groom. The reason is that this canto celebrates the glories of love itself, and of the wedding, rather than the specific individuals involved. As described above, the allusion to "Solomon" adds splendor to the canto and elevates a wedding to the status of a royal event.

10 It is very difficult to be certain about what parts of the palanquin are being described. Still, it is clear that this is an extravagantly expensive piece of work. עמודיו, "its pillars," refers to posts that hold up a canopy over the sedan chair. רפידה is a *hapax legomenon*, but it seems to be related to רפד, "to spread out." I take it to be the framework that supports a canvas canopy over a sedan chair. If correct, this probably means that the wooden framework that supported the canopy had an overlay of gold. Of itself, תוך means "middle," but here it evidently refers to some part of the interior of the sedan chair. Although a *hapax legomenon*, it seems fairly clear that רצוף means "inlaid" or "fitted." Murphy (149) observes that Akkadian and Syriac parallels support this interpretation. The noun רִצְפָה in Ezek 40:17–18 means "pavement," and thus רָצַף would seem to describe the joining of objects together. The LXX actually has λιθόστρωτον, "pavement," here in the Song.

The significance of אַרְגָּמָן, "purple," is that the item in question was made of material dyed purple with the secretions from certain mollusks found in the eastern Mediterranean (any one of four species of mollusks could be used). Tyre and Sidon were the principal sources of this material. The color was highly prized, and items colored with this dye were extravagantly expensive (it required some eight thousand mollusks to produce a single gram of this dye, according to *ISBE* 3:1057, "purple"). It goes without saying that one would not normally use this dye for upholstery.

The significance of אַהֲבָה, "love," is obscure here. Numerous scholars propose emendations. Fox (*Song of Songs,* 126) emends to אֲבָנִים, "stones." While אבנים can refer to precious stones (often with a modifier), this seems an awfully flat term to use in a book that revels in its rich vocabulary. The word אבנים normally just refers to rocks. At any rate, evidence for this emendation is wanting. Murphy (149) notes that some scholars emend to הָבְנִים, "ebony." This makes better sense than "stones," but it too suffers from being purely conjectural. G. R. Driver (*JBL* 55 [1936] 111) suggested that אַהֲבָה here means "leather" on the basis of an Arabic cognate, but this suggestion has found little favor with scholars. In short, no emendation is fully persuasive. If, however, one is willing to understand an implied preposition such as בְּ with אַהֲבָה, one might take it to mean, "inlaid with (the word) love," or one might regard "love" to be the metaphorical material from which this part of the palanquin is made. Some scholars suggest that the interior of the palanquin is inlaid with ivory tiles depicting erotic motifs, but there is no parallel for using אַהֲבָה in this way. Even granting the possibility that Hebrew would employ an abstract term like "love" to denote erotic art, the word used would almost certainly be דֹּדִים and not אַהֲבָה. Although poetry does drop particles and prepositions, it is not clear that this is the case here. Also, there is little warrant for translating it adverbially as "lovingly" (NASB, NIV).

No emendation or rendition of the text is convincing or able to gain wide acceptance. I therefore suggest that "its interior is fitted together" is used absolutely. This line refers only to the quality of the craftsmanship of the vehicle and says nothing about the materials used, much less about any graphical art. That is, the pieces of the sedan chair are not fastened together with nails, ropes, or other materials but by means of carefully carved interlocking joints. This understanding of רִצְפָה is appropriate given what we know of the word. If this is correct, then the word אַהֲבָה stands alone, without any clear grammatical link to any other word in the passage. If this is the case, then אַהֲבָה, "love," might be read to be a kind of suspended predicate in apposition to the entire account. That is, the whole entourage is called "love" because the gorgeous and opulent palanquin, the fragrance of the incense, and the royal guard together depict the meaning of the event. A profound marvel—the love of a man and a woman—is being honored in the ceremony. If this usage of אַהֲבָה seems peculiar, one should note that later the man, in the middle of an extensive *wasf* on the manifold beauty of the woman, declares her to be אהבה בתענוגים, "love with the delights" (Song 7:7 [ET 7:6]).

The way the text draws upon the language of theophany and worship lends credibility to this interpretation. The materials of the sedan chair—wood from

Lebanon, silver, and gold—together with the fact that Solomon "made" it, forces the thoughtful reader to recall the building of the temple (1 Kgs 5–6). The purple fabric recalls the fabric of the tabernacle (e.g., Exod 35). The sedan chair is almost a kind of shrine or an ark of the covenant. But the woman inside is not deified or made an object of worship. The text says nothing about the woman and almost nothing about the man. All attention is on the spectacular and opulent entourage, where אהבה, "love," is honored as a wonderful and mysterious gift.

מבנות ירושלם: Because of the preposition מן, translations often render this as "by the daughters of Jerusalem." It is better, however, to treat the מ as an emphatic, enclitic מ with אהבה, "love," in the previous line and leave it untranslated. See Pope (446) and Murphy (150). Even if the מ were taken to represent the preposition מן here, it still would not follow that מבנות ירושלם must be linked to line 3F. The מן could be taken as a partitive. Either way, the phrase is vocative; it goes with the exhortation that follows in v 11 and is matched by בנות ציון, "daughters of Zion," in line 4B.

11 The chorus calls on the girls of Jerusalem to come out and view "Solomon" but says little about the man himself. Instead, their words draw attention to (1) the crown he wore on his wedding, (2) his mother, and (3) the joy that filled his heart at his wedding. As suggested already, "Solomon" here is not a character in a story but serves as a symbol of regal majesty, a quality that every groom (ideally) partakes of.

The עטר, "crown," here is not necessarily a crown of state but may be some kind of wedding garland. Even if it were a wedding garland, however, the fact that it is on Solomon's head gives it royal status. In effect, the wearing of the wedding garland gives every groom such status. If postbiblical Jewish customs are a guide, it is likely that Israelite grooms at this time wore wedding crowns and that their brides were in fact brought to them on palanquins. *B. Soṭah* 49a begins (Epstein edition translation, 1985): "During the war with Vespasian they [the rabbis] decreed against [the use of] crowns worn by bridegrooms and against [the use of] the drum. During the war of Quietus they decreed against [the use of] crowns worn by brides and that nobody should teach his son Greek. During the final war they decreed that a bride should not go out in a palanquin in the midst of the city, but our rabbis permitted a bride to go out in a palanquin in the midst of the city." See also 3 Macc 4:8 and *m. Soṭah* 9:14. Of course, it is possible that these practices were derived from Song 3:5–11, but in light of how obscure this passage is, it is more likely that the Song alludes to an ancient practice than it is that a later custom grew out of the Song.

This text also implies that the mother of the groom placed the wedding garland on his head. The historical mother of Solomon was the famous Bathsheba. It is difficult for the informed biblical reader to encounter this text and not recall her history with David, although it is unlikely that David's notorious crimes are the point of this allusion. Nevertheless, recollection of the story brings to mind that Bathsheba had been a woman who bathed on the roof and who by her alluring beauty almost brought down a king. Although now given the ceremonial task of crowning her son at his wedding, she had once been a woman of powerful sexuality. The mother, the very image of domesticity, had once been an alluring woman. Elsewhere, the Song presents the sexual experience of the man and the woman as a renewal of the experience of their mothers (Song 8:2,

5). They would complete the circle by entering the mystery through which they had themselves been engendered by their mothers. Also, the presence of the mother at the wedding is a reminder that in ancient Israel a wedding was not simply a private matter between a man and a woman but also involved the extended families, and in particular the family of the groom.

The joy of "Solomon" at his wedding reminds the audience of the celebratory nature of the event. The joy is not simply a matter of the impending wedding night but is also a result of the exaltation of the bride and groom and of love itself. The young women of the city are called out to experience the excitement.

Explanation.

The marriage of a man and woman is here represented as an event that is both regal and divine. Of themselves, the man and woman are ordinary mortals, but the ceremonial bringing of the bride to the groom exalts both of them to the status of royalty. One might suggest that a marriage reenacts the story of Gen 2, when God brought the woman to Adam, the first "king." It reminds us of the ideal that we were intended to fulfill and of this creation miracle, the union of man and woman, that was not altogether spoiled by the fall. The ceremonial trappings of the entourage convey the reality that the joining of man and woman is a thing of great glory. It is a celebration of love.

The fact that we have here a canto about a bride's arrival does not mean that Song of Songs was performed at weddings or that it was the text of a wedding liturgy. Rather, the Song seems to draw on the wedding rituals of ancient Israel in order to orient the audience to what was happening in the course of the songs. That is, by inserting a canto on the arrival of a bride, the poet tells the audience that the Song is moving toward the consummation of the marriage of the man and woman.

A distinctive motif of this canto is the abundance of royal trappings. The bride arrives in a lavish sedan chair belonging to the groom, the entourage has a large military escort, and the man is called a king. Twice the text refers to "Solomon." Even so, this does not establish either that the Song of Songs describes actual events from the life of Solomon or that Solomon is a character in the Song. Instead, "Solomon" is just as much a lyrical motif as is the stag, the vineyard, or the shepherd. Some scholars speak of the groom as playing the role of Solomon. This is not inaccurate, but it is perhaps more precise to say that Solomon functions as a metaphorical figure who brings out aspects of the ideal bridegroom. The motif of the gazelle in Song 2:9 portrays the beauty, grace, and vigor of the idealized young man; the figure of Solomon presents him as magnificent—a king who greets the arrival of a bride when she comes in the palanquin and with the entourage that he has provided. A groom on his wedding day is thus a virtual king in that he is elevated above his companions, dressed more splendidly than any other man, and gives a royal reception to his bride. On this one day, a young man is a "Solomon in all his glory" (Matt 6:29 RSV).

An interesting parallel to what happens here is in Jesus' parable of the wise and foolish virgins (Matt 25:1–13; against some interpreters [e.g., Schweizer, *Good News according to Matthew*, 466] I consider the entire parable to be dominical [cf. Davies and Allison, *Gospel according to Saint Matthew*, 392–94]). In that passage, ten virgins (παρθένοι) remain outside waiting for the arrival of a groom. He is evidently expected to appear sometime during the evening since the girls who will receive him all have torches (this is probably preferable to "lamps"; see Gundry, *Matthew*, 498–500 for a discussion of this issue), and actually he does not show up until the middle of the night. At that point, someone in the distance shouts that he is approaching, and the girls scurry about to get their torches prepared and accompany him into the house. Only those girls with burning torches are recognized to be part of the wedding party and are admitted. Jeremias (*Parables of Jesus*, 172–74) argues on the basis of nineteenth-century accounts of Palestinian weddings that this picture is not an artificial construct but that in all essential details is an accurate portrayal of what happened in weddings of ancient Judea. Even so, Jesus' parable leaves a great deal out, including information about where the groom was going, where the bride was at the time, and at what stage of the wedding celebration all this took place. Beyond the information Jeremias has documented, details relevant to the wedding customs described in the parable are lost to us. F. W. Beare (*Gospel according to Matthew*, 480) notes that NT scholars are reduced to conjectural reconstructions of wedding customs of this period in order to interpret the text.

There were almost 1,900 years between the Palestinian weddings Jeremias describes and the NT, and a considerable space of time (some 900 years, in my estimation) between the NT and the composition of the Song. Still, comparison is useful. In both the Song and the NT, a group of young, unmarried women announces and greets an arriving party. In Matthew, the bridegroom arrives; here, it is the bride. In contrast to the parable, the palanquin with the bride approaches during the day (as is established by the observation that people can see a column of smoke or dust at a distance, v 6). We also have no indication that the girls in the Song have torches. On the other hand, the customs described in the Song (that the woman comes riding in a palanquin and the man is wearing a wedding crown) have strong attestation in early postbiblical Judaism (see *Comment* on 3:11).

One can account for the differences between the Song and Matthew in several ways. First, neither text purports to give an exhaustive account of contemporary wedding customs. It may be that the two texts allude to different events that took place in the course of normal wedding festivities. If so, there may have been one arrival for the groom (at the middle of the night) and one for the bride (the next day?). Second, the temporal and cultural distance between tenth-century B.C.E. Israel, first-century Judea, and nineteenth-century Palestine cannot be brushed aside. Jeremias points out that even in nineteenth-century Palestine wedding customs differed from village to village. The practice described in Jesus' parable may not have existed in the cultural context of the Song. Third, the Song may be drawing upon an incident such as the arrival of Pharaoh's daughter as Solomon's bride (1 Kgs 3:1) for its imagery. Again, this would not mean that this is a canto *about* this incident; it would only mean that the incident furnished a picture of grandeur at a wedding that served as a motif for the Song. Fourth, both the Song and Jesus manipulate their presentations of wedding customs for their own rhetorical purposes.

In Jesus' parable, half of the girls are out of oil when the groom finally arrives. One need not assume that this was a routine occurrence in actual weddings;

presumably, girls would bring enough oil if it were normal that the groom did not arrive until the middle of the night. Jesus no doubt created the unusual situation of girls without oil for the sake of the message of his parable.

This points to a significant difference between the two presentations. In Matthew, the focus is on the ten virgins and their preparedness or lack of the same. The bridegroom himself receives little attention while his retinue (if he has any) and means of transportation receive none at all. In the Song, by contrast, *all attention is on the nature of the bridal entourage,* which is described under the rubric of a royal visitation. Nothing is said of the bride herself. The details of this canto are drawn as much from the cultural trappings of royalty as from contemporary wedding practices. Put another way, this is probably not a presentation of how a normal bridal procession in ancient Israel would have actually looked. It is an idealized image of a wedding procession under the metaphor of royal splendor.

C. Tenor: The Flawless Bride I (4:1–15)

Bibliography

Brown, J. P. "The Mediterranean Vocabulary of the Vine." *VT* 19 (1969) 146–70. **Crim, K. R.** "'Your Neck Is like the Tower of David' (The Meaning of a Simile in Song of Solomon)." *BT* 22 (1971) 70–74. **Eichrodt, W.** *Ezekiel.* OTL. Philadelphia: Westminster, 1970. **Garrett, D. A.** *Hosea, Joel.* **Honeyman, A. M.** "Two Contributions to Canaanite Toponymy." *JTS* 50 (1949) 50–52. **Lichtheim, M.** *Ancient Egyptian Literature.* Vol. 2, *The New Kingdom.* Berkeley: Univ. of California Press, 1976. **Lyke, L. L.** "The Song of Songs, Proverbs, and the Theology of Love." In *Theological Exegesis.* Ed. C. Seitz and K. Greene-McCreight. Grand Rapids: Eerdmans, 1999. 208–23. **Waldman, N. M.** "A Note on Canticles 4:9." *JBL* 89 (1970) 215–17.

Translation

FIRST STANZA

TENOR

1 *How beautiful you are, my companion,*	1A
how beautiful you are!	1B
Your eyes are doves behind your veil.[a]	1C
Your hair is like the flock of goats	2A
skipping[b] *from Mount Gilead.*	2B
2 *Your teeth are like a shorn flock*	3A
that comes up from washing	3B
in which every one has a twin:	3C
not one among them is bereft of its partner.	3D
3 *Your lips are like scarlet thread,*	4A
and your speech is lovely.	4B
Your cheek is like a split pomegranate behind your veil.	5A

⁴	*Your neck is like the tower of David,*	6A
	built in courses.	6B
	A thousand shields hang upon it,	6C
	all of them the armaments of warriors.	6D
⁵	*Your breasts are like two fawns,*	7A
	twins of a gazelle, that feed among the lotuses.	7B
⁶	*Until the day comes to life*	8A
	and the shadows flee,	8B
	I will get me to Myrrh Mountain	8C
	and to Incense Hill.	8D

Second Stanza

⁷	*You are beautiful all over, my companion,*	9A
	and you do not have a single flaw.	9B
⁸	*Come ᵃ from Lebanon, O bride!*	10A
	Come ᵃ from Lebanon, make your way!	10B
	Venture ᵇ from the summit of Amana,	10C
	from the summit of Senir and Hermon!	10D
	from the dens of lions,	10E
	from the lairs ᶜ of leopards!	10F

Third Stanza

⁹	*You leave me breathless, my sister, my bride.*	11A
	*You leave me breathless with one of your glances,*ᵃ	11B
	with one strand of your necklace.	11C
¹⁰	*How beautiful are your caresses,*ᵃ *my sister, my bride!*	12A
	*How much better are your caresses*ᵃ *than wine,*	12B
	and the aroma of your perfume than any balsam!	12C
¹¹	*Your lips drip honey, my bride!*	13A
	Honey and cream are under your tongue!	13B
	*The aroma of your clothes is like the aroma of Lebanon.*ᵃ	13C

Fourth Stanza

¹²	*An enclosed garden is my sister, my bride,*	14A
	an enclosed pool, a sealed fountain.	14B
¹³	*Your growth is a paradise:*	15A
	pomegranates with choice fruit,	15B
	henna with spikenard,	15C
¹⁴	*nard and saffron,*	15D
	calamus and cinnamon,	15E
	with every incense tree,	15F
	myrrh and aloes	15G
	with all the best balsam.	15H
¹⁵	*Garden fountain!*	16A
	Well of living water,	16B
	and flowing from Lebanon!	16C

Notes

1.a. For MT לצמתך מבעד, "from beyond your veil" (see *Comment*), LXX has σιώπησις, "silence" or "taciturnity," for צמה, "veil," in the very peculiar phrase, ἐκτὸς τῆς σιωπήσεώς σου, "beyond your taciturnity." Vg. *absque eo quod intrinsecus latet*, "besides what lies hidden within." σ´ κάλυμμα, "veil."

1.b. LXX translates with ἀπεκαλύφθησαν, "revealed," while Vg. has *ascenderunt*, "ascend."
8.a. MT אִתִּי, "with me," but the ancient versions (LXX, OL, Syr., and Vg.) give strong support for reading this as אֱתִי, "come!" a fem. sg. impv. from אתה. LXX δεῦρο, "come," and Vg. *veni*, "come." Murphy (155) argues for MT on the grounds that it makes sense and therefore need not be set aside. This requires that we take תבואי to be a "double-duty" verb, but it would be odd for the verb תבואי, "make your way," to be doing double duty from the end of the second line of two lines. Normally, a double-duty verb is at the beginning of a gapping structure, as in the second half of this verse, where תשורי, "venture," governs everything that follows it. Keel ([1994] 154) accepts אִתִּי on the grounds that it is the more difficult reading, but he translates the verse with ellipses indicating that he thinks it is corrupt; this is not a helpful solution. It is simplest to follow the versions and read אֱתִי, as many scholars do (e.g., Pope, 474).
8.b. Taking שׁוּר as "to travel" and not "to gaze," contrary to BDB. See Fox, *Song of Songs*, 135.
8.c. Emending MT מֵהַרְרֵי, "from the mountains of," to מֵחֹרֵי, "from the lairs of," in parallel to מִמְּעֹנוֹת, "from the dens of." Cf. Nah 2:13: חֹרָיו וּמְעֹנֹתָיו, "his lairs and his dens," in reference to the dens of lions.
9.a. As Murphy (156) notes, עַיִן, "eye," is fem., but here the text uses the masc. form of the word בְּאַחַד, "one" (but Q emends this to בְּאַחַת). The disagreement in gender may be accounted for by the fact that it is not strictly one of her eyes that disarms him but one of her glances (cf. Keel [1994] 71).
10.a. For MT דֹּדַיִךְ, "your caresses," both times LXX has μαστοί σου, "your breasts," reading שָׁדַיִךְ; cf. Vg. See *Comment*.
11.a. It is possible that the phrase כְּרֵיחַ לְבָנוֹן, "like the fragrance of Lebanon," should be emended to כְּרֵיחַ לְבֹנָה, "like the fragrance of frankincense," to match מִכָּל־בְּשָׂמִים, "than any balsam," in v 10. MT is intelligible, however, and need not be changed.

Form/Structure/Setting

In the context of the Song, the bride has been brought to the bridegroom in the sedan chair (Song 3:6–11), and now they are ready to consummate their wedding. Terms of endearment—רעיתי, "my companion"; אחתי, "my sister"; and כלה, "bride"—dominate this canto as the groom now tenderly persuades the bride to yield herself to him.

The canto is divided into four stanzas, each marked by a declaration of affection for the bride in the opening line. In v 1, the man declares, "How beautiful you are, my companion!" and the first stanza continues through v 6. In v 7 he says, "You are beautiful all over, my companion" and continues the second stanza through v 8. The third stanza, vv 9–11, begins with the man calling her "my sister, my bride" in line 11A, but it also has a declaration of her beauty in the first line of the second strophe of the stanza (line 12A): "How beautiful are your caresses, my sister, my bride!" The fourth stanza, vv 12–15, also begins with the man calling her his sister and bride. Together, the four stanzas present the bridegroom alternatively praising the bride and declaring her to be inaccessible to him (see figure 8). The obvious point is that he cannot have her until she voluntarily yields to him; it is a decision she must make. Division of such a large canto into strophes is difficult. Of course, one could simply make each of the four stanzas into strophes, but this would lead to some massive strophes and obscure the interrelationships among some of the lines. The discussion above suggests that there are sixteen strophes in all.

Strophes 1–8 make up the above first stanza. A *waṣf* (a song of praise to one's beloved), it is governed by the description of the parts of the woman's body. The first strophe (1A–C) repeats the strophe found in Song 1:15. The second and third strophes (2A–3D) begin every line with the letter שׁ (in line 3D it is preceded by a conjunction). The fourth, fifth, and sixth strophes concern three topics: the mouth (4A–B), the cheek (5A), and the neck (6A–D). Each strophe is marked by beginning a line with the preposition כ, "like." The seventh strophe describes the breasts under the metaphors of two fawns (7A–B) and two hills (8A–D).

α	The pleasures of the bride: her beauty (vv 1–6 ["my companion"])
β	The inaccessible pleasure: the bride as mountain goddess (v 7–8 ["bride"])
α´	The pleasures of the bride: her affection (vv 9–11 ["my sister, (my) bride"])
β´	The inaccessible pleasure: the bride as locked garden (vv 12–15 ["my sister, (my) bride"])

Fig. 8. Alternating themes of canto VIc

The second stanza is made of two strophes (vv 7–8, lines 9A–10F). Strophe 9 could be read as an inclusion that concludes the first stanza, but for reasons outlined above, it is the opening of the second stanza. Strophe 10 employs line-initial repetition in lines 10A–B (אתי מלבנון), which should be read as feminine imperatives, "come from Lebanon." Line 10B ends with תבואי, "make your way!" which is matched at the beginning of line 10C by תשורי, "venture!" both modal second feminine singular imperfects. Lines 10D–F are dependent on 10C and employ matching via the fourfold repetition of prepositional phrases with מן in 10C–F.

The third stanza is made of three strophes (11A–13C, in vv 9–11). Each strophe is in three lines, and all three have the same pattern: the "B" lines, via repetition or matching, to some degree parallel the "A" lines, and the "C" lines, in syntactical dependence on the "B" lines, conclude the strophes. Strophe 11 begins with repetition (לבבתני, "you leave me") in 11A–B. There is also consonance in the second word of 11A (אחתי, "my sister") and 11B (באחת, "with one"). Line 11C is bound to 11B by dependence and matching (באחת, "with one," in 11B, באחד, "with one," in 11C). Strophe 12 likewise begins with repetition (מה, "how," in 12A and 12B, with דדיך, "your caresses," also repeated). Line 12C is bound to 12B by a simple conjunction. Strophe 13 does not begin with literal repetition, but lines 13A and 13B each begin with a word that means "honey" (נפת and דבש). Line 13C is bound to 13B by another conjunction. Other elements also link the lines of this stanza together. For example, lines 12C and 13C each begin with וריח, "and the fragrance." Finally, all three strophes have the same logic: two lines describe the intoxicating power of her lovemaking, and a third line describes something delightful that she is wearing. In strophe 11 (v 9), two lines state that she "leaves him breathless," and a third line speaks of her necklace. In strophe 12 (v 10), two lines speak of how wonderful her caresses are, and a third mentions her perfume. In strophe 13 (v 11), two lines speak of the sweetness of her kisses, and the third speaks of the fragrance of her clothes. All these elements mark this stanza as having three strophes of three lines.

The fourth stanza is also made up of three strophes (vv 12–15, strophes 14–16). The first strophe begins with two lines that use repetition (גן נעול, "enclosed garden" [14A], and גל נעול, "enclosed pool" [14B]). Strophe 14 thus begins with two lines that use repetition or matching and thus seems to be following the same pattern that the three strophes of the previous stanza employ. However, it breaks off this pattern, and strophe 15 is altogether different. Strophe 16 returns to the pattern of two lines that employ matching, followed by a third line dependent on the second line. Like strophe 13 of the previous stanza, strophe 16 uses synonymous terms to achieve a kind of repetition for lines A and B: מעין גנים, "spring of gardens," and באר מים חיים, "well of living waters." Line 16C depends on 16B via another conjunction.

Comment

1 The metaphor of the woman's eyes being doves is difficult to unpack; see *Comment* on 1:15. In this verse, however, it seems that the point of comparison is that her eyes are partially hidden behind a veil, much as a dove hides in the cleft of a rock (see Song 2:14 and Jer 48:28). He finds the way her eyes seem to be hiding behind her veil to be very alluring.

The idiom מבעד לצמתך, "behind your veil," appears here and at 4:3 and 6:7. The meaning of צמה as "veil" is open to question. The problem is further complicated by the fact that the compound preposition מבעד ל (מן + בעד + ל) also occurs only in these verses, and צמה occurs elsewhere only at Isa 47:2. G. Gerleman (144) suggests that LXX σιώπησις, "silence" or "taciturnity," has misread the verb as צמת, "to destroy, to silence," here. The Vulgate is equally obscure (see *Note* 4:1.a.). Some translate צמה as "locks (of hair)," but evidence supporting this is inadequate. The sixteenth-century Spanish Hebraist Luis de León argued that Jerome was using a euphemistic paraphrase, because צמה actually refers to female pudenda (J. Barr, "Luis de León," 231–33). This interpretation is possible in light of Isa 47:2, a taunt of the "virgin daughter of Babylon," where גלי צמתך could be taken to mean "expose your pudenda" rather than "take off your veil." The first clause of Isa 47:3 is תגל ערותך, "your nakedness will be exposed." But it is almost impossible to make sense of the line עיניך יונים מבעד לצמתך, "your eyes are doves behind your," in the Song with this interpretation of the word צמה. Pope (457) observes that Symmachus has κάλυμμα, "veil," here and that in Aramaic verbs from the root צמם are used of veiling the face. Hence, the translation "veil" is retained here.

Her hair, which may be dark and wavy, reminds him of a flock of goats leaping down the side of a mountain. The root גלש only appears here and again in precisely the same phrase at Song 6:5. Its meaning is uncertain. The versions are of little help and differ in their interpretations (see *Note* 4:1.b.). Pope (459–60) observes that two suggestions have been made from cognate languages. An apparently foreign word in the Egyptian text Papyrus Lansing, verso 1,9, *kʾ-pʾ-šw*, seems to mean "skip." On the other hand, a Ugaritic fragment (2001.1.5) contains the phrase *wtglṯ thmt*, which might be taken to mean, "and the abyss was roiled." Given the minimal state of our information, it is probably best to take גלש here to mean that the flock is skipping down the mountain and so from a distance resembles a turbulent, sensual mass of hair. (See *HALOT* גלש.) For a shepherd people, this would have been high praise, and the compliment connotes vitality in the woman.

In addition, the praise of the woman is particularized in that the goats are leaping down "Mount Gilead." The location of Mount Gilead is unknown. It may be not a single mountain but the ridges in the Transjordan opposite Samaria.

Judg 7:3 does refer to מהר הגלעד, "the mountain of the Gilead," but a number of scholars regard that text as suspect and emend to "Mount Gilboa" or render the phrase as "Mount Galud." Interpreted as "Galud," it would refer to Ain Jalud, to the west of the Jordan and south of Jezreel (cf. *ISBE* 2:470, "Gilead, Mount"). Here in the Song, however, there is no intrinsic reason to doubt the text. Probably מהר גלעד is either the slopes of Gilead generally or is a name attached to some specific site in Gilead that is now lost to us.

It is noteworthy that the man often praises the woman in terms of the places, flora, and fauna of the Levant. Elsewhere, he compares her features to a tower that David built (4:4), to Lebanon (4:11), to Tirzah and Jerusalem (6:4), to the pools of Heshbon (7:4), and to Carmel (7:5). The text abounds in references to goats, to sheep that have just been shorn, to gazelles feeding, and to vineyards, local flowers, and fruits.

2 The woman has all of her teeth! This may seem like a rather droll bit of praise to the modern, Western reader, but we live in an age of highly sophisticated dentistry and orthodontics. Until very recently, a beautiful, healthy smile with no missing teeth was hardly something people could take for granted. The fact that the teeth are like shorn lambs that come up from washing obviously implies that they are clean and white. Although data on קצב is scarce, 2 Kgs 6:6 is fairly strong evidence that the rare root קצב means to "cut off," or with reference to sheep, "shorn."

The fact that every one has a twin means that no teeth are missing. The root תאם with the sense to "double" or "have a twin" appears in Exod 26:24 and 36:29 (in both cases the noun תּוֹאָם) and in Song 6:6, which virtually repeats the present text. In this case, the *hip̄'il* מַתְאִימוֹת cannot mean "bear twins," in which case three sheep would be in view (the mother and her twin lambs). Rather, it means to have a twin sibling or to be in pairs. One could take "twin" to refer to the correspondence of upper and lower teeth, but probably it means that each tooth on the right side of the face has a matching tooth on the left side. That is, for the upper right canine tooth there is a matching canine on the upper left, and so forth.

The adjective וְשַׁכֻּלָה would normally mean "childless" or refer to the bereavement suffered as the result of the death of one's children. The point here is that every lamb has a twin and not that every sheep has twin children. Note also the assonance in the words וְשַׁכֻּלָה, "bereft," and שֶׁכֻּלָּם, "which every one."

Shorn lambs leaping up from their washing connote vigor and health, just as a good smile is a sign of good health. The image of lambs at shearing time would have evoked deep feelings of appreciation for the joys of pastoral life in a people who knew this life well.

3 The idea that her lips are "like a scarlet thread" is not particularly attractive to us, since it seems to imply that she has thin lips. This is certainly not the point. The obvious visual link between the metaphor and the lips is the color red, a feature still regarded as attractive for women's lips in many cultures. For the reader of the biblical canon, it is noteworthy that the phrase חוט השני, "scarlet thread," is precisely the same as that used to describe the "scarlet thread" by which Rahab signaled to the Israelites which house was hers (Josh 2:18). Is it coincidence that Rahab, a prostitute, had such an item readily available in her home? Possibly; but a scarlet thread may have had some kind of sexual significance and thus have been a kind of trademark for prostitutes. Keel ([1994] 143) suggests that a prostitute would have attached the red cord to her door as a symbol of her profession. If so, the red cord may not have of itself signaled prostitution; it could have been a symbol for love (like the "heart" shape today) that was co-opted by prostitution. In any case, the point may be that the man sees her lips as an invitation to love.

"Your speech is lovely." Interpreters routinely take מדבר here to mean the "mouth as the organ of speech" on the basis of its pairing with שפתתיך, "your lips." It is more likely that מדבר here refers to speech itself rather than to the organ of speech. The Song frequently avoids parallelism that is fully redundant. Also, the adjective נאוה, "lovely," does not refer exclusively to visual beauty; see Ps 147:1, נאוה תהלה, "praise [to God] is lovely." Elsewhere in the Song the man sings of his delight in the sound of her voice (2:14). Fox (*Song of Songs*, 130) suggests that ומדבריך נאוה is a wordplay that could be heard to mean "and your wilderness is an oasis," meaning that even her blemishes are beautiful. But the man regards her as flawless (v 7), and it is at any rate unlikely that he would use "wilderness" to mean "blemish."

The noun רקה, "cheek," appears five times in the Bible, including here and a parallel text in Song 6:7, as well as in Judg 4:21–22; 5:26. The latter three texts all describe how Jael drove a tent peg through the temple of Sisera. The word probably refers to the side of the head, including what we would call the temple and the cheekbone. In describing her cheeks as halves of pomegranates, he may mean one of two things. He could be saying that she has high cheek bones, analogous to how a pomegranate half bulges out on its rounded side. It is more likely, however, that he means that the parts of her cheeks that are visible above her veil have a pinkish color, like the interior of a split pomegranate. He has already spoken of the redness of her lips, and the point here seems to be that she has a youthful glow. Also, the interior of a pomegranate connotes sweetness and sensual pleasure.

4 The military language employed to describe the "tower of David" indicates that the main point of comparison is not that her neck is long and slender, like a high tower (notwithstanding the fact that Egyptians considered long necks attractive). Obviously there is a superficial resemblance between a tower and a neck, but height, delicacy, and proportion do not figure in the language here. Keel ([1994] 147) observes that ancient Near Eastern towers tended to be massive rather than slender. Also, not every tower is adorned with armaments as this one is.

The meaning of לתלפיות (a *hapax legomenon*) is uncertain. LXX reads it as a proper name. Most treat it as a noun from the root לפא*, meaning "to lay in courses" (Gerleman 148). Thus בנוי לתלפיות is routinely translated "built in courses." BDB has the conjectural "armory" and Crim (*BT* 22 [1971] 74) the dubious interpretation "Your neck is like the tower of David, / round and smooth. // A thousand famous soldiers / surrender their shields to its beauty." The phrase "built in courses" may mean that it is built with ashlar—that is, with stone that could be precisely cut and thus tightly fitted together (cf. *HALOT* תַּלְפִּיוֹת). Aesthetically, this makes for a more admirable tower, and it also probably had some military advantage, since a foe could not easily scale or pry apart the stones.

The word שלט appears seven times in the OT (2 Sam 8:7 [ǁ 1 Chr 18:7]; 2 Kgs 11:10 [ǁ 2 Chr 23:9]; Jer 51:11; Ezek 27:11; and here). It is usually translated "shield" (here in the Song it is paired with מגן). On the other hand, "shield" is not appropriate in Jer 51:11, where it seems to mean a "quiver (for arrows)," and only in the two texts in Samuel and Kings (with parallels) is "shield" likely. Fox (*Song of Songs*, 131) makes a good case that שלט simply means "military equipment." Ezek 27:11 has a most remarkable parallel to this text: "the Gammadim were in your towers. They hung their weapons on your walls [בְּמִגְדְּלוֹתַיִךְ הָיוּ שִׁלְטֵיהֶם תִּלּוּ עַל־חוֹמוֹתַיִךְ] all around; they perfected your beauty." That text is a lament over Tyre, and the identity of the "Gammadim" is uncertain (Eichrodt, *Ezekiel*, 379, takes it to mean "watchmen"). It is clear, however, that the Gammadim are allies and defenders of the city who both adorned and protected the walls with their arsenal. Precise translation is not possible for שלט, but it definitely is military in nature.

Even if we assume that the shields and weaponry are in some sense metaphorical for necklaces and other jewelry worn about the neck, the martial connotation of depicting her neck in these terms cannot be set aside. The association of the neck and tower with David, Israel's great warrior king, enhances the military tone of the text. The language of Ezek 27:11 is very close to that of this verse. There is a kind of beauty associated with military hardware, but it is a beauty that connotes strength. Applied to walls and towers, this language connotes impregnability. The man's adoration of the woman arises in part from the fact that he cannot take her at will. He speaks tenderly to her, hoping that she will give him willingly what he cannot take by force. Furthermore, his words imply respect for how she deports herself and possesses her beauty. She is not weak in her beauty but strong.

5 There is obviously no visual resemblance between her breasts and twin fawns other than that both come in pairs. A number of scholars follow W. Rudolph (147), who contends that one can see only the rounded backs of the two fawns protruding above tall flowers as they feed, and that this accounts for the simile here. But as Keel ([1994] 150) points out, this does not work in the shorter version of the simile at Song 7:3. Nor do we need to imagine that the woman is wearing a wreath of flowers around her breasts (Fox, *Song of Songs*, 131). Rather, it seems that the comparison is another example of how gazelles in the Song connote playfulness, energy, and sexuality (e.g., Song 2:7, 9). The picture of fawns feeding among lotus flowers (so taking בשושנים) seems unnatural; the lotus is a water lily. Of course, the image need not be one of fawns standing *in* the water and *eating* water lilies; it is more likely that they are understood to be feeding on grass near the edge of ponds where lotuses grow. It is in this sense, standing on dry ground, that they are "among" the lotuses. Or, it may be that שושנים connotes both lilies and lotuses (see *Comment* on 2:1–2, 16 above). But the juxtaposition of lotuses and fawns is significant. Both connote beauty, sexuality, and life. The woman can compare the man's lips to lotuses (Song 5:13) and call herself a lotus (Song 2:1). For the man, her breasts are a focal point of her sexuality.

6 For the translation of עד שיפוח היום as "until the day comes to life," see *Comment* on 2:17 above.

Having described her breasts, the man abruptly breaks off from the description and declares his intentions. He is determined to get himself to "Myrrh Mountain" and "Incense Hill," and the meaning of his words is hardly obscure: the two hills are obviously her breasts. They are not literal mountains in Israel or elsewhere, nor are they simply the "make-believe world of love poetry" (Murphy, 159). Scholars sometimes cite the Cairo love songs to the effect that a man in his woman's arms imagines himself in the land of Punt, the domain of the gods (cf. Keel [1994] 152). In my view, the analogy to the Egyptian text here is overworked. "Myrrh Mountain" and "Incense Hill" are not the proper names of some mythological paradise like Punt or the Elysian Fields, nor are they literal hills in the terrain of Israel. They are a straightforward metaphor for breasts. In Song 7:7–8, the man does much the same thing he does here. In the course of a *waṣf* (praise of the woman), he comes to the woman's breasts and suddenly interrupts his description of her beauty and expresses a keen desire to enjoy her breasts; in 7:7 he says that they are like clusters in a palm tree, and in 7:8 he says that he will climb the tree and lay hold of those clusters. The breasts are here given the names "Myrrh Mountain" and "Incense Hill" obviously because their shape is mountainlike but also because they give exotic pleasure, much as spices do. In addition, the Israelite bride may have literally perfumed her breasts with myrrh and incense; in Song 1:13, the woman describes the man as a pouch of myrrh between her breasts, a metaphor that may reflect an actual bridal practice. In saying that he intends to get himself to these mountains "until the day comes to life and the shadows flee," the man means that he intends to make love to her all night long. The language of love is often hyperbolic.

7 This verse concludes the *waṣf* with a summation that fairly says everything the man wants to get across: the woman is absolutely flawless.

8 However this verse is translated (see *Note* 4:8.c.), one should not take it to mean that the man is with the woman in her mountain lair. It could mean that he is calling her down from her mountain lair so that she could accompany him from Lebanon, a reading that would still retain אִתִּי, "with me," but emendation is better.

This strophe depicts the woman in goddesslike terms. She is high in the mountains of the north where she dwells with lions and leopards. Keel ([1994] 155) points out that the Anti-Lebanon range is the highest in the vicinity of Israel, attaining to a height of 3,088 meters above sea level. Hermon and Amana are two mountains of this range, although the location of Amana is disputed. According to Deut 3:9, Hermon and Senir are one and the same mountain. Keel ([1994] 155–57) also notes that cylinder seals from the Akkad period (ca. 2200) depict Ishtar ascending a mountain or standing with her foot on the back of a leashed lion, and he reproduces an Egyptian image of a nude goddess standing on a lion. Also, a gold pendant of ca. 1350 from Minet el-Beida, the harbor of Ugarit, is most illustrative. It depicts a naked goddess wearing only a necklace (v 9); she stands on a lion and holds a gazelle (v 5) in each hand (see Keel [1994] 91). An analogous piece is a stamp seal from Minos in Knossos (ca. 1500) that portrays a bare-breasted goddess standing on a mountain peak flanked by two lions (see Keel [1994] 160).

In the Christian era, a young man who praised the woman of his dreams as an "angel" was not literally asserting that she was superhuman, nor was he composing devotional literature. Similarly, although the Song here depicts the woman in goddesslike terms, she is not a goddess and this is not a hymn fragment. In addition, we should not regard it as intolerable that she is suddenly described in these terms or see this as an interruption in the Song or an incongruous insertion. Traditional images of goddesses have been pressed into service here to provide a metaphorical vision of how the woman seems to him. The point of the text is that she is wonderful, powerful (in her sexuality), and inaccessible. As such, this text appropriately responds to what has gone before in vv 1–7. The man sees her as a beauty surpassing hope and imagination, and at the very moment that he and she are near to coming together he wonders if she will actually make her way to him. She is goddesslike to him in that possessing her seems as magical and impossible as possessing a goddess—and we do well to remember that many a goddess from the ancient world carries the epithet "Virgin." Once again, the virginity of the woman asserts itself and sets her far beyond his reach. She will be his only if she chooses to come down from her mountain lair.

Here for the first time the woman is called כלה, "bride" (the word can also mean "daughter-in-law," but context excludes that meaning here). The word appears six times in the Song; astoundingly, these come in five successive verses (4:8, 9, 10, 11, 12) with the sixth appearing nearby in 5:1. A number of scholars regard כלה as merely a term of endearment that does not imply that a wedding has or will take place. While the use of the term does not demonstrate that the Song is an epithalamium—much less a kind of wedding liturgy—there is no reason to assert that "bride" does not have its normal meaning here. In the quasi-story that stands behind the Song, the man and woman are newly married. It is true that he also calls her "sister," but this term is well known to be a term of affection a man may use for a woman, and it functions like רעיתי, "my companion." But it would be peculiar to use כלה, "bride," as a term of affection for a woman who was not in fact one's bride.

Furthermore, we need to account for the surprising cluster of uses of the term כלה, "bride," here and only here. As suggested above, this canto depicts a bridegroom calling his new bride on their wedding night to their first union. He tenderly woos her, in effect seducing her rather than simply claiming his right as husband to her body. Even so, he repeatedly calls her "bride" in this context to gently remind her that she has entered this relationship with him, and that a bride is not truly a bride until she has consummated her marriage. Calling her "bride" is not simply demanding sex from her on the grounds that she is now his wife, but it is a tender reminder of the nature of their relationship. Five times in a row addressing her by this epithet, he declares how beautiful and delightful she is to him while yet speaking of her as a goddess on a mountain (Song 4:8) or a locked up garden (Song 4:12). The point is that to truly be a bride she must descend to him and open her garden to him. Finally in Song 5:1, at the celebration of their sexual union (as I interpret it), he calls her "bride" for the last time. From that point forward, she is no longer a bride but a wife.

9 "You leave me breathless." The *pi'el* denominative לבבתני may be understood as either to take away someone's heart (i.e., to leave one feeling shaken and weak) or to give someone heart (i.e., to energize or even arouse sexually). Interpreters have given their opinions and support to either side of this issue. Pope (479–80) observes that Sumerian and Akkadian analogues imply that the root *lbb*, "heart," can refer to male sexual arousal. See also Waldman (*JBL* 89 [1970] 215–17), who argues that לבב means "to rage" and from that "to be sexually aroused" on the analogy of ὀργή, "fury," and ὀργάω, "to arouse." Fox (*Song of Songs*, 136) rejects this interpretation on the grounds that the Akkadian material in question deals with impotence, which is not a matter of concern here. This is a weak objection; the fact that the specific Akkadian texts that we possess deal with impotence when they use *lbb* in a sexual sense does not mean that *lbb* connotes arousal only in a context of treating impotence. The *pi'el* לבב only occurs four times in the Bible; two are in this verse and two are in 2 Sam 13:6, 8, where it means to "bake bread" from a homonymous root. Scholars have naturally set these instances aside as irrelevant, but they may be in one sense germane to the issue here. In the 2 Samuel verses, Amnon is asking that Tamar come and "bake bread" (לבב) in his sight so that he might eat from her hand. It may be that the Hebrew reader would have seen a wordplay between the two meanings and have taken that to be representative of a debauched aristocrat amusing himself with his own prurient cleverness. In the Song, however, it remains unclear how we should take לבב. It is possible that the word itself is ambiguous and connoted both the arousal and the emotional slaying of a man by a woman. For this reason, I have left the ambiguity in place with the rendition, "You leave me breathless." It is at any rate clear that the woman has all his attention.

The noun ענק, "strand," appears in the form הָעֲנָקוֹת in Judg 8:26, where it refers to decorative bands about the necks of camels. In Prov 1:9, וַעֲנָקִים describes some kind of necklace, whether made of many strands, beads, or chain links. Here, עֲנָק either means a single bead or a strand of a necklace of many strands. A single glance or a single strand or bead of her necklace, in other words, the slightest action on her part or the most insignificant detail of her jewelry, is sufficient to captivate him. In the ancient Near East, goddesses were sometimes portrayed as naked except for jewelry.

The use of אחתי, "my sister," as a love term has naturally provoked scholarly interest. The term is found in Egyptian love poetry and even in Sumerian love poetry, and some interpreters, influenced by the practice of consanguineous marriage in the Egyptian royal house, thought that this was a common practice. In reality, it was probably quite rare. The term here does not mean that she is literally his sister. Still, we must ask why the Song would use a love term that seems to imply incestuous love (cf. Lev 18:9). The significance of the term as an affectionate expression of licit love is not unrelated to its literal meaning. A brother and sister are members of the same family and household. As close relatives, the emotional bond between them is very strong. In an ancient Israelite family, to be sure, kinship and its duties were not taken lightly. In calling her his "sister," the man implies that they have become one family. The canonical analogue is Adam's declaration that the woman was bone of his bone and flesh of his flesh (Gen 2:23). In Wisdom literature, by contrast, the prostitute or adulteress is the "foreign woman" or "stranger" (נכריה; e.g., Prov 2:16; 5:20; 6:24; 7:5). In calling her sister, he declares that the two of them are bound as by having common flesh and blood.

10 This strophe opens with a recapitulation of the praise of her body but moves into a celebration of the joys of receiving affection from her. The metaphors here relate to sensations rather than to physical objects. Wine, perfume, balsam, honey, and milk all connote not the items themselves but their tastes and smells. Also, metaphors that are liquids rather than solids (such as towers, mountains, goats, or sheep) more readily lend themselves to the celebration of an action—her lovemaking—rather than to the praise of her physical body.

Balsam is an aromatic resin that flows from a plant after an incision has been made in a stem. It is used in the preparation of perfumes and incense, and the word בשם in the Song refers to perfumes made from balsam. Classical literature also refers to the balsam tree (τὸ βάλσαμον). The exotic qualities of its oil gave rise to interesting legends. According to Pausanias, *Description of Greece* 9.28.3, the balsam tree grew in Arabia and was frequently the nesting place of vipers that would have to be driven away before the resin could be harvested. The danger of this activity was not as great as one might think, Pausanias assures us: "Since the vipers feed on the most fragrant of perfumes, their poison is diminished and less deadly." The word is sometimes rendered as "spices," but this is misleading because that term in English seems to imply leafy herbs and ground peppercorns, which are certainly not meant here. The Queen of Sheba brought balsam with her when she visited Solomon (1 Kgs 10:2, 10). At least in very wealthy households, people used balsam as a beautification treatment for women (Esth 2:12).

The language of this verse fairly dramatically reworks but reflects a verse of praise that was heaped upon the man in Song 1:2-3: "Indeed your caresses are better than wine, / better than the fragrances of your perfumes. / Your very name is like perfumes poured out." In the Song of Songs, the focal point of adoration progressively moves from the man to the woman.

11 The assonance and consonance of the phrase נֹפֶת תִּטֹּפְנָה שִׂפְתוֹתַיִךְ, "your lips drip honey," underscores the sensuality of this verse. The Song invokes every kind of sensual experience, from the fragrances of perfume, balsam, and the cedars of Lebanon to the sweetness of honey and the richness of milk, to convey something of the pleasures the woman gives. Milk and honey are of course formulaic for the abundance of the land of Israel (Exod 3:8), and it may not be accidental that the pleasures of this Israelite woman are extolled in terms reminiscent of the glories of the land itself (see *Comment* on 4:1).

12 In the fourth strophe, the woman is an enclosed garden and pool. The word גל, "pool," basically means "heap," and it is used either for a pile of rocks or a wave. Attempts to force this meaning into the text are futile (e.g., "rock garden" in the NASB). There is ample evidence for emending גל to גן, "garden," including the LXX, Vg., Syriac, and several Hebrew manuscripts. On the other hand, Pope (488–89) has accumulated a good bit of evidence for taking the root *gll* to connote "pool" here. Note that גלה means "bowl" in Zech 4:3 and Eccl 12:6; the plural means "springs" in Josh 15:19 and Judg 1:15. I would suggest that the Song uses גַּל as a rare word for "pool" here because the assonance with גַּן links it to the preceding metaphor, but its meaning links it to the following metaphor, "fountain."

The garden of the ancient Near East was something of a small park rather than a simple flower or vegetable garden. Numerous texts from the Bible and elsewhere attest to how highly such gardens were prized and regarded as sources of pleasure. A prime example is Eccl 2:4–6, where the author devotes three verses to a description of the extent of his gardens. Those gardens included vineyards, fruit trees, and pools of water. In Papyrus Harris 500, a girl describes herself as a garden with a stream in it. In the Lichtheim translation (*New Kingdom*, 192), it reads: "I am your sister, your best one; / I belong to you like this plot of ground / That I planted with flowers / And sweet smelling herbs. / Sweet is its stream, / Dug by your hand, / Refreshing in the north wind." The image of the pleasures of the woman as a fountain also looks back to Prov 5:18–20, where the "wife of your youth" is called a "fountain" and the young man is exhorted to let himself be satiated by her breasts.

L. Lyke ("Song of Songs") seeks to forge a link between the Song and the patriarchal stories at the point of the motif of the "betrothal to a woman at a well" (Gen 24:10–61; 29:1–20; Exod 2:15b–21). He observes that the language of wells and watering evokes the image of the female and fertility (also in connection with Prov 5:15–18). From this, Lyke goes on to conclude that "a result of the complexity of its metaphors is that the theological register of its individual and particular language can be projected to the whole of the Song. Therefore, while always the poetry of human love, it simultaneously can be understood in terms of the ancient idiom that understands humans' relation to God via the same metaphors. It is this expansion of the collective intuitions about its language that leads to the sense that the Song, *as a whole*, can be read allegorically" (italics original). He further concludes that the "influence of the 'secondary' theological register on the 'primary' human register of the language is to provide one of the means by which it becomes possible to articulate the sanctity of human love" ("Song of Songs," 223).

There are several problems with Lyke's analysis. First, it is not at all clear that the Song, where the woman *is* a sealed fountain, directly alludes to the Genesis and Exodus texts, where a woman is *encountered at* a well or spring. Second, it is not likely that the significance of the spring or well can be subjected to the kind of totality transfer that Lyke seems to suggest. Third, it is not clear from Lyke's article what the "theological register" is in the metaphor of the spring, nor how it can be transferred to the Song. Fourth, like many other scholars, Lyke suggests that "as a whole" the Song can be legitimately allegorized. But the problems are in the details. The constant assertion that the love between humans "in some sense" is a figure of the love between God and humans is an empty sentiment unless one can show how it is done in the reality and the particulars of the text. The usage of the metaphor of the well found in the Song and elsewhere (especially Prov 5) suggests that in the Bible a well or spring can represent the sexuality of a woman both in terms of the pleasure she gives and her fertility; beyond that, one cannot safely go.

In this verse the notable feature of the metaphor is that she is a "locked" garden and "sealed" fountain. The point is not that she is locked to all others but open to him. Rather, it is that she is as of yet still virginal and out of even his reach. Like the prior metaphor of the goddess on a mountain, this strophe presents her as inaccessible. He appeals to her to open herself to him.

13 The word שלחיך, "your growth," is generally translated "your shoots." Evidence that the word actually means this is less than one could hope for. The noun שלח normally means "weapons" or "projectiles," as in Neh 4:11, 17 (ET 4:17, 23). Some interpreters argue that the word means "pool" or "tunnel" in Joel 2:8, but this is certainly wrong (see Garrett, *Hosea, Joel,* 341 n. 34). Keel ([1994] 176) argues that the term means "canals" here and that it is metaphorical for the vagina, but he has limited evidence to support this claim. He cites the proper name ברכת השלח, "Pool of the Shelah," in Neh 3:15, but usage in a proper name cannot establish the meaning of a word. The name Valley of Achor, for example, does not imply that *Achor* means something related to "valley" (it means "trouble"). Keel takes שלח to mean "shaft" in Job 33:18 in parallel to שחת, "pit."

This enjoys some modern support (a number of scholars see a reference to the River Styx here), but the traditional translation "sword" may well be correct (the LXX takes it as metonymy for "war"). Keel does note that *shalch* in Arabic can mean "vagina," but this does little to support the notion that the Hebrew word here literally means "canal." Furthermore, if the man is here singing about her vagina under the metaphor of a canal, why would he use the plural form ("your canals")? Finally, to give such an elaborate depiction of her vagina by describing it in terms of no less than twelve different words for varieties of fruit, spices, and perfumes is simply in bad taste. The text being what it is, scholars have suggested numerous ways to emend the text, such as that it should be read as שלחך, with ש being the relative pronoun and לחך being the noun לֵחַ, "freshness," with a pronoun suffix. So interpreted, it is "your freshness" (see Rudolph, 151). Probably the traditional interpretation is correct, that this word refers to the parts of a plant that "shoot" out (i.e., roots and stems) on the basis of the root שלח, "to send out." See the usage of the verb שלח in Jer 17:8 and Ps 80:12 (ET 80:11) and the noun שלחותיה, "its shoots," in Isa 16:8. The word here refers to the growth of plants generally and not to branches of a single plant.

In short, the phrase "your growth" does not refer to any parts of the woman's body. Rather, it refers to the variety of plants found in her "garden," a metaphor for the pleasures of her lovemaking. This verse does not catalog parts of her anatomy under the metaphor of plants; still less does it focus on her vagina. It uses an assortment of aromatic plants to communicate the idea that her love gives manifold and diverse pleasures. Her affection is to him an Eden ("paradise"), a garden-park with every kind of exotic, delicious, and wonderful kind of plant. Loving her could never be boring.

I have translated פרדס here as "paradise" because it seems to me that this communicates best to the English reader what is meant by the term. In American English, *park* connotes a public area with trees and recreation areas, but no spices or edible plants, and *grove* connotes a place where apples or oranges are intensively cultivated. *Garden* connotes a small piece of ground with cultivated flowers or vegetables. Even the term *paradise* is not fully adequate since to many people it suggests a tropical island. פרדס conveys the idea of a place that is intensely beautiful, and parklike in that it contains trees of all kinds but gardenlike in that it has spices, flowers, and edible plants. Also, notwithstanding the cantillation in the received text, there is no reason to regard פרדס as a construct here. It should be followed by a minor pause, marking a colon break.

Seven lines follow after פרדס, "paradise," with the preposition עם, "with," serving to help demarcate the units. There are five pairs of items; the first two employ עם (15B–C), but 15D, 15E, and 15G are without עם. Lines 15F and 15H employ עם with a plurality of items marked by כל, "all." Thus, lines 15B–H form a structured list (see figure 9).

14 Nard originated in India; saffron came from regions around the Caspian and Black Seas. קנה basically means "cane" or "reed." The calamus is a kind of aromatic reed and seems to be what is meant here. Jer 6:20 links aromatic cane to frankincense and says that it was imported from a distant land. Exod 30:23 indicates that it was used for cultic purposes and also links it to cinnamon. Calamus was probably a variety of sweetcane imported from northern India (cf. *ISBE* 1:573, "Calamus"), and cinnamon came from India and Sri Lanka. Frankincense came from southern Arabia, and "aloes" probably came from the eaglewood, a tall, slender tree found in India and Malaya (*ISBE* 1:99, "Aloes"). Scholars have pointed out that the variety of plants described here is so diverse that it is hard to imagine how a single garden might contain them all. Thus it is sometimes regarded as a kind of fantasy garden. It is at least clear that only the very wealthy would be likely to have such a garden. At any rate, this is not meant to be taken as a literal garden.

"Pomegranates with choice fruit,"	עם פרי מגדים	רמונים	15B
"henna with spikenard,"	עם־נרדים	כפרים	15C
"nard and saffron,"	נרד וכרכם		15D
"calamus and cinnamon,"	קנה וקנמון		15E
"with every incense tree,"	עם כל־עצי לבונה		15F
"myrrh and aloes,"	מר ואהלות		15G
"with all the best balsam,"	עם כל־ראשי בשמים		15H

Fig. 9. Structure of canto VIc, lines 15B–H

15 In Song 4:12, the beginning of this strophe, the man had sung of her under the two metaphors of the garden and the spring. In vv 13–14 he focused on the garden, but he concludes here by turning to the spring. As mentioned above, in Wisdom literature the woman as fountain signifies the giving of sexual pleasure (Prov 5:18–20). On a literal level, a fountain or well in a garden has two purposes: it waters the plants, and it gives refreshment to people in the garden. It may be significant that the source of water is a spring or well rather than a cistern, which simply collects water brought to it. The spring or well, by implication, has sources within itself and never runs dry. The woman continually draws from resources within herself all that is needed to maintain the pleasures of the garden and the refreshment she gives. She is the counterpart to the righteous man of Ps 1 or Jer 17:8, who is like a tree planted by streams of water and thus flourishes continually.

Explanation

Together, the four stanzas present the bridegroom tenderly persuading the bride to yield herself to him. He alternately praises her and declares her to be inaccessible to him. The obvious point is that he cannot have her until she voluntarily yields to him; it is a decision she must make. This text recognizes the place for tender speech in love, particularly as directed from the man to the woman. Such speech is not here manipulative or coercive. It is a subordination of the man's physical desire to the emotional needs of the woman. It also acknowledges that sex is first the joining of two hearts and only then the joining of two bodies. Finally, it is marked by an unwillingness to use force or claim one's legal rights as husband. In the context of the Song, the bride has been brought to the bridegroom in the sedan chair (3:6–11), and now they are ready to consummate their wedding.

A number of motifs are present. Scholars routinely refer to the song of admiration (especially as seen in vv 1–7) as a *wasf*, a song in praise of one's beloved.

The motif of pining over one's inability to reach the beloved is also common in Egyptian love poetry. There, however, the pining is more literal in that the two lovers are physically separated. Here, the two are in one another's presence but separated by the bride's virginity. The motif of the woman as a garden of delights appears elsewhere in the Song and in ancient Near Eastern poetry. The portrait of the woman as a goddesslike figure, high on a mountain and surrounded by lions, draws upon a motif familiar from ancient artwork. Here, as elsewhere, the Song skillfully manipulates and recasts traditional motifs and images to create a text that is altogether unlike its contemporary analogues.

A man from the southern United States might well compare his beloved's beauty to that of a magnolia blossom or declare that his love for her is as enduring as the flow of the Mississippi. A man from Colorado or Alberta might in his mind merge his love for his wife with his love for the Rocky Mountains. A man from the coast of Maine might experience something of the same feelings when he looks at waves breaking into stony cliffs or smells the sea air as when he looks upon his wife or smells her fragrance. This does not mean that the woman is an allegory for these regions or that the local natural history is an allegory for the woman. Still less does it mean that the woman actually looks like or smells like the regional metaphors. One's love of homeland is often localized in particulars—the bluebonnet flowers of Texas, the desert flora of Arizona, or the magpies of Korea. When a man loves his wife and loves his homeland, the two loves can merge in a way that is complementary and not competitive. So strong is this bond that a soldier at war in a distant land may perceive himself to be fighting to protect wife and country almost as though they were one and the same.

We should not regard it as a given that the male singer of the Song would use so many particular images from the Levant. He could have easily used metaphors that were more universal, albeit not without occasionally falling into cliché. But the woman to whom he sings is not any woman from any place. She is, after all, an Israelite woman, and her appearance, mannerisms, and fragrance evoke feelings that are not unlike the sentiments aroused by the places, activities, and natural history of Israel. For us who are outsiders to the ancient land of Israel and its pastoral ways, many of these comparisons sound strange if not comical. But for the audience that knew and loved this land and its ways, his praise of her would have been evocative of deep sentiments and thus would have told them why the man so loved this woman. Love for one's spouse, like love for one's homeland, is specific and bound to particulars. At the same time, however, the local color of describing her in terms familiar to an Israelite does not make this a patriotic or nationalistic tract. National identity as such plays no role in the Song.

VII. Soprano, Tenor, and Chorus: The Consummation (4:16–5:1)

Translation

TENOR
¹⁶ Awaken, north wind, and come, south wind! — 1A
Breathe on my garden and let the scent of its balsam waft! — 1B
SOPRANO
Let my lover come to his^a garden — 2A
and eat its choice fruits. — 2B
TENOR
^{5:1} I come^a to my garden, my sister, my bride. — 3A
I pick my myrrh with my balsam. — 3B
I eat my honeycomb^b with my honey. — 3C
I drink my wine with my milk. — 3D
CHORUS
Eat, friends! — 4A
Drink and be drunken with lovemaking!^c — 4B

Notes

16.a. Two MSS of LXX^A have κῆπόν μου, "my garden." But MT's change of speaker makes good sense and should be kept.

5:1.a. The pf. forms do not always refer to the past, least of all in poetry. Here, a present translation is more appropriate than the English present pf. found in many versions.

1.b. MT יערי, "my honeycomb." LXX (and Vg.) αρτον μου, "my bread."

1.c. It is difficult to tell whether דודים is a vocative here meaning "lovers" (parallel to רעים, "friends") or is direct object of שתו ושכרו and is an abstract pl. used for "lovemaking." The term often appears in the Song in the sg. with a pronoun suf. as a term for the man (e.g., דודי, "my lover," in Song 1:16 and דודך, "your lover," in 5:9). However, it appears six times in the pl. (Song 1:2, 4; 4:10 [2x]; 7:13; and here). In every other case where it is pl. it refers to lovemaking rather than to lovers.

Form/Structure/Setting

The garden in this canto is the woman's body. Since Song 4:16b speaks of "my garden" but 4:16c speaks of "his garden," it appears that the man sings 4:16ab and the woman sings 4:16c. In 5:1 the man speaks of "my wine," "my balsam," and "my myrrh," all in reference to the delights of the woman's body and affection. Thus, the man also sings of her as "my garden." Of course, it is possible that the woman sings all of v 16, first speaking of her body as "my garden" and then as "his garden," but it is not possible that the man sings 4:16c.

Similarly, it is clear that the man sings lines 3A–D in Song 5:1, but it seems that the chorus sings 4A–B at the end of 5:1; this final pair of lines addresses "friends" and exhorts them to drink deeply of love. That is, it appears that the chorus in 5:1c is telling the two lovers to enjoy their time together.

If the lyrics are as I have arranged them, they form a neat symmetry. Each of the four strophes is held together by matching, albeit with some variation, as in strophe 1. In strophe 3 each line begins with a first-person perfect verb; this verb is always followed by a noun that is the object of the action (in every case the noun has a first singular suffix). The only variation is that line 3A ends with "my sister, bride," whereas the other three lines all end with a prepositional phrase using עם, "with."

In the structure of Song of Songs, this piece is the center of a large chiasmus that spans the whole of the work. Often, in a biblical chiasmus, the central text governs and provides the hermeneutical key to the whole text. In this case, the centerpiece is the sexual union of the man and woman. This moment is the pivot point for the whole book, and this commentary suggests that the bridal event, the movement from virgin to wife, is the theme of Song of Songs.

Comment

16 The text uses the terms צפון, "north wind," and תימן, "south wind," but avoids the term רוח. This word means "wind," but it also is the divine Spirit that brooded over chaos in Gen 1:2 and arouses the dead bones in Ezek 37:9. In not using רוח, the text avoids any possibility of presenting the sexual act as a sacramental event. The man does invoke these winds to breathe life into his garden, an act that recalls God breathing life into the body of the first man in Gen 2:7. While the text does not treat the sexual act in mythological terms or "sacralize" the moment, it does invoke something of the mystery and quasi-religious power of sexual ecstasy.

5:1 The language of this verse looks back to the song of admiration in Song 4:1–15, with its pairs of fragrances and flavors linked by the preposition עם, "with"; see especially 4:13–14. The myrrh, balsam, honey, wine, and milk are all now qualified by the pronoun "my." The woman is no longer that distant, untouchable marvel, the virgin. She is his. The chorus closes this canto with an exhortation to enjoy this moment. They do not counsel restraint. The verb שכר means to drink deeply; it frequently means to become drunken (e.g., Gen 9:21; 1 Sam 1:14; Jer 25:27). They should partake of this pleasure to the fullest.

Explanation

The Hebrew Bible elsewhere speaks of wind blowing from the north and then from the south, in contrast to the movement of the sun, which is from east to west (Eccl 1:5–6). Here, the wind stirs up the fragrances of the exotic plants of the garden. The force of the wind is not described, but one would expect the coming together of the north wind and south wind to be a rather stormy event. Obviously the wind in view here would not be so severe as to be destructive to the metaphorical garden or to carry fragrances away, but it is not necessarily a gentle puff of a breeze. The blowing of powerful winds on a garden conveys the idea that the garden has been seized by an external power, such that the trees seem to move of their own accord and the resins and oils of the plants are released. It is an appropriate metaphor for sexual passion in the woman.

The man desires his new wife to experience passion and give herself to him, but the "magic" of sexuality to seize, arouse, and open his wife to him is beyond his power to control. He can only invoke it as an outside force. Hebrew wisdom does not deify this power under names such as Eros or Aphrodite, but it does understand that the emotional fervor of sexuality seems to be a powerful force that seizes control of us.

The woman responds that the man should come into his garden and eat his choice fruit. In the language of the Song of Songs, this is a straightforward invitation for him to enter her sexually. In the structure of the Song of Songs, this is the centerpiece and crescendo. All of the Song focuses on this, the union of the new husband and wife.

VIII. Three Wedding-Night Songs (5:2–6:10)

A. Soprano, Tenor, and Chorus: Pain and Transformation (5:2–8)

Bibliography

Alden, R. "רדיד." *NIDOTTE* §8100. **Black, F. C.** "Beauty or the Beast? The Grotesque Body in the Song of Songs." *BibInt* 8 (2000) 302–23. **Bright, J.** *Jeremiah.* **Exum, J. C.** "A Literary and Structural Analysis of the Song of Songs." *ZAW* 85 (1973) 47–79. **Hess, R.** "רסס." *NIDOTTE* §8272. **Holladay, W. L.** *Jeremiah 2.* **Israelit-Groll, S.** *The Art of Egyptian Love Lyrics.* CahRB 49. Paris: Gabalda, 2000. **King, P.,** and **L. Stager.** *Life in Biblical Israel.* **Phipps, W. E.** "The Plight of the Song of Songs." *JAAR* 42 (1974) 82–100. **Thomas, D. W.** "*Kelebh* 'Dog': Its Origin and Some Usages of It in the Old Testament." *VT* 10 (1960) 410–27. **Walsh, C. E.** "A Startling Voice: Woman's Desire in the Song of Songs." *BTB* 28 (1998) 129–34.

Translation

FIRST STANZA

SOPRANO
2	I am asleep, but my heart is awake.	1A
	The voice of my lover, pounding: ᵃ	1B

TENOR
	Open to me!	2A
	My sister, my companion, my dove, my perfect one!	2B
	Now that my head is full of dew,	2C
	my locks are full with the drops of the night!	2D
3	I have stripped off my tunic!	3A
	How can I put it back on?	3B
	I have washed my feet!	3C
	How can I defile them?	3D

SECOND STANZA

SOPRANO
4	My lover puts his hand through ᵃ the opening,	4A
	and my womb rages against it.	4B
5	I arise to open for my beloved,	5A
	and my hand drips myrrh;	5B
	even my fingers are running with myrrh,	5C
	on the handles of the bolt.	5D
6	I open to my lover,	6A
	and my lover has lost interest! ᵃ He has moved along!	6B
	I expire when he speaks.	7A

I seek him and do not find him;	8A
I call him and he does not answer!	8B
Third Stanza	
⁷ *The guards that go about the city find me.*	9A
They beat me, they wound me,	9B
they take my veil from me,	9C
the guards of the walls.	9D
Fourth Stanza	
⁸ *I call upon you to swear, daughters of Jerusalem,*	10A
if you find my lover,	10B
what should you say to him?	10C
That I am wounded by love.	10D

Notes

2.a. LXX adds ἐπὶ τὴν θύραν, "on the door."
4.a. The prep. מן here evidently means "through" as in Song 2:9.
6.a. Omitted in LXX. α´ σ´ Syr. are like Vg. *declinaverat*, "avoids (me)."

Form/Structure/Setting

This text is a jolt to the harmony of the Song of Songs. After the rhapsodic praise of the glories of the woman and the delicate portrayal of their union in 4:1–5:1, we abruptly have a barely coherent canto of the man pounding at her door and running away followed by the woman taking a beating at the hands of the city guards. As the following comments will try to demonstrate, this is not by any means to be interpreted as an actual story involving a real door or guards or a physical beating of the woman. It is instead a symbolic representation of the woman's loss of virginity.

This canto is the first part of the second of the wedding-night cantos and corresponds to Song 3:1–5. Where 3:1–5 dealt with the woman's anxiety over the wedding night, this part concerns the actual event. I differ from most interpreters in that I regard v 3 to be the man's rather than the woman's lyrics; see the *Comment* on 5:3 below.

This canto can be easily divided into four stanzas. The first stanza begins with a two-line strophe (lines 1A–B) that describes the man's desperate attempt to get in her door; this strophe uses only verbless clauses. Strophe 2 uses very terse language; line 2B is simply four vocatives! In strophe 3, lines 3A–B match lines 3C–D.

The second stanza (vv 4–6), like the first, begins with a two-line strophe (lines 4A–B) that suggests a somewhat violent, invasive act on the part of her lover. Several strophes describing the opening of the door follow. First, she describes the bolt and her dripping fingers (lines 5A–D), the abrupt "disappearance" or loss of interest on her lover's part (lines 6A–B), her despair when he speaks (line 7A), and her inability to find him (lines 8A–B). These strophes employ syntactic dependence (strophes 4, 5, and 6), repetition (5B–C), and matching (strophe 8).

The third and fourth stanzas introduce two unexpected groups: the guards (v 7, strophe 9) and the Jerusalem girls (v 8, strophe 10). Each strophe has four lines. Like Song 2:7; 3:5; and 8:4, strophe 10 begins with the formula of adjuration directed toward the girls of Jerusalem. Here, however, the promise she elicits from them is not that they will not arouse love before it is ready but that they will tell her lover that she is wounded by love. The text actually calls attention to the fact that this is an unexpected use of the adjuration: the girls in v 9 ask her why she does this.

Many interpreters draw attention to the similarity that this section has to the *paraklausithyron*, the song of complaint by a lover who stands outside his girlfriend's house and pleads to be allowed admission. References to a door between lovers occur throughout ancient love poetry. It is found in Roman works (e.g., Lucretius, *De rerum natura* 4.1177–79), in the Egyptian Papyrus Chester Beatty I, and in the Akkadian British Museum 47507. While the comparisons are educational, they can lead the interpreter astray. The Song is not like other poems; it takes traditional motifs and weaves them into patterns that are altogether different from what we see in other literature. Murphy (169) has correctly observed that the essence of *paraklausithyron* is complaint by the excluded lover against the door itself and his girlfriend but that this element is absent here. In fact, however, there is no standard use for the image of the door between lovers in ancient poetry; different texts use the image in altogether different ways.

For example, in Lucretius, the lover pining at his girlfriend's door is an illustration of the madness of emotional passion. In British Museum 47507, it is actually the female lover (Ishtar) who wants the door to be open. In Papyrus Chester Beatty I, it is a foolish young man who has forgotten that the prostitute does not really love him and that he must pay for her services. In addition, the Egyptian song is a fairly straightforward piece about a boy trying to get into a brothel to gain access to a prostitute. The details have some referential and symbolic elements: when he says he will bring a sacrifice to the door, he means that he will bring gifts to the owners of the brothel; when he says he will pay a carpenter to build a grass door, he is using hyperbole to express the lengths he will go to in order to gain admission to the brothel.

This canto of the Song of Songs goes far beyond the referential language of the Egyptian piece. It is surreal, and it is impossible, I will argue, to give this passage a literal reading without the text becoming nearly incomprehensible. Even if one should claim to make sense of the literal gist of these lyrics, one is left with a love song that is horrifying: A man pounds at his lover's door; after some hesitation, she arises to let him in, but he has already run away; she frantically looks for him, but the night watchmen find her, strip her, and beat her up! As a love song (if taken literally), this is a monstrous parody. The only way to interpret this material meaningfully is to take its surreal imagery and incongruous twists for what they are: a metaphor symbolizing something altogether different from the quasi-story on the surface of the text. In short, the device of the *paraklausithyron* has been taken, radically modified, and exploited to convey a message quite different from what the Egyptian or Latin poets created.

It is important to realize that, with the exception of the relatively innocent נשק, "kiss," in Song 1:2, the Song never uses direct language to describe a sexual act but always works under the veil of metaphor. Typical biblical terms for sexual acts (e.g., to lie [שכב] with a woman, to enter [בוא] a woman, to know [ידע] a woman, to uncover the nakedness [גלה ערוה] of a person) do not occur in the Song, and straightforward language such as בתולים, "virginity," is similarly avoided.

Even where the text appears to be fairly ribald, it still employs metaphor (e.g., Song 7:8–9a [ET 7:7–8a]: "This is what your full physique is like: a palm tree. / And your breasts are its clusters. / I said, 'I will climb the palm tree, / I will hold its panicles of dates.'" What we find here is an account of the woman's first sexual event, which is likewise told in metaphor.

Comment

2 אני ישנה ולבי ער, "I am asleep, but my heart is awake," does not necessarily mean that she is having a dream; none of the typical Semitic vocabulary of dreaming is present (Pope, 510–11). The word ער, "awake," may connote arousal, as does the root עור in Song 4:16 (cf. Exum, *ZAW* 85 [1973] 61). "I am asleep" may mean little more than that she is in bed. Dealing with this episode, as with Song 3:1–5, one should not dismiss it as a dream. Taken literally, the man is pounding at her door so that, even if she had been asleep, she would soon be wide awake (unless one argues that the man himself is part of a dream and that the whole episode is unreal). It is true that this text is surreal in its imagery and that many peculiar things happen, but symbols should be interpreted and not dismissed. Of course, dreams are often odd and highly symbolic (Gen 40–41; Dan 2); it may be that "I am asleep, but my heart is awake" is a signal to the reader to expect a text that is dreamlike in its use of bizarre but emblematic images. Also, being both asleep and awake at the same time implies that the woman is both numb and alert. If this is the moment of her loss of virginity, it may be that her mind has shifted into something of a state of shock as she tries to come to terms with the experience.

The verb דופק connotes "pounding" or driving hard. דפק appears in Gen 33:13, where Jacob warns that the cattle will die if they are driven hard, and in Judg 19:22, where the men of Gibeah attempted to batter down the door of a house. Fox (*Song of Songs*, 143) follows ibn Ezra and argues that the word here means "entreating," but the meaning attested elsewhere in the Hebrew Bible is to be preferred. One would expect עתר or חלה if the intended meaning were "entreat." Clearly this is not "knocking" in any polite sense. Taking the analogy of Judg 19:22, it is closer to trying to batter down a door. The syntax of this line can be taken in one of two ways. The word קול can be taken to be an exclamation, as, "A voice!" and thus paraphrased as "Listen!" as in the NRSV. Alternatively, קול דודי can be read as a construct chain, "the voice of my lover," with דופק as the predicate. Grammatically, the latter is more likely. Probably the audience is to understand that he is pounding at the door and that this physical pounding on the door is matched by how he speaks. In the lines that follow, the man uses words in a staccato, pounding fashion that characterizes his desperation to get in.

The man's words have something of an air of desperation about them: "Open to me! My sister, my companion, my dove, my perfect one!" This rapid-fire string of affectionate terms implies that the man is trying to be as tender as possible but is in a desperate hurry for her to "open." If I have interpreted the text correctly, this is the moment of the consummation of their wedding. It appears that he will now complete sexual union with her but that she is now resistant. Her resistance is not a sudden rejection of him but is the reality of her virginity. For his part, the man can scarcely restrain himself. The text implies that the man and the woman enter the wedding night with very different physical impulses and concerns. The man feels an overwhelming need to complete the physical union and attain sexual relief, but the woman feels dread and hesitation at crossing the culturally conditioned psychological barrier of her virginity, together with fear of the physical pain that this may entail. To the man, the woman is strangely hesitant and unenthusiastic. To the woman, the man is demanding and insensitive. The wisdom of the Song prepares both parties to face the unexpected behavior of their partners with understanding.

Although these words obviously belong to the man, it may be that in the performance of the Song they were actually sung by the soprano in a caricature of the man's voice. The terms of affection, piled upon one another as they are in line 2B, lose their sweetness.

The reason the man gives for his appeal is as follows:שראשי נמלא־טל קוצותי רסיסי, לילה "my head is full of dew, my locks are full with the drops of the night." The metaphor obviously portrays him standing outside the door of a house and pleading to be let in on the grounds that he is getting wet with dew. Taken literally, the stated reason is weak; one might complain about standing outside in the rain, but not about standing outside in the dew. The referent for the "head" that is wet with the "drops of the night," is not literally dew on the hair of the head. רסיס appears only here meaning "drop." In Amos 6:11 the word means "fragments" or "something chopped up," but this appears to be an unrelated form (cf. *HALOT*). In Ezek 46:14, the root רסס means "to moisten," which accords well with a meaning "drop" here, and has cognates in Arabic and Syriac. Cf. Hess in *NIDOTTE* §8272. The man is pleading that his sexual stimulation is so strong at this point that further delay is unbearable for him. In modern English parlance, *head* is sometimes a euphemism for the penis, and this text seems to be employing the same circumspection in its language. The "drops of the night" refer to semen.

(As an aside, I would suggest that this understanding of ראש might explain an enigmatic text and provide further evidence that "head" can refer to the penis. In 2 Sam 3:6–7 we read that, after the death of Saul, Abner took Saul's concubine Rizpah for himself. Ish-bosheth [Ishbaal] read this as a political act directed against himself. The fact that Abner could take his father's concubine made Ishbaal look pitifully weak in his struggle against David, and he challenged Abner to give an explanation. Abner gave the outraged reply, הראש כלב אנכי אשר ליהודה, "Am I a dog's head that belongs to Judah?" [2 Sam 3:8]. The meaning of "dog's head" has mystified scholars. Most take it to be a kind of insult, which it surely is, but it is not clear why the head of the dog should be the focus of the aspersion. D. W. Thomas [*VT* 10 (1960) 417–23] argues that a "dog's head" is a baboon, but this is not persuasive, and at any rate it is not clear why Abner would ask if he were a "baboon belonging to Judah." But if "head" is itself slang for "penis," then "dog's head" is a special kind of slur, one reserved for a male prostitute. In this case, Abner is asking Ishbaal if he thinks that the Davidic party ["Judah"] has hired him as a male prostitute to bed Rizpah and so embarrass Ishbaal. This interpretation becomes all the more plausible when one recognizes that "dog" by itself was a term for a male prostitute [Deut 23:18–19 (ET 23:17–18), where context requires that the "wages of a dog" are monies earned by male prostitutes]. Professional soldier that he is, Abner uses language that is doubly graphic when he asks if Ishbaal thinks he is a "dog's head.")

It is not at all difficult to imagine that an Israelite audience would have heard a sexual reference in the man's remarks about his "head." In addition, analogy suggests that they would have understood the "drops of the night" to be a seminal emission; Deut 23:11 (ET 23:10) describes a man's nocturnal emission as a מקרה־לילה, an "event of the night," a phrase that is less suggestive than the "drops of the night" we have here, but still quite clear. At any rate, it is apparent that the man's primary concern is not that his hair is getting wet with dew. Rather, his words symbolically describe an urgent desire for sexual release.

3 This verse is almost always taken to be part of the soprano's lyrics. Interpreters generally assert that she is making the excuse that she cannot get up to open the door because she has already gone to bed. This is improbable, however, since the man is not asking her to come outside; he wants to come inside. She would have no reason to claim that she had washed her feet and therefore could not get them dirty. There is no indication that these words are anything but a continuation of the man's lyrics. That is, they are further entreaties for her to let him in. We should note that the כתנת, "tunic," is rarely women's clothing; it is more frequently used of male apparel in the OT (e.g., Gen 37:3; Exod 28:4; 40:14; 2 Sam 15:32; Isa 22:21; Ezra 2:69).

Taken as the man's words, the phrase that he had washed his feet may imply that he had washed them with a basin of water provided outside the door and did not want to go back out on the street, having just gone through the trouble of washing his feet. We should also note that רֶגֶל, "foot," in the dual is also used as a euphemism for the genital area; cf. *HALOT* רֶגֶל. The statement that he had stripped off his tunic gives the startling image of him standing naked outside the door. This is of course absurd if taken literally, but it is comprehensible if the text here blurs the metaphor of the man outside the door and the signified meaning of the man at the very moment of consummating his marriage. The reality is that he is naked as he seeks to join himself to her; the metaphor is that he is standing outside the door. The sense of urgency implied in the metaphor is all the more vivid if one imagines him standing naked outside the door and desperately trying to come in.

Even if the words were taken to be the woman's, the sexual significance of the line would still be present. The only place where כתנת, "tunic," is specifically a woman's garment is in the story of Tamar, where the כתנת she wears is the emblem of her virginity (2 Sam 13:18)! If the words do belong to the woman, they could mean "(If) I take off my כתנת, how shall I put it back on," meaning that she hesitates because she knows that loss of virginity is irreversible. Still, in my view, it is better simply to ascribe this verse to the man.

4–5 Many interpreters take this verse to mean that the man reached his hand through the latch opening to open the door (cf. NIV, NJB). But there is no evidence that חר can mean "latch opening" (see Pope, 518–19; G. L. Carr, 134; Fox, *Song of Songs*, 144). The word חר simply means "hole" (e.g., Ezek 8:7; 2 Kgs 12:10), although it can sometimes refer to a cave (e.g., Job 30:6). Keel ([1994] 190) comments that "Keyholes were apparently rare and made in such a way that it was not possible to put a hand through them," but he proposes the more absurd idea that the man was trying to stick his hand through a peephole in the door. The intended significance, the sexual union of the man and woman, is at the surface of the text. Even if in an Israelite house there was a hole that a man would put his hand through in order to open a door, and even if the word חר refers to such a hole, the sexual implications are clear (cf. King and Stager, *Life in Biblical Israel,* 31–33).

The word יד, "hand," is well known to have a euphemistic significance as "penis" (Isa 57:8, 10; cf. Ugaritic text 52:33–35 [found in UT 409]; *HALOT* יָד). The Qumran Manual of Discipline prescribes punishment for allowing one's יד, "hand," to be exposed (1QS 7:13). As early as the Sumerian love poetry, "hand" appears to represent the male organ; in the song of King Shu-Sin's beloved, she asks her bridegroom to put his "hand" on the "cup" in an evident euphemism for sexual union (*CS* 1:542). Although it is true that often a hand is just a hand, in this case it is impossible to escape the significance of his putting his יד, "hand," in the חר, "hole."

The woman adds, "my womb raged against it." מעים, "womb," can refer to the inner organs or guts of a person, the most personal, private parts, and can sometimes refer to emotions. Used of a woman, however, the word almost always refers to the womb and it often has בטן as a parallel. For example, עליך נסמכתי מבטן ממעי אמי, "I have relied upon you from birth, from the womb of my mother" (Ps 71:6), and עמי העוד־לי בנים במעי, "Do I still have sons in my womb?" (Ruth 1:11 NIV). The verb המה means to groan, growl, roar, or be in tumult. The best analogy for its usage with על is in Pss 42:6 (ET 42:5), 12 (ET 12:11); 43:5, where the psalmist asks his own discouraged soul (נפש), "Why do you groan against me?" The woman thus declares that her womb is roaring or raging against him, her lover. At the moment of their union, the woman's sexual parts seemed to fight within her against the event. For her, the moment of the consummation of their marriage has become something less than ecstasy. מעים, "womb," is more than just the sexual organs themselves. It seems to her that her "insides" struggle against the event.

Fox (*Song of Songs,* 144–45) rejects the view that this is a metaphorical account of the sexual union of the man and woman. His significant arguments are as follows. First, he contends that the man's putting his "hand" through the "hole" only means that he put it in her window. Fox asks, "One wonders how the poet could have said 'he put his hand in through the hole' in such a way as to prevent [a sexual] reading." Second, Fox asserts that v 5, where the woman says that she arose and opened for him, makes no sense if v 4 implies that intercourse has already taken place (so also D. Bergant, 64). Third, Fox contends that one should not read this text as a "gynecological conceit, in which each part of the door lock represents a specific part of the female genitals." Fourth, he says that it is in poor taste and ruins the tone of the love song for the man to have sexual union with her and then abruptly get up and run out the door (v 6). Fox argues that the couple would have had sexual union had she opened the door in time, but she was too slow.

Regarding the first objection, one must observe that the Hebrew Bible never uses חר, "hole," to mean "window." The question "How could the poet have said 'he put his hand in through the hole' without sexual innuendo?" is not appropriate because there was no reason for the poet to make such an odd statement, using such provocative language, *unless he intended a sexual meaning.* If the poet had actually meant "window," he could have used the very common term חלון, which would not have any sexual overtones, least of all as a symbol of the woman's genitals. Even if one acknowledges that the Israelite house had either a kind of hand-sized keyhole or large peephole, it does not follow that a poet who only meant to say, "he attempted to open the door," was at a loss to find a way to communicate this without sexual overtones. The clause "he put his hand through the opening" is sexual, and a poet as skillful in the subtleties of language as this one would surely have known to avoid it if that were his intent. We should note that King and Stager (*Life in Biblical Israel*, 32), in their account of what they call the "Egyptian" key and keyhole system, add that in Song 5:4-6, "the poet's double entendre is transparent throughout this passage."

Fox's second objection arises from a confusion of the signifier and the signified. The signifier (the metaphor) is of a man trying to gain admission to a house. The signified is a man trying to attain sexual union with his new wife. When the woman says that she arose, she is, on the level of the metaphor, saying that she got up to open the door. Getting out of bed to open a door, however, is not part of the signified event (the sexual union). One should not take details from the signifier and apply them literally to the signified. The question, "Why would she jump out of bed to open the door for him right after their sexual union?" is like asking, "If the 'mountains of spices' in Song 8:14 refer to the woman's breasts, why does she ask her beloved to be like a 'gazelle' on them? Does she want him to trample on her breasts?"

Her getting up may signify that she finally comes to the moment of full acceptance of the event. The arising could signify arousal on her part, but it need not. It indicates that she now embraces the man and this moment. The verb קום, "to arise," often implies that one carries out the action that he or she is expected to perform (e.g., Gen 37:35, "All his sons and all his daughters rose up to comfort him" [RSV]). Literal standing up is not required, and the verb is an auxiliary. In the *metaphor* (the signifier), her "arising" is part of her going to open the door. The language of arising may be no more than part of the metaphor of the door, and it may not signify anything at all, and as such, needs no explanation.

The details that follow, "and my hand drips myrrh; / even my fingers are running with myrrh, / on the handles of the bolt," support this interpretation. One need not read this as a "gynecological conceit" (Fox) or claim that every part of the door represents part of the female anatomy to see that something beyond the literal meaning of opening a door is going on here. It is peculiar that her hands should be so soaked in myrrh—a very expensive product—that they should be dripping with it. A modern woman, by analogy, would not put a tablespoon of expensive perfume on her hands. J. Munro says in her analysis of the imagery of the Song (*Spikenard and Saffron*, 49), "Normally one would not let myrrh, imported at great cost from Arabia and India, simply drip (*nṭp*), for myrrh was a highly valued commodity, and among other things, a component of holy oil (Exod. 30.23-25). The image of dripping myrrh is therefore one of conspicuous abundance." I would argue, however, that the dripping is not an image of abundance (which is not a topic in Song 3:1-5). Rather, such excess implies that the image is not to be read literally.

Murphy's suggestion (171) that the man had left a quantity of myrrh on the bolt as a token of his love is impossible (the woman's fingers drenched the bolt, and not vice versa). Murphy's opinion appears to be derived from Lucretius, where a love-sick male puts flowers on his beloved's threshold, scented oil on her doorposts, and kisses on the door itself (*De rerum natura* 4.1177–79). As described above, the *paraklausithyron* is used in various ways in ancient poetry, and Song of Songs has taken this image and shaped it in a distinctive manner; one cannot use Lucretius or the Egyptian poems to determine the meaning of this sequence in the Song. Those who regard the sexual interpretation as prurient must explain why the poet would include such an unnatural detail in the account. The picture of a woman with her hands drenched in myrrh, who thereby saturates the bolt of a door, is not to be taken literally.

It is probable that the *significance* of different elements of the metaphorical door do not cohere in a simple or logical manner to the *sequence of events* or to *individual elements* of the story. This is not an allegory, where a story follows a sequence of events in which each event coherently and sequentially has an allegorical meaning (as in *Pilgrim's Progress*). Rather, it is a series of metaphors, and the metaphors are not logically consistent. For example, the man pounding on the door and desperate to get in represents a man who is eager to achieve sexual union with his new wife; that is, he wants to enter her. This does not mean, however, that every part of the door represents a different part of her anatomy, or that every subsequent symbolic element will be logically coherent with the first. When the woman's fingers drip with perfumed oils, they get the bolt of the door wet. It is difficult to avoid the conclusion that the ואצבעתי, "fingers," represent the woman's genitals, that the oils suggest vaginal fluids, and that the מנעול, "bolt," suggests the man's penis. It does not matter that at one moment the door represents the woman's body or that the pounding man speaks of his desire to come inside her, and that at another moment the bar on the door represents part of the man's anatomy. (This is not a "gynecological conceit" [Fox].) This interpretation does not require that we demonstrate that biblical Hebrew elsewhere uses "fingers" as a euphemism for a woman's genitals. It is not a stock metaphor; it is driven by the symbolism of the context, that is, by the image of a woman opening a door. Sexual intercourse involves bodily fluids. In this case, מור, "myrrh," might suggest a woman's natural fluid since myrrh connotes sexual pleasure in the Song (1:13; 4:6, 14; 5:1, 13). The metaphor implies that the woman now fully accepts the entrance of the man into herself. The woman getting up to open the door to the man suggests as much.

One should also take note of a recent feminist interpretation, that the woman's wet fingers tell us that she is masturbating and that this is a "biblical wet dream" (C. Walsh *BTB* 28 [1998] 129–34; also Walsh, *Exquisite Desire*, 105–14; F. C. Black, *BibInt* 8 [2000] 314–15). On this view, the man vanishes because he was only a dream anyway. This interpretation is conceivable if one affirms that this canto describes a woman's dream. I have argued, in the *Comment* on v 2, that there is no reason to regard this text as an account of a dream. In addition, this interpretation of the passage is illegitimately selective. One part of the text is a "dream" (the man at the door) and is dismissed as unimportant, while another part is what really happened (her fingers got wet) and is the focus of the whole text. In this interpretation, the reference to the man's "hand," implying that he had sexual relations with her, is brushed aside as the woman's fantasy. The man who is at the door, who calls to her, who puts his hand through the hole, and who disappears, and whom she then seeks, is far more important in the text than her fingers, and there are no grounds for treating the latter as real and everything else as fantasy. This is not a passage about female masturbation.

6 The opening words of this verse, "I open to my lover," tell us that she has given her body to her new husband. It is probably significant that פתחתי אני, "I opened," here has no direct object (J. C. Exum "In the Eye of the Beholder," 83–84); it is the woman herself who opens. More than that, she has yielded her heart, her identity, and her former life to him. She has given up the status of virgin to him and in a real sense placed herself in his hands. It is at this moment that she expects and needs his complete devotion and affection. The next words, however, are jolting: her lover loses interest (or perhaps, "wanders off")! חמק is often translated "goes away," but that interpretation needs some explanation. The root appears elsewhere only in Jer 31:22: "How long will you dillydally [תִּתְחַמָּקִין], unfaithful girl? For Yahweh has created a new thing in the earth: A woman will surround a man." In context, תתחמקין means that the girl has trouble making up her mind among her boyfriends; Bright (*Jeremiah*, 276) has appropriately proposed the translation "dillydally." Holladay (1989:194) notes that the Arabic *ḥamiqa/ḥamuqa* means "stupid" or "silly." The primary significance of התחמק seems to be indecision and silly, flirty behavior rather than physical movement from place to place. Here in the *qal* stem it does not signify that the man is going from woman to woman. It probably suggests a loss of interest. The point is not that he has physically run out the door but that his interest has abruptly dissipated. In the metaphorical story, of course, he disappears, and she must search for him in the streets. This brings us to Fox's fourth objection, that it is unseemly for the man to have sexual relations with her and suddenly get up and leave. Once again, this objection reflects a fundamental confusion of the signifier with the signified. The signifier is her man frantic to come in, putting his hand through a hole, and abruptly leaving. The signified is the first sexual union of a bride and groom, and how the bride perceives the experience. The details of the symbolic tale of the man at the door and the signified event of the consummation of a marriage should not be mixed together. Even if one were to translate חמק as "depart," the metaphorical departure of the man in the metaphorical story does not mean that, in the actual event (the signified), the man literally jumped out of bed and ran down the street after having sexual relations with the woman.

The man's sudden "loss of interest" would seem to be nothing else but that he has experienced sexual release. As such, his ardent passion and desire have abruptly abated. This does not really mean that he has ceased to love her or to desire her, much less that he has bounded out the door. From the man's perspective, one might suggest, he has not behaved in an unusual or cold-hearted manner. One cannot expect him to be as passionate after the event as he was before his sexual release. From the woman's perspective, however, he seems to have suddenly abandoned her. In an instant, his passion has cooled, and that just as she has opened to him. He has עבר, "moved along," in the sense of behaving as though he were finished with lovemaking and could move on to something else. The verb עבר is often rendered "departed" or "gone," but this does not seem to be precisely correct. For "depart," Hebrew can employ a number of verbs (בוא, עלה, הלך). But עבר generally means "to cross over," and it is often used for the crossing of rivers or for crossing through territory. Metaphorically, it often means to cross a moral boundary, i.e., to "transgress." A good analogy for the usage of עבר in this text is in Gen 18:5, where Abraham tells his visitors they should eat and then they can move along (עבר) since they have visited him while passing through (עבר). Hence, the word in Song 5:6 means something like "to move along" or "to continue with a journey." A simple departure does not seem to be the main point (as it would have been with הלך); the word here conveys the idea "he went about his business." Loss of interest, not mere physical absence, is implied. For her, this is a cruel joke, especially if she is in physical and emotional pain.

The woman thus says that she expired when he spoke. The only helpful example we have for understanding נפשי יצאה, "my soul expires," is Gen 35:18, where the metaphor means "to die." Here, the woman does not mean that she died. The phrase means "the breath to go out." It could be analogous to what English speakers mean when they say "was totally deflated" and refer to the experience of heartbreak or of having one's hopes dashed. At the same time, we cannot assume that this expression would not have been jolting to an Israelite audience, who may have heard it to mean "I died." "To expire" is an appropriate translation.

בדברו, "when he speaks": If the man is speaking to her, he is obviously not literally absent. The speaking here denotes a return to prosaic speech and an end to the actions and words of passionate love. He has left the realm of ecstatic eros and has returned to the ordinary. She feels deflated and crushed—worse than that, she says she has died. If as some suggest דבר in this context can mean, "turn away" (see *Note* 5:6.a.), the point is even more forceful: he has simply stopped making love to her and turned over! I do not, however, consider "turn away" to be a likely meaning of the word on the basis of Akkadian and Arabic cognates (e.g., Murphy, 165; Pope, 526). *HALOT* s.v. I דבר lists several examples of דבר in the *pi'el* meaning "turn away" or "drive away," but these examples are either intelligible with the normal meaning of "speak" (e.g., Ps 75:6 [ET 75:5]) or are based on conjectural emendations (e.g. Ps 56:6 [ET 56:5]). It is possible that an ancient Israelite audience would have recognized בדברו to mean, "when he turned away," but this is far from certain. Translators feel that the usual meaning, "when he spoke," is impossible because the man has supposedly run off into the night. This commentary argues that the account of the man who pounds at the door and runs away is merely the signifier, a symbolic account meant to represent something entirely different. As such, some of the details are impossible or absurd if read literally. While the meaning "he turned away" would suit this interpretation, I am not convinced that the word has this meaning in biblical Hebrew. It is better to take the word in its normal sense of "speak" and understand that at this point the text is not working within the confines of the metaphor of the man at the door (cf. NRSV).

7 It has already been suggested that the guards of the city are a metaphor for the woman's virginity. In Song 3:1–5, the woman confronts her anxiety over losing her virginity. In this text, she loses it. The guards' beating is the searing pain she has after her husband withdraws.

It seems somewhat peculiar that the Song says the guards took away the רדיד. The meaning of the term רדידי is uncertain; it may mean "my shawl" or "my veil." It only occurs elsewhere in Isa 3:23, where it is included in a list of clothing and accessories used by women and probably was some kind of a thin veil (cf. Alden, רְדִיד, *NIDOTTE* §8100). Thus, רדיד seems to be exclusively an item of women's clothing in biblical Hebrew. It may also have been a garment that was associated particularly with young women. The Isaiah text castigates the "daughters of Zion" (Isa 3:16–17; see also Isa 4:4) for their jewelry, clothing, and provacative mannerisms. In light of the fact that the term "daughters of Zion/Jerusalem" appears in the OT only here and in the Song, it would seem that Isaiah is speaking of young, fashion-minded women rather than of wealthy, older women. That the metaphorical phrase "daughter of Zion/Jerusalem" refers to the "virgin" Jerusalem further implies that Isaiah's "daughters of Zion/Jerusalem" were actual young women.

If biblical Hebrew associates the רדיד with young women—with women who were supposed to be virgins—רדיד in this text may be representative of virginity itself. Otherwise, there is no clear reason for the text to point out that the guards took it away. This detail is not the poet's way of making the assault more vivid; actual soldiers presumably had little use for women's veils. As a poetic metaphor, however, soldiers stripping away the woman's veil is a removal of the outward sign that she belongs to the "daughters of Zion." As a woman who has lost her virginity, she no longer belongs among those women, as subsequent texts and the woman herself will make plain.

Although ancient love poetry has no analogy to the guards, Keel ([1994] 195) does cite an intriguing provision of the Middle Assyrian law code (twelfth century) as follows: "A prostitute dare not veil herself; her head remains uncovered. Anyone seeing a veiled prostitute should arrest her, gather witnesses, and bring her to the entrance of the palace. Her jewelry may not be taken, but the one who arrests her receives her clothing. She should be given fifty blows with a club and have asphalt poured on her head." Several significant differences between this text and the Song stand out. The woman of the Song is not a prostitute, and she is not arrested but simply assaulted. The guards do not receive her clothing after a judicial procedure but simply take her veil by force. The Assyrian text describes the role not of guards but of any common citizen. Nevertheless, the Assyrian text tells us that a veil may be representative of the status of the woman in an ancient Near Eastern culture. This may also imply that, in the symbolism of this text of the Song, the woman feels that she has lost her purity, notwithstanding that she lost her virginity in a lawful manner. That is, in a culture that gives so much emphasis to preserving virginity until marriage, the virgin inevitably has special status.

The beating of the woman by the guards represents the physical and emotional trauma of losing her virginity. One should not expect chronological precision in relating the parabolic story to the signified loss of virginity. The parabolic story represents different aspects of the event; it is not a precise, moment-by-moment account.

An objection that has been raised against this interpretation of the text is that the woman "hasn't been a virgin for quite some time" and thus cannot have just lost her virginity (Longman, 130). There is no indication whatsoever that she had lost her virginity prior to the consummation at Song 4:16–5:1. To review, the woman begins by singing of her longing for the man and of her self-consciousness (1:2–8). The woman and man then sing of their devotion to each other (1:9–2:7). The language is sexually charged (he is like a bundle of myrrh between her breasts, 1:13), but there is no statement to the effect that they have attained sexual union. Song 2:8–17 is the invitation to depart, and again the desire for sexual fulfillment is clear, but there is no indication that the desire has been achieved. Song 3:1–4:15 is the beginning of the "wedding-night songs" that lead directly to the moment of fulfillment in 4:16–5:1. In short, the language of 1:2–4:15 is charged with sexual anticipation and as such strongly implies that the consummation has *not* occurred. W. E. Phipps observes (*JAAR* 42 [1974] 83), "It would be anachronistic to interpret the Song of Songs as infatuations and sexual experimentation of promiscuous youth."

Longman recognizes that 5:2–8 is erotic in nature ("The door is clearly a euphemism for the woman's vagina" [166]), and yet of this verse, where the guards beat the woman, Longman resorts to describing the beating as a "dream" and suggests by way of interpretation that it symbolizes "the unfriendly urban-public gaze" (169). But why are people unfriendly to her? Why does the text use such violent language to make this point? Does the hostility of the "urban-public gaze" have any larger function in the Song, or is it isolated to this text, and if so, why? This verse is stunning to the reader, and it cannot be set aside with an isolated, *ad hoc* interpretation. Readers need to know why this astonishing verse is in the Song. I suggest that the only reading that makes sense in the context of the book is that it is the moment when she ceases to be a virgin.

In summary, to assert that there is no sexual symbolism in this canto is to refuse to see how odd and contrived the details of the story are when it is given a superficial, literal reading: The man's reason for needing to come in the house is the flimsy and peculiar excuse that his hair has dew in it; the man (as argued above) is standing naked outside the door; the woman has an enormous quantity of expensive, perfumed oils on her fingers; she has drenched her hands in perfume before going to bed even though she is not expecting the man to come and is initially unwilling to let him in; when the woman begins to open the door, the man abruptly runs away; to top it all off, the woman, the heroine of a romantic, sensual love song, gets beaten up by city guards! It is difficult to imagine that the poet intended us to hear the canto on this level. Gledhill (*Message of the Song of Songs*, 178, italics original) wants to read the story literally, but seems to be trying to avoid the scandal of the text by saying that "in her struggle to free herself, her flimsy garments were torn from her, leaving her battered, *bruised*, shivering, and half naked." But the text says, "They beat me, they wound me, / they take my veil from me." That is, this is not a tussle that got out of hand; it is a beating. In a book where every text is dominated by symbolism (the man is an apple tree, a shepherd, a king, a gazelle; the woman is a palm tree, a garden, a peasant, a princess), why would the poet suddenly tell a literal but bizarre story? Gledhill (*Message of the Song of Songs*, 181) can only justify the text by suggesting that it has moral lessons to teach: the canto tells how the woman suffered for being coquettish ("She is deliberately withdrawing her affection, perhaps as a punishment for some supposed slight or lack of appreciation"). Besides the fact that this explanation is entirely extraneous to the text, one needs to remember that on a literal reading, the couple is not married. They do not live in the same house. In that case, would letting him in be the right thing to do? Would refusal to let him in be "coquettish"?

By contrast, many interpreters who do see sexual imagery here are quite inconsistent. Walsh is selective about which elements are a dream and which are reality. Other interpreters see many sexual references in the early part of the sequence, but then, when the woman is beaten by the guards, lapse into the "dream" interpretation.

8   Once again, the woman calls on the girls of Jerusalem to make a promise. It is possible with Fox (*Song of Songs,* 146) to translate, "Do not tell him that I am wounded by love," although the analogies Fox suggests (1 Kgs 12:16; Job 16:6) are not very close. This translation would be correct if the text had used אם, "if," or even למה, "why," but with מה, "what," it is only a possibility. It is more likely that she is asking them to convey the message to her beloved that she is wounded by love. She does not comprehend his behavior and feels abandoned by him. She has had to endure the ordeal alone. This is not a girl sending a message to her lover via some friends. It is a poetic device that uses an address to the chorus to convey information about the woman's condition to the audience. It indicates that at the moment of her trauma she thinks of herself still as a girl who seeks the comfort and companionship of her friends in dealing with an emotional trial. She has not yet completed the emotional transition from girl to wife. The friends, however, will remind her of her love for him and enable her to complete her transformation (Song 5:9). But we must remind ourselves again that this is a song and not a dramatic play or history. The interaction of the singers is not to be understood as the dialogue of actors, and the lyrics do not make up a "story" as we understand the term. The woman did not run from her beating to her friends. The question, "Why would she suddenly start talking to her old girlfriends?" misunderstands the genre.

The final line, that she is wounded by love, repeats a line from Song 2:5. There her pain came from the fact that she was yearning for a sexual relationship with her lover but was at the same time filled with dread. Here, her hurt is more real; what she both wanted and dreaded has come to pass.

Explanation

In the interpretation that I am proposing, the entire sequence is a metaphorical story: the man pounds at her door; she opens to him but finds that he is gone; she looks for him and she gets beaten up by guards. The peculiar elements in the story (the dew on the hair, the oils on the fingers, and so forth) are understood to be contrived by the poet in order to develop the symbolism. On the symbolic level, the entire sequence relates that a new husband desperately wanted inside of his new wife, that she experienced sexual excitement, that he seemed to lose interest after sexual release, that she felt abandoned and experienced the pain of the loss of her virginity.

Understood this way, the woman's search for the man is metaphorical; she does not literally plunge into the night after her lover. She instead feels emotionally abandoned. She wonders where his love for her has gone. She feels that he has no sense of how strong is her need for passion and affection at this moment; it is as though he were not there at all. Her search for him in the night is thus emblematic of her yearning.

Scholars sometimes draw a parallel between the woman's quest for her beloved and the quest of Isis for Osiris or the quest of Anat for Baal. In these myths, the god (Osiris, Baal) is in a battle with an evil god (Seth, Mot, Yam). The good god is killed, but his goddess-consort (Isis, Anat) seeks his body in order to resurrect him. The significance of the parallel between this mythological motif and this part of the Song is easy to exaggerate. In Song of Songs, the man and woman are not deities, the man is not in a battle with an evil deity, he does not die, and the woman does not resurrect him. If anything, it is the woman who falls into mortal danger (with the guards of the city), rather than the man.

A more fruitful area for drawing parallels to the quest of the woman after the man is in the heroic literature of the ancient world. Heroic figures (Gilgamesh, Herakles, Orpheus, Jason, and so forth) must go on a quest in order to achieve their desired goals. In those tasks, they face great dangers. The quest can be a transformative event, although in the ancient legends the transformation is in a tragic context.

In the Song, the protagonist is the woman. She must go out and face terrifying dangers in the night in order to possess love. Ancient stories of women who take heroic quests are more rare, but they are not unknown. The myth of Psyche is possibly the best example. In the version of Apuleius, a jealous Venus commanded Cupid to make the ravishing beauty Psyche fall in love with the most grotesque of men. Instead, Cupid himself fell in love with Psyche and took her to a remote island where he visited her only at night. Despite his warnings that she should never look on his face, she came with a lamp to see him while he lay asleep. While she gazed at his beauty, a drop of oil from the lamp fell on him and woke him. He rebuked her and fled away; she thereafter roamed the earth in search of him. Venus imposed harsh tasks on her, but Cupid was touched by her repentance, and Jupiter finally made her a goddess.

We need to take one more look at the clause in v 6 that is usually rendered "I was crushed when he departed" or the like but which is translated above as "I expired when he spoke." This is, in one sense, a kind of spiral into despair when her new husband appears to have abruptly moved from intense passion to prosaic speech. But the words may signify something more. The expiration of the woman may reflect the theme that is common in stories of the heroic quest, namely, the hero's "death" and "resurrection" (in quotation marks because it is not a literal death here). A descent into Hades is a decisive break with the old self, and the return is a birth of the new self. Thus, the words may imply a motif of transformation. The Song, like the myths, sends the protagonist out on a heroic quest where she faces harrowing dangers. She leaves her security behind and exposes herself to danger and pain for the sake of attaining her beloved. There is no journey out into the streets of the night, but the image portrays her determination to have her beloved, in the face of what it costs her, an act of courage and devotion.

This interpretation is fruitful both on the literary and the practical levels. It indicates that a young man and a young (virgin) woman enter a wedding night with fundamentally different sexual natures. For the man, the desire for sexual union is an uncomplicated, albeit urgent, matter. For the woman, however, it is a more complex affair and involves both physical trauma and the need for emotional support and tender affection. Both man and woman do well to approach their marriage with an understanding of the mindset of the other. The suggested parallel between the woman's quest for her lover in the Song and the hero's quest in epic literature to fulfill an appointed task indicates that the woman's courage to face this moment for the sake of her beloved places her on a heroic level. She confronts a trauma that the man cannot know, and in doing so, she is the valiant and heroic protagonist of the Song.

B. The Bride Recovers the Groom (5:9–6:3)

Bibliography

Hill, A. E. "תַּרְשִׁישׁ." *NIDOTTE* §9577. **Lee, G. M.** "Song of Songs 5:16, 'My Beloved Is White and Ruddy.'" *VT* 21 (1971) 609. **Martínez, F. G.** *The Dead Sea Scrolls in English.*

Translation

First Stanza

CHORUS
9 What makes your lover better than other lovers,	1A
most beautiful of women,	1B
what makes your lover better than other lovers,	1C
that you would have us swear such an oath?	1D

SOPRANO
10 My lover is radiant and tan;	2A
he is outstanding[a] among ten thousand.	2B
11 His head is pure gold.	3A
His hair is like the spathe,[a]	3B
black as a raven.	3C
12 His eyes are like doves	4A
beside streams of water,	4B
washed in milk,[a]	4C
sitting on basins filled with water.	4D
13 His cheeks are like a bed of balsam;	5A
they are trellises of aromatic herbs.	5B
His lips are lotuses,	6A
dripping with flowing myrrh.	6B
14 His arms are rods of gold	7A
set with the golden topaz.	7B
His loins are a piece of ivory	8A
hung with sapphires.	8B
15 His thighs are alabaster pillars	9A
set on pedestals of pure gold.	9B
The effect he gives is like Lebanon;	9C
he is as choice as the cedars.	9D
16 His mouth is sweetness itself.	10A
Every part of him is desirable!	10B
This is my lover, this is my companion,	10C
O daughters of Jerusalem!	10D

Second Stanza

CHORUS

6:1 Where has your lover gone,   11A
    most beautiful of women,   11B
    where has your lover turned,   11C
    that we may seek him with you?   11D

SOPRANO

2 My lover went down to his garden   12A
    to beds of balsam,   12B
    to graze in his gardens   12C
    and to gather lotuses.   12D
3 I am my lover's and my lover is mine,   13A
    he who grazes among the lotuses.   13B

Notes

10.a. MT דָּגוּל is from דגל, to "hoist a banner," a root that reappears in Song 6:4, 10. Here it seems to mean "marked as special" and hence "outstanding." LXX Vg. Tg. render it "chosen."

11.a. The meaning of MT תַּלְתַּלִּים, a *hapax legomenon*, is uncertain. It is sometimes rendered "wavy" on the analogy of תל, a "mound," but this seems to be little more than a conjecture. LXX renders it ἐλάτα, which is usually rendered "palm-fronds," and some prefer this translation here. LSJ, however, indicates that ἐλάτη means either "silver fir" or the "spathe of the date inflorescence." The spathe is the part that encases the blooms or spadix of certain plants, such as the jack-in-the-pulpit.

12.a. Rudolph (158) proposes inserting שִׁנָּיו, "his teeth," after בחלב, "with milk," on the grounds that it was lost through haplography. Thus, "his teeth are bathed in milk." This is unlikely.

Form/Structure/Setting

In this segment, questions by the chorus lead into songs by the bride. The subject matter is metaphorically the finding of the lost groom, but in reality it deals with the bride's reflections first on her love for the groom and second on his love for her. She does not so much find the groom as she rediscovers herself and the reasons she married him. In the larger structure of the book, Song 5:9–6:3 corresponds to Song 3:6–11, where the chorus hails the arrival of the bride. In the earlier text the bride comes to the groom, while in the latter text the bride metaphorically finds the groom. In both passages, the chorus has a decisive role. Precious materials dominate the imagery in both. In 3:6–11 gold, silver, wood from Lebanon, and purple fabric make up the palanquin. In 5:9–6:3 the man is described in terms of gold, ivory, sapphires, and alabaster.

Song 5:9–6:3 consist of two stanzas, each headed by questions posed by the chorus. In each case, the questions take the form of a four-line strophe (5:9; 6:1), and in each case the bride replies with a lengthy declaration of the glories of the man she loves.

The first strophe of the first stanza (5:9, sung by the chorus) has matching pairs of lines (line 1A is repeated in line 1C). In the soprano's part that follows (vv 10–16), she sings a series of short strophes governed by the descriptions of the parts of the man's body. The first strophe of the second stanza (6:1, again sung by the chorus) is another matching pair of lines (lines 11A–B match lines 11C–D). The soprano responds with two strophes (6:2–3); both of these strophes are held together by syntactical dependence.

This text uses the familiar *wasf*. Under the literary guise of the woman describing her beloved to a group of girls so that they can help her search for him, the woman actually reminds herself of all the things that she finds extraordinary about him (5:9–15). Her love for him allows her to move beyond the pain of 5:2–7. Then, under the guise of telling the girls where to find the man, the woman proclaims that he is in love with her and delights himself in the pleasures that she gives (6:2–3). She triumphantly concludes that she and the man belong to one another (6:3) and so completes the healing process occasioned by her loss of virginity.

Comment

9 The chorus is asking the woman what makes her beloved so special that they should make such a promise to her. This question forces the woman to recall why she loves her husband. In effect, the choir's question calls the woman back to reflect on the fundamental reason that she gave her virginity to this man. Thus, the woman's love for the man completes her transformation. She is transformed not simply because she has lost her virginity but because the event was for her a heroic quest carried out in a context of loving and being loved (see *Explanation* to 5:2–8 above). She can therefore cope with the pain of the experience and realize that he has not abandoned her at all.

10 In contrast to ancient standards of female beauty, where white skin was highly valued (see *Comment* on 1:5), the ancients seemed to prefer dark, tanned skin for men. Tan skin apparently was considered masculine. David was regarded as attractive for his reddish skin (1 Sam 16:12). Her claim that he is "outstanding among ten thousand" restates more prosaically what she had said in Song 2:3.

11 In this *wasf*, she works her way down from his head to his legs. She speaks of the head before speaking of the hair even though the latter is on top. The head (and face) imply the personality and individuality of the man, and this has precedence over the hair. Put another way, it is not simply his anatomy she loves; it is the man himself.

The spathe (see *Note* 5:11.a.) encloses the blooms of certain plants, such as the jack-in-the-pulpit. Gerleman (173–74) argues that this part of the palm is dark on the outside but white on the inside. Its dark exterior makes it an apt counterpart to the comparison to a raven. Black hair implies youth and vigor; this is in contrast to gray hair, which naturally connotes age and experience (see Prov 20:29). Ancient peoples regularly lampooned baldness (cf. 2 Kgs 2:23). The comedies of Aristophanes frequently subjected bald men to taunts or made reference to this stock comic device (e.g., *Clouds* 540: "she does not ridicule bald men or dance lewd dances"). The woman's beloved is neither bald nor gray!

12 The comparison of eyes to doves is something of a stock metaphor, although the point of comparison between the eyes and doves remains a mystery. Here, however, it is the washing of the dove that is the focus rather than the dove itself. This implies that his eyes are moist and sparkling. To put it negatively, the man does not have a dry, dead stare. The fluttering of birds when they bathe perhaps implies that his eyes have a lively, dancing movement. חלב, "milk," simply gives the metaphor in a more exaggerated form since milk implies richness. There is obviously no reason that a bird would actually bathe in milk.

יֹשְׁבוֹת עַל־מִלֵּאת, "sitting on basins filled with water," is difficult. Some render it as "mounted like jewels" (cf. NIV) on the basis of the fact that the *piʿel* of מלא can be used for setting jewels (Exod 28:17; cf. also the noun מִלֻּאָה, "setting"). But Gordis (90) calls this an inept rendering. Murphy (166) understands the man's teeth to be the topic here and renders it "set in place," but this is not persuasive. In light of the fact that doves appear to be the operative metaphor here, it seems best to take מלאת to refer to basins full of water above which the birds are perched rather than as settings for jewels or gums for the teeth. The LXX reads ἐπὶ πληρώματα ὑδάτων, "above basins of water." So also Keel ([1994] 199–201), and note especially his figures of vessels from Cypress and Hadrian's villa near Rome that portray doves perched above vessels.

13 The line "towers [מִגְדְּלוֹת] of aromatic herbs" strikes interpreters as such a harsh metaphor that it is often emended to מְגַדְּלוֹת, the *piʿel* participle, and rendered something like "putting forth aromatic blossoms" (Murphy, 166). But while the *piʿel* of גדל is used of rain that causes plants to grow (Isa 44:14; Ezek 31:4) or of a person who tends growing plants (Jonah 4:10), it is not elsewhere used of a place where plants grow. Keel ([1994] 201) follows Gerleman (175) and takes it to refer to cones of fat mixed with spices that Egyptians apparently wore on their heads at drinking parties. However, to describe the man's *cheeks* as a spice cone that one would normally place on *top of the head* seems a grating turn of an image even by the standards of the Song. The best solution seems to be that the מִגְדְּלוֹת are not military towers but banks of flowers that are towerlike because of their height (cf. NJB and NASB). It appears that the מגדלות מרקחים are trellises of aromatic flowers and herbs.

The description of the man's cheeks as like balsam or trellises of spices possibly relates to his beard, although the word לְחִי, "cheeks," tells us that her focus is more on his skin than on his beard. He may well have scented his beard with some kind of perfume, but this, too, is not necessarily the point of the metaphor. The word מֶרְקָחִים is a *hapax*, but it probably means something like "herbal spices" after the root רקח (thus, *HALOT*), which is found in words concerning spiced ointments. Spices and perfumes in the Song generally imply something that is sensually pleasurable whether the spices are literally present or not. The lips, similarly, are described as lotuses, not because they in any sense look like lotuses but because they are almost magical in their rejuvenating or pleasure-giving power. The lotus was a symbol of life to the Egyptians. In addition, she may mean that his kisses have a sweet taste. Herodotus in his *Histories* 2.92.2–3 reports that the Egyptians gathered lotus flowers, crushed the poppylike centers, and baked bread. He also tells us that the root of the lotus has a sweet flavor. In *The Odyssey*, Odysseus encounters the "Lotus Eaters" (Λωτοφάγοι) in his wanderings across the Mediterranean. Eating the lotus caused a person to enter a blissful, forgetful state, as described in *Odyssey* 9.91–97 (W. B. Stanford, ed., *The Odyssey of Homer*, 2d ed. [London: Macmillan, 1959] 134).

οἱ δ' αἶψ' οἰχόμενοι μίγεν ἀνδράσι Λωτοφάγοισιν.
οὐδ' ἄρα Λωτοφάγοι μήδονθ' ἑτάροισιν ὄλεθρον
ἡμετέροις, ἀλλά σφι δόσαν λωτοῖο πάσασθαι.
τῶν δ' ὅς τις λωτοῖο φάγοι μελιηδέα καρπόν,
οὐκέτ' ἀπαγγεῖλαι πάλιν ἤθελεν οὐδὲ νέεσθαι

ἀλλ' αὐτοῦ βούλοντο μετ' ἀνδράσι Λωτοφάγοισι
λωτὸν ἐρεπτόμενοι μενέμεν νόστου τε λαθέσθαι.

And they, straight away setting out, mingled with the Lotus-eating men.
The Lotus-eaters plotted no ruin to the companions
Of us, but gave to them lotus to eat.
But whoever ate of the sweet fruit of the lotus
No longer wanted to come give a report or even to return,
But they wished with the Lotus-eating men
To remain plucking lotus, and to forget about going home.

Other classical writers also speak of the blissful forgetfulness of eating the lotus. Thus, she may be suggesting that his lips move her into a dreamy bliss. Of course, we cannot be sure that the λωτός of classical literature and the Hebrew שׁוּשָׁן are the same, although LSJ does list "Egyptian Lotus" as one of the meanings for λωτός. The woman adds that his lips are dripping with flowing myrrh, combining a phrase she had used of herself in Song 5:5 with the image of the lips dripping with pleasant liquids (Song 4:11). As in these texts, the metaphor connotes sexual excitement and pleasure (see also *Comment* on 2:2, 16 above).

14 יָדָיו, "his hands," by metonymy apparently refers to his arms since it makes little sense to describe hands as rodlike, unless one were referring to the fingers. There is absolutely no unanimity among scholars regarding the identity of the gemstone תַּרְשִׁישׁ. I have chosen "golden topaz" with *NIDOTTE* §9577. But this is the only place in the Hebrew Bible where תַּרְשִׁישׁ has the definite article. This may imply that she has a single stone in mind for each hand rather than that they are covered with gemstones.

מֵעֶה, "loins" (found as dual מֵעַיִם or plural מֵעִים), refers to the lower abdominal part of the body (internally). It can refer to the intestines (2 Sam 20:10). Since this area was thought to govern emotions, the term often refers to one's emotional state (Isa 16:11; Lam 1:20). The Aramaic מְעֵה refers to the external abdomen in Dan 2:32, but it is not clear that this meaning applies in Hebrew. The word often refers to the genitals, be it of a man or a woman (Gen 15:4; 25:23; 2 Sam 7:12). The word is obviously not describing his internal organs or his emotions; it refers either to his abdominal region generally or his genitals specifically. The English word *loins,* although archaic, best captures this range of meaning.

עֶשֶׁת, "a piece," is given an enormous number of interpretations. Many render it something like "plate" or "panel"; the NJB has "block." This interpretation follows the LXX, which has πυξίον, "tablet." The more common Hebrew terms for "plate" or "tablet" are צִיץ, גִּלָּיוֹן (Isa 3:23 and 8:1), and especially לוּחַ. Some take עשׁת to mean "smoothness" or "shine" after Jer 5:28, where the root עשׁת is paired with שָׁמַן, "to be fat." It is not at all clear that the form in Jer 5:28 is related to the word here, however, and attempts to create a translation on that analogy are really no more than conjecture. A more likely parallel is in the Copper Scroll from Qumran, 3Q15 I, 5; II, 4, where עשׁת זהב means "bar(s) of gold" (Martínez, *Dead Sea Scrolls in English,* 461, renders it "gold ingots"). Gerleman (176) suggests that ingots of gold would have taken the shape of bricks or disks; this can be taken to be support for the translation "plate." On the other hand, while a brick, disk, or plate shape may be appropriate for gold, it hardly seems appropriate for ivory. In addition, the parallel to "gold ingots" suggests that עשׁת here refers to ivory in an unfinished state, just as "gold ingots" differ from gold jewelry or inlaid gold in that ingots have not yet been artistically fashioned. The natural shape of an ivory tusk indicates that "bar" is a more likely translation. On the other hand, we should not take this to be a complete tusk of ivory, for which Hebrew would probably use קרן here (see Ezek 27:15, where שן קרנות = "tusks of ivory"). Murphy, curiously, translates these two lines as, "His belly, a work of ivory / covered in sapphires" (164). But in a footnote in his introduction (75 n. 305), he gives the lines a more thorough treatment and renders it, "his loins, a shaft of ivory, ensconced in lapis lazuli." He also notes that rabbinic sources suggest that עשת refers to a pillar or column "comparable to the shape of a scroll." The word is therefore almost certainly used as a metaphor for the penis, but I have given עשת the more neutral translation "piece."

The usage of עלף, "hung," is somewhat of a mystery. The LXX has ἐπὶ λίθου, "upon stone," but Pope (544) is probably correct that the LXX is guessing here. In Isa 51:20 (*pu'al*), Amos 8:13 (*hitpa'el*), and Jonah 4:8 (*hitpa'el*), it means to "faint." In Gen 38:14 it is used (*hitpa'el*) of Tamar draping a large garment over herself in order to conceal her identity. An occurrence of the root in Ezek 31:15 should also be vocalized as a *pu'al* (*HALOT*) and translated "wilted." Here in the Song (*pu'al*), it describes the metaphorical ivory (שן here treated as a feminine noun) somehow having sapphires attached to it. Some scholars deny that עלף, "faint, wilt," and עלף, "drape," are from the same root, but in light of how consistently עלף appears in the *pu'al* and *hitpa'el*, we are probably dealing with a single root. The basic idea of the root is probably to "droop" or "hang." This would account for the meaning "faint" or "wilt," since the person or tree in this state stands feebly with limbs hanging and is on the point of collapse, and it would also account for the meaning "drape" in Gen 38:14 (i.e., Tamar draped or hung a large veil over herself). It is difficult to see how מעלפת could mean "inlaid" here in the Song, as though sapphires were imbedded in the ivory. A translation "covered with sapphires" is also unlikely, since the sapphires do not seem to have obscured the ivory in the way that Tamar's cloak hid her face. The main point of עלף seems to be that something hangs, not that something covers something else. In keeping with other usage of עלף, it would appear that the ivory has sapphires hung from it.

The similarity between arms and rods is obvious. Once again, she speaks of him as זהב, "gold." A number of interpreters point out that she seems to be describing a statue, and thus they postulate that this was originally a hymn to an idol. This is altogether unnecessary. The "gold" conveys the idea of high value, and it also reflects the fact that she has already described him as having a deep tan. It is noteworthy that she describes the parts of his body that would normally be exposed to the sun (head, arms, and lower legs) as gold but describes those parts that would be hidden (loins and thighs) as ivory and alabaster (i.e., pale by comparison). She is not describing an image; she is describing a man's body metaphorically using precious materials.

The meaning of מעיו עשת שן מעלפת ספירים, "his loins are a piece of ivory hung with sapphires," is transparent, and one is tempted to hide behind a more innocuous, traditional translation (e.g., "his belly is a plate of ivory inlaid with sapphires"). As far as I can tell, however, evidence indicates that this is indeed a piece of ivory hung with sapphires. This naturally suggests the male genitals, and one might well look at this and wonder if there is the kind of phallic humor going on here that one would expect to find among the Greek comedians. This imagery, however, does not relate to having an enormous penis, as in Greek comedy (as described above, the word עשה does not mean "tusk," contrary to Longman, 164). Instead, the woman describes his private parts as having high value to her. She does not focus any more on these parts than she does on his eyes, arms, or legs, and she uses precious metals and gems to describe these body parts as well. It is not inappropriate for a woman in love to take pleasure in the anatomy of her husband, including his sexual parts. The tone here is not comic.

15 The word אדני here should be translated "pedestals" rather than "sockets." In the metaphor, these are what the thighs rest upon. His thighs are the pillars, and his lower leg region or feet are the base or pedestals for the pillars.

As mentioned above, the whiteness of his upper thigh (alabaster) stands in contrast to the golden color of his lower legs, but she highly values every part of him. The total effect of the man's appearance on her is like that of Lebanon. He is in her eyes magnificent to look upon. She here abandons the language of bodily parts being like precious materials to compare him to a forest. It should be clear by now that she is not describing an idol. She employs the comparison to Lebanon because the trees of the forest are both strong and beautiful (yet without excessive floral coloring) and so are an appropriate symbol of male beauty. In Song 2:3 also she declares him to be the finest among the trees (i.e., among men). The parable of Jotham (Judg 9:7–15) also compares men of different qualities to trees.

16 She returns to the pleasures of his mouth as an allusion to the pleasure of his kisses (Song 1:2). There is a triumphal, joyful note to this verse that heals the despair of Song 5:2–7. As a counterpart to Song 1:4 ("Rightly they love you!"), she in effect says, "No wonder I love him!" Here alone the woman uses רעי, "my companion," of the man; elsewhere he routinely speaks of her with this term. She has fully set herself apart from the girls of Jerusalem; her true companion now is not they but he.

6:1 The second question of the chorus serves as a bridge to the soprano's next part. Their question may give the impression that they are so intrigued by the beauty of this man, as she has described him, that they want to see him for themselves. At most, however, this question only superficially has that function. Once again, the point of this text is not that a woman is literally asking her friends to join a search party and find her truant husband. Rather, this question allows her to complete the process of transformation through the realization of the full force of her husband's love for her. The first question (Song 5:9) allowed her to reflect on how much she loves him. This question allows her to acknowledge how much he loves her.

2-3 The man is not lost; she knows exactly where he is. Where is he? He is making love to her! As in Song 4:16, the גן, "garden," that belongs to the man is the body of his wife. In Song 5:13, she had described his cheeks as beds of balsam, but now she is the bed of balsam that he takes pleasure in. They belong to one another and mutually take pleasure in one another. Under the metaphor of the gazelle, he is feeding among the plants of the garden. Like a gardener, he is picking lotuses from his garden.

All of this makes for narrative chaos if read in any literal way. If one imagines the woman to be standing outside asking her friends to help find her beloved, he cannot be at that moment in process of making love to her. Even her metaphors are mixed and somewhat incoherent. He enters the garden both as a gardener and as a grazing animal, and he gleans among the lotuses (an unusual crop for an ancient Israelite!). As the parts of a canto, however, the lyrics wrap images of love around the audience. The soprano sings of the reality and presence of the man's love.

Contrary to those who interpret the Song from the standpoint of the fertility cults, going down (ירד) hardly connotes a descent to Sheol. There is nothing of "love and death" in this verse (see Pope, 210–29). Keel ([1994] 209) notes that until Greco-Roman times settlements in Palestine were always on hills and that gardens were in the valleys. Thus, someone going to a garden would of necessity "go down."

Explanation

Once again, I must remind the reader that this is a song and not a drama or history. This is not a real woman actually talking to girlfriends about a lover who mysteriously ran off in the night. And as before, we must not mix the signifier with the signified and so imagine that the young bride, immediately after having consummated her marriage, is standing outside looking for help from the girls in finding her vanishing husband. Also, we are not to suppose that a young bride would actually give such a detailed account of her husband's anatomy to her girlfriends. No "storyline" is present here, only the musical presentation of the transformative power of love.

"I am my lover's and my lover is mine": the woman has been able to move beyond the trauma of Song 5:2–7 through the realization that she is now both lover and beloved and that all of the man's desires are fulfilled in her. Her transformation from virgin to wife is complete. She now sees herself fully bound to the man in affection and commitment, and she possesses him just as he possesses her. There can be no question of the love described here being anything other than monogamous. The woman's claim upon the man here is the counterpart to the man's claim in Gen 2:23 that she is "bone of my bones and flesh of my flesh" (RSV). The two have become one flesh.

C. Tenor and Chorus: The Flawless Bride II (6:4–10)

Bibliography

Stern, E. *Archaeology of the Land of the Bible.*

Translation

TENOR
4   You are beautiful, my companion, like Tirzah,[a]   1A
    lovely, like Jerusalem,   1B
    awesome, like panoplied cities.   1C

⁵ *Turn your eyes away from me,*	2A
for they excite me!	2B
Your hair is like the flock of goats	3A
*skipping from Gilead.*ᵇ	3B
⁶ *Your teeth are like a flock of lambs*	4A
that comes up from washing,	4B
in which every one has a twin:	4C
*not one among them is bereft of its partner.*ᵃ	4D
⁷ *Your cheek is like a split pomegranate behind your veil.*ᵃ	5A
⁸ *There are sixty queens*	6A
and eighty concubines	6B
and girls without number,	6C
⁹ *but she is unique—my dove, my perfect one;*	7A
she is unique to her mother,	7B
flawless to the one who gave her birth.	7C
The girls see her, and they reckon her blessed;	8A
the queens and concubines see her and praise her:	8B
CHORUS	
¹⁰ *Who is this,*	9A
looking down like dawn?	9B
Beautiful as the moon,	9C
bright as the sun,	9D
*awesome as the panoply of heaven.*ᵃ	9E

Notes

4.a. LXX (followed by the versions) ως ευδοκια, "like satisfaction." The context mentioning other cities supports MT.

5.a. See *Note* 4:1.b. and *Comment* on 4:1.

6.a. See *Comment* on 4:2.

7.a. See *Comment* on 4:3.

Form/Structure/Setting

The phrase אימה כנדגלות, "awesome like the panoplied cities/heavens," in vv 4 and 10 serves as an inclusion to demarcate the boundaries of this text. The man begins this section by singing of the woman being as awesome as the great cities of his day and concludes it by comparing her to the heavenly host. The three lines in v 10 ("Beautiful as the moon, / bright as the sun, / awesome as the panoply of heaven") answers the three lines of v 4 ("You are beautiful, my companion, like Tirzah, / lovely, like Jerusalem, / awesome, like panoplied cities."). It is not absolutely necessary to read v 10 ("Who is this . . .") as belonging to the chorus; the tenor could sing this strophe as well. On the other hand, a choral response is appropriate after v 9b declares that girls, queens, and royal concubines all praise her. For that matter, it is possible that v 10 is sung by both the tenor and chorus together.

The *wasf*, as is common, uses a number of small strophes governed by the individual body parts under discussion. Still, there are some very nice touches. The matching three-line strophe at v 8 (strophe 6) is answered by another matching three-line strophe at v 9 (strophe 7).

This section repeats many of the themes and metaphors of the *wasf* of Song 4:1–15; in some cases we have verbatim repetition. Both 4:9 and 6:5 speak of how her eyes excite and intimidate him, albeit they use different expressions. Using almost identical language, both texts describe her hair as goats skipping down Gilead (Song 4:1b; 6:5b; the latter lacks the word הר, "Mount"). The comparison of her teeth to pairs of lambs, v 6, is identical to Song 4:2 except that 4:2 has הקצובות, "the shorn [sheep]," where 6:6 has הרחלים, "the lambs." The terminology in the two comparisons of her cheeks to sliced pomegranate (4:3b; 6:7) is the same. Some metaphors are similar in theme but different in content. In Song 4:8 the woman is a goddess high on a mountain among the lions, and in 4:12 she is a locked garden, but in 6:4 she is an armed city, and in 6:10 she is the armies of heaven. On the other hand, each text develops distinctive ideas. In Song 6:8–9, all other women compare unfavorably to her and even sing her praise, a theme lacking in 4:1–15. On the other hand, the motif of the garden dominates much of 4:1–15 but it is altogether absent from 6:4–10. Finally, 4:1–15 is much more detailed and elaborate as it poetically praises parts of her anatomy.

The language of the garden has been dropped here probably because this metaphor focuses heavily upon sexual pleasure. In this canto, the tenor sings of his continuing devotion to her rather than of his sexual desire for her.

Comment

4 The very first words from the man after his "absence" are "You are beautiful, my companion" (with יפה, "beautiful," coming first). They serve to reassure her of his continued devotion to her. He does not play the role of Amnon, who humbles the woman, then loses interest in her (2 Sam 13:15). More than that, he continues to hold her in awe: "lovely, like Jerusalem, awesome, like panoplied cities." It is not correct to describe his attitude toward her as one of fear (against Murphy, 177), but surely there is amazed awe. The metaphor of the woman as unassailable city (like the virgin Zion; Isa 37:22) is not dropped after they have consummated their marriage. She is no more a virgin, but she remains inviolate.

According to A. F. Rainey (*ISBE* 4:860–61; see also the discussion by A. Chambon in Stern, *Archaeology of the Land of the Bible*, 2:433–40), the city Tirzah seems to be associated with Tell el-Faʿrah (north), near the Wadi el-Faʿrah and eleven kilometers north-northeast of Shechem. R. de Vaux excavated the site between 1946 and 1960 and found evidence of settlement from as early as the Neolithic age. A city with defensive ramparts, straight streets, and rectangular houses existed here in the Early Bronze Age but was abandoned around 2600 B.C.E. A new city stood here during MB IIA and IIB, and evidence indicates that the city lasted until the thirteenth century. De Vaux described three major strata for the Iron age. The earliest (stratum III) belonged to the period of David and Solomon and suffered a destruction around 900 B.C.E. Depending on how one reads the badly damaged stele of Sheshonq (Shishak) from Karnak, it is possible that Pharaoh Shishak sacked the city during his campaign in the latter half of the tenth century (K. A. Kitchen, *ISBE*, 4:489). Stratum II, the next major phase of the city, de Vaux dated to the eighth century; it suffered a violent end. The last phase (stratum I) was much more meager and belongs to the period after the Assyrian destruction of Samaria in 722.

The Bible tells us that the Israelites under Joshua took the city (Josh 12:24). 1 Kgs 14:12–17 implies that Jeroboam made it his capital after the breakup of the united kingdom. Tirzah remained the capital of the northern kingdom until the brief reign of Zimri. According to 1 Kgs 16:17–18, Omri trapped Zimri in Tirzah and laid siege to the city. When the defenses of the city were breached, Zimri burned the royal palace down around his head and died in the flames. Omri then moved the capital to Samaria.

The data tell us that Tirzah was a major city during the united monarchy, was an enemy city during the early days of the divided kingdom, and was a marginal or abandoned city afterwards. All in all, it is noteworthy that the Song places Tirzah on the level of a northern counterpart to Jerusalem. It is not likely that the Song would have celebrated the city if it had been written in Jerusalem after the secession of the northern kingdom (or that the Song would have celebrated Jerusalem if it had been written in the northern kingdom). As Keel ([1994] 213), says, "[S]uch a reference would be difficult to imagine during that period given the extremely tense relations between the two capitals (cf. 1 Kgs. 15:6, 16)." After the exile, Tirzah simply ceased to have any significance. For a poet at that time to create such a parallel would make no sense. Of course, one can always argue that a postexilic poet created the parallel as a kind of deliberate archaizing, but such an interpretation would clearly be ad hoc. Tirzah did not leave behind the kind of legacy that would prompt a postexilic poet to remind his audience of Tirzah's former glory, nor did it serve as a type for a fabulous citadel (such as Camelot is for the English). Taken at face value, the parallel plainly implies that the Song was written during the narrow window of history when Tirzah had prominence in the north but was not yet the domain of an enemy state. Such boundaries set the text squarely in the Solomonic period.

"Panoplied cities": The word דגל is associated with military regiments, as in its frequent use in Num 2 for the banners around which military units were organized. Here, the feminine plural *nipʻal* participle refers to the cities Tirzah and Jerusalem made awesome by the presence of defending armies with all their military pomp.

5–7 The root רהב means to show insolence in Isa 3:5, and in Prov 6:3 it means to importune someone boldly (both *qal*). At Ps 138:3 (*hipʻil*), it means to make someone bold. Here (*hipʻil*), translators often take it to mean "to humble, overwhelm, or make someone ashamed," a meaning that is the opposite of what we see elsewhere. However, in the remainder of the man's canto here (vv 6–9) he praises her; he does not seem to be embarrassed in her presence. The point here is probably that her eyes so excite him that he can hardly keep a cool head and not that she makes him feel ashamed. So רהב in the *hipʻil* should be taken to mean "embolden" or "excite" rather than "embarrass." The meaning seems to be that he can hardly keep his head when near her; everything about her sweeps him away.

In 5b–6, the tenor essentially repeats material from Song 4:1–3. Again, one should not regard this repetition as merely the use of stock metaphor with no further significance. It conveys the message that the man's desire for the woman is undiminished. She is, in his eyes, as beautiful and mysterious as she was while he still was awaiting the consummation of their marriage.

8–9 The point of these two verses, that the man regards his beloved as better than all other women, is self-evident. Readers naturally wonder if the queens and concubines refer to Solomon's legendary harem (1 Kgs 11:3); Delitzsch ([1877] 111) argued that the relatively "small" numbers reflected a period early in Solomon's reign! The rounded numbers, however, indicate that this is an artificial device for the sake of a hyperbolic comparison. The device is similar to the numerical pattern in Wisdom literature, "there are three things . . . , there are four" ("sixty" and "eighty" represent 3 x 20 and 4 x 20). In addition, princesses and concubines are reputedly the most beautiful of women (princesses because they were raised in a pampered setting and concubines because they are chosen specifically for their beauty). In the fashion of Wisdom literature, the man is proclaiming that however many other women of whatever status there may be, his beloved is still by far the best. Other women may be sixty, eighty, or countless in number, but his companion is אחת, "one."

10 Although אימה כנדגלות is precisely the same phrase as that found in v 4, "awesome as panoplied cities," the context is different. There, the woman is likened to a fortified city; here, she is likened to heavenly bodies, and the נדגלות must be the stars here personified as heavenly armies, "awesome as the panoply of heaven."

This verse looks back to Song 1:5–6, where the woman says she was darkened (שחורה) by the sun because of the anger (נחרו, from the root חרה, "to be hot") of her brothers, yet was still beautiful (יפה). Here, she looks down like the dawn (שחר), is beautiful (יפה), and is as dazzling as the sun (כחמה, literally "like the heat"). Where v 4 had described the woman's awesome beauty under the metaphor of the fortified cities, this text describes her as splendid under the metaphor of heavenly bodies.

The dawn was not just a time of day but a kind of heavenly body. Pagan literature identified the dawn as a goddess; students of Homer are familiar with the "rosy fingered Dawn" (ῥοδοδάκτυλος Ἠώς). The choice of the word לבנה for "moon" in this text (as opposed to the common ירח) may have been driven by the fact that לבנה is the feminine of לבן, "white." The point of comparison is the splendor of the woman with the bright light of a full moon. Similarly, the choice of חמה for "sun" (instead of the normal שמש) may be due to its similarity to חם, "heat" (another reflection on the woman's radiance). Also, the poet may have wanted to avoid שמש and ירח precisely because of their associations with pagan deities. While the woman receives extravagant, hyperbolic praise, she is not divinized (nor is this a hymn in praise of a goddess). As described above, the phrase אימה כנדגלות here refers to the heavenly hosts—i.e., the stars. The military nature of this personification (the stars as an angelic army with banners) again indicates that the woman is awesome in her beauty.

Explanation

The verbatim or near-verbatim repetition here of certain lines from chap. 4 is more than the use of formulaic expressions. By repeating his previous words of admiration for her, the man implies that his desire for the woman is undiminished by his having consummated the relationship with her. She is still as desirable to him as ever before. The fact that Song 6:4–10 is not as detailed or fulsome in describing her body is primarily for aesthetic reasons—the Song would be rather tedious if this section mechanically worked its way through all the details of the *waṣf* in Song 4:1–15. The repetition of a few items of praise—

for her hair, teeth, and cheeks—is enough to signal to the audience that he still feels the same way about her. On the other hand, the lengthy praise of her beauty in 4:1–15 serves a specific purpose. There, the man is persuading her with words of admiration and love to give herself to him. He is in effect tenderly *seducing* her, if one may rightly speak of a groom seducing his bride on their wedding night. In Song 6:4–10 it is enough for him to reaffirm his desire for her.

The change in metaphors from goddess on a mountain and locked garden in Song 4:1–15 to grand cities and heavenly host in Song 6:4–10 is significant. The operating motif behind the goddess and the locked garden is that she is *inaccessible*. By contrast, the operating motif of the grand cities and the heavenly array is that she is *awesome*. A mighty city is inaccessible only in time of war, and he has come to her in peace (cf. Song 8:10). And although one might speak of the heavenly host as inaccessible, this is not the implication one would ordinarily draw from the metaphor. Rather, comparison of her to the hosts of heaven implies that she is awe-inspiring.

She is no longer a mountain goddess or a locked garden to him for the simple reason that she is no longer a virgin; he has deflowered her. But deflowering need not connote humiliation or loss of status. In his own mind, he has not humbled her at all; she is as awesome as ever, if not more so. His love for her has matured from urgent passion to profound devotion.

IX. Soprano, Chorus, and Tenor: Leaving Girlhood Behind (6:11–7:1 [6:13])

Bibliography

Bloch, A. A., and **C. Bloch.** "From *In the Garden of Delights*." *Judaism* 44 (1995) 36–63. **Deckers, M.** "The Structure of the Song of Songs and the Centrality of *nepeš* (6.12)." In *A Feminist Companion to the Song of Songs*. FCB 1. Ed. A. Brenner. Sheffield: Sheffield Academic Press, 1993. 172–212. **Paul, S. M.** "An Unrecognized Medical Idiom in Canticles 6,12 and Job 9,21." *Bib* 59 (1978) 545–47.

Translation

SOPRANO

¹¹ I came down to the nut[a] grove	1A
to see the young plants by the river,	1B
to see if the vines were budding,	1C
the pomegranates blooming.[b]	1D
¹² I do not know my own soul;	2A
it has set me among the chariots of Ammi-nadiv![a]	2B

CHORUS
⁷:¹ Come back, come back, O Shulammite![a]	3A
Come back, come back, that we may gaze on you!	3B

TENOR
Why would you gaze on the Shulammite,	4A
as on the "Dance of the Two Companies"?[b]	4B

Notes

11.a. Although a *hapax legomenon* in the Hebrew Bible, the meaning "nut" (or more specifically, "walnut") is well established for אגוז from postbiblical Heb. and from cognates. See Pope, 574–79.

11.b. The Gk. here adds ἐκεῖ δώσω τοὺς μαστούς μου σοί, "There I will give you my breasts."

12.a. See *Comment* on v 12 for a full discussion of the meaning of this proper name.

7:1.a. There are no grounds for emending this to "Shunammite" (i.e., Abishag, the woman of 1 Kgs 1:3, 15; 2:17–22).

1.b. The word הַמַּחֲנָיִם is literally "the two camps." As a proper name, מַחֲנַיִם refers to the place in Gilead on the Jabbok named by Jacob (Gen 32:3 [ET 32:2]). As a place name, the term appears thirteen times in the Bible, but never with the def. art.

Form/Structure/Setting

The singer of vv 11–12 is evidently the woman since v 12 seems to speak of this person being taken away in a chariot, and, immediately after that, the chorus proclaims the line "Come back, O Shulammite!" (Song 7:1a [ET 6:13a]), which, with its plural form ונחזה־בך, "that we may gaze upon you," belongs to the chorus. Song 7:1b (ET 6:13b), a reply to the chorus in behalf of the Shulammite, belongs to the male singer.

This brief section quickly moves through three singing parts, and this rapid change of singers is indicative of a transformation in the woman's situation. It begins with calm, pastoral imagery (the woman strolls down to see how her plants are growing), but suddenly introduces a jolting shift of scene (she can hardly comprehend how she came to be among the chariots of *Ammi-nadiv*, "My-beloved-is-a-prince"). The Song abruptly indicates that the woman is leaving, much to the distress of her companions. Finally, the groom issues a mild rebuke to the women to the effect that they should not call on her to stay so that they can continue to look at her.

Comment

11–12 The metaphor of the garden almost always refers to female sexuality (e.g., Song 4:12–5:1), and some evidence indicates that the walnut, like the apple, symbolized sexuality in the ancient world. A place called Caryae (Καρύαι, "walnut trees") in Laconia was the site of an image to Artemis Caryatis ("Artemis of the Walnut"). Here every year the Lacedaemonian maidens held chorus-dances in a festival called the Καρυάτεια (Pausanias, *Description of Greece* 3.10.7). In this passage of Song, however, the woman has simply gone down to look at her walnuts and other young, growing plants, and no festival is in view. The language of these lines connotes not activity but expectation. By describing herself as going down to check on these plants, she indicates that this is a metaphorical flashback to her earlier days, when she was awaiting the time of love. In the words of the oath she called on the Jerusalem girls to take, she would not "awaken the passions of love until they are ready" (Song 2:7). In v 12, however, she suddenly finds her situation dramatically changed.

12 The phrase לא ידעתי is often translated "before I knew it," but there is little justification for this. One would expect something like בטרם אדע if that were the intended meaning. On the analogy of Job 9:21 (לא־אדע נפשי), one should understand לא ידעתי נפשי to mean, "I do not know myself." It probably connotes "I can hardly keep my composure" or "I am beside myself with joy." S. M. Paul (*Bib* 59 [1978] 545–47) compares this to usage in Mesopotamian medical texts, where to "not know oneself" implies partial loss of consciousness due to overstimulation of the emotions.

One all but despairs of making sense of the second line of v 12 (cf. Pope, 584–91). The verse has given rise to an enormous number of emended and conjectural readings. None of them works. For example, switching the consonants of מרכבות, "chariots," to מברכת, "blessed one" (Murphy, 177; cf. NAB), is hardly persuasive (Murphy himself says, "None of the many emendations proposed by scholars is really convincing"). Another far-fetched proposal is that of A. A. and C. Bloch (*Judaism* 44 [1995] 57–58), who switch the letters around from עמי־נדיב to נדיב־עמי, "the nobleman of my people," and so render it very freely as "She sat me in the most lavish of chariots." The translations in the ancient versions suggest that they were working with the same text that we have in the MT, and that they had as much difficulty making sense of it as we do. One must therefore try to interpret it with minimal emendation. The most natural way to take שמתני מרכבות is as "she [i.e., my נפש, "soul"] has set me (among) chariots." Taking the path of least resistance for עַמִּי־נָדִיב, one could take it simply as a proper name. This route is taken by the LXX, Vulgate, and some Hebrew manuscripts, although they read the more familiar "Amminadab" for "Amminadiv." The principal problem with this translation is that, unless "Amminadiv" had some significance for the ancient Israelites that is totally lost on us, it appears to make no sense. The name Amminadiv is altogether unknown. Reading it as Amminadab does not really help matters; there is no Amminadab of great repute in the Bible. The name is found in Exod 6:23; Num 1:7; 2:3; 7:12, 17; 10:14; Ruth 4:19–20; 1 Chr 2:10; 6:7 (ET 6:22); 15:10–11. None of these is of sufficient stature to give significance or symbolism to the chariots here. Pope (587) is correct when he asserts that the "expedient of taking unintelligible words as proper names has produced some bizarre results in the Bible and elsewhere." If an emendation is to be employed, one might read עַמִּי־נָדִיב as עִמִּי נָדִיב, "a princely man is with me." Still, this is little more than a conjecture. The best solution, however, is not to emend but to regard עַמִּי־נָדִיב as the woman's sobriquet for her beloved. Support for this interpretation is a mere two verses away, in 7:2 (ET 7:1), where the man calls the woman בַּת־נָדִיב, "daughter of a prince," i.e., "my lady." In עַמִּי־נָדִיב, the woman has substituted עַמִּי for the more familiar דּוֹדִי, "my beloved," a term she frequently uses in texts such as Song 1:13–14. דּוֹד means "my uncle" but can also be used affectionately to mean "my love," and עַמִּי likewise means "my uncle." It is commonly used in proper names, such as עַמִּיזָבָד (1 Chr 27:6) and עַמִּיאֵל (Num 13:12). Thus it seems that by extension עַמִּי has also taken on the meaning "my beloved." Therefore עַמִּי־נָדִיב is indeed a proper name, albeit an artificially created one, "My-beloved-is-a-prince."

The woman is dumbfounded that her own soul (נפשׁ) had carried her away and that she now stands among the chariots of "My-beloved-is-a-prince" (i.e., her new husband). This description of her situation may have had a literal counterpart in the wedding ceremonies of ancient Israel when the groom departed with his new bride, perhaps on the day following the wedding night. In any case, she is now being taken away to a new life.

7:1 As noted above, the two halves of this verse belong to different parts since the first line calls the woman back "that we may gaze on you" while the second is a mild rebuke, asking why they want to do this. The plurality of the first half implies that it belongs to the chorus, and thus the second half belongs to the groom (it is not likely that the woman is speaking of herself in the third person). The fact that תֶּחֱזוּ, "would you gaze," is masculine plural could imply that there is a male chorus that takes part in the Song. On the other hand, Hebrew is not consistent in its use of the second feminine plural but sometimes uses the second masculine plural form with a feminine plural subject (e.g., Ruth 1:8). More to the point, the Song never uses the second feminine plural form, even when women are clearly being addressed (Song 1:6; 2:7; 3:5; 5:8; 8:4). No male chorus is really indicated.

The women want the bride to remain with them so that they may enjoy her beauty and companionship. This is simple delight in the bride and not sexual leering (as might be implied by a male chorus).

Rather than leave her to answer for herself, however, the groom speaks up for his bride. His words imply that the time for staring at her is over. Her great beauty was that of a bride in all her array, but now the wedding is over. The precise meaning of the "Dance of the Two Companies" is unknown, but one can presume that it was a dance familiar to the audience of the Song. If it involved two companies of dancers, it must have been quite complex and have received the rapt attention of spectators. The noun מחלה, "dance" (from חול, "to whirl"), seems to imply a particularly exuberant kind of dancing (Exod 15:20; 32:19; Judg 21:21; 1 Sam 29:5); it was perhaps something similar to the ecstatic dancing of the "whirling dervishes" of Turkey. The groom is telling them not to stare at her as though she were such a show. There is no need to see something of combat between two armies here, as does Keel ([1994] 229).

Explanation

In the structure of Song of Songs, this section answers Song 2:8–17, where the groom invites the woman to depart with him. That section also has pastoral imagery (the lover as a gazelle and the flowering of the landscape in spring). More significantly, the man in Song 2:10 calls the woman to come away with him, but the chorus in Song 7:1 (ET 6:13) cries out, "Come back! Come back!" and is mildly rebuked by the tenor. In the psychology of the Song, the chorus wants the woman to stay in their world, but she cannot do this because she has crossed the threshold from virgin to wife.

X. Tenor and Soprano: The Second Song of Mutual Love (7:2 [1]–8:4)

Bibliography

Black, F. C. "What Is My Beloved? On Erotic Reading and the Song of Songs." In *The Labour of Reading: Desire, Alienation, and Biblical Interpretation*. Ed. F. C. Black, R. Boer, and E. Runions. Atlanta: Society of Biblical Literature, 1999. **Brenner, A.** "Aromatics and Perfumes in the Song of Songs." *JSOT* 25 (1983) 75–81. ———. "'Come Back, Come Back the Shulammite' (Song of Songs 7:1–10): A Parody of the *wasf* Genre." In *A Feminist Companion to the Song of Songs*. FCB 1. Ed. A. Brenner. Sheffield: Sheffield Academic Press, 1993. 234–57. ———. "A Note on *bat-rabbîm* (Song of Songs VII 5)." *VT* 42 (1992) 113–15. **Joffe, A., J. P. Dessel**, and **R. Hallote**. "The 'Gilat Woman.'" *Near Eastern Archaeology* 64.1–2 (2001) 8–23. **King, P.**, and **L. Stager**. *Life in Biblical Israel*. **Stern, E.** *Archaeology of the Land of the Bible*. **Trible, P.** *God and the Rhetoric of Sexuality*. Philadelphia: Fortress, 1978.

Translation

FIRST STANZA

TENOR

2(1) *How beautiful are your feet in sandals, Bath-nadiv!* [a]	1A
The curves of your hips are like rings,	1B
the work of an artist! [b]	1C
3 *Your navel is like a rounded goblet*	2A
that never lacks [a] *for mixed wine!* [b]	2B
Your belly is like a heap of wheat	3A
hedged about [c] *with lotuses.*	3B
4 *Your two breasts are like two fawns,*	4A
twins of a gazelle.	4B
5 *Your neck is like the Tower of Ivory.* [a]	5A
Your eyes are like the pools of Heshbon	6A
at the gate of Bath Rabbim. [b]	6B
Your nose is like the Tower of Lebanon	7A
looking toward [c] *Damascus.*	7B
6 *Your head creates the effect of Mount Carmel,*	8A
and the strands of your hair are like rich, purple cloth;	8A
a king could get caught in that "loom" of yours! [a]	8B

SECOND STANZA

7 *How beautiful you are! How pleasant you are!*	9A
You are love with all its delights!	9B
8 *This is what your full physique is like: a palm tree.*	10A
And your breasts are its clusters:	10B
9 *I said, "I will climb the palm tree;*	10C
I will hold its panicles of dates, [a]	10D
that your breasts may be like the clusters of grapes	10E
and the fragrance of your nipples [b] *like apples."*	10F

Third Stanza

TENOR
¹⁰ Your mouth is like the finest wine — 11A
SOPRANO
going smoothly^a to my lover — 11B
TENOR
gliding past my lips and teeth!^b — 11C
SOPRANO
¹¹ I belong to my lover, and his desire is for me. — 11D

Fourth Stanza

SOPRANO
¹² Come, my lover, let us go to the field! — 12A
Let us spend the night among the henna! — 12B
¹³ Let us go early to the vineyards! — 13A
Let us see if the vine has budded, — 13B
if the grape blossom has opened, — 13C
if the pomegranates are in bloom. — 13D
There I will give you my love! — 13E
¹⁴ The mandrakes give forth a fragrance, — 14A
and at our doorways are all manner of choice fruits. — 14B
New things as well as old, — 14C
my lover, I treasure up for you. — 14D

Fifth Stanza

^{8:1} If only I could treat you like my brother, — 15A
one who sucked at the breasts of my mother! — 15B
I would find you in public and kiss you, — 15C
and no one would scorn me! — 15D
² I will lead you, I will take you, — 16A
to the house of my mother who used to teach me! — 16B
I will let you drink wine (the spiced variety!)^a — 16C
and the sweet wine of my pomegranate!^b — 16D

Sixth Stanza

³ His left hand is under my head, — 17A
and his right hand embraces me. — 17B
⁴ I call on you to swear, daughters of Jerusalem, — 17C
that you will not arouse or awaken the passions of love — 17D
until they are ready. — 17E

Notes

2.a. Lit., "daughter of a prince" (בַּת־נָדִיב), this is a sobriquet for his beloved. See *Comment* on 6:12.

2.b. The word אָמָּן is a *hapax legomenon*, but its meaning is not in doubt. It is related to the Akkadian *ummānu*, "artisan," and is rendered τεχνίτης in LXX and *artifex* in Vg. Cf. *HALOT*. Prov 8:30 and Jer 52:15 have the related אָמוֹן.

3.a. The negated impf. has an almost adj. role. Thus אל־יחסר should be rendered "that never lacks" and not as a juss., "may it never lack."

3.b. מזג is a *hapax legomenon* but is probably related to ממסך, "mixed wine," found in Isa 65:11 and Prov 23:30. It is some kind of mixed or spiced wine.

3.c. סוג is another *hapax legomenon* in biblical Hebrew, but its meaning as "hedged" or "fenced in" is well established from Mishnaic Hebrew and cognate languages. Cf. *HALOT*, סוג II.

Form/Structure/Setting

5.a. Numerous scholars have noted that a line appears to be missing after צַוָּארֵךְ כְּמִגְדַּל הַשֵּׁן, "your neck is like the Tower of Ivory," but evidence is lacking for us to determine what, if anything, is missing, and speculative emendations are unpersuasive.

5.b. Read בַּת רַבָּה in reference to Rabbah, the Ammonite town not far to the northeast of Heshbon. See A. Brenner, *VT* 42 (1992) 113–15.

5.c. פְּנֵי דַמָּשֶׂק would normally mean "the face of Damascus," but here פְּנֵי seems to be short for לִפְנֵי, "toward" or "facing."

6.a. בָּרְהָטִים is enigmatic. Elsewhere, רַהַט is a "drinking trough" (Gen 30:38, 41; Exod 2:16). It may, however, refer to some part of a loom, such as the beams to which the cords of the warp were fastened (cf. *HALOT*, רַהַט). Context supports this interpretation, and for the sake of simplicity I have simply rendered it "that 'loom' of yours" without trying to specify a certain part of the loom.

9.a. The word סַנְסִנָּה seems to mean the "panicle of the date" after the Akkadian *sissinnu*. See *HALOT*, סַנְסִנָּה.

9.b. אַף regularly means "nose" (e.g., Gen 24:47; 2 Kgs 19:28; Job 40:24, 26; Prov 30:33), but it is peculiar that the tenor would sing of the "fragrance of your nose." Murphy (183) contends that אַף here means "breath," but אַף never has this meaning unless one were to argue that the use of אַף for "anger" suggests this idea. On this basis, Keel ([1994] 246) takes אַף to mean "heavy breathing and the scent produced by passion." This is possible, but there is no evidence that the word was used for erotic passion as well as for anger. The normal Heb. words for "breath" are רוּחַ and נְשָׁמָה, but never אַף. 2 Sam 22:16 speaks of the "breath of his nose" (רוּחַ אַפּוֹ), but this means that the nose *has* breath, not that it *is* breath. When Heb. wants to speak of the smell of one's breath, it uses רוּחַ for "breath" (Job 19:17). Pope (636–37), on the analogy of Ugaritic *ap*, "entrance," suggests that it here means "vulva." This is quite far-fetched. In *UT* 52.24, 59, 61 ("The Birth of Dawn and Dusk"), the gods suck "on the nipple of the breast" (*bap dd* or *bap zd*). Akkadian *appu* could also be used for the nipple. If the Hebrews sometimes used אַף in the manner attested in the Ugaritic and Akkadian texts, they would have taken it in this context to mean "nipple."

10.a. דּוֹבֵב is a *hapax legomenon*. Most scholars take it to be a *qal* ptc. of דבב, but that root elsewhere in the Hebrew Bible connotes speaking or spreading a rumor. *HALOT* (דבב) connects this occurrence in the Song to the Arabic *dabba*, "to crawl," but this is hardly persuasive. Murphy (183–84) more plausibly links it to the root דוב, which he says means to "flow" but which *HALOT* connects to the Arabic *dwb*, to "dissolve." Notwithstanding the difficulties, *HALOT* (דבב) suggests that דּוֹבֵב here means something like "trickle."

10.b. For שִׂפְתֵי יְשֵׁנִים, "lips of sleepers," read שְׂפָתַי וְשִׁנָּי, "my lips and my teeth," with LXX χείλεσίν μου καὶ ὀδοῦσιν, Syr., and Vg.

8.2.a. יַיִן הָרֶקַח is often translated "spiced wine," although one might expect יַיִן to be either in const. with הָרֶקַח or in grammatical agreement with it if that were the meaning. It is more likely that הָרֶקַח is in apposition as "from wine, the spiced variety."

2.b. A number of MSS have the pl. רִמּוֹנִים, "pomegranates," here rather than the first sg. suf. This is the easier reading ("from sweet wine of pomegranates"), but in language as sexually charged as this, "my pomegranate" is correct.

Form/Structure/Setting

Song 7:2 (ET 7:1)–8:4 is a massive canto in six stanzas. The first two stanzas, Song 7:2–9 (lines 1A–10F), are a *wasf*, a descriptive song of praise of the woman's beauty. The first stanza, sung by the tenor, opens with "How beautiful are your feet in sandals," and a description of the woman's body follows. The description moves upward from the feet to the head. This part of the canto has nine small strophes, each describing a body area in turn (feet and legs, strophe 1; navel and belly, strophe 2; belly, strophe 3; breasts, strophe 4; neck, strophe 5; eyes, strophe 6; nose, strophe 7; head and hair, strophe 8). The second stanza is marked by "How beautiful you are" in 7:7, echoing "How beautiful are your feet in sandals" at 7:2. After this exclamatory praise of the woman (lines 9A–B), the tenor sings a longer, single strophe in praise of the full body of the woman and in particular of her breasts (lines 10A–F). The two stanzas thus mirror each other in that both are exclamations of the woman's beauty, but stanza 1 gives a detailed, area-by-area description of her beauty, while the latter describes her body in a more holistic fashion but focused on her breasts.

In the third stanza (7:10–11), the tenor and soprano sing four lines antiphonally (lines 11A–D). The feminine singular suffix on וחכך, "and your palate," implies that the tenor sings line 11A. Line 11B uses the word לדודי, "to my beloved," which is the woman's sobriquet for the man; it indicates that this line is sung by the soprano. Line 11C contains no suggestion of who the singer is but is assigned to the man. Line 11D again refers to דודי and thus is sung by the soprano. This exchange makes a nice transition from the man's praise of the woman (7:1–9) to the woman's songs of longing for the man (7:12–8:4).

The fourth and fifth stanzas (7:12–8:2), describing the woman's longing for the man, are her response to the tenor's words in the first two stanzas. In the fourth stanza (7:12–14 [lines 12A–13D]), the woman proclaims her desire for the man's affection in the metaphorical terms of the vineyard and garden, which echo his description of her as a palm tree, a grape vine, and an apple tree in 7:8–9. This stanza has three strophes. The first strophe, 7:12 (lines 12A–B), is an invitation to the fields and the henna. The second strophe, 7:13 (lines 13A–E), calls the man to the vineyards. The third strophe, 7:15 (lines 14A–D), focuses on the mandrake blossoms at their door. In the fifth stanza (8:1–2 [lines 15A–16D]), she yearns to be able to show affection for her lover in public (first strophe, lines 15A–D) but instead asserts that she will take him to the "house of my mother" (second strophe, lines 16A–D).

The sixth stanza substantially repeats Song 2:6–7 and closes off this canto. The whole is arranged with the man singing of his love for the woman in two stanzas, a transitional exchange between the singers, the woman singing of her love for the man in two stanzas, and a conclusion with the familiar adjuration for the maidens.

The fourth canto (Song 1:9–2:7), which stands opposite this canto in the larger structure of Song of Songs, also features the *waṣf* as a dominant formal element and is also made up of six stanzas.

The poet's art is also in evidence in the construction of the individual strophes. In strophe 2, assonance links the two lines (אגן הסהר, "rounded goblet," and אל־יחסר, "does not lack"). In strophes 14 and 15 (7:14 [ET 7:13]–8:1) each has something of an inclusion. Line 14A begins with הדודאים, "the mandrakes," which sounds like דודי, "my lover," at the beginning of 14D. In strophe 15, both lines 15A and 15D end with לי, "to me." Still, the construction of the strophes here does not have the elaborate artistry seen in other parts of Song of Songs, probably because much of this material is governed by the catalogue of body parts in the *waṣf*.

Comment

2 It is curious that he begins by speaking of her feet "in sandals" since through the rest of the song it appears that her entire body is exposed to him. The description of the curves of her hips does not definitively say that her hips are exposed, but it would seem to imply it. If the understanding of חלי as something like the rounded curve of a gold earring is correct, it is an apt metaphor for a woman's bare hip. Certainly her navel is exposed to him in v 3. Thus, it seems, the woman in this *wasf* is portrayed as having little or no clothing. But, of course, a song is not always consistent about these things. It may be that a sandal, which is an article of clothing that leaves most of the foot bare, is something of a tease. Keel ([1994] 231), on the basis of a portrayal of exiles in a relief from the palace of Sennacharib, suggests that Judean women normally went barefoot. If so, then the sandal may convey the idea that she is dressed up in a way that is particularly alluring to him. Also, as Keel suggests, the wearing of sandals may give her a dignity above the common woman.

At Song 6:12, both Ammi-nadiv and Bath-nadiv ("My-beloved-is-a-prince" and "Daughter-of-a-prince") are taken to be hypocorisms (pet names) for the man and woman. These are evidently not their given names but sobriquets they have bestowed on one another. That is, each regards the other as regal and praiseworthy. These names do not imply that either is actually of the royal household.

The word חֲלִי appears only here and at Prov 25:12 in the Hebrew Bible, although Hos 2:15 has the similar חֶלְיָה. The generic translation "ornament" is not too helpful. Some render it "jewel," but this seems unlikely if by "jewel" one means "gemstone," since the point of the comparison is that her thigh is smooth and rounded, which of course a gemstone is not. The Proverbs text has חלי paired with נזם, "earring," and indicates that a חלי was often made of gold, which implies that חלי is also some kind of ring-shaped (or perhaps ball-shaped) piece of jewelry.

3 In Ezek 16:4 the שׁר is the umbilical cord, and in Prov 3:8 it is apparently the navel and by metonymy stands for the health of the body (parallel to לעצמותיך, "to your bones"). Pope (617) observes that the Arabic *surr* also means "umbilical cord" but notes that the Arabic word *sirr* means "pudenda" or "fornication," and suggests that the word refers to female genitals. Many commentators regard the "navel" here to actually be the woman's vagina, and thus they suggest that the assertion that it "never lacks for mixed wine" refers to the moisture of an aroused woman (thus apparently Pope, 620, and Murphy, 185). On the other hand, there is no reason to translate שררך as "your valley," as Murphy (182) has done. Evidence cited above that it means only "navel" is quite clear. Furthermore, the round goblet is a fitting metaphor for the navel but a somewhat peculiar one for the vagina. Of course, it may well be that the navel itself suggests the woman's genitals euphemistically (Longman, 195). On the surface at least, her belly and navel are the focus of the man's admiration here.

The אגן is a fairly large mixing bowl or goblet analogous to the Greek *krater*, that is, a big, two-handled bowl. Pope (618) notes that the sanctuary of Hirbet Semrin has yielded nine specimens of stone bowls, some of which have the inscription, "This krater [*'gn' dnh*] so-and-so dedicated to such-and-such a deity," and that an image of a bowl carved into a cliff at Petra has an inscription that identifies it as an *'gn*. It seems odd that a field of wheat would be hedged about with lilies or lotuses, but it may be the woman's belly and not the wheat that actually has the flowers. In other words, she may be wearing a chain of flowers about her waist. But even this may not be necessary; it may well be that the flowers are present in the text simply to enhance the portrayal of the beauty of the "heap of wheat" imagery, and that the flowers have no special significance or literal counterpart.

What may be the significance of the wine and the wheat here? We have already noted that several authors take מזג, "wine," to be vaginal moisture. Longman (195) suggests that the חטים, "wheat," is pubic hair; this interpretation requires that we take the word בטן, "belly," to mean specifically "pubic hair," which is rather far-fetched. Prior to Longman, Brenner ("Come Back," 247) suggested that the heap of wheat was pubic hair, but she saw a reference to both belly and pubic hair in the language. Brenner's exegesis is quite peculiar here; she claims the verse tells us that the woman of the Song is "frankly, fat" ("Come Back," 248). The text speaks of the navel and all the abdominal area and not only or specifically of the genitals. "Wheat" does not suggest obesity.

This verse speaks of wine and wheat, products of the field and vineyard, in association with the woman's body. חטים, "wheat," occurs only here in the Song of Songs, although "wine" (here מזג, elsewhere יין) is used several times for the pleasures of love. In keeping with usage elsewhere in the Song, "wine" usually refers not to some specific bodily fluid (vaginal moisture, saliva, etc.) but to the delights of love generally (see Song 1:2, 4; 2:4; 4:10; 5:1; 8:2).

Wheat, along with barley, beans, and lentils, is a staple of the Israelite diet, but unlike sweet fruits, honey, and wine, it is not associated with rapt pleasure or lovemaking. Some suggest that the color of the woman's belly may be similar to that of wheat; this may partially explain the language, but it does not seem to be an adequate explanation. It may be that the curvature of bound sheaves of harvested wheat suggest the curvature of the woman's waist. It would be more certain that this was the meaning if the poet had used the word אלמה, "sheaf," instead of the more ambiguous ערמה, "heap." On the other hand, אלמה only occurs in two verses in the Hebrew Scriptures (Gen 37:7; Ps 126:6), and it may be that ערמה sometimes referred to a sheaf. A sheaf of wheat stalks bound at the middle could certainly suggest a woman's waist. (For a description of the Israelite harvest practices, see King and Stager, *Life in Biblical Israel*, 89–91.)

Still, the use of חטים, "wheat," here is striking. Since wheat, along with the other staples of the Israelite diet, was essential for life and could be regarded as the primary fruit of the field, it may be that "wheat" obliquely alludes to the woman's distinctive reproductive power, the ability to grow a child in her "belly" (or "womb," בטן). For the ancient Israelite, the birth of the first child was not a long-deferred blessing, much less something to avoid; it was the much-desired fulfillment of a marriage. Couples desired the first pregnancy to come as soon as possible. Thus, it is possible that the man here is also celebrating the power of the woman's "belly" to produce fruit. The association of wheat, the staff of life, with this power seems appropriate.

The Hebrew בטן, "belly, womb, stomach, " is an ambiguous term, and it appears that this verse makes much of its ambiguity. On one level, the verse speaks of the simple beauty of her navel and curved waist, like a bound sheaf of wheat. On another level, it suggests her genital area as well as sexual arousal. On a third level, it speaks of her as one who has the power of fertility in her "belly." In other words, the meaning of the verse should not be limited either to the woman's navel and waist or simply to her vagina and to sexual arousal but should encompass her whole "belly" with all its beauty, sexuality, and fertile power.

4 This verse repeats, in abbreviated form, Song 4:5 (see *Comment* there). This repetition reminds the reader that much of the language of the Song is formulaic. Thus, one should be careful about reading too much into a metaphor. The image of the breasts as two fawns is striking, but it is not necessarily laden with multiple meanings.

5 Despite the presence of the definite article, translations almost always render כמגדל השן as "like *an* ivory tower" instead of "like *the* ivory tower." It is unlikely, of course, that the text refers to a tower actually made of ivory or even covered in ivory. The expense would be prohibitive. Like the "houses of ivory" in Amos 3:15, the tower described here may have had some ivory in or on it, or it may have simply looked like ivory.

Could the poet be speaking of an imaginary object? This is not likely, since unreal objects make for poor similes and it is not a normal strategy of the Song. The article, moreover, suggests that it is a real tower (contrast the idealized, indefinite "palaces of ivory" in Ps 45:9 [ET 45:8]). It probably had the name simply because it was whitish in color. Other items used for similes and metaphors in this context (Bath Rabbim, Heshbon, Carmel) are real objects and proper names. By the same token, כמגדל הלבנון is "like the tower of Lebanon" and should not be translated as an indefinite noun. Inasmuch as this tower is said to be looking toward Damascus, it is a specific tower.

The "Tower of Ivory" is both like and unlike the "Tower of David" with which the man describes the woman in Song 4:4. In both cases, the point is not that there is some visual correspondence between the woman's neck and the aforementioned towers, although the similarity of a neck to a tower no doubt suggested the metaphor to the poet. Rather, the dignity and awesomeness of the towers is applied to the woman. On the other hand, "Tower of David" in 4:4 presents the audience with something like a fortress, and the term there connotes impregnability. The name "Tower of Ivory," by contrast, implies a tower of striking beauty and craftsmanship—a tower that is beautiful in its creamy white coloration. The change in metaphor is significant. She is no longer impregnable to him, and the military language has disappeared. But she is not bowed. She remains a tower of strength and elegance. It goes without saying that the usage does not refer to the arrogant and aloof scholar implied in the English term, "ivory tower."

Heshbon was located in the Transjordan west of the northern edge of the Dead Sea. It is identified with Tell Hesban. Archaeological research has to date yielded little material remains from the Iron Age, although evidence for occupation goes back to at least 1200 B.C.E. The biblical narrative indicates that Heshbon was occupied earlier than that; Num 21:25–34 identifies it as the city of King Sihon of the Amorites. There are a number of reservoirs in the area; one of these could have been the pools that the Song mentions. Stratum 17 (ninth to eighth centuries) of Tell Hesban in particular has yielded a large reservoir on the south side of the Tell. It was fifteen meters to a side and had a capacity of about two million liters. L. T. Geraty ("Heshbon," *ABD* 3:181–84) suggests that this may have been the reservoir of Song 7:5, although, if the date for the Song that this commentary suggests is correct (tenth century), another pool is probably meant. Geraty also describes an egg-shaped cistern from the twelfth or eleventh century (in Stern, *Archaeology of the Land of the Bible*, 2:628). Heshbon apparently underwent a violent destruction at the end of Stratum 16 (seventh to sixth century). Apparently the site was abandoned for about three hundred years, from ca. 500 B.C.E. to ca. 200 B.C.E. (L. T. Geraty in E. Stern, *Archaeology of the Land of the Bible,* 2:628), and was rebuilt in the Hellenistic era.

The eyes suggest pools of water to poets because they are moist and reflective and have depth. A reservoir also connotes the drinking of water, and thus the line may imply the idea of drinking in her beauty. Her eyes are a particular focus of adoration for the man, and he describes them in a series of metaphors and expressions. They are like doves (Song 1:15; 4:1); they excite him (4:9) and arouse him (6:5). It was suggested above that the prior references mean that she is sexually attractive. On the surface, at least, this final metaphor seems different since pools of water do not in any obvious way suggest sexual arousal—unusual in the context of a *wasf* filled with sexually charged language. This stanza moves upward from the feet but really gravitates toward the face and head. This focus on her head implies his love for the distinctive beauty of her face and indeed for the person that her face represents. He is excited by her, but even in his awareness of her breasts and perhaps genitals, v 3, he has not lost sight of her face.

The proclamation that her nose is like the tower of Lebanon may seem comical to the modern reader and suggests that she has an unusually long nose. This is certainly not the poet's intention. Again, the מגדל, "tower," connotes dignity and strength. Also, a tower can add great symmetry and beauty to a landscape and will focus a viewer's attention on itself. In the same manner, the woman's nose perfectly sets off the symmetry of her face and elicits the man's admiration.

6 ראשך עליך ככרמל is literally "your head upon you is like Carmel," which sounds peculiarly crude. But עליך probably implies the effect that her head and hair as she has arranged it have on her overall appearance, and not just to the fact that her head sits on her body.

Her head has no visual similarity to Mount Carmel (the "Carmel" here is the headland ["Mount Carmel"] that juts into the Mediterranean north of the plain of Sharon and not the village Carmel in Judah). The fact that the Hebrew ראש, "head," is also used for both the peak of a mountain (2 Sam 15:32) and the hair of the head (Isa 7:20) may have suggested this comparison to the poet. The name *Carmel* means "orchard" or "vineyard," but the word is not used as a common noun in the Song. The region has fertile ground for olives, grain, and grapes, which makes it all the more fortuitous as a representation of the woman. Carmel was also a sacred site from at least the second millennium and thus was an appropriate setting for the contest between Elijah and the priests of the fertility gods Baal and Asherah (1 Kgs 18); cf. H. O. Thompson, "Carmel, Mount," *ABD* 1:874–75. Mount Carmel is not especially tall (about 550 meters [1800 feet]), but its prominence above the plains and the sea make it all the more strikingly beautiful. This line primarily indicates that her head/hair completes the beauty of her body just as Carmel gives special beauty to the landscape in which it sits, but the comparison suggests her fecundity as well.

The only analogue to דלה "strands of hair," as used here is in Isa 38:12, where it is the warp of a fabric. It is from the root דלל, "to hang down," and thus means locks or strands of hair. The word ארגמן usually refers to cloth dyed deep reddish-purple from the shell of the murex shellfish. Here, it seems to refer to threads that have been dyed this color but that have not yet been woven into cloth. Perhaps the audience is meant to understand that the woman literally has deep reddish-black hair; even so, this particular word, אַרְגָּמָן, was probably chosen because the dye was very costly and fabrics made with this coloring were highly prized.

The metaphor of the loom implies that her feminine power is greater than the most vigorous form of masculine power, that of a king. Weaving was in the ancient world often considered to be the quintessential woman's work. The ideal wife of Prov 31:19 stretches out her hand to the distaff (by contrast, it was a disgrace for a man to work with the distaff according to David's curse in 2 Sam 3:29). There were exceptions to this rule; the craftsmen who fabricated the tent of meeting included men who were skilled at weaving (Exod 35:34–35), implying that there was a professional guild of men who included weaving in their skills. Even so, throughout the ancient world, the loom and distaff were almost invariably associated with women. Inasmuch as weaving complex patterns involved a good deal of skill as well as an ability to make calculations, weaving is associated with cunning and intelligence in women. This theme appears repeatedly in Greek mythology. Ariadne, a Cretan princess and daughter of King Minos, enabled Theseus to escape the labyrinth by giving him a skein of thread. Penelope, wife of Odysseus, had to contend with suitors who sought to persuade her that her husband was dead. She bought time for herself by telling them that she would choose a new husband as soon as she finished weaving a shroud, but every night she unraveled the work of the previous day. The story of Arachne shows how much pride women could take in their skills. Arachne was so accomplished at weaving that she challenged the goddess Athena to a competition; she won, but the spiteful goddess changed her into a spider. In the Bible, the crafty Delilah sought to undo Samson's strength by weaving the strands of his hair into a loom (Judg 6:13–14). Thus, it is not surprising that the tenor associates the woman's ability to subdue him with the cunning skills of the loom. Here, the banter is loving and joyful, and there is no hint of malice or suspicion.

7 This verse begins a new stanza in the tenor's part of this canto. The opening line "how beautiful you are" corresponds to "how beautiful are your feet" at the opening of the first stanza. The opening strophe (Song 7:7, lines 9A–B) is brief and abstract; the much longer second strophe of this stanza (7:8–9, lines 10A–F) concretely (albeit metaphorically) describes the woman's body and his desire to make love to her. Murphy (186) takes 7:7 as the conclusion to the first stanza, regarding it as an inclusion with 7:2. This is possible, but taken this way, the second stanza or *wasf* begins quite abruptly and without any lead-in.

אהבה בתענוגים is literally "love with the delights" ("you are" is implied). One could take אהבה to refer to the woman herself (an abstract for concrete) and thus render it "beloved." Some further develop this interpretation by reading with the Syriac and Aquila בַּת תַּעֲנוּגִים, "delightful girl," for בַּתַּעֲנוּגִים. But אהבה is never concretized in this way elsewhere in the Song (it occurs eleven times over ten verses). Since אהבה is a common abstract noun and the phrase is intelligible as it stands, I take it to be an exclamation about how thrilled he is with his relationship to her. Therefore, line 9B should not be translated "O loved one, delightful daughter" (so Murphy, 80), but in context as "(You are) love with all its delights." He does not simply use the abstract אהבה as a concrete noun, as "O loved one" would have it. Rather, he asserts that the abstract quality of love is made concrete in the woman's body. She is, for him, the incarnate form of the delights of love.

8 קוֹמָתֵךְ, lit. "your height," here refers to the impression conveyed by the woman's entire body when viewed from head to toe, hence "your full physique."

The תָּמָר, "date palm," is among the oldest cultivated fruit trees. According to I. Jacob and W. Jacob ("Flora," *ABD* 2:803–17), it was a marvelously useful plant in that every part of it could be put to use in construction and weaving. Furniture, fences, ropes, wigs, baskets, and many other items could be produced in the ancient Near East from the raw materials of this tree. In addition, its flowers are white and fragrant and its fruit very sweet. The tree had long been associated with women in the Levant; תָּמָר (Tamar) is a woman's name in Gen 38:6 and 2 Sam 13:1. The tree is also quite grand and can grow to one hundred feet in height. Thus, the man's chosen metaphor is both suitable and highly complimentary. No visual similarity is implied between the signified and the signifier.

Keel ([1994] 242–43) also observes that the date palm is associated with fertility goddesses throughout the ancient world and that it also is regarded as the pattern of the holy tree. In Mesopotamian cylinder seals, for example, the date palm appears alongside images of Ishtar. This association is important, but it is possible to make too much of it. I cannot agree with Keel ([1994] 246) that "the man's plan to climb the palm and lay hold of its date clusters (or breasts) has the aura of a sacral act." Again, contrary to many modern interpreters, the Song does not ritualize sexuality or treat sexual intercourse as a sacred event. Similarly, the adoration of the woman stops short of deifying her. Still, the fact that the date palm in ancient thinking was laden with significance as a metaphor of female sexuality no doubt helps to direct the choice of symbols used here. The woman (not the goddess) is for him the expression of sexual power and pleasure that the date palm represents.

The comparison of her breasts to the clusters of dates does not mean that she is imagined to be many-breasted, like Artemis of Ephesus, whose chest is covered with breasts (or, perhaps, with eggs). The fruit of the date palm is sweet, and it is the fruit that especially draws people to the tree. So also the breasts of the woman give pleasure and strongly attract the man. Also, individual dates are rather small, but the date clusters that grow on date palms are rounded in a manner that somewhat resembles a woman's breast.

9 אָמַרְתִּי, "I said," indicates the man's resolve to enjoy the woman's body. This indication of resolve works well with a metaphor of climbing a date-palm tree. In light of the height that these trees could attain, as well as the primitive nature of any climbing equipment that the ancient orchard farmer might have possessed, going up a date palm to get the fruit would have been no small task. This does not mean that making love to the woman requires some heroic show of strength on his part; it only means that desire to enjoy her pleasures is equal to the desire and determination one would need in order to scale the date palm for its fruit.

The focus on the woman's breasts as a source of pleasure recalls the exhortation of Prov 5:19: "Let (your wife's) breasts satisfy you at all times; be exhilarated with her love always" (my translation). Keel ([1994] 246) observes that this focus on the breasts is reminiscent of the "pillar goddesses" from ancient Israel (especially eighth to sixth century B.C.E.). These are female figures, nude but sometimes with few clearly defined anatomical details except for a pair of large breasts. As Keel notes, earlier statuary often gave emphasis to the female genitals but paid little or no attention to the breasts. Noteworthy in this regard is the "Gilat woman," a fourth-millennium figurine found in the Beer-sheba basin (see Joffe, Dessel and Hallote, *Near Eastern Archaeology* 64.1–2 [2001] 8–23). This representation of a nude woman is quite primitive; she has a barrel-shaped torso and a round head with small points representing the ears. Her face is crudely painted on. Her arms and legs are sticklike pieces. Strangely, however, although her breasts are insignificant points on her chest, her genitals are the most realistic element of her entire body, even to the point of representing her pubic hair with a series of carefully done incisions in the crotch area of her terra cotta body. No such attention is given to the hair of her head. Keel ([1994] 250) has reproductions of second-millennium scarabs from Gezer, Lachish, and elsewhere that likewise focus all attention on a naked woman's crotch but give no attention to the breasts. Thus, it is possible that the shift from a focus strictly on the woman's genitals to a focus on the breasts speaks of a shift away from an emphasis strictly on fertility and reproduction to a focus on the pleasures of sexuality. Be that as it may, it is at least clear that the attention on the breasts here and in Prov 5 indicates that sexual activity is for pleasure also and not simply for reproduction.

Line 10D, אחזה בסנסניו, "I will hold its panicle of dates," could be rendered with "I will grab" or "seize." This seems a violent term, and it could be taken by the woman to be a crude if not painful action on his part. However, all must be read in context, and the verb simply describes his enthusiasm about her breast. In the larger context, in which both man and woman are exhilarating in their joy of love, this verb need not be taken to be an offensively aggressive action.

The metaphors shift in lines 10E, where her breast is like a bunch of grapes, and 10F, where her nipple has the fragrance of apples. The comparison of lovemaking and especially of the woman's body to fruit is not unusual.

10 This and the next verse make an antiphonal transition to the soprano's part. כיין הטוב, lit. "like the wine of the good," is the wine of a very good vintage and thus more than just "good wine." Wine is associated with the act of kissing in Song 1:2, and the references to lips and teeth (as in the proposed emendation) further imply that kissing is the focus of this stanza. The antiphonal singing of these lyrics implies that the activity is equally delightful for both the man and the woman.

11 In Song 2:16 and 6:3, the woman simply sings that she belongs to her lover and her lover belongs to her. Here, she sings, "I belong to my lover, and his desire is for me." Why does she not assert that he belongs to her? Certainly it is still true that he belongs to her; the ownership has not become a one-way street. Nevertheless, the changed language may be significant. The locus of love and desire here is the woman's body; all possessiveness and desire are directed toward her. While it is still true that the man and woman mutually possess one another, it is the woman's body that is the domain of their love.

Like the English word *desire*, the Hebrew תשוקה can be healthy or pathological. It appears three times in the Hebrew Bible, at Gen 3:16 and 4:7 and in this verse. In Gen 4:7 sin is metaphorically presented as some kind of crouching beast that desires to ambush and carry away Cain as its prey; there, the "desire" is clearly evil. The interpretation of Gen 3:16 is debated, but in that context as well, the desire should be regarded as pathological. The relevant line, "Your desire will be for your husband, and he will rule you" (NIV), grammatically matches Gen 4:7 and so probably should be given the same reading, that the desire is a negative desire (contrast Trible, *God and the Rhetoric of Sexuality*, 160). In the context of Gen 3:16, moreover, God is describing the pain and conflict that will enter the woman's life because of sin. Neither the desire of the woman nor the rule by the man can be interpreted in that context as positive or healthy. Because of the fall, the ideal of marriage is in Gen 3 portrayed as shattered and deadly. The woman will "desire" the man, but it will be an unhealthy, clinging, and controlling desire. The man, likewise, will "rule" the woman not in a benevolent fashion but as a cold oppressor.

Nevertheless, this usage is not determinative for the meaning of תשוקה in Song 7:11. In the Song, the ideal of love and marriage is represented almost as though the fall had never happened. One should not transfer the meaning of תשוקה in Genesis to the Song. Song of Songs presents love, sexuality, and the pleasures of a man and woman as compassionate as well as robust and healthy.

12 It is difficult to know what to make of בכפרים. Most versions ancient and modern take כְּפָרִים to mean "villages" (e.g., LXX: κώμαις). Why would she want to go to the villages unless "villages" here simply means "countryside"? On the other hand, כפרים meaning "henna" is one of the delights of love in Song 1:14 and in particular of the woman's body at Song 4:13. Inasmuch as this is an invitation to love (v 13: "there I will give you my love"), it seems best to take כפרים to refer to henna. In 1:14, her lover and the love he has for her are like henna blossoms that adorn her beauty. In 4:13, the man uses henna as part of a metaphorical description of the manifold pleasures that her body gives him. Thus, to spend the night among the henna is self-evidently an invitation to him to enjoy love with her.

Her invitation to him to go to the fields is probably a double entendre. No doubt lovers did literally go out into the fields to enjoy their love in privacy. The level of privacy one could find out in the fields, in contrast to the close quarters in the confines of cities and villages, to say nothing of houses with extended families, is evident in the rape legislation of Deut 22:23–27. At the same time, the fields, like the gardens, vineyard, and meadows of the Song of Songs, symbolize the pleasures of love.

13 As Murphy (187) observes, נשכימה, "let us go early," does not denote a second round of journeys but is parallel to the invitation in the previous verse. The soprano is the singer. Lines 13B and 13D repeat verbatim two lines found in Song 6:11; the woman is the singer there as well. At 6:11, the woman's words signify expectation. Her words are followed by her being swept away on the chariot of Ammi-nadiv. Song 6:11–7:1 continues the transition of the woman from maiden to wife. In Song 7:13, in contrast to 6:11, the woman does not go down to the gardens alone but invites the man to go with her. The motif of 6:11 is the reflections of a young woman on her own blossoming and transformation, while the motif of 7:13 is joint exploration and discovery. Thus, although it is correct to say that there is a sexual meaning behind her words, there is more to it than simply another invitation to a tryst under the guise of a garden. The garden had been an arena of waiting and expectation, but now it is where she and her man explore the delights of love together. Here, too, there is a double entendre. While the vineyards and groves symbolize sexuality and sexual discovery, they are also literal vineyards and groves that young lovers explore together.

14 This is the only place in the Song of Songs where mandrakes are mentioned. The only other place they appear in the Bible is in the famous episode of Leah's mandrakes (Gen 30:14–16). A great deal of superstition and folklore surrounds the mandrake. Its roots can somewhat resemble a human form (similar to ginseng, which is also called "Asian mandrake"), and legend says that it screams when uprooted and that its screams can cause death or insanity. It is regarded in folklore as having curative or fertility powers, and it has been used as a narcotic (it can in fact be quite toxic). According to Jacob and Jacob ("Flora," *ABD* 2:803–17), it has a "bluish-violet, bell-shaped flower." It is noteworthy, especially in light of the supposed powers of the mandrake root, that the woman actually makes no mention of the root but only refers to its flower and the fragrance that the flower gives. However, Keel ([1994] 257–59) suggests that the fragrance of the mandrake was thought by the ancients to possess aphrodisiac powers. Most significantly, he points to a painted relief from Tell el-Amarna (fourteenth century) in which an Egyptian queen holds mandrakes under the pharaoh's nose in order to arouse his sexual interest. The Cairo love songs, similarly, regard the smelling of mandrakes to be a prelude to lovemaking.

The soprano sings that all manner of choice fruits are at their doorways. The doorway could be taken to be another symbol of the woman's genitals, but this is unlikely since she speaks of "our doorways." The picture is of a house that is grand enough to have more than one doorway and that has varieties of fruit-bearing or flowering plants at the doorways. The doorways also suggest the Hebrew concept of "going in and coming out," an idiom for engaging in daily activity of all kinds (e.g., Deut 28:6). In addition, חדשים גם־ישנים, "new things as well as old," is a merism for "all kinds of things." The language thus suggests that the home of the couple is richly endowed with delights of every kind, both familiar and new. Sexuality is not absent from this image—certainly the context is charged with sexual language—but the sexuality is set in an idealized portrait of domestic happiness.

The affectionate giving of the woman's body to her man is represented in the last lines of the two strophes found in vv 13–14. Strophe 14 (v 13) ends with "There I will give you my love" (line 13E), and strophe 15 (v 14) ends with "my lover, I have treasured (these) for you" (line 14D). The woman stands at the center of a joyful, loving home.

8:1 The woman's wish that her man could be her brother sounds most peculiar to modern ears, as though she had a strange desire for incest. The reader must, however, bear two things in mind. First, *brother* and *sister* were common terms of endearment between lovers in the ancient Near East, as is indicated by the frequent use of the terms in the Egyptian love poetry. Second, she is not wishing that she could make love to him in public, but she is wishing that she could be more public about her affection for him. Apparently any public show of affection between a man and woman, even a husband and wife, was severely censured in Israelite society at this time. One could publicly kiss a close blood relative, however, without arousing the ire of the community (Gen 29:11). Thus, her desire is not to kiss her brother but to make known unashamedly her love for her husband. The sexual life of a couple is properly kept private, but this very privacy prevents the woman from in any way expressing openly the joy she has found in her man's love. One should add that she is no more exhibitionist than she is incestuous, but she would like to kiss in public to let everyone know how she feels about him. A female singer in the sixth stanza of Papyrus Chester

Beatty I group A expresses exactly the same desire to be able to kiss her "brother" without fear of reproach.

The language with which the woman of Song of Songs describes the man as "brother," however, is arresting: "one who sucked at the breasts of my mother." This line looks back to the end of the man's piece, in which he spoke of his determination to get to the woman's breasts (Song 7:9), and it also looks ahead to the next verse, where she says that she will lead him to her "mother's house."

2 The verbs of the first line of this strophe (line 16A) should not be given an optative or subjunctive translation. The imperfect forms אנהגך אביאך do not continue the optative construction of the previous verse. The actions expressed here—such as giving her lover wine—are not unattainable wishes but are the kinds of things she can do with him. The use of two verbs side by side indicates determination to carry out her intention toward her lover.

They should be rendered, "I will lead you, I will take you." She is not saying that if he were her brother she would take him to her mother's house. Rather, the placement of the two verbs in asyndeton is emphatic and speaks of her determination. This use of two or more imperfects in asyndeton to suggest resolve is not uncommon. For example, in Exod 15:9 we read, "The enemy said, 'I will pursue, I will overtake, I will divide [ארדף אשיג אחלק] the spoil'" (RSV). Thus, contrary to Keel ([1994] 261), she is not saying that she wishes he were her brother so that she could sneak him into her mother's house. Rather, she declares that since she cannot give him any affection openly, she will more than make up for it with the affection she gives him in private.

The line אל־בית אמי תלמדני, "to the house of my mother who used to teach me," calls for attention. Why would she desire to take him to her mother's house? Many interpreters assume that the couple is unmarried and that she wants to take him there for a sexual rendezvous. Elsewhere, however, she seems to have no trouble in finding an occasion to make love to him, so why would she now want to take him to her mother's house for a tryst? If the relationship were illicit, what location would be more fraught with danger than her parents' home? And if one goes back to the view that she wants him to be her brother so she can take him home and be his lover, the logic is so bizarre, not to say perverse, that it goes well beyond the bounds even of ancient poetic license.

The verb תלמדני could be translated "you will teach me." The reference to her "mother's house," however, suggests that the verb is a third feminine singular (referring to her mother) rather than a second masculine singular. The form is ambiguous, and many interpreters regard it as a second masculine since it is unlikely that at this stage the woman's mother would teach her. However, the sense need not be future, and "she teaches me" could mean, "she serves as my example." Probably, however, the word here is a historical imperfect and has the sense "she used to teach me" and, thus, "she was my teacher." Elsewhere in the book she is not in the position of looking to the man to be her teacher in love, so it seems odd that she would describe her relationship to him in such terms here. In addition, line constraints require that we treat אל־בית אמי תלמדני, "to the house of my mother who used to teach me," as a single line. We cannot drop אביאך from line 16A to line 16B since that would leave line 16A with a single unit (too short). We cannot treat lines 16A–B as a single line since that would give us a line with five constituents (too long). Also, contrary to several interpreters, we cannot move the verb תלמדני to line 16C and translate it "You will teach me so that I may give you a drink of spiced wine" (thus Keel [1994] 261–62). This move places two simple imperfects of different person side by side, which is quite harsh. If the meaning were "you would teach me so that I might give a drink to you," the verb אשקך would certainly have the conjunction. In addition, line 16B is syntactically bound to line 16A. All of this strongly suggests that אמי, "my mother," is the subject of the verb תלמדני with an implied relative pronoun. A number of scholars (e.g., Pope, 659) advocate emending to תלדני, "she bore me," but this is unwarranted. Even if she is his wife, it is not at all clear why she would want to go to her mother's house. Throughout the whole Song we see the transformation of the woman from a girl at home under the domination of her family—of her "mother's sons" (Song 1:6)—to a woman who in the love of her husband is free from their control. Hence, a desire to go make love in her mother's home is surprising.

The "house of my mother" occurs elsewhere in the Song only at 3:4. There, I suggested that the house of her mother and the chamber of the woman who conceived her can only be the womb. Here the meaning is even clearer. In Song 8:1–2 she self-evidently is taking him to a night of lovemaking, and no explanation for doing this in her mother's literal house is satisfactory. The "mother's house" is thus here a euphemism for the female genitals, and it is appropriate as a designation of the place of procreation.

The phrase "my mother . . . who used to teach me" therefore suggests that her mother was her first teacher and example in the ways of sexuality. In ancient Israel the mother was no doubt the girl's primary teacher in matters of puberty, menstruation, sexuality, childbirth, and lactation; there would have been no middle-school lectures on human sexuality. Unless she were the youngest in the family, an Israelite girl may well have been present at the births of some younger siblings and certainly would have seen her mother or her mother's peers nursing the younger children. Of course, an Israelite peasant girl would also have assisted her mother in matters involving animal husbandry. In summary, the ancient girl would have grown up with a much more intimate awareness of the sexual life of her mother than her modern counterpart does, and she would rightly call her mother "my teacher" in these things.

There is something beautiful in this picture. She is not, in entering the world of sexuality, doing something that is alien and abhorrent to her. She is emulating what she has seen and heard all of her life in the person who, up to this time, has been the closest to her. More than that, as her mother made love to her father and so gave birth to daughters and sons, she will do the same and become the teacher of her daughters.

עסיס is a kind of sweet or fresh wine. The word occurs in Isa 49:26; Joel 1:5; 4:18 (ET 3:18); Amos 9:13 and here. Her promise to give her man wine and sweet pomegranate wine to drink is another fairly obvious promise to give him her favors. Keel ([1994] 263) illustrates a relief from the time of Ramses III in which nude women of the harem give a man pomegranates and mandrakes, a fairly clear display of the sexual significance of these items.

3-4 These verses repeat Song 2:6–7 except that there is no adjuration to swear by the gazelles here. Again, the woman is at rest in her man's love, and she again calls on the girls not to arouse love until the right time.

Explanation

First, the man gives an admiring description of various parts of the woman's anatomy; he then graphically describes his strong intention to make love to her. Notwithstanding the attention he gives to her breasts in the second stanza, vv 7–9, the movement here from the feet upward is meaningful. The goal and focal point of the first stanza are her face and head. This focus conveys an appreciation for the person and personality of the woman since the face, more than any other part of the body, physically presents a person's individuality. Then the woman uses beautiful but for the most part indirect language to speak of the pleasures of love; but in the last stanza, she much more boldly asserts that she will make love to him. Thus, the first and fourth stanzas are preludes to the second and fifth, which should be taken to be the focal points of this canto. The point is that the lovers are now free to engage in sexual play, and they are intent on doing so. This song concludes with the woman expressing her happiness at being in the arms of her beloved and warning the other girls not to squander their affection and hearts.

XI. Chorus and Soprano: Claiming the Beloved (8:5–7)

Bibliography

Albright, W. F. "Archaic Survival in the Text of Canticles." In *Hebrew and Semitic Studies*. FS G. R. Driver, ed. D. W. Thomas and W. D. McHardy. Oxford: Clarendon, 1963. 1–7. **Murphy, R. E.** "Dance and Death in the Song of Songs." In *Love & Death in the Ancient Near East*. FS M. H Pope, ed. J. H. Marks and R. M. Good. Guilford, CT: Four Quarters, 1987. 117–19. **Tromp, N. J.** "Wisdom and the Canticle. Ct 8, 6c–7b: Text, Character, Message and Import." In *La Sagesse de l'Ancien Testament*. Ed. M. Gilbert. Gembloux: Duculot, 1979. 88–95. **Watson, W. G. E.** "Love and Death Once More (Song of Songs VIII 6)." *VT* 47 (1997) 385–87.

Translation

	First Stanza	
CHORUS		
5	Who is this	1A
	coming up from the wilderness,[a]	1B
	leaning on her lover?	1C
SOPRANO		
	Under the apple tree I aroused you.[b]	2A
	That is where your mother conceived you;[b]	2B
	that is where she conceived, she gave you[b] birth.	2C
	Second Stanza	
6	Set me like a seal upon your heart,	3A
	like a seal upon your arm.	3B
	For love is strong, like death.	3C
	Jealousy is severe, like the grave.	3D
	Its spark[a] is a blaze of fire! It is a mighty flame!	3E
7	Many waters are not able to extinguish love,	3F
	and rivers cannot overwhelm it.	3G
	If a man were to give all his worldly possessions[a] for love,	3H
	his offer would be utterly scorned.	3I

Notes

5.a. MT המדבר, "the wilderness." LXX λελευκανθισμένη (supported by OL) = מתבררה, "purifying herself."

5.b. The Syr. renders the second sg. suf. in this verse as fem. and so requires that this be taken as the man's lines, and some interpreters have followed suit. The Syr. alone, however, is slender basis for making the emendations, notwithstanding the extensive discussions on the part of some scholars (e.g., Murphy, 191). The Heb. is clear and widely supported; in these circumstances, emendation is ill advised. It appears that some interpreters found the notion that the woman would intentionally arouse the man to be offensive.

7.a. את כל הון ביתו, lit. "all the wealth of his house."

Form/Structure/Setting

This canto has two stanzas; the first is made of two similar strophes, and the second is made of a single long strophe. It has a choral introduction (8:5a), but the body of the canto is given to the soprano (8:5b–7). The choral strophe could be taken to be two lines, but since we have a matching pair of lines in 1B and 1C (participle followed by prepositional phrase), it is probably best to let 1A stand alone as a complete line.

The soprano's part has two strophes, one quite short and the other very long. Song 8:5b, "under the apple tree," is the first strophe. As in the choral strophe, there are three lines, with line 2C closely matching line 2B. Thus, the canto opens with two three-line strophes, and each has an opening line followed by two matching lines in syntactic dependence on the first.

The second stanza has an unusually long strophe—nine lines. Of course, one might argue for breaking this into smaller strophes, but there does not appear to be any clear reason to do so. The entire strophe appears to be bound together by the notion of the power of love. Lines 3F and 3H are unusually long, and they are answered by two very short lines (3G and 3I). One wonders how this would have sounded when performed.

Formally, this canto begins as inquiry (sung by the chorus) but quickly turns from that to a song on the power of love (the soprano). In this respect this unit looks back to Song 3:6–11. Both cantos speak of the coming of the bride. However, whereas the tenor responded to the chorus's canto in 3:6–11 with a song tenderly alluring his bride in Song 4:1–15, the soprano here responds with a canto on the power and jealous fury of love (Song 8:5b–7). That is, where the woman's arrival *before* their union was followed by his appeal for her to give herself to him, the woman's arrival here *after* their union is followed by her claim to his absolute devotion.

In the structure of Song of Songs, however, this unit looks back to 1:7–8, the Song of Finding the Beloved. There, the soprano despaired of finding her beloved and asked him where he might be, adding that she did not want to be a woman "picking fleas" among the flocks. The chorus in turn told her to go out to where the shepherds may be found. Here, however, instead of telling her to go out to the pastures, the chorus sings of the arrival of the woman. She begins her part with lyrics addressed to the man, "Under the apple tree I aroused you." That is, instead of seeking her lover, she sings of where she found him. Furthermore, in Song 1:7 she asked where he made his flocks lie down at the heat of noon, but in 8:6 she sings of the heat of love, declaring it to be an unquenchable fire. Most importantly, whereas 1:7–8 describes her somewhat desperate desire to find her beloved, in this text she demands that he permanently set her as a seal on his heart and arm. She will never lose him again.

Comment

5 Lines 1A–B repeat verbatim a text from Song 3:6 ("Who is this coming up from the wilderness?"). The following line, however, is radically different. Where 3:6 has the theophanylike description "like a pillar of smoke," the present text continues with "leaning on her lover." The earlier text depicted the bride arriving with regal splendor where this text presents an image of the woman at peace drawing security and stability from her man. Also, where the former text moved into a section in which the chorus gave an elaborate portrayal of the military entourage of the Solomonic groom (Song 3:7–11), here the arrival imagery is dropped as quickly as it is mentioned. Instead, the woman sings of the passionate love that binds her to her husband. The motif in 3:6–11 was the man and woman in a formal ceremony; the motif here is of the man and woman in passionate love.

The verb עור appears nine times in the Song of Songs, and four of these times, as here, it is in the *po'lel* stem. In the *qal*, the verb means to "awaken" (cf. Song 4:16; 5:2). In the *nip'al* it means to "be woken up." The *hip'il* means to "awaken" or more frequently to "set in motion" (e.g., Isa 41:2, 25; 45:13; Ezr 1:1). In the *po'lel* it means to "set in motion," "disturb," or "arouse" (Ps 80:3; Job 3:8; Prov 10:12; Zech 9:13). The *po'lel* frequently suggests arousing some kind of fury or passion. The three other *po'lel* occurrences in the Song are in 2:7; 3:5; and 8:4, where the woman exhorts the Jerusalem girls not to "arouse" (*po'lel*) or "awaken" (*hip'il*) love. In short, the woman is not saying here that she simply woke the man when he was napping under an apple tree. Rather, "arouse" is the proper translation.

The woman's canto concerns fiery passion, possession, and pain. She begins with the straightforward assertion that she aroused him under the apple tree, characteristically a metaphor of physical love. She then declares that this place, the apple tree, was where the man's mother conceived him, went into the pains of labor, and gave birth to him. Scholars have made much of this language, but few surpassed W. F. Albright ("Archaic Survival," 7), who suggested that "the mother of the beloved was a mythical figure, possibly a girl who had escaped to the desert after becoming pregnant by a god." This is not the point of this canto. The significance of the "apple" was discussed in the *Comment* on 2:3, but the specific place of arousal—under the apple tree—calls for comment. Why was it not under a datepalm tree, or in the vineyards? There are many other fruit and garden metaphors for sexuality in the Song besides the apple. It may be that the appearance of the apple tree is significant. A peculiarity of many apple trees is that they appear gnarled and twisted and, especially in winter, have more of an aged look than do many other trees. Nevertheless, they produce luscious fruit that, with its reddish coloration, full and rounded shape, and juicy flesh, seems to be the very image of youth. The branches of the tree fork in many directions; there is nothing linear about an apple tree (in contrast, for example, to the date palm). All of this suggests that the apple tree symbolizes not merely sexuality but sexuality as it continues from generation to generation. The old give birth to the young, and the "family tree" continues to spread and grow through the years.

One can hardly doubt that עוררתיך, "I aroused you," refers to sexual and reproductive activity, but the woman does not literally mean that all this took place under an apple tree. Rather, under the metaphor of the apple tree she speaks rather directly of sexual intercourse and what follows it, conception and birth. Sexual union and giving birth are times of intense physical and emotional pleasure and trauma. The woman has entered this kind of intense physical relationship with her husband, and she recapitulates the experience of their mothers.

There is some question regarding whether this *pi'el* of חבל means to "give birth" or to "conceive" a child (cf. *HALOT*, and note that חֵבֶל means "labor pains" [e.g., Isa 13:8; 26:17]). The only other place where this form is used in connection with pregnancy is in Ps 7:15 (ET 7:14), הנה יחבל־און והרה עמל וילד שקר, "Consider! He conceives wickedness and is pregnant with trouble and gives birth to deception." The Ps 7 text supports taking it to refer to conception or pregnancy rather than to childbirth. Still, the Song seems to exploit some of the ambiguity of the term here. See below.

6 In the ancient Near East, seals were made with the use of wood, clay, or stone stamps impressed into lumps of clay or wax. In addition to the stamped seal, the cylinder seal could be rolled over a lump of clay to produce an image. The distinctive Egyptian seal, the scarab, was also widely used in Palestine. Finger rings might also include a seal or scarab (as was the case apparently with the ring that the pharaoh gave to Joseph in Gen 41:42). Seals could be engraved with pictorial images, written text, or both.

Seals were especially important for indicating ownership or maintaining security. One would use a seal called a bulla to secure a treasury, to guarantee the authenticity of a royal edict or a deed, and to protect the contents of a scroll (Deut 32:34; Esth 3:12; Jer 32:10; Isa 29:11). The telltale seal (a scarab?) of Judah in Gen 38:18 was proof that he had been with his daughter-in-law. The breastplate with twelve stones representing the tribes of Israel had the engraved seal "holy to Yahweh" (Exod 28:36), indicating that the tribes of Israel were the special possession of God. Jezebel was able to send letters in Ahaz's name by using his seal (1 Kgs 21:8).

In this text, the woman calls upon the man to set her as a seal on his heart and arm. This is a sign of covenant commitment to marriage and is analogous to the wearing of phylacteries as tokens and reminders of Israel's covenant fidelity to Yahweh (Deut 6:4–9; 11:13–21). In the Song, the חותם, "seal," could refer to the wearing of a seal around the neck or on an armband, but it is more likely to be purely metaphorical. We do not have evidence that people in the ancient Near East had standard tokens of love or marriage analogous to the modern wedding ring. In Gen 24, the servant of Abraham gives a ring and bracelets to Rebekah as signs of his desire to take her back to be Isaac's wife, but even here it is not clear that any of the jewelry would have been understood to connote marriage in the specific way the modern wedding ring does. Murphy (191) comments that the "practice of wearing something that belongs to one's beloved is of course widespread." Still, it does not appear that the woman here alludes to some commonly practiced custom of men wearing jewelry or clothing that represented their love for their wives or girlfriends. The scribes who copied and preserved the Song would no doubt associate this line with the bullae with which they routinely closed up scrolls and marked them as their own. This may be the key to the metaphor. As a scroll is closed up and sealed tight against all but the indicated owner of the bulla, so the man is to be closed up toward every other woman.

It is from this perspective that one should interpret the following lines, "For love is strong, like death. / Jealousy is severe, like the grave." This does not refer to a funerary cult (Pope, 228–29 and *passim*), nor does it mean that love is an apotropaic amulet meant to ward off death (cf. Pope, 666–67, and Keel [1994] 272–74). In addition, one should not seek the key to this line in fertility myths concerning Isis and Osiris or Baal and Anat. The stories of heroic women who saved their men in times of trouble that Keel ([1994] 274–75) alludes to (e.g., Michal in 1 Sam 19:9–17) are another false trail. The woman is not here promising to fight for her husband or preserve his life.

Love in this text is not in *a battle with* death but *is compared to* death (see also Murphy, "Dance and Death," 118). N. J. Tromp ("Wisdom and the Canticle," 94) argues that 8:6b–7c is a Wisdom teaching that conveys the following message: "Love is represented here as a force which is able to overcome the negative forces that threaten the very existence of the world and mankind. In other words, Love gains the victory over chaos and creates wholesome order and life." But, contrary to Tromp, there is no reason to suspect that this is a secondary editorial addition, and to isolate it from its context (where the issue at hand is the possessiveness of love) is unwarranted. There is no indication here of love gaining a "victory" over death. These, love and death, are conceptually bound yet polar opposites. It is not likely that "love is strong, like death" refers primarily to the power of sexuality and regeneration to preserve the family line in the face of death (Watson, *VT* 47 [1997] 385–87). While that is no doubt true, and there are some allusions to reproduction in the Song and even in the previous verse, the following lines make it clear that she is here speaking of the passion and jealousy of love rather than its reproductive function.

רֶשֶׁף appears to mean "spark" in Job 5:7 but seems to refer to lightning in Ps 78:48. In Deut 32:24 and Hab 3:5 it is a plague. In Ps 76:4 (ET 3), רִשְׁפֵי־קָשֶׁת, "flames of a bow," seems to mean arrows. The root idea of flames seems to be behind all of these uses. Hence, "spark" is the most reasonable translation at this point. The word רֶשֶׁף does not of itself mean "arrow" and should not be translated that way in the absence of the qualifying noun "bow." There is no allusion here to something like Cupid's arrows. Also, there is no compelling reason to suppose that lightning is meant here.

The word שלהבתיה occurs only here, but it is probably a combination of the noun שַׁלְהֶבֶת, "flame," and the shortened form of the divine name יהוה. Alternative explanations, e.g., that it is a third feminine singular pronoun suffix (as in the LXX), are not persuasive. The colorful LXX rendition, περίπτερα αὐτῆς περίπτερα πυρός φλόγες αὐτῆς, "encircled by a colonnade of her, encircled by a colonnade of fire, her flames," is not a sound basis for either emending or interpreting the Hebrew text. At the same time, שלהבתיה should not be taken as an actual reference to the name of God. The ending here has virtually lost all theological significance, and it simply functions adjectivally for "mighty" or the like.

The assertion that the flame of love is like a mighty flame does not allude to a weather god casting a thunderbolt while in battle with Yamm or Mot. The language describes the furious power of love. The noun שלהבת, "flame," appears in Job 15:30, where it describes God's destruction of the wicked, and in Ezek 21:3 (ET 20:47), where God threatens to consume the trees of the Negev with fire. In both cases, the fire is metaphorical for divine wrath. The word is never used in the Bible for literal fire; rather, it connotes jealous anger. It is the fire of wrath, not the fire of compassion, that is in view here (*contra* Murphy, 197). The language describes the ardor and exclusivity of the bond of love between man and woman. In this verse, although it has a divine counterpart, the "flame" of jealousy is a human attribute.

7 The contrast between fire and water is so obvious that one hardly need look to mythological images of the waters of primordial chaos for an explanation of this line. The fury of the fire of love is so great that even great volumes of water cannot quench it. One cannot easily escape its power after one has entered this realm. Those who have admitted this fire into their lives will find it impossible to douse.

Explanation

Why does this canto begin with an arrival motif? It does not seem a necessary or even congruous introduction to the somber analysis of the power of love that follows. But on close inspection, it is an appropriate prelude to the woman's song. The previous arrival canto (Song 3:6–11) gave the couple a grand and heroic status. Much the same is true here, where it is the woman who is the object of attention and who is placed in high esteem. The fact that she is "leaning on her lover" does not diminish her position but suggests to the audience that this is a woman who knows love. The choral prelude informs the audience that the woman has sufficient stature and experience to make the profound pronouncements on love that follow.

The Song's fixation on the mother (v 5) is important. Not one time does the Song refer to the father, but seven times it mentions the mother (Song 1:6; 3:4, 11; 6:9; 8:1, 2, 5). The woman's premarital domestic life was governed by her "mother's sons" (1:6). Solomon was crowned by his mother (3:11), and the bride is the beloved daughter of her mother (6:9). The intimate connection between brother and sister is defined by the fact that they both nursed at the breasts of one mother (8:1). The "mother's house" is a metaphor for the woman's womb with its sexual and reproductive functions (3:4; 8:2). Here in 8:5 the passions of the wife/mother bind her and her husband together. Taken together, the reason for the dominance of the mother and the silence about the father are not difficult to explain: against the passionate depth of her experiences in losing virginity, entering pregnancy, giving birth, and nursing children, the man's sexual experiences are rather trivial by comparison. The woman is the domain of sexual and domestic love.

The woman's name is metaphorically stamped upon the man's arm, his breast, and indeed upon his soul. As the woman had sung of the man as a sachet of myrrh hanging between her breasts (Song 1:13), she now sings of herself as stamped into the body and mind of her husband. This can only mean that she possesses him as her own and now demands his complete fidelity. The bond is of course a bond of love, but she is unashamedly possessive and exclusive about it. Since man and woman were from the beginning meant to be "one flesh," infidelity and even polygamy are here excluded. The terms in which the woman claims possession over the man are very strong; it is striking that the Song closes with the woman, rather than the man, making this claim to exclusive ownership.

She claims that love, like death, is inescapable. The love the man and woman have experienced has bound them together permanently. The passion of their love for one another holds them as relentlessly as does death, and only death itself can actually separate the two lovers. Fury and destruction are implicit in these words. Those who passionately love are passionately possessive. One cannot trifle with love or with one's lover. Yahweh himself is a jealous God (Exod 20:5). Although there are those who are paranoid about infidelity, neurotically dependent, or wrongly jealous (exemplified in literature by Othello), exclusivity is not of itself corrupt or oppressive. It is wrong, indeed perverse, for the lover to be indifferent to the presence of rivals. Also, jealousy in this context need not refer to the paranoid suspicion that one's lover is faithless. If the jealousy of Yahweh over Israel is the model, the term refers to a proper possessiveness in the setting of a wholesome relationship. Rightly experienced by healthy souls, this exclusivity is part of the glory of love and further indicates the seriousness of entering this relationship.

The comparison to death probably has another implication: to marry is to give one's life to another, and whoever marries has died to all others. Analogous to Jesus' teaching that one must "die" in order to experience true freedom and life in the gospel (John 12:24), one must die to all extramarital sex in order to experience the joy of marital sex.

No one should lightly or thoughtlessly enter into a love or sexual relationship. To do so is to invite emotional catastrophe—love has great power over one's own soul as well as over the soul of the other. Those who think that they can lightly enter love but then quench its fires at will create turmoil within their own hearts and invite trouble from their lovers. It is hardly out of character for the woman's part to give the audience such warnings about the power of love. She has already three times called on the Jerusalem girls not to arouse love before it is ready (Song 2:7; 3:5; 8:4).

This is not to say, however, that love is a bad thing. It is an exquisite, soul-consuming experience that humans yearn for. To have this kind of passion for another person is a gift; it cannot be bought or sold. When the woman sings of someone giving his money for love, she is not referring to buying sexual favors (which certainly can be done) or even to gaining a wife with wealth, which is also fairly common. She rather is speaking of the experience of love itself, something that can never be bought.

In addition, this text intersects with other biblical Wisdom literature. Love is here valued above wealth and possessions, and it cannot be bought. Prov 16:16 proclaims, "To get wisdom, how much better it is than gold! / And to get understanding is preferable to silver!" Love, like Lady Wisdom, exceeds the value of gold (Prov 8:19). It is important to observe that in Song 8:7 it is the woman who demands fidelity of the man. In the ancient Near East it was a given that adultery by a wife was a heinous offense, but expectations of men were far less in this regard. Yet here, as in Prov 5:7–23, sexual devotion is demanded of the husband. The bride makes the same kind of claim on him as Lady Wisdom does on the young man (Prov 1:20–33). Fidelity to one's bride is equated with fidelity to Wisdom; holding to the one preserves love, and holding to the other preserves life.

XII. Chorus and Soprano: The Virgin's Education II (8:8–12)

Bibliography

Alden, R. L. "Song of Songs 8:12a: Who Said It?" *JETS* 31 (1988) 271–78. **Arbel, D. V.** "'My Vineyard, My Very Own, Is for Myself.'" In *The Song of Songs: A Feminist Companion to the Bible*. FCB 2d ser. 6. Ed. A. A. Brenner and C. R. Fontaine. Sheffield: Sheffield Academic Press, 2000. 90–101.

Translation

First Stanza

CHORUS
8 We have a sister, a little girl   1A
  (she has no breasts).   1B
  What shall we do for our sister   1C
  on the day that she is engaged?   1D
9 If she is a wall,   2A
  we will build her a tier^a of silver.   2B
  If she is a door,   2C
  we will enclose her with a plank of cedar.   2D

SOPRANO
10 I was^a a wall, and my breasts were like towers;   3A
   then^b in his^c eyes I was one^d who finds peace.   3B

Second Stanza

CHORUS
11 There was a vineyard belonging to Solomon in Baal Hamon.   4A
   He leased the vineyard to tenants.   4B
   Each would pay from his crop a thousand pieces of silver.   4C

SOPRANO
12 My vineyard, the one that belongs to me, is in my power.^{a} 5A
   The thousand are for you, Solomon,   5B
   but two hundred for those who tend the crops.   5C

Notes

9.a. LXX OL Syr. and Vg. make this pl. Read a sg. with MT.

10.a. Contrary to most translations, it is not necessary to translate the verbless clause אֲנִי חוֹמָה in the present tense. The temporal particle אָז implies that this verse concerns the past.

10.b. LXX reads ἐγώ [i.e., אֲנִי], "I," for MT's אָז, "then." Read MT.

10.c. LXX^B "in their eyes."

10.d. The ptc. כְּמוֹצְאֵת means "like one finding," but "like" (כ) here relates to the metaphor of the walled city. If "like" is included in the translation, one should understand it to mean "I was like a city finding peace." Otherwise, the כ should be left untranslated as in the *kaf veritatis*.

12.a. לְפָנַי means not only "before me" but "in my power." A parallel is Gen 34:10: שְׁבוּ לִפְנֵיכֶם תִּהְיֶה וְהָאָרֶץ וּסְחָרוּהָ וְהֵאָחֲזוּ בָהּ, "and the land will be available to you; settle down and trade in it and acquire property in it."

Form/Structure/Setting

This text is composed of two stanzas; the first has three strophes, and the second has two. In each stanza, the chorus sings first with lyrics describing some particular issue that relates to a third party (the proper care for the "little sister" in strophe 1, and the care for the vineyard of Solomon in strophe 4). Then, in each stanza, the soprano responds by describing her own situation vis-à-vis the issues the chorus has raised. The choral strophes 1 and 2 are each of four lines, and the woman's response in strophe 3 is two lines. In stanza 2, both the chorus and the soprano sing a single strophe of three lines.

This canto is thus unusual for the fact that the majority of the lyrics are sung neither by the tenor nor the soprano but by the chorus. One might say that the concerns and questions of the community rather than the rapturous love of the man and woman dominate this canto. On the other hand, the movement from a stanza heavily dominated by the chorus (Song 8:8–10) to one in which the lines are balanced and the soprano has the last word (Song 8:11–12) implies that the woman has in some measure triumphed over the world around her.

This unit clearly relates to "The Virgin's Education" in Song 1:5–6. Catchwords that link Song 1:5–6 to 8:8–12 are שלמה, "Solomon"; נטר, " tend, tenants"; and כרמי, "my vineyard." The point of this text is that she has left childhood behind and entered the freedom and responsibility of womanhood.

Interpreters often assert that Song 8:8–9 belongs to the brothers. Nowhere else in the Song, however, does one find any indication that there is a male chorus functioning as "brothers." This is the result of thinking of Song of Songs as a drama rather than as a Song. Even the female chorus only very loosely plays the part of the Jerusalem girls; their main role is to provide a third voice in the Song. They interact with the two principal singers and allow for more freedom and complexity in the libretto than a song of only two parts would allow. There is no need to ask about the relationship between the little girl of 8:8–9 and the chorus, as though these were actual characters in a drama or history. The whole point behind introducing the little girl is to provide a vehicle that allows the Song to elaborate on the transformation from virgin to wife.

One should also add that the plural forms in Song 8:8–9 are fairly clear indicators that these lyrics belong to the chorus and not to the soprano or the tenor. It is of course possible that we could have something more complex going on here (e.g., the soprano and tenor singing together in vv 8–9), but, in the absence of clear evidence to the contrary, it is best to go with the simplest solution, that the first-person plural forms imply that the chorus is singing. The singer of 8:12 is undoubtedly the same as the singer of 8:10, the woman (see also Alden, *JETS* 31 [1988] 271–78).

Comment

8 The chorus describes the little sister by saying that she has no breasts. She could therefore be anywhere between a small child and a preadolescent. The sexual nature of the depiction is striking; it defines her in terms of her sexual maturity. This contrasts with the more typical way of defining childhood in terms of mental capacity, as in Isa 7:15–16 (ability to make moral choices), Isa 8:4 (ability to say "father" and "mother"), Jer 1:6 (ability to speak with eloquence), and

Jonah 4:11 (ability to distinguish left from right). But the description is appropriate because it is precisely the sexual life of the girl that is the focus of the chorus's concern.

1 Sam 25:39, וידבר באביגיל לקחתה לו לאשה, "and he spoke for Abigail to take her to himself as his wife," indicates that the idiom שידבר־בה refers to the betrothal of a woman. Although strict grammar would imply that ביום שידבר־בה, "on the day that she is engaged," means that they want to know what they should do on that specific day, the actual meaning may not be quite so precise. That is, instead of asking what they should do specifically on the child's day of engagement, they may be asking what they should do *with regard to* her future engagement. On the other hand, if the cultural practice in view here involves a girl becoming betrothed while she is still a small child and long before her actual wedding, the grammar can be applied more literally. Either way, the chorus appears to be asking what they should do for her in light of the fact that she will someday marry.

9 Interpreters frequently see an antithesis here between the חומה, "wall," and the דלת, "door," with the wall representing chastity and the door representing a tendency toward promiscuity. That is, one could take these alternatives to refer to the girl's moral character, specifically in the sexual realm. On the surface this appears to be reasonable, but several factors make it an unlikely interpretation. First, it is not clear that one can or should predetermine whether a prepubescent girl will be chaste in later years. Second, the apodosis after each alternative is pretty much the same; in both cases, they intend to fortify the girl against assault (i.e., take steps to maintain her chastity). Third, the word for "door" here describes not an access but a barrier. If the intent had been to describe her as not resistant to the sexual desires of males, the text would have probably used the term פתח, "doorway" or "opening," rather than דלת, "the door itself"; cf. Keel ([1994] 279). It is more likely that the two alternatives introduced by אם, "if," mean "if we use the analogy of the wall" and "if we use the analogy of a door." In both cases, the analogy has nothing to do with the girl's moral disposition but looks back to the picture of the virgin as a walled city. With both analogies, the chorus asserts that they will take steps to insure that the young girl remains a virgin until her wedding.

The term טירה, "tier," almost always means "encampment" (Gen 25:16; Num 31:10; Ezek 25:4; Ps 69:26; 1 Chr 6:39). One time it means a row of stones in a wall (Ezek 46:23, where it is used in conjunction with טור; a course or row of jewels, beams, statues, or stones in Exod 28:17–20; 39:10–13; 1 Kgs 6:36; 7:2, 4, 12, 18, 20, 42; 2 Chr 4:13). The word here is often taken to mean "turret" or "battlement," but there is no clear analogy for this usage. If טירה is fundamentally a variant of טור, this could explain how it could mean either "encampment" (in which there is a row of tents) or a row of stones in a wall. But the notion that this is some kind of battle tower is difficult to justify.

The translation of נצור here is difficult. The verb צור sometimes means to "secure" money in a bag, as in Deut 14:25; 2 Kgs 5:23; Ezra 5:3. This usage is parallel to צרר, "tie up," and some scholars take the form here to be a variant of צרר. But one does not "tie up" something with cedar, and this interpretation should be rejected. The LXX has διαγράψωμεν, a verb that means to "delineate" or "mark off with lines." This implies that the Septuagintal translators read צור with a meaning of "to chisel, form, or engrave" (see Exod 32:4; 1 Kgs 7:15). This is a biform of צר. Taken this way, it would imply that the "door" was decorated or engraved with cedar carvings. צור can also mean to harass or fight, as in Exod 23:22 and Deut 2:9, 19, but that usage is out of the question here. צור often means to "besiege," as in Deut 20:12; 2 Sam 11:1; 20:15; 1 Kgs 15:27; 16:17; 20:1. In all these cases it is used with the preposition על; indeed, used with על, the verb צור elsewhere always means to "besiege" (20x). This is very strong evidence, and one must assume that same meaning prevails here. However, the purpose of a siege was not just to break into a city. A siege was, first of all, a stratagem meant to keep anyone from getting into or out of a city. Hence, we should take this to mean "besiege" not in the sense of "assault" but in the sense of "enclose."

The טירת כסף, "tier of silver," and the לוח ארז, "plank of cedar," are both meant to fortify the castle (the virgin) against assault (loss of virginity). The metaphor does not concern how she might lose her virginity (whether by force or by consent); it only indicates that the chorus intends to prevent loss of virginity. Silver and cedar, however, are ornamental; they are not materials one would typically use for defensive bulwarks. This is self-evident in the case of silver, but cedar is associated with palatial dwellings as well (e.g., 2 Sam 7:2, 7; Jer 22:14–15; 1 Kgs 5–7; Ezra 3:7). The implication of using expensive and decorative materials (as opposed to iron, stone, or generic wood) to secure the virginity of the girl is that her status as virgin is to be honored and maintained in a way that enhances her dignity. She is not placed in a prison like a criminal; she is protected like a precious treasure. The historical analogy is how the virgin daughters of David were honored with decorative clothing (2 Sam 13:18).

10 The soprano turns the image of the wall in an unexpected direction by describing her breasts as the towers on the wall. This obviously conveys the fact that, unlike the little sister, she has attained sexual maturity and has full breasts. But it also indicates her resistance to seduction. In the defense of a city, the towers are the proud symbols of its resistance to all attackers; the taking of the towers implies that the last vestiges of resistance have collapsed and the city is in the hands of its enemies.

By בעיניו, "in his eyes," she does not only mean, "in his estimation" or "in his opinion." She also means that she has found in his eyes peace for herself.

11–12 The location of Baal Hamon is unknown. An old speculation is that Baal Hamon is to be identified with Balamon of Judith 8:3, a city that, according to that text, was near Dothan (north of Samaria). Pope (686–88) notes the similarity between Baal Hamon and *Baal-ḥammo,* the name of a Carthaginian deity mentioned in votive inscriptions. He suggests that הָמוֹן be emended to חַמּוֹן, the name of a town mentioned in Josh 19:28. He also notes that the name Ḥammon occurs in the *Ma'ṣub* inscription, which mentions that some citizens dedicated a shrine to Ashtarte in the shrine of the god of *Ḥammon*. He argues on the basis of some texts of dubious interpretation that *Baal-ḥammon* was itself a place name. In addition, since Ashtarte was associated with the motif of guarding a vineyard in Ugaritic Text 2001.2.1, he suggests that this text and Song 1:6 may allude to a shrine to Ashtarte at *Ḥammon*. Apart from the fact that emendation is unsupported, the connections Pope proposes are too tenuous to be persuasive.

The name Baal Hamon may be purely fanciful. It means "lord of uproar," "lord of wealth," or perhaps even, "husband of a mob." This could be a playful allusion to Solomon's wealth and infamous harem. A vineyard represents real property and wealth, but in the Song it also represents female sexuality. Thus, many interpreters see Solomon's vineyard as a very thinly veiled allusion to his harem. In the analogy, the tenants would be guardians of the harem. Some see here a joke at Solomon's expense: the two hundred shekels that go to the tenants (v 12) imply that some of the officials who are in charge of Solomon's harem receive sexual favors from its women (this assumes that not all of the keepers of the harem were eunuchs). If this interpretation is correct, one would probably regard the man as the singer of v 12. He would be saying that, unlike Solomon with his mob of women, he has one single vineyard, his wife, for himself.

If one presses the above interpretation, it appears that "Solomon's vineyard" is describing a brothel rather than a harem. If in his vineyard are women under the control of tenants from the vineyard who paid him one thousand pieces of silver and earned two hundred for themselves, it can only be a brothel; a harem does not turn a profit. But this is not what the text implies. If the vineyard of Solomon is simply his harem, the metaphor of profit is ill conceived and at best quite awkward.

There are compelling reasons, however, for regarding this interpretation as somewhat superficial and ultimately as simply wrong. The woman is the singer in Song 8:12 because it relates back to Song 1:6, in which she complains that she could not keep her own vineyard while under her brothers' authority. In 8:12 we see the redemption and transformation of the woman whereby she now has control over her own vineyard. This symmetry is destroyed and the relationship between the two passages is obscure if at 8:12 her husband simply declares his authority over her, the vineyard. The problem here is not that the modern reader refuses to accept the ancient understanding of the relationship between husband and wife; it is that the text itself requires some kind of balance. This balance is not achieved by the man declaring that he possesses his own vineyard, however true that may be.

While the vineyard of Solomon may allude to his harem, it is not exclusively or even primarily that. The key to interpreting this metaphor is in the woman's use of the term in Song 1:6, where her lack of freedom to tend her own vineyard is emblematic of her servile status. There, she could not tend her own vineyard because of the duties imposed on her by her brothers. Solomon, by contrast, does not tend his own vineyard by choice. He has voluntarily allowed servants to take his place in caring for a vineyard and watching it flourish.

Explanation

In Song 1:5–6, the woman sang of her life in the home of her mother, where her brothers treated her as a slave. She was forced to work in the family vineyards and had no opportunity to cultivate her own. She was in effect an outsider in that she was given no freedom to find and develop her interests. Nevertheless, she was made strong by the experience and is ready to take her place as a woman.

This text, Song 8:8–12, also deals with the education of the virgin. First, the singers of the chorus ask what they should do with their little sister and rhetorically answer their own question (vv 8–9). The woman then sings of her transformation from virgin to wife under the metaphor that the chorus has employed, the wall (v 10). Previously she had been like one ready for war where men were concerned. Her defenses were up, and she was the walled city surrounded by the guards of the wall (Song 3:3), her virginity. With him, however, she found peace. That is, looking into his eyes, she found one whom she could fully trust. She was no longer a town under siege; she could open the gates freely. The "towers" now belong to her lover, but not by conquest or force. His banner flies over the city, and it is a banner of love (Song 2:4).

In v 11, the chorus sings of the vineyard of Solomon, a motif that obviously looks back to the vineyard of Song 1:5–6. Solomon has in effect cut himself off from the pleasures of direct involvement in life and converted the process into a financial transaction. The agrarian ideal of tending a garden and having the joy of eating grapes from vines that one has cared for with one's own hands is lost on Solomon as he sits sequestered in Jerusalem taking in accounts receivable. The text alludes to his harem here in the sense that the true meaning of sexual love is lost on Solomon as well. For him, a vast harem was a political necessity and a visible sign that he was a great and wealthy monarch. But he had no experience of love as the singer of this canto experienced it: "My lover is mine and I am his." Solomon was the *Baal Hamon*, the lord of a mob. He owned a great many things and people but knew them only from a distance.

The woman responds that she would rather have personal control over her own vineyard than be in Solomon's position, that is, be the absentee landlord over vast estates. In contrast to Solomon, the woman experiences life and her one lover directly.

XIII. Tenor, Chorus, and Soprano: The Farewell (8:13–14)

Bibliography

John of Ford. *Sermons on the Final Verses of the Song of Songs.* Trans. W. M. Beckett. Kalamazoo, MI: Cistercian, 1977. **Tournay, J. R.** "The Song of Songs and Its Concluding Section." *Imm* 10 (1980) 5–14.

Translation

    TENOR AND CHORUS
13 O lady^a who inhabits the gardens,   1A
    while friends listen for your voice,^b let me hear you!   1B
    SOPRANO
14 Hasten away, my lover,   2A
    and make yourself ^alike a gazelle^a   2B
    or a young stag on the mountains of balsam!   2C

Notes

13.a. "Lady" is implied by the fem. sg. ptc. הַיּוֹשֶׁבֶת, "one inhabiting." The LXX has the masc. sg. ὁ καθήμενος and Syr. reads masc. pl., but emendation of the MT is not called for. Cf. Murphy, 194.

13.b. The word לקולך, "to your voice,Ó could do double duty as object of both מקשיבים, "listening," and השמיעיני, "let me hear."

14.a-a. Missing in LXX and some MSS of Syr.

Form/Structure/Setting

This text is composed of two short strophes. In v 13 the male, or the chorus, or both together, call out to the woman, and in v 14 the woman answers. Scholars are unsure about who the singer is in v 13, but, since the woman is the focus and protagonist of the Song, the chorus and tenor are understood to sing together to her here. They in effect throw the spotlight on her in order to celebrate her transformation. This blending of voices is the counterpart to the introduction in Song 1:2–4, where the soprano and chorus compete with one another in declaring their admiration for the man. The woman responds in v 14 by calling on the man to resume his role as lover under the guise of the stag on the mountains of balsam. As the Song had begun with a call for the man to "kiss me with the kisses of his mouth" (1:2), it ends with a call for him to exult in the love of the woman.

Comment

13 In Song 2:14 the woman's voice is surpassingly sweet to the man, and he desires to hear her speak. In this verse, everyone has fallen in love with her. If it is correct that both the tenor and chorus sing this together, the combination of their voices signals to the audience that everyone wants to hear her speak. The lyrics declare that "friends listen for your voice." חברים, "friends," occurs elsewhere only in the Song at 1:7, where it refers to her lover's associates, the other shepherds. In that text, the woman sang of her hesitation about appearing in the midst of his friends, a situation in which she would have been an outsider. Here, she is the man's wife and is admired by all—husband, girls, and shepherds. She has replaced the man as the object of admiration (see Song 1:2–4).

The appellation given to her as היושבת בגנים, "the lady who inhabits the gardens," is significant. In the Song, the metaphor of the garden or of fruit regularly refers to sexual pleasures generally or to the woman's body specifically. Here, as the lady who inhabits the gardens, she is the domain of love. The joys and desires of love have her at the center and all look upon her in wonder. Certainly the man is enchanted by her. (The line "let me hear you" may have been sung by the tenor alone.)

14 The woman responds only to the man and seems unconcerned about the chorus or the "friends." This stands in contrast to Song 1:7, where she was mortified at the thought of being among the companions of the man. Here she focuses her attention wholly on him and ignores all others. When she tells him to ברח, "flee," she does not mean that he should run away from her. Under the metaphor of the stag on the mountains, she is calling on him to come away from the crowds and give all his attention to her. The phrase הרי בשמים, "mountains of balsam," refers to the woman's breasts and by metonymy to her whole body (with focus on her sexuality). She is calling on him to make love to her.

Explanation

This is the third time a canto or stanza has ended with reference to the man experiencing her breasts under the metaphor of mountains. The canto of the invitation to depart (Song 2:8–17) concludes with her inviting him to be like a deer or gazelle "on the cleft mountains" (2:17). At Song 4:6, the man ends a stanza by saying that he will get himself "to Myrrh Mountain and to Incense Hill." Here, the entire Song of Songs ends with a call for him to experience the "mountains of balsam." The mountain is obviously a favorite image for the breast in the Song, but there is more to be said than that. Another image for the breast in the Song is a cluster of dates or grapes (Song 7:9 [ET 7:8]). But mountains, apart from their obvious visual similarity to breasts, are not consumable or transient in nature. To the contrary, they connote grandeur and permanence. As such, perhaps mountain is a preferred metaphor because it shows that sexual love transcends any one couple's experience. It is an abiding universal of the human experience. It has dignity, like the mountains, and Song of Songs itself is also, like the mountains, an abiding statement of its beauty and dignity. By placing the call to the mountains at the end of various parts and at the end of the entire opus, the text makes the mountains the special focus of attention. This focus on the breasts as the region of lovemaking is in keeping with Prov 5:19 and suggests that the Song rightly belongs in the Wisdom corpus. It further suggests that the woman's body (and especially her breasts) is the locus of the couple's love. Finally, *mountains* in its literal sense suggests a pastoral setting in the hill country of Israel, and so provides an image of an ideal setting for young lovers. The man and woman thus depart into the countryside and leave the audience, and the reader, with a distant, wistful vision of love.

Lamentations

Author's Preface

If I recall correctly, I first discussed with John Watts the possibility of undertaking this project in the fall of 1996. David Hubbard had passed away without completing the work on Lamentations, and John was looking for someone to take Dr. Hubbard's notes on chapter 1 and incorporate them into a commentary on the book. I never had the privilege of meeting Dr. Hubbard, but I have met many influenced by his ministry. I accepted this assignment sometime in 1997, and the end result is before you. It is an honor to have had the chance to work once again with my "Father Doctor," John Watts, who prepared the metrical notations for this volume, and with my friend James Watts. Their editorial expertise made this a better book, as did Melanie McQuere's.

This commentary was written in a variety of places and with the help of many people. Some initial work was accomplished at The Southern Baptist Theological Seminary from 1997 to 1999. I am particularly grateful to Bruce Keisling of Boyce Centennial Library, who conducted bibliographical searches for me.

Further work was undertaken on the project while I was teaching at Trinity Episcopal School for Ministry from 1999 to 2001. Besides enjoying unqualified support from my faculty colleagues, our dean, Gavin McGrath, and our president, Peter Moore, I was greatly helped by having Sarah Lebhar as my research assistant. Sarah made certain that I had needed resources, a task made easier by Dr. Robert Munday and the staff of the Trinity library. During the summer of 2001 I taught at Beeson Divinity School, where I used the Samford University Library and wrote the introductory chapter.

Since 2001 I have served on the faculty of Wheaton College, a place that supports its faculty members' writing efforts admirably. I have received research assistance from Stephen Webster, Amber Stone, Keith Williams, and Greg Goss. I have also benefited from the help of the staff at Buswell Memorial Library. During the summer of 2002 I was given an Aldeen Grant by the college to do research and writing on the commentary at Moore Theological College in Sydney, Australia. While in residence there, I was encouraged by Old Testament colleagues Barry Webb and Paul Williamson, as well as by John Woodhouse, principal of Moore College, himself an Old Testament scholar. The college librarians were unfailingly cheerful and helpful. Archbishop Peter Jensen and Phillip Jensen, Dean of St. Andrew's Cathedral, Sydney, made the arrangements for our stay and offered superb hospitality. The Jensen brothers are good, gracious, and encouraging friends, as are their wives, Christine and Helen.

Besides the friends already mentioned, I have received constant support from long-time friends and from family members. Richard Bailey, Kyle McClellan, Mike Tucker, Tom Jones, and Greg Thornbury offered specific encouragement on the project and on life. In 1998 Ben Mitchell, who has the gift of mercy, was with me during very hard times, and my oldest and wisest friend, Jim Dixon, guided me through some tough decisions associated with those times. Ben and Jim have a high theology of friendship. As always, Scott Hafemann informed, encouraged, and inspired me throughout the writing process. In fact, Scott was the one who first advised me to accept the project. Only God can give you friends like Scott. My sister Suzanne Kingsley and her husband, Gordon, shaped my views on lament and hope more than they will ever know.

Most of all, my wife, Heather, and my daughter, Molly, have contributed their love, laughter, and expertise to this project. Heather, a professional theological editor, offered advice alongside love and encouragement. She also provides an atmosphere in our home that is as conducive to scholarly writing as I can imagine. Molly rejoiced in every finished stage. She also shared the difficult changes that occurred in the last several years. She is currently concluding undergraduate studies in biblical studies and will pursue graduate studies in New Testament at Oxford University next year. I am grateful for her commitment to our Lord. Though it would be appropriate to dedicate this project in honor of David Hubbard, I believe he would agree with my decision to dedicate it to Molly. After all, he gave his life to preparing people like Molly for the Lord's work, and I share at least a measure of his commitment.

For these and other kindnesses, I am very grateful.

PAUL R. HOUSE

Wheaton College
Easter 2003

Commentary Bibliography

In the text of the commentary, references to commentaries on Lamentations are by author's name only.

Aalders, G. C. *De Klaagliederen.* Kampen: Kok, 1952. **Adeney, W. F.** *The Song of Solomon and the Lamentations of Jeremiah.* New York: Funk & Wagnalls, 1900. **Alshekh, M.** *The Book of Lamentations: Solace amidst the Ashes: The Commentary of Rabbi Mosheh Alshich on Megillath Eichah/Lamentations.* Jerusalem: Feldheim, 1993. **Ash, A. L.** *Jeremiah and Lamentations.* The Living Word Commentary. Abilene, TX: Abilene Christian UP, 1987. **Berlin, A.** *Lamentations.* OTL. Louisville, KY: Westminster John Knox, 2002. **Bettan, I.** *The Five Scrolls: A Commentary on the Song of Songs, Ruth, Lamentations, Ecclesiastes, Esther.* Cincinnati: Union of American Hebrew Congregations, 1950. **Boecker, H. J.** *Klagelieder.* Zurich: Theologischer Verlag, 1985. **Bonaventure.** *D. Bonaventvræ S.R.E. Episcopi Card. . . . In librvm sapientiæ & lamentatinoes Ieremiae Prophetae pia & erudite expositio.* Venice: Apud Petrum de Franciscijs, 1574. **Brandscheidt, R.** *Das Buch der Klagelieder.* GSAT 10. Düsseldorf: Patmos, 1988. **Budde, K.** "Die Klagelieder." In K. Budde, A. Bertholet, and D. G. Wildeboer, *Die Funf Megillot.* KHC 17. Freiburg, Leipzig, and Tübingen: Mohr (Siebeck), 1898. **Bugenhagen, J.** *In Ieremian Propetam Commentarium.* Vitebergae: In Officina Petri Seitz, 1546. **Bullinger, H.** *Threnorum, seu, Lamentationum beati Ieremiae prophetae breuis explicatio.* Tiguri: Excudebat Froschouerus, 1561. **Calvin, J.** *Commentaries on the Book of the Prophet Jeremiah and the Lamentations.* Trans. J. Owen. Calvin's Commentaries 11. 1563. Reprint, Grand Rapids, MI: Baker, 1996. **Castro, C. de.** *Commentariorum in Ieremiæ Prophetias, Lamentationes, et Baruch.* Paris: Apud Michaëlem Sonniom, 1609. **Cheyne, T. K.** *Lamentations.* London: Funk & Wagnalls, 1913. **Coffman, J. B.** *Ecclesiastes, Song of Solomon, Lamentations.* Abilene, TX: Abilene Christian UP, 1994. **Crowley, E. J.** *The Books of Lamentations, Baruch, Sophonia, Nahum, and Hebacuc: With a Commentary.* New York: Paulist Press, 1962. **Dalglish, E. R.** *Jeremiah, Lamentations.* Nashville: Broadman, 1983. **Davidson, R.** *Jeremiah II and Lamentations.* Daily Study Bible. Philadelphia: Westminster, 1985. **Del Rio, M. A.** *Commentarivs litteralis in Threnos, id est, Lamentationes Ieremiæ prophetæ.* Lvgdvni: Svmptibvs Horatii Cardon, 1608. **Deursen, F. van.** *Ruth, Klaagliederen, Esther.* Amsterdam: Duijten & Schipperheijn, 1991. **Dobbs-Allsopp, F. W.** *Lamentations.* IBC. Louisville, KY: Westminster John Knox, 2002. **Droin, J. M.** *Le Livre des Lamentations: "Comment?": Une traduction et un commentaire.* Geneva: Labor & Fides, 1995. **Ellicott, C. J.** *The Book of Jeremiah and Lamentations.* Grand Rapids, MI: Zondervan, 1961. **Ellison, H. L.** "Lamentations." In *Expositor's Bible Commentary.* 12 vols. Grand Rapids, MI: Zondervan, 1986. 6:695–733. **Ewald, H.** *Die Psalmen und die Klagelieder.* 3d ed. DAB. Göttingen: Vandenhoeck & Ruprecht, 1866. **Exell, J. S.** *Jeremiah, the Lamentations of Jeremiah.* 1900. Reprint, New York: Revell, 1981. **Figueiro, P. A.** *Paraphrases in Praophetias Ieremiæ, Commentarios in eiusdem Lamentationes.* Lyon: Suptibus Horatii Cardon, 1615. **Fuerst, W. J.** *The Books of Ruth, Esther, Ecclesiastes, the Song of Songs, Lamentations.* CBC. Cambridge: Cambridge UP, 1975. **Gaab, J. F. von.** *Beiträge zur Erklärung des sogenannten Hohenlieds, Koheleths und der Klagelieder.* Tübingen: Heerbrandt'schen, 1795. **Gelin, A.** *Jérémie—Les Lamentations—Le Livre de Baruch.* La Sainte Bible de Jérusalem. Paris: Cerf, 1951. **Gerstenberger, E. S.** *Psalms, Part 2, and Lamentations.* FOTL 15. Grand Rapids, MI: Eerdmans, 2001. ———. *Zu Hilfe, mein Gott: Psalmen und Klagelieder.* Neukirchen-Vluyn: Neukirchener Verlag, 1989. **Ghislerius, M.** *In Ieremiam propetam commentarii . . .* Jugduni: Laurentii Durand, 1623. **Gordis, R.** *The Song of Songs and Lamentations.* New York: Ktav, 1974. **Gosdeck, D. M.** *Jeremiah, Lamentations.* Milwaukee: Northwestern, 2000. ———.

Jeremiah, Lamentations. St. Louis: CPH, 1995. **Gottwald, N. K.** "Lamentations." In *Harper's Bible Commentary*. Ed. J. L. Mays et al. San Francisco: Harper & Row, 1988. 646–51. **Gross, H.** *Klagelieder*. Würzburg: Echter, 1986. **Guest, J.** *Jeremiah, Lamentations*. Communicator's Commentary. Waco, TX: Word, 1988. **Guinan, M. D.** "Lamentations." In *The New Jerome Biblical Commentary*. Ed. R. E. Brown et al. Englewood Cliffs, NJ: Prentice Hall, 1990. 558–62. **Habel, N. C.** *Jeremiah and Lamentations*. St. Louis: Concordia, 1968. **Haller, M.** "Die Klagelieder." In M. Haller and K. Galling, *Die Funf Megilloth*. HAT 18. Tübingen: Mohr (Siebeck), 1940. **Hamon, M.** *Commentaire sur les Lamentations de Jérémie*. Paris: Chez Le Clere, 1790. **Hardt, H. von der.** *Threnos*. Helmstadii, 1712. **Harrison, R. K.** *Jeremiah and Lamentations*. TOTC. Downers Grove, IL: InterVarsity Press, 1973. **Henderson, E.** *The Book of the Prophet Jeremiah and That of the Lamentations*. Andover: Draper, 1868. **Hillers, D. R.** *Lamentations*. AB 7A. New York: Doubleday, 1972. ———. *Lamentations*. 2d ed. AB 7A. New York: Doubleday, 1992. **Hinton, L. B.** *Jeremiah and Lamentations*. Basic Bible Commentary. Nashville: Abingdon, 1988. **Hitzig, J.** *Das Hohe Lied: Erklärt von d. Ferdinand Hitzig. Die Klaglieder. Erklärt von d. Otto Thenius*. Leipzig: Hirzel, 1855. **Huelsemann, J.** *D. Joh. Hulsemanni in Jeremian & Threnos Commentarius posthumus*. Frankfurt: Sumptibus Johannis Herebordi Klosii, 1696. **Huey, F. B.** *Jeremiah and Lamentations*. NAC. Nashville: Broadman Press, 1993. **Jensen, I. L.** *Jeremiah and Lamentations*. Chicago: Moody Press, 1966. **Kaiser, O.** "Klagelieder." In H. Ringren and O. Kaiser, *Das Hohelied/Klagelieder/Das Buch Ester*. 4th ed. ATD 16.2. Göttingen: Vandenhoeck & Ruprecht, 1992. **Keil, C. F.** *Jeremiah, Lamentations*. Trans. J. Martin. Commentary on the Old Testament 8. 1872. Reprint, Grand Rapids, MI: Eerdmans, 1980. **Kent, D. G.** *Lamentations: Bible Study Commentary*. Grand Rapids, MI: Zondervan, 1983. **Knabenbauer, J.** *Commentarius in Danielum prophetam, Lamentationes et Baruch*. Paris: Lethielluex, 1891. **Knight, G. A. F.** *Esther, Song of Songs, and Lamentations*. TBC. London: SCM Press, 1955. **Kodell, J.** *Lamentations, Haggai, Zechariah, Malachi, Obadiah, Joel, Second Zechariah, Baruch*. Wilmington, DE: Glazier, 1982. **Kraus, H. J.** *Klagelieder*. 3d ed. BKAT 20. Neukirchen-Vluyn: Neukirchener Verlag, 1968. **Kuist, H. T.** *The Book of Jeremiah; the Lamentations of Jeremiah*. Richmond, VA: John Knox, 1960. **Lamparter, H.** *Das Buch der Sehnsucht: Das Buch Ruth, das Hohe Lied, die Klagelieder*. Stuttgart: Calwer, 1962. **Löhr, M.** *Die Klagelieder des Jeremia*. HKAT 3.2.2. Göttingen: Vandenhoeck & Ruprecht, 1906. **Lowth, W.** *A Commentary upon the Prophecy and Lamentations of Jeremiah*. London, 1728. **Lundmark, J.** *In Threnos Jeremiae dissertation: Cujus partem primam*. Upsala: Edman, 1799. **Mayer, F.** *Die Klagelieder Jeremias: Ein Evengelium für Mühselige und Beladene*. Stuttgart: Quell, 1934. **McGee, J. V.** *Jeremiah and Lamentations*. Pasadena, CA: Thru the Bible Books, 1978. **Meek, T. J.**, and **W. P. Merrill.** "Lamentations." *IB*. 12 vols. Nashville: Abingdon, 1956. 6:3–38. **Moskowitz, Y. Z.** "Lamentations." In *Five Megillot*. Da'at Miqra Series. Jerusalem: Mosad Harav Kook, 1990. **Müller, H. P.** *Das Hohelied, Klagelieder, das Buch Ester*. Göttingen: Vandenhoeck & Ruprecht, 1992. **Nägelsbach, C. W. H.** *The Book of the Prophet Jeremiah: Theologically and Homiletically Expounded*. Edinburgh: Clark, 1871. **O'Connor, K. M.** "Lamentations." *NIB*. Nashville: Abingdon, 2001. 6:1013–72. ———. "Lamentations." In *The Women's Bible Commentary*. Ed. C. A. Newsom and S. H. Ringe. Louisville, KY: Westminster John Knox, 1992. 178–82. **Oecolampadius, J.** *In Hieremiam Prephetam Commentariorum libri tres*. Argentinae: In Officina Matthia Apiarii, 1533. **Oettli, S.** "Die Klagelieder." In *Kurzgefaszter Kommentar zu den heiligen Schrisften Alten und Neuen Testaments*. Ed. H. Strack and O. Zöckler. A: Altes Testament 7. Abteilung: Die poetischen Hagiographen. Nördlingen, 1889. 199–224. **Origen.** *Jeremiahomilien; Keleliederkommentar; Erklärung der Samuel- und Königsbücher*. Reprint, Berlin: Akademie, 1983. **Paffrath, T.** *Die Klagelieder*. Bonn: Hanstein, 1932. **Paschasius Radbertus.** *Commentaria in Lamentationibus Ieremie prophete*. Basel: Balilien, 1502. ———. *In Lamentatioes Ieremiæ prophetæ quæ ut quinque capitibus continent, ita in quing redegit libros, opus certe aureun, nunquam antehac uisum, nec typis excusum*. Cologne: Ex officina Eucharii, 1532. **Peake, A. S.** *Jeremiah and Lamentations*. Vol. 2, *Jeremiah XXV to LII*,

Lamentations. Century Bible. London: Caxton, 1911. **Piscator, J.** *In Prophetam Jeremiam et ejusdem Lamentationes Commentarius.* Herbornae Nassoviorum: Ex Officina typographica Christophori Corvini, 1614. **Plöger, O.** "Die Klagelieder." In O. Plöger et al. *Fünf Megilloth: Ruth, Das Hohelied, Esther, Der Prediger, Die Klagelieder.* (HAT 1.18, 2d ed. Tübingen: Mohr (Siebeck), 1969. **Provan, I.** *Lamentations.* NCB. Grand Rapids, MI: Eerdmans, 1991. **Re'emi, S. P.** "The Theology of Hope: A Commentary on the Book of Lamentations." In R. Martin-Achard and S. P. Re'emi, *God's People in Crisis: A Commentary on the Book of Amos and A Commentary on the Book of Lamentations.* ITC. Grand Rapids, MI: Eerdmans, 1984. **Renkema, J.** *Lamentations.* Trans. B. Doyle. HCOT. Leuven: Peeters, 1998. **Ricciotti, G.** *Le Lamentazioni de Geremia.* Turin and Rome: n.p., 1924. **Ringgren, H.** *Das Hohe Lied, Klagelieder, Das Buch Esther.* Göttingen: Vandenhoeck & Ruprecht, 1981. **Rudolph, W.** *Das Buch Ruth, Das Hohe Lied, Die Klagelieder.* 2d ed. KAT 17.1–3. Gutersloh: Mohn, 1962. **Salters, R. B.** *Jonah and Lamentations.* Old Testament Guides. Sheffield: JSOT Press, 1994. **Schneider, H.** *Das Buch Daniel. Das Buch der Klagelieder. Das Buch Baruch.* Frieburg: Herder, 1954. **Smit, G.** *Ruth, Ester en Klaagliederen.* Groningen: Wolters, 1930. **Smith, J.** *Jeremiah and Lamentations.* Joplin, MO: College Press, 1972. **Stoll, C. D.** *Die Klagelieder.* Woppertal: Brockhaus, 1986. **Streane, A. W.** *Jeremiah, Lamentations.* Cambridge Bible for Schools and Colleges. Cambridge: Cambridge UP, 1881. **Strobel, A.** *Trauer um Jerusalem: Jeremia, Klagelieder, Baruch.* Stuttgart: Katholisches Bibelwerk, 1973. **Tarnow, J.** *In Threnos Jeremiae commentarius.* Hamburg: Sumptibus Sam. Heilii & Joh. Gottf. Liebezeit, 1707. **Thenius, O.** *Die Klagelieder.* Leipzig: Mohr (Siebeck), 1855. **Tobiah ben Elieser (Toviyahu ben Eli'ezer).** *Tobia ben Elieser's Commentar zu Threni (Lekach Tob.): Zum ersten male nach ms. München.* Berlin: Druck von H. Itzkowski, 1895. **Udall, J.** *A Commentarie upon the Lamentations of Ieremy.* London, 1900. **Vaihinger, J. G.** *Der Prediger und das hohelied.* Stuttgart: Besler, 1858. **Weiser, A.** "Klagelieder." In H. Ringren, A. Weiser, and W. Zimmerli, *Spruche/Prediger, Das Hohe Lied/Klagelieder, Das Buch Esther.* 2d ed. ATD 16. Göttingen: Vandenhoeck & Ruprecht, 1962. **Westermann, C.** *Lamentations: Issues and Interpretation.* Trans. C. Muenchow. Minneapolis: Fortress, 1994. **Wiesmann, H.** *Die Klagelieder.* Frankfurt am Main: Philosophisch-theologische Hochschule Sankt Georgen, 1954. **Wright, J. S.** *Lamentations, Ezekiel, Daniel.* Grand Rapids, MI: Eerdmans, 1970. **Yamamuro, G.** *Eremiya-ki; Eremiya aika.* Tokyo: Kyuseidan Shuppan oyobi Kyokyubu, 1941. **Ziegler, J.** *Jeremias. Baruch. Threni. Epistula Jeremiae.* 2d ed. Göttingen: Vandenhoeck & Ruprecht, 1976. **Zlotowitz, A.** *Lamentations: A New Translation with a Commentary Anthologized from Talmudic, Midrashic, and Rabbinic Sources.* New York: Mesorah, 1977.

General Bibliography

Ahuvyah, A. "*ykh yšbh bdd hʿyr rty ʿm* (Lam 1:1)." *Beth Miqra* 24 (1979) 423–25. **Albrektson, B.** *Studies in the Text and Theology of the Book of Lamentations.* Lund: Gleerup, 1963. **Alexander, P. S.** "The Textual Tradition of Targum Lamentations." *AbrN* 24 (1986) 1–26. **Alter, R.** *The Art of Biblical Poetry.* New York: Basic, 1985. **Anderson, G. A.** *A Time to Mourn, a Time to Dance: The Expression of Grief and Joy in Israelite Religion.* University Park, PA: Pennsylvania State UP, 1991. **Barthélemy, D.** *Critique textuelle de l'Ancien Testament.* Vol. 2, *Isaïe, Jérémie, Lamentations.* OBO 50.2. Fribourg and Göttingen, 1986. **Baumgartner, W.** *Die Klagegedichte des Jeremias.* BZAW 32. Giessen: Töpelmann, 1917. **Begrich, J.** "Zur hebräischen Metrik." *TRev* 4 (1932) 67–89. **Benjamin ben Aaron of Zalozce.** *Tore zahav: ʿal Hamishah humshe Torah gam ʿal Megilat Ekhah u-Megilat Ester.* Jerusalem, 1988. **Berlin, A.** *The Dynamics of Biblical Parallelism.* Bloomington: Indiana UP, 1985. **Bosman, H. J.** "Two Proposals for a Structural Analysis of Lamentations 3 and 5." In *Bible et Inromatique.* Paris: Champion, 1992. 77–98. **Bouzard, W. C., Jr.** *We Have Heard with Our Ears, O God: Sources of the Communal Laments in the Psalms.* SBLDS 159. Atlanta: Scholars Press, 1997. **Bracke, J. M.** *Jeremiah 30–52 and Lamentations.* Louisville: Westminster John Knox, 2000. **Brandscheidt, R.** *Gotteszorn und Menschenleid: Die Gerichtsklage des leidenden Gerechten in Klagelieder 3.* Trier: Paulinus, 1983. **Brooks, R.** *Great Is Your Faithfulness.* North Darlington: Evangelical Press, 1989. **Brug, J. F.** "Biblical Acrostics and Their Relationship to Other Ancient Near Eastern Acrostics." In *Scripture in Context: The Bible in the Light of Cuneiform Literature.* 3 vols. Ed. W. W. Hallo et al. Lewiston, NY: 1990. 3:283–304. **Brunet, G.** "Une Interpretation nouvelle du livre biblique des Lamentations." *RHR* 175 (1969) 115–17. ———. *Les Lamentation contre Jérémie: Réinterpretation des quatre premières lamentations.* Paris: Presses Universitaires de France, 1968. **Budde, K.** "Das hebräische Klagelied." *ZAW* 2 (1882) 1–52. ———. "Poetry (Hebrew)." In *A Dictionary of the Bible.* Ed. J. Hastings. 5 vols. Edinburgh: T & T Clark, 1902. 4:2–13. **Cannon, W. W.** "The Authorship of Lamentations." *BSac* 81 (1924) 42–58. **Caro, H. I.** *Beiträge zur ältesten Exegese des Buches Threni mit besonderer Berücksichtigung des Midrasch und Targum.* Berlin: Itzowski, 1893. **Cohen, A.** *Midrash Rabbah: Lamentations.* London: Soncino, 1939. **Cohen, C.** "The 'Widowed' City." *JANESCU* 5 (1973) 75–81. **Cohen, M. E.** *The Canonical Lamentations of Mesopotamia.* 2 vols. Potomac, MD: CDL, 1988. ———. *Sumerian Hymnology: The Eršemma.* Cincinnati: Hebrew Union College Press, 1981. **Cohen, S.** "The Destruction from Scripture to Midrash." *Proof* 2 (1982) 18–39. **Cowles, H.** *Jeremiah and His Lamentations.* New York: Appleton, 1880. **Dahood, M.** "New Readings in Lamentations." *Bib* 59 (1978) 174–97. **De Hoop, R.** "Lamentations: The *Qinah*-Metre Questioned." In *Delimitation Criticism. A New Tool in Biblical Scholarship.* Ed. M. C. A. Korpel and J. M. Oesch. Assen: Van Gocum, 2000. 80–104. **Dennison, J. T., Jr.** "The Lament and the Lamenter." *Kerux* 12 (1997) 30–34. **Dobbs-Allsopp, F. W.** "The Effects of Enjambment in Lamentations (Part 2)." *ZAW* 113 (2001) 370–85. ———. "The Enjambing Line in Lamentations: A Taxonomy (Part 1)." *ZAW* 113 (2001) 219–39. ———. "Linguistic Evidence for the Date of Lamentations." *JANESCU* 26 (1998) 1–36. ———. "The Syntagma of *bat* Followed by a Geographical Name in the Hebrew Bible: A Reconsideration of Its Meaning and Grammar." *CBQ* 57 (1995) 451–70. ———. "Tragedy, Tradition, and Theology in the Book of Lamentations." *JSOT* 74 (1997) 29–60. ———. *Weep, O Daughter of Zion: A Study of the City-Lament Genre in the Hebrew Bible.* BibOr 44. Rome: Pontifical Biblical Institute, 1993. **Dori, Z.** *Megilat Ekhah: tirgumah u-midrashah.* Kiryat Netafim: Dori, 1984. **Dorsey, D. A.** "Lamentations: Communicating Meaning through Structure." *EvJ* 6 (1988) 83–90. **Durlesser, J. A.** "The Book of Lamentations and the Mesopotamian Laments: Experiential or Literary Ties." *Proceedings, Eastern*

Great Lakes Biblical Society 3 (1983) 69–84. **Eichler, U.** "Der klagende Jeremia." *TLZ* 103 (1978) 918–19. **Eissfeldt, O.** *The Old Testament: An Introduction.* Trans. P. Ackroyd. New York: Harper and Row, 1965. **Everson, A. J.** "Days of Yahweh." *JBL* 93 (1974) 329–37. **Ferris, P. W., Jr.** *The Genre of Communal Lament in the Bible and the Ancient Near East.* SBLDS 127. Atlanta: Scholars Press, 1992. **Fitzgerald, A.** "The Mythological Background for the Presentation of Jerusalem as Queen and False Worship as Adultery in the OT." *CBQ* 34 (1972) 403–16. **Follis, E. R.** "The Holy City as Daughter." In *Directions in Biblical Hebrew Poetry.* Ed. E. R. Follis. JSOTSup 40. Sheffield: JSOT Press, 1987. 173–84. **Freedman, D. N.** "Acrostic Poems in the Hebrew Bible: Alphabetic and Otherwise." *CBQ* 48 (1986) 408–31. ———. "Acrostics and Metrics in Hebrew Poetry." *HTR* 65 (1972) 367–92. **Gadd, C. J.** "The Second Lamentation for Ur." In *Hebrew and Semitic Studies.* FS G. R. Driver, ed. D. W. Thomas and W. D. McHardy. Oxford: Oxford UP, 1963. 59–71. **Garr, W. R.** "The Qinah: A Study of Poetic Meter, Syntax and Style." *ZAW* 95 (1983) 54–75. **Gordis, R.** "A Note on Lamentations ii 13." *JTS* 34 (1933) 162–63. **Gottlieb, H.** "Das Kultische Leiden des Königs: Zu den Klageliedern 3, 1." *SJOT* 1 (1987) 121–26. ———. *A Study on the Text of Lamentations.* Acta Jutlandica 48, Theology Series 12. Arhus: Arhus UP, 1978. **Gottwald, N. K.** "The Book of Lamentations Reconsidered." In *The Hebrew Bible in Its Social World and in Ours.* SBLSymS. Atlanta: Scholars, 1993. 165–73. ———. "Lamentations." *Int* 9 (1955) 320–38. ———. *Studies in the Book of Lamentations.* Rev. ed. SBT 1.14. London: SCM Press, 1962. **Gous, I.** "A Survey of Research on the Book of Lamentations." *OTE* 5 (1992) 185–205. **Graetz, N.** "Jerusalem the Widow." *Shofar* 17.2 (Winter 1999) 16–24. **Gray, G. B.** *The Form of Hebrew Poetry.* 1915. Reprint, New York: Ktav, 1972. **Green, M. W.** "The Eridu Lament." *JCS* 30 (1978) 127–67. **Grossberg, D.** *Centripetal and Centrifugal Structures in Biblical Poetry.* SBLMS 39. Atlanta: Scholars Press, 1989. **Grossfeld, B.** "The Targum to Lam. 2:10." *JJS* 28 (1977) 60–64. **Guest, D.** "Hiding behind the Naked Woman in Lamentations: A Recriminative Response." *BibInt* 7 (1999) 413–48. **Gunkel, H.** *Introduction to Psalms: The Genres of the Religious Lyric of Israel.* Ed. J. Begrich. Trans. J. Nogalski. 1933. Reprint, Macon, GA: Mercer UP, 1998. ———. "Klagelieder Jeremiae." In *Die Religion in Geschichte und Gegenwart.* 2d ed. Tübingen: Mohr (Siebeck), 1929. 1049–52. **Gwaltney, W. C., Jr.** "The Biblical Book of Lamentations in the Context of Near Eastern Lament Literature." In *Scripture in Context II: More Essays on the Comparative Method.* Ed. W. Hallo, J. Moyer, and L. Perdue. Winona Lake, IN: Eisenbrauns, 1983. 191–211. ———. "Lamentations, Book of." *DBI* 2:44–48. **Ha'adni, M.** *Perush le-sifre Tehilim, Pirke Avot, Rut, Ekhah, Ester.* Tel-Aviv: Afikim, 1997. **Hallbäck, G.** *Prædikerens Bog og Klagesangens: Fortolket.* Copenhagen: Danske bibelselskab, 1993. **Hallo, W. W.** "Lamentations and Prayers in Sumer and Akkad." In *Civilizations of the Ancient Near East.* 4 vols. Ed. J. Sasson. New York: Charles Scribner's Sons, 1995. 3:1871–81. **Helberg, J. L.** "The Incomparable Sorrow of Zion in the Book of Lamentations." In *Studies in Wisdom Literature.* Ed. C. W. van Wyk. Hercules, S. Africa: NHW Press, 1973. 27–36. ———. "Land in the Book of Lamentations." *ZAW* 102 (1990) 372–85. **Hillers, D. R.** "History and Poetry in Lamentations." *CurTM* 10 (1983) 155–61. ———. "Lamentations, Book of." *ABD* 4:137–41. ———. "Observations on Syntax and Meter in Lamentations." In *A Light unto My Path.* FS J. M. Myers, ed. H. M. Bream et al. Philadelphia: Temple UP, 1974. 265–70. **Horgan, M. P.** "A Lament over Jerusalem ('4Q179')." *JSS* 18 (1973) 222–34. **Hunter, J.** *Faces of a Lamenting City: The Development and Coherence of the Book of Lamentations.* BEATAJ 39. Frankfurt am Main: Lang, 1998. **Jacob ben Hayyim Feivush, ha-Kohen.** *Zera' Ya'akov: . . . perush . . . 'al . . . Shir ha-Shirim, Ekhah, Yonah . . .* Warsaw: Di-defus Yisrael be-Reb Yosef ha-Kohen Alapin, 1878. **Jahnow, H.** *Das hebräische Leichenlied im Rahmen der Volkerdichtung.* BZAW 36. Giessen: Töpelmann, 1923. **Johnson, B.** "Form and Message in Lamentations." *ZAW* 97 (1985) 58–73. **Joseph Hayyim ben Elijah al Hakam.** *Sefer Nehamat Tsiyon: perush be-derekh ha pardes 'al Megilat Ekhah.* Jerusalem: Yeshu'an ben David Salem, 1987. **Joyce, P.** "Lamentations and the Grief Process: A Psychological Reading." *BibInt* 1 (1993) 304–20. ———. "Sitting Loose to History: Reading the Book of Lamentations without Primary Reference to Its Original Historical Setting." In *In Search of True Wisdom*. FS R. E. Clements, ed. E. Ball. JSOTSup 300. Sheffield: JSOT Press, 1999. 246–62. **Kaiser, B. B.** "Poet as Female Impersonator: The Image of Daughter Zion as Speaker in Biblical Poems of Suffering." *JR* 67 (1987) 164–82. **Kaiser, W. C., Jr.** *A Biblical Approach to Suffering*. Chicago: Moody Press, 1982. **Kartveit, M.** "Sions dotter." *TTKi* 1–2 (2001) 97–112. **Kasser, R.** *Jérémie 40, 3–52, 34, Lamentations, Épître de Jérémie, Baruch 1,1–5,5*. Cologne: Biblioteca Bodmeriana, 1964. **Klein, J.,** ed. "Lamentations." *Encyclopedia Olam Hatanakh* 16A. Ramat Gan: Revivim, n.d. 107–59. **Kohen Stedek, B.** *Alon Bakhut: be'ul 'al megilat kinot*. 1711. Reprint, Brooklyn: Ahim Goldenburg, 1991. **Kramer, S. N.** "The Weeping Goddess: Sumerian Prototypes of the Mater Dolorosa." *BA* 46 (1983) 69–80. **Krašovec, J.** *Reward, Punishment, and Forgiveness: The Thinking and Beliefs of Ancient Israel in the Light of Greek and Modern Views*. VTSup 78. Leiden: Brill, 2000. ———. "The Source of Hope in the Book of Lamentations." *VT* 42 (1992) 223–33. **Lanahan, W. F.** "The Speaking Voice in the Book of Lamentations." *JBL* 93 (1974) 41–49. **Landa, N. H. S.** *Sefer Ahavat Tsiyon*. 1893. Reprint, Bruklin: Goldenburg, 1993. **Landy, F.** "Lamentations." In *The Literary Guide to the Bible*. Ed. R. Alter and F. Kermode. Cambridge, MA: Belknap, 1987. 329–34. **Langedult, P.** *Aantekeningen of Verklaaringer Over het geheele Nieuwe Testament: Als mede over de Klaagliederen van Jeremias*. Amsterdam: Pietersz, 1687. **Lee, N. C.** *The Singers of Lamentations: Cities under Siege, from Ur to Jerusalem to Sarajevo*. Biblical Interpretation 60. Leiden: Brill, 2002. **Levine, E.** *The Aramaic Version of Lamentations*. New York: Hermon, 1976. **Linafeldt, T.** "Margins of Lamentations." In *Reading Bibles, Writing Bodies: Identity and the Book*. Ed. T. K. Beal and D. M. Gunn. London: Routledge, 1997. 219–32. ———. "Surviving Lamentations." *HBT* 17 (1995) 45–61. ———. *Surviving Lamentations: Catastrophe, Lament, and Protest in the Afterlife of a Biblical Book*. Chicago: Univ. of Chicago Press, 2000. **Löhr, M.** "Alphabetische und alphabetisierende Lieder im Alten Testament." *ZAW* 25 (1905) 173–98. ———. "Der Sprachgebrauch des Buches der Klagelieder." *ZAW* 14 (1894) 31–50. **Marcus, D.** "Non-recurring Doublets in the Book of Lamentations." *HAR* 10 (1986) 177–95. **McDaniel, T. F.** "The Alleged Sumerian Influence upon Lamentations." *VT* 18 (1968) 198–209. ———. "Philological Studies in Lamentations, I." *Bib* 49 (1968) 27–53. **Michalowski, P.** *The Lamentation over the Destruction of Sumer and Ur*. Winona Lake, IN: Eisenbrauns, 1989. **Mintz, A.** "The Rhetoric of Lamentations and the Representation of Catastrophe." *Proof* 2 (1982) 1–17. **Moore, M. S.** "Human Suffering in Lamentations." *RB* 90 (1983) 534–55. **Nathansohn, J.** *Dibere Shaul ăl ha-Tora we-hamesh Me-gillot min*. Lemberg: Suess, 1875. **Neusner, J.** *Israel after Calamity: The Book of Lamentations*. The Bible of Judaism Library. Valley Forge, PA: Trinity Press International, 1995. **O'Connor, K. M.** *Lamentations and the Tears of the World*. Maryknoll, NY: Orbis, 2002. **Pham, X. H. T.** *Mourning in the Ancient Near East and the Hebrew Bible*. JSOTSup 302. Sheffield: Sheffield Academic Press, 1999. **Pick, S.** *Das dritte capitel der Klagelieder in seinem sprachlichem verhältniss zu den Weissagunger Jeremias*. Breslau: Schatzky, 1888. **Porteous, N.** "Jerusalem-Zion: The Growth of a Symbol." In *Verbannung und Geimkehr*. FS W. Randolph, ed. A. Kuschke. Tübingen: Mohr (Siebeck), 1961. 235–52. **Raabe, A.** *Die Klagelider des Jeremias und der Prediger des Salomon im Urtext nach neuester Kenntniss der Sprache dehandelt (erstere metrische) übersetzt: Mit Anmerkungen und einem Glossar versehen neuer Gesichtspuckt für hebräisches Versmaas eröffnet*. Leipzig: Fernau, 1880. **Renkema, J.** "The Literary Structure of Lamentations (I–IV)." In *The Structural Analysis of Biblical and Canaanite Poetry*. Ed. W. van der Meer and J. C. de Moor. JSOTSup 74. Sheffield: JSOT Press, 1988. 294–396. ———. "The Meaning of the Parallel Acrostics in Lamentations." *VT* 45 (1995) 379–83. **Reyburn, W. D.** *A Handbook on Lamentations*. UBS Handbook Series. New York: United Bible Societies, 1992. **Robinson, T. H.** "Once More on the Text of Lamentations." *ZAW* 52 (1934) 309–10. **Rudolph, W.** "Der Text der Klagelieder." *ZAW* 56 (1938) 101–22. **Ruppert, L.** "Klagelieder in Israel und Babylonien: Verschiendene Deutungen der Gewalt." In *Gewalt und Gewaltlosigkeit im Alten Testament*. Ed. N. Lohfink. Freiburg: Herder,

1983. 111–58. **Ryken, P.** *Jeremiah and Lamentations: From Sorrow to Hope.* Wheaton, IL: Crossway, 2000. **Salters, R. B.** "Searching for Patterns in Lamentations." *OTE* 11 (1998) 93–104.
———. "Using Rashi, Ibn Ezra and Joseph Kara on Lamentations." *JNSL* 25 (1999) 201–13. **Selms, A. van.** *Jeremiah deel III en Klaagliederen.* Nijkerk: Callenbach, 1974. **Shea, W. H.** "The *qinah* Structure of the Book of Lamentations." *Bib* 60 (1979) 103–7. **Shelomoh, D.** *Sefer Mesos kol ha-mit'ablim: perush 'al Megalit Ekhah bi-shene ofanim, ha-rishon be-derekh yagon va-anahot veha-sheni be derekh sova' semahot.* Jerusalem, 1988. **Slavitt, D. R.** *The Book of Lamentations: A Meditation and Translation.* Baltimore: Johns Hopkins UP, 2001. **Sorotzkin, Y.** *Megilat Rut: 'im perush Rinat Yitshak; Megilat Ekhah: 'im perush Rinat Titshak.* Wickliffe, OH: Sorotzkin, 1989. **Tanhum ben Joseph of Jerusalem.** *Tanchumi Kierosolymitani Commentarii araicus in Lamentationes e codice unico bodleiano literis hebraicis exarato descripsit charactere arabico et edidt Gulielmus Cureton.* London: Madden, 1843. **Taylor, R. R.** *Studies in Jeremiah and Lamentations.* Abilene, TX: Quality, 1992. **Thomas, W.** *Scriptures Opened and Sundry Cases of Conscience Resolved, in Plain and Practical Answers to Several Questions, upon the Proverbs of Solomon, Ecclesiastes, Jeremiah, Lamentations, Ezekiel, and Daniel.* London: Sampson Evans, 1675. **Thompson, J. A.** "Israel's 'lovers.'" *VT* 27 (1977) 475–81. **Tigay, J.** "Lamentations, Book of." *EncJud.* 10:1368–75. **Tossanus, D.** *Lamentationes Ieremiase prophetæ, lamentabili hoc et lugubri tempore perecessariæ.* Frankfurt: Apud Andream Wechelum, 1581. **Van der Heide, A.** *The Yemenite Tradition of the Targum of Lamentations: Critical Text and Analysis.* Leiden: Brill, 1981. **Vermigli, P. M.** *In Lamentationes Ieremiae Prophetae.* Tiguri: Bodmer, 1629. **Vital, B. ha-Cohen.** *Alon Bakhut: Be'ur 'al megilat Kinot.* Venice: Nella Stamparia Bragadina, 1711. **Waltke, B.,** and **M. O'Connor.** *An Introduction to Biblical Hebrew Syntax.* Winona Lake, IN: Eisenbrauns, 1990. **Weintraub, N.** *Elyashiv: perush 'al megilat Ekhah.* Jerusalem: Defus Erets Yisra'el, 1945. **Weissblueth, S.** "Mipî 'elyôn lō' tēṣē' hārā'ôt wehaṭṭôb." *Beth Miqra* 32 (1986–87) 64–67. **Westermann, C.** *Praise and Lament in the Psalms.* Trans. K. Crim. Atlanta: John Knox, 1981. **Wiesmann, H.** "Der plamnäszige Aufbau der Klagelieder des Jeremias." *Bib* 7 (1926) 146–61. ———. "Der Verfasser des Büchleinds der Klagelieder ein Augenzeuge der behandelten Ereignisse?" *Bib* 17 (1936) 71–84. ———. "Der Zweck der Klagelieder des Jeremias." *Bib* 7 (1926) 412–28.

Introduction

Considering Lamentations

Bibliography

Alter, R. *Art of Biblical Poetry.* **Barth, K.** "The Strange New World within the Bible." In *The Word of God and the Word of Man.* Trans. D. Horton. 1957. Reprint, Gloucester, MA: Peter Smith, 1978. **Berlin, A.** *Dynamics of Biblical Parallelism.* **Kugel, J. L.** *The Idea of Biblical Poetry.* New Haven, CT: Yale UP, 1981. **Lowth, R.** *Lectures on the Sacred Poetry of the Hebrews.* Trans. G. Gregory. [Originally *De Sacra Poesi Hebraeorum: Praelectiones Acadamiae Oxonii Habitae.* 2 vols. Oxonii, Italy: Typographo Clarendoniano, 1753.] Andover: Codman, 1829. **O'Connor, J. M.** *Hebrew Verse Structure.* Winona Lake, IN: Eisenbrauns, 1997. **Smart, J.** *The Strange Silence of the Bible in the Church.* Atlanta: John Knox, 1980. **Westermann, C.** *Praise and Lament in the Psalms.*

One of the least controversial comments that one could write about Lamentations is that it has not received the sort of critical and popular attention that has been afforded many other OT books. There have been several significant contributions to Lamentations studies, but this book still remains fairly obscure to many scholars and general readers. And it is fairly easy to understand why this is the case, given the current interests of the academy and the Western church.

The book conveys pain, indeed agony, caused by divine punishment in response to human sin, which is hardly a popular topic these days. Though ancient tradition associated Lamentations with Jeremiah, the book is anonymous. Thus, students and scholars cannot with certainty tie it to a great figure of the past or to a specific school of thought, which may inhibit certain kinds of historical analyses. Lamentations describes one of Israel's greatest failures, not one of God's great saving acts in history, a fact that may discourage some biblical theologians from including it in their reflection. The book follows a particular poetic pattern, the acrostic, for four chapters, only to break that pattern in its final chapter. The poems have fewer obvious unifying principles than many other books, so redaction critics may be frustrated in their search for distinctive theological strands and form critics hampered in their struggle to discern how the poems fit into the lament forms found in the psalms. The book has been used in Jewish liturgical life to mark the destruction of the temple and in Christian worship during Holy Week, yet it is seldom preached in churches. All these facts tend to obscure whatever worth Lamentations may have for twenty-first-century readers.

Given this situation, it is necessary to stress the potential scholarly and ecclesiastical value of Lamentations. Though the list could be extended, there are four basic reasons that Lamentations needs to be considered by the Christian church and the academy. I say *considered* rather than *reconsidered* because I do not think that the book has ever truly been embraced even by those normally most committed to biblical studies. Each of these four reasons stems from the growing and meaningful scholarly tradition concerning Lamentations. I hope that each reason also provides ways that this tradition may be effectively expanded, especially as they have been spelled out in this Introduction and in the commentary itself.

First, paying attention to Lamentations may aid a heightened appreciation for the power and relevance of OT poetry, especially poetry that addresses harsh subject matter. OT studies have long benefited from careful, insightful analyses of Hebrew poetry. From Lowth's seminal work in the eighteenth century *(Lectures on the Sacred Poetry of the Hebrews)* to those by Alter *(Art of Biblical Poetry)*, Berlin *(Dynamics of Biblical Parallelism)*, Kugel *(Idea of Biblical Poetry)*, J. M. O'Connor *(Hebrew Verse Structure)*, and others in the twentieth century, the discipline has gained much valuable ground in the attempt to understand non-narrative Hebrew texts. To be sure, one could argue that even more ground has been gained in the analysis of Hebrew narrative, but that possibility should not dampen one's gratitude for the work done on poetry. Nor should the fact that older notions of the poetic genre have been challenged mar this appreciation. Sound ideas often grow out of the shattering of hoary consensus. At the same time, older conceptions that have stood the test of time need not be discarded simply because they had the poor taste to be offered decades or centuries ago. Notions born in different eras can form suitable and fruitful partnerships.

Taken together, the poems that make up the book of Lamentations display a linguistic and conceptual power rarely seen even in biblical literature. Their power grows out of their subject, structure, dramatic presentation, irony (particularly the irony of reversal), shifting tone, historical setting, theological weight, and paradoxical imagery. This power is definitely evident when the book is read aloud, yet this power is even more obvious when the book is read and reread silently. As a written text, Lamentations uses the eye to move the intellect and emotions. As a written text the poems create a telling logical and psychological impression. As a written text the poems have significant individual and collective weight, for they offer a sustained, detailed, and realistic sense of the terror of individual and corporate punishment for sin. Since the book comes to us as a written text, it is appropriate to give the text as it stands close attention without negating whatever life the poems have had as oral presentations.

Second, considering Lamentations could lead to a deepening of Christian scholarship and worship. Claus Westermann has rightly argued that the poems of Lamentations must be interpreted and appreciated as *laments*. They must not be reinterpreted to fit current conventions or preferences. He asserts that until the church rediscovers how to lament not only will the book of Lamentations remain largely unread; the church's ability to *pray* as the Bible instructs it to pray will remain impaired. Conversely, a renewed willingness to study and use laments may deepen the church's theological base and enhance its relationship to the living God of the Bible. Thus, in Westermann's opinion, the scholarly exercise of determining the literary form, historical setting, exegetically demonstrated meaning, and theological significance of Lamentations is more than a necessary and vital *scholarly* exercise. It is also a service to *the church* and for those who currently live outside the Christian community, waiting to see if the church has a sense of reality in a harsh world. Therefore, Lamentations research involves technical tasks that can have very important ramifications in our own life setting.

The Christian community in the West may not have totally forgotten how to lament over sin, but it is certainly well into the process of forgetting how to do so, even in light of shattering world events. This slide into theological amnesia results in part from a general failure to read and interpret the whole of the Bible consistently, carefully, realistically, and theologically. Traditionalists are as guilty as nontraditionalists in this matter. Conservative scholars and pastors are now sending out the sort of distress signals about lack of biblical knowledge that characterized books and articles written by mainline denominational scholars a generation ago.

But there is another reason for this amnesia. The Western church has gotten addicted to success and wealth and is influencing Two-Thirds-World Christians to do the same. People who value ease and monetary success will tend to ignore the Bible's statements on suffering and grief. They will avoid confessing sin since to do so would be to admit that they do not deserve to be happy and satisfied. A lack of reality pervades this sort of Christianity, and its adherents are not likely to become very interested in Lamentations. They might well ask, "Why read about defeat when we can bask in victory?"

Considering Lamentations could bring the church back into the real world depicted in Scripture. In Lamentations, sin is destructive; it must be confessed, or there is no forgiveness for it. In Lamentations, sin has consequences. In Lamentations, God cares about sin, suffering, and depravity and does something about them. In Lamentations, there is no ease regardless of what the people of God do. In Lamentations, God is fair, tough, caring, and ultimately faithful. Without question, these and other themes found in Lamentations are biblical ideas that course through the whole of Scripture. If so, then one's attitude toward this book may be an indication of how one views much of the rest of the Bible's teachings. Thus, accepting this small book could well lead to the embracing of a more thoroughly biblical Christian worldview.

Third, a study of Lamentations may well aid the study of the genre of psalms at certain key points. For instance, both Hermann Gunkel *(Introduction to Psalms)* and Claus Westermann *(Praise and Lament in the Psalms)* state that laments began as fairly simple forms and then were adapted into more complicated forms as time passed. When writing about Lamentations, both conclude that the book contains many mixed forms of psalms. Johan Renkema, in many ways the master commentator on Lamentations, asserts that Lamentations brings together a variety of poetic forms from sacred and secular circles. If so, then it is impossible to analyze laments and praises as if they are consistently uniform compositions. It is impossible to treat the so-called hybrid psalms as if they are quite unusual. Thus, one must delve further into the nature and purpose of the psalms, as well as into the way they are conceived, shaped, and handed down to the community of faith.

Fourth, a study of Lamentations will give more depth, reality, and historical substance to OT theology. Without question, the Writings, of which Lamentations is a part, is the least treated of the sections of the Hebrew canon. There are many reasons for this situation, but the fact is that this situation needs to be addressed. Closer examination of Lamentations may aid an understanding of the role of the exile, of personal frustration and pain, of liturgy, of faith, and of hope in the OT. It could also help theologians realize the enormity of themes such as the day of the Lord and God's wrath. After all, it is in Lamentations that the results of the many divine threats found in the Law and the Prophets unfold. It is also here that psalms dealing with the temple's destruction (see Ps 74) and the loss of the Davidic dynasty (see Ps 89) are echoed. Perhaps through this process literary analysis may become more closely wedded to historical data and to theological reflection, a result that is long overdue in scholarly circles.

Obviously, this commentary can only be a very small down payment on the goals noted above. Still, working along these lines may well make a small contribution to the reaching of them. Thus, this commentary attempts to participate in this process. It will do so first by offering a fairly traditional introduction to the book, then by examining the text, form, structure, meaning, and theology of each section of Lamentations. Thus, it is not so much through new methods that this volume hopes to help the reader understand Lamentations better but through the application of established approaches in a manner complementary to the subject matter.

Text

Bibliography

Albrektson, B. *Studies in the Text and Theology.* **Alexander, P. S.** "The Textual Tradition of Targum Lamentations." *AbrN* 24 (1984) 1–26. **Allegro, J. M.,** and **A. A. Anderson.** *Qumran Cave 4, I (4Q158–4Q186).* DJD 5. Oxford: Clarendon, 1968. **Dahood, M.** "New Readings in Lamentations." *Bib* 59 (1978) 174–97. **Driver, G. R.** "Hebrew Notes on 'Song of Songs' and 'Lamentations.'" In *Festschrift Alfred Bertholet.* Ed. W. Baumgartner et al. Tübingen: Mohr, 1950. 134–46. ———. "Notes on the Text of Lamentations." *ZAW* 52 (1934) 308–9. **Gottlieb, H.** *Study on the Text of Lamentations.* **Horgan, M. P.** "A Lament over Jerusalem ('4Q179')." *JSS* 18 (1973) 222–34. **Levine, E.** *Aramaic Version.* **Robinson, T. H.** "Notes on the Text of Lamentations." *ZAW* 51 (1933) 255–59. ———. "Once More on the Text of Lamentations." *ZAW* 52 (1934) 309–10. **Rudolph, W.** "Der Text der Klagelieder." *ZAW* 56 (1938) 101–22.

Like virtually every other commentary on Lamentations, this volume bases its translation and comments on the Masoretic Text (MT) of the Hebrew Bible as it appears in *Biblia Hebraica Stuttgartensia (BHS)* and its earlier version *Biblia Hebraica Kittel (BHK).* Variations found in relevant ancient translations will be examined and incorporated where such changes are deemed appropriate. These emendations will be few in number since experts on the Hebrew, Greek, Syriac, and Aramaic versions of the book tend to agree that these translations usually stick very closely to a Hebrew text very much like the MT. A brief history of the discussion provides the rationale for this course of action.

Prior to 1963, when Bertil Albrektson's *Studies in the Text and Theology of the Book of Lamentations, with a Critical Edition of the Peshitta Text* was published, scholars tended either to accept the MT as it stood or to offer relatively few emendations. These emendations were sometimes based on the commentator's views of how much the text of Lamentations diverged from the commentator's view of how *qinah* meter (see "Poetic Meter" below) ought to operate. At other times they were more connected to a close comparison of the Greek and Syriac versions. With the publication of Albrektson's monograph, however, the discipline received its first full-scale treatment of the text-critical issues in Lamentations. Albrektson concludes that the Greek "translation is on the whole quite literal, in several places even extremely slavish. Almost every verse in Lamentations shows that the translator attempted to render faithfully every single word of his Hebrew text, and there are numerous examples of a striking literalism" (*Studies in the Text and Theology*, 208). As for the Syriac, Albrektson writes, "Like LXX the Syriac translation is based on a Hebrew text which must have been almost identical with MT. On the whole P (the Peshitta or Syriac text) is a faithful rendering of this *Vorlage* [the Hebrew Text that it translated], though some characteristic peculiarities can be observed" (210). In his opinion, when the Syriac varies from the MT, it is usually to render a clear and plausible meaning in the translation. Thus, these variations do not indicate a manuscript tradition different from the MT (211). He also concludes that the Syriac and Greek translations are based on the same version of the MT because of the ways that the two vary from one another (212).

In his thorough and carefully argued 1978 monograph, *A Study on the Text of Lamentations*, Hans Gottlieb basically affirms Albrektson's viewpoints, though Gottlieb does offer several corrections and refinements of Albrektson's work. He writes, "In my view Albrektson's approach to the text-critical problems in Lamentations is correct in principle, and in most instances I agree with him on the solutions of the individual problems" (*Study on the Text*, 4). Despite this significant agreement, Gottlieb does attempt to correct what he thinks are mistakes Albrektson makes in Lam 3 and elsewhere. He also assesses the observations Mitchell Dahood (*Bib* 59 [1978] 174–97) makes on the Northwest Semitic background to some words in Lamentations (*Study on the Text*, 14). Gottlieb's text-critical methodology is sound and will be consulted in this commentary's translation, translation notes, and exegetical statements.

The Dead Sea Scrolls offer limited insight into the textual tradition of Lamentations. There are only a few "small portions" of Lamentations in the whole of the Scrolls (Hillers [1972], xxxix), but there are several quotations from the book in 4Q179, a lamentation over the city of Jerusalem that incorporates passages of Scripture from a variety of OT books (J. M. Allegro and A. A. Anderson, *Qumran Cave 4, I (4Q158–4Q186)*, 75–77). Maurya Horgan writes that this manuscript may be dated prior to 30 B.C.E. because of its script and suggests that the reign of Antiochus IV may be the background for its composition (*JSS* 18 [1973] 222–23). She further observes, "It is striking that there is nothing in this fragmentary Qumran writing which demands an origin in an Essene community. There is neither reference to specific tenets of the Essene sect, nor is there mention of persons or events prominent in the history of Qumran. Furthermore, though the text consists largely of biblical allusions, a commentary or interpretation, such as is frequently found in Qumran literature which relates to Scripture, is absent" (223). The fragment's chief value for textual criticism is in its quotations of various verses in Lamentations. Their existence allows one to check any potential errors against these quotations. The fragment may also offer insight into the role of lament in Second Temple Judaism since it demonstrates how the whole of Scripture could be used to form texts useful for individual or corporate mourning of national calamity and/or sin.

Aramaic versions of Lamentations have some value for textual criticism, though these versions may be even more valuable for what they reveal about liturgical practices that transpired long after the destruction of 587 B.C.E. In *The Aramaic Version of Lamentations* (1976), Etan Levine summarizes the value of the

Lamentations Targum by writing, "Were the Aramaic version of Lamentations merely a translation of a biblical work into Aramaic, its value would be largely limited to philological aspects. However, the *targum* has virtually rewritten the book, and its subject matter includes the fall of the Second Temple as well as the First Temple! Further, it presents polemics as to the reason(s) for the Exile, and the process of eventual salvation. It deals with theodicy, exhortation and messianism, countering Christian exegesis and theology. By emendation, elaboration and paraphrase it fuses the *Oral Torah* and the *Written Torah*" (9). Thus, the Targum is part translation, part commentary, part polemical tract, and part inspirational book. P. S. Alexander notes that there are two basic recensions of the Targum text, one from the west and one from Yemen, and that it is impossible to ascertain their dates (*AbrN* 24 [1986] 6–8). He also stresses the Targum's value for understanding ancient liturgy (1) and asserts its value for textual criticism based on his conviction that from chap. 3 "onwards, with brief lapses it offers a more or less word-for-word rendering of the original" (1).

Though there have not been numerous monographs devoted to text-critical matters in Lamentations, there have been a surprising number of translations of and comments on the text of the book. Of course, in the past fifty years several translations of the whole Bible have been published, such as RSV, NEB, NASB, NIV, NRSV, REB, and ESV. Besides these popular translations, Norman K. Gottwald, Robert Gordis, Delbert Hillers, Johan Renkema, Claus Westermann, Adele Berlin, and others have offered translations of Lamentations that typically include text-critical commentary. Thus, there are a number of analyses of specific textual issues, and much of this material will be utilized in this commentary's translation and exegesis.

Given this very brief survey, it is appropriate to use the MT as the foundational Hebrew text of Lamentations. This conclusion does not mean that the text never requires emendation, but it is fair to say that such alterations ought not to be large in number. Many solid contributions to this field have been made in the past few decades, and one of the goals of this commentary is to bring some of the more significant of these achievements together in one place.

The translation in this commentary follows a few basic principles. First, as was stated in the preceding paragraph, it follows the MT. It alters the text in places where the evidence strongly warrants such a change, and it takes suggestions made by Albrektson, Gottlieb, Rudolph, and Levine very seriously. Second, it tries to be an essentially literal translation. That is, it tries to translate one word for one word, one phrase for one phrase, and so on. Third, it attempts to present each line as it unfolds in its two parts. Echoes and parallelism are perhaps rendered more clearly in this system. Fourth, it attempts to translate terms consistently so that themes and linguistic connections are more evident. Fifth, it makes no effort to translate metrical elements. This method is not the only valid one that can be employed, but it is a valid approach.

Authorship and Date

Bibliography

Cannon, W. W. "The Authorship of Lamentations." *BSac* 81 (1924) 42–58. **Childs, B. S.** *Introduction to the Old Testament as Scripture.* Philadelphia: Fortress, 1980. **Craigie, P. C.** *The*

Old Testament. Nashville: Abingdon Press, 1986. **Dillard, R. B.**, and **T. Longman III.** *An Introduction to the Old Testament.* Grand Rapids, MI: Zondervan, 1994. **Dobbs-Allsopp, F. W.** "Linguistic Evidence for the Date of Lamentations." *JANESCU* 26 (1998) 1–36. **Driver, S. R.** *An Introduction to the Literature of the Old Testament.* 1897. Reprint, Gloucester, MA: Peter Smith, 1972. **Eissfeldt, O.** *Old Testament.* **Gadd, C. J.** "The Second Lamentation for Ur." In *Hebrew and Semitic Studies.* FS G. R. Driver, ed. D. W. Thomas and W. D. McHardy. London: Oxford UP, 1963. **Gwaltney, W. C.** "The Biblical Book of Lamentations in the Context of Near Eastern Lament Literature." In *Scripture in Context II: More Essays on the Comparative Method.* Ed. W. Hallo, J. Moyer, and L. Perdue. Winona Lake, IN: Eisenbrauns, 1983. 191–211. **Harrison, R. K.** *Old Testament Introduction.* Grand Rapids, MI: Eerdmans, 1969. **Jahnow, H.** *Hebräische Leichenlied.* **Kaiser, O.** *Introduction to the Old Testament: A Presentation of Its Results and Problems.* Trans. J. Sturdy. Minneapolis: Augsburg, 1975. **Kramer, S. N.** *Lamentation over the Destruction of Ur.* Chicago: Univ. of Chicago Press, 1940. ———. "Lamentation over the Destruction of Ur." In *ANET,* 455–63. ———. "Lamentation over the Destruction of Nippur." *Acta Sumerologica* 13 (1991) 1–26. **LaSor, W. S., D. A. Hubbard,** and **F. W. Bush.** *Old Testament Survey: The Message, Form, and Background of the Old Testament.* 2d ed. Grand Rapids, MI: Eerdmans, 1996. **Lee, N. C.** *The Singers of Lamentations.* **McDaniel, T. F.** "The Alleged Sumerian Influence upon Lamentations." *VT* 18 (1968) 198–209. **Rendtorff, R.** *The Old Testament: An Introduction.* Trans. J. Bowden. Philadelphia: Fortress, 1986. **Young, E. J.** *An Introduction to the Old Testament.* Rev. ed. Grand Rapids, MI: Eerdmans, 1964.

Determining the author and date of the book of Lamentations depends on several factors, each of which contains beguiling difficulties. When the data have been assessed, it is hard to escape the fraternal twin conclusions that no author can be established with certitude but that the date of composition can be fixed with some confidence. These seemingly contradictory results are justified when one considers the wealth of material offered in the scholarly literature on these subjects. Though the following survey of Lamentations research is by no means exhaustive, it touches upon some of the main aspects of the field of study. This survey unfolds by examining different genres of OT criticism.

INTRODUCTIONS TO THE OLD TESTAMENT

Lamentations itself does not contain even one reference to a named author, nor does any other book of the Bible make a statement about the author's identity. But the book describes the fall of Jerusalem, an event commonly dated 587–586 B.C.E., which leads some scholars to feel fairly confident about the book's date. Jewish tradition associated Lamentations with Jeremiah, an eyewitness to the fall of Jerusalem, as early as the era in which the Septuagint was translated. Though it is impossible to know for certain, several experts believe this decision may have been based in part on 2 Chr 35:25, which states, "Then Jeremiah chanted a lament for Josiah. And all the male and female singers speak about Josiah in their lamentations to this day. And they made an ordinance in Israel; behold, they are also written in the Lamentations" (NASB). The Syriac and Latin versions of the OT followed this tradition, as have most English translations. Since Lamentations clearly deals with the fall of Jerusalem, it is hard to see how the laments mentioned in 2 Chronicles could be those in Lamentations. Thus, perhaps from this passage itself the ancient community of faith knew that Jeremiah composed laments and thereby deemed it likely that he was responsible for the poems in Lamentations. They probably also noted similarities between some of Jeremiah's laments and those in the book, and no doubt depended upon the knowledge that Jeremiah is the prophet most associated with the fall of Jerusalem. Whether this passage sparked the belief in Jeremianic authorship or some tradition did, the fact remains that for centuries Jeremiah was routinely accepted as the book's author. Thus, it is wholly appropriate to explore the accuracy of this tradition. To do so, one must examine evidence offered by introductions to the OT, commentaries, monographs, and articles.

In recent times scholars writing introductions to the OT have only rarely agreed with the ancient belief in Jeremianic authorship. Generally, scholars across the theological spectrum have expressed a reverent agnosticism on the matter. For example, Otto Eissfeldt writes, "It would be an idle task to endeavour to discover the actual poet or poets" (*Old Testament*, 505). Though he can see how Jeremiah could come to be associated with laments over Jerusalem's demise, he does not think it likely that the same Jeremiah who looked to a bright future for Jerusalem (see Jer 30–33) would lament as the writer(s) of Lamentations does. Similarly, Raymond Dillard and Tremper Longman conclude that the Jeremiah "tradition is certainly not impossible, but neither is it certain. Further, it is not worth argument, since the text does not insist on it and its interpretation does not depend on it"(*Introduction*, 304). Though they express their conclusions in different ways, S. R. Driver (*Introduction*, 461–65), R. K. Harrison (*Old Testament* 1070), Otto Kaiser (*Introduction*, 355), Brevard Childs (*Introduction*, 592–93), Rolf Rendtorff (*Old Testament*, 269), Peter C. Craigie (*Old Testament*, 240), and William S. LaSor, David A. Hubbard, and Frederick W. Bush (*Old Testament Survey*, 527) take the same approach. Even E. J. Young, one of the ablest of the conservative writers of OT introductions, states, "In light of these arguments it seems most likely that Jeremiah did compose Lamentations. Of this, however, we cannot be certain, and it seems best to admit that we do not really know who the author was" (*Introduction*, 344). Clearly, these scholars do not minimize the importance of establishing a book's author when that can be done; they simply do not think that they can do so in the case of Lamentations. Despite their reticence on the subject of authorship, however, they tend to argue that the detailed emotional descriptions in the book lead to the conclusion that the poems were written by an eyewitness shortly after the fall of Jerusalem.

It must be noted that these experts do weigh certain evidence for Jeremianic authorship. In particular, though he does not assert that Jeremiah wrote Lamentations, S. R. Driver takes special care in examining specific literary qualities shared by the books of Jeremiah and Lamentations, so I will use him as a representative early scholar on this matter. He lists four basic categories of similarities between the two.

First, he writes that the books have a shared tone. The fact that each is "profoundly sympathetic in national sorrow, and ready to pour forth its emotions unrestrainedly, manifests itself both in Lam. and in Jer. (e.g. c. 14–15)" (*Introduction*, 462). It must be said that this shared tone holds in the lament segments of Jeremiah, yet not in the book as a whole.

Second, Driver (*Introduction*, 462) concludes that both books attribute the nation's demise to the same causes. Judah falls as a result of national sin (compare Lam 1:5, 8, 14, 18; 3:42; 4:6, 22; 5:7, 16 to Jer 14:7; 16:10–12; 17:1–3; and so on), sinful prophets and priests (compare Lam 2:14; 4:13–15 to Jer 2:7–8; 5:31;

14:13; 23:11–40; 27:1–28:17), and vain confidence in weak and unreliable allies (compare Lam 1:2, 19; 4:17 to Jer 2:18, 36; 30:14; 37:5–10).

Third, Driver observes that the two books use many of the same metaphors and figures of speech (*Introduction*, 462). For example, both portray Jerusalem as the "virgin daughter of Zion broken with an incurable breach" (compare Lam 1:15; 2:13 to Jer 8:21ff.; 14:17). Both appeal to the Lord for the defeat of their enemies (compare Lam 3:64–66 and Jer 11:20), and both expect that their foes will someday be as desolate as Jerusalem (compare Lam 4:21 and Jer 49:12).

Fourth, Driver lists eleven phrases in the books that are nearly identical (*Introduction*, 462).

1. Jerusalem's lovers offer her no comfort (Lam 1:2; 1:8b–9; Jer 30:14; 13:22b, 26).
2. Jerusalem's eyes and Jeremiah's eyes are running down with tears (Lam 1:16a; 2:11a, 18b; 3:48–49; Jer 9:1, 18b; 13:17b; 14:17).
3. Jerusalem's breach has been great (Lam 2:11, 13; 3:47–48; 4:10; Jer 6:14; 8:11, 21).
4. Israel's priests and prophets have sinned (Lam 2:14; 4:13; Jer 2:8; 5:31; 14:13ff.; 23:11).
5. Israel's women eat their own children during a siege (Lam 2:20; 4:10; Jer 19:9).
6. Israel has terrors all around her (Lam 2:22; Jer 6:25; 20:10).
7. The speaker in Lam 3:14 says, "I have become a derision," a phrase also found on Jeremiah's lips in Jer 20:7.
8. Both books use the terms "wormwood" and "wormwood and gall" (Lam 3:15; Jer 9:15; 23:15).
9. Both books use the terms "fear and the snare" (Lam 3:47; Jer 48:43).
10. Both books use the phrase "they hunt me" (Lam 3:52; Jer 16:16b).
11. Both books use the term "the cup" (Lam 4:21; 5:16; Jer 13:18b; 25:15; 49:12).

It is fair to say that these parallels are not accidental. At the very least the author or authors of Lamentations used language similar to Jeremiah's, which, among other things, means that the two books share a linguistic and theological point of view.

At the same time, Driver also states the differences between Lamentations and Jeremiah that lead him to claim that the books were probably not written by the same person. He argues that certain stylistic variations exist between the two, for Lamentations includes several words not used in Jeremiah, a much longer work. He finds it hard to believe that "a writer, who, in his literary style, followed, as Jeremiah did, the promptings of nature, would subject himself to the artificial restraint implied by the alphabetical arrangement of c. 1–4" (*Introduction*, 463–64). He thinks the variation in the acrostic order in Lam 2–4 means that they were not written by the author of Lam 1, which in turn means that Jeremiah could not have been the author of the whole of Lamentations.

More importantly, Driver identifies what he perceives to be theological differences between Lamentations and Jeremiah (*Introduction*, 463). In particular, he concludes that Jeremiah would be unlikely to express his desire that his/Israel's enemies be judged by the Lord, as the author of Lam 1:21–22 and 3:59–66 does. He doubts that Jeremiah would both consider Babylon the Lord's instrument of judgment on Judah and hope God would judge the Babylonians. Also, Driver does not think that Jeremiah would state that visions have ceased from the prophets, something Lam 2:9 claims. Further, Lam 4:17 says that the author and the people waited for a nation that could not save them, which Driver considers a direct contradiction to Jer 37:5–10. Finally, Driver does not consider it plausible that Jeremiah would have spoken as favorably about Zedekiah (the last king of Judah) as Lam 4:20 seems to do.

Much of Driver's critique does not hold up under close scrutiny, though several of his ideas have merit. On the positive side, he correctly identifies vital differences in the phraseology of Lamentations and Jeremiah. Some of the divergences could be due to differing subject matter, yet where one could logically expect similarities in syntax, one does not always find them. On the negative side, it is impossible to argue with certainty exactly what sort of tone and poetic approach Jeremiah might have taken toward the fall of Jerusalem in acrostic laments. An author makes use of whatever genre or tone best suits the literary need. It is therefore equally impossible to determine from slight variations in acrostic forms that one author did not write all four poems. Such evidence seems highly inconclusive at best.

Driver's theological differences are even harder to sustain. On more than one occasion the prophet did indeed ask the Lord to punish his enemies, especially in Jer 11–20, the location of his famous "confessions" (see Jer 12:1–4; 17:18; 18:18–23). It was not always his practice to intercede for the straying nation. Likewise, though a prophet himself, Jeremiah was extremely critical of prophets with whom he disagreed (Jer 23:11, 33–35; 27:1–28:17; and others). And though Jeremiah does indeed understand Babylon to be the instrument of God's wrath, he also marks the Babylonians for divine punishment (Jer 50:1–51:64). Clearly, then, the book of Jeremiah, which accurately portrays the theology of the prophet, includes a more diverse, yet balanced, approach to the topics Driver mentions than Driver himself discusses in detail.

Even more than a hundred years after it was written, Driver's survey still conveys many of the main lines of thought in Lamentations studies. Driver's helpful analysis reveals, for instance, why the majority of writers of OT introductions take a rather agnostic position on the question of authorship. The linguistic differences are sufficient to make one pause before settling on Jeremianic authorship. At the same time, the linguistic similarities make one admit that the two books share a theological vocabulary and a theological viewpoint. Therefore, many of these scholars think it best to remain as neutral as the book itself on the matter of authorship. But it is necessary to probe much further than most of these experts do into the theological and literary perspectives that the books have in common. It is these common elements that expose the canonical unity of Lamentations with Jeremiah and the Deuteronomistic literature, and it is these differences that should keep Lamentations from being forgotten in the wake of the greatness of Jeremiah's theological and literary weight.

COMMENTARIES, MONOGRAPHS, AND ARTICLES

The commentary, monograph, and scholarly article tradition bears much the same result as the introduction to the OT tradition, though it takes the discussion into many subtle and detailed paths of its own. Since the authors who accept Jeremiah's authorship of Lamentations are in the minority, perhaps it is best to survey them first. Some, though not all, of the adherents of this point of view wrote before the ascendancy of the historical-critical method as practiced by Wellhausen, Gunkel, and other scholars who became prominent in the latter half of the nineteenth century and the first half of the twentieth century. Therefore, they were more likely to operate within traditional boundaries than was the historical-critical school, but they did offer historical, linguistic, and theological reasons for their conclusions. They did not simply restate what the church had always said about the book. Every scholar who accepts Jeremianic authorship of Lamentations holds two basic convictions: Lamentations is a unified construction probably penned by one person, and Lamentations is close enough in content to Jeremiah that the books were probably both written by the prophet. Thus, they believe that the book was written shortly after 587 B.C.E.

For instance, John Calvin (1509–1564) wrote a substantive (two hundred pages in English editions) translation of and commentary on Lamentations in 1563. Though he concludes that Jeremiah wrote Lamentations, Calvin does not do so without dealing with some of the same basic issues commentators still discuss. For instance, he disagrees with Jerome's contention that Lamentations was written to mark and mourn Josiah's death (299). He also denies that Jeremiah wrote about the fall of Jerusalem in predictive fashion in Lamentations, mainly because in Lamentations Jeremiah's "manner of stating things is wholly different from that used in prophetic writings" (299). This quotation indicates that Calvin was aware of differences in word usage between Jeremiah and Lamentations and believed that the book was written after the fall of Jerusalem. Finally, Calvin concludes that the theology of Lamentations is a unified work intended to instill repentance and hope in the people. He writes, "We now in a measure understand for what purpose this Book was written by JEREMIAH: his object was to show that though nothing in the land appeared but desolation, and the temple being destroyed, the Covenant of God appeared as made void, and thus all hope of salvation had been cut off, yet hope still remained, provided the people sought God in true repentance and faith; and he thus proceeded in the course of his calling, and made it evident that his doctrine would not be without benefit" (300). In other words, Calvin claims that the book's theology revolves around themes such as God's judgment, human repentance, hope in the Lord, and prayer offered in confidence in God's mercy (300). These and related ideas Calvin then expounded in his exposition of the Hebrew text.

Though one can certainly find fault with parts of Calvin's analysis, he lays a solid foundation for further studies in this, one of the first historically and linguistically based works on Lamentations. He asserts that Jeremiah is the book's author, that the fall of Jerusalem is the book's historical setting, that repentance and renewal form its core theology, and that exegetical work must inform all conclusions on these subjects. In other words, Calvin came to traditional conclusions about the authorship of the book, but he did not do so blindly. His exegetical and theological insights continue to aid valid exegesis of Lamentations to this day.

By the time C. F. Keil (1872) and A. W. Streane (1881) published their commentaries on Lamentations, a decided shift against Jeremiah being the book's author had already begun to emerge. Indeed, having duly noted that the Septuagint, Vulgate, Syriac, Arabic, and Targumim considered Jeremiah the author of Lamentations, Keil found it necessary to chart the history of the debate in some detail (see 339–50). Beginning with Hermann von der Hardt's 1712 work, which was the first to question Jeremiah's authorship of Lamentations, stretching through Thenius (1855) and Ewald's (1866) commentaries, Keil examined and sought to refute three basic reasons scholars had rejected the traditional view of the book's authorship.

First, Keil cites the notion that there are statements in Jeremiah that are contradictory to some made in Lamentations. Chief among these contradictions is the one between Lam 5:7, which states that the people have suffered for their fathers' sins, and Jer 31:29–30, which inveighs against the proverb, "The fathers have eaten sour grapes, and the children's teeth are set on edge." Keil argues that the Lamentations passage makes a statement of fact similar to those found in Exod 20:5 and Jer 16:11. He claims that these texts indicate that one can indeed cause one's descendants to suffer as a result of one's own sins, and that the Jeremiah passage deals with persons who refuse to take responsibility for their own sins. In other words, one can suffer for the sins of one's parents, but simply because one is suffering is no guarantee that such is the case (341–42). Surely Keil is correct in his analysis. Whether or not Jeremiah wrote Lamentations does not rest on this evidence alone.

Second, Keil deals with the assertion that Lamentations could not have been written by Jeremiah because the book of Lamentations quotes Ezekiel, which was written after 571 B.C.E. He finds that what appears to be a connection between Lam 2:14 and other passages in Ezekiel is best explained by the text's connection with Jeremiah and Jeremiah's possible familiarity with one or more of Ezekiel's oracles (342–44). At the very least, Keil denies that there is any direct quoting of Ezekiel in Lamentations. Thus, he rejects this reason for not accepting Jeremiah's authorship, though only after fairly extensive analysis of the problem.

Third, Keil examines proposed stylistic and linguistic differences between the book of Jeremiah and Lamentations. After an initial survey, Keil admits that "the language and mode of representation in these poems certainly exhibit much that is peculiar; and we find in them many words, word-forms, and modes of expression which do not occur in the prophecies of Jeremiah" (346). He continues, "But it must also be borne in mind that the Lamentations are not prophetic addresses intended to warn, rebuke, and comfort, but lyric poetry, which has its own proper style of language, and this is different from prophetic address" (346). Therefore, Keil attributes the seeming oddities in Lamentations to the genre and subject matter of that book.

Having dealt with these objections, Keil concludes his discussion of authorship with an impressive list of stylistic similarities between the two books like those noted by Driver (see Keil, 345 n. 1, 348 n. 1, 349). He does not simply fall back on tradition or depend upon harmonization techniques to make his case. Rather, he attempts to base his conclusions on linguistics and reasonable discourse. His analysis demonstrates that there are solid points of contact between the books. Even if one disagrees with his conclusion, one still has to deal seriously with the probability that Lamentations borrows phrases and theological themes from Jeremiah or from those who share his point of view.

For his part, Streane (1881) notes and challenges the same objections, though in much less detail than Keil. Perhaps Streane's most significant contribution is his own compilation of linguistic, tonal, and theological similarities between Lamentations and Jeremiah (see 356–57). Again, these passages lead to the conclusion that there are definite theological and linguistic correspondences between the books. One may not be as certain as Streane that "Jeremiah was beyond question" the author, but neither can one ignore the areas of agreement. As is true of Calvin and Keil, Streane does take the traditions about Jeremianic authorship seriously when drawing his conclusions, but he makes his decision about authorship at the very least partly based on exegetical, theological, and historical analysis, not solely on the basis of tradition.

Very few twentieth-century authors advocated Jeremianic authorship of Lamentations. One exception to this rule was W. W. Cannon. In an article published in 1924 (*BSac* 81 [1924] 42–58), Cannon assessed opposition to Jeremianic authorship and disputed its findings based on nine considerations.

1. The book was most likely written by an eyewitness and therefore written near 587 B.C.
2. The first four poems are *qinoth*, or funeral laments, a literary form also found in Jer 9:9b–11, 9:20–21, 22:6–7, and 22:21–23.
3. Jeremiah cared deeply about Judah's fate.
4. Jeremiah and Lamentations share significant theological and linguistic connections.
5. The linguistic and theological differences between the books are not so detailed or unusual to preclude Jeremiah being the author of both books.
6. It is likely that one author, not several, wrote Lamentations.
7. It is unlikely that the poems were written at radically different times.
8. The connection between Lamentations and Ezekiel is not so telling as to render Jeremianic authorship of Lamentations impossible.
9. Jeremiah had the time and opportunity to write Lamentations after the fall of Jerusalem. (*BSac* 81 [1924] 43–58)

Cannon concludes his analysis by admitting that his arguments cannot be considered infallibly conclusive. Still, he writes, "But the writer does claim to have shown that the tradition that Jeremiah was the author of these poems is possibly true, and that as much or more may be said in favor of his authorship than can be adduced on behalf of any other view" (*BSac* 81 [1924] 58).

Cannon's article is carefully crafted and argued. It includes as good a summary of the arguments for Jeremianic authorship to that time as is possible. Most of the ideas he forwards are shared by Keil or noted by Driver. Of particular importance, however, are his comments on the *qinoth* in Jeremiah. These texts demonstrate that Jeremiah and Lamentations share an art form that helps create theology in both books. Therefore, reading these passages alongside one another may help illuminate the theological and linguistic emphases in each.

Perhaps chief among advocates of Jeremiah's authorship of Lamentations in the twentieth century was Hermann Wiesmann, who published his *Die Klagelieder* in 1954 after having penned several key articles on the subject in the 1920s and 1930s. Like Calvin, Keil, and Streane before him, Wiesmann argued that the linguistic and theological connections between Jeremiah and Lamentations indicate that the books are by the same author, and that this author was Jeremiah. He also denied that the placement of Lamentations in the Writings section of the Hebrew canon means that the book could not have been written by Jeremiah and offered the suggestion that Lamentations was placed in the Writings for liturgical purposes (56–84). Unlike his predecessors, Wiesmann presented his evidence over a period of thirty years and in several venues. Wiesmann's work demonstrates once again that even if Jeremiah is not the author of Lamentations, one must take seriously how specific words, phrases, and concepts similar to those found in Jeremiah influence Lamentations. It is not enough to use this information to decide whether Jeremiah wrote Lamentations. This evidence must be used to help interpret the latter book.

Though he did not argue for Jeremianic authorship of Lamentations, Wilhelm Rudolph suggested in his *Die Klagelieder* (2d ed., 1962) that Lam 3 sounds like it has been placed in Jeremiah's mouth as a literary device (227–45). He also observed that Lamentations has verbal connections with Ezekiel, Isaiah, and Psalms, not just with Jeremiah. Thus, Rudolph concludes that the central poem in Lamentations bears the marks of Jeremiah's legacy as the prophet of the remnant, yet he does not think that this evidence is sufficient to argue for Jeremianic authorship. Still, he seeks to find a means whereby the connections with Jeremiah can be important, which is no small quest. He also tries to link Lamentations to the broader biblical material, which is vital for the placing of Lamentations within the OT's canonical theological structure.

Finally, F. B. Huey cautiously posits Jeremianic authorship of Lamentations in his 1993 commentary. Huey writes that the tradition that Jeremiah penned Lamentations is quite old and widely attested, that Jeremiah was an eyewitness to Jerusalem's destruction, that the unity of the book can be defended, and that the arguments against Jeremianic authorship based on logical and theological grounds are not compelling (see 442–43). Therefore, he concludes that it is certainly plausible to decide that Jeremiah wrote the book. In fact, he states that "there is no reason to doubt that Jeremiah uttered these laments, thus making him the author" (443). At the same time, he asserts, "However, inspiration and the value of scripture do not depend on certain identification of the human author or authors" (443). In other words, Huey finds that it is likely that Jeremiah wrote Lamentations, yet he realizes that the fact that no author is named in the book means that no specific biblical truth claim is at stake in the discussion. Like some of his predecessors, Huey's main contribution to Lamentations studies is in his linguistic and exegetical work. It is in these areas that he points out connections to Jeremiah and the whole of the OT canon that make Lamentations more recognizable as a participant in the OT's teachings about sin, suffering, judgment, and hope.

As is true of all scholarly traditions, the one just surveyed has both strengths and weaknesses. The strengths have already been stated. For example, these scholars exhibit a high degree of linguistic and exegetical skill. Their consistent drawing of linguistic and theological connections between Jeremiah, other OT books, and Lamentations keeps Lamentations from being treated in isolation from its canonical context. These scholars' convictions about the book's unity keep Lamentations from being treated as a collection of loosely related poems. Their commitment to historical context keeps Lamentations from being treated in a vacuum.

Nonetheless, it is appropriate to suggest a few weaknesses as well. For instance, they may lean too heavily on the extrabiblical tradition that ties the book to

Jeremiah. If so, they are placing a great deal of emphasis on a tradition that has no actual biblical attestation. Also, their desire to note connections between Lamentations and Jeremiah may well lead them to limit their discussion of differences between the books. Finally, given their convictions about the connections between the books, they could spend more time defining how Lamentations clarifies theology in Jeremiah and vice versa. Even with these and other weaknesses duly noted, however, this tradition makes a significant contribution to Lamentations research, and it is one that is too often neglected.

Without question, the majority of Lamentations scholars over the past two hundred years have disagreed with Calvin, Keil, Streane, Cannon, Wiesmann, and Huey. They have done so largely because of their acceptance of what have become traditional historical-critical objections to Jeremianic authorship of Lamentations such as those listed by Driver. They have also done so because many of them believe that one author did not write all five of the poems and because those who do think one author wrote all five poems do not consider it necessary to conclude that Jeremiah was the poems' author.

Starting with the nineteenth-century commentators, the historical-critical tradition in biblical studies has accepted certain specific reasons for rejecting the notion of Jeremianic authorship of Lamentations. Several of these reasons have already been noted in the discussions above. For example, Thenius (1855), Ewald (1866), and Budde (1898) argued that Jeremiah was not the author of Lamentations because Jeremiah would not have agreed with the sentiments expressed in Lam 4:17 or 5:7; because Lamentations is placed in the Writings in the Hebrew canon, not with the prophets; and because Lam 2:14 and other texts seem to cite Ezekiel. Budde also concluded that the differences in the thematic contents of the five laments in the book are significant enough to determine that there are multiple authors at work. Budde's commentary supplemented his groundbreaking 1882 essay on the poetic meter of Lamentations (*ZAW* 2 [1882] 1–52); in this essay he stressed the sameness of the meter in the poems and the differences in the content of the poems. Thus, Budde helped popularize the idea that the book's poems were written by several authors and collected over a long period of time for liturgical purposes. Historical critics did not accept all these commentators' conclusions about the authorship and the date of the editing of Lamentations, but their arguments against Jeremianic authorship became an established part of the historical-critical tradition of scholarship.

During the first half of the twentieth century, historical-critical scholars continued to discuss the authorship of Lamentations along the lines established by Budde; these discussions were also supplemented by key form-critical studies. For example, commentaries by Max Löhr (1906; rev. ed. 1923), A. S. Peake (1911), Wilhelm Rudolph (1939; 2d ed. 1962), and Max Haller (1940) accepted the basic premises of Budde and others' conclusions on the improbability of Jeremianic authorship. While doing so, however, they did not agree on the number of authors the book did have. On the one hand, Löhr and Haller concluded that the diversity of expressions and emphases in Lamentations means that it is unlikely that one author penned the book. Haller suggested that the book's authors were influenced by prophetic thought and that those authors may have been temple singers (94). On the other hand Rudolph thought that the poems share a consistent theological vision held together by the confession of God's nature in Lam 3. These scholars wrestle with unity in a different way, then, from the adherents of Jeremianic authorship. They tend to debate how a group of poems do or do not hold together thematically and linguistically and what these differences mean for the book's composition and redaction instead of examining solely how the language and theology of Lamentations are like or unlike those found in Jeremiah. These scholars seek new paradigms of internal literary and theological coherence because they have abandoned Jeremianic authorship. Their insights are crucial, for coupled with the insights offered by their more conservative colleagues they offer elements of unity as well as checks and balances on overly zealous views of unity.

Two crucial form-critical works published during this era heavily influenced future Lamentations research. In 1923 Hedwig Jahnow published a study of Hebrew laments *(Das hebräische Leichenlied im Rahmen der Volkerdichtung)* that concluded that the laments in Lamentations originated in funeral laments, or dirges, such as those found in 2 Sam 3:33–34 and Jer 38:22 (124–62). She noted the various elements of these dirges and stated that Lamentations adapted the form for the death of a city, in this case Jerusalem. Earlier scholars and contemporaries, such as Budde and Cannon had already commented on the use of funeral themes and funeral meters in Lamentations, but Jahnow systematized the literary elements of the dirge in much more detail. She also emphasized that the writer of Lamentations had turned a secular form (funeral dirge) into a religious form of expression about Jerusalem's fall.

In 1933, Hermann Gunkel, Jahnow's professor, then cited her research as evidence that Lam 1, 2, and 4 are dirges, that Lam 3 is of mixed genre, though largely an individual lament, and that Lam 5 is a community lament. Concerning the historical process involved in the composition of Lamentations, Gunkel writes, "In a late period of the Psalms, the transformation of the dirge is conducted with several motifs of the common complaint, as transpires in Lam 1, 2, and 4 which H. Jahnow has exquisitely described. . . . This type of melding is all the more noteworthy since the dirge and complaint are a world apart in terms of their type. On the other hand, both genres do have a certain, distant relationship that dominates the complaints. Moreover, the dirge normally concerns the death of an individual, but in Lamentations it is related to Zion's misfortune. Thus, it has been filled with political elements, thereby coming closer to the communal complaint. Thus, several elements, which were originally characteristic of communal laments, found their way into Lamentations" (*Introduction*, 95–96). Clearly, Gunkel considers Lamentations a collection of poems shaped over time, albeit in a creative fashion. Concerning the religious elements added to the dirge form, Gunkel asserts, "The element in which YHWH is occasionally the subject was normally not possible in the dirge (cf. 1:5c, 12e, 13–15, 17–18; 2:1–9, 17–19, 21f; 4:11, 16). This reference to YHWH is clear in the *'summons'* using his name (1:9e, 11e, 20a; 2:20a); the *petition* to him to look upon Zion's suffering and to listen to its moaning (1:9e, 11e, 20e, 21a, 2:20a); the *'curse'* of the enemies (1:21f, 22a) with the *petition* against them (1:22b); the *confession of sin* (1:18b, 20d; 4:6, 13) combined with the theodicy (1:18a); and finally, several of the complaints proper follow the subject of the communal complaint more closely than the dirge (cf. especially 1:9f, 20a, b, c, 21a). In this manner, the originally *secular* genre of the dirge has been transformed into a *religious* poem (H. Jahnow)" (*Introduction to Psalms,* 96 [emphasis original]).

Given his conclusions, he found it necessary to assign different authors to the various genres, to interpret the poems separately from one another as one might do in a strict form-critical work on Psalms, and to date them later than the sixth century B.C.E. As the century progressed, Jahnow's work fueled further analyses of Lamentations within its ancient context, while Gunkel's observations informed work on the genre and unity of Lamentations. Gunkel's influence was particularly evident in works written between 1950 and 1970, whether those works argued for the unity or composite nature of Lamentations. Interestingly, though, his view on the date of Lamentations was not as readily accepted as his views on their literary diversity.

Whatever one may think of Gunkel's ideas, one of the benefits of his analysis is that the artistry of Lamentations is much more evident. From Gunkel's analysis, as well as from those of Keil, Budde, and Cannon, it is appropriate to conclude that Lamentations meshes more than one poetic type and uses more than one sort of poetic meter to achieve its results. In other words, Lamentations is in many ways artistically diverse, even brilliant. At the very least, then, the author or editors of the book were able to achieve a high creative level. How this fact affected future consideration of the authorship and date of Lamentations depended on the scholar in question.

Several stimulating volumes and articles devoted to Lamentations appeared between 1950 and 1975. Key articles stressed historical connections between Lamentations and the use of dirges in the ancient world. Significant commentaries continued to address matters raised in earlier years. At least two groundbreaking monographs related to the theology of Lamentations were published. Thus, more attention was paid than in previous eras to how history, exegesis, and theology intersect in the book. Despite this progress in Lamentations studies as a whole, however, the main issues in the discussion of authorship remained nearly the same as before. Still, as these years unfolded, a preference for a unified approach to Lamentations became more common in the discussions, as did the belief that the book was written close to the time of the events it describes.

Several articles and monographs in this era were devoted to examining possible connections between Lamentations and other ancient Near Eastern laments. S. N. Kramer was in many ways the pioneer in this field, for over a fifty-year span he wrote several comparative studies of Sumerian laments for the destruction of cities and the book of Lamentations. His conclusion was that there are several similarities between laments over Ur written in the second millennium B.C.E. and the book of Lamentations. He then argued that these similarities mean that the author of Lamentations transformed the Sumerian forms into poems about Jerusalem (see *Lamentation over the Destruction of Ur;* "Lamentation over the Destruction of Ur," 455–63; *Acta Sumerologica* 13 [1991] 1–26). C. J. Gadd basically agreed with Kramer, claiming that the Sumerian songs at least influenced the Hebrew author ("Second Lamentation for Ur," 61). In his careful critique of Kramer and Gadd's conclusions, T. F. McDaniel argued that there was too much time between the writing of the Sumerian laments and Lamentations for such a connection to be possible. Thus, he contended that there was no specific connection between sixth-century B.C.E. Judah and ancient Sumeria (*VT* 18 [1968] 209). More specifically, McDaniel wondered how authors working in Judah in the mid-sixth century B.C.E. could have known the Sumerian literature (*VT* 18 [1968] 207). Based on these conclusions, McDaniel placed the date of Lamentations within a few decades after the fall of Jerusalem. Based on what he considers evidence McDaniel did not possess, W. C. Gwaltney, Jr., defended Kramer's assessments in his 1983 treatment of the topic ("Biblical Book of Lamentations," 191–211). Gwaltney posits that, during their time in Assyria and Persia in the sixth century B.C., Jewish exiles did in fact have the opportunity to learn earlier Sumerian literary forms (210–11). Thus, the time and opportunity gap noted by McDaniel is not relevant. Regardless of the validity of Gwaltney's opinions on the connection between Sumerian laments and Lamentations, he agrees with McDaniel's assessment of when Lamentations was written. Both scholars take the years immediately after Jerusalem's fall as their starting point for the book's date.

Though clearly aware of their own fallibility, the authors of historical-critical commentaries on Lamentations in the 1950s generally focused on the diversity of the book's material. For instance, George A. F. Knight (1955) and T. J. Meek (1956) state that only Lam 2 and 4 seem to be by the same author. The rest of the book shows signs of being written by several authors over a number of years, though both scholars date the completed book soon after the exile (see Knight, 116; Meek, 5). Meek concludes that the poems were written in Palestine and brought together for cultic purposes (5), while Knight determines that they were penned by eyewitnesses who were well aware of the prophecies of Jeremiah and Ezekiel (116). Their comments leave open several possibilities concerning the poets' identity, life setting, and professions, but they agree that the book was written fairly shortly after the exile.

Though more open to the possibility of a single author of Lamentations than Knight and Meek, H. J. Kraus (1st ed. 1956; 3d ed. 1968) and Artur Weiser (1st ed. 1958; 2d ed. 1962) also considered the divergences between chaps. 1, 2, and 4 and the rest of the book. In particular, both writers viewed chap. 3 as different from the other poems and as strategic to the book's message as a whole. Though noncommittal about the exact identity of the author or authors of the book, both Kraus and Weiser suggest that the poems were composed and gathered by persons involved in the Jerusalem cult shortly after the exile (see Kraus [1968], 13–15, and Weiser [1958], 40–42). Therefore, their considerations of authorship brought them very close to the conclusions offered by Knight and Meek, and helped establish cultic functionaries working in Jerusalem after the city's defeat as viable candidates for the book's authors.

Two key works on the theology of Lamentations also made vital contributions to the discussion of the book's authorship. In his 1954 (2d ed. 1962) monograph *Studies in the Book of Lamentations*, Norman Gottwald offered a translation, introduction, and theological assessment of Lamentations. Frustrated with the seemingly perennial debates over whether Jeremiah wrote the book, Gottwald argued that what was needed was an analysis of the theology of Lamentations. As for the book's authorship, Gottwald writes, "In order to clear the way for fruitful study, the author wishes to make it plain that he does not believe that Jeremiah wrote Lamentations, nor is he satisfied with the usual critical alternative: three or more authors over a period of perhaps two centuries. He believes that at least the first four poems (which correspond to the first four chapters) are the work of a single poet. With respect to the concluding poem it is impossible to be dogmatic. All of the poems, however, are to be understood as stemming from the exilic period between 587 and 538 B.C. The uniform historical setting, the similarities of style and vocabulary, and the community of thought which they share make it possible to speak of *the theology* of the Book of Lamentations" (21 [emphasis original]). Gottwald's subsequent analysis of the theology of Lamentations (see "Theological Purposes in Lamentations" below) reveals an author skilled in mixing psalm forms (33–46) who asks why Judah has been punished so severely when the people had repented during Josiah's reign (47–62). Gottwald's volume properly pushes for theological, not just historical, analysis of Lamentations. His assertion that Lamentations mourns defeat in the face of reform, however, does not square with any biblical account of how the nation was acting at the time of Jerusalem's demise.

Bertil Albrektson expressed a similar frustration with the state of Lamentations studies and a desire to chart a more theological course in his *Studies in the Text and Theology of the Book of Lamentations, with a Critical Edition of the Peshitta Text* (1963). Like Gottwald, Albrektson laments that earlier commentators spent so much time on whether Jeremiah wrote Lamentations and so little time on the book's theology (214). As is true of Gottwald's volume, Albrektson's monograph does not offer many specific declarations about the author of Lamentations, yet it too makes statements that contribute to a portrait of the author. Stated briefly, Albrektson believes that the book had a single author who was reared in the temple traditions of Jerusalem (223). This author was influenced by two streams of thought: the Zion tradition that Jerusalem was God's elect city and could never fall, and the Deuteronomistic tradition that emphasized the centralization of the cult (238). The author then blended these traditions in an effort to work through in a theological fashion the fact of the city's devastation (238–39). Albrektson's study has much to commend it, particularly its emphasis on the blending of Deuteronomistic and Jerusalem theology (see "Theological Purposes in Lamentations") and how that blending helps define the author's thought. Taken together with Gottwald's study, Albrektson's work aids the attempt to describe the author even if that author's identity cannot be asserted with full authority, and both works correctly argue that any assessment of the authorship of Lamentations ought to take theology into account.

Commentaries written by Otto Plöger (2d ed. 1969), Delbert R. Hillers (1972; 2d ed. 1992), and Robert Gordis (1974) reinforced older opinions on authorship and date and charted new approaches to the subject. For instance, Plöger stated that all five poems might have come from a single author, yet he also noted that chaps. 1, 2, and 4 differ from chaps. 3 and 5 in content and form. Though not dogmatic about his position, Plöger concluded that the book probably arose in cultic circles (see 129–30). Gordis, on the other hand, determined that the differences in the book's "theme and . . . standpoint make it clear that the various elegies do not emanate from a single author" (126). Given these divergences, he claims chaps. 2 and 4, both of which offer graphic descriptions of Jerusalem's fall, were probably written by eyewitnesses close to 570 B.C.E. The other three poems, which seem more distant from the destruction, were likely completed by

530 B.C.E. (see 126–27). Gordis offers no specific statement on the circles in which the author operated. Unlike Plöger or Gordis, Hillers interprets "the poems as an intelligible unity, whether or not this unity results from one author or from an editor who ordered originally separate works" ([1972], xxii; see Hillers [1992], 14, for similar conclusions). He does so in part because he finds the evidence put forth through the years to be inconclusive and perhaps in part because of a desire to work with the text as it stands. Hillers believed that Lamentations was written in Palestine soon after the fall of Jerusalem, but states no opinion on the author's personal circumstances or school of thought. Though scholars continued to work along lines adopted by Plöger and Gordis, many authors decided to take the path Hillers chose and spend less time discussing matters of authorship and date.

A survey of commentaries and articles on Lamentations written during 1975–2002 illustrates the tendency of scholars to choose one of the earlier approaches to authorship and date. Otto Kaiser (4th ed. 1992) argued that all the poems come from a later date than the fall of Jerusalem, claiming that the earliest poems were penned about 450 B.C.E. and the latest about 300 B.C.E. (109–10). Thus, he agrees with many of the late nineteenth-century critics on the book's date.

S. Paul Re'emi (1984) took a theological approach to the book, as was fitting for the series in which his book appeared. He accepts the reasons given through the years by historical-critical scholars for why Jeremiah could not have written Lamentations, but he does not choose to comment further on the subject except to state that the author does not come from priestly or prophetic circles (80–81). So Re'emi differs from many historical-critical exegetes on that point. He also follows in the footsteps of Gottwald and Albrektson in his attempt to highlight the theology of Lamentations.

Writing in the conservative *Expositor's Bible* commentary series, H. L. Ellison (1986) states that it is best to consider the arguments for and against Jeremianic authorship "fairly evenly balanced" and concludes that arguments for Jeremianic authorship seem "to be mainly sentimental" (696). Like most commentators, Ellison held that the book was written in Palestine within a few decades of the events it describes.

After a careful and closely argued discussion, Iain Provan (1991) asserts that there is "insufficient evidence, when the literary character of the poems in Lamentations is taken into account, to decide questions of authorship and place of composition" (19). Provan reached this conclusion because he deemed it possible that the book was written long after the events it commemorates, that one author or many could have been involved, and that the book's original purpose cannot be recovered with accuracy. His opinions are not reached in a cynical or cavalier manner. Rather, they reflect the state of the discipline as a whole. If opposing positions are plausible, he argues, then it is impossible to state with full confidence which approach is correct. In this way, like Ellison, Provan follows Hillers's approach to the subject of authorship.

Claus Westermann (1990; ET 1994) sought to examine and emphasize the meaning and significance of laments in his important commentary. As a prelude to his own analysis of Lamentations, Westermann charts much of the history of Lamentations research, though he focuses upon how writers have or have not taken laments seriously as vital biblical materials. As for authorship and date,

Westermann thinks that the poems reflect a later written expression of an earlier oral response to the fall of Jerusalem. Therefore, it is impossible to recapture the first voice in the poems, though it is possible to conclude that this voice was that of an eyewitness. It is also likely that the poems arose by 550 B.C.E. based on parallels with Isa 40–55, but Westermann considers it possible that chap. 3 ought to be assigned to a later date. Finally, Westermann thinks it likely that the poems originated in Palestine (100–105). While Westermann's greatest insights are on the subject of the nature and purpose of laments (see below), he demonstrates the difficulty of assigning dates and authors to original oral and written sources at this stage of Lamentations research.

Johan Renkema (1993; ET 1998) offers readers a masterful historical, exegetical, and structural commentary on Lamentations. Indeed, this volume may be unsurpassed in its nearly indefatigable commitment to explicating the book's meaning. As is true of many previous scholars, Renkema asserts that the book emerged in temple circles soon after the destruction of Jerusalem. In fact, he argues that the poems came from temple singers, a guild that remained active after the temple's razing. He writes that the "people did not need tens of years to arrive at a *modus vivendi* with the downfall. Rather, the intense emphasis on the dreadful famine points to a more recent experience" (54). It is important to note that Renkema reaches his decision based on close analysis of the text itself. At every point he submits textual evidence for why he argues as he does. Thus, at the very least one has to take his assertions seriously even when one does not adopt his opinions.

Erhard Gerstenberger offers a form-critical study of Lamentations in his 2001 commentary. In many ways he stands at the center of historical-critical research on the book. For example, after noting the history of the interpretation of the book in Jewish and Christian traditions he concludes, "For linguistic, historical, generic, and thematic reasons, modern scholarship cannot accept the authorship of the prophet Jeremiah" (468). He then proceeds to stress the importance of reading Lamentations in light of parallels between the book and Mesopotamian dirges (469). In other words, he has great appreciation for the work conducted by Jahnow, Gwaltney, Hillers, Westermann, and others. Next, he notes the difficulty of establishing the book's meter with exactitude and spends almost no time on acrostics as a genre (469–71). Then, having written freely of "redactors," "authors," and "transmitters" (471), he concludes that the poems "seem to fit into one liturgical sequence" that seeks God's favor and help, most likely at yearly mourning festivals (473). Finally, he decides that there is not enough evidence to pinpoint the time and place of the book's origins, yet at the same time he underscores its role in communal worship (473–75). He then interprets the book in light of these fundamental conclusions.

Kathleen O'Connor's 2001 commentary maintains contact with older approaches to the book, yet it also reflects some new trends in theological analysis of the book. She believes that the book most likely addresses the 587 B.C.E. debacle but does not consider it possible to determine the exact setting or number of authors involved ([2001] 1013–16). Still, she "assumes a unity of the material in the book's present form" ([2001] 1016). She notes the way acrostics bring order to "various voices, images, and perspectives" in individual poems (1019) and charts the importance of alternating speakers ([2001] 1020). Perhaps most significantly, she stresses how the poems "create a space where communal and personal pain can be re-experienced, seen, and perhaps healed. . . . Indeed, its recovery in our communal lives could lead to a greater flourishing of life amid our own wounds and the woundedness of the world" ([2001] 1013). She asserts, "The book functions as a witness to pain, a testimony of survival, and an artistic transformation of dehumanizing suffering into exquisite literature. In the process, it raises profound questions about the justice of God" ([2001] 1024). Clearly, O'Connor insists that the book helps people to voice their pain, an emphasis Westermann made repeatedly in his 1994 volume. Just as clearly, she is open to the notion that God's justice is probed and should be probed today. In this way she connects here and in a 2002 volume (see "Theological Purposes in Lamentations" below) with newer perspectives.

F. W. Dobbs-Allsopp has offered both linguistic and theological studies of Lamentations. In 1998 he published "Linguistic Evidence for the Date of Lamentations" (*JANESCU* 26 [1998] 1–36), in which he examined the vocabulary, syntax, and orthography of Lamentations. He concluded that Lamentations exhibits at least seventeen aspects of postexilic Hebrew and asserted that the book was probably written by 540–520 B.C.E. Thus, he agrees with the majority of experts on the book's date. In his 2002 commentary he affirms his earlier conclusion on the book's date and then states that "the widely observed unity of form and point of view, rhythmic dominance of the *qinah* meter, and general resemblance in linguistic detail throughout the sequence are broadly suggestive of the work of a single author" (5). Therefore, though he admits the difficulties associated with this conclusion, he prefers to write about a single poet's work rather than that of several poets.

Nancy Lee's 2002 monograph, *The Singers of Lamentations,* offers a creative and helpful contribution to issues of authorship, date, and application of Lamentations. Besides analyzing Lamentations closely, she compares the book to lament literature in the ancient and contemporary worlds. As part of her analysis of Lamentations she compares what she considers authentic oracles of Jeremiah (see *Singers,* 46) to Lamentations and concludes that this person speaks in Lamentations (129). Thus, Lamentations is a sort of extension of the book of Jeremiah, even though the prophet is more of a co-sufferer in Lamentations than he is in Jeremiah (145–46). As for the book's theological perspective, she decides that Lamentations "holds in tension that there can be both individual innocence and corporate guilt. However, the book does nuance corporate guilt in the end by laying more blame upon the political and religious leaders of its capital city" (198). Perhaps her argument for Jeremiah's potential role in Lamentations will incite future research on that possibility. At the very least, her careful drawing of connections between Jeremiah and Lamentations makes that process essential for future treatments of Lamentations. Jeremiah's thought must be examined for Lamentations to be understood.

Adele Berlin's 2002 commentary in many ways represents the mainstream of Lamentations scholarship on authorship and date. For instance, she agrees with Dobbs-Allsopp's conclusions on the book's date (no later than 520 B.C.E.; see Berlin, 34–35). Further, she agrees with Lee's comments about the use of a Jeremiah persona in the book (30–32) and finds it unnecessary to posit several authors for the book. Finally, she mirrors the trend toward more theological analysis than appeared in past Lamentations commentaries (7–22), yet she does not fail to observe the parallels between Lamentations and other ancient laments (26–30). In other words, her volume offers an excellent report of the state of Lamentations scholarship and produces crucial insights that go well beyond this consensus (see commentary below).

At this point in the discussion it is appropriate to summarize some of the main emphases offered by scholars who do not accept Jeremianic authorship of Lamentations. First, like their counterparts, they carefully scrutinize linguistic, theological, and literary data to make their conclusions. Unlike their counterparts, however, they do not agree on the results of their research. On the one hand, several of these experts assert that the five poems that constitute Lamentations are a connected whole, which means that a single author/redactor is certainly a strong possibility. On the other hand, many of them hold that the material is too diverse to draw such a conclusion. Thus, they suggest a variety of options for the author or authors. These options include the possibility that several persons of unknown origins and commitments wrote and collected the poems, that persons influenced by prophetic circles penned and gathered them, or that a group associated with cultic practices (for example temple singers) composed and adapted them for worship. This variety of possibilities has, over time, led several scholars to decide that the matter simply cannot be solved with anything approximating certainty.

Second, like their counterparts these scholars basically agree that Lamentations was in its present literary form within a few years after the fall of Jerusalem. Of course, there are exceptions to this consensus, but during the last century more and more experts came to this conclusion. Therefore, their opinion on the era of the book's emergence agrees with the historic position of the versions of Lamentations and with writers holding to Jeremianic authorship.

Third, many of the works help reveal the literary artistry of the book's author. Though their counterparts are hardly deficient in this area, overall the form-critical and historical-critical scholars have delved into these matters in the most depth. Such studies do not claim to reveal the exact identity of the author of the book, but they do help explicate that author's approach to the book's subject matter. They also aid in the assessment of how many writers may have been involved in the production of Lamentations.

Thus, though this tradition of scholarship has not decisively determined the author and date of Lamentations, it has aided the drawing of a portrait of that author and has supplemented the traditional view of the date. According to this tradition, the author was one knowledgeable of the worship practices and theology associated with the temple. Most likely, the author also lived through the horrors of the destruction of Jerusalem, or at the very least knew persons who did. The author believed that Israel's pain stemmed from knowing that they had sinned against God and suffered the consequences of their actions, though this author also implies that the pain has been sufficient for the crime and hopes that relief should come soon. The author was highly skilled in the writing of laments and was particularly adept at mixing traditional psalm forms to create fresh laments that kept contact with earlier artistic expressions. At the same time, however, this author remains an anonymous, at times enigmatic, figure. Since this anonymous person's past cannot be uncovered, one must be careful when drawing conclusions about the setting for this author's work. Though adherents of Jeremianic authorship are more decisive about the book's author, it is fair to say that their overall authorial portrait does not differ greatly from that of their counterparts.

CONCLUSION

Given the lack of consensus on the matters of authorship and date, it is tempting to suggest a brand new proposal or to argue vehemently for one of the options already expressed. After all, the field seems wide open to these possibilities. Despite such temptations, however, this commentary adopts a much simpler approach, though one hopes an approach based on the evidence that the text itself offers. Lamentations was most likely written by an individual of faith committed to explaining why Jerusalem fell, what its effects were on the populace, and how the people could return to the Lord they had abandoned. This individual also wished to help the people find expressions for their pain that led to theological and therefore realistic wholeness, and this person was committed to helping Israel restore its relationship with God. The book was most likely written within a few decades after the destruction of the city, but this possibility is just that—a possibility.

Why an individual and not a group of persons? Though one must be humble and cautious when answering this question, it seems most plausible to me that one person clearly could have written Lam 1, 2, and 4, given the similarity in their linguistic and thematic contents and the many intertextual connections in the book (see *Comment* sections). It is equally plausible that the same person or someone of like mind wrote Lam 3, especially given the flow of the book (see *Comment* section). Still, chap. 3 is the most distinct in style and point of view among the poems, as has been well documented by Westermann and others. It is certainly true that Lam 5 is stylistically unique among the five poems, but it is a community lament, which is hardly a rare form of Hebrew poetry. The same person could have written it and the other poems. Lam 1, 2, 3, and 4 employ acrostic patterns, and Lam 5 mirrors acrostic forms. The poems' differences exist within a very consistent and unified framework.

Further, as a group the five poems have a discernible progression, as the discussion of the book's structure offered below indicates. The first two poems set forth the people and problems that concern the book. A narrator who speaks in third person, Zion, and a first-person speaker are the chief characters; and the extremity, causes, and avenues of relief from suffering are among the key themes. Chap. 3 offers a soliloquy by a representative of the community of faith, who may well be the first-person speaker of chap. 2. This representative has suffered with the people, and he counsels the people how they, like he, may come to a better relationship with their covenant God. Chap. 4 continues to detail the nation's pain; then chap. 5 concludes the book with a community lament that indicates that the nation at least partly takes the advice given in chap. 3.

Several verbal and thematic correspondences/echoes occur between particular parts of chapters, probably indicating intentional authorial design. The differences in the poems imply that either a single person composed them separately and brought them together as a group or that a single person brought together five poems by various authors because they express a unified theology. The many similarities in the poems hint that they are the work either of one person or of a group of like-minded individuals. In other words, they are not a disparate collection of loosely related pieces. They have a pattern, though that pattern is not like that found in many other biblical texts. It is possible that such patterning reflects group activity, but it seems more likely that such a small collection was not the product of a large group working over a long period of time. It is more likely, at least on the face of things, to posit a single writer/collector who formed the book we now possess.

It is impossible to state with accuracy the identity of this individual. One must recall that the text itself does not reveal the author, which means that at a very basic level the text is meant to be read as an anonymous work, perhaps so that it might be considered the prayers of many, not just one person. This conclusion is not meant as a dismissal of other viewpoints. The Jeremianic authorship tradition has pointed out significant interfaces between Jeremiah and Lamentations. Indeed, this tradition has established the advisability of treating the style and theology of Lamentations in light of Jeremiah. Other traditions have indicated the need to seek to understand the book's diversity and to consider different potential origins. They have also stated possible beliefs that the author or authors may have held, as was stated above. Still, this commentary will comment on what it deems *an author* has done, not what *a group* has done, while at the same time attempting to make good use of clarifying material written by persons from the opposite viewpoint. It will also consider the overall authorial portrait gleaned from the Jeremianic and non-Jeremianic traditions noted above to be basically accurate. With the exception of naming a particular person, in many ways various representatives of the two traditions agree on the sort of author the book probably had.

As for the date, it is not necessary to conclude that the sort of lament found in Lamentations must have been penned within days after the events. The fact that the poems are acrostics indicates that great care and crafting went into their composition. It is hard to imagine the eyewitnesses of the fall of the city spontaneously crying out in acrostic verse! It is also true that their subject matter remained a concern long after the events they depict.

Still, the acrostic form and the contents of Lamentations do not necessitate a late date, since it hardly takes centuries to memorialize an event and include it in worship services. In fact, mournful worshipers came to the temple soon after the destruction of the city (see Jer 41:5 and Zech 7:1–4). Haggai indicates that worship continued on the temple site before the new temple was constructed. Clearly, the desirability of and opportunity for laments of the type found in Lamentations existed soon after 587 B.C.E. Just as clearly, these opportunities existed for centuries afterwards, and in many ways continue to the present day. The immediate need, however, strongly implies that the book was composed reasonably close to the time of the fall of Jerusalem and has been used ever since. Perhaps the Septuagint's ascription of Lamentations to Jeremiah is also evidence of early usage of the book in mourning over the temple's destruction because of the people's sins.

Given these cautious conclusions, this commentary considers Lamentations the work of one person. This person wrote linguistically connected poems and placed them in the order we now have. These poems reflect the theological perspective (found in Jeremiah and other prophets who loved Zion) that the Lord would not spare even the place where he had placed his name if Israel rebelled over a long period of time, for she knew the covenant curses found in the Law. They also reflect the lament traditions found in Psalms, particularly those laments that mix various types of material to make their point, and even more particularly those psalms that deal with the fall of Jerusalem and its implications. The author loved the people of God very much and was grieved by their troubles, even though (or especially because) they were self-inflicted woes. Perhaps most importantly, this author shared the sorrows of God's covenant people, and he ministered to them in and through his poems as one of God's faithful. This is an involved author, one who thinks, writes, and feels with the best of the biblical poets. Certainly this author could have been Jeremiah, a temple singer, a prophetically oriented priest, or some other faithful member of the believing community. For whatever reason, this person chose to remain anonymous, which forces interpreters to deal solely with his poems and their theology, despite the desire for his name and circumstances. This decision pushes readers toward the book's message; it presses readers to cease trying to avoid the book's expressions of pain and confessions of sin, which in turn forces them away from normal Western religious and cultural practice.

Liturgical Uses

Lamentations has had a long history of liturgical usage. Though it was almost certainly used in worship from its date of origin, the contours of those early services are now lost to us. We do know, however, that for centuries the reading of the book has been part of the ceremonies surrounding the commemoration of the destruction of the temple. A survey of highly possible and currently known usages may allow contemporary liturgists some insight into how Lamentations may be used in worship today.

The OT indicates that services of mourning over Jerusalem's demise occurred almost from the time of the destruction itself and continued for many years. Jer 41:4–8 recounts mourners coming to the city with beards shaved, clothes torn, and bodies cut and with offerings in hand soon after the Babylonian governor Gedaliah was murdered. Their actions may have been impromptu, but they do not seem to be described as unusual. Thus, mourning rituals of some sort were considered a form of piety from the outset of the exile.

Some six or seven decades later, mourning and fasting were undertaken during the fifth and seventh month, according to Zech 7:3–5 and 8:19. These practices are described as having been observed since the destruction of the city, but these passages do not explicitly state whether the city's destruction was the source of the mourning. Still, the months coincide with those listed in 2 Kgs 25:8 and Jer 52:12–30 as the time of the destruction, so the connection is likely. If so, then Israel marked the loss of temple structure and national independence from earliest times, strongly implying that the people reflected upon the theological and historical importance of this event from the time it happened.

Based on these ancient observances, later Judaism used Lamentations in public mourning exercises taking place "on the 9th of *Ab*, the fifth month, which falls in July or August according to the modern calendar. The 9th is chosen in preference to strict adherence to either of the two biblical dates (II Kings 25:8–9 gives the 7th of *Ab;* Jeremiah 52:12 gives the 10th) because of the tradition that the *second* temple fell to Titus on the 9th of *Ab*, and that Bar Kokhba's fortress Betar fell on that date in A.D. 135" (Hillers [1972], xli [emphasis original]). The 587 B.C.E. fall of Jerusalem was not the only event marked at this service of mourning. As Etan Levine writes, "Jewish tradition . . . attributes five calamities to the Ninth of Ab: the decree that none of the Hebrews who left Egypt, except Caleb and Joshua, should enter the Promised Land; the destruction of both the First Temple and the Second Temple; the fall of Bethar, the last fortress during the Bar Kokba rebellion; the ploughing over of Jerusalem by the Romans. Consequently, this day is considered most important of all fast days" (*Aramaic Version*, 13). In this somber festival, then, Lamentations came to be used as a book that is able to describe all sorts of national and personal disasters, not just the Babylonian destruction of Jerusalem.

The details of the Ninth of Ab are interesting for their liturgical history and for their potential links to later Christian usage of Lamentations. Levine notes that Lamentations was at first read only privately during the festival but that in time it came to be incorporated into synagogue services. He also states that eventually this observance "saw the synagogue bared of all ornament, the curtain of the Holy Ark itself stripped away, all lights extinguished except for small reading candles, and the congregants sitting on the floor or on stools, barefoot, chanting in subdued voices. The chant's musical scale has no parallel in traditional Jewish repertoire, but it is found among the Syrian Christians (Maronite and Jacobite) and among the Copts in Egypt" (*Aramaic Version*, 13). These practices highlight the importance and seriousness with which these mourning ceremonies were conducted. They also provide a clear parallel with Christian usage of Lamentations during the Lenten season on Maundy Thursday, Good Friday, and Holy Saturday, given such Christian practices as stripping the altar, mourning over sin, and waiting patiently for God to act. Both traditions include Lamentations in what amounts to the most reflective and penitential rites of the liturgical year.

Throughout the centuries, then, Lamentations has been utilized in significant ways at important times. The book was most likely written for or at least quickly incorporated into worship services devoted to using the fall of Jerusalem as a paradigm for mourning one's sins and life's disasters. There is no question that in later centuries Lamentations was appropriated for calamities unconnected to the Babylonian invasion of Jerusalem. This appropriation at least suggests that later worshipers felt free to apply Lamentations to settings that fit the book's basic context. Christian usage of the book during Holy Week makes the same point. Believers in Jesus Christ have found it beneficial to use Lamentations to express one's deepest sins and greatest life agonies. They have not found the book to be too mournful, too negative, or too challenging of God's authority when taken into proper context. This willingness to use Lamentations in these settings may well lead to a re-examination of how the book can be used in current calamitous situations, which could in turn lead to a deepening of contemporary worship and popular theology.

Place in the Canon

Bibliography

Childs, B. S. *Introduction to the Old Testament as Scripture.* Philadelphia: Fortress, 1980. 590–97. **House, P. R.** *Old Testament Theology.* Downers Grove, IL: InterVarsity Press, 1998. 483–89.

There has never been serious opposition to the canonicity of Lamentations. At the same time, the book has been placed in more than one position in the various versions of the canon. These differences indicate preferences for certain views of authorship and date (the Greek, Latin, and English versions of the canon), as well as emphasis on thematic content (the Hebrew version).

As was stated above in the section on authorship and date, the Septuagint cites Jeremiah as the author of Lamentations. Thus, it is not surprising that the Greek tradition places Lamentations directly after the book of Jeremiah. Since the Vulgate (Latin) follows the Septuagint, and the English Bible follows the Vulgate, both those versions place Lamentations after Jeremiah. This practice has continued, despite the questions about the book's authorship over the past several decades.

The Hebrew order of books reflects at least two thematic concerns. First, it indicates a liturgical concern, since Lamentations was joined with four other books associated with festivals: Song of Songs (Passover), Ruth (Feast of Weeks), Ecclesiastes (Feast of Tabernacles), and Esther (Purim). These five books, called the Megilloth, were recited at their respective festivals, and were usually kept together in canonical arrangements, though they did not always appear in the same place in each canonical list. Second, in the MT, Lamentations introduces the exile in the Writings and then is followed by Esther and Daniel, both books that deal with the trials associated with exile. This exilic theme continues until Ezra, Nehemiah, and Chronicles address the problems endemic to the return to the Promised Land that marked the end of the exile and the fulfillment of Jeremiah's predictions (Jer 29:10–13). Thus, Lamentations stands at the head of a group of books dedicated to exploring matters crucial to living for the Lord under difficult, sometimes excruciating, circumstances. The book aids a proper understanding of why the exile occurred and how one may turn to the Lord in the aftermath and ensuing years of the exile.

Poetic Form and Meter

Bibliography

Budde, C. "Das hebräische Klagelied." *ZAW* 2 (1882) 1–52. **Freedman, D. N.** "Acrostic Poems in the Hebrew Bible: Alphabetic and Otherwise." *CBQ* 48 (1986) 408–31. ———. "Acrostics and Metrics in Hebrew Poetry." *HTR* 65 (1972) 367–92. ———. "Acrostics and Metrics in Hebrew Poetry." In *Pottery, Poetry, and Prophecy: Studies in Early Hebrew Poetry.* Winona Lake, IN: Eisenbrauns, 1980. 51–76. **Garr, W. R.** "The *Qinah:* A Study of Poetic Meter, Syntax, and Style." *ZAW* 95 (1983) 54–75. **Grossberg, D.** *Centripetal and Centrifugal Structures in Hebrew Poetry.* SBLMS 39. Atlanta: Scholars Press, 1989. **Heater, H.** "Structure and Meaning in Lamentations." *BSac* 149 (1992) 304–15. **Hillers, D.** "Lamentations, Book of." *ABD*, 4:137–41. ———. "Observations on Syntax and Meter in Lamentations." In *A Light unto My Path*. FS J. M. Myers, ed. H. M. Bream et al. Philadelphia: Temple UP, 1974, 265–70. **Johnson, B.** "Form and Message in Lamentations." *ZAW* 97 (1985) 58–73. **Shea, W. H.** "*Qinah* Meter and Strophic Structure in Psalm 137." *HAR* 8 (1984) 199–214. ———. "The *qinah* Structure of the Book of Lamentations." *Bib* 60 (1979) 103–7.

The form and structure of Lamentations are among its most distinctive and creative features. Shaped as a series of four acrostic poems and one concluding acrosticlike poem, the book utilizes older set literary forms to forge a new type of literature. This creative brilliance is not always evident at first glance, particularly because the more recognizable set forms often arrest the reader's attention. A brief examination of the book's use of acrostic format, meter, echoing techniques, general structure, and mixing of genres will at least offer some glimpses into the artistic excellence of the book of Lamentations.

ACROSTIC FORMAT

Lamentations consists of five clearly delineated poems, each of which is governed by the fact that the Hebrew alphabet has twenty-two letters. The first four poems are acrostics, which means that each succeeding line or set of lines begins with the subsequent letter of the Hebrew alphabet. Even in his use of this format the author demonstrates flexibility. As Hillers writes concerning the book's acrostics, "Chapters 1 and 2 are of a relatively simple type, in which each stanza has three lines, and only the first line of each is made to conform to the alphabet, so that stanza one begins with *aleph*, stanza two with *beth*, and so on through the twenty-two letters of the Hebrew alphabet. Chapter four is of the same type, but here each stanza has only two lines. Chapter three is more elaborate: each stanza has three lines, and all three lines are made to begin with the proper letter, so that there are three lines starting with *aleph*, three with *beth*, and so on. . . . Chapter five is not an acrostic, but has exactly twenty-two lines and thus conforms to the alphabet to a lesser degree. Other biblical poems with twenty-two lines exist—Pss 33, 38, 103—and it is reasonable to suppose that in all these cases the number of lines is chosen intentionally, though none are acrostics" ([1972], xxiv–xxv). One thing should be added to Hillers's excellent description, which is that Lam 1 and 2 differ in one small way. Though both follow the alphabet, Lam 1 follows the order of *ayin* then *pe*, while Lam 2 (as well as Lam 3–4) follows the order of *pe* then *ayin*. Both alphabetic orders occur in other ancient Hebrew literature, with the former order occurring in texts like Ps 119 and the latter in Prov 31 (on this point see Renkema, 48–49).

For as long as there has been biblical scholarship, experts have proposed theories to explain biblical writers' use of acrostics. First, a few writers have suggested that the authors used the format because they thought it had magical powers. This option seems unlikely given the systematic rejection of magic in the OT. Second, more scholars have concluded that the system aided memory retention in a largely nonliterate society. This notion has merit, though sometimes the acrostic format is elaborate enough to make one wonder if it was simpler to learn the acrostic pattern or the material itself. Third, other experts have claimed that the format allows for aesthetic beauty and artistic expression. Of course, other writers have found the acrostic systems to be forced and unnatural, so this situation may be a case of beauty being in the eye of the beholder. Still, the extensive use of various sorts of acrostics in Lamentations indicates that the book's author possessed great skill in this ancient art form. Thus, this third possibility has obvious merit, though it is probably not the only reason the author used acrostics. Fourth, many commentators have decided that the use of acrostics means that the author intends to convey a sense of completion, a sense that everything "from A to Z" is included in the text. This idea also has some merit, for Lamentations does indeed offer a rather comprehensive account of the nature and variety of suffering associated with the fall of Jerusalem and its aftermath. It is probable that options three and four are the best suggestions. It is therefore advisable to start with these possibilities and develop them as needed.

The aesthetic option may lead to further helpful observations on the book's structure and contents. For example the book's acrostics exhibit various differences in length of line, frequency of identical letters, and slight variation in alphabetic ordering, which creates distinct poems by means of the acrostic form (see Renkema, 48). Though such differences are hard to see in translation, they were evident to the book's original audience. These variations mark the poems as different yet very much connected works, a fact that has ramifications for determining the book's message (see "Theological Purposes in Lamentations" below). They also indicate that the subtle differences between the poems are original to the text (contra Westermann, 63), which has implications for the book's unity and authorship (see "Authorship and Date" above).

It is quite possible that the separate yet integrated acrostics among the poems of Lamentations also help structure the book as a whole. Scholars have long observed that Lam 3 is not only the numerical center of the book but the thematic and logical center as well. That is, the problems stated in chaps. 1 and 2 find at least a tentative solution in chap. 3, which in turn affects the contents of chaps. 4 and 5 (see Westermann, 63–76, for a survey of opinions). Bo Johnson (*ZAW* 97 [1985] 62) argues that the individual acrostics in the book may create an acrostic structure for the whole book that coincides with the book's message. He notes that chaps. 1 and 2 consist of twenty-two three-line segments whose first line begins with successive letters of the alphabet, that chap. 3 also consists of twenty-two three-line segments, but that each line begins with the appropriate letter of the alphabet, that chap. 4 consists of two-line segments that begin with the successive letters of the alphabet, and that chap. 5 has twenty-two segments of two lines each, none of which begins with the successive letter of the alphabet. Given this scheme, the book's acrostic forms intensify from chap. 1 to chap. 3, for chap. 3 is the most acrostic of all the poems (65). After this midpoint of the book, the acrostic forms lessen in intensity in chap. 4, which has a series of two-line segments, then fade out completely as chap. 5 has twenty-two lines but no alphabetic succession.

This format focuses the reader's attention on the flow of the book's message by careful use of poetic form. It guides readers toward an increased interest in the centrality of chap. 3, which in turn causes them to reexamine how chaps. 1 and 2 lead to that central point, and how chaps. 4 and 5 do or do not bring resolution to the issues raised earlier in the book. In this way the book's form and function merge.

Johan Renkema suggests a further way that the acrostics help shape the book's structure. He notes that at several places the particular acrostic segments correspond to one another. In other words, for example, the contents of the *alef* lines are similar. He asserts that 1:1, 2:1, 3:1, and 5:1 are linked by imagery associated with widowhood, misery, darkness, and disgrace (Renkema, 39). He offers similar poetic echoes for the *bet* and succeeding sections (39–40). Though one can dispute some of Renkema's linkages, his thesis is sound. Thematic connections do exist between the particular parts of the book's acrostics. Once more, then, the book connects form and message. What occurs here is not an instance of aesthetics for aesthetics sake but aesthetics in the service of the book's message.

So the acrostic form does many things in Lamentations. It helps create the five poems, and it helps readers distinguish one from the other. It helps the specific parts of the book relate to corresponding parts. It aids readers in focusing on the message of what at first seems to be five separate poems. It gives readers the sense that a thorough treatment of pain and sorrow has appeared in the book. In other words, the acrostic form is more than an artificial device. The acrostics make the book artistic and functional at the same time.

POETIC METER

Anyone attempting to discuss the poetic meter in Hebrew poetry cannot hope to proceed with anything close to scholarly consensus. In fact, in recent years the whole question of the nature of non-narrative OT texts has been raised again. Experts discussed the pros and cons of using terminology like parallelism, meter, and poetry. I will not rehearse or debate those matters here but will simply note that this commentary accepts the validity of using such terminology and at the same time gladly references ways in which the debate has brought important refinements to the discipline.

Though there is debate on the matter, there is a general scholarly consensus that there is some regularity in the meter of Lamentations that allows its readers a bit more certainty about its principles than is afforded interpreters of several other poetic books. This rhythm has typically been referred to as *qinah* meter, a term described in detail by Budde in his seminal 1882 article on Lamentations (*ZAW* 2 [1882] 1–52).

Budde writes that in Lam 1–4 (the strictly acrostic poems) the standard poetic line consists of two unequal segments, with the first segment being longer by one word than the second (5). He claims that the normal sequence was three words followed by two (3:2 meter), though he also observes that there are several verses in Lamentations that employ a different pattern (6). After surveying the use of this meter in Lamentations and related texts such as Isa 14 and Ezek 27 (6–23), Budde concludes that this poetic form was most likely used to mourn the dead (24–25). He states that Lamentations does not always use normal Hebrew poetic parallelism, yet he observes that the second of two lines often echoes the first (19). Thus, Budde argues that Lamentations has a recognizable genre (funeral lament), a clear meter (3:2, called *qinah*), and a fairly consistent pattern of parallelism (echoing technique). Refinements and discussions of Budde's work have been offered since the publication of this article, but the general outline of Budde's thesis remains the general outline of the discussion of the form, meter, and purpose of Lamentations to this day.

One particular refinement is in the area of the purpose of the 3:2 meter. Budde's article could leave the impression that the appearance of the 3:2 meter always signaled a funereal lament. Delbert Hillers states that "it seems less certain that this rhythm was necessarily associated with laments in ancient Hebrew usage, for laments occur without this rhythm (e.g., 2 Sam 1:17–27) and the rhythm occurs outside of laments" ("Lamentations, Book of," *ABD*, 4:139). David Noel Freedman's careful analysis of the language of acrostics indicates that Lamentations does indeed have the shorter second line, yet he also demonstrates that this meter exists in laments that are not strictly funeral laments (*HTR* 65 [1972] 392). Therefore, the 3:2 meter usually appears in texts that have lament as their main content, but this lament may not be a funeral lament. This point becomes important when discussing the historical connection between Lamentations and other ancient Near Eastern laments over fallen cities (see below).

The *qinah* has a distinct syntactical structure. In his analysis of the poetic syntax of Lamentations Delbert Hillers compares the book's poetic lines to the narrative syntax in Genesis. He discovers that in clauses with verbs Lamentations follows a standard verb-subject-prepositional-phrase format about two-thirds of the time (Hillers, "Observations on Syntax and Meter," 267–68). In the remaining cases the sequence of verb-prepositional phrase-subject or verb-direct object-prepositional phrase appears, though Hillers does not state in his article why these differences happen (268). Still, Hillers's study demonstrates that the poetic sentence structure of Lamentations generally follows what amounts to narrative syntax, though the book diverges from that norm slightly about one-third of the time.

In his 1983 article W. Randall Garr seeks to discern why these divergences occur on *qinah* meter, syntax, and style. After a careful and basically accurate treatment of these components in Lamentations, Garr reaches the following conclusions. First, the initial line (Line A) in the two-part poetic lines usually has the verb first but then employs several post-verb syntactical possibilities (*ZAW* 95 [1983] 73). This approach allows the author of Lamentations flexibility within what at first glance appears to be a very stringent 3:2 meter within an acrostic poem format. Second, the second line (line B) "is highly dependent upon the A line" (74). This means that "the B line functions as a modifier or as a statement adjunct to the first" (74). Thus, line B strengthens, elaborates upon, heightens, softens, or clarifies the point begun in line A. This echoing technique is made possible in part through the second part of the 3:2 meter being shorter than the first. Third, variations in the normal syntax occur so that the author may emphasize "one word or a group of words," as is the case when writers of narrative alter standard word order (74). Garr's observations help spell out how *qinah* syntax works. They especially aid interpreters' understanding of the relationship between the parts of individual poetic lines. More work needs to be done on how individual lines connect to one another to create whole poems, but Garr's article places such studies on firmer ground than would have been possible previously.

William H. Shea attempts to demonstrate that the *qinah* format's role in Lamentations exceeds that of the basic line. Indeed, he claims that the 3:2 sequence shapes the whole of the book. Shea first notes that the first three chapters of Lamentations are acrostics based on three-line segments and that the last two chapters are poems formed by two-line segments. He then writes, "As far as the two major blocks of poetic materials in Lamentations are concerned, therefore, they can be divided into sections of three chapters (1–3) and two chapters (4–5) each, or the 3:2 *qinah* pattern on so grand a scale that it encompasses the entire book of Lamentations" (*Bib* 60 [1979] 106). This theory also takes into account the longstanding "problem" that the first four chapters are acrostics but the last chapter is not. Shea argues that, though chap. 5 is not an acrostic, the chapter still has the same basic *qinah* meter as the other chapters. As for the unity of the book, Shea concludes, "Such a structure obviously presents a strong argument against the view that chapter five should be attributed to a later author than the first four acrostic chapters. To separate chapter five from the preceding four chapters would disrupt the very precise *qinah* structure in which the book was written as a comprehensive unit" (107). Though one could dispute parts of Shea's comments about authorship, Renkema is correct when he observes that Shea's proposal makes it unlikely that extensive editing of the book is the best explanation of the authorship of Lamentations (Renkema, 38).

Thus, Shea's article claims that the *qinah* form partners with the acrostic structure to make the book a coherent whole. Taken with Johnson's findings on the structure of the book of Lamentations (*ZAW* 97 [1985] 58–73), Renkema's conclusions on the connections between the acrostic segments, and Budde's discoveries concerning the *qinah* line, Shea's proposal aids an understanding of the author's artistic achievement. Unity of line, chapter, book, and message exists in Lamentations. At the same time, diversity occurs in ways calculated to demonstrate distinct poems and important poetic lines. As a whole, then, the book operates as a consistent, coherent, subtle unity, but not as a grindingly same unity, and its poetic meter plays a strong role in this artistic achievement.

Lamentations and Ancient Near Eastern Parallels

Bibliography

Ferris, P. W., Jr. *Genre of Communal Lament.* **Green, M. W.** "The Eridu Lament." *JCS* 30 (1978) 127–67. ———. "The Uruk Lament." *JAOS* 104 (1984) 253–79. **Gwaltney, W. C.** "The Biblical Book of Lamentations in the Context of Near Eastern Lament Literature." In *Scripture in Context II: More Essays on the Comparative Method.* Ed. W. Hallo, J. Moyer, and L. Perdue. Winona Lake, IN: Eisenbrauns, 1983. 191–211. **Jahnow, H.** *Hebräische Leichenlied.* **Kramer, S. N.** "Lamentation over the Destruction of Nippur." *Acta Sumerologica* 13 (1991) 1–26. ———. *Lamentation over the Destruction of Ur.* Chicago: Univ. of Chicago Press, 1940. ———. "Lamentation over the Destruction of Ur." In *ANET,* 455–63. **McDaniel, T. F.** "The Alleged Sumerian Influence upon Lamentations." *VT* 18 (1968) 198–209. **Michalowski, P.** *Lamentation over the Destruction of Sumer and Ur.* **Walton, J. H.** *Ancient Israelite Literature in Its Cultural Context: A Survey of Parallels between Biblical and Ancient Near Eastern Texts.* Grand Rapids, MI: Zondervan, 1989.

As was stated in the section on authorship and date (see above), over the past several decades scholars have noted similarities and differences between Lamentations and ancient Sumerian laments, especially those offered for fallen cities. Since this discussion is a vast and vital one, it is necessary to determine which parts of the debates are most relevant to Lamentations studies. This determination is made all the more difficult because anything one can learn about ancient laments has the potential to contribute to a more accurate interpretation of Lamentations. Still, given that these comparative studies typically stress either the nature of lament in general or laments over cities in particular, it makes sense to choose to examine the evidence related to laments over cities, since that is the clearest parallel to Lamentations. It is also appropriate to probe the extent (if any) to which Lamentations is dependent upon other ancient cultures for its form and content.

There are five Sumerian/Babylonian city laments that have been excavated in more than fragmentary form and translated into English. These texts include *Lamentation over the Destruction of Ur, Lamentation over the Destruction of Sumer and Ur, The Nippur Lament, The Eridu Lament,* and *The Uruk Lament* (Walton, *Ancient Israelite Literature,* 160). The laments over Ur are the most famous of these texts. They describe the destruction of Ur, an event that occurred ca. 2000 B.C.E., and may well date from the first three centuries of the second millennium B.C.E. (see Kramer, *ANET,* 455; Michalowski, *Lamentation over the Destruction of Sumer and Ur,* 16; Walton, *Ancient Israelite Literature,* 160). Since their publication, these texts have been compared to Lamentations to determine what literary elements the pieces might have in common. Generally speaking, there have been those who have argued that the texts are fairly similar and those who have claimed that the texts are part of the same general ancient milieu, but hardly identical in content, structure, and form.

S. N. Kramer has taken the former position. Beginning with his seminal 1940 monograph *(Lamentation over the Destruction of Ur),* Kramer argued that Sumer was the mother of Near Eastern lament, an art form that appeared as early as "the 24th century B.C." ("Lamentation over the Destruction of Nippur: A Preliminary Report," *ErIsr* 9 [1969] 89). Having translated at least the city laments for Ur and for Sumer and Ur, Kramer claimed that these poems might be dated "sometime in the first half of the second millennium B.C." (*ANET,* 455). Kramer also concluded that the lamentations for Ur served as prototypical laments for other fallen cities. Finally, he claimed that "the biblical *Book of Lamentations* owes no little of its form and content to its Mesopotamian forerunners, and, that the modern orthodox Jew who utters his mournful lament at the 'western wall' of 'Solomon's' long-destroyed Temple, is carrying on a tradition begun in Sumer some 4,000 years ago"(*ErIsr* 9 [1969] 89).

As could be expected, not all scholars have agreed that there is a clearly discernible historical connection between second-millennium B.C.E. Sumer and sixth-century B.C.E. Judah. Few if any have doubted that Sumerian lament preceded Israelite lament or that in some manner Israelite lament came to reflect this earlier tradition. But this agreement does not necessarily lead to the conclusion that Lamentations was directly influenced by these earlier poems. Kramer himself offers no explanation for how the connection took place.

Thomas F. McDaniel argues that it is difficult, if not impossible, to show dependence on an art form prevalent 1400 years prior to the time of the writing of Lamentations (*VT* 18 [1968] 200). He also refuses to place much emphasis on vocabulary and other linguistic likenesses between Lamentations and the Sumerian texts since the subject matter is so similar. Rather, he finds it more likely that Lamentations is closer in form to other biblical laments over cities (cf. Ezek 27). Thus, he prefers to "speak not so much of parallel literary motifs but of the common experience of the vanquished at the hands of the victor" (200–201). Delbert Hillers does not discount Sumerian influence altogether, but he also finds it hard to consider Lamentations the direct literary descendant of the Sumerian city laments ([1972], xxix).

In more recent works, W. C. Gwaltney, Jr. (1983), Piotr Michalowski (1989), and Paul W. Ferris, Jr. (1992), have examined the evidence offered by both schools of thought and come to different conclusions. Despite their disagreements, however, their studies of the subject are significant because they highlight the actual literary correspondences between Lamentations and the earlier Sumerian city laments, not just their potential historical connectedness.

Gwaltney's article ("The Biblical Book of Lamentations in the Context of Near Eastern Literature") has two basic purposes: to examine how Sumerian forms might have influenced Lamentations and to note similarities and dissimilarities between Lamentations and Sumerian city laments. On the first point, Gwaltney surveys the development of Sumerian/Babylonian laments and decides that the ancient city laments were written ca. 1925 B.C.E. and that they were never fully incorporated into the stock poems of the nation's liturgy (196). He then proceeds to argue that first-millennium Babylonian laments were composite in nature but that they still maintained elements of the city lament (203–5). Next, he compares Lamentations and finds what he considers several striking similarities and differences (see below). Finally, he notes that "Jewish clergy" could have encountered laments in Babylonian cultic activities and that "the exiles of the Northern Kingdom also had similar opportunities in the cities of Assyria to observe or participate in these rituals" (210). Clearly, Gwaltney thinks that it is important for historical and genetic reasons to maintain a close interpretational tie between Babylonian lament and Lamentations.

Gwaltney's literary analysis of Sumerian city laments, first-millennium Babylonian laments, and Lamentations is thorough and clear. For convenience' sake he divides his discussion into four parts: ritual occasions, form/structure, poetic techniques, and theology ("Biblical Book of Lamentations," 205). On the question of cultic context he notes that "we are without documentation to inform us" (209). In other words, there is insufficient evidence about the cultic usage of either Lamentations or the Babylonian texts to draw any solid conclusions. As for structure and organization, Gwaltney observes little sameness between how the texts unfold in the two traditions (209).

It is in poetic technique and theology that Gwaltney finds what he considers definite correspondences between Lamentations and Babylonian lament. He argues that common poetic techniques include the interchanging of first-, second-, and third-person speakers, the use of cries of woe and of interjections, and the use of tightly organized parallelism ("Biblical Book of Lamentations," 209). One might add to his list the appearance of phrases such as "How long?" and common pleas for the deity to look carefully at what has happened to the sufferer (see 206). Theological commonalities he lists include the deity causing the city's demise for some specified reason, the notion that the deity has abandoned the city, and the concept that the deity is all-powerful (208). Despite these theological similarities, Gwaltney also observes that Babylon includes such features as calls for the deity to awaken and the presence of a goddess mourning for the city that are not present in Lamentations. Thus, he does not claim that the two traditions are close to being identical.

In his *Lamentation over the Destruction of Sumer and Ur*, Piotr Michalowski offers a basic analysis of the city laments as a group. He finds no extensive correspondences between the city laments and Lamentations, a subject he does not really address. He also does not find many likenesses between one city lament and another. He writes, "From the formal point of view the texts that have been grouped together under the label of 'city laments' are not homogeneous. Except for the fact that they depict in great detail the fall and destruction of cities and states, as well as a decision by the gods to undo the disaster, they have little in common. All the known examples are divided into sections called *kirugu*, but the number and size of these sections differ in individual compositions, although the fragmentary state of *LE [The Eridu Lament]* and *LW [The Uruk Lament]* makes it difficult to generalize in this matter" (5–6). M. W. Green, who translated *The Eridu Lament*, makes a similar statement about the diversity in the city laments. She comments, "These five major compositions constitute a distinctive literary genre with a characteristic thematic content, but considerable stylistic and structural variety" (*JCS* 30 [1978] 127). Given Green's and Michalowski's observations about the city laments, then, it is difficult to determine how the genre could necessarily affect Lamentations in more than a general way. After all, the extent of borrowing between the Babylonian city laments themselves may be an open question.

Ferris examines a wide range of ancient laments, so his work is much broader than most of those cited above. Still, he treats city laments in some detail and interacts critically with Gwaltney's opinions. In his analysis of city laments, he observes that they all share a few basic structural components, such as a complaint of abandonment, a supplication to a deity, and an appeal for restoration. He also observes that more than one of the poems contain a description of the devastation (*Genre of Communal Lament*, 28–36). Thus, there are some elements of the Babylonian city laments that do appear in Lamentations. The question is whether those elements are enough alike to warrant considering Lamentations dependent on the earlier texts.

After a thorough examination of Hebrew individual and communal lament, Ferris addresses Gwaltney's assertions. Though he clearly respects the level of Gwaltney's scholarship, Ferris disagrees with Gwaltney's two major conclusions that the theology of the city laments and the poetic techniques they employ are similar enough to Lamentations to suggest that the biblical book was influenced by the Babylonian compositions. On the first of these points, Ferris admits that Gwaltney is correct in arguing that both the city laments and Lamentations depict their respective deities as powerful, as in charge of the relevant city's destruction, and as possessing anthropomorphic characteristics (*Genre of Communal Lament*, 170–71). But he argues that such divine traits exist in all sacred literatures, not just lament, and that the nature of lament would include the supplicants asking for help and bemoaning a calamity of some magnitude. On the second point, Ferris believes that Gwaltney skews the results by limiting his discussion to Lamentations, for Hebrew laments appear elsewhere as well. Therefore, Gwaltney's synthesis has the effect of allowing one to survey all the city laments, pick any of the elements that may be close to Lamentations, and argue for a close relationship between the two when a fuller analysis would display more generic differences. Thus, after a long and thorough examination of the relevant poems and viewpoints about them, Ferris concludes, "A close look at the data available just does not seem to support the theory that lament was something learned directly from the Babylonians during the exile. The Hebrew communal laments are sufficiently distinct and demonstrate an almost unique flexibility of form and style" (174). At the same time, he adds that the Babylonian and Hebrew poems come out of a common culture and share some features even if direct dependence cannot be proven (173–74).

Given the diverse nature of opinion on this subject and the possibility of further evidence being unearthed, one must be cautious in stating conclusions. Still, five matters deserve noting. First, Lamentations does stand in a long and honored line of city laments. That a Hebrew poet would consider Jerusalem worthy of such attention testifies to the status the city held in the author's mind. After all, it is given treatment afforded such great cities as Ur and Tyre. Second, Lamentations does have some thematic and poetic likenesses to Sumerian/Babylonian laments. These likenesses include a high view of the relevant deity, divine displeasure as the cause of the city's demise, lengthy descriptions of the city's devastation, and cries for divine aid. Third, there are major differences between the Babylonian laments and Lamentations. Polytheism reigns in the Babylonian account, while strict monotheism is the theological viewpoint expressed in Lamentations. Therefore, prayer itself has a different function and focal point in the two traditions. Fourth, there is not enough literary or historical evidence to link the Babylonian texts to Lamentations. This fact does not negate the strong likelihood that Israelite lament is in some manner historically dependent on earlier lament traditions. Fifth, one appropriate way of utilizing Babylonian parallels is as a dialogue partner for Lamentations. That is, reading the Babylonian city laments alongside Lamentations may allow interpreters to understand better what the author and audience of Lamentations may have experienced and expressed in their own setting. It may also demonstrate the distinctive faith of Israel as it emerged in the most terrible of times.

Genre: Lament and Acrostic

Bibliography

Ferris, P. W., Jr. *Genre of Communal Lament.* **Gunkel, H.** *Introduction to Psalms.* **Westermann, C.** *Praise and Lament in the Psalms.*

Given the preceding description of the acrostic format, poetic meter, and place of Lamentations in the ancient lament tradition, it is both easier and harder to determine the book's genre. On the one hand, the book's contents clearly mark Lamentations as a series of laments in acrostic form that include both individuals and the community of faith as a whole. Just as clearly, these laments are not standard, straightforward laments, if such texts exist in the OT. Rather, they are poems that mix forms, a fact recognized by Gunkel decades ago (see *Introduction to Psalms*, 82–98). In fact, Lamentations does not simply adapt and blend poetic forms. Rather, the author even employs narrative techniques, such as the appearance of an informed, if not omniscient, narrator; narrative syntax; description of events; and dialogue. In other words, the author crafts a book out of poems that effectively present Jerusalem's predicament by meshing standard poetic and selected narrative components.

Of course, lament studies have long been a staple of biblical criticism in general and form criticism in particular for many years. Thus, scholars have often described the fundamental literary elements of laments. For example, Gunkel claims that the main categories of community laments include: "1. a lamenting *complaint* over the misfortune; 2. a supplicational *petition* to YHWH to change the misfortune, whereby; 3. all types of thoughts appear in which one reproaches one's self for consolation or speaks before YHWH in order that he will hear and intervene" (*Introduction to Psalms*, 88 [emphasis original]). Claus Westermann, who has written as effectively as anyone on the nature of praise and lament, adds that communal laments regret "suffering and the disgrace of suffering" (*Praise and Lament in the Psalms*, 179) and that they often include questions such as "Why?" and "How long?" (176). He also stresses that the book of Lamentations is a plaintive lament, rather than a funeral dirge, for "the plaintive lament is directed towards God" rather than toward a community (95). Given these various elements, Ferris offers the following working definition of communal lament: "A communal lament is a composition whose verbal content indicates that it was composed to be used by and/or on behalf of a community to express both complaint, and sorrow and grief over some perceived calamity, physical or cultural, which had befallen or was about to befall them and to appeal to God for deliverance" (*Genre of Communal Lament*, 10). His analysis of Hebrew laments indicates that a variety of structural possibilities may be used to convey the necessary sorrow and grief.

As for individual laments, Gunkel lists four basic components: summons, complaint, petition, and assertion of confidence in the Lord (*Introduction to Psalms*, 152–80). Westermann basically agrees with Gunkel's categories, though he refines them into the following five segments: address (and introductory petition), lament proper, a turning toward God (confession of trust in the Lord), a petition, and a vow of praise (*Praise and Lament in the Psalms*, 170). Of course, there are several situations that may lead to the writing of laments, and the structural arrangements suggested by Gunkel and Westermann are basic, not universal, as they both freely admit.

One quickly realizes that no one particular type of lament predominates in the book of Lamentations. Based on Jahnow's work (*Hebräische Leichenlied*), Gunkel considers Lam 1, 2, and 4 communal complaints that have been transformed from dirges (*Introduction to Psalms*, 95). He classifies Lam 3 as a mixture of private and public complaints (94) and Lam 5 as a fairly straightforward communal complaint (82). Clearly, he treats all five poems as mixed forms rather than as standard individual or community laments. Though Westermann emphasizes that Lamentations is a series of poems that creates a communal complaint rather than a group of personal dirges, he basically agrees with Gunkel's comments on the form of the poems. They include elements associated with laments, but they do not share a set structural format (Westermann, 95–98). Therefore, Delbert Hillers correctly assesses the situation when he writes that the author of Lamentations "had no liturgical or literary models he followed slavishly. On the other hand, in language and imagery he follows tradition rather closely" ([1972], xxviii).

This analysis indicates that where genre is concerned the book of Lamentations has no exact biblical or ancient Near Eastern parallels. As Renkema observes, "Since there is nothing similar to Lamentations in terms of size in the OT, we are forced to assume that its five closely related songs are a unique literary creation" (41). This book is more than a mixing of forms that may reflect good or bad editing. This book is a masterful combining of related literary material. When one considers that this book meshes *qinah* meter and overall structure, combines individual and community lament, combines the basic syntax of narrative and poetry, uses the structure of acrostic without making all the acrostics the same, and provides thematic continuity from first poem to last, then one has to be impressed with the book's artistry even if one cannot put a specific name to the book's genre. The exegesis of Lamentations offered below will take these various parts of Lamentations into account but will not attempt to force the book into a specific known genre of biblical texts.

At the same time, it is appropriate to consider carefully what it means to interpret laments on their own merits, something Westermann in particular has tried to do in his work on Lamentations. He correctly states that over time laments have come to be devalued in scholarship and in formal worship settings: "This devaluation of the lament does not directly stem from the interpreters of the texts themselves; it is rooted in a pre-understanding. It is thought inappropriate to lament before God; lamentation is not compatible with proper behavior toward God. Lament disturbs or detracts from a pious attitude toward God" (81). Of course, this approach to Scripture, which Westermann deplores, removes readers of Scripture from much of the Bible. It removes reality from the theological equation and leads to spiritual dishonesty or disillusionment. A restoration of the lament genre to common worship could have many good effects, but Westermann offers the most important one: laments allow hurting people to use the language of suffering to come directly to God (89–91). There is no need to recover, then report back to God how one felt. There can be a direct approach to the one who can help and a restoration of relationship.

If the language and purpose of lament can be recaptured, then the genre itself will be redeemed for new audiences. Lamentations is the clearest representation of lament theology in the OT. It keeps faith with the past by using older forms and keeps pace with the future by forging new ways to make consistent forms fresh and sufficiently creative. Thus, it may have great potential for making lament a viable genre for today's people of faith.

Theological Purposes in Lamentations

Bibliography

Albrektson, B. *Studies in the Text and Theology of the Book of Lamentations.* **Childs, B. S.** *Introduction to the Old Testament as Scripture.* Philadelphia: Fortress, 1980. 590–97. **Ferris, P. W.** *Genre of Communal Lament.* **Gottwald, N. K.** *Studies in the Book of Lamentations.* **House, P. R.** *Old Testament Theology.* Downers Grove, IL: InterVarsity Press, 1998. 483–89. **Linafeldt, T.** *Surviving Lamentations.* **O'Connor, K. M.** *Lamentations and the Tears of the World.* **Preuss, H. D.** *Old Testament Theology.* Trans. L. G. Perdue. 2 vols. Louisville, KY: Westminster John Knox, 1991, 1992.

As the survey of opinions on authorship and date has demonstrated, virtually every major work on Lamentations has made some theological comments about the book. At the same time, many of these comments do not necessarily draw out the book's theological implications. Indeed, Westermann states that these observations may be boiled down to two basic positions: the book states why the nation has suffered and how it may find relief from this suffering (76). Therefore, it is appropriate to analyze the theology of Lamentations a bit further to discover its distinct witness and its role in the overall theology of the OT. This analysis reveals that Lamentations utilizes texts on covenantal curses and blessings, prophetic warnings and exhortations, and psalmic reflections on Jerusalem's fall to establish God's righteousness and faithfulness, on the one hand, and on human sinfulness, contrition, puzzlement, legitimate questioning, patience, and worship, on the other. Adaptation of well-known forms provides the literary means by which the acrostics present these ideas.

Gottwald's and Albrektson's monographs have been formative in the study of the theology of Lamentations. They summarize and assess previous theological opinions on the book and in turn have been cited themselves in most subsequent works. Thus, these volumes are pivotal in the field. They invite further writing on the subject.

Gottwald (*Studies in the Book of Lamentations,* 51) argued that at the heart of the theology of Lamentations lies a single question: Why did Israel suffer so greatly so soon after the reforms instituted by Josiah ca. 622 B.C.E.? (51). He concludes that this question is asked "at the point in Israel's life where the tension between history and faith is, for the first time, most sharply posed" (51). How so? Because at this point in their history the people had been schooled by adherents of Deuteronomistic theology to expect that reform would bring blessing. Thus, when defeat and destruction followed reform, the people sought an explanation. Israel expresses its dismay in Lamentations by using themes of reversal that depict past glory and present pain and its hopes for the future by declaring that God can once again reverse their fortunes, this time in a positive direction (53–60). In this way the nation states its pain, its faith in God, its belief in meaningful history, and its belief in God's lordship over history (62). Overall, then, the book participates in the great tradition of Israelite prophetic thought yet also unites the priestly concern for liturgy with the prophetic desire for covenantal faithfulness (114–19).

Obviously, there is much to commend in Gottwald's work. In fact, at the risk of overstatement, it is possible to conclude that virtually all he writes is true except for his central historical point that the people had been faithful reformers and thus had reason to wonder why they were forced to suffer so greatly. After all, this historical point is not verified by Lamentations itself or by the overall witness of the OT. Indeed the opposite point seems to be made by both sources. At the same time, Gottwald's description of the literary and theological means the author employs is largely accurate. The book does focus on past and potential future reversal. It does maintain continuity with prophetic and priestly emphases, and it does steer a course between feelings of doom and expressions of hope. The author of Lamentations believes that the nation has a present and a future with God, not just a past. In other words, the theological gains Gottwald makes should not be obliterated solely by important disagreements about his basic historical conclusions.

Similar sentiments can be expressed about Albrektson's monograph. After an excellent discussion of the text of Lamentations, which includes detailed comparisons of the Hebrew and Syriac versions, Albrektson interacts extensively with Gottwald's volume. He concludes that Gottwald's strengths are considerable, especially in the areas of content analysis. At the same time, he also disagrees with Gottwald's assertion that the question of how Israel could suffer so greatly after Josiah's reform is the key to the theology of Lamentations. He thinks that Deuteronomistic theology is prevalent in Lamentations and draws particular attention to the links between Deut 28 and Lamentations (*Studies in the Text and Theology*, 234). He concludes, with Gottwald, that Deuteronomistic theology is one major strand in Lamentations theology, even though he thinks that the people had reason to expect the covenant curses, not the covenant blessings (see Deut 27–28).

To this Deuteronomistic strand Albrektson adds a Zion emphasis that he believes is integral to the book. He notes that Psalms of Zion such as Pss 46, 48, and 76 stress Jerusalem's inviolability; he then observes that passages like Lam 2:15; 4:12, 20; and 5:19 include images similar to those in the Zion psalms (*Studies in the Text and Theology*, 220–29). Next, he asserts, "'The key to the theology of Lamentations is in fact found in the tension between specific religious conceptions and historical realities: between the confident belief of the Zion traditions in the inviolability of the temple and city, and the actual brute facts" (230). Then Albrektson cites the many questions and descriptions of pain in Lamentations as evidence that the Israelites had thought that the city was inviolable. Finally, he states that the Deuteronomistic and Zion traditions are conjoined in Lamentations by a common interest in the central sanctuary. It is this linkage, according to Albrektson, that makes the author's interpretation of history allow for God's sovereignty on the one hand and the people's need to reach out to their God through prayers, confessions, and questions on the other (235).

Albrektson's achievement is, like Gottwald's, considerable. His emphasis on the connection between Deuteronomistic and Zion theology is necessary for one to grasp the full achievement of the theology of Lamentations. His rejection of Gottwald's central historical question is appropriate, and his identification of Israel's questions about Zion's fall is helpful for tracing the book's structure and argument. Overall, then, this volume adds certain significant elements to the discussion.

Despite these advances, however, there are a few places where Albrektson either overstates or understates aspects of the theology of Lamentations. The chief overstatement is in his conclusions about the inviolability of Jerusalem. Though one can hardly write an indisputable statement on this subject, it is fair to question whether the inviolability of Zion and the impregnability of Jerusalem are necessarily the same thing in OT theology. After all, Zion is God's home where he dwells with his redeemed people unhindered by sin or rebellion in Pss 46, 48, and 76. Similar themes exist in Isa 25, where the word ציון, "Zion," does not appear, but the concept of God's mountain certainly does. Zion cannot be overthrown because God, Zion's king, cannot be overthrown. Zion's people are safe because they live where death has been eradicated (Isa 25:6–12) and where Jerusalem has been transformed along with all creation (Isa 65:17–25). Jerusalem, on the other hand, is the place where God has chosen to put his name (see Deut 12:8–12; 1 Kgs 9:3; and so on), yet also a place that can become a heap of ruins if disobedience becomes a way of life for the people (1 Kgs 9:6–9). In short, Zion is often portrayed as a glorified Jerusalem, but Jerusalem is not always designated as Zion.

God's choice of Jerusalem and threats against Jerusalem are particularly clear in the "temple sermons" in Jer 7 and 26. Further, in Lamentations itself the belief among the people and some of their enemies that the city could not be taken (4:12), though related in the book, should not be equated with the views of the author. The author has great sympathy with the people's plight and with the results of their tendency to believe the lies told them by their priests, kings, and prophets (Lam 2:9–10; 4:13) but does not seem utterly surprised that sin has led to judgment. In other words, the author views things much as the prophet Jeremiah did. Thus, Albrektson's assessment of the connection between Deuteronomistic theology and Zion theology in the OT as a whole needs refinement, which means that his conclusions about Lamentations do as well. This assessment is not intended to diminish his contribution to Lamentations studies, though, since his work provides the grounds for such discussion and disagreement.

As for the commentary tradition, surveys by Westermann (76–81), Provan (20–25), and Renkema (58–63) have shown that commentators usually take one of three basic viewpoints on the theology of Lamentations. They conclude that the book offers an explanation for Jerusalem's suffering, that it points to a way out of the suffering, or that it provides a way by which worshipers may express their pain to God and to one another. Of course, these ideas often overlap in the various discussions. Though Westermann, Provan, and Renkema do not find excessive fault with the first two of these emphases, they stress the need to go beyond these issues to consider the implications of the third option more fully. Westermann in particular wishes to raise awareness of the importance of "complaint," or "lament," in biblical faith (see Westermann, 81). Provan hopes that the effects of suffering, such as feelings of abandonment, isolation, and rejection, will be taken into consideration (see Provan, 24). Renkema maintains that the nation's puzzlement over the cause of their plight and what it meant was at the heart of the book's theology and that this puzzlement is expressed by the prayers found in the book (Renkema, 62–65).

These emphases in the commentary tradition are not dissimilar to those found in Gottwald and in Albrektson. The first concern, the need to find a reason for the destruction, coincides with Gottwald's statements about the correlation between expectations associated with reform and the reality of the city's demise, as well as with Albrektson's comments on the people's concerns about the inviolability of Jerusalem. These agreements seem to rely in part on interpreting the people's questioning as unjust in some way. In other words, the people are asking why they have suffered when they have been faithful to some degree or why the city has been sacked when God promised such a catastrophe could never occur. A divine promise seems to have been vacated.

One problem with this viewpoint is that the book itself does not make such claims. The people do mourn their losses. They do consider them perhaps more than sufficient for the crimes committed. They most emphatically want their pain to cease, and they definitely consider their enemies to be as worthy of punishment as they. But these assertions are not accompanied by claims of innocence, as is often the case in similar passages in Psalms (see Pss 3–7). In fact, there seems to be an acceptance of guilt and a need to confess sin. The people in Lamentations lay their woes at the feet of their own nation's sins, yet they continue to reach out to the God who alone can deliver them from the present horrible distress. In this way, the book operates somewhat like the book of Job, but in reverse. It demonstrates that those who suffer because of their own sins may cry out to God as readily as innocent sufferers do.

The second concern stated by commentators, the need to find a way out of the suffering, is not dealt with as extensively by Gottwald and Albrektson, yet it is not absent altogether. Gottwald, Albrektson, and the commentators agree that Lam 3 is crucial for grasping how Israel may come through this time of trouble. This chapter offers an extensive reflection by an individual inextricably linked to the nation as a whole. The individual admits his own sin, confesses God's faithfulness, and prays a community prayer for return to God and punishment of the nation's enemies. Afterwards, chap. 5 concludes the book with a communal prayer that the Lord will restore the people. Albrektson notes that these passages indicate that the nation must cease trusting in God supposedly enthroned in an inviolable temple and learn to trust in God who reigns supreme and unfettered in history (239). Gottwald also expresses the importance of God's sovereignty in history and adds that Lam 3:31, which states that God "does not afflict from his heart," is "the high watermark of Lamentations' understanding of God" (*Studies in the Book of Lamentations,* 99). As long as Israel believes that the Lord does not gladly or arbitrarily judge human beings, there is a theology of hope that can sustain the people and lead them to a new and stronger relationship with the God of history, who is also their covenant God.

Surely these points of agreement between the commentators and the theologians are sound. Lamentations does base its theology of hope, its theology of pressing beyond the current situation, on the character of God. Because God is just and righteous, the people have suffered for their covenant breaking. This suffering has been shared by the faithful and unfaithful in Israel. In effect, God's faithfulness to the covenant has required that the nation receive the penalty of its own unfaithfulness (see Deut 28:15–68). At the same time, the covenant also promises forgiveness and renewal when repentance occurs (see Deut 30:1–10), so the nation can now count on the faithfulness of God in a more congenial and positive way. All hope does rest in the Lord, the one who rules history. What remains unclear at the end of Lamentations is exactly how the Lord of history will choose to live up to his faithfulness at this juncture in Israel's national history, which means that faithful individuals must likewise wait to learn how the Lord will work in their personal circumstances.

The third concern stated by the commentators, that Lamentations expresses the language of complaint and sorrow, is clearly shared by Gottwald and Albrektson, but it is the commentators who press this matter the most vigorously. This may be the case because of the strong form-critical tradition shared by several of these writers. If so, then it is not surprising that Westermann has made a particularly strenuous effort to show the importance of treating the laments in Lamentations as laments, not simply as comments about God, Israel, or the intersection of history and theology. He opposes what he believes is the general devaluation of laments as a valid expression of biblical faith, either through overt statements of their unsuitability for current prayer or indirectly through the turning of the laments into mere confessions of human sin or of God's nature (81–84). Instead, Westermann affirms, "The real significance of laments resides in the way they allow the suffering of the afflicted to find expression" (81). He wishes to keep alive the validity of lament as a Christian way of praying so that the church will not give way to triumphalism, pride, and unwillingness to see the pain inherent in human existence (82). He also wishes to stress the many ways laments express human suffering, which in turn impacts human relationships and human-divine relationships (96).

Westermann is not alone in these concerns. Provan states that Lamentations seeks to draw readers into the suffering depicted in the book. He adds, "We are further being invited to learn from their experience, to participate in their attempt to relate their experience to the reality of God. The book reminds us in a forceful way of the challenge of suffering to faith, and invites us to feel and to ponder its significance" (Provan, 24). To enter into the book's message in this way one must learn to speak the book's language, not just read it to find a swift way out of pain.

Renkema appreciates Westermann's theological reclamation of the lament as a legitimate form of prayer. At the same time, he concludes, "Westermann's obsession with the original form of Lamentations as complaints of the people during the great distress of 587 prevents him from seeing what actually happened: not distress followed by lament-prayer—as was usually the case—but distress followed by disillusionment!" (Renkema, 60). This disillusion stemmed from their amazement at the difference between the events of 587 and what the people thought they knew about God's character (62). They did not think that God's punishment would be so severe. Thus, it seems unjust to them now. At the same time, their belief in God's essence and God's deeds in history, especially his kingship over nations, provided a mental framework for a theology of hope (66–69). This belief, forged in adversity, is best stated in Lam 3, where theology and reality particularly come together (70). Through these emphases Renkema accepts Westermann's basic premise about the value of lament yet pushes beyond literary form to theological principles stated by means of that form.

Recently, some volumes committed more to theological reflection on Lamentations than to traditional verse-by-verse technical analysis of the book have taken new paths toward understanding its theology. Based in part on concern for issues related to evil and suffering in a post-Holocaust, post-World-Trade-Center-bombings world, and in part on Westermann's insistence that Lamentations voices pain and demonstrates human survival more than it explains human suffering, these scholars openly discuss God's abuse of and violence against Jerusalem.

Tod Linafelt examines Lam 1–2 and compares these texts to ancient and contemporary materials he considers survival literature. He highlights three ideas in Lam 1–2 (*Surviving Lamentations*, 18). First, he believes current readers need to find "strategies for surviving the book's harsh and violent, as well as theologically challenging, images and language." Second, he agrees with Westermann's "brief aside" that survival is the main issue in Lamentations (see Westermann, 81). Third, he argues that the survival of Zion's children is a major issue in Lam 1–2 and also concludes that the book's female characters deserve more scholarly treatment than they have received in the past. Survival is not easy according to Linafelt, since it truly only occurs in the afterlife of Lamentations, where readers fill in the gap that God's absence in the book leaves (*Surviving Lamentations*, 61).

Both Kathleen O'Connor (*Lamentations and the Tears of the World*, 110–24) and F. W. Dobbs-Allsopp (44–46) discuss what they call the "abusing God" and "divine violence," respectively, before moving on to describe what hope the text offers. O'Connor asserts that Lamentations offers a "chorus of contradictions" about God, for the book speaks both of God's goodness and of God's willingness to torture and abuse human beings (111–13). Given the difficulties related to this observation, O'Connor writes that readers often justify or ignore divine violence and texts about violence or consider God both loving and abusive yet beyond censure because of divine sovereignty (116–19). She decides to pursue another path, which is to read Lamentations as a book whose power as the word of God must emerge from the community, whose members "must reincarnate the revealed word in [the community's] own context" (121). In fact, she believes that the book models this process since it reveals differing perspectives on God. At the end of the day, O'Connor concludes that the book leaves readers with the slender hope expressed in Lam 3:33 that God does not judge from the heart. She hopes that God's silence at the end of the book reveals that "God has no ready explanation for the catastrophes facing the beloved people. Instead God suffers as the whole community accuses God of evil, hateful deeds. Maybe God's silence veils God's innocence rather than reveals divine calculated destruction. I want it to be so" (124).

Dobbs-Allsopp offers related comments. He writes that the ultimate reason for God's violence must remain shrouded in mystery, yet some observations can be made (44). For example, "violence is part of the scriptural witness to God," the chief example of which is Jesus' crucifixion; "violence cannot be treated in isolation from other language about God"; confronting violence in God will force readers to confront violence in general; and believers cannot justify violence but must admit that it exists (44–46). Like Linafelt, Dobbs-Allsopp believes that hope resides somewhat in survival as long as survival means "projected life" (46). Further, he locates hope in human dignity that "reasserts the goodness for which God created human beings" (47). Like O'Connor, he also focuses on Lam 3:19–24 and 3:25–39, but he cautions against using these verses to the extent that they trivialize horrible events such as the Holocaust (48). Thus, the book includes "theodic and antitheodic poles" that need to be maintained. Still, Dobbs-Allsopp concludes that whatever hope exists resides in God and, agreeing with Jon Levenson, asserts that time spent asking God to blast away evil may be better spent than time spent attempting to explain why evil exists (48).

These volumes are just three of several that may well signal a new development in studies in OT theology in general and Lamentations theology in particular. They reflect a hermeneutical shift not just from the text to the community of faith but from the community to the current reader as the basis of the text's meaning as well. Interestingly enough, these scholars use the text as their authority for leaving the text. They do so for a good reason, which is to find ways to comfort hurting people. Thus, if one disagrees with them, it can hardly be on the basis of their intentions. Rather, it must be on the basis of their method and on the results that method does or does not produce. If they are wrong in their method, then they may not achieve this worthy goal.

These recent writers make several important theological contributions. First, they take Lamentations seriously as a book that has much to contribute to current theological-ethical issues. Second, they treat the nature of God as a serious contemporary moral issue. Their approach to theology is theocentric, not just anthropocentric. Third, they take the questions normal suffering people ask quite seriously. In doing so they push the limits of traditional theological constructs. Fourth, they indeed take laments seriously as laments. They do not fail to attempt to take the poems as poems that express pain.

At the same time, there are problems with their approaches to the theology of Lamentations. First, they do not note that the different speakers in Lamentations agree about what has happened to Jerusalem. There are indeed alternating and distinctive voices in the book, yet these are complementary, not competing, voices. Every character agrees that Israel's sin has caused this pain, that God has brought this pain, and that the pain is severe. Second, they do not accept the book's own statements about the original context. That is, they do not fully believe the book's speakers when they state that all the book's sufferers are not innocent sufferers. Of course, they correctly observe how the speakers in Lamentations mourn the treatment of innocent children, and this issue deserves to be addressed. At the same time, it is more than an open question whether one should consider God abusive at this point or the Israelites the most negligent parents imaginable. The biblical testimony is that these parents ignored warning after warning before the Babylonians came. Third, they treat Lamentations in isolation rather than in the context of biblical theology. Of course, this critique is open to the countercritique of why one should give the whole biblical witness priority, but it is difficult to understand the book's genre, purpose, or setting without recourse to those texts. Fourth, they seem to focus on who should be blamed for the pain rather than on the restoration of the relationship between God and Israel, which is a major point of the third chapter. They correctly note God's silence, but blame is not the point there either. What matters is how that silence may be bridged, a fact that the people's earnest prayers in chaps. 4 and 5 attest.

Given the insights found in Gottwald's and Albrektson's monographs and the theological comments on Lamentations found in Westermann, Provan, Renkema, Linafelt, K. M. O'Connor, and Dobbs-Allsopp, it is appropriate to take their conclusions into consideration when summarizing the theology of Lamentations. Stated briefly, they establish the importance of blending Deuteronomistic, Zion, and lament themes. They also demonstrate the necessity of examining the nature of God and the nature of the Israelites as these portraits develop in Lamentations, and the appropriateness of positing how the people affected by Jerusalem's fall understood God and his acts in history. To pull these and other thematic elements together, the following summary of the theology of Lamentations uses four centering themes: God and the people of God, God and Jerusalem, God and the nations, and God and prayer. From these categories a portrait of God in Lamentations will be drawn.

GOD, THE PEOPLE OF GOD, AND THEIR SUFFERING

Readers encounter God in Lamentations through the people of God, through the words and prayers of Israelites affected by the destruction of their nation's capital. It is therefore reasonable to begin a discussion of the theology of Lamentations with an examination of how the Lord relates to Israel in the book. Several features emerge from the text, not all of them immediately flattering to God or to the people.

First, several passages depict the Lord as the harsh judge of perpetually sinful Israel. For instance, the first four verses of the book describe Jerusalem as a woman who has suffered great reversal and horrible deprivation (Lam 1:1–4). Then Lam 1:5 states why this suffering has occurred—Israel has sinned against God, which has led the Lord to cause her tremendous grief. Later, Lam 1:12 indicates that the grief and pain are the result of God's fierce anger. At the same time, the book confesses that God's fierce anger is a result of his righteousness, not an impulse in opposition to that righteousness (Lam 1:18). As the book proceeds, these themes become regular parts of the laments, particularly those found in chaps. 1, 2, and 4, and indeed the book ends with a plea to God for relief from the horrors of the devastation (Lam 5:19–22). God has punished as thoroughly as Israel has sinned, a horrible conclusion to a long era of the nation's history.

Second, the book indicates that harsh punishment has come in part because the Lord is a God who keeps the promises he makes to his people. God is faithful to his word and indeed rules the world by means of his word (Lam 3:37–38). Jerusalem's demise comes as the fulfillment of God's word (Lam 2:17). Herein lies one of the book's many ironies: the same truthfulness and dependability that bring the people hope in Lam 3:22–23 also bring them destruction. This point underscores the multifaceted nature of Deuteronomistic theology. God is always loving and truthful, which means God must always be willing to punish the very sins that make a relationship between Israel and God marred or temporarily broken, for love requires the protection of a crucial relationship.

Third, Lamentations states that the Lord is the one to whom Israel may and must pray. God sees (1:11; 1:20; 3:59), hears (3:56), remembers (3:19; 5:1), and delivers (3:26, 57–58), so God is the one to whom the people turn for help. Those who pray to the Lord expect that he is compassionate, faithful, and willing to exercise lovingkindness (3:22–23). They realize that God's first impulse is not to judge, for he does not judge "from his heart" (3:33). They accept that their sins, not God's failure as a covenant partner, have caused their tragedy. They also count on their relationship with God to have an effect on his willingness to hear, forgive, restore, and renew (2:20).

Without question, one thing that makes the laments so excruciatingly poignant is that God's people utter them. The situation is tragic, for God has caused this grief to envelop the very ones he has loved and cared for since the days of Abraham, the very ones he has loved and elected (Deut 7:7–8). The situation is also tragic because God's people have pushed their loving God to the necessity of demonstrating love by exercising severe punishment (Deut 7:9–11). In fact, this punishment is awful enough that the people ask their God to remember whom he has judged (Lam 2:20). Despite this extraordinary situation, it is the relationship itself that causes the people to hope in God, for it is the relationship that has revealed and established the nature of God in Israelite history. The fact that God has punished Israel does not negate the covenantal relationship. God's people remain God's people.

GOD AND JERUSALEM/ZION

Albrektson's monograph *(Studies in the Text and Theology)* highlights the need to understand God's attitude toward Jerusalem/Zion and correctly asserts that the theology of Lamentations is greatly concerned with the city's demise and future status. One must remember, however, that the city itself is not God's main concern. The people have this primary importance. Still, the city's role is vital and is best understood as standing as the visible symbol of God's ongoing love for the nation, whether that ongoing love is in the near, distant, or eschatological future. In this way the book once again keeps faith with Deuteronomistic theology.

Jerusalem's destruction symbolizes the defeat of the nation as a whole. As is true of other ancient laments for cities, the lament for Jerusalem is powerfully significant because the capital city represents all the other cities that have been overrun. If Jerusalem has fallen, then what has happened to all the less significant places in the land? If Jerusalem, the nation's strongest citadel, has been breached, then surely the whole land lies in ruins. Without this visible symbol of national prowess, the populace could easily lose heart.

Of course, more than this basic important theme is included in Jerusalem's demise. In Deuteronomistic texts God promises to choose one specific place for sacrifices and worship (Deut 12:5–14). Early in Israelite history this place was Shiloh (see Josh 18:1; Judg 18:31; 1 Sam 1–2; Jer 7:12–15), but David later placed the ark of the covenant at Jerusalem as a means of centralizing worship there, an act God blesses (see 2 Sam 6–7). Solomon transferred the ark to the newly built temple early in his reign (1 Kgs 8:1–13), and God promised to put his name there forever, unless the nation turned from serving their God (1 Kgs 9:1–9). Jeremiah's temple sermons (see Jer 7; 26) are basically messages on the ideas found in 1 Kgs 9:1–9. Thus, the temple represented the place where the Lord placed his name, so it is a very special edifice; yet it is a place that God may well vacate (see Ezek 10:1–22) if the nation no longer obeys the covenant stipulations for continuing relationship. God may act in righteous freedom. It is not a building that will stand no matter how its occupants act, so Jerusalem is not a city that cannot be breached no matter what its people and leaders do.

Without question, many Israelites seemed to have a different notion from the one presented in this literature. Indeed, Jeremiah's temple sermons attempt to correct persons who break the covenant and believe that as long as the temple stands they are safe in God's promised land (Jer 7:1–15). How did the people acquire such a misconception? Though it is impossible to say for certain, some scholars have suggested that this belief arose from Zion theology such as that reflected in Psalms and Isaiah. If this is the source, then one must assess the accuracy of their conclusions about those sources. Does the Bible contain conflicting Zion/Jerusalem theologies? If so, on which side does Lamentations stand?

To begin to answer these questions for the context of Lamentations it is necessary to note a few foundational principles. First, Isaiah, Jeremiah, and Psalms all agree that Jerusalem/Zion is a place specially used by God. It is on Mount Zion, adjacent to Jerusalem, that the temple was built. Therefore, it was on Zion that the people praised God; lamented to and before the Lord; offered appropriate, atoning sacrifices; and generally experienced communion with God and community with one another (see H. D. Preuss, *Old Testament Theology*, 2:46). All this was possible because God had chosen this place for these purposes. Every strand of OT theology agrees on this basic premise.

Second, Isaiah, Jeremiah, and Psalms all agree that God rejects Jerusalem and hands it over to its enemies (see Isa 1:4–9; 3:16–26; 8:5–15; 29:1–4; Pss 74; 79; Jer 7:1–15; 52; see Preuss, *Old Testament Theology*, 2:44–46) because the people of God refuse to serve their God. The importance of Jerusalem/Zion as a place does not protect even it from the results of the nation's sinful behavior. Significance and inviolability must not be mistaken for the same thing. Lamentations may present the most obvious evidence of this principle.

Third, Isaiah, Jeremiah, and Psalms also agree that God will once again choose Jerusalem to be a special place (see Preuss, *Old Testament Theology*, 2:50–51). There remains a future role for Jerusalem/Zion within the history of Israel. This role is associated with the people's resettling in the land (Isa 14:1; Jer 32:1–15; Ps 126; and so on) and with their renewed worship at the old site (see also Hag 1–2). Thus, Jerusalem is not like Shiloh, the first central place the Lord chose (Jer 7:1–15), for it never loses its prominence.

Fourth, Isaiah, Jeremiah, and Psalms stress that there is an eschatological future for Jerusalem/Zion. It is this theme that most clearly includes what are generally considered inviolability elements. In this Jerusalem/Zion there is no more death (Isa 25:6–12) or sickness, for it is a completely recreated Jerusalem (Isa 65:17–25). This Jerusalem/Zion is associated with the new covenant, which is an eternal covenant (Jer 31:31–40). This Jerusalem/Zion is the headquarters of the Davidic messiah (see Ps 2). Therefore, this Jerusalem/Zion is a purified and glorified city, a place where the holy God of Israel reigns over the faithful from all nations forever (see Isa 25:6–12). It is the capital of an eschatological kingdom. In this way Zion theology ultimately removes the effects of sin brought to light through Deuteronomistic theology.

Given these principles, then, it is important to note the difference between what the OT itself teaches and what some Israelites may have believed. Some Israelites no doubt believed that the sinful city of Jerusalem could be equated absolutely with Zion, the holy city in which the Lord dwells with his people. Thus, they probably thought that their city could never be breached. They may have read past deliverance, such as the one during the Sennacherib crisis of 701 B.C.E., as evidence for the validity of their convictions. If so, then they were not in concert with the canonical witness of the whole of Scripture. They did not grasp the confluence of Deuteronomistic and Zion theology. To the extent that the original audience of Lamentations believed a false, or at least incomplete, theology, that audience suffered disillusionment. Likewise, their future comfort depended on the extent to which they accepted a more balanced approach to Jerusalem theology, and Lamentations presses them to accept this type of theological thinking.

GOD AND THE NATIONS

Lamentations does not offer the sort of extensive treatment of the nations found in books like Isaiah, Jeremiah, or the Twelve, but elements of the relationship between God and the nations appear nonetheless. Most of these elements refer to God's role as judge of the whole earth more than to his role as the redeemer of people from all lands. Still, it is essential to note that, as judge, God treats Israel and the nations the same. Neither entity may live as it pleases and escape the Lord's wrath. Both are responsible to the covenant God of Israel.

To illustrate the consistency of God's actions with Israel and the nations in Lamentations, it is appropriate to turn briefly again to God's work with Israel. Obviously, in Lamentations the Lord has grown weary of Israel's sin and chosen to judge that sin. God's judgment takes the form of an invasion of Jerusalem by a foreign army, of terrible suffering resulting from the city's defeat, and of agony associated with living in a devastated place. Lamentations indicates that the Lord does not spare the covenant people any of the pain that comes from ignoring the judge of all the earth. It also asserts that the Babylonians are God's agents of punishment, for God sent them.

Having noted how God has treated Israel, one can see that the Lord deals with the nations in a similar manner. Though most of the information about the nations emerges in the book's prayers, this information still stands as *the author's* convictions. Having expressed pain, sorrow, and contrition, the book calls upon the Lord to judge the wickedness of Israel's enemies in Lam 1:22. At this point the book asserts that the enemies are God's messengers of punishment, yet at the same time it recognizes that the invaders have sinned by committing atrocities (see also Lam 5:11). Similar sentiments are stated in chap. 3, for there the "man who has seen affliction" intones that God does not afflict willingly; nor does God approve of injustice (Lam 3:33–36), which probably refers to the actions of Israel's enemies. He also prays that Israel's enemies will be judged (Lam 3:64–66). In Lam 4:22, the text states that Zion's miseries are nearly over, but those of Edom are about to begin. Again, the reason for the punishment is the foreign nation's sins. At every juncture the poet asks the Lord to punish such sin, and at every juncture the expectation is that God will comply.

Clearly, the book of Lamentations expects that God will apply the same standards of justice to the invaders as he has to Israel. Those who sin through committing injustice, atrocities, and other acts of violence cannot escape divine wrath. There is no concrete expression of hope for the nations, such as occurs in Isa 19:21–25 or Zeph 3:8–9, but such hopes for Israel are not exactly trumpeted in the book either. Hope is possible, even probable, yet hardly an overt part of the book's message. Still, if one can expect that the God who judges Israel will also renew Israel, then one can likewise expect that he has similar plans for the nations as well.

GOD AND PRAYER

In its final written form Lamentations is nothing if it is not a book of prayer. This fact forces readers to deal with the nature, purpose, and boundaries of prayer, especially those of lament. Doing so involves readers in wrestling with the nature and acts of God, issues that are inextricably linked to prayer and its components. The prayers in Lamentations indicate that there is only one God to whom one may pray. They confess that this God is fully righteous; that this God hears and answers prayer; that this God is willing to hear and respond to hard-hitting, complaint-oriented prayer; and that this God is constantly compassionate and faithful to the covenant people. In short, this God rules over the whole of creation and of history.

It is striking, given the ancient context of lament, that Lamentations addresses all its concerns to one God. Other nations' laments often sought aid from a secondary or tertiary deity when a primary god did not respond favorably (see Ferris, *Genre of Communal Lament*, 28–45). In the OT, however, there is no other deity to whom the people may turn. As is true in Psalms, Job, and other suffering texts, Lamentations offers a clear monotheistic faith. If the author believed that another deity could help, surely that deity would be invoked. Surely if there was ever a time when persons of faith might seek another deity, it would be when life was far from what one wished it to be. In all these texts, however, the faithful indicate that they have nowhere else to turn. They have no other god to whom they can pray or to whom they wish to pray. Their relationship is *with the Lord*, the *very one* who has brought these terrible times upon them, albeit for their sins. Their confession is that there is no other god, and their guiding hope is that the God who punishes is also the God who restores (see House, *Old Testament Theology*, 489–90).

When the people pray to the one God with whom they have a long-term relationship, they can expect that, for good or ill, this God is righteous. Indeed, Lam 1:18 states this belief explicitly. What this confession means for prayer is that the Lord can be expected to do the just and right thing. The problem with this conviction is that the people are not sure how and when God's righteousness will turn from their destruction to that of their tormentors. They know that a righteous God who judges sin must have judged them and must in due time judge those who commit atrocities against them, but "how long" such deliverance through means of punishment will tarry remains a question only God can answer. Still, grasping the truth that God is righteous gives the nation some hope that the one God who rules history will not be silent forever (see Lam 3:33–36).

There seems to be no question in the worshipers' minds that God hears and answers prayers, even prayers of lament. The book's several invocations make this point. Israel may call upon God to "see" (for example, Lam 1:9; 1:11; 1:20; 2:20; and so on), "remember" (for example, Lam 3:19; 5:1), and "restore" (Lam 5:21) because it is within God's nature and power to grant such requests. Just as God has seen, remembered, and torn down, so the opposite may also occur. The tone of the prayer does not seem to have a bearing on the Lord's willingness to act on the people's behalf. Jerusalem's current state is extreme, so the tone of the prayers is extreme. There is no reason to pretend that all is well, that the people are not suffering, that the nation has behaved well, or that God appears particularly kind at the moment. It is realistic and honest to state the stark facts and ask the Lord to treat the people as before, given their confession and contrition. Indeed, real hope can only grow out of this sort of realism. Anything less might be an admission that the nation has not understood what has happened and why.

Lamentations also confesses that the God to whom the people pray is endlessly faithful and compassionate (Lam 3:22–23). This statement of faith is the cornerstone of the book's central chapter and serves as a reference point for the nation's hope in the midst of lament. Because the Lord is compassionate and faithful, the narrator in chap. 3 can bear the affliction that has been laid upon him (Lam 3:19–38). Because the Lord is consummately compassionate as well as fully righteous (Lam 1:18), the "daughter of Zion" can believe that God will punish the people no longer (Lam 4:22). Because God has not afflicted willingly (Lam 3:32–33), surely the Lord will act favorably on Israel's behalf. Certainly the Lord has done so in the past (Lam 5:21). Thus, the book's prayers make sense. They are not simply desperate wishes.

Finally, when the people pray, they know that they are speaking to the God who rules the world. They seek help from the God who sees their sin (Lam 1:8), who sends armies to conquer them and punish those sins (Lam 1:18), and who can in turn punish their tormentors (Lam 4:22). This God is the one who rules the world by the power of his word (Lam 3:37), from whose mouth comes both well-being and calamity (Lam 3:38), and whose throne endures forever (Lam 5:19). In Lamentations, prayer is speaking with utter frankness with the ruler of all things about the things that concern the worshiper. Such prayer is not simple resignation to a higher power. It is a humble, yet substantive, grappling with the current situation in light of the nature of God. Incredibly, this grappling is done with the ruler of the universe, and the book's form, tone, and contents reflect the seriousness and quality necessary for this type of prayer.

CONCLUSION

Though further theological reflection will be offered in the *Explanation* sections of the commentary, it is appropriate to draw some conclusions about the book's portrait of God at this point. From the preceding discussion it is clear that the Lord is righteous, just, powerful, kind, severe, compassionate, faithful, and willing to hear and answer prayer. There is no question that the Lord is a thorough, severe, and unstinting judge of thorough, ingrained, consistent sin. At the same time, it is plain that these characteristics are not the primary facets of God's nature, for these are not constant actions derived from that character. God's lovingkindness, faithfulness, and ruling power are the Lord's ongoing traits, so the covenant people have hope for the future.

As Brevard Childs notes, this theology serves as the basis for hope in each successive generation of the community of faith. He writes that through Lamentations the community is "summoned to faith in God, but at the same time to lift up its devastation in corporate prayer" (*Introduction to the Old Testament as Scripture*, 595). As the faithful do so, confession and hope replace dirge and despair. The presence of the book of Lamentations in the Bible thus gives each new generation the chance to apply God's faithfulness and ruling power to their situation (see House, *Old Testament Theology*, 488). It also gives them the opportunity to use laments to do so.

How She Dwells Alone! (1:1–22)

Bibliography

Ahuvyah, A. "*ykh yšbh bdd h'yr rty 'm* (Lam 1:1)." *Beth Miqra* 24 (1979) 423–25. **Biddle, M.** "The Figure of Lady Jerusalem: Identification, Deification, and Personification of Cities in the Ancient Near East." In *Scripture in Context: The Biblical Canon in Comparative Perspective.* Ed. K. L. Younger et al. Lewiston, NY: Mellen, 1991. 4:173–94. **Cohen, C.** "The 'Widowed' City." *JANESCU* 5 (1973) 75–81. **Cross, F. M.** "Studies in the Structure of Hebrew Verse: The Prosody of Lamentations 1:1–22." In *The Word of the Lord Shall Go Forth.* FS D. N. Freedman. Ed. C. L. Meyers and M. O'Connor. Winona Lake, IN: Eisenbrauns, 1983. 129–55. **Dahood, M.** "New Readings in Lamentations." *Bib* 59 (1978) 174–97. **Dobbs-Allsopp, F. W., and T. Linafelt.** "The Rape of Zion in Thr 1,10." *ZAW* 113 (2001) 77–81. **Driver, G. R.** "Hebrew Notes on 'Song of Songs' and 'Lamentations.'" In *Festschrift Alfred Bertholet.* Ed. W. Baumgartner et al. Tübingen: Mohr (Siebeck), 1950. 134–46. **Ewald, H.** *Die Psalmen und die Klagelieder.* **Ferris, P. W., Jr.** *Genre of Communal Lament.* **Follis, E. R.** "Zion, Daughter of." *ABD,* 6:1103. **Gottlieb, H.** *Study on the Text of Lamentations.* **Gottwald, N. K.** *Studies in the Book of Lamentations.* **Gunkel, H.** *Introduction to Psalms: The Genres of the Religious Lyric of Israel.* **Hillers, D. R.** "Roads to Zion Mourn (Lam 1:4)" *Per* 12 (1971) 121–34. **Hurowitz, V.** "*zwllh* = peddler/ tramp/vagabond/beggar: Lamentations i 11 in Light of Akkadian *zilulû.*" *VT* 49 (1999) 542–45. **Jahnow, H.** *Hebräische Leichenlied.* **Kaiser, B. B.** "Poet as 'Female Impersonator.'" *JR* 67 (1987) 164–83. **Linafeldt, T.** *Surviving Lamentations.* **McDaniel, T. F.** "Philological Studies in Lamentations, I." *Bib* 49 (1968) 27–53. **O'Connor, K. M.** *Lamentations and the Tears of the World.* **Praetorius, F.** "Threni I, 12. 14. II, 6. 13." *ZAW* 15 (1895) 143–46. **Provan, I.** "Reading Texts against an Historical Background: The Case of Lamentations 1." *SJOT* 1 (1990) 130–43. **Renkema, J.** "Literary Structure of Lamentations (I–IV)." In *The Structural Analysis of Biblical and Canaanite Poetry.* Ed. W. van der Meer and J. C. de Moor. JSOTSup 74. Sheffield: JSOT Press, 1988. 294–396. **Robinson, T. H.** "Anacrusis in Hebrew Poetry." In *Werden und Wesen des Alten Testaments.* BZAW 66. Giessen: Töpelmann, 1936. 37–40. **Rudolph, W.** "Der Text der Klagelieder." *ZAW* 56 (1938) 101–22. **Salters, R.** "Lamentations 1:3: Light from the History of Exegesis." In *A Word in Season.* FS W. McKane. Ed. J. D. Martin and P. M. Davies. JSOTSup 42. Sheffield: JSOT Press, 1986. 73–89. ———. "Structure and Implication in Lamentations 1?" *SJOT* 14 (2000) 293–300. **Seow, C. L.** "A Textual Note on Lamentations 1:20." *CBQ* 47 (1985) 416–19.

Translation

א	1 a	How [b] she dwells [c] alone!	(3)
		The city great with [d] people [e]	(3+2)
		has become like a widow.	
		(The city) great among the nations,	(2+2+2)
		princess among the provinces,	
		has become a vassal.	
ב	2	She weeps bitterly in the night,	(3+2)
		and her tears [a] are on her cheeks. [b]	
		There is no one comforting her	(3+2)
		out of all her lovers.	
		All her friends have dealt treacherously with her;	(4+3)

		they have become her enemies.	
ג	3	Judah has gone into exile under affliction,	(3+2)
		and under harsh servitude.	
		She dwells among the nations;	(3+3)
		she does not find rest.	
		All her pursuers overtook her	(3+2)
		between the straits.[a]	
ד	4	The roads to Zion mourn,	(3+3)
		for none are coming to the festival.	
		All her gates[a] are desolate;	(3+2)
		her priests are groaning.	
		Her virgins are grieving,[b]	(2+3)
		and she suffers bitterly.	
ה	5	Her foes have become (her) master;	(3+2)
		her enemies prosper.	
		For the LORD has made her grieve	(3+3)
		because of her numerous transgressions.	
		Her children have gone away,	(2+3)
		captives before the foe.	
ו	6	And has gone out[a] [b]from Daughter[b] Zion,	(4+2)
		all her majesty.	
		Her officials have become like deer;	(3+3)
		they have not found pasture.	
		They have fled without strength,	(3+2)
		before their pursuers.	
ז	7	Jerusalem remembers	(2+3)
		(in) the days of her affliction and her wanderings,[a]	
		[b]All her precious things	(2+2+2)
		that were	
		from days of old,[b]	
		When her people fell into the hand of the foe,	(4+3)
		and there was no one helping her.	
		Her enemies saw her; they laughed	(3+2)
		because of her annihilation.	
ח	8	Jerusalem sinned greatly;[a]	(3+3)
		[b]therefore[b] she became impure.[c]	
		All who honored her despised[d] her,	(3+3)
		for they saw her nakedness.	
		She herself groaned	(3+2)
		and turned away.	
ט	9	Her uncleanness was in her skirts;	(2+3)
		she took no thought for her future.	
		Thus she went down[a] amazingly;[b]	(2+3)
		there was no one comforting her.	
		"See, O LORD, my affliction,[c]	(3+3)
		for my enemy has triumphed."[d]	
י	10	The enemy has stretched out his hand	(3+3)
		over all her precious things.	

		For she has seen the nations	(3+2)
		enter her holy place,	
		whom you commanded not to enter	(4+2)
		into your assembly.	
כ	11	*All her people are groaning,*	(3+2)
		seeking bread.	
		They trade their precious things ᵃ *for food,*	(3+2)
		to revive their strength.	
		"See, O LORD, and consider,	(3+3)
		for I am despised."	
ל	12	*Is it nothing to you,*ᵃ	(2+2)
		all you who pass by?	
		Consider, and see	(2+3+3)
		if there is any sorrow like my sorrow,	
		which was brought (severely) upon me,	
		which the LORD made (me) grieve,	(3+3)
		on the day of his fierce anger.	
מ	13	*From on high he sent fire*	(3+2)
		*into my bones, and it trampled them.*ᵃ	
		He spread a net for my feet;	(3+2)
		he turned me back.	
		He left me desolate,	(2+3)
		faint all day.	
נ	14	*He bound* ᵃ *a yoke of my transgressions;*	(3+2)
		by his hand they were fastened together.	
		They went up ᵇ *upon my neck;*	(3+2)
		he caused my strength to fail.	
		The Lord ᶜ *gave me into the hands of*	(3+3)
		(those before whom) I am unable to stand.	
ס	15	*He has scorned* ᵃ *all my strong men—*	(3+2)
		*the Lord in my midst.*ᵇ	
		He has proclaimed a festival against me	(3+2)
		to shatter my chosen ones.	
		The Lord has trodden the wine-press	(3+3)
		for the virgin daughter of Judah.	
ע	16	*For these things I am weeping;*	(4+4)
		my eyes, my eyes ᵃ *flow with tears*	
		because a comforter is far from me,	(4+2)
		one to restore my soul.	
		My sons are desolate	(3+3)
		because the enemy has prevailed.	
פ	17	*Zion stretches out her hands;*	(3+3)
		there is no one comforting her.	
		The LORD has commanded concerning Jacob	(3+3)
		that his neighbors become his foes.	
		Jerusalem has become	(2+2)
		*an unclean thing in their midst.*ᵃ	
צ	18	*The LORD is indeed righteous,*	(3+3)

		for I have rebelled against his word.	
		Listen, please, all peoples,[a]	(4+2)
		and see my sorrow.	
		My virgins and my young men	(2+2)
		have gone into captivity.	
ק	19	*I called to my lovers;*	(2+2)
		they deceived me.	
		My priests and my elders	(2+2)
		perished in the city	
		while they sought food for themselves	(4+2)
		so they might revive their souls.[a]	
ר	20	*Look, O LORD, for I am in distress;*	(3+2)
		my inward parts are in turmoil.	
		My heart is cast down within me	(3+3)
		because I have been very rebellious.	
		In the street the sword bereaves;	(3+2)
		in the house it is like death.[a]	
ש	21	*They heard*[a] *that I am groaning;*	(4+3)
		there was no one comforting me.	
		All my enemies have heard of my calamity.	(4+4)
		They rejoice that you yourself have done it.	
		You have brought[b] *the day you announced,*	(3+2)
		but let them be as I am.	
ת	22	*Let all their evil (deeds) come before you;*	(4+2)
		now deal (severely) with it,	
		just as you have dealt (severely) with me	(3+3)
		for all my transgressions,	
		because many are my groans,	(3+2)
		and my heart is faint.	

Notes

1.a. LXX (followed by Vg.) prefixes this sentence: καὶ ἐγένετο μετὰ τὸ αἰχμαλωτισθῆναι τὸν Ισραηλ καὶ Ιερυσαλημ ἐρημωθῆναι ἐκάθισεν Ιερεμιας κλαίων καὶ ἐθρήνησεν τὸν θρῆνον τοῦτον ἐπὶ Ιεροσαλημ καὶ εἶπεν. Hillers ([1992] 64) translates, "And it came to pass after Israel had been taken captive and Jerusalem had been laid waste, Jeremiah sat weeping and lamented this lament over Jerusalem, and he said."

1.b. איכה, "how," is set off on a line to itself in *BHS*, perhaps to mark the book's title (see Robinson, "Anacrusis in Hebrew Poetry," 37–40). Kraus (22) rightly objects that the word is characteristic of lament style (cf. Lam 2:1; 4:1; Isa 1:21; 14:4; Jer 48:17).

1.c. ישבה, "sits, dwells." A pf. is used to describe a present condition that is quite fixed in nature.

1.d. רבתי, "great with, full of," retains the י of early case endings, as does שרתי, "princes," below (GKC §90.1).

1.e. עם, "with people." Kraus (22) asserts that Syr. adds "with," which means that perhaps the text should read בעם. Albrektson (*Studies in the Text and Theology*, 55) disagrees, arguing that "with people" is "a natural rendering of MT."

2.a. ודמעתה, "her tear," sg., apparently in a collective sense.

2.b. MT לחיה, "her cheek," also a collective. LXX, Syr., Vg. make it pl., while two Heb. MSS make it dual.

3.a. בין המצרים, lit. "between the narrows," from מצר, "a narrow place" (BDB, 865). LXX τῶν θλιβόντων αὐτὴν, "the one compressing it," perhaps wrongly saw the Heb. as *hip'il* ptc. of צרר, "tie up, restrict" (BDB, 869). Syr. and Vg. "between the narrows" translates correctly.

4.a. MT כל שעריה, "all her gates." *BHS* emendation שעריה is unnecessary.
4.b. נוגות, "are grieving" (*nip'al* ptc. from ינה). LXX reads ἀγόμεναι, "ones dragged off, kidnapped," apparently translating נהוגות, "led away." Based on the verse's probable parallelism, MT is followed.
6.a. ויצא, "has gone out," is act. (*qal* impf. 3 m. sg., יצא), but *BHS* offers a conjectural reading of LXX, καὶ ἐξῄρθη, a pass. ("is removed"; repointing the Heb. as a pass.; see *BHS* footnote). There is little difference in meaning.
6.b-b. מן בת ציון, "from daughter Zion." A few versions of the Qere eliminate the נ and read מבת. No change in meaning results.
7.a. MT reads "and her wanderings." The *BHS* note would make the word a ptc. (see LXX ἀπωσμῶν, "wanderings"). No change in meaning results.
7.b-b. In chaps. 1–3, 1:7 and 2:19 are the only four-line verses. Scholars who suggest omitting a line differ over which line should be eliminated. Hillers ([1992] 68) and Kraus (22) would leave out the second line. Renkema (128) argues for the coherence of the text as it stands. No ancient version omits any line, and emendations based on divergences from the normal poetic patterns in Lamentations assume a singularity of form that the book simply does not display. Thus, MT is followed.
8.a. חטא חטאה, "sinned greatly." This translation emends חֵטְא to חָטֹא to make the first word an inf. abs. Even if MT vowels are retained, the sense of the verse is not altered, for the twofold use of forms of "sin" emphasizes Jerusalem's wickedness.
8.b-b. *BHS* note suggests deleting for the sake of meter. Read MT.
8.c. לנידה, "impure," is a *hapax legomenon*. If it is a partial writing of נִדָה (BDB, 622), it may mean "impurity" as in v 17 below. But if it is derived from נוד (BDB, 626–27), it means "fluttering, a quivering."
8.d. הזילוה, "despise her." If this is a *hip'il* pf. from נזל, it means "cause her to flow." But if it is a *hip'il* pf. from זלל, it means "make light of her, despise her" (BDB, 273). See GKC §67y. The latter meaning makes more sense in context.
9.a. ותרד, "thus she went down." *Qal* impf. 3 f. sg., plus *vav* consec. The *BHS* note suggests ותורד, a *hop'al* impf. 3 f. sg., "she was brought down." This reading follows σ´: καὶ κατήχθη (pass.), "she was brought down." Vg. also reads as a pass. (*deposita est*). Since the emendation requires adding a *vav* and the form makes sense as it stands, it seems defensible to retain MT.
9.b. פלאים, "amazingly, or extraordinarily." This m. pl. noun is a pl. of amplification or intensification. See GKC §124a-f.
9.c. עני, "my affliction." Note the shift to first-person speech here. The Boharic version and Ambrose, following OL, fail to note the change and thus read "her affliction."
9.d. הגדיל, "has triumphed"; literally, "has become great, or magnified." Waltke-O'Connor states that here "the subject causes himself to be regarded as great" (440).
11.a. מחמדיהם, "their precious things." Some MSS indicate that the Qere reading omits the *vav*. There is no significant difference in meaning.
12.a. לוא אליכם, "Is it nothing to you?" This phrase is extremely difficult to translate into idiomatic English. This translation turns the phrase into a question. LXX simply translates the words literally. See Albrektson (*Studies in the Text and Theology*, 66–69) for a discussion of options.
13.a. וירדנה, "and it trampled them." MT presents this form as a *qal* impf. 3 m. sg. from רדה. LXX and Syr. "have interpreted the Hebrew verb as a Hiphil from the root ירד ('descend')" (Albrektson, *Studies in the Text and Theology*, 72). Gordis (157) cites parallels such as Joel 4:13 (MT) as evidence that MT makes sense as it stands. Driver ("Hebrew Notes," 137), Keil (370), and Albrektson (*Studies in the Text and Theology*, 72) agree.
14.a. נשקד, "he bound," is a *hapax legomenon* whose root appears only here in the OT. LXX reads ἐγρηγορήθη ἐπί, "He is attentive to," a Heb. text of שקד על, which requires a change from ש to שׁ and the altering of vowel points in the second word (על to עֹל). Renkema (164) rejects the idea that difficult forms require emendation and agrees with Albrektson's (*Studies in the Text and Theology*, 74) positive assessment of Ewald's (329) suggestion that שקד may well be "a technical term for putting on a yoke." The context seems to be that the Lord creates a yoke made of Judah's sins, and that this yoke then brings them to their knees.
14.b. עלו, "they went up, rose." V 14 contains על two times and עלו once. V 5 contains על and עולליה, while v 22 has עולל. Thus, the meanings "upon," "go up," and "yoke" interact in a way that has probably confused the versions. Here LXX^L reads τὸν ζυγὸν αὐτοῦ, "his yoke," which equates עֻלּוֹ. In LXX^B the text reads ἀνέβησαν, "they go up," which corresponds to עָלוּ. MT's play on words should be retained (see Albrektson, *Studies in the Text and Theology*, 74–75).
14.c. אדני, "the Lord [Adonai]." *BHS* suggests reading יהוה, "LORD [Yahweh]." Rudolph (207) and Hillers ([1992] 74) discuss the matter, with Hillers concluding that the variation between the two follows no particular pattern. Thus, there is no compelling reason to accept the *BHS* suggestion.

15.a. סלה, "he has scorned." This form (pi'el pf. 3 m. sg.) only appears here in MT. Hillers ([1992] 74) suggests that a scribe has confused סלה and סלל, "he has heaped up." He argues that this reading connects contextually with the harvest imagery in 1:15c. Renkema (168–69) agrees with Hillers, but Keil (372) reads סלה as "lift up, take away." The versions vary widely, which probably indicates their efforts to translate a rare verb whose root can carry various meanings.

15.b. בקרבי, "in my midst." LXX reads ἐκ μέσου μου, "from my midst," and is followed by Vg. A ב may have been confused with a מ in LXX.

16.a. עיני עיני, "my eyes, my eyes." According to Gottlieb (Study on the Text, 18), five Heb. MSS, LXX, Syr., and Vg translate only one of the words. Most modern translations follow their lead. Still, Gottlieb (Study on the Text, 19) also notes "it is a by no means rare phenomenon for a word to be repeated in a Semitic text, so that it should thereby be given greater emphasis." Renkema (172) and Keil (373) agree, but Hillers ([1992] 75) considers the phrase "a clear case of dittography," as does Albrektson (Studies in the Text and Theology, 77).

17.a. ביניהם, "in their midst." BHS suggests reading בעיניהם, "in their eyes." Either reading makes sense contextually, but without textual support it is not necessary to change.

18.a. כל עמים, "all peoples." Several Heb. MSS, LXX, and Tg. read with the Qere: העמים, "the peoples." Little if any interpretive importance hinges on this variation.

19.a. LXX and Syr. add "and they found nothing." Kraus (22) accepts this reading as probable, but Albrektson (Studies in the Text and Theology, 80), Hillers ([1992] 76), and Renkema (186) rightly consider the phrase an explanatory gloss on a very difficult text. Tg. does not include the phrase.

20.a. בבית כמות, "in the house it is like death." Albrektson (Studies in the Text and Theology, 81) observes that these words "are an ancient crux." Syr. may be based on a tradition that reads בבית מות, "in the house of death," but Albrektson (81) thinks it just as likely that the Syr. translator "prefers a clear and readable rendering to a literal but obscure translation of the Hebrew text, and P's text is exactly the sort of translation we should expect of a difficult passage." Gordis (159–60) and Gottlieb (Study on the Text, 20) conclude that the כ is an "asseverative Kaph" that makes the best reading "without, the sword bereaved; within, there was death" (Gordis, 159). This comparison between what is outside and what is inside is the most important component to preserve.

21.a. שָׁמְעוּ, "they heard." LXX reads ἀκούσατε, which is a pl. impv. equal to שִׁמְעוּ, while Syr. renders the form a sg. impv. Albrektson (Studies in the Text and Theology, 83) considers MT original, based on contextual grounds and also on his conclusion that the Syr. translator typically smooths out difficult texts. Gottlieb (Study on the Text, 20–21) agrees and adds that the sg. and pl. forms are often interchangeable in the Syr.

21.b. הבאת, "you have brought." BHS suggests accepting Syr., which amounts to הָבֵא אֶת, "bring." Albrektson (Studies in the Text and Theology, 83–84) thinks that the translator could easily have misread הבאת as את הבא. Gottlieb (Study on the Text, 21–22) disagrees, for he thinks יום קראת refers to hopes for restoration, not to the destruction of Jerusalem. Given the verse's emphasis on the enemies, Albrektson's reading seems more probable.

Form/Structure/Setting

Virtually every scholar who comments on the genre of Lam 1 considers the poem to be of *mixed form*. That is, they conclude that the text combines elements of more than one type of poetry. For example, in her groundbreaking work on the form of Lamentations, Jahnow (*Hebräische Leichenlied*, 168–91) states that Lam 1 includes a few of the basic characteristics of the dirge. Based in part on the findings in her monograph, Gunkel claims that Lam 1 adapts motifs from the dirge to transform Lam 1 into a religious poem (*Introduction to Psalms*, 95). Though he does not accept Jahnow's and Gunkel's historical reconstruction of the composition of Lam 1, Westermann agrees that certain features of the dirge do appear in the poem. He cites the occurrence of a mournful cry at the outset of the poem, a description following the mournful cry, and the presence of a reversal motif as examples of dirge elements used in the poem (117). He also discerns clear connections to communal complaint (see below). Similarly, Re'emi writes that confessions of sins (1:5, 8, 14, 18, 20) and individual laments (1:9c–

11c, 12–16) are part of Lam 1 (79), and that when the poet addresses the Lord the dirge turns into prayer (84). The list could be extended, but the point has been made. Scholars do not think that Lam 1 is a "pure" form of any genre.

Despite his own caution about assigning Lam 1 to a particular genre, Westermann argues that the poem exhibits several aspects of the communal lament. He lists the following characteristics as motifs found in communal laments: invocation, accusation against God, community's direct complaint, complaint about enemies, acknowledgment of guilt, avowal of confidence or retrospection, plea for God to take heed, plea for intervention, and petition for reprisal against enemies (118–19). Therefore, of what he considers the main elements of communal lament, he notes that only two do not appear in Lam 1: the avowal of confidence and the plea for intervention on behalf of the covenant people. He conjectures that these may be absent because "the shock of the catastrophe went so deep as to forestall their articulation" (119). Westermann admits that the communal elements that do appear do not unfold in the clear, specific order that marks standard community laments and suggests that this is the case because the acrostic structure was imposed on the original oral material at a later stage of editing (100–104). In other words, in his opinion the elements of communal complaint are evident, but they are mixed with other literary aspects because of the text's compositional history.

Renkema questions the possibility of establishing a genre for the passage as it stands or in any theoretical earlier form. This conclusion is consistent with his conviction that the book as a whole cannot be assigned to a single genre. Though he agrees with Westermann's cataloging of community lament motifs, he questions Westermann's historical reconstruction of the chapter's composition (92). He asserts that the lack of traditional communal lament order, coupled with the fact that alphabetic poems are not used to express community laments elsewhere, means that there is no way to confirm a genre for the poem (92). Interpreters must take motifs from known genres into account, but chap. 1, like the book as a whole, must be treated as a unique composition (Renkema, 92).

Given this diversity of opinion among these important representative interpreters of the book, it is appropriate to seek new ground from which to work, yet new ground that maintains contact with the solid observations about genre that have been made in the past. One way to achieve this goal is to view the acrostic format as more than a convenient way to present the material or as an imposition on the material. Many cultures have poetic types that require poets to prove creativity within set structures. Without question, the acrostic was such a genre for the author of Lamentations. It encouraged subtlety, use of several literary and thematic motifs, and variety in meter. Only the basic order of the alphabet was fixed; all else was open for authorial development. Westermann has rightly argued that laments must be taken seriously as laments. It is just as accurate to argue that Lamentations ought to be taken seriously as an acrostic. In this way both the book's thematic and its structural components may be emphasized in effective, appropriate ways.

The long acrostic form requires a commitment to comprehensiveness. Thus, the author of Ps 119 had to determine to expound the full range of ideas related to the value of the Law, while the author of Lamentations had to chart the detailed paths of national and personal sorrow and whatever grounds for hope existed (see Gottwald, *Studies*, 32). In doing so, the author of Lamentations could employ personal and communal lament motifs, as well as those of the dirge. Indeed the poet was forced to do so because of the scope of the subject matter. This poet was also virtually compelled to employ repetition of theme, sound, meter, and vocabulary in this process, for again the genre requires comprehensiveness of expression and subject matter. The comments below offer a brief analysis of the way the poet pursued this basic goal through the blending of genre, the artful deployment of structure, and the obvious use of verbal repetition. Gottwald was correct when he wrote, "If artistic achievement is to be judged by the correspondence between intention and execution, then the author of Lamentations, within the limits he set for himself, was an artist of the first rank" (32).

Blending of Literary Forms in Acrostic

As has been stated, elements of the dirge appear in Lam 1. The initial evidence of this occurs in the very first word of the book, when the narrator exclaims, "How . . ." Other OT texts use this exclamation of woe to express unbridled grief. For instance, Isa 1:21 exclaims concerning Jerusalem, "How the faithful city has become a whore!" (NRSV). Jer 48:17 states concerning Moab, "How the mighty scepter is broken, the glorious staff!" (NRSV). A shorter form of the word occurs in OT dirges with approximately the same force in 2 Sam 1:19–27 in David's funeral lament for Saul and Jonathan, in Jer 2:20–21 when the prophet mourns Judah's descent into spiritual whoredom, and in Mic 2:4 where the prophet reports a taunt song. Obviously, the use of איכה, "how," at the outset of Lamentations could take the reader's mind in a variety of generic directions, though each direction includes mourning of some kind.

The use of tragic reversal is another funereal/dirge element prominent in Lamentations. This motif begins with the opening "how" and continues to sound throughout vv 1–11, where the poet highlights the dramatic contrast between past glory and present calamity. Besides the samples cited above from Isa 1:21 and Jer 48:17, this type of reversal occurs in 2 Sam 1:19, 25, and 27:

> How the mighty have fallen!
>
> How the mighty have fallen
>   in the midst of the battle!
>
> How the mighty have fallen,
>   and the weapons of war perished! (NRSV)

These short bursts of despair are more than matched by the lengthy contrasts in Ezekiel's songs of lamentation over the kingdom and ruler of Tyre in Ezek 27. Here the prophet offers an extended dirge *(qinah)* in poetry and prose that emphasizes that Tyre's glorious history of sea trade (Ezek 27:1–25a) has been shipwrecked (Ezek 27:25b–36), and concludes with a detailed description of mourning rites for the great city (Ezek 27:30–32).

Lam 1:1–11 itself offers several dramatic statements of reversal. Both sides of these contrasts often appear in the same verse, perhaps as a result of the acrostic format. These reversals include the following instances:

1:1 "The city great with people has become like a widow... princess among the provinces, has become a vassal."
1:2 "All her friends... have become her enemies."
1:4 "The roads to Zion mourn, for none are coming to the festival."
1:6 "And has gone out from Daughter Zion, all her majesty."
1:7 "Jerusalem remembers... days of old."
1:8 "All who honored her despised her."
1:10 "For she has seen the nations enter her holy place."
1:11 "They trade their precious things for food."
1:17 "Zion stretches out her hands; there is no one comforting her."
1:18 "My virgins and my young men have gone into captivity."
1:20 "My heart is cast down within me."

Such passages clearly emphasize a situation of then versus now. Like Tyre, Jerusalem has become what she never thought she would be. She has fallen from heights that she had taken years to reach. And all these reversals have occurred because she has sinned. Thus, her funereal comments are tragic in part because they need not ever to have been uttered. Her reversal is of her own making.

Besides the usage of exclamatory איכה, "how," language and reversal terminology, the author of Lamentations employs the dirgelike element of lengthy description of the city's pain, especially in 1:1–11. Jerusalem weeps bitterly (1:2); her children are in exile (1:3); her roads mourn (1:4); her foes rule her (1:5); her leaders have fled (1:6); her foes gloat (1:7); Jerusalem groans (1:8); and her people groan and seek for bread (1:11). Even more elaborate descriptions of misery appear in chaps. 2 and 4, so the motif is well established in the book as a whole. Jerusalem's pain is not stated in solely general terms. Rather, the agony becomes as real to the reader as the author can make it.

As the first eleven verses unfold, the text increasingly recognizes that God has caused the pain because Judah has sinned. Though God is not addressed directly, Yahweh is acknowledged as the ultimate agent of punishment and Judah's transgressions as the ultimate cause of judgment in 1:5. In 1:8, the fact that "Jerusalem sinned greatly" led to her vicious and treacherous enemies acting as God's emissaries of punishment. Though the focus of 1:11 continues to be the people's horrible pain, this agony begins to make a specific kind of theological sense to readers.

As was stated at the beginning of this discussion, the author also incorporates various elements of the communal lament in chap. 1 and in subsequent chapters. First, there are clear requests from the personified collective city for Yahweh to ראה, "see," Judah's condition and situation (1:9c, 11c, 20a). Similar petitions for Yahweh to pay attention occur in standard psalms of complaint (see Pss 5:1; 13:3; 17:1; 31:2; 80:14; 86:6; 88:2; 102:1; 130:2; 141:1; 143:1). These pleas directed to the Lord demonstrate that the shattered city has yet a spark of life and a thread of hope. Funereal language is the dramatic vehicle that conveys the city's despair and desolation, but the fact that *complaint* language occurs as well staves off a sense of total hopelessness. As long as the people reach out to God, there may yet be a way out of the current horrible circumstances.

Second, after a dramatic cry to people passing by to grasp her incomparable sorrow (1:12a–b), the city launches into an accusation against God in 1:12c–15. Such accusations are staples of communal laments in Pss 44:9–16, 74:9–11, and 80:12–13. In Lam 1:12c–15 the complaints against the Lord are addressed not to him directly but rather to anonymous persons. Still, the Lord is mentioned, albeit in the third person, so the text probably implies that the Lord could hear and act on the city's behalf. One must wonder whether the speaker does not think the Lord wishes to hear such a petition directly, because divine wrath has been poured out, or the speaker is so angry at the Lord that the speaker does not wish to address the Lord.

Third, there are complaints against old foes that have remained hostile (1:21b) and old friends who have become recent foes (1:17b, 19a). Fourth, the city acknowledges the people's guilt (1:14a–b, 20b; see also 1:5b, 8–9) and also offers a justification of God (1:16, 20a–b, 21a), which may also serve as a confession of trust, however muted that confession may be because of the pain the city endures. Fifth, these elements of communal lament are supplemented by the city's pleas for someone to share her pain (1:12, 18b), by her complaints about lack of comforters (1:16b, 17a, 21a), and by descriptions of agony (1:16b, 20a–b, 21a).

Sixth, and finally, the chapter concludes with the city once again asking Yahweh to "see" (ראה, 1:20a; see 1:9c, 11c) what has occurred. Unlike 1:9c and 11c, however, the city also petitions the Lord to punish the foes who have ravaged Jerusalem (1:21–22). Though the city may earlier have feared or simply not wished to speak to the Lord openly about the people's sins, now she addresses the Lord directly and forcefully. Judah's enemies have sinned greatly themselves, so they deserve God's wrath. Surely the same God who judged the sins of the covenant people will have the same response to wicked Gentiles.

As was noted above, Westermann thinks Lam 1 contains virtually all the components found in communal complaints. He also argues that dirge elements combine with the normal characteristics of the communal lament to make the chapter a virtual encyclopedia of pain resulting from invasion. Through these observations he goes a long way toward explaining the genre of this text. But again the significance of the acrostic form must not be forgotten. It is the acrostic that requires as complete a depiction of the city's pain as is possible. It is the acrostic form that forces readers to endure all the pain that an alphabet can express. It is the acrostic form that leads to the incorporation of elements of dirges, community laments, and other expressions of pain. Thus, though Renkema is correct to stress the impossibility of deeming this chapter and the whole of Lamentations anything except an acrostic, it is important to examine and report what this poetic form may entail.

Structural Patterns

Lam 1 exhibits structural unity. Though not the first to discover a concentric pattern in Lam 1 (see A. Condamin, *Poemes de la Bible* [Paris, 1933]), Renkema (295–97) has offered the most complete analysis of this type of verbal repetition in Lam 1. According to Renkema, this pattern is determined by the poem's acrostic structure and by the change of speaking voices that occurs in 1:12. He has also shown that the chapter's fairly clear linear movement augments this concentric pattern (85). The concentric pattern Renkema conceives revolves around 1:11–12, verses he considers the "kernel" of the chapter, both because they are at the heart of the alphabet and because they declare the chapter's main theme: "God, men! Look at our misery" (297).

Form/Structure/Setting

Based on similarities in phraseology or vocabulary, the verses are paired from the two halves of the poem, with the result that the matched verses are the same distance from the central point of the poem. For example, he argues that vv 1 and 22 are matched by the inclusion of the word רבתי/רבות, "full" or "great"; vv 2 and 21 are paired by the inclusion of the phrase אין־לה מנחם/אין מנחם לי, "no one comforting her/me"; and so forth throughout the entire chapter (see Renkema, 296–97). Renkema notes that vv 8 and 15 do not have a strong common link (296), but he still makes a very strong case for intentional linking of the opposite verses in the acrostic structure. Despite the potential question mark at v 8 and v 15, this is a remarkable pattern. The fact that chap. 2 most likely exhibits a similar concentric patterning makes it difficult to consider the linkages sheer coincidence or somehow necessary to the acrostic format. Rather, they are more likely the result of intentional literary artistry.

Lam 1 also displays unity in its repetition of thematic elements. Perhaps the most prominent of these themes is Jerusalem's lack of comfort and help:

1:2	"There was no one comforting her."
1:7	"And there was no one helping her."
1:9	"There was no one comforting her."
1:16	"Because a comforter is far from me."
1:17	"There is no one comforting her."
1:21	"There was no one comforting me."

The changes in syntax help emphasize the theme and add variety to its emphasis. Each half of the poem has three instances of the theme, and both the narrator and Jerusalem raise the complaint. Given the regularity of this theme, it must be taken into account in any summary of chap. 1. The main theme of the chapter may be Jerusalem's misery, but that misery is made greater by the lack of aid and human kindness.

The constant appearance of כל, "all," in the chapter also binds the poem together. Sixteen times in thirteen separate verses the poet intones the encompassing "all," and both the narrator and Jerusalem use the term. Note the following list:

1:2	"all her lovers"
1:2	"all her friends"
1:3	"all her pursuers"
1:4	"all her gates"
1:6	"all her majesty"
1:7	"all her precious things"
1:8	"all who honored her"
1:10	"all her precious things"
1:11	"all her people"
1:12	"all you who pass by"
1:13	"faint all day"
1:15	"all my strong men"
1:18	"all peoples"
1:21	"all my enemies"
1:22	"all their evil"
1:22	"all my transgressions"

Renkema writes that this constant refrain works with the acrostic format to convey a picture of the totality, the comprehensiveness, the completeness of the disaster (307). Even a cursory glance at this list indicates that every significant theme in the chapter is magnified by the use of כל, "all." Thus, every problem that Jerusalem faces is stated in terms of totality. The people face total oppression by enemies, total loss of property, total loss of cultic activity, total loss of leaders, total lack of sympathy from their formal allies, total surrender of prestige and dignity, and total guilt before God for their sins. All weaknesses have been exposed, and all hope for avoiding catastrophe has been dashed.

These linguistic details point to an aesthetic structural unity in Lam 1. At the same time, the chapter also exhibits a discernible thematic progression that revolves around changes in speakers at strategic points. This movement from third-person description of Jerusalem's woes to direct first-person speech about them allows the chapter to emphasize the extraordinarily personal nature of the devastation. The acrostic's determination to exhibit the totality of Jerusalem's agony thereby includes personal and national pain that is both felt and observed.

Changes in speakers occur at 1:9c, 1:11c, and (perhaps) 1:12a. In 1:1–9b a very observant and sympathetic third-person narrator describes the reversal of Jerusalem's fortunes (1:1–3), the desolation in Jerusalem proper (1:4–6), and the reason for Jerusalem's defeat (1:7–9b). At this point in the poem a first-person cry for the Lord to "see . . . my affliction" (ראה . . . את־עניי; 1:9c) breaks into the heartfelt description. The narrator continues in 1:10–11b, noting how the city's enemies have so drained her resources that her people must sell treasured possessions merely to have enough bread to sustain life. Once again, at this juncture the narrator's depiction of events is stopped by a plea for God to ראה, "see," how the city is being despised. Thus, these two first-person interjections act more as punctuation marks—and exclamation points at that—than as interruptions or breaks in a smooth speech. In effect, the invocations at 1:9c and 1:11c indicate that the narrator has accurately described Jerusalem's terrible predicament, for the first-person character is moved to call out to God based on what has been said about the people's experience.

In 1:12–22 the first-person speaker and third-person narrator switch roles. The first-person speaker implores those passing by to consider the enormity of the pain the Lord has brought upon her in 1:12–16. Certainly sin caused the grief (1:14), but this admission adds to the grief rather than diminishing it (1:16). At this point, the third-person narrator agrees with his counterpart. Zion has no comforter, God has brought these disasters, and Jerusalem has been defiled (1:17). These facts are indisputable. Finally, in 1:18–22 the first-person speaker freely admits that Yahweh has been "righteous" (צדיק הוא יהוה) in this matter (1:18) and claims that Jerusalem's למאהבי, "lovers," have deceived her (1:19). In such dire straits Jerusalem asks the Lord to ראה, "see" (1:20), her pain and thus deal with her opponents' sins as he has dealt with hers (1:22).

As in 1:1–11, one speaker's speech serves as a clarifying interjection for the other. Both speakers are in agreement about the cause, scope, and horror of the city's devastation and its aftermath. The poem includes, then, a comprehensive effect that involves and includes tight, thorough description by two representative speakers, one that offers Jerusalem's viewpoint and one that offers the viewpoint of any sympathetic witness to the scene. These facets join with the linguistic connections noted above to produce an integrated, comprehensive literary portrait of loss, its results, its horrors, and its solution. In other words, the poem succeeds in fulfilling the goals and possibilities inherent in the acrostic form.

Given these preliminary observations, the following basic structural/thematic elements are evident in chap. 1. Chap. 1 may be divided into two major parts: vv 1–11, which stress Jerusalem's devastation, and vv 12–22, which highlight the city's cries for help. Within these two main headings lie several subheadings, including Jerusalem's reversals (1:1–3), emptiness (1:4–6), uncleanness (1:7–9), groaning (1:10–11), acute sorrow (1:12–16), understandable pain (1:17), and prayers to the Lord (1:18–22). Two persons speak in this chapter: a sympathetic third-person narrator (1:1–11b, 17) and Jerusalem herself (1:9c, 11c, 12–16, 18–22). Obviously, the change in speaker helps determine the changes in subject matter. Lam 1:1–11 covers the first half of the alphabet and 1:12–22 uses the second. Thus, a break in main speakers occurs at the halfway point in the alphabetic format.

The poem's setting was discussed in the Introduction. Though it is impossible to ascertain with absolute certainty when the poem was composed, it is clear what scene it describes. Jerusalem has fallen because of her sins, and although Babylon is not mentioned by name in these verses, the destruction of 587 B.C. is the context here. Provan correctly observes that the text is general enough to fit more than one devastation (11–13), yet the Bible tends to focus on this one particular defeat. Therefore, the 587 situation serves as the most logical setting for this poem and for Lamentations as a whole.

As was noted above, Westermann (98–105) has sought to discern the process by which the text came into its present form. Like numerous other commentators, he considers the poem's language to be so raw, open, fresh, and telling that it must have emerged soon after the city's fall (102). He accounts for the highly structured nature of the poem by arguing that the acrostic format was imposed, or at least used as a secondary resource, at a later date (100). Of course, Westermann's approach requires the adoption of a much more negative assessment of the acrostic than this commentary takes. Given its value as a form particularly suited for comprehensive statements, it is just as likely that a poet wishing to express the absolute impact of the city's demise would frame raw, eyewitness speech in an acrostic format as in some other form. In fact, probably no other biblical poetic form allows for as much thorough reporting of impressions and events in so compressed a space as the acrostic.

Thus, whenever the poem was composed, and this commentary treats it as written relatively soon after 587 B.C.E. (see above in the Introduction), the acrostic form contributes to, rather than detracts from, its effective presentation. Westermann is correct to emphasize the immediacy of the poem's language. He rightly refuses to consider these texts merely stylized works by a detached author. But his insistence that the acrostic format somehow clouds the laments' power and purpose is unfounded. In fact, focusing on the acrostic as the most adequate form for the author's subject matter helps readers do what Westermann desires most: let laments be taken seriously as laments. The author of Lamentations took lament so seriously that he chose a comprehensive lament form, and most likely did so from the very start. Horrible circumstances rarely stifle all literary artistry, structural or otherwise, and indeed historically they have quite often had the very opposite effect.

Comment

1–3 The first section of the chapter describes the isolation of העיר, "the city," which remains unnamed until 1:4. Above all, the city's plight amounts to a series of horrible reversals in fortune in these verses. Past abundance and prominence are contrasted with terrible present bereavement, humiliation, and devastation (1:1). Past friendships and alliances are contrasted to present abandonment and treachery (1:2). Past strength of numbers in the chief city of the land is compared to expulsion and loss of inhabitants. Simply stated, Judah has gone into exile, leaving the land, including Jerusalem, devoid of population and obvious hope for the future.

1 The acrostic poem begins with איכה, "how," a word often associated with funereal language for nations or cities (see Isa 1:21; Jer 48:17). Gordis writes that this word "is the longer and more poetical form of the adverb איך, 'how,' the hallmark of the Hebrew elegy. Both forms are used to express the incredulity and grief of the poet at the disaster he is bewailing (cf. e.g. *Isa.* 1:21 and *Jer.* 2:21). The usage also occurs in prose, as in Koheleth's outburst at the same fate befalling the sage and the fool (*Ecc.* 2:16)" (153). Here the word stands as both a subject title for the book as a whole and as the first letter of the alphabet. Thus, the comprehensive treatment of Jerusalem's pain begins with an exclamation that the rest of the poem explains.

Currently Jerusalem "dwells" or "sits" by herself. Here the Hebrew perfect form (ישבה) describes a condition quite fixed in nature. At this point the city is in a static, prolonged mood of uncomfortable solitude. She dwells בדד, "alone." This word is a noun that may serve as an adjective but is often an adverbial accusative that does not change form in a feminine context. It occurs frequently with words meaning "to dwell," whether ישב (Lev 13:46; Jer 15:17) or שכן (Num 23:9; Deut 33:28; Jer 49:31; Mic 7:14), and it has a range of significations. Usages include God's uniqueness—"You alone, O LORD, make me lie down in safety" (Ps 4:9 [ET 4:8] NRSV)—and "safety" or "security" in times of isolation (Deut 33:28; Jer 49:31; Mic 7:14). If the latter passages frame the sense of בדד for the poet here, then the thrust of the text must be extremely ironic since the city is hardly safe and secure (cf. Hillers, [1992] 64). Given the context, however, it is more likely that "isolated" is the intended meaning. Jerusalem is as isolated as the leper depicted in Lev 13:46, another בדד passage. Thus, Jerusalem dwells as lonely as a leper. She has no allies (1:2) and few if any inhabitants (1:3). This declaration that Jerusalem dwells alone, in isolation, acts as a heading that the rest of the verse expounds.

The descriptions of these clear reversals begin. The city was once filled with many people, but is now like a widow. She was once great among the nations, but has become a vassal. Thus, though בדד may or may not be intended as an ironic comment, these phrases constitute a horrible, ironic situation. A place that was "great" once no longer occupies that position.

The three expressions of the city's former glory testify to the abundance of her population (רבתי עם, "great with people"), to her prominence among neighboring nations (רבתי בגוים, "great among the nations"), and to her leadership qualities and status among the neighboring nations (שרתי במדינות, "princess among the provinces"). Indeed the third image intensifies the second, thereby highlighting both how high Judah had risen in regional esteem and how far she has fallen.

The first positive image is that of a prosperous, full, mother of the nation. McDaniel suggests that based on Phoenician and Ugaritic parallels רבתי may mean "mistress" rather than "great" or "full" (*Bib* 49 [1968] 29–31). He notes (30) that Wiesmann at least implied this honorific meaning in his commentary (see Wiesmann, 103, 107). Renkema agrees to some extent since he translates the phrase "that city, that Lady among her people" (96). But Hillers is probably right to emphasize that biblical parallels like Isa 1:21 ("How she has become a whore, the faithful city!") and 1 Sam 2:5 (ורבת בנים—"having many sons") "seem to make the traditional understanding preferable to the otherwise attractive suggestion of T. McDaniel" ([1992] 64). At an earlier time Jerusalem was "great with people" in the sense of having many inhabitants.

The second positive image is of a city "great *among* the nations." Kraus suggests that this phrase may refer to the years prior to the catastrophe of 597 B.C.E. (26). It is true that at least during the latter years of Josiah's reign (640–609 B.C.E.) the nation carved out a leading role for itself. It is also true that the Babylonian threat of 605 B.C.E. and the Egyptian domination of Judah's political scene immediately after Josiah's death had devastating effects on the small nation. Though Kraus correctly identifies one of the times by which Judah had lost prior prominence, it is not possible to settle upon 597 B.C.E. as the most likely reference. It remains most plausible to conclude that Jerusalem's defeat in 587 B.C.E. best fits the context. Prominence was indeed achieved from time to time, but whatever glory days occurred in the past are definitively just that—in the past.

The third positive image in effect heightens the second. Not only was Jerusalem prominent, or "great" (רבתי), she was also in fact a "princess," a noble (שׂרתי) among them (במדינות). She was more than simply one nation among equals. Perhaps the poet remembers back to the time when she was a leader in regional alliances against the mighty international powers (Isa 7:1–16), or when her king stood against Assyria and survived (2 Kgs 18:1–37), or even when her king opposed Egypt and paid with his life (2 Kgs 23:28–30). Regardless, at times Judah attempted to be more than a passive smaller nation. The poet recalls these times and marks their passing.

Two contrastive images express Jerusalem's reversal of fortunes. First, she היתה כאלמנה, "has become like a widow." As with ישׁבה, the perfect-tense verb here relates an apparently permanent condition. The noun כאלמנה conveys more than one connotation. It can indeed mean that she is without a husband. After all, several OT texts use the metaphor of Israel as God's spouse (cf. Isa 54:1–8; Ezek 16, 23; Hos 1–3), and this imagery includes Israel either leaving God or God turning Israel over to her sins. This phrase may also drop the personified city into the class of the marginalized along with the orphan and resident alien (cf. Deut 10:18; 16:11; Isa 1:23; Jer 7:6–7; Ps 94:6; Lam 5:3). Such persons often had no effective advocate, so their rights were ignored and the justice due them perverted. God's promised protection of the widow (cf. Pss 68:6 [ET 68:5]; 146:9) must have seemed distant indeed to the bereft city. Like Naomi, who lamented her change from being full to being empty and from being pleasant to becoming bitter (Ruth 1:20–21), Jerusalem must have felt the sting of this reversal.

Second, the "princess among the provinces has become a vassal." The repetition of רבתי, "great with," "great," in the sense of "many," reinforces the picture of lost grandeur. It also anticipates the final verse of chap. 1, which states כי רבות אנחתי,

"many are my groans." What was once an abundance of people and prestige has become an abundance of groans and faintings. The narrator, who speaks in 1:1, and the city, who speaks in 1:22, agree on this point.

Jerusalem is described as a former "princess." This word is less precise than its English translation, for it is used in the plural to describe the courtly women who waited vainly with Sisera's mother for the Canaanite commander to return (Judg 5:28), the seven hundred wives of Solomon in contrast to the concubines in his harem (1 Kgs 11:3), the royal women who will nurse the restored Israel (Isa 49:23), and the wives of Persian nobility (Esth 1:18). In the form שרה the word is the name given Sarai as the mother of a significant nation yet to be born (cf. Gen 17:15–21; Isa 51:2). In the past Jerusalem was a truly significant city.

Jerusalem's significance was particularly noteworthy when compared with "the provinces" in the region. In 1 Kings מדנה refers to an administrative district (see 1 Kgs 20:14–15, 17, 19), while in Esther (about thirty times), Dan 8:2 and 11:24, Ezra 2:1, and Neh 1:3, 7:6, and 11:3 it describes a "province" or "satrapy." By the time Jerusalem was destroyed, nations like Judah, Ammon, Tyre, Sidon, and Philistia had become virtual provinces of Babylon, and before that many of them had been just as subservient to Assyria. At times Judah exercised some autonomy, which may explain her perceived prominence. It is also true, as Hillers ([1992] 81) points out, that the poet may be echoing themes of Jerusalem's lofty power and beauty such as those found in Pss 48:2–4 (ET 48:1–3) and 87:1–3. For Judah's citizens, Jerusalem was politically, spiritually, geographically, and aesthetically significant. Now she is like everyone else.

What was once a privileged position has become one of subservience, for she is currently היתה למס, "a vassal," or "one required to do forced labor." This phrase recalls earlier instances of oppression, especially those in Egypt (Exod 1:11) and those under Solomon (1 Kgs 4:6; 9:15–21). The Egyptian reference may serve as a reminder that the Babylonian exile was often viewed as a reversal of the exodus. Slavery, or nearly that, not freedom, had become Jerusalem's lot in life.

2 The poet now focuses on the city's loneliness and lack of comfort. As Re'emi writes, "The theme of the widow is developed further; heartbroken, she weeps in the night under the burden of her suffering. There is no one to comfort her, those who loved her in the time of her prosperity have deserted her, some have even betrayed her (cf. Jer. 16:5; Job 2:11)" (84–85). She is bereft of her "people" in v 1, and here she is without her אהביה, "lovers," and רעיה, "friends."

Her sorrow is expressed emphatically. The phrase "she weeps bitterly" consists of an infinitive absolute (בכו) and an imperfect-tense verb of the same root (תבכה), a common way of intensifying an action. Her weeping occurs בלילה, "in the night," which underscores her lonely, lingering grief. Her tears are ודמעתה על לחיה, "on her cheeks," or perhaps "constantly on her cheeks," so her grief has a permanent quality to it. It stays with her at all times, for she has no apparent hope of consolation.

Such weeping is a standard part of Israel's vocabulary of complaint and lament (see Pss 69:11 [ET 69:10]; 78:64; 126:6; 137:1). It is central to Israel's expression of humanity. OT writers record without embarrassment many instances of weeping, from Hagar's sorrow (Gen 21:16) to that of the people who hear the Law read in Neh 8:9. Likewise, the word דמעתה, "tears," occurs regularly in laments, particular in Psalms (6:7 [ET 6:6]; 39:13 [ET 39:12]; 42:4 [ET 42:3]; 56:9 [ET 56:8]; and so on), yet also in Jeremiah (8:23 [ET 9:1]; 9:17 [ET 18];

13:17; 31:16). Jerusalem's pain is not unique. As the text proceeds, her sorrow does reach depths seldom expressed in the language of lament.

Jerusalem's agony is as solitary as it is bitter. She might reasonably have expected help from מכל אהביה, "all her lovers," or from כל רעיה, "all her friends/allies," yet if so she has been utterly disappointed. This disappointment echoes throughout chap. 1; it is expressed again in 1:9, 16, 17, and 21. She has no one who is אין לה מנחם, "comforting her." Westermann comments, "The Hebrew verb *niham* has a broader range of meaning than the English 'console.' *Niham* . . . also refers to actions that alleviate or mollify suffering. This fuller range of meaning lies behind the reference to Job's friends, when they are said to come to console Job. It is also the thrust of the opening clause of Deutero-Isaiah's proclamation 'Comfort, comfort my people!'" (125). Westermann adds that in the ancient world even "the realities of ethnic conflict and inter-group hostility" do not negate the fact "that people are essentially neighbors to one another" (125). If one could be expected to experience grief over little or no help from strangers, even enemies, how much more pain emerges from old friends standing aloof in times of trouble?

Who are these אהביה, "lovers," and רעיה, "friends"? Provan asserts that "all that love her" is preferable to "lovers," since Israel's sin is not introduced until 1:5 (36). Hillers agrees that betrayal by friends is a common theme in Hebrew and Babylonian literature ([1992] 81), but he also observes, "In the metaphorical language familiar especially from Hosea, Jeremiah, and Ezekiel, Israel, the wife of Yahweh, has been unfaithful to him by entering into an alliance with other nations and gods (e.g., Hos 8:9–10; Ezek 16:28–29; 23:5–21). These paramours in the end forsake her (Hos 2:9[=7E]; Jer 22:20–22; 30:14) or turn against her (Ezek 16:37–41; 23:22–29; cf. also v 19 below)" ([1992] 82). Though one should be cautious at this point, it is likely that this reference to "lovers" alerts readers that this weeping woman may not be as innocent as she first appears. Future revelations are foreshadowed here. Her "friends" are most certainly neighbors with whom Jerusalem made a treaty to ward off Babylon (cf. Jer 27:1–22). These weak allies could not deliver her; only God could have done so, but the people refused this option (cf. Jer 25:1–38). Worse still, they בגדו, "betrayed, dealt treacherously," with her and היו לה לאיבים, "became her enemies." Against the backdrop of 605–587 B.C.E., it seems that Egypt was an ally unable or unwilling to help Judah, while Edom was a neighboring nation happy to loot the stricken Jerusalem (see Obad 10–14).

3 Having depicted the city's bitter loneliness in 1:2, the poet now offers the book's first descriptions of Judah's descent into exile. The need for a word beginning with *gimel* prompts the use of גלה to introduce the exile theme. Exile is not an overtly major motif in Lamentations, a fact that may indicate the book's Palestinian provenance. The verb גלה only appears here and in 4:22, where the end of exile is anticipated, and the noun גולה does not occur in the book. Exile is the reason Jerusalem sits alone, weeps, and hopes for restoration. The author chooses to make exile a constant background image rather than an openly obvious foundational one.

Judah's serving as the subject of the exile expands the poem's scene and its scope of suffering. Now both capital city and national name have become personified. As is true of most personifications, this one operates as hyperbole (see Rudolph, 210; Provan, 38), for it does not describe the exile of the whole nation (see Jer 40–42). Rather, it highlights the forced exit of many citizens, among them skilled tradespeople, leaders, and ordinary citizens who had not been deported in 597 B.C.E. when Ezekiel went there. The terrible and numerous deportations sharpened mother Jerusalem's loss, loneliness, and abandonment. This sense of comprehensive loss indicates that this exile is the one in 587 B.C.E., and not the invasion of 597 B.C.E., as Rudolph suggests (193).

"Affliction and harsh servitude" characterize Jerusalem's exile. Her מעני, "affliction," may refer back to the forced labor implied in Jerusalem's vassal status (1:1), and it certainly becomes a constant theme, recurring in 1:7, 9 and 3:1, 19. ומרב עבדה, translated "harsh servitude," literally means "abundance of work." She works all the time. Such unceasing labor evokes memories of Israel's Egyptian bondage (see Exod 1:14; 2:23; 5:11; 6:6, 9). Judah's suffering may be equal to what was endured in Moses' era, but readers have to wonder already if their innocence is equal to that of their ancestors.

If exodus imagery lies behind 1:3a, then the fact that Judah "dwells among the nations" and "does not find rest" becomes even more poignant. שבה, "she dwells," echoes 1:1a, so the duration of the city's loneliness matches the length of the exiles' stay among the nations. Here בגוים, "nations" probably means "Gentiles." Judah now lives out among the nations, dispersed from the land of promise. Inevitably she finds no מנוח, "rest," a term used only here in Lamentations. The word's sister noun מנוחה and its verb family are used often in the OT to depict God's act of settling Israel safely in the promised land (see Deut 12:9; 25:19; 2 Sam 7:1, 11; and so on). Part of the pain and shame of exile resulted from the loss of rest that the Lord gave the people under Joshua, David, and Solomon. God's people have reverted back at least as far as pre-exodus days.

Judah tried to avoid exile by fleeing her enemies. This flight was unsuccessful, for "all her pursuers overtook her between the straits." The phrase כל רדפיה, "all her pursuers," indicates a thorough, well-staffed action. This pursuit imagery appears again in 1:6, 3:43, 3:66, 4:19, and 5:5. The fact that these pursuers השיגוה, "overtook her," echoes the account of Zedekiah's attempt to leave Jerusalem as the Babylonians were entering the city's breached walls. Both 2 Kgs 25:1–7 and its parallel passage, Jer 52:1–11, use forms of רדף and נשג to describe the pursuing and overtaking of Zedekiah, his warriors, and his officials. Thus, it is likely that the poet reflects the Babylonian invasion, which indeed came after Judah's allies abandoned or dealt treacherously with her (1:2). Just where the invaders overtook the city is harder to determine since המצרים, "the straits," is rare. Keil writes, "This word denotes 'straits,' narrow places where escape is impossible (Ps. cxvi.3, cxviii.5), or circumstances in life from which no escape can be found" (361). Therefore, the word may indicate a simple completion of Babylon's invasion, or it may be a reversion to a description of emotions. That is, it may either simply mean, "The Babylonians captured us in the narrow places in the cities and hills," or it could mean, "The Babylonians captured us in the midst of our distress." Most likely the poet uses this word because of its elasticity. This choice allows for a historical referent to take on evocative force.

So far the text has announced Jerusalem's pain and situation. The poet has compared the city to a widow, noted her terrible reversal from noblewoman to vassal laborer, described the depth of her sorrow, divulged that her neighbors and lovers have acted unfaithfully, and revealed that her children have gone into exile. Her historical circumstances also have theological ramifications. Judah has left the land of promise for a place of no rest among the nations. These foundational matters are revisited throughout the book, so it is difficult to overemphasize their importance for understanding the book as a whole.

4–6 This section is closely linked to vv 1–3 by several factors. First, the use of personification expands to include the city's דרכי, "roads," and שעריה, "gates," (1:4bc). Second, the city, before now unnamed, is identified as Zion (1:4a, 6a). Third, the city remains the center of attention, since it is mentioned twice by name and ten times by the pronouns "she" or "her." Fourth, צריה/איביה, "foes/enemies," continue to be a significant factor. Fifth, these foes' work is once again depicted as רדף, "pursuit" or "hunting" (compare 1:3c and 1:6c). These verses expand the portrayal of the city's damage and distress by highlighting the plight of specific sites—roads, gates (1:4ab)—and of certain segments of the population—priests, young women (1:4bc), children (1:5c), and nobility (1:6b).

All these sad descriptions are facets of Zion's paralyzing loss, which leaves her steeped in bitterness (1:4c), stripped of authority (1:5a), afflicted with grief by Yahweh (1:5b), bereft of children (1:5c), robbed of splendor (1:6a), and deprived of leadership (1:6bc). The exile introduced in 1:3 is described further in 1:5–6, where Zion's children go into captivity with the enemy pressing them, and with their leaders, like half-starved stags, feebly trying to dodge the enemy's arrows. The acrostic form continues to do its job. More descriptions of sorrow, sin, and suffering emerge, yet now almost always based on what has already been said. All types of reality, whether emotional, physical, or spiritual, are brought into the poem. Thoroughness already marks the composition.

4 Continuing the pattern of personification, the poet writes, "The roads of Zion mourn." This phrase clearly identifies the city for the first time. As Renkema observes, "The name itself is not simply a synonym for Jerusalem. It is a unique term, rather, for Jerusalem as the location of the cult, as the temple city, the dwelling place of YHWH" (112). Though a common designation for the capital city, ציון, "Zion," never lost its connotation as the holy mountain on which David placed the ark of the covenant and Solomon built the temple. Its importance was evident because the house of God and the house of the king stood there. ציון, "Zion," is the poet's favorite word for Jerusalem. It occurs three times in chap. 1 and seven times in chap. 2. ירושלם, "Jerusalem," appears seven times in the poems, all in chaps. 1–2. עיר, "city," is used six times, four of them in chaps. 1–2. In comparison, in chaps. 3–5 ציון occurs only three times (4:11; 5:11; 5:18) and עיר only twice (3:51; 5:11). The city's woes are emphasized more in the book's early poems than in its later ones, when the people's woes, confessions, and petitions take precedence.

The word דרכי, "roads," stresses the centrality of worship for the whole of Judah, for all roads led to Jerusalem and God's temple. All the paths to Jerusalem are empty now, however, and so no one comes to Zion for festival, prayer, or sacrifice. These desolate roads mourn (אבלות) in a manner similar to the grief expressed by the "land" in Hos 4:3 and Jer 12:4 and 23:10, the "ground" in Joel 1:10, and the "gates" in Isa 3:26 and Jer 14:2 (see Budde, 80). These inanimate objects come alive with grief thrust upon them by forces and causes so far unspecified.

Zion's שעריה, "gates," share the roads' sorrow. Though "desolate" captures the sense of שוממין, it is also possible to translate the word as "appalled," or "stunned," as is evidenced by the use of its verbal form in Jer 2:12 ("Be appalled, O heavens"). Both reaction and result must be kept in mind. Desolation implies here both a psychological feeling and a current social status.

This shared grief stems from the fact that מבלי באי מועד, "none are coming to the festival." The word מועד can have a range of meanings, including appointed time, place, or meeting (BDB, 417–18). All three possibilities and combinations of them occur in Lamentations. In 1:4 (cf. 2:6b, 7, 22) it refers to festive occasions appointed by Israel's historic calendar of feasts (see Lev 23; Deut 16) centered in Zion. In 2:6a it stands for the temple, the divinely appointed meeting place, and in 1:15 it may refer to a meeting between parties. Its constant usage in Exodus, Leviticus, and Numbers indicates how important the concept was in Israel's worship and what pain would be caused by the disruption of these mandated events. Joel 1:8–9, 1:13, and 1:16 illustrate the agony associated with the loss of worship activity, while Pss 122 and 125 portray the joy and exhilaration of ongoing adoration of Yahweh.

In the second half of the verse the roads and gates are joined in their grieving by כהניה, "her priests," and בתולחיה, "her virgins." Of course, the priests are the temple's chief functionaries. They are supposed to teach the people and help them with prayers and sacrifices. Because no one comes to the temple they נאנחים, "are groaning." Forms of this word are used elsewhere to express Israel's groaning under Egyptian bondage (Exod 2:23), Ezekiel's moaning at the prospect of Yahweh's wrath (Ezek 21:6–7 [MT 21:11–12]), and the noise made by starving cattle (Joel 1:18). In Lam 1, אנח in the *nipʿal* stem conveys the voicing of horrible pain by the priests (1:4), Jerusalem (1:8c), the people (1:11a), and the city (1:21a). As for the virgins, it is likely that they "had some kind of special involvement in the liturgical life of the temple" (Renkema, 116). Provan (40) notes that young women are highlighted in several OT passages: (1) they dance at Shiloh's annual festival (Judg 21:19–21); (2) they participate in joyful processions (Ps 68:24–25 [MT 68:25–26]); and (3) they rejoice and dance in restored Israel (Jer 31:4), a gladness they will share with the priests (Jer 31:13–14). Thus, it is clear that at the very least these women's normal role was to express joy during religious celebrations. So their נוגות, "grieving," is a tragic reversal of their cherished activity. Forms of the verb יגה also appear in 1:5, 12 and 3:32, 33. Their grief is significant, unexpected, and brought about by others (see *NIDOTTE*, 2:397). The priests have no worship service, and the virgins have no joy.

Zion herself והיא מר לה, "suffers bitterly." This phrase embraces and summarizes all the suffering—the mourning, grieving, and groaning. Mother Zion's situation is created by what her children experience, and the sum total of these experiences can only be described as bitter. Like Naomi, who in the midst of her pain asked to be called "Bitter" instead of "Pleasant" (see Ruth 1:13, 20), Zion's current situation leads to this conclusion.

5 The poet has introduced several characters vital to the whole book: the city, Zion, the foes, the unfaithful lovers and allies, the priests, and the virgins. Now Yahweh, the book's most significant character, enters the picture. Readers learn that all the misery depicted in 1:1–4 stems from the Lord's activity. God has caused it. Of course this fact leads to yet another significant issue, which is why God has done so, and then to still another important matter, which is how Israel will react to the Lord's actions.

Before introducing Yahweh, however, the author states, "Her foes have become (her) master; her enemies prosper." This information goes beyond that offered in 1:2–3, for it expresses a settled, current situation. The fact that Zion's enemies have become לראש, "her master," or more literally "her head," may echo Deut 28:13, 44, where Moses declares that Israel's status as "head" or "tail" among the nations depends on obedience to or disobedience of God's covenant. In contrast to herself, Zion's foes שלו, "prosper." They live well from the misery of others. In his first "confession" (12:1), Jeremiah asks why the treacherous שלו, "prosper." In Ps 122:6 (NRSV) the writer prays, "May they prosper who love you" (ישליו אהביך). Clearly the irony of this situation is that those who hate God's people receive the blessing usually reserved for those who love them. Everything seems to be turned upside down. Or is it?

At this point the author reveals one of the book's most significant theological concepts: what has happened to Judah has occurred because of her sins. How did the foe become her master? Why do they prosper? "For the LORD has made her grieve because of her numerous transgressions." Deut 28:52–57 promises invasion, siege, and capitulation for constant sin against God and God's word, and Deut 28:58–63 threatens terrible affliction, diminishment of population and influence, and exile for the same reason. These covenantal warnings have become reality for the current generation.

The particle כי expresses cause here and introduces the fact that Yahweh has made Jerusalem grieve (יהוה הוגה). This information serves several contextual functions. First, it gives a brief reason for the main character's pain. Second, it places all authority for the people's life in God's hands. Third, it verbally connects the grieving in 1:4 to the causer of grief in 1:5. Fourth, it foreshadows the need to confess sin that recurs throughout the book. The mentioning of רב פשעיה, "her numerous transgressions," alerts readers to Israel's behavior through a general term for sin (פשע). This word is frequently used to describe the willful breaking of God's laws. It acts as a catchword in the first poem (see 1:5, 14, 22), and its verbal form appears in 3:42. In Amos it sets the tone for the indictments against Israel's neighbors and against Israel itself (Amos 1:3, 6, 9, 11, 13; 2:1, 4, 6). It is used to depict political rebellion in 1 Kgs 12:19 and 2 Kgs 1:1 and 3:5, 7. Such occurrences indicate that the poet highlights God's people's rebellion against his divine authority. These crimes against God's authority were as numerous as they were serious. The word רב, "numerous," suggests abundance, even multiplication (see Hos 8:11, 14; 10:1). Zion's rebellions were not sporadic, rash acts that disrupted a general pattern of obedience. Disobedience eroded God's patience with their activity over a long period of time. Jer 5:6 expresses the same opinion. Judah's enemies will overcome them because כי רבו פשעיהם, "they multiply their transgressions."

The verse's final segment—"Her children have gone away, captives before the foe"—reprises the theme of exile from 1:3 and prefaces the more elaborate picture in 1:6. Here the word עולליה, "children," seems not to refer to a specific age group but to the populace as a whole, so it is parallel to יהודה, "Judah," in 1:3a. All the captives, whatever their age or station in life, were Zion's children, and their departure leaves their mother bereft, bitter, and virtually alone. The phrase שבי לפני־צר, "captives before the foe," indicates that the people were marched into exile one heavy step at a time. Though שבי, "captives, captivity," is at first glance general enough to leave one guessing at the exiles' destination, the fact that the densest uses of the word are in Jeremiah (15:2; 20:6; 22:12; 30:10, 16; 43:11; 46:27; 48:46) and Ezra-Nehemiah (Ezra 2:1; 3:8; 8:35; 9:7; Neh 1:2–3; 7:6; 8:17) strongly suggests that the Babylonian exile is meant.

6 V 6 closes this section (1:4–6) by summarizing and reinforcing its two major emphases: Zion's desolation (1:6a) and the exile of a host of her people (1:6bc). It does so by adding the city's officials to the list of those who have been driven out by the Babylonians. Without such leaders, it seems unlikely that the city will be able to regroup effectively and rebuild any time soon.

This *vav* line of the acrostic begins with the phrase ויצא מן־בת־ציון כל־הדרה, "and has gone out from Daughter Zion, all her majesty," which once again underscores Jerusalem's favored status and corresponding significant loss. The genitive force of the construct בת־ציון is appositional: the daughter and Zion are one and the same (see Provan, 41; Westermann, 110, 112; Hillers, [1992] 85). Whose daughter is she? According to Follis (*ABD*, 6:1103) "Daughter Zion" acts as "an image of the unity between place and people within which divine favor and civilization create a setting of stability and home." In other words, Zion is God's daughter, and as such she stands as a comforting and nurturing symbol to the rest of the land. Thus, that she has lost כל־הדרה, "all her majesty," signals doom for all other places in Judah, or may indicate that their fate was sealed before hers.

What "majesty" is meant here? The psalmists use forms of הדר as a synonym for God's glory and majesty (see Pss 96:6; 145:5). Renkema notes that the word also denotes Yahweh's kingship (Pss 104:1; 111:3; 145:5, 12) and Yahweh's majesty in creation (Ps 29:4; see Isa 35:2). He also observes that God bestowed הדר on Jerusalem in Ezek 16:6–13, 14 (Renkema, 122). Isaiah's declaration of woe against Jerusalem in 5:13–14 may offer a clue about the word's force here. Isaiah threatens exile for the nation and כבודו, "its leaders," which is literally "its glory." Further, in a dramatic comparison of exile to *sheol*, Isaiah states that Jerusalem's "nobility," which literally is "her majesty" (הדרה), will "go down" into the grave of exile. The verbal and conceptual affinities between Isa 5:13–14 and Lam 1:5–6 suggest that הדרה, "her majesty," is not an abstract picture of Jerusalem's beauty or status but a concrete reference to her people and leaders. Jerusalem's leaders were part of the majesty God bestowed on the city, and now that majesty has gone away to exile along with the city's beloved children. In other words, the covenant people have been exiled.

Like the people, Judah's שריה, "officials," have endured siege and its attending loss of food. Thus, they have become כאילים, "like deer," who לא־מצאו מרעה, "have not found pasture." Consequently, when the enemy came, וילכו בלא כח, "they fled [or 'went away'] without strength." They became easy prey for their persistent רודף, "pursuers." These שריה, "officials," appear again in 2:2, 2:9, and 5:12. The word has a range of uses in the OT (see BDB, 978–79), but here probably describes political, military, and civil leaders. Renkema writes that such persons were often wealthy and well dressed, so this verse describes quite a reversal of fortunes (124). Their lack of strength is evident, for their foes overtook them as one overtakes a starving animal. This description of their capture echoes 2 Kgs 25:5 and Jer 52:8, for both state that the Chaldeans וירדפו, "pursued," the king and his army and easily overtook them. Not even the הדר, "majesty," of Judah, its best leaders, could save the nation. The leaders could not even save themselves.

7–9 So far the poet has depicted the city's reversal of fortunes (1:1–3) and Zion's desolation and emptiness (1:4–6). The city is a widow bereft of children, allies, and lovers, while Zion is a treasured place emptied of human and liturgical majesty. In 1:7–9 the bereaved main character is called ירושלם, "Jerusalem," for the first time. Under this name the grieving capital is portrayed as an unclean place whose sin led to her demise. Thus, the theme of Zion's sin begun in 1:5 grows in this section, which has the effect of removing any lingering doubts about the root cause of the nation's woe. Judah's problems in real space and time stem from theological errors, not just from political mistakes or historical contingencies.

7 Lam 1:7 and 2:19 are the only verses in chaps. 1–3 that have four lines instead of three. Hillers ([1992] 68), Kraus (22), Wiesmann (110), and others suggest dropping the second line—כל מחמדיה אשר היו מימי קדם, "All her precious things that / were from days of old"—to reinstate the normal three-line verse because the verse still makes sense without it. Though they are correct that such an excision does leave a meaningful verse, they are not necessarily correct in asserting that a differently constructed verse must be corrupt. The poet offers several variations on normal forms in the book, so the text is not uniform throughout. It is also true that 2:19 also has four lines. Though one can argue that both texts are corrupt, it is also possible to argue that the poet intentionally has one four-line verse in each of the first two poems.

Albrektson (*Studies in the Text and Theology,* 62–63), Haller (96), Gottlieb (*Study on the Text,* 13), and others conclude, on the other hand, that it is the third line, not the second, that ought to be removed. Again, the verse can be read without the third line and make sense. But again no textual evidence against the line exists. Albrektson writes, "The fact that all four lines are found in both LXX and Syr is of course not a conclusive argument against the theory of a gloss, as there are several centuries between the time when the book was written and the time when it was translated" (62). Given this lack of textual evidence, Albrektson rests his case "on the empirical observation that all the other stanzas have only three lines" (62). If the argument for the necessity of three lines is the chief reason for omitting the verse, then this is insufficient cause in a book like Lamentations. The verse makes sense as it stands. Given the lack of contrary evidence and the verse's readability, then, this commentary treats the MT.

זכרה ירושלם, "Jerusalem remembers," right now, during ימי עניה ומרודיה, "the days of her afflictions and her wanderings," what she has lost. The text's lack of clear temporal markers forces one to decide whether Jerusalem currently suffers pain or that agony is in the past. Renkema argues that the force of זכר is "pondering," not simply recalling events, and that 1:7ab details what she ponders at the present time (126–27). What she ponders now is partly what happened in her recent past, for she recalls בנפל עמה ביד־צר, "when her people fell into the hand of the foe," which was partly caused by her lack of any strong helper (ואין עוזר לה). She also reflects upon the utter shame of her enemies' scornful laughter (ראוה צרים שחקו על־משבתה, "her enemies saw her and laughed over her [or 'because of her'] annihilation"). This past laughter rings in her ears, causing present pain. But this present memory of recent horrible events is made still worse by her recollection of כל מחמדיה, "all her precious things," which parallels כל הדרה, "all her glory," from 1:6. Just as "her glory" probably refers to Israel's exiled leaders, the fact that היו מימי קדם, "all her precious things were from days of old," means that the poet thinks of "the times of Moses and Joshua, of David and Solomon" (Keil, 364). Jerusalem remembers days of victory, days of great leaders, and days of wealth. All these are connected to her glorious past, just as misery, wandering, defeat, and contempt are part of her terrible, depressing present. Her thoughts range from the distant past, to the recent past, to the present moment. Each one has its part in her current state of mind. All covenant blessings seem lost.

8 At this point the narrator turns from Jerusalem's state of mind to the reason for her descent from past prominence and glory to present agony and shame. The text states bluntly that "Jerusalem has sinned greatly." Her sin is made emphatic by the infinitive absolute followed by the perfect tense (חטא חטאה, "has sinned greatly"). This declaration partners with 1:5, which asserts that Jerusalem's פשעיה, "transgressions," a word that emphasizes rebellions of various types (see *NIDOTTE*, 3:706-10), led the Lord to make her grieve. The root חטא expands Jerusalem's iniquity beyond rebellion against God. As Renkema explains, "The actual content of the root חטא points more towards a breach of community relationships, thus placing the accent on the fact of the transgression rather than on the inclination to transgress. Where norms and rules exist in a community then the root חטא implies their transgression" (132). Jerusalem has both rebelled against God and sinned against herself by her inhabitants, sinning against one another. By using multiple words for wrongdoing, the poet continues to use the acrostic format effectively. In this instance a thorough treatment of Jerusalem's sin leads to a thorough understanding of why she has fallen.

As a result of this great sinning (על כי, "therefore"), Jerusalem היתה, "became," and remains לנידה, "impure." Keil writes that this word "signifies in particular the uncleanness of the menstrual discharge in women, Lev. xii.2, 5, etc.; then the uncleanness of a woman in this condition, Lev. xv.19, etc.; here it is transferred to Jerusalem personified as such an unclean woman, and therefore shunned" (365). כל מכבדיה, "all who honored her," in the past now הזילוה, "despise(d) her," a word that re-emphasizes how drastically her fortunes have changed and highlights the depths of the shame she must now endure. Why? כי ראו ערותה, "because/for they saw her nakedness." Hillers explains this phrase: "The motif 'they saw her naked' is meaningful at several levels. It is primarily an expression of the utter contempt with which Zion is treated. Exposure of one's body, especially the genitals, was to the ancient Israelites an almost immeasurable disgrace, a shame they felt much more deeply than most moderns would" ([1992] 86). Renkema adds, "Disgrace of this kind was also used in the portrayal of the fate of certain (personified) cities who had undergone YHWH's judgement, for example, Nineveh (Nah 3:5f) and Jerusalem (Jer 13:26)" (134). Her former admirers have seen "her bloodstained clothing" (Provan, 45), the results of her impurity, firsthand. Her nakedness here includes her sins, her exposure to invasion, and her defeat. When others see her sins and their results, they despise her, then turn away in disgust. She is left utterly alone, so she "groaned [נאנחה] and turned away [ותשב אחור]." God has judged her, and her friends have abandoned her, but she has brought the situation on herself.

9 The first part of this verse continues the uncleanness and nakedness imagery begun in 1:8. Now the poet states that "her uncleanness [טמאתה] was on/in her skirts [בשוליה]." In other words, it clung to her. As Westermann asserts, "She cannot free herself of this uncleanness; it is out in the open where everyone can see it" (129). Leaving this condition unattended indicates that לא זכרה אחריתה, "she took no thought for her future." Or, as Renkema translates the phrase, "she was not prepared for such an outcome" (136). She did not think things would turn out as they did. Clearly, she did nothing to amend her ways, either because she thought she had done nothing wrong or because she mistook God's patience for indifference. Either way she reached the wrong conclusion.

Jerusalem's consistently sinful action had two basic consequences: her coming down, or destruction, and her loneliness. Indeed, ותרד פלאים, "she went down amazingly." The root ירד occurs in Deut 20:20 in the context of the fall of a city, in Isa 47:1 to describe the future defeat of Babylon, and in Ezek 30:6 to depict Egypt's demise (Provan, 45). Thus, the phrase here most likely refers to Babylon's victory in 587 B.C.E. Jerusalem's fall was פלאים, "wondrous," or "spectacular." It was no typical military setback. On the day of Jerusalem's greatest loss אין מנחם לה, "there was no one comforting her." No one came to console her.

Perhaps given this desolation, the city now, at last, cries out to God. Did she do so when her priests were busy, her virgins happy, her leaders in place, and her admirers near? Apparently not. Did she do so when her uncleanness clung to her skirts? Again, apparently not. Instead, she looked for other relationships. Only when other comforters were missing did she turn to the Lord. But now she implores Yahweh to ראה, "see," עניי, "my afflictions." This use of ראה echoes again in 1:11, 1:20, and 2:20. Westermann writes that in communal and individual laments a plea usually comes after the lament, often includes an invocation to God, and exists in laments but not in dirges. Lam 1:9, 11, and 20 "could just as well stand in one of the many psalms of lamentation in the psalter" (130). Whatever she has done in the past, Jerusalem looks to the Lord now. She calls attention to afflictions she has suffered, which connects her plea to the narrator's description of her woes in 1:3, 7. It also connects her to the distant past, when God "saw" Israel's pain and moved to deliver them (Exod 2:23–25). Further, she asks God to notice that her afflictions are caused by the fact that her enemy has הגדיל, "triumphed," or more literally "been made great" (*hipʿil* perfect third masculine singular). So far she states the obvious, but does so to God, the only one who can help her. More involved statements come later.

10–11 This section depicts Jerusalem's groanings and continued cries for Yahweh to ראה, "see," what has happened to her. It also extends the reason for the groaning to include the violation of the holy place and its utensils by the invading Babylonian armies. Skillful repetition of words already used in 1:1–9 links this section to what precedes it, and its inclusion of first-person speech by Jerusalem prepares readers for the city's impassioned pleas in 1:12–16 and 1:18–22.

10 The narrator resumes the third-person detailing of Jerusalem's situation. In doing so he chooses language similar to that in 1:7. He states that "the enemy has stretched out his hand." The word for "enemy" is the same in both places (צר), and each text emphasizes the enemy's power through the use of a form of "hand" (ביד in 1:7, and ידו in 1:10). Further, v 10 explains that the "enemy has stretched out his hand over all her precious things." Both 1:7 and 1:10 use the same word for "precious things," with 1:7 reading מחמדיה and 1:10 מחמדיה. In 1:7 these "precious things" are not identified overtly, though they could be either items or people. Here the reference is almost certainly to the Babylonians' plundering of the temple (Kraus, 30). Much to her dismay, Jerusalem ראתה, "saw," Gentiles (גוים) enter (באו) מקדשה, "her holy place," the temple.

This entering violates Deut 23:3–6, which forbids Moabites and Ammonites from coming into the "assembly of the LORD" because of treachery against Israel (O. Kaiser, 126). Apparently the passage came to be applied to Israel's enemies, to Gentiles, or to both. Of course, by the era of the Maccabees the rule was applied to Gentiles in general, though converts were granted some access to the holy site. The close verbal connections between Deut 23:4 and Lam 1:10 indicate that this is the commandment the poet has in mind. Both texts include a prohibition that they or he "shall not go" (לא יבאו in 1:10 and לא יבא in Deut 23:4) as well as a designation of the "assembly of the LORD" (Deut 23:4, בקהל יהוה) or "your assembly" (Lam 1:10, בקהל לך) as the prohibited place. This linking of Deut 23:4 to the fall of Jerusalem highlights the notion that when Jerusalem and its temple were violated, the Lord was likewise violated.

11 Besides the mental anguish of seeing the temple defiled (1:10), the people have endured practical, physical pain. Due to Jerusalem's demise, "all her people [כל עמה] groan/are groaning [נאנחים]" for a very specific reason—they are forced to seek constantly (מבקשים) for bread (לחם). Hunger and the difficulty of finding bread become a regular theme from this point forward. In fact, as Renkema claims, "Structural analysis reveals that in their [the poets'] conception of the five songs the famine took a literally central position" (147). After all, 2:11 stresses "the desperate hunger of the little children," 3:16 underscores the lack of food, 4:10 reveals that women ate "the corpses of their children" (see also 2:20), and 5:9–10 describes "the hunger raging in the land" (147). Add to these texts the famine theme found in 1:19, 2:19, 4:3–5, 4:7–9, and 5:6 (147) and one senses the urgency and reality of the problem. No wonder constant groaning may be heard. The people endured famine and siege and must now scrape together nourishment in a devastated city.

In such desperate times the people sell what they have to get enough to eat. To describe their desperation the poet uses the familiar "their precious things" (מחמדיהם following the Qere reading of the MT). Used in 1:7 to describe precious leaders and a precious heritage and in 1:10 to describe precious items in the temple, the word now portrays whatever precious possessions the people can sell באכל להשיב נפש, "for food, to revive their strength/soul." Hillers even contends that the precious things are her children ([1992] 87–88). If so, the pain must be magnified accordingly. Thus, the poet uses one word to depict a comprehensive portrait of desperation and thereby demonstrates how conciseness contributes to the thoroughness inherent in the acrostic form.

As in 1:9c, the city breaks into the narrator's moving description with a plea that Yahweh ראה, "see," their horrible situation. Indeed, she intensifies her plea by adding והביטה, "and consider," to ראה. Earlier she asked that Yahweh ראה, "see," her affliction and the way their enemies had triumphed. Now she wants Yahweh to "see and consider" how she is being זוללה, "despised," which echoes the claim in 1:8 that those who once honored her now have הזילוה, "despised her." Her reversal of fortunes gnaws at her, and the shame associated with it causes her added anguish. The repetition of key concepts underscores the severity of her situation and the earnestness of her plea.

12–16 This passage begins the chapter's second major section. Having introduced Jerusalem's devastation by detailing her reversals (1:1–3), emptiness and desolation (1:4–6), uncleanness (1:7–9), and groaning for sustenance (1:10–11), the poet turns to the city's specific, heartfelt calls for help and understanding. Jerusalem expresses her acute, seemingly unique, sorrow (1:12–16) and her acknowledgement of sin and prayers to Yahweh (1:18–22). In 1:17, the narrator sympathizes with Jerusalem's plight and attests to the validity of her statements.

Vv 12–16 introduce certain key concepts that grow in importance as the book proceeds. Here Jerusalem admits that God has been the one who punished her (1:12), and here she speaks of her sins for the first time (1:14). Here the city herself first describes the pain she and her children feel (1:14) and the pain and shame her enemies bring upon her (1:14, 16). These details are carefully elaborated as the text continues. This passage is only a beginning point, yet it is a memorable and telling beginning point.

12 Jerusalem cried out to Yahweh in 1:9c and 1:11c but now asks the opinion of כל עברי דרך, "all you who pass by." Whereas she wants God to ראה, "see," and והביטה, "consider," in 1:11c, she asks the same of everyone (הביטו וראו) in 1:12. Renkema observes, "As she had hoped that YHWH would look upon her as a helper so her hope continues that when the passers-by see her affliction they will be moved to help her" (154). Of course, looking for aid from someone other than the Lord has been a long-standing error committed by Jerusalem. Thus, it may well be that the city has yet to turn to God alone for deliverance, or it may be, as Westermann suggests, that 1:12–16 "is a fervent lament directed toward God" (132). Either way help can only come from the Lord now, and Jerusalem's awareness of personal guilt and trust in Yahweh will determine if such help is forthcoming.

Jerusalem attempts to gain the onlookers' sympathy by explaining the enormity of her situation. On the one hand, the implied notion that there has never been אם יש מכאוב כמכאבי, "any sorrow like my sorrow," seems self-serving. Other cities had endured the Babylonians' reign of terror. Therefore, one can certainly consider this phrase hyperbole for the sake of gaining the hearer's attention. On the other hand, Jerusalem's extraordinary pain may be explained by 1:12c— "which the LORD made (me) grieve on the day of his fierce anger." That is, there may be no pain like hers because it is her God who has sent this devastation upon her. She suffers at the hands of the one she expected to save her. One must wonder, however, on what grounds she had a right to assume such deliverance.

Lam 1:12c echoes 1:5b in a way that adds to these questions concerning Jerusalem's statements earlier in the verse. The narrator claims in v 5b that Yahweh caused grief על רב פשעיה, "because of her numerous transgressions" (v 5). In other words, the narrator exonerates God in the matter of Jerusalem's grief. The city has yet to be so explicit. At this point she asks those passing by to consider whether there has ever been sorrow like that which אשר הוגה יהוה, "the LORD made (me) grieve." The use of the same subject and verb in both places and the lack of the specific explanatory phrase about Jerusalem's sins make a comparison of stated causes inevitable.

Jerusalem does say that God has caused this grief ביום חרון אפו, "on the day of his fierce anger." Of course, the mentioning of Yahweh's "day" brings to mind many texts concerning the great and terrible "day of the Lord." For instance, in a judgment oracle against Babylon, Isa 13:13 uses nearly the same phrase as 1:12c to describe the time of that nation's destruction—וביום חרון אפו (see Kraus, 31). Isa 13:14–16 then portrays Babylon's people like frightened sheep and gazelles, and tells the awful truth that their children will be killed and their wives raped. Obviously, such imagery is similar to that in Lam 1:6–7, 11; 2:12–15, 20; and 5:11–14, to name just a few texts. Such is the horror of God's day of fierce wrath on Jerusalem,

Babylon, or any other place. Judgment has come, and it has been thorough. What remains to be seen is whether Jerusalem will grasp why these events occurred and how prayer, repentance, and renewal work together as a redemptive whole.

13 Descriptive judgment imagery continues in this verse. The fact that ממרום שלח אש, "from on high he sent fire," reminds readers of divine judgment of such places as Sodom and Gomorrah (Gen 19:23–29), and also of predictions of destruction by fire of Damascus, Gaza, and elsewhere in Amos 1:3–2:5 (see Löhr, 6). The mention of fire from on high reinforces, then, the poet's connection of Jerusalem's plight to imagery of the day of the Lord. Her devastation was horrible and thorough, and it had a divine origin.

This judgment came from God, but it took the form of human force against human flesh. Jerusalem experienced this wrath in a personal way, for the fire went בעצמתי, "into my bones." Of course, this phrase echoes Jer 20:9, where the prophet laments that when he tries to forget God and not speak, the message is "like a burning fire [כאש בערת] shut up in my bones [עצר בעצמתי]" (NRSV). Though each text has its own particular emphasis, both passages stress the intensely personal way in which God's will exerts itself on the character. Jeremiah and Jerusalem both receive internally God's displeasure. The result of the burning is also thorough. This fire "trampled" Jerusalem's bones, and forced Jeremiah to speak. The translation "trampled" (וירדנה) is not without problems (see *Note* 13.a. above and Renkema, 161), but works well in at least two ways. First, it depicts a disease/fire that devastates the city's bone structure. This fire has had a clearly disabling effect. Second, it reminds readers that Babylon was God's fire in this case and that their marching trampled the city, its inhabitants, and its temple. Thus, the use of וירדנה gives the poet flexibility in describing metaphorically what has occurred.

Not only did God send fire, he also פרש רשת, "spread a net," to trap any who managed to flee. As Provan explains, "Elsewhere in the OT the image of 'spreading the net' is often used of the enemy's assault on the righteous (e.g. Ps 35:7) or of Yahweh's action against his enemies (Hos 7:12). That Jerusalem should be the object of Yahweh's attention in this respect is a shocking reversal of the norm, emphasizing the dire plight in which the city finds itself" (49). This net insured that escape was impossible. Jerusalem confesses that השיבני אחור, "he [God] turned me back." God sent them back to the fire, back to the trampling.

Faced with fire and fleeing, the city could not cope. She was left שממה, "desolate," and דוה, "faint." This latter word may mean either "faint" or "sick," and it occurs with לב, "heart," in Isa 1:5 and Jer 8:18, as well as in Lam 1:22 and 5:17 (see Hillers, [1992] 89). Clearly, the city is in no condition to fight or flee now. Her energy is gone, as is her overall health. Again, God has caused this condition. Harrison summarizes the situation when he writes, "The fire burns into the inner recesses of the city, the net prevents anyone from escaping, and the idea of faintness completes the picture of a demoralized community" (210).

14 As if the fire and net were not enough, the Lord took further action. Stunned, faint, and facing the enemy, Jerusalem had a על, "yoke," placed upon her by God himself. This yoke was made of interesting material—Jerusalem's sins (פשעי, "my transgressions"). God took this yoke and ישתרגו, "fastened (it) together," בידו, "by his own hand." In Jer 27:8, the prophet reports that God has decided to place Judah and the surrounding countries בעל מלך בבל, "under the yoke of the king of Babylon." The false prophet Hananiah predicts in Jer 28:2–3 that God will shatter this yoke in two short years, but Jeremiah counters that claim in 28:5–17. This yoke was fashioned by Israel's sins and placed on the neck by God's decision to punish those transgressions. Babylon is the fire that tramples Jerusalem's bones in Lam 1:13a, the net that traps her feet in 1:13b, and the yoke that burdens her neck in 1:14a.

When this God-fashioned, sin-forged, Babylon-produced yoke עלו על צוארי, "went up upon my neck," Jerusalem says, the result was predictable. She was unable, as a yoked, snared, and diseased individual, to withstand her enemies. Once again, however, Babylon may have been the fire, snare, and yoke, but it was God who sent Babylon. Jerusalem asserts that הכשיל כחי, "he caused my strength to fail," and follows that declaration with the explanatory phrase "The Lord gave me into the hands of (those before whom) I am unable to stand." Renkema notes that this initial use of אדני, "Lord" or "Adonai," instead of the normal יהוה, "LORD" or "Yahweh," here is not simply for variety's sake. When the latter term appears in Lamentations "we are left either with the context of his oppression . . . or it is said in general terms that he executes judgement" (167). Both 1:5 and 1:9 represent the oppression imagery, while 1:17; 2:6, 17, 22; and 4:11, 16 represent the general judgment theme. Further, the אדני, "Lord," texts include harsher terminology, for in those passages the Lord hands over (1:14c), piles up (1:15a), treads (1:15c), engulfs (2:1), destroys (2:2), becomes like an enemy (2:5), and casts out (2:7; 3:31) (167). In other words the appearance of this particular version of the divine name may well signal to readers that a tougher God, seemingly less personal to Israel, is at work. Put another way, this name for God signals the Lord's punishing sovereignty instead of his congenial sovereignty. At the very least the use of this particular name indicates specific, not general, types of judgment. Under such judgment the people simply cannot bring themselves to a standing position (לא אוכל קום).

15 Readers might well wonder where Israel's fighters were when Babylon swept through Jerusalem. Was there no resistance? Jerusalem states סלה כל־אבירי, "he has scorned all my strong men," which indicates that God defeated the soldiers. Provan notes that the root סלה, "he has scorned," is comparatively rare in the OT, appearing only here, in Ps 119:118, and in Job 28:16. He concludes, "In the latter reference, it is used of measuring the worth of something (wisdom) in gold. In the former, it seems to have the sense of 'to evaluate negatively,' i.e. 'to have contempt for, to scorn.' . . . Like an enemy commander, God has weighed up the opposition and found them of no account" (51). Ps 119:118 is also part of a longer passage on judgment (Ps 119:118–20). God did not consider Jerusalem's forces a viable army. Even their אבירי, "strong men," or "valiant men," a word used to denote fighting men (Jer 46:15; Judg 5:22 [ET 5:23]) and stubborn men (Isa 46:12), were useless in this conflict.

This scorning felt like betrayal to Jerusalem. Her own Lord (אדני), the one in her own midst (בקרבי), has מועד . . . קרא, "proclaimed a festival," against her (עלי). This calling of a festival is like the calling of a sacrificial meal on the day of the Lord in Zeph 1:7–8 (see also Jer 46:10; Isa 34:6; Ezek 39:17–30). In both texts God sets Judah apart for the day of judgment. Here God's purpose was לשבר בחורי, "to shatter my chosen ones," whereas in Zephaniah it was for the like purpose of פקד, "visiting," or "punishing," the wicked. Instead of gathering Israel for one of their traditional festivals where the people would at least speak of God, the Lord has called for a new festival, one that destroys the nation's choicest young men. Apparently this festival replaces those lost in 1:4!

Having used judgment imagery similar to that found in Ps 119:118–20 and Zeph 1:7–8, the poet now uses metaphors like those in Isa 63:1–6. God has scorned the tough men and has called a festival of destruction against the choice young men. Now he treads them as wine for the assembled guests. As Meek explains, "The figure is a lurid one; the wine for the feast was the blood squeezed out of human bodies, conceived of as grapes (cf. Isa. 63:3)" (14). The לבתולת בת יהודה, "virgin daughter of Judah," was the object of this treading. Jerusalem did not suffer alone, for the whole land endured the Babylonian assault. As Renkema writes, "Daughter Judah is forced to endure the same judgment as daughter Zion" (170). Thus, this verse expresses the totality of the destruction of the populace. Jerusalem has lost both her young men and her young women, a comprehensive concept stated even more explicitly in 2:21–22 (see O. Kaiser, 127).

16 Jerusalem concludes her speech by invoking images quite reminiscent of the narrator's comments in 1:1–3. Because of what she has described in 1:12–15 (על אלה), she understandably says, אני בוכיה, "I am weeping." Indeed, in a very emphatic statement about her eyes (עיני עיני) she says that they ירדה מים, "flow with tears." Her crying is constant and heartfelt, just as the narrator reported in 1:2a.

Loneliness and isolation compound her sorrow. Once again the issue of a מנחם, "comforter," which was first voiced in 1:2b, arises. In the earlier text the missing "comforters" are the city's אהביה, "lovers," and רעיה, "friends, neighbors." In this passage, however, the comforter's identity is not stated explicitly, though 1:17, a verse spoken by the narrator, indicates that the same comforters may be in view. Still, this is Jerusalem's speech, so she may have the Lord in mind. Renkema writes, "Others may observe that there is no one to comfort and help daughter Zion (1:2b, 7c, 9b), but she herself keeps open the possibility that YHWH will look upon her in the moment of distress" (173). At least her statement does not preclude the Lord, especially since she has asked him to ראה, "see," her affliction in v 9c and v 11c and asks him to do so again in v 20. She needs a constant comforter to bring constant restoration of her life, or soul (משיב נפשי), for both מנחם, "comforting," and משיב, "restoring," are participles. Such is the depth of her predicament. In v 11b the people search for food להשיב נפש, "to revive their strength," while here the comforter is supposed to achieve this goal.

Instead of this needed comforter, however, Jerusalem encounters enemies who become stronger and stronger until they prevail (כי גבר אויב). These are the same enemies who in 1:2 and 1:5 deal treacherously with Jerusalem and succeed in their plans. Hoping for divine deliverance, Jerusalem received instead human deception and cruelty. Therefore, her בני, "sons," אבירי, "strong men," בחורי, "chosen ones," and לבתולה, "virgin daughter," from 1:15 are as שוממים, "desolate," as Zion's gates in 1:4b (שוממין). Her assessment of her own situation in 1:12–16 is as bleak as the narrator's in 1:1–11a.

17 The narrator provides a summarizing bridge between Jerusalem's two major speeches. It is retrospective because it concisely states what both speakers have found to be true. It is also prospective because it mentions Yahweh. It invites Jerusalem to attempt again to gain Yahweh's ear. From this point on the Lord becomes a major topic of the book.

In 1:10 the narrator reports that Jerusalem's foe צר פרש ידו, "has stretched out his hand," and captures the temple's precious items. Now he divulges that פרשה ציון בידיה, "Zion stretches out her hands." Hers is not an acquisitional stretching out; it is an imploring one. She is like a supplicant, or a beggar. There is no one available to comfort her (אין מנחם לה), so her stretching out is futile (see Jer 4:31). This assertion about the lack of a מנחם, "comforter," mirrors 1:16b.

Next, the narrator explains why her efforts are futile, and in doing so renews the book's explicit theological discussion: "Yahweh has commanded" (צוה יהוה) something specific ליעקב, "concerning Jacob" or "for Jacob." The use of the patriarchal name is significant. Jerusalem, Zion, and Jacob are all considered synonymous at this point (see Plöger, 139). This linking, which recurs in 2:2–3, means that all Israel (see 2:3), all the patriarch's descendants, not just Judah, have been part of God's decree. Though the fall of Jerusalem is the book's main focal point for discussing divine judgment, the whole of Israelite history from 722 to 587 B.C.E. must also be kept in mind. Not only has the northern kingdom been surrounded by foes (סביביו צריו); Judah has now been as well. Whatever relief may eventually result must also be for the whole people, not just Judah or Jerusalem.

God commands the foes to surround Jacob for the same reason as those who once honored her turned away from her in 1:8–9. Her sins have made her filthy, unclean (לנידה היתה, 1:8), and she has become recognized as unclean by her neighbors (לנדה ביניהם, 1:17). This word for uncleanness appears in Isa 30:22 and 64:5, Ezek 7:19, and Ezra 9:11 (Ash, 342), illustrating its common usage in judgment-related passages. This assertion reinforces the narrator's conviction that the city, Judah, and the whole of the people have suffered for their own sins. Individual exceptions may well exist, but as a group the people of Israel have not been the righteous victims of a marauding enemy. Rather, they are facing the consequences of years of sin and resultant uncleanness.

18–22 The final section of the book's first acrostic poem records Jerusalem's initial detailed prayer directed to Yahweh. She no longer solely calls out to those passing by (see 1:12–16), but now she also beseeches the only one who can truly help her (Renkema, 175). Now Zion summons Yahweh to participation and offers prayers for "God's gracious intervention" (Westermann, 136). What remains to be seen is whether these prayers reflect the repentance and renewal required for the restoration of their relationship with their God and whether these prayers reflect a sole dependence on their God for relief.

18 Jerusalem begins her speech/prayer with an emphatic declaration of God's righteousness in the matter of her punishment. The poet places a characteristic of God and a pronoun for God prior to the name for God (צדיק הוא יהוה) thereby creating the emphatic phrase "the LORD is indeed righteous." Of course, the Lord has been righteous in the matter of his command against Jacob, as was related by the narrator in 1:17b. This admission is similar to the psalmist's confession in Ps 51:6 (ET 51:4) that the Lord is righteous in speaking against the psalmist (למען תצדק בדברך). God has not punished without cause. In fact, Jerusalem proceeds to confess כי פיהו מריתי, "for I have rebelled against his word," or more literally "against his mouth." Renkema asserts that this expression "is always used for resistance to a particular command given in a particular situation, but never for disobedience with respect to commandments which have eternal validity" (181). He concludes that the reference is probably to Jerusalem's rejection of God-sent prophets like Jeremiah (see also Kraus, 33). By rejecting God's mouthpiece, the prophets, the people have also rejected the Lord, who sent them.

Having stated her guilt, Jerusalem now calls upon all peoples to hear and see her sufferings. Hillers ([1992] 76) notes that an "appeal to 'all peoples' is fairly rare," and comments that Ps 49:2 (ET 49:1), Mic 1:2, and 1 Kgs 22:28 offer the closest parallels. The psalm is a wisdom poem that calls all nations to hear how God will deliver the author from "the power of Sheol" (Ps 49:16 [ET 49:15]). Mic 1:2 warns the nations that God is coming to judge, while 1 Kgs 22:28 reports Micaiah's use of the phrase to emphasize the validity of his prophecy against Ahab. Interestingly enough, these usages offer specific insight into Lam 1:18b. After all, the nations will ראה, "see," that the devastation detailed in 1:18c comes from Jerusalem's refusal to heed (שמע, "hear") the prophetic word themselves. Further, the nations are summoned to "see" and "hear" both Jerusalem's judgment and (potentially) their own. Indeed Amos 1:2–2:16 and Jer 46–51 indicate that the day of the Lord will fall on the nations, not just on Israel. Finally, in an ironic twist on Ps 49, the city stresses how God refuses to deliver when the one praying remains unrepentant.

Jerusalem states that her grief (מכאבי) stems from the exile of her choice sons and daughters. Their going away בשבי, "into captivity," echoes the narrator's reference to captivity in 1:5c. The mention of בתולתי ובחורי, "my virgins and my young men," references the same groups as those introduced in 1:5c and 1:15. Jerusalem has lost those she presumably cares for the most. Her lack of attention to God's words on repentance have led her to cry out for attention to her plight. One has to wonder if her chosen audience will listen any more carefully than she herself has done.

19 Jerusalem picks up images first offered by the narrator. In 1:2 the narrator comments that there is no one comforting her מכל אהביה, "from all her lovers," and here Jerusalem states that "I called to my lovers; they deceived me." Meek writes that the המה, "they," "is pleonastic and accordingly emphatic" (15). Jerusalem states in a very strong way, a very personal way, what the narrator offers in a more matter-of-fact manner. She seems at least disappointed, if not absolutely outraged.

Who are these lovers, and how have they deceived her? As was stated in the comments on 1:2, these lovers are her faithless former allies (Peake, 311). They are those she hoped would deliver her from the Babylonian siege (Keil, 375). Renkema argues that the use of the *pi'el* participle for "lovers" (למאהבי) is "clearly negative. It is used exclusively to designate the adulterous character of the relationship in question. In the context of Hosea it is used directly to indicate improper love for the Baalim [Hos 2:7, 9, 12, 14, 15]. Elsewhere it refers to the inappropriate placing of one's trust in one's allies and their gods [Jer 22:20, 22; 30:14; Ezek 16:33, 36, 37; 23:5, 9, 22]" (183). This last option best fits the context here. Jerusalem admits that she has pursued her lovers instead of heeding God's word (see 1:18). At the same time, she does not take full responsibility for her actions, for she claims she was deceived. They pledged military help, then left her all alone. Their treachery compounded her own disobedience.

To make matters worse, her own leaders could not aid her. She says, כהני וזקני בעיר גועו, "My priests and my elders perished in the city." They have succumbed to hunger כי בקשו אכל למו, "while they sought food for themselves." In this phrase the

כי, "while," expresses temporality instead of causality (see Hillers, [1992] 63, 77; Keil, 375). They were so faint that they perished while in the very act of looking for sustenance. Clearly, anyone in such a state of deterioration was in no position to comfort Jerusalem, or anyone else for that matter. They could only try to find something למו, "for themselves."

20 Jerusalem once again asks God to ראה, "look," at her situation. As in 1:9c and 1:11c, the call to see leads to a description of misery. This verse offers the most heartrending depiction yet. In 1:9c the city claims that God should see how the enemy has triumphed, and in 1:11c how Jerusalem is despised. Here Jerusalem claims to be in distress (כי צר לי). The word for distress (צר) is so similar to the word for enemy (צר) in 1:10 that one is reminded that the foe and the pain are nearly identical. This distress is so palpable that it seems like her inner parts (מעי) are glowing red (חמרמרו) or searing hot (see Lam 2:11; Job 16:16; Keil, 376). Her emotional state could hardly be more devastating and she still have the ability to communicate.

Further, she adds, נהפך לבי בקרבי, "My heart is cast down (or turned upside down) within me." Her heart has been overthrown (הפך). The poet returns to the overthrowing of cities in 4:6 and 5:2, and to the overthrowing of individuals and their hearts in 3:3 and 5:15. Emotions are as vulnerable as exposed cities here.

Three words between descriptions state the cause of all this emotional burning and upheaval. The poet follows the purpose particle כי, "because," with an infinitive absolute and a first-person perfect verb (מרו מריתי, "I have been very rebellious"), which makes the phrase strongly emphatic. She is beginning to come to her senses (Harrison, 212). This word for rebellion (מר) not only accurately depicts her condition; it also sounds like the word used to describe her turmoil (חמרמרו). Her distress and enemy sound nearly identical, as do her rebellion and inner turbulence.

Where can she go for safety? Nowhere. She has already learned that she has no helpful allies and no leaders able to assist her. She states, "In the street the sword bereaves; in the house it is like death." The first half of the line (מחוץ שכלה חרב) is quite similar to Deut 32:25 (מחוץ תשכל חרב), and also to other judgment-threatening texts such as Lev 26:22–25, Jer 15:1–9, and Ezek 5:17 and 14:15–17 (see Ash, 343; Renkema, 181). All these texts *threaten* the sword and the death of loved ones. Jerusalem has *experienced* the reality the threat *foreshadows,* and she understands that this reality came about because of her lack of response to such warnings. The second half of the line is notoriously difficult (see *Note* 20.a.), but the sense is clear. Terror and death are resident in the houses as surely as they roam the streets. Jerusalem is not safe anywhere (see Westermann, 137–38).

21 Several themes from earlier verses come together here. First, Jerusalem states, שמעו כי נאנחה אני, "They heard that I am groaning"—the very thing she asks the unfriendly nations to do in 1:18b (שמעו נא כל עמים). Second, they have heard, and they know that she has no comforter (אין מנחם לי), which the narrator (1:17a) and the city (1:16b) have both already noted. Third, when all her enemies (כל איבי; see 1:2, 5, 9, 16) שמעו, "heard," of her רעתי, "calamity," they of course did not become her comforter. Rather, ששו, "they rejoiced," at her dilemma. Her "lovers" are useless and her "enemies" are effective (see 1:2, 5, 9, 16). Fourth, Jerusalem admits to God כי אתה עשית, "that you yourself have done it," which corresponds to her confession of rebellion in 1:20b (כי מרו מריתי). Both clauses express the cause of the presence of enemies, lack of comforters, and loss of life. Israel's rebellion against God's word (1:18a; 1:20b) has led to the righteous God's (1:18a) punishment of a rebellious people. Fifth, she recognizes that הבאת יום קראת, "you have brought the day you announced," which invokes imagery of the day of the Lord from 1:12 and from the prophetic literature (see Isa 2:12; Amos 5:18; Zeph 1:14–18; and others). Jerusalem has ignored such warnings, so she feels the effects of her willful ignorance. At the same time, she recalls the universal nature of God's day of wrath (see Isa 13–23; Jer 46–51; Amos 1:3–2:3; and others), and therefore asks God to make her wicked foes ויהיו כמוני, "as I am." They are agents of judgment, not beneficiaries of righteous behavior. Such prayers against enemies are fairly standard in psalms of lamentation (see Pss 79:12; 83:14–15; Westermann, 138). They are also prominent in psalms like Pss 74 and 137 that discuss how Israel has been defeated because of her sins.

22 Jerusalem continues her prayer against her foes. Having said הבאת, "you brought," the day, she now asks, תבא כל־רעתם לפניך, literally, "let come all their evil before you." Having repeated forms of בוא in successive lines, Jerusalem now uses עלל, "deal," in the next two phrases. She wants God to ועולל למו, "deal with it (the evil)," just as, or in the same manner as (כאשר), the Lord has dealt with her (עוללת לי). She feels her enemies deserve "the day" as much as she. As she does in 1:20b and 1:21b, in 1:22b Jerusalem confesses that her sins have caused her pain (על כל פשעי). Each of these comments occurs in the second half of the second line of the verse, and each unfolds in terse, three-word phrases. Repetition of word and structure mark 1:20–22.

One final set of repetitions concludes the passage. Jerusalem asks for this judging of enemies so that her many groans and faintness of heart may stop. She was once רבתי עם, "great with/full of people," and רבתי בגוים, "great among the nations" (1:2), but now she is full of groanings (כי רבות אנחתי). Of course, the word for groanings is the same as the one used in 1:21. The mentioning of her heart echoes her downcast heart in 1:20b. Thus, she prays that all this groaning and all this faintness of heart leave her and go to her enemies. It is important to note that Jerusalem makes no mention of her own innocence. Thus, she pins her hopes on God's justice alone (Harrison, 213). Westermann summarizes, "In other words, the traditional theme of a plea for reprisal against enemies has indeed been adopted, but here it is associated with an awareness of the singular set of circumstances. The plea for reprisal grows directly out of the experience of having been decimated. No one yet dares voice a plea for Israel's restoration" (138). Such pleas will come later in the book (see 5:21–22).

Explanation

Chap. 1 is introductory, for it sets forth the entire book's format, tone, and themes. This powerful acrostic lament declares that Jerusalem is desolate, devoid of the normal group of people (1:1). It describes how her friends have forsaken her (1:2–3), her roads and gates are desolate (1:4), her festivals are unattended (1:4), and her enemies have triumphed (1:5–6). The city's fall has been spectacular (1:9), and it has led to devastating results (1:11–16). This chapter also addresses why such disaster has befallen the chosen city. God has sent the day of the Lord on the people for their sins against his word (1:5, 8–9, 12, 14, 18–22).

Covenant breaking has led to covenant curses such as the loss of people (1:1–3), land (1:3, 18), and sanctuary (1:10). Groaning and death are everywhere (1:20–22). Though this poem is first and foremost an acrostic and a thorough treatment of a subject, it also contains many of the basic elements of communal laments. The city addresses the Lord (1:9, 11), describes the calamity her enemies have brought upon her (1:10–16), confesses that God has brought the disaster because of her sins (1:12–15, 18), and asks that her enemies be punished (1:21–22).

The city's grief is compounded by the realization that it need not have happened. The people sense that their affliction is self-inflicted to an extent. God has punished their sin, just as the covenantal blessings and curse texts (see Lev 26; Deut 27–28) promised. They understand that the God who protected them in the past has forsaken this role because of their disobedience. Their wounds are their own fault. God has not forsaken them for no reason. The whole chapter seeks to describe how God afflicts and forsakes the people who have rejected his word and have forsaken their covenant commitments. Two speakers, a narrator and Jerusalem, express this main theme, and each main section contributes to this overriding idea. At the center of the poem (1:12) stands the belief that this suffering is part of the day of God's wrath.

The first speaker, the narrator, only uses third-person indirect speech. Readers are informed about Jerusalem's situation (1:1–9b, 10–11) and the narrator's knowledge about the reason for her desperate situation (1:17) in this manner. The second speaker, Jerusalem/Zion, expresses herself through first-person indirect and first-person direct speech. She speaks apparently to readers in 1:12–16 and 1:18–19 (indirect) and to Yahweh (direct) in 1:9c, 1:11c, and 1:20–22. These alternating speeches help move the poem from description to agreement between speakers, to confession, and finally to pleas for relief from enemies.

Zion acknowledges that God has brought the day announced by those whose word she rejected (see 1:18). This day is God's time of judgment, the day referred to elsewhere in the OT as the "day of the Lord" (see Amos 5:18–20), "a day" (see Isa 2:12), "that day" (Hos 2:21), "the days of punishment" (Hos 9:7), or some similar variation. This day was announced by God's prophets (see Amos 3:1–7), and the people either return and seek the Lord (see Joel 2:12–27; Mal 3:16–18) or face punishment. Zion realizes that this day has overcome her, and she prays that her enemies will be similarly punished (1:21c). She asks that their evil deeds be punished as hers have been (1:22). Only then will they leave her alone and her hurts be healed (1:22c). Only then will the day of the Lord be complete. She wants God to punish the wicked nations as Joel 3:1–21, Amos 1:3–2:3, Zeph 2:4–15, and other prophetic texts indicate that he will. Again, until God acts in this manner she will have no relief.

This chapter sets forth the wise narrator's views on reversals (1:1–3), emptiness (1:4–6), uncleanness (1:7–9), and groanings (1:10–11). It does reveal Jerusalem's own acute sorrow (1:12–16) and prayers for help (1:18–22). But this poem is not merely descriptive. It does not only paint a portrait of suffering, though it does fulfill that important task. It also begins the book's discussion of how those who have brought suffering on themselves and those they love may deal with this difficult situation. So far Jerusalem accepts the reason for the events and prays that the one who brought these circumstances reverse her fortunes once again. God's righteousness is the key to relief no less than it was the key to punishment. Ironically, punishment of others is her best hope for freedom. The wicked may be divine instruments of punishment for a time, but eventually those who turn to the Lord must have release from the grip of oppression. Otherwise, God's righteousness does not guide human events.

How the Lord Has Clouded the Daughter of Zion! (2:1–22)

Bibliography

Albright, W. F. "A Catalogue of Early Hebrew Lyric Poems." *HUCA* 23 (1950–51) 1–39. **Buccellati, G.** "On Lam. 2,5." *BeO* 3 (1961) 37. **Buchanan, A.** "The Role of Protest in Lamentations." Th.M. thesis, Australian College of Theology, Kensington, 2001. **Dahood, M.** "New Readings in Lamentations." *Bib* 59 (1978) 174–97. **Daiches, S.** "Lamentations ii 13." *ExpTim* 28 (1917) 189. **Ferris, P. W., Jr.** *Genre of Communal Lament.* **Gordis, R.** "A Note on Lamentations ii 13." *JTS* 34 (1933) 162–63. **Gottlieb, H.** *Study on the Text of Lamentations.* **Grossfeld, B.** "The Targum to Lam. 2:10." *JJS* 28 (1977) 60-64. **Gous, I.** "Exiles and the Dynamics of Experiences of Loss: The Reaction of Lamentations 2 on the Loss of the Land." *OTE* 6 (1993) 351–63. **Heim, K. M.** "The Personification of Jerusalem and the Drama of Her Bereavement in Lamentations." In *Zion, City of Our God.* Ed. R. S. Hess and G. J. Wenham. Grand Rapids, MI: Eerdmans, 1999. 129–69. **Jahnow, H.** *Hebräische Leichenlied.* **Kaiser, W. C., Jr.** *Biblical Approach to Suffering.* **Lee, N. C.** *Singers of Lamentations.* **Linafeldt, T.** *Surviving Lamentations.* **McDaniel, T. F.** "Philological Studies in Lamentations, II." *Bib* 49 (1968) 27–53. **Meinhold, J.** "Threni 2,13." *ZAW* 15 (1895) 286. **Miller, C. W.** "Poetry and Personae: The Use and Function of the Changing Speaking Voices in the Book of Lamentations." Ph.D. dissertation. Iliff School of Theology and University of Denver, 1996. **O'Connor, K. M.** *Lamentations and the Tears of the World.* **Praetorius, F.** "Threni I, 12. 14. II, 6. 13" *ZAW* 15 (1895) 143–46. **Provan, I.** "Feasts, Booths and Gardens (Thr 2,6a)." *ZAW* 102 (1990) 254–55. **Renkema, J.** "The Literary Structure of Lamentations (I–IV)." In *The Structural Analysis of Biblical and Canaanite Poetry.* Ed. W. van der Meer and J. C. de Moor. JSOTSup 74. Sheffield: JSOT Press, 1988. 294–396. **Rudolph, W.** "Der Text der Klagelieder." *ZAW* 56 (1938) 101–22.

Translation

א	1	How the Lord has clouded [a] with his wrath the daughter of Zion!	(3+2)
		He has cast down from heaven (to) earth the splendor of Israel.	(3+2)
		Indeed, he has not remembered his footstool on the day of his wrath.	(4+2)
ב	2	The Lord has swallowed up, he has not [a] shown mercy, to all the pastures of Jacob.	(2+2+3)
		He has overthrown in his fury the fortresses of the daughter [b] of Judah.	(2+3)
		He has brought to the earth, he has defiled,[c] her kingdom [d] and her officials.	(3+2)
ג	3	He has cut down in his burning wrath [a] all the might of Israel.	(3+3)
		He has withdrawn his right hand	(3+2)

		from the face of the enemy.
		Indeed he has burned in Jacob, (2+2+2)
		like a blazing fire;
		it has consumed all around.
ד	4	He has bent his bow like an enemy, (3+2)
		setting his right hand.
		Like a foe indeed he has killed (2+3)
		all the eye's delight.
		In the tent of the daughter of Zion, (3+3)
		he has poured out like fire his fury.
ה	5	The Lord was like an enemy; (3+2)
		he swallowed up Israel.
		He swallowed up all her palaces; (3+2)
		he laid in ruins his strongholds.
		Indeed he has multiplied in the daughter of Judah (3+2)
		mourning and lamentation.
ו	6	Indeed he has done violence to his booth as to a garden;ᵃ (3+2)
		he has laid in ruins his place for appointed festivals.
		The LORD has brought to an end in Zion (3+2)
		festival and Sabbath.
		Indeed he has spurned in his indignant wrath (3+2)
		king and priest.
ז	7	The Lord has rejected his altar; (3+2)
		he has disowned his holy place.
		He has delivered into the hand of the enemy (3+2)
		the walls of her palaces.
		They have given voice in the house of the LORD, (4+2)
		as on a day of festival.
ח	8	The LORD determinedᵃ to lay in ruins (3+3)
		the wall of the daughter of Zion.
		He stretched out a measuring line— (2+2+2)
		he did not return
		his hand from swallowing up.
		Indeed he caused rampart and wall to lament; (3+2)
		they languish together.
ט	9	Her gates have sunk to the ground; (3+3)
		ᵃhe has ruined and shatteredᵃ her bars.
		Her king and her officials (are) among the nations; (3+2)
		ᵇthere is no law.ᵇ
		Even her prophets (2+4)
		have not found a vision from the LORD.
,	10	They sitᵃ on the ground, they are silent,ᵇ (3+2)
		the elders of the daughter of Zion.
		They throw dust on their heads; (3+2)
		they put on sackcloth.
		They bow their heads down to the ground, (3+2)
		the virgins of Jerusalem.
כ	11	My eyes are worn out by weeping; (3+2)

		my inward parts are in turmoil.	
		My liver^a is cast down to the ground	(3+3)
		because of (the) shattering of (the) daughter of my people,	
		Because infants and nursing babes faint	(3+2)
		in the open places of the city.	
ל	12	They say to their mothers,	(2+3)
		"Where is (the) grain and wine?"	
		as they faint like wounded men	(2+2)
		in the open places of the city,	
		as their lives are poured out	(2+3)
		on their mothers' bosom.	
מ	13	What can I repeat to you^a—	(2+3+2)
		what can I compare for you,	
		O daughter of Jerusalem?	
		^bWhat can I liken for you that I may comfort you,^b	(4+3)
		O virgin daughter of Zion?	
		For great as the sea^c is your shattering.	(4+3)
		Who can heal you?	
נ	14	Your prophets envisioned for you	(3+2)
		vanity and worthlessness.	
		Indeed they did not expose your iniquity	(4+2)
		to avert your captivity.^a	
		Indeed they envisioned for you	(2+3)
		burdens of vanity and enticement.	
ס	15	They clap (their) hands against you—	(3+3)
		all who pass (your) way.	
		They hiss and wag their heads	(3+3)
		against the daughter of Jerusalem.	
		"Is this the city that ^awas called 'perfection of beauty,	(5+3)
		the joy of all the earth'?"^a	
פ	16 a	They have opened their mouth against you—	(3+2)
		all your enemies.	
		They hiss and they gnash (their) teeth;	(3+2)
		they say, "We have swallowed (her) up.	
		Surely this is the day we have waited for!	(4+2)
		We have found (it)! We have seen (it)!"	
ע	17	The LORD has done what he purposed;	(4+2)
		he has carried out his word,	
		which he commanded from days of old;	(4+3)
		he has thrown down and not shown pity.	
		And now (the) enemy rejoices over you;	(3+3)
		he has raised up the horn of your foes.	
צ	18	Their heart^a cried out to the Lord:	(4+3)
		"O wall of the daughter of Zion,	
		make tears descend like a torrent	(3+2)
		day and night.	
		Do not give yourself relief;	(4+4)
		do not let grow still (the) daughter of your eyes."	

ק	19	*Arise! Cry loudly in the night*^a	(3+2)
		at the beginning of the watches.	
		Pour out your heart like water	(3+3)
		before the presence of the Lord.	
		Lift up your hands to him	(3+3)
		for the lives of your little ones,	
		^b*who are fainting from hunger*	(2+3)
		at the head of every street.^b	
ר	20	*Look, O* LORD, *and consider:*	(3+3)
		whom have you ever treated thus?	
		Should women eat their offspring,	(4+2)
		the little ones of their tender care?	
		Should one be killed in the sanctuary of the Lord,	(4+2)
		priest and prophet?	
ש	21	*They lie in the dust of the streets,*	(3+2)
		young and old.	
		My virgins and my choice men	(2+2)
		^a*have fallen by the sword.*^a	
		You have killed on the day of your anger;	(3+3)
		you have slaughtered without^b *pity.*	
ת	22	*You invited as to the day of an appointed feast,*	(3+2)
		my terrors^a *on every side.*	
		And there was not on the day of the LORD's *wrath*	(5+2)
		fugitive or survivor.	
		Those whom I tenderly care for and raised,	(3+2)
		my enemy has made an end of them.	

Notes

1.a. Albrektson (*Studies in the Text and Theology*, 85–86) notes that this *hapax legomenon* is probably derived from עב, "cloud," though some commentators believe it derives from the Arabic root for "blame" or "revile." LXX and Syr. support Albrektson's contention.

2.a. LXX and MT read לא, "not." The Qere and some MSS of Syr., Tg., and Vg. read ולא, "and not." Either reading is possible, though the latter reading is followed here. See Gordis (169) for a brief discussion.

2.b. Vg. reads *virginis* (בתולה). No other ancient version offers this reading.

2.c. Albrektson (*Studies in the Text and Theology*, 88) notes, "Unlike LXX ἐβεβήλωσε and T אפיס, the Syriac translation has not taken the Hebrew word as a finite verb but has vocalized it as a form of חלל 'pierced, slain' (cf. 2:12; 4:9)." He suggests that "the translator read the first מ of this word as the last letter of the preceding word." Given the lack of other MS evidence, Albrektson's conclusion is accepted and MT is retained. For an opposing viewpoint, see Dahood, *Bib* 59 (1978) 179–80.

2.d. The LXX reads βασιλέα αὐτῆς, "her kingdom," as does Syr. Albrektson believes the Syr. reading is due to "the first מ being connected with the preceding word . . . and the rest of it being pointed מַלְכָּהּ" (*Studies in the Text and Theology*, 89). Gottlieb (*Study on the Text*, 24–25) argues that, based on contextual difficulties and the fact that "the personal sense, 'king,' for the word ממלכה does not occur with certainty in any other passage in the OT, it is improbable that it occurs here in Lam. 2:2." Albright (*HUCA* 23 [1950–51] 34), Dahood (*Bib* 59 [1978] 179), and Hillers ([1992] 93) read "her king." Given Albrektson and Gottlieb's arguments, the MT reading seems preferable.

3.a. LXX, Syr., and some Vg. MSS read "his wrath" (אפו), and this reading is adopted here.

6.a. LXX reads ὡς ἄμπελον, "like a vine, vineyard." This reading is possible, yet no clearer than MT (see Gottlieb, *Study on the Text*, 28).

8.a. LXX reads καὶ ἐπέστρεψεν, "and he turned." It is possible that the translator mistook a ח for a ה. See Albrektson, *Studies in the Text and Theology*, 100–101.

9.a-a. *BHS* notes that this stich has three words while the regular meter for the second stich in a line has only two. Thus, it recommends deleting one word. Such absolute consistency is not reflected in Lamentations as a whole, so MT is retained.

9.b-b. אֵין תּוֹרָה, "there is no law." Tg. make this phrase causal, "because of not following the law," which interprets the reason for the devastation. Gottlieb (*Study on the Text,* 30) also understands the phrase as priestly instruction, yet he finds it unnecessary to emend the text.

10.a. MT reads יֵשְׁבוּ (impf.), but LXX, Syr., and Vg. read יָשְׁבוּ (pf.). No significant change in translation results.

10.b. דָּמַם may mean either "silent" or "mourn" (see BDB, 199). Despite arguments to the contrary (see McDaniel, *Bib* 49 [1968] 38–40), Gottlieb (*Study on the Text,* 31–32) concludes that the context best fits "silent."

11.a. כְּבֵדִי, "my liver" (see BDB, 458). LXX reads δόξα μου, "my glory," which means it translates כְּבֹדִי, a reading Syr. follows (see Kraus, 38). Albrektson considers this pointing "a very natural mistake" (*Studies in the Text and Theology,* 105) and deems "liver" a natural parallel to מֵעַי, "my inward parts."

13.a. The Qere reads אֲעִידֵךְ (*qal* impf. 1c sg. from עוד), "I bear witness." Vg. reads *comparabo te* (אֶעֱרָךְ), "I will compare you." It seems that these possibilities may well be efforts to render a difficult MT reading easier (see Gottlieb, *Study on the Text,* 32; Albrektson, *Studies in the Text and Theology,* 107–8).

13.b-b. LXX reads τίς σώσει σε καὶ παρακαλέσει, "who will save you and comfort you?" which equals מִי יוֹשִׁיעַ לָךְ וְנִחֲמָךְ. Rudolph (*ZAW* 56 [1938] 108) suggests that LXX offers a freer rendition of the MT, while Albrektson (*Studies in the Text and Theology,* 109), following Ziegler's suggestion, posits a corruption of the original LXX. Once again the variant seems to attempt to offer an interpretation of a difficult MT reading.

13.c. LXX reads ποτήριον, "cup," for כַּיָּם, "sea." Thus כּוֹס is read for כַּיָּם. LXX treats "cup" as a construct rather than as a simile for the extent of the devastation.

14.a. The reading "to avert your captivity" renders the Kethib rather than the Qere (see Hillers, [1992] 95; Westermann, 142). For the opposite view see Provan, 73–74; Keil, 394; Albrektson, *Studies in the Text and Theology,* 111.

15.a-a. *BHS* and several commentators suggest that this line is too long and thus in need of emendation. Rudolph thinks that the line is lengthened because the verse quotes Ps 48:3 (ET 48:2) (*ZAW* 56 [1938] 108). Albrektson correctly states, "The fact that the author is quoting titles of distinction for Jerusalem may well be a sufficient ground for the exceptional length" (*Studies in the Text and Theology,* 114).

16.a. Some versions of Heb., Gk., and Syr. transpose 2:16 after 2:17 to maintain the פ-ע alphabetic order. Renkema (48) argues persuasively that the author's breaking of the normal alphabetic order created a clear distinction between chaps. 1 and 2, which are otherwise virtually interchangeable.

18.a. *BHS* and several commentators have rightly found this line difficult to translate in the passage's context. Thus, despite any strong textual evidence, they find the line corrupt and offer emendations. Though the passage is obscure, it probably reflects a rare literary form, not a textual corruption. For a survey of difficulties, see Gottlieb, *Study on the Text,* 35–37. For suggested emendations, see Albrektson, *Studies in the Text and Theology,* 115–18.

19.a. The Qere reads בַּלַּיְלָה, which reflects the normal spelling of the form.

19.b-b. Many commentators remove this line because it makes the verse longer than the others in chap. 2. Since chap. 1 also has one four-line verse (1:7), the presence of a four-line verse here is more likely a stylistic decision rather than a gloss or addition.

21.a-a. LXX expands this line to read ἐπορεύθησαν ἐν αἰχμαλωσίᾳ ἐν ῥομφαίᾳ καὶ ἐν λιμῷ, "they went away by captivity, by the sword, and by famine." Provan argues that this reading reflects an attempt to link v 20 and v 21 more closely (78), and Albrektson considers the reading "yet another instance of an inner-Greek corruption" (*Studies in the Text and Theology,* 123).

21.b. Many MSS of Syr., Latin, and Aram. versions read וְלֹא, "and not." No significant change in meaning results.

22.a. LXX reads παροικίας μου κυκλόθεν, "my sojourners," thus reading the text as God calling for sojourners, not terrors, to come to the feast. MT connects with similar texts in Jeremiah (see Jer 6:25; 20:3, 10; 46:5; 49:29) and should be retained. See Albrektson, *Studies in the Text and Theology,* 124–25, and Gottlieb, *Study on the Text,* 37–38.

Form/Structure/Setting

Approaching the form, structure, and setting of Lam 2 requires interpreters to keep in mind details from Lam 1 and to consider data peculiar to the second poem. This observation may seem simplistic at first, yet it is not so when one recalls that some experts treat Lamentations as five essentially separate poems, on the one hand, or read Lam 1 and 2 as essentially identical, on the other. Lam 2 does have distinct features that mark it as a creative achievement in its own right, but these features are joined to common ones that allow this set piece to interact with the other four chapters in a way that produces movement in the message of the book as a whole.

As was true of Lam 1, Lam 2 is composed of more than one literary type. Lam 2 contains elements of the dirge, communal lament, and individual lament. These elements have been merged so carefully that they are not easy to extract without doing damage to the interpretation of the whole. Still, such dirge elements as the description of horrible results of the city's demise (2:11–12, 20–22) and such lament elements as the Lord's ultimate responsibility for Israel's defeat (2:1–10, 17) and the people's plea for help (2:20–22) are plain enough. Certain dirge elements are missing, the most significant of which may be, as Linafelt points out, "the announcement that someone has died" (*Surviving Lamentations*, 36, 38). But a terrible *near*-funeral has occurred. Similarly, significant lament features are absent, the most important of which may well be the lack of a clear statement of faith in God's future saving activity based on God's benevolence in the past. Such "gaps" are only gaps if one wishes the poem to be other than what it is. The text *as it stands* is a masterful blending of literary types and techniques. The dirge elements allow for a funereal tone without pronouncing Jerusalem dead, while the lament elements allow the poem's speakers (see below) to discuss the effects of devastation on the people's relationship to God.

Like Lam 1, 3, and 4, Lam 2 is an acrostic poem, following an alphabetic sequence. It uses the same format as Lam 1 except that it switches the *ayin-pe* sequence. An acrostic poem's purpose is to create an intentionally thorough description or argument, not simply to create a poem with a built-in memory device. Lam 1 offers a thorough, heartrending description of "How she (the city) sits/dwells alone!" (1:1). Lam 2 builds on this description in order to highlight "How the Lord has clouded with his wrath the daughter of Zion!" (2:1). God is the subject of punishment-oriented verbs no less than twenty-eight times in the first eight verses alone. This drumbeat of what God has done is not so much a series of accusations as it is a thorough statement of fact. Lam 2:11–19 describes reasons for pain related to Jerusalem's predicament in painstaking and pain-inducing detail. The alphabetic sequence marks an amazingly complete description of God's actions and their effects unfolding before the reader.

Besides these formal aspects normally associated with the psalms, Lam 2 also has some particular affinities with prophetic forms. Like Lam 1, this poem features alternating speakers. Such alternating of speakers is fairly common in Jer 2–6, 8:4–10:25, and 11–20, as well as in Zephaniah. It is also true that the theology found in Lamentations and those books is quite similar.

These likenesses intensify in chap. 2. Now either three speakers appear or one of the two speakers from the previous poem takes on a new role. Once again a narrator details Jerusalem's situation in third-person indirect discourse in 2:1–10. As before, Jerusalem addresses Yahweh directly in first-person speech in 2:20–22. Between these passages there is first-person speech that appears to speak of Jerusalem in third-person terms (2:11–12). There is also first-person speech that addresses Jerusalem directly (2:13–19). The speaker in 2:11–19 has great sympathy for Jerusalem and therefore urges her to seek the Lord (2:18–19). To explain this shift in rhetorical tactics, scholars have suggested that the narrator may have become converted to the city's point of view (K. M. O'Connor, *Lamentations and the Tears of the World*, 31–34), the Lord may now speak to Jerusalem (Gerstenberger, [2001] 487–89), or Jerusalem may speak in 2:11–12 and the narrator in 2:13–19 (Miller, "Poetry and Personae," 111–15).

Lee is bolder in her suggestion. She asserts that Lam 2, and to a lesser extent Lam 1, is so close in its rhetoric to Jer 4, 8, and 10 that one can identify the speaker in 2:1–19 with Jeremiah and the speaker in 2:20–22 with a "Jerusalem poet" (*Singers of Lamentations*, 132–62). She claims that Jer 4, 10, and Lam 1–2 all focus on how God destroys like an enemy, causing Jerusalem's fall, and how Jerusalem's children have been harmed (161–62). She concludes, "In sum, Lam 1 and 2 belong together as a rhetorical piece, suggestive of oral performance of two poets in the crisis of a particular context, continuous with much in the poetry of the book of Jeremiah and their utterances there" (162). Her careful linguistic work indicates that, at the very least, Lam 2 must be read against the background of Jeremiah, and the commentary below will attempt to make good use of many of her insights.

This acrostic poem includes elements of dirge, lament, and prophetic dialogue. It integrates these related, yet hardly identical, literary types into a comprehensive statement on God's wrath and its effects on Israel. It takes aspects found in chap. 1 and intensifies and expands them, which results in thematic movement from description and plea to involvement and accusation. Lam 1 and 2 both begin with איכה, "how"; both have twenty-two verses composed of three lines each; both have changing speakers; and both may stand alone as poetic pieces (see K. M. O'Connor, *Lamentations and the Tears of the World*, 30–31). At the same time they are sufficiently different to contribute to the whole book's consistent movement from description to urgent prayer.

Given the shift in speakers noted above, it is best to begin the charting of the chapter's structure according to those shifts. Lam 2:1–10 clearly details what God has done to Israel, apparently as an explanation of what 1:21 describes as "the day you announced." This section ends with a description of this day's impact on Jerusalem. Though Westermann (159–60) and K. M. O'Connor (*Lamentations and the Tears of the World*, 31–35) consider 2:1–10 a series of accusations, Gerstenberger ([2001] 485–87) and Hillers ([1992] 102–6) are correct to treat these verses as clear theological description. Second-person address seems more likely in accusatory speech, though it is far from impossible for third-person speech to appear in such a role. In 2:1–10 what God has done includes showing no mercy (2:1–3); treating Israel like an enemy (2:4–5); and laying waste the temple (2:6–7), city defenses (2:8–9a), and national leaders (2:9b–10). Johnson considers this segment the "fact half" of the chapter, with 2:11–22 serving as the "interpretation half" of the poem (*ZAW* 97 [1985] 64–65).

Lam 2:11–19 is easy enough to set apart from 2:1–10 and 2:20–22, yet it is quite challenging in its specific elements. As Miller ("Poetry and Personae," 111–15) points out, most scholars consider the "I" in this passage to be the narrator, though he and a few others think Jerusalem is the speaker in 2:11–12 and the narrator the speaker in 2:13–19. Of course, these approaches are based on the opinion that only two speakers exist in chaps. 1 and 2. Gerstenberger breaks with this consensus and argues for a third speaker, concluding that God is this speaker ([2001] 487).

The third-speaker hypothesis makes the most sense for three reasons. First, it seems unlikely that the narrator would change from third-person to first-person speech with no intervening speech to signal this change. K. M. O'Connor thinks that 2:1–10 prepares readers for this switch (*Lamentations and the Tears of the World*, 31–35) but that the rhetoric of 2:1–10 does not warrant this conclusion. Still, she is right to argue that 2:11–22 does diverge from 2:1–10. Second, as Lee asserts, the language in 2:11–22 is very close to the two-person prophetic dialogue found in Jeremiah. Though Lee (*Singers of Lamentations*, 132–62) also considers 2:1–10 very close in style to Jeremiah, she finds more parallels between 2:11–22 and the prophet's style. Third, chap. 3 begins with first-person speech by one who has suffered yet also advises Israel how to react to what God has done. It is possible that the two non-Jerusalem first-person speakers in chaps. 2 and 3 are the same.

Despite the difficulty of sorting out the voices in this segment, the message of these verses is clear. The speaker weeps over the destruction of his people, paying particular attention to the fate of Jerusalem's children (2:11–12). Next, the speaker mourns Israel's acceptance of false prophets and status as object of scorn (2:13–17). Finally, the speaker counsels the people to turn to the Lord (2:18–19). Though Gerstenberger's suggestion that God speaks here is appealing, the character's mourning and advising fit the prophets more closely. No identification here is without problems, but this conclusion is plausible given Lee's analysis. Lam 2:20 uses the command/appeal to ראה, "see," that first occurs in 1:9c and 1:11c, a fact that helps identify the speaker here as Jerusalem. The mentioning of "my young women and my young men" (2:21) and "my terrors" (2:22) provides contextual evidence for the same conclusion. Like 1:20–22, 2:20–22 calls on Yahweh to "see." But 1:20–22 admits sin and asks God to judge enemies, while 2:20–22 asks God to consider who he has judged and how horribly he has done so. Both texts reference God's יום, "day" (1:21; 2:22), so these differences make it possible to chart a variety of implications of that "day." Indeed 2:1 begins the poem with God's "day," and 2:22 concludes the piece with a reference to this event. The whole poem must be read with this theme in mind (see the *Comment* for chap. 2).

Besides this clear structural framework based on shifting speakers, the poet also uses interlocking rhetorical devices as in chap. 1. Renkema (307–8) notes the following connections:

2:1 and 2:22 stress "the day of his anger."
2:2 and 2:21 mention God's lack of mercy.
2:3 and 2:20 include "consuming" imagery.
2:4 and 2:19 use the phrase "pour out."
2:5 and 2:18 are connected by the use of "Lord/Adonai."
2:6 and 2:17 use the name "LORD/Yahweh."
2:7 and 2:16 mention Israel's enemies.
2:8 and 2:15 use the word "daughter."
2:9 and 2:14 mention prophets and visions.
2:10 and 2:13 mention "daughter Zion."
2:11 and 2:12 describe fainting in the street.

These likenesses are too striking to be accidental. Thus, the poet adds interlocking verbal connections to the acrostic pattern and the unfolding speeches to create a cohesive whole.

As if these structural and verbal markers were not enough to establish structural unity, the poet includes thematic emphases that tie Lam 1 to Lam 2. First, 1:21c asserts that God has brought the promised "day," which can be nothing less than the day of Yahweh threatened in Isaiah, Amos, and elsewhere. Then 2:1 continues this emphasis by explaining God's cloud of wrath as "the day of his wrath." Finally, 2:22 concludes the poem with the fact that Jerusalem has experienced "the day of the LORD's wrath." Second, 2:20 echoes 1:9c, 1:11c, and 1:20 by imploring God to ראה, "see," what has happened and change the situation. This plea sets up an interesting tension, for Jerusalem knows that sin has caused the "day" to come (1:18–22), yet she asks the very God who brought the calamity to "see" what he has done. How God "sees" the "day" continues to be a major issue in the book. Third, much of the same destruction imagery from chap. 1 occurs again in chap. 2. The toppling of walls, cleansing of worship, and destitution of people appear especially in the narrator's speeches in 1:1–11 and 2:1–10.

The poet uses structural, verbal, and thematic elements to create a poem that can stand on its own yet also serve as the next stage of a connected whole. There are several possible implications of this conclusion. Lam 2 may serve as part two of a five-part exercise in lamenting, confessional, imploring prayer. It may also stand on its own as a prayer that recognizes that the day of the Lord has come yet also calls God to "see" and act based on the worshiper's sense of unexpected horrors related to the "day." It may then lead to other poems that deal with further, related aspects of complaint, confession, contrition, and coping.

Chap. 2 may be divided into three sections based on the alternating speakers: vv 1–10, in which the narrator describes how the Lord has covered Jerusalem with a cloud of wrath on "the day of his wrath"; vv 11–19, where a voice like the prophet Jeremiah's expresses grief over the city's woes and counsels her to cry out to God for help; and vv 20–22, where Jerusalem asks God to "see" what terrors the day of wrath has brought on the chosen people. These major sections have several subsections. In 2:1–10 the text stresses God's merciless attack (vv 1–3), God's treating Israel like an enemy (vv 4–5), and God's devastation of temple (vv 6–7), defenses (vv 8–9a), and leaders (vv 9b–10). In 2:11–19, the speaker notes the horrifying fate of Jerusalem's children (vv 11–12), regrets Israel's trust of false prophets and role as byword of the nations (vv 13–17), and urges Jerusalem to call on the Lord (vv 18–19). In 2:20–22, Jerusalem notes the suffering of children, priest, and prophet (v 20), then asserts God's lack of pity (v 21), and finally remarks on the totality of the day of wrath (v 22). From start to finish the poem charts what it means to experience God's direct, purposeful, unstinting judgment. It also moves readers from description (2:1–10), to concern and counsel (2:11–19), to direct address of God (2:20–22).

What was said about the setting of Lam 1 largely applies to Lam 2. Traditionally scholars generally dated the poem soon after the destruction of Jerusalem in 587 B.C.E. (see for example Haller, 93; Wiesmann, 146; Weiser, 322; Kraus, 44; and others), though more recently some experts have preferred not to commit to an exact date (see Provan, 7–19; Hillers, [1992] 10–15), or have committed to a slightly later date than immediately after Jerusalem's downfall (Westermann,

61–63; Renkema, 54–57). Of course, each scholar's views on the authorship and date of the whole book affect their views on this chapter. At any rate, the presence of 2:7 and its temple destruction imagery at least negates a pre-587 B.C.E. date for virtually every interpreter.

The chapter's contents are not particularly helpful for determining how long after the temple's destruction the poem may have been written. Clear day-of-the-Lord theology appears, yet such theology existed well before 587 B.C.E. and continued well after that time. Dirge and lament forms have been adapted, but again these literary types easily pre-date and easily post-date Jerusalem's fall. Given the lack of any reference to a new temple or renewed activity in Jerusalem, however, it is also possible to interpret the poem as having been written between 587 and 515 B.C.E. There is no solid reason to suppose that reflection on destruction did not begin immediately after it occurred, a likelihood Jer 41:4–8 attests. Given the lack of reference to exilic life, it is also probable that the poem was composed in Palestine. The setting *in the text* is the fall of Jerusalem and its immediate consequences. The commentary will stress that setting in its interpretive statements.

Comment

1–3 This section begins the chapter's depiction of God clouding "with his wrath the daughter of Zion" (2:1a). More than twenty examples of what this general phrase entails follow in 2:1–8. Even when the governing images change, the effect is the same: Israel has been in the way of God's wrath, so the people have endured the full brunt of that wrath. Consequently the nation has been left physically and emotionally spent.

1 As in 1:1, the narrator begins this poem with the dirgelike exclamation איכה, "how." Whereas the former verse introduced Jerusalem's desolation, this text indicates that she may be alone but she has not been *left* alone. God has indeed visited her, yet only with fierce judgment, not with acts of deliverance or even relief. In fact, he has covered or "engulfed her" (Renkema, 216) with a cloud of wrath (יעיב באפו). Thus, this wrath is everywhere. It is what she sees and what she feels and what she experiences. Though Jerusalem is "the daughter of Zion," God's chosen one, she has been the recipient of the Lord's fiercest anger. Privilege has not shielded her. Rather, it has put her in this position.

Two destructive phrases follow this general announcement. First, "He has cast down from heaven (to) earth the splendor of Israel" (2:1b). Renkema (217) notes that the *hip'il* usage of שלך with Yahweh as the subject almost never has a positive connotation. The form clearly marks the Lord's actions as *purposeful*. Jerusalem's fall has been spectacular: from heaven (משמים) to earth (ארץ). Yet even this terrible fall is not fatal. As Peake (313) comments, "Exalted to heaven, it had been thrust down to earth, not to Sheol; its ruin is not irretrievable." The תפארת ישראל, "splendor of Israel," *has* fallen. This splendor is Jerusalem itself, given the mention of "the daughter of Zion" in 2:1a (Streane, 368), but Jerusalem's general splendor consisted of several specific constituent parts, such as the temple, the fortifications, the officials, the populace, and so forth (Provan, 59). Taken together as a whole, when Jerusalem fell, the whole nation's splendor fell with it.

Second, God "has not remembered his footstool on the day of his wrath." These two phrases carry heavy theological freight. In Exod 2:24 and 6:5 when God remembered his covenant with the patriarchs, he acted on Israel's behalf. In psalms of praise (Ps 98:3) and in historically reflective psalms (Ps 105:8) the poets celebrate God's never-failing remembering of the covenant with Israel. Therefore for God *not* to remember (ולא זכר, "he has not remembered") Israel in any way marks a significant reversal in the people's fortunes because of a reversal in their relationship with God. The Lord has not remembered הדם רגליו, "his footstool." Though this phrase probably refers to the ark in Ps 99:5, Ps 132:7, and 1 Chr 28:2, here it refers to the city in general or the temple in particular, since the ark was destroyed prior to 587 B.C.E. (Hillers, [1992] 97). God's not remembering Israel is not a passive forgetfulness, for he has made Jerusalem the object of his anger ביום אפו, "on the day of his wrath." This terrible day had been promised since at least as early as the eighth century B.C.E. (see Isa 2:1–4:1; Amos 3–5) and had been threatened more recently by Jeremiah (see Jer 4:5–31) and Zephaniah (see Zeph 1:3–3:8). Now it has come, as 1:21 has already recognized, and Jerusalem experiences it as the opposite of covenantal mercy.

2 Five more verbal clauses describe the day of God's wrath. Each one gives particular definition to the rather general phraseology in 2:1, and each one attests to the totality of divinely induced destruction.

The first two phrases denote how completely the Lord's attitude has changed concerning Israel: "The Lord [Adonai] has swallowed up [בלע אדני], he has not shown mercy [ולא חמל]." The first verb hardly ever appears with Yahweh, Adonai, or Elohim as its subject. As Lee observes, the term usually refers to enemies who devour a person. In Jer 51:34 the verb describes Nebuchadnezzar's consumption of Jerusalem. Thus, Lam 2:2 indicates that the Lord has done what enemies normally do, and that indeed the Lord sent Babylon to do the swallowing (Lee, *Singers of Lamentations*, 135). This verb (בלע, "swallow up") becomes a standard way of describing God's judgment in this chapter (see 2:2, 5, 8, 16). The second verb (חמל, "show mercy") likewise reflects God's change of attitude toward Israel. In Joel 2:18 it describes God's mercy on a repenting people, and in 2 Chr 36:15 it is used in connection with the Lord's motive in sending prophets to warn the people to change. For God to not have this mercy means that the time for sending warning prophets has ended. It may also indicate that God's warning mercy has ceased because no repentance like that found in Joel 2:1–18 has occurred. Israel has enjoyed God's mercy for centuries but does not do so at this point in time.

The result of this swallowing up and lack of mercy is that the whole of the land has been affected. All of Jacob's pastures (כל־נאות יעקב) have suffered in the day of judgment. Devastated land is a staple of day-of-Yahweh imagery (see Joel 1:2–2:11; Amos 4:6–13; Zeph 2:4–15), so it is not surprising to find it here. Historically speaking, Babylon's incursion into the land included several destroyed cities and much devastated land before it ever reached the capital city. Jerusalem's woes did not occur in isolation; in fact, בת־יהודה, "the daughter(s) of Judah," suffered well before בת־ציון, "the daughter of Zion," did.

Having used two familiar verbal images to describe the devastation of Jacob's pastures, the poet now uses another one to depict the fall of "the fortresses of the daughter of Judah" (מבצרי בת יהודה). God has "overthrown in his fury" (הרס בעברתו). The verb הרס, "overthrow," appears five times in Jeremiah. It is part of God's programmatic "to pluck up and break down, to destroy and to overthrow, to build and to plant" in the call story (Jer 1:10). It is used by Yahweh in Jer 45:4 to describe his judgment of Israel, whom he built up over time. The term appears with the others from Jer 1:10 in Jer 24:6, 31:28, and 42:10 in texts that promise the reversal of Israel's negative fortunes. Outside the book of Jeremiah the verb occurs in promises of punishment in Mal 1:4 and Ps 28:5, as well as in Mic 5:10 (ET 5:11), where God says, "I will overthrow all your fortresses" (והרסתי כל מבצריך), which is a near equivalent of Lam 2:2b. In other words, the narrator uses a verb connected with texts referring to the day of the Lord. God has overthrown, just as he threatened in Micah, Jeremiah, and Psalms.

The final two verbs also connect 2:2 to other judgment texts. God has "brought to the earth" (הגיע לארץ); indeed "he has defiled [חלל], her kingdom and her officials [ממלכה ושריה]." The first verb in the *hipʿil* stem is part of judgment language in Isa 25:5, 12 and Ezek 13:14. Most significantly, Isa 25:12 includes the word ומבצר, "fortress," a form of which (מבצרי, "the fortresses of") appears in Lam 2:2b. The second verb (חלל, "defile") is used in several punishment passages, such as Isa 43:28, Isa 47:5–6, and Ezek 22:16 (Renkema, 226), with the latter two texts including the Babylonian destruction as a historical background. Finally, Ps 89:39–41 (ET 89:38–40) includes חלל, "defile," and מבצר, "fortress," in its statements about how God has dishonored the king's crown and ruined his fortresses (see Lee, *Singers of Lamentations*, 137). Of course, Ps 89 summarizes the fall of Jerusalem and highlights the covenantal implications of the loss of the Davidic ruler. Lam 2:2c participates in this tradition that questions what God had in mind after 587 B.C.E.

Read in isolation, 2:2 may be understood to indicate surprise or accusation on the narrator's part. But given the context of 2:1–2 (the day of the Lord) and the usage of these same words in other judgment texts, it is much more likely that the narrator reports, albeit with true sympathy, that God has acted according to what the prophets and psalms threaten/promise. Such reports are horrible even when placed in canonical context, yet this context indicates they do have a theological and historical basis behind them.

3 This verse's three sections continue the process of placing Israel's current situation within historical/textual context, for the narrator uses judgment imagery drawn from the Law, Prophets, and Writings. Thus, the text continues to spell out the effects of the day of the Lord on Israel. By doing so the poem divulges the results of Israel's sin, which have already been confessed by Jerusalem in 1:18–22 and pointed out by the narrator in 1:5 and 1:8–9.

The first segment connects readers to the Law. Lam 2:3a states that God has "cut down [גדע] in his burning wrath [בחרי אף] all the might of Israel [כל קרן ישראל]." Forms of the term for "burning" (בחרי) only occur five times in the OT, and this passage and Deut 29:22–23 (ET 29:23–24) are the only two that have God for its subject. In Deut 29:22–23 the text describes a burnt out land so devastated by God's wrath (אף) that foreigners marvel at its devastation. The inclusion of both האף, "the anger," and חרי, "burning wrath," in this text make it a likely candidate for precursor to 2:3a, as does the fact that it comes after the judgment announced in Deut 28, which mirrors the context of 2:3a. Also, the ruined pastures of 2:2a and the scorched earth of 2:3c match the devastated land in Deut 29. It appears, then, that 2:3a describes the carrying out of the covenant threats concerning long-term, deep-seated rebellion by Israel.

God has cut down Israel's might. The word קרן, translated "might," literally means "horn," a metaphor that denotes pride and strength (Hillers, [1992] 97). Provan (61) observes, "To have one's 'horn' exalted by God was to be given power or honour by him (2:17; 1 Sam. 2:10; Ps. 112:9). To exalt one's own 'horn' was to trespass on God's prerogative and thus to behave arrogantly (Ps. 75:4–5 [MT 75:5–6])." Once again Ps 89 provides a backdrop for the poem, for in 89:18, 25 (ET 89:17, 24) the writer confesses to God that "by your favor our horn is exalted" (ESV), and the Lord has promised, "My faithfulness and my steadfast love shall be with him, and in my name shall his horn be exalted" (ESV). In Ps 89 the קרן, "horn," is the power of the Davidic ruler, and given 2:2c the same is probably true here. In destroying the kingdom and officials the Lord has cut off the קרן, "horn," of Israel. The threats found in the Mosaic covenant have specific effects on the continuation of the Davidic covenant.

The second segment also begins with an image connected to the Law and to Ps 89. God has השיב אחור ימינו, "withdrawn his right hand," with the result that the enemy has conquered Jerusalem. Hillers ([1992] 98) suggests that God has pulled back Israel's hand, and Provan (61) suggests that the phrase may signify "simply that God in a general way has rendered Israel powerless." In chap. 2, however, God is so actively involved that it seems unlikely that he is not the subject. If so, then this withdrawal reverses what the Lord did at the Red Sea, where the people confess that God's right hand shattered the enemy (Exod 15:6) and caused the earth to swallow the Egyptians (Exod 15:12). Interestingly, a form of בלע, "swallow," is used in Exod 15:12, which may form a contextual connection with Lam 2:2, 5, 8, and 16. It may also be the case that the poet again reflects Ps 89, since 89:14 (ET 89:13) praises the power of the creator—God's right hand. Either or both contexts fit. The removal of God's right hand leads to judgment, or the opposite of exodus deliverance, while the acknowledgment of God's power (right hand) in a poem like Ps 89 that asks God for relief may lead to a similar response in Lam 2.

The third segment uses common prophetic metaphors for judgment, though it should also be noted that Ps 89:47 (ET 89:46) likewise reflects on God's burning wrath. God "has burned in Jacob [ויבער ביעקב] like a blazing fire [כאש]," and the result is that "it has consumed all around" (אכלה סביב). The terms בער, "burn," and אש, "fire," and אכל, "consume," are all used elsewhere to depict the full force of divine wrath. For example, בער, "burn," appears in Jer 4:4, 7:20, 21:12, and 44:6 to describe judgment that has begun and will not be quenched until the whole land has felt its heat. Amos 5:6 expresses the same image, and Amos 1:2–2:4 uses אש, "fire," and אכל, "consume," imagery to describe the judgment of Israel, Judah, and their neighbors.

Once again the narrator chooses phraseology that brings together various passages related to the day of the Lord. Coupled with the covenant threats from the Law and reversal imagery from the Law and Ps 89, the day-of-the-Lord metaphors provide a powerful, canonical description of Israel's current situation.

4–5 This section continues the poem's overall emphasis on the day of the Lord, the cloud of God's wrath, and the fire of God's anger. It does so, however, by stating explicitly what 2:1–3 more than implies, that the Lord has become "like an enemy" to Israel. Once again images from earlier texts are used, especially divine-warrior metaphors, and once again these images express the reversal of fortunes Israel has experienced.

4 Lam 2:3b notes that God has withdrawn ימינו, "his right hand," from the enemy. This verse begins by asserting that God has purposefully, actively used his right hand to shoot arrows at Israel. This is because he has become כאויב, "like an enemy," which means he seems like those mentioned in chap. 1 who sacked, looted, oppressed, and scorned Zion.

With God's enemy status established, 2:4b comments that "like a foe [כצר] indeed he has killed [ויהרג] all the eye's delight [כל מחמדי עין]." This last phrase, which is used to describe the best of one's household in 1 Kgs 20:6 and Ezekiel's wife in Ezek 24:16, most likely refers to loved ones and precious items here.

This interpretation of 2:4b is supported by 2:4c, for the phrase באהל בת ציון, "in the tent of the daughter of Zion," refers to the very places where people live with their beloved family members among their life's possessions. Jer 10:20 uses tent imagery in this manner in a judgment passage. Such personal activity against the people is one more indication that God has "poured out like fire his fury" (שפך כאש חמתו). To turn again to Jer 10, in v 25 the prophet urges God, "pour out your fury on the nations" (שפך חמתך על הגוים), which resembles 2:4c very closely. Jeremiah continues, noting that "they have consumed" (אכלו) Jacob, the very thing 2:3c ascribes to God's burning wrath. In other words, 2:4c and Jer 10:17–25 indicate that the Lord's and the nations' activities have been one and the same, a point made clearly in 1:5 and 1:8–10. God's acting like an enemy includes sending or even leading foreign enemies, a fact that causes Jeremiah to cry out to the Lord in Jer 10:25 and likewise causes the prophetic voice to counsel Jerusalem to do the same in Lam 2:18–19.

5 This verse continues themes from vv 1–4 by reusing key words from those texts. In fact, few words in v 5 have not been used previously. This repetition of concepts marks v 5 as a summary of 2:1–4, so it states decisively what it means to be under God's wrath and thereby have God as an enemy.

Two memorable phrases link 2:5a to 2:1–4. The Lord was "like an enemy" (כאויב), and "he swallowed up Israel" (בלע ישראל). Since בלע, "swallowed up," is normally reserved for enemies' activities, it is not unusual to find it associated with אויב, "enemy," here. The reference to "enemy" not only reminds readers of 2:4; it may also take them back to the covenant curses found in Lev 26 and Deut 28. Though Lev 26:21–26 does not call God Israel's enemy, it does state that if Israel does not turn from long-term sin that God will *himself* strike Israel, bring a sword on the people, let them be besieged, and turn them over to their enemies. Then 26:27–39 states the horrors their enemies will perpetrate against them, and 26:40–45 stresses forgiveness based on confession of sin. Similarly, Deut 28:20–68 states what God *will do directly* to punish Israel for their sins. Both texts emphasize the turning over of Israel to enemies (Lev 26:17, 25, 34, 36, 37, 38, 39, 41, 44; Deut 28:25, 31, 68). God is "like an enemy" because he has become *for* their enemies. At this point in time, Israel has experienced nothing less than the covenant curses themselves, which is another way of saying they have experienced the day of the Lord.

In 2:5b the narrator continues the בלע, "swallow(ed) up," imagery by stating that God has "swallowed up all her palaces" (בלע כל ארמנותיה). This phrase reverses positive Zion imagery such as that found in Ps 48:4 (ET 48:3), where God himself protects "her palaces" (בארמנותיה). Now that God has withdrawn his right hand (2:3b) and become like an enemy (2:4a; 2:5a), these palaces have no defense. Besides this swallowing up of palaces, the Lord has "laid in ruins his strongholds" (שחת מבצריו). Presumably these are the same strongholds as in 2:2b.

The result of this swallowing up and destroying is that God has "multiplied in the daughter of Judah [וירב בבת יהודה] mourning and moaning/lamentation [תאניה ואניה]." Again, this mourning and lamenting have been caused by God himself, yet only as the direct result of what the Israelites themselves have done. The two truths go together, a fact that is easy to forget in chap. 2, given the lack of direct references to Israel's sin.

6–7 These two verses continue to detail the implications of the day of wrath and God acting like an enemy, but the emphasis is on what has happened to the temple and its related festivals and Sabbaths. Lam 1:4 has already stated that such observances have ceased. Lam 2:6–7 asserts that God has directly caused this cessation.

6 The Lord's actions against Zion and the temple environs receive priority. The first line is difficult to translate, but its force is easily understood. God "has done violence [ויחמס] as to a garden [כגן]" to "his booth [שכו]." Renkema (239–40) notes that some commentators find it difficult to accept that the Lord is the subject of חמס, "do violence," since the term normally reflects wrongdoing (BDB, 329). This linking of God and חמס, "do violence," is not impossible at all, though, given the difficult terms already attached to Yahweh. Again, the issue is how the day of the Lord comes upon and is experienced by the Israelites. Given the mention of festivals later in 2:6a, the mention of God's booth (שכו) probably does double metaphorical duty. Yahweh's booth is most certainly the temple, and the demolishing of his booth also means there will be no Festival of Booths, or any other festival for that matter. The rest of the line confirms this reading. God "has laid in ruins [שחת] his place for appointed festivals [מועדו]." This use of שחת, "ruin," echoes the one in 2:5b, where the strongholds are destroyed, while the presence of מועד, "appointed festival," reminds readers of 1:4a, which expresses similar desolation. The temple lies in ruins.

With the temple demolished, Yahweh has effectively "brought to an end in Zion" both מועד, "festival," and שבת, "Sabbath." The first term refers to Israel's great annual festivals (Deut 16:1–17), while the second refers to weekly Sabbaths and to special Sabbaths associated with the festivals. Lam 2:5 asserts that God has done what 1:4 has observed as reality. Yahweh brought these festivities to an end.

The Law and the Prophets warn of such losses. Lev 26:34–35 stresses that when the people are driven from the land the ground will enjoy its Sabbaths from the people. Isa 1:2–20 states that Jerusalem was left "like a booth in a vineyard" (Isa 1:8) partly because of the unrepentant hearts of those who frequented the temple. Jer 7 and 26 warned that the temple would be destroyed in part because of the wickedness of its constituents. Sadly, Israel has now felt the full force of these threats/promises.

The narrator returns to God's wrath as an explanation for what has occurred. In a phrase nearly as stunning as "he has done violence," the narrator asserts that God has "indeed spurned [וינאץ] in his indignant wrath [בזעם אפו] king and priest [מלך וכהן]." Three texts from Jeremiah help set נאץ, "spurned," in context. Jer 14:13–22, a passage that addresses lying prophets before pleading with God, implores Yahweh, "Do not spurn us" (אל תנאץ). Jeremiah bases this plea on the glory of God's name, the covenant, and God's reputation among the nations' gods (14:19–22), all reasons given by Moses when he interceded for Israel after the golden-calf incident (see Exod 32:11–13). God responds in 15:1–2 that even if Moses or Samuel were interceding he would not spare Israel.

In Jer 23:16–17 the Lord condemns prophets who tell those who "spurn the word of Yahweh" (למנאצי דבר יהוה), that all is well. Clearly, Israel has spurned God's word, and their false prophets have comforted them in this spurning. This verse parallels Ps 107:11, which attributes Jerusalem's fall in part to spurning God's word.

Jer 33:23–25 records that the people claim God has "spurned them" (ינאצון) from being a nation (Jer 33:24). Unlike Jer 15:1–2, the Lord responds by stating that he will restore them because of his covenant with Abraham, Isaac, and Jacob (Jer 33:26). Thus, any spurning of Israel is not permanent. It is disciplinary.

Given this background it is no wonder that the narrator singles out the priest and king here and adds the prophets in 2:9. The kings, priests, prophets, and people opposed Jeremiah (see Jer 1:17–19), and it is these same groups that God has spurned. Still, even this spurning is not final, no matter how much it seems so now. King, temple, and festivals are not finished.

7 This verse may offer the book's clearest expression of the actual destruction of the temple. God "has rejected his altar" (זנח אדני מזבחו), the very place where he placed his name, yet on the condition of obedience (1 Kgs 9:1–9). Lacking obedience, not even sacrifices are worth having (see Isa 1:2–20). The verb זנח, "reject," is fairly rare, but it appears in Ps 74:1, a verse that also mentions God's wrath. This psalm includes a description of enemies in the sanctuary, so it may be part of this text's background. Ps 89:39 (ET 89:38) uses the verb to describe how God has rejected the Davidic dynasty. The two psalms depict the effects of 587 B.C.E. on priest and king.

This rejection of the altar means that God "has disowned his holy place" (נאר מקדשו). The verb only appears here and in Ps 89:40 (ET 89:39), where it states that God has rejected his covenant with David (נארתה ברית עבדך). A form of the noun appears in Ps 74:3 (בקדש), as do familiar words such as אויב, "enemy," and מועד, "festival" (see Ps 74:2–3). Apparently the narrator reflects the rejected temple dilemma of Ps 74 and the rejected monarchy dilemma of Ps 89. At the same time, he makes use of Mosaic covenant threats with prophetic prayers and predictions of disaster and renewal. The narrator reflects a whole canon theology, not just one aspect of a canonical theology.

The concrete result of God's disowning the temple is that "he delivered into the hand of the enemy [הסגיר ביד אויב] the walls of her palaces [חומת ארמנותיה]." The enemies mentioned so prominently in chap. 1 have received God's help. They have not simply achieved Jerusalem's destruction on their own. Of course, the word for "palaces" is the same here and in 2:5b. In the former verse Israel and Judah provide the frame of reference, whereas in this instance the temple itself is in view. God has seen to it that what happened to the nation generally and the kingship particularly has happened to the temple. Indeed "king and priest" (2:6c) have felt the force of the day of wrath, the rejection of the Lord (2:7a).

Israel's enemies revel in their victory: "They have given voice [קול נתנו] in the house of the LORD, [בבית יהוה] as on a day of festival [כיום מועד]." In other words, they raise their voices in God's house as if they are having a party. Renkema (249) explains, "As we can see from the song-response (1:7), צרים שחקו 'the enemies laugh,' these noisy invaders are expressing their joy." God has allowed those who should not enter the temple to enter the temple (see 1:10; Renkema, 249–50). Once there, in the place where God cut off מועד, "festivals" (2:6b), the Lord allows the enemy to have their own sort of מועד, "festival." As Provan (67) observes, "God has enabled Israel's enemies to engage in a parody of this worship in the very temple itself!" This concern for the enemy's actions in the temple is similar to Ps 74:4–8, though that text describes roaring, cutting, and burning, in more detail. Still, both texts state what is unthinkable if Zion theology is not placed under the broader rubric of covenantal blessings and consequences (see Lev 26; Deut 27–28; 1 Kgs 9:1–9): the nations have conquered the land, entered the temple, and burned both as if they were no more significant than any other place they had destroyed.

8–9a These lines make it plain that God's destruction of Jerusalem was a conscious, calculated act, not something that took him by surprise. They also attest to the thoroughness of the destruction. The walls and whole of Jerusalem have been shattered, not just the temple.

8 At some specific point in time Yahweh "determined/thought/decided [חשב] to lay in ruins [להשחית] the wall [חומת]" of Zion. The first verb (or a form of it) appears six times in Jeremiah. In Jer 18:11 (part of the "potter vision"), 26:3 (the second "temple sermon"), and 36:3 (part of the sermon Jehoiakim burns in the fire), the word is used to describe the Lord's plans to judge Judah. The latter two texts offer repentance as a way to avoid God's plan. Jer 29:20 and 50:45 announce God's plans to judge Edom and Babylon respectively. On a more positive note, Jer 29:11 announces God's good plans for the remnant already in Babylon. Thus, the word can have either positive or negative connotations, yet only negative ones for unrepentant people, which is the context here. Obviously, what God "determined" God has done. Jerusalem's wall is "in ruins."

Further proof of God's deliberate action comes in 2:8b: God "stretched out a measuring line" (נטה קו). The same sort of imagery occurs in Amos 7:7–9, where the Lord measures the high places of Israel for destruction, though the word for the measuring instrument there is אנך, not קו as here. So extensive was the plan for destruction that the Lord "did not return his hand from swallowing up" (לא־השיב ידו מבלע). In other words, whatever God marked would be "swallowed up," a term found in 2:2, 5, and 16 as well, and he kept stretching out his hand farther and farther, thus marking the whole city for destruction.

As a consequence of this measuring for the purpose of demolishing, or swallowing up, God causes the חל וחומה, "rampart and wall," the city's defenses, to ויאבל, "lament/mourn," and אמללו, "languish/wither." These same two verbs are used in combination to describe the mourning of Jerusalem and the withering of her gates in Jer 14:1–2. Elsewhere they are often used in judgment texts (see BDB, 5, 51). The city's defenses mourn and wither at the heat of battle, and it must be remembered that God sees that they do so.

9a The narrator completes his description of the city's destruction. Three vigorous verbs state what has occurred. Jerusalem's "gates have sunk to the ground" (טבעו בארץ שעריה), presumably as a result of the withering of the walls (2:8c). God "has ruined and shattered her bars" (אבד ושבר בריחיה). אבד, "ruined," can also commonly mean "destroyed" or "perished" (BDB, 1–2). Together these verbs depict total destruction. The city lies devastated and defenseless, without temple or fortification.

9b–10 At this point the narrator moves from the demolition of walls and buildings to human devastation. Kings, prophets, priests, officials, and people (see Jer 1:17–19) have been affected. Their absence means even worse societal conditions than when they were present.

9b–c Given the context of the day of the Lord (1:12c; 1:21c; 2:1c), this passage is not an abstract description of what has happened to disinterested parties.

These groups have a past that relates to what has happened to them in the present.

The king, his officials, and Israel's prophets have all suffered from the Babylonian invasion. Indeed, מלכה ושריה, "her king and her officials," categories already referred to in 2:2c (see 1:6b for שריה, "officials," by themselves), are בגוים, "among the nations." This text parallels 1:3, where the narrator states that "Judah has gone into exile" (גלתה יהודה) and "she dwells among the nations" (היא ישבה בגוים). The king and officials share the people's fate.

Further, אין תורה, "there is no law." This phrase is difficult to interpret in context. Zlotowitz (79) notes that the MT could lead one to read the passage as "the kings and officials are among the nations where there is no divine law," and the midrash does so. He argues, however, that the phrase refers to the loss of proper instruction in God's word, which is the way most scholars interpret the phrase. Renkema (259) observes that 2:6c links king and priest, which indicates "the royal guarantee to maintain the said cult. With the loss of king as protector, an important pillar of the liturgy also disappeared, a fact which also had serious consequences for the priestly teaching associated therewith." Albrektson (*Studies in the Text and Theology*, 103) considers the phrase parallel to the ones about the kings, officials, and prophets. Thus, as Keil (500) summarizes the matter, "The law is the summary of the rule of life given by God to His people: this exists no more for Judah, because, with the destruction of Jerusalem and of the temple, the divinely appointed constitution of Israel was abolished and destroyed." In Jer 18:18 people, resentful of the prophet's message, declare that the law will not perish from the priest. Yet this very thing has occurred.

It is important to consider the activities of the priests at or near the time of destruction. According to Jeremiah the priests participated in idolatry with the kings, officials, and prophets (Jer 2:26–28; 8:1–3; 19:1–15), as well as in seeking unjust gain (Jer 6:13; 8:10). At some future point in time, however, the Lord will restore the priests, who will then function appropriately (Jer 31:14; 33:17–18). Thus, the loss of priest and law was justified yet not permanent. At one level this loss is a massive one, yet at another level it is hardly a loss at all. Like the kings, the priests had functioned so poorly in the present that only future hope remained.

Things get even worse, for "even her prophets [גם נביאיה] have not found [לא מצאו] a vision from the LORD [חזון מיהוה]." This lack of finding mirrors that of Judah not finding rest in 1:3b and the officials not finding pasture in 1:6b. Once again Jeremiah proves helpful. Yahweh declares in Jer 14:14 that he has not sent the prophets who proclaim peace and safety, so their vision is a חזון שקר, "false vision," built on lies formed in their own deceitful minds. Jer 23:16 takes a similar approach, for there Yahweh asserts that such prophets "speak a vision of their hearts" (חזון לבם ידברו), or that which is "not from the mouth of Yahweh" (לא מפי יהוה). At the same time, Jeremiah himself faithfully related God's word. Could he, then, speak of the prophets in this manner? Indeed he does so in the passages noted above and in others. As Lee writes (*Singers of Lamentations*, 146 n. 53), "In the book of Jeremiah, Jeremiah often refers to the other prophets as נבאים [prophets] though he is set apart from them." Since he is also a priest (Jer 1:1–3), the same goes for that role. Lam 2:9 states the general case, as does the Lord and the prophet in Jeremiah: as a class of people the prophets have not been faithful, and because of this they receive no vision from Yahweh, which is an earmark of what happens on the day of the Lord (see Amos 8:11–12).

10 With the king, officials, and people "among the nations," and the priests and prophets impotent to teach and envision, it is no wonder that the elders and virgins mourn among the rubble. Every element of society suffers under God's wrath.

Zion's elders sit silently (ידמו), clothed in sackcloth (חגרו שקים), and "throw dust on their heads" (העלו עפר על ראשם). They are in mourning because of what has occurred, and they are silent because they have no wisdom to share or verdict to render, which was their role in society. They have no more to offer than the priests or prophets (Provan, 70). In fact, 1:19 indicated that many elders and priests have already perished from hunger, which demonstrates that they have not even been able to save themselves.

Likewise, the בתולת, "virgins," who have not, like some of their sisters, already gone into exile (see 1:18) "bow their heads to the ground" (הורידו לארץ ראשן). This posture most certainly coincides with the mourning done by the elders. These virgins normally have a cultic role of singing, dancing, and expressing joy (see Renkema, 266). Rather than singing, they bow their heads to the ground with sadness. Jeremiah never associates this group with sinful practices, but in Jer 31:13–14 he states that when God restores Jacob's fortunes the old men, young men, priests, and virgins will exchange their weeping for joy.

The day of the Lord has had horrible effects, according to the narrator. City, temple, defenses, king, officials, priests, prophets, elders, and virgins have felt its force. That such things were threatened in the Law and the Prophets makes what has occurred more understandable yet no easier to endure. Such knowledge could increase the pain. The issue of what the people should do now comes to the fore.

11–12 At this point the poem turns from third-person description to first-person statements directed toward the reader. Before turning to first-person comments directed at Jerusalem in 2:13–19 (Miller, "Poetry and Personae," 114–17), this first segment serves the purpose of having the speaker identify directly and sympathetically to Jerusalem and her plight (see O. Kaiser, 143). This speaker is no interloper. He shares her pain and expresses ways to proceed now.

11 This speech's syntax is so similar to some found in Jeremiah that the speaker must be identified as Jeremiah or as a person that has thoroughly embraced his theology. Lee (*Singers of Lamentations*, 147–48) offers several reasons for opting for the former conclusion. First, "Jeremiah's personal expressions of weeping (8:23; 13:17; 14:17) are found in poetry in the book of Jeremiah several times." Second, in those passages "he uses not only the common terms 'eyes' and 'weep,' but in both 8:19–23 and 14:17 *five times* he also uses his favored term of endearment for Jerusalem, 'Daughter of My People' (בת עמי), for whom he weeps"(emphasis original). Third, the word מעי, "my inward parts," appears in 2:11 and is also used in Jer 4:9 twice. Keil (501) adds a fourth link: שבר בת עמי, "(the) shattering of (the) daughter of my people," found in 2:11b "is a genuine Jermianic expression (cf. 6:14; 8:11, 21; etc.) which again occurs in v. 13, 3:47, 48, and 4:10." This prophetic figure weeps for the people as only one who has ministered to them can.

This weeping is thorough and heartfelt and very much like Jerusalem's in 1:20–22. The speaker states that his "eyes are worn out by weeping" (כלו בדמעות עיני). A similar phrase occurs in Ps 69:4 (ET 69:3), so the speech draws on psalmic lament language as well as prophetic lament imagery. Further, his "inward parts are in turmoil" (חמרמרו מעי). This verb is fairly rare, and typically refers to fluid fermenting or foaming (BDB, 330). It appears in 1:20, where the phrase appears with the verb and noun reversed. This reusage of the phrase indicates the speaker's identification with the people and their pain. He feels like they do about the loss of the children, though he confesses no sin.

Again the speaker expresses his pain, this time by asserting that his "liver is cast down to the ground" (2:11b). This reference to לארץ, "the ground," echoes the usage of this same form in 2:10c. The speaker's liver, or emotions, is cast down as low as the virgins' heads. Why? "Because of (the) shattering [על שבר] of (the) daughter of my people [בת עמי]." Therefore the speaker identifies himself specifically as one of them. Once again, such a description fits a prophetic figure such as Jeremiah or someone who shares his viewpoint. After all, the prophets had to live between the Lord and the people to fulfill their calling. Jeremiah's life was particularly hard in this regard (see Jer 11–20).

This shattering takes on specific, human form in 2:11c–12. Already the elders and priests' plight has received attention. Now the speaker states that "infants and nursing babes [עולל ויונק] faint [בעטף]" in the city's open places. Jer 10:20 lists the loss of children as one of the woes the nation faces. Deut 28:41, 50, and 53–57 indicate that the nation that conquers the unrepentant Israel will have no mercy on the young, will take the children into captivity, and will besiege the people until they eat their own children rather than face starvation. The speaker understands that the children's plight is one more horrifying proof that the covenant curses have not only come upon the people; they continue with horrifying results. It is therefore an indication of how the people's sins affect their children. Failure to serve the Lord meant, among other things, failure to teach their children about God as Deut 6:4–9 directs. It also meant that children would be killed in invasions or sent into exile or forced to die of malnutrition. This suffering could have been averted by parental faithfulness.

12 The images only get more horrifying. "They say to their mothers, 'Where is (the) grain and wine?'" So the infants (עולל) ask their mothers for food and drink, but their mothers can do nothing for them. These calls for food must be decreasing in volume, for the calls are given "as they faint like wounded/pierced men" (בהתעטפם כחלל). This comparison is apt, since such men perished in the city a few verses earlier. Whereas they were pierced by arrows or spears, these children have been pierced by hunger and want. Their homes, perhaps razed in the loss of battle, are no longer available to them, so their suffering occurs "in the open places of the city" (ברחבות עיר), the location already mentioned in 2:11c.

Their crying out is to no avail. One final image completes their suffering. The last line of v 12 reveals that they speak to their mothers, in the open places, while their lives slowly drain away on their mothers' bosom. The same verb (שפך) describes the casting down of the speaker's emotions in 2:11b and the slow casting away of life here. Sadly, the verb begins with the little ones speaking לאמתם, "to their mothers," and ends with them dying אל חק אמתם, "on their mothers' bosom." This terrible inclusio defines the depths of sorrow the speaker attempts to convey.

These images of starvation and death are meant to be moving. Westermann (153–54) writes, "The precipitating event was the 'day of wrath' on which Israel experienced the punishment of God. Although the event was recognized as punishment, it remained incomprehensible in its severity. . . . With the perishing of young children by starvation, something unspeakable has taken place. The explanation that this was a divine punishment does not suffice, for what is the place of small children in that!" Renkema (276) comments, "What kind of struggle could the smallest ones have put up?! Where adults are forced to fight for their lives (cf. 1:11a, 19bc), the smallest ones are left with little say and helplessly they 'pour out their lives on their mothers' lap.'" Calvin (365) adds, "When, therefore, the Prophet says that children cried to their mothers, he means to represent a sad spectacle, which ought justly to produce horror in the minds of all." Concerning the speaker, K. M. O'Connor (*Lamentation and the Tears of the World*, 38) observes that he "has entered her space, her world, her horror; he *sees*." To feel nothing when faced with such misery is truly to be numb or dead inside, and the speaker is neither. Knowing that the parents' actions have led to devastating results for their children, he will speak kindly to these parents, then urge them to seek the Lord in 2:13–19.

13–17 Sorrow and regret mark this passage. The speaker feels inadequate to comfort the people's understandably deep pain. Yet he attempts to do so by noting their prophets' failures, their political friends' treachery, and their enemies' boasting. The destruction was not all the people's fault. They had help. He reminds them that God has done what he said he would do; then he counsels them to seek the Lord. Apparently he firmly believes that Yahweh will respond favorably.

13 Despite identifying with and sharing her pain, the speaker does not know exactly what to say to "daughter of Jerusalem," to "virgin daughter of Zion." This verse is punctuated with three instances of מה, "what," and one of מי, "who," joined by the causal clause כי, "for."

The first "what" asks "What can I repeat to you?" The verb אעידך is very difficult to translate (see *Note* 13.a.); it probably means something like "What familiar soothing words can I say to you?" The speaker has no pat phrases that will work here.

The second מה queries "What can I compare for you [מה אדמה־לך]?" There is no way to compare her situation to another in a way that will make sense or alleviate the pain she feels. Coupled with the preceding מה, v 13a indicates that there are no sayings and no similes that match the needs of this situation.

The third מה wonders "What can I liken for you [מה אשוה־לך] that I may comfort you [ואנחמך]?" It seems that the speaker cannot achieve his goal of comforting hurting Jerusalem. The first verb normally means "to be like, resemble" (BDB, 1000), so the speaker confesses the unusual nature of Jerusalem's suffering. The second verb appears in participial form five times in chap. 1 (1:2, 9, 16, 17, 21), each time to grieve that Jerusalem has no one to comfort her. Now it seems that yet another speaker confirms this lack of comfort, so her hopes fade more by the moment.

Why is her pain so far beyond comfort? The כי clause answers this question: "For great as/like the sea [כי גדול כים] is your shattering [שברך]." In fact, her shattering is so great that the speaker asks, "Who can heal you [מי ירפא לך]?" Jer 19:10–11 recounts a symbolic act in which Jeremiah is told to "shatter" a vessel and tell the people "I will shatter this people" (אשבר את העם הזה), and "no one will be able to heal/mend it" (לא יוכל להרפה). Since both שבר, "shatter," and רפה, "heal/mend," appear in close contextual proximity in Lam 2:13c and Jer 19:10–11, it is likely that a similar concept applies both places, if in fact v 13c does not have Jeremiah in mind. God has done what Jer 19:10–11 stated that he would do; yet the fulfillment of this prophecy, when actually seen and experienced, stuns the speaker.

14 Lam 2:9c states that as a result of the city's demise the prophets have not seen visions, and Lam 2:20 indicates that priests and prophets were killed in the very sanctuary of the Lord. Here the prophetically oriented speaker states flatly that Israel's prophets "envisioned [חזו] . . . vanity and worthlessness [שוא ותפל]." False prophets appear regularly in Jeremiah, though שקר is the normal word for false statements instead of שוא. Jeremiah uses שוא, "vanity," in texts about false gods (Jer 6:29; 18:15) and in ones about Israel trying to make herself beautiful for her lovers (Jer 4:30), and uses תפלה, "worthlessness," in a text about false prophets (Jer 23:13). Both words are used in Ezek 13:1–16, one to describe falsehood (שוא) and one to depict words that amount to "whitewash" (תפל) of sin.

Several implications arise from 2:14a. First, Lamentations agrees with prophets like Hosea (see Hos 4:5), Jeremiah (see Jer 14:13–22; 23:9–40; 27–29), and Ezekiel (see Ezek 13:1–19), who lay part of the blame for Israel's destruction on prophets who refuse to speak God's hard words to a rebellious people. Of course, the people share the blame, for they had to accept what was preached. As Calvin (368) writes, "We now perceive the design of the Prophet: he says that the Jews had indeed been deceived by the false prophets; but this had happened through their own fault, because they had not submitted to obey God, because they had rejected sound doctrine, because they had been rebellious against all his counsels." At the same time, v 14a is part of a text emphasizing comfort and counsel, so the people's blame is here left implicit.

Second, in Jer 14:13–22 the prophet allows the false prophets to stand as a reason for intercession. He knows he is a prophet yet speaks of "the prophets" as a group separate from himself. Therefore the criticism of the prophets in Lamentations is not proof that Jeremiah did not write the book, nor proof that Lamentations does not highlight prophetic theology. True prophets considered criticism of false prophets part of their task.

Third, Lam 2:14a uses either Ezek 13:1–16 or stock phrases known in the religious culture. This fact does not rule out Jeremiah as author of Lamentations since Ezek 13:1–16 may well have been delivered and/or written down well before Jerusalem's fall. Regardless of the dating, the oddity of the words in question appearing together probably indicates that the author of Lam 2 knew Ezek 13, just as he knew Pss 73, 74, and 89, as well as multiple passages in Leviticus, Deuteronomy, and Jeremiah. In other words, the author had knowledge of passages that span the OT canon. One cannot name the author of Lamentations from these observations, but one can learn more about the book's theology.

Fourth, the comments about false prophets in 2:14a and elsewhere do not negate the value of faithful prophets in Israelite history. 2 Kgs 17 and 25 and Jer 52 all make it clear that God sent true prophets to turn Israel from their sins. Though some people responded to their message, these constituted only a remnant of Israel.

Sadly, the false prophets did the opposite of what was needed. They "did not expose [ולא גלו] your iniquity [עונך]." There is wordplay at work here. The word for "exposed" comes from the same root as "exiled" (גלה), so the concept here is that failing to expose sin meant the nation was exposed to exile. The purpose of exposing sin was להשיב שביתך, "to avert your captivity." The root of השיב is שוב, a word that means "to turn, return." שוב may also mean "repent." Only repenting could turn their hearts and avert disaster, but unlike Jeremiah, who spoke of repentance over a hundred times, the prophets in question preached vanity, whitewash, nothing useful. The Qere form of the text (שׁבוּתֵךְ) makes the phrase parallel the words of Amos 9:14. In fact, their visions were "burdens/sermons [מַשְׂאוֹת] of vanity [שָׁוְא again] and enticement [וּמַדּוּחִים]." This latter word comes from נדח, which in the *hipʿil* stem has the sense of allurement (see Deut 13:14; Prov 7:21; Provan, 288). Rather than leading the people back to God, their message enticed them toward covenant disobedience of the type that Hos 1–3, Jer 2–6, and Ezek 16, 20, and 23 consider spiritual adultery. Their sermons led the daughter of Zion toward lovers (see 1:2, 19) who could not comfort instead of toward the covenant God who could heal. Their sermons could hardly have done more damage to an erring (1:5, 18) people.

15 Slowly, inexorably, the speaker leads the people toward his counsel that they seek the Lord (2:18–19). He does so in part by eliminating other sources of comfort. Having identified with the lowest depths of their pain (2:11–12) and having removed their prophets as a source of true knowledge of God's will (2:14; see 2:9), he now eliminates those passing by as possible helpers. Later he will likewise strike the enemies from the list (2:16). Soon the Lord will be their only hope for relief.

In 1:12 Jerusalem asked "all those passing by" (כל עברי דרך) to "see" (ראו) the extent of her pain and, presumably, act on her behalf. Now the speaker uses the identical phrase to refer to the same group but adds that "they clap (their) hands against you" (ספקו עליך כפים). The verb may mean to slap one's thigh in remorse (Jer 31:19; Ezek 21:17), strike hands in anger (Num 24:10), slap someone (Job 34:26), strike or splash (Jer 48:26), or mock (here and Job 27:23; BDB, 706). Thus, physical abuse could be meant, but in context the meaning is probably derisive in nature, since those passing by also "hiss [שׁרקו] and wag their heads [וינעו ראשׁם]" against Jerusalem, terms normally associated with mocking (see Keil, 503; Gerstenberger, [2001] 489). Provan (74) writes that this mocking is not sheer mirthful scorn but rather mocking undertaken with hostility.

They contemptuously ask, "Is this the city that was called 'perfection of beauty, the joy of all the earth'?" This final line is unusually long (see *Note* 15.a-a.), which has the effect of lengthening the mocking. Löhr (13) observes that the phrase כלילת יפי, "perfection of beauty," also appears in Ezek 27:3 and 28:12 in laments over Tyre's demise. In the OT the term describes more than one marvelous city marked for destruction. The phrase משׂושׂ לכל הארץ, "the joy of all the earth," however, appears only here and in Ps 48:3 (ET 48:2), a passage that speaks of the glory of Zion and the great power of the Lord. Whether those passing by wish to mock what has become of Jerusalem's beauty and significance as a city or as a worship site, they are able to do so. At this time Jerusalem is impressive neither as a capital city nor as a place that highlights God's power over other kingdoms. Or so the mockers think, for 2:17 will highlight God's sovereignty over world events.

16 Before this emphasis occurs, though, the speaker continues his description of those who mock Israel. This time he comments that אויביך, "your enemies," a noun used for God in 2:4 and 2:5, and for those to whom God gave Jerusalem in 2:7, "have opened their mouth against you" (פצו עליך פיהם). As those passing by did in 2:15b, these enemies "hiss" (שׁרקו) like a great wind and "gnash (their) teeth" (ויחרקו שׁן). This latter term appears in Pss 35:16 and 37:12 and Job 16:9, and "is here an expression of rage that has burst out" (Keil, 503). As in 2:15, the mockery takes on a vicious, violent character (Provan, 297). These enemies could hardly be more pleased.

The reason for their joy is their belief that they have caused Israel's pain. Four first-person common plural verbs express their joy and self-congratulation. First, they claim, "We have swallowed [her] up!" (בלענו). In other words, they claim credit for what 2:2, 5, 8, and 16 assert that Yahweh has done. God has used them as an instrument, but they see things differently. Second, they exult, "Surely this is the day we have waited for" (שקוינהו). Indeed קוה carries the force of waiting for something eagerly, not merely standing by until something occurs. They can hardly believe that the time has come.

Third, they exclaim, "We have found [it]!" (מצאנו). Unlike Judah, who has found no resting place (1:3), or Jerusalem's leaders, who have found no food (1:6), or Israel's (false) prophets, who have found no vision (2:9), the enemies have found exactly what they were seeking. It is as if they have found great treasure. Fourth, the enemies rejoice in what they have seen (ראינו). Of course, the narrator states in 1:8–9 that those who once honored Jerusalem now turn away from her because they have "seen" (ראו) her nakedness. In 1:10 the narrator notes that Israel has "seen" (ראתה) the nations go into the temple. Given these woes, she asks God to "see" in 1:9, 11, and 20, and even asks those passing by to "see" in 1:12, 18. Tragically, the enemies have seen, and they are the only ones in the book of Lamentations who like what they have seen.

17 Regardless of what Jerusalem or her opponents think, what has occurred has happened because of Yahweh's plans and commands. No one else has had ultimate authority over the city or its people. All Jerusalem's opponents' success may be traced back to God's relationship with Israel.

Stated simply, "Yahweh has done [עשה יהוה]" exactly "what he purposed [זמם]." This second verb may be used for plans in general, yet it often appears in prophetic judgment texts (BDB, 273). For instance, in Jer 4:28 it expresses the need to mourn over coming judgment, for God says, "I have spoken, I have purposed [זמתי], and I will not relent, and I will not turn from it." Similarly, in Jer 51:12 the text states that Babylon will be judged, "for Yahweh has indeed purposed, indeed he has done [כי גם זמם יהוה גם עשה] what he spoke against the inhabitants of Babylon." Taken together, these passages express a clear theology of Jerusalem's destruction providing evidence of God's sovereignty in history. This observation is confirmed by the rest of v 17a, for it explains that God "has carried out his word/threat" (בצע אמרתו). The verb has violent overtones to it (BDB, 130–31), which makes contextual sense. God's threats made through the prophets concerning Jerusalem's demise could not be carried out in a merely symbolic fashion.

God's plans and their violent fulfillment continue to be emphasized in 2:17b. Not only has God done what he purposed; he commanded them from days long ago (צוה מימי קדם). Jerusalem's destruction was no act of random violence. Rather, it was a specific act by God intended to punish the long-term sins of a specific nation, Israel. Thus, this verse has a very specific frame of reference and should not be applied to every city's fall. Israel has known since the days of Moses the cost of centuries of rebellion (see Lev 26; Deut 27–28), though the fulfillment of those threats only came upon Jerusalem in 587 B.C.E.

Lam 2:2 stated that God "has thrown down/overthrown [הרס]" the city (see Jer 1:10; 24:6; 31:28; 42:10; 45:4). The verse also stated that he has done so without showing mercy (ולא חמל). Once the destroying process began, there was no turning back, especially since no general penitent response came from the people. As a result, the much-mentioned (see 1:2; 2:3, 4, 5, 7) אויב, "enemy," has rejoiced over Israel (וישמח עליך). Their gloating, hissing, and clapping of hands (see 2:15–16) has turned into sheer joy.

This joy does not come from something they have done, for God "has raised up [הרים] the horn/power [קרן] of your foes [צריך]." The verb, a *hip'il* that expresses causative action here, has not appeared previously in the book. The two nouns have occurred, with "horn" having been used in 2:3a when the narrator describes the demise of Israel's power, and "foe" having been used in 1:5, 7, and 10 to describe those who have destroyed the city and temple. In other words, the "foes" are the Babylonians, whose "horn," or power, the Lord has made to grow greater and greater.

Jerusalem may blame her foes for her terrible situation, but God sent the foes, just as the prophets said he would if the covenant people did not change. Jerusalem may hope that those passing by or her old prophets may bring her a word other than the ones brought by Hosea, Amos, Zephaniah, and Jeremiah, but God has already given the word they must hear. Their situation is a result of a divine word about human sin. In a similar text, Zech 1:1–6 uses every main verb used in Lam 2:7 to assert that judgment has come because of sin. The prophets foretold as much, and the people's appropriate response now is repentance. For such to occur, Jerusalem needs to continue to talk to God, just as she has done in 1:20–22.

18–19 To effect this renewed relationship between the Lord and the people, the speaker urges the people to seek the Lord. The motive for doing so is found in the needs of her children. It is as if the plight of the infants should move Jerusalem to act in appropriate ways that instruction, exhortation, and warning never could.

18 The first line of v 18 is very difficult to translate (see *Note* 18.a.). As Gordis (166) explains, "The suffix of *libbam* has no antecedent. It obviously cannot refer to the previously mentioned foes." Thus, he suggests emending the text to צקי לבך, "pour out your heart," rather than צעק לבם, "their heart cried out," a suggestion that Hillers follows ([1992] 101). Provan (75) notes that every ancient version supports the MT, so he thinks לבם, "their heart," refers to the inhabitants of Jerusalem. Keil (504) concludes that the speaker proceeds as if the people are already crying out, so he summons them to more and better approaches to the Lord. Renkema (308) argues that the hearts of the children are crying out, which is why their parents need to intercede for them. Renkema's conclusion makes the best sense, given the introduction of the children's vast suffering in 2:11–12 and the mentioning of intercession for them in 2:19.

The hearts of Jerusalem's children "cried out [צעק] to the Lord [אל אדני]," presumably in concert with the cries they made to their parents in 2:12. As they cry out, they address their plea to the "wall of the daughter of Zion" (חומת בת ציון). Given the differences of opinion on who the speaker is here, it is hardly surprising that there is a similar level of disagreement on the identity of the wall of Jerusalem. Gordis (167), Lee (*Singers of Lamentations*, 156–57), and Keil (504) consider the wall the totality of the city. This has certainly been the meaning of the term so far in the book. Renkema (311), Provan (76), and Gottwald (*Studies*, 11), however, conclude that God is the wall, or defense, of Jerusalem. They base this conclusion partly on Zech 2:9 (ET 2:5), which describes Yahweh in this way.

Once again it is necessary to be humble in one's opinions on such matters. It seems best in context to read the children calling out to their city in its totality, including their parents, to pray and grieve. Then the speaker urges the parents to do the same in 2:19. The Lord is the ultimate recipient of the parents' prayer, so God's role in this section cannot be forgotten.

Zion is asked to "make tears descend like a torrent" (הורידי כנחל דמעה) both "day and night" (יומם ולילה). The word translated "torrent" can denote "a mountain stream, rushing down its rugged channel" (Streane, 373), so it implies a large source of water coming with force. Clearly, this image stresses urgency and power. Jer 14:17 states, "My eyes flow down [תרדנה עיני] with tears night and day [דמעה לילה ויומם]," and the walls are encouraged to do the same now. They are to take no rest (אל תתני פוגת לך) nor allow their eyes to grow still (אל תדם בת עינך), for the matter is extremely urgent. The water must not stop flowing for any reason, for the children's lives are on the line, and the nation's future is at stake.

19 Now the speaker continues the pleading begun by Jerusalem's children. This verse has four parts instead of the normal three, so some commentators delete a line. As was the case in 1:7, though, no textual evidence exists for such a deletion. The adding of a line draws attention to 2:19, so its meaning is vitally important. In this case the people's need to pray for their offspring should take high priority in their lives. Little else matters in the current situation. They need divine help.

The speaker employs a series of four imperatives. First, he commands Jerusalem, "Arise! Cry loudly in the night." The two initial imperatives (קומי רני) indicate the need for "unprecedented intensity. In the wake of all that Zion has had to undergo, to plead for God once again to take heed no longer appears as a matter of course" (Westermann, 157). This intensity is shown in the instruction to those who arise and cry out to be as earnest as watchmen, as involved as those who stand guard "at the beginning of the watches" (לראש אשמרות). Provan (76) notes that "we are probably to understand this as implying renewed effort at the commencement of each watch rather than a fresh start in prayer after sleep (cf. Ps. 63:6 [MT 63:7])." In fact, the urgency of the situation hardly leaves room for sleep at all.

In the third command, the speaker counsels Jerusalem, "Pour out your heart like water" (שפכי כמים לבך). The verb שפך, "pour out," has become a staple in the book, having already appeared in 2:4, 11, and 12. In 2:4 it is used to describe how God has poured out, or cast down, his fury. In 2:11–12 the narrator states that his inward parts have been cast down, or poured out, and also states that the lives of Jerusalem's children are now being poured out, or cast down, on their mothers' breasts. Now the people should pour out their hearts like the speaker poured his out, or, more to the point, like their children had their lives poured out. The intercession should match the need.

The location of this pouring out is clear—נכח פני אדני, "before the face/presence of the Lord." As Calvin (382) notes, the people must seek God "so as to seek alleviation from him, which could not have been done, were they not convinced that he was the author of all their calamities; and hence, also, arises repentance, for there is a mutual relation between God's judgment and men's sins." They have nowhere else to go, so as Davidson (187) comments, "It is now all or nothing: a total pouring out of grief to the God who is the source of their trouble, but the God in whom alone any hope rests."

The final imperative completes the speaker's description of earnest prayer. Having risen up, raised their voices, and poured out their hearts, they are now told, "Lift up your hands to him" (שׂאי אליו כפיך). Westermann (157) writes that this phrase "connotes both lamentation and supplication." God must fill their hands, for they cannot do so themselves. These hands must be raised for "the lives of your little ones" (על נפש עולליך), for the very ones taken into captivity (1:5), fainting in the streets (2:11), and crying out for their parents to pray (2:18). If they are truly grieved, and how could they be otherwise, they must plead the cause of their children. Again, their "life" (נפש, see 2:12) is at stake, since they are "fainting from hunger" (העטופים ברעב) in the streets. A similar scene unfolds in 2:12, where the children faint like warriors pierced in battle.

God declares in Jer 6:11 and 9:20 (ET 9:21) that wrath will come that will "cast down children in the street" (שׁפך על עולל בחוץ) and "cut off children from the street" (להכרית עולל מחוץ). Lam 2:11–12, 18–19 indicate that these unheeded warnings have become reality. The same parents who did not obey God's word must turn and pray for their children. Past disobedience must not lead to present pride, stubbornness, and a resultant unawareness of danger.

This whole section underscores the difficulty of discussing the elements of sin and punishment in Lamentations. On the one hand, it is absolutely true that the vast majority of Israel's adults chose not to follow the covenantal standards attached to their nation's relationship with God. Thus, they have suffered for their own sins. On the other hand, the children have suffered gravely because of their parents' unwillingness to believe texts such as Deut 28 or warnings like those in Jer 6:11 and 9:20–21 that relate directly to the effects their sins will have on their own children. One could blame God for the whole situation, since he sent the Babylonians, but if God never punishes Israel, then wickedness must go unpunished, an option hardly favorable to anyone. The children suffer for the sins of others, in this case their parents and the Babylonians. People have suffered for the sins of others since Abel died at Cain's hand. This does not change the children's suffering, but it may change readers' question from "How could *God* do such a thing?" to "How could *those parents* do that to their children?" It may also lead one to marvel that a renewed relationship is possible at all between God and people who ignore warnings about their children's safety. According to 2:11–19 such a new beginning is not only possible; it is the way for the parents to redeem themselves and spare their offspring further agony.

20–22 As in chap. 1, Jerusalem offers this chapter's final speech. She has heard from the narrator and the prophetic speaker, and now she responds. In 1:9, 11, and 20 she asked God to ראה, "see," her situation, and she does so again now. Previously she described her awful situation and her grief (1:12–16); then she confessed her sin and asked God to judge her enemies on the day of wrath as he had judged her. In other words, she proceeded through some basic elements of the lament (see Westermann, 139–40). Now she responds to the previous speaker's counsel and calls on Yahweh. Her earlier comments should be kept in mind; this speech should not be read in isolation from her others.

20 Jerusalem's opening "Look, O LORD, and consider" echoes 1:11c perfectly (ראה יהוה והביטה). This plea has the effect of asking God one more time to do what he has not yet done. Having made this opening plea, she launches into a series of statements about what God has done; these statements parallel similar comments made by the narrator in 2:1–10. The assertions would amount to mere accusations if they were not offered in a prayer in which "see" means "do something." To encourage God to see she uses one interrogative and two hypothetical particles.

First, she asks, "Whom have you ever treated thus?" (למי עוללת כה). The verb here provides "word play . . . with עלל (children) in vs 19" (Lee, *Singers of Lamentations,* 159) and reflects back to 1:12, where Jerusalem asks those passing by if there has ever been sorrow like that the Lord "brought [severely]" (עולל) on her, and 1:22, where Jerusalem asks God to "deal severely" (ועולל) with her enemies' sin just as he has "dealt severely" (עוללת) with her transgressions. Here Jerusalem repeats the verb, this time to raise the issue of her relationship with God and the justice of what he has done.

Second, she queries, "Should women eat their fruit/offspring [אם תאכלנה נשים פרים], the little ones of their tender care [עללי טפחים]?" Without question, the answer to this question is "No! Such things should not occur."

But such things did occur in wartime (see 2 Kgs 6:24–31), and Lev 26:29, Deut 28:52–57, Jer 19:1–9, and Ezek 5:10 warn that such will occur when the covenant people rebel against God for a sufficient number of years (see Renkema, 321). Perhaps Jerusalem means at this point in the book, "Given my previous admissions of guilt, should such things continue?" Either way, she does what the prophetic speaker told her to do: she takes her children's case before Yahweh.

Third, she wonders whether "priest and prophet" (כהן ונביא) should "be killed [אם יהרג] in the sanctuary of the Lord [במקדש אדני]." These two groups have been mentioned previously, the former in 1:4, 1:19, 2:6, and (implied) 2:9, and the latter in 2:9 and 2:14. Such things should not be. Priests should teach God's word and aid God's people in worship (Deut 33:8–11; Mal 2:1–9), and they should be honored for doing so. Prophets should accurately convey God's word (see Deut 13:1–5; 18:15–22), and they should be obeyed. However, careless and wicked priests often meet a bad end (Lev 10:1–7; 1 Sam 4:12–22), as do false prophets (see Jer 28:1–17). Such were some of the priests and prophets Lamentations mentions. Still, Jeremiah was a good prophet, and others existed as well (see Jer 26:20–23). God needs to see those and any new faithful ones who have arisen. One wonders whether Jerusalem counts on her new-found confession or fails to understand yet the implications of her former actions.

21 This verse may well contain the highest concentration of previously used words in the entire book. In fact, only שכבו, "they lie," and טבחת, "you have slaughtered/killed," have not already appeared. The text serves as a summary of what has already been stated as true or prayed for as a need. The intensity on Jerusalem's part is thereby evident, so it may well be that she attempts to pray with the urgency called for in 2:13–19. Such a concentration of images and the themes associated with them further testifies to the poetic skill of the author of Lamentations.

Jerusalem continues her prayer by stating a terrible fact: "They lie in the dust of the streets [שכבו לארץ חוצות], young and old [נער וזקן]." Earlier לארץ, "to the dust," occurs to denote how far the rulers of Israel have fallen (2:2c), how far Jerusalem's elders have fallen (2:10a), and how desperately Jerusalem mourns (2:10c). Now the term depicts the resting place of the city's young and old. That the streets constitute the place of death or dying has already been stated in 1:20, and that the elders are part of the dying is confirmed by 1:19, whereas 2:10 has them mourning on the ground (לארץ). Thus, these elders die where they once lamented. This line indicates that Jerusalem apparently agrees with the narrator's assessment of the situation, and she uses this information to pray fervently as the prophetic speaker has advised.

Though starvation was certainly a cause of death during this era, it was not the only one. The most direct means was the edge of the Babylonians' swords. Therefore, Jerusalem continues praying, "My virgins and my choice men [בתולתי ובחורי] have fallen by the sword [נפלו בחרב]." Jerusalem's virgins have already appeared in 1:4, 1:18, and 2:10. In 1:4 they have been afflicted, in 1:18 they have gone into captivity, and in 2:10 they bowed their heads in mourning. Now Jerusalem reveals that some of them have died as well. They were joined in death by the "choice men," the young men old enough and able enough for battle. These are depicted as shattered in battle in 1:15, as taken into captivity with the virgins in 1:18, and as killed here. That Jerusalem has fallen has been asserted in 1:7, while 1:20 reported that the sword has robbed her of her children and leaders. As in 1:20, Jerusalem asks God to see such things and act now. Jer 15:1–2 and a host of other judgment texts warn of the use of the sword as an instrument of punishment. Jerusalem has seen such threats come to fruition, and she prays against future occurrences of the same.

Jerusalem believes that God has done these things. Drawing once again on day-of-the-Lord imagery, Jerusalem states, "You have killed on the day of your anger" (הרגת ביום אפך). The verb occurs in 2:4, where the Lord acts like an enemy by killing Jerusalem's family members, and in 2:20, where Jerusalem asks if prophets and priests should be killed in the sanctuary. Here Jerusalem associates this killing with the day of God's anger, a term found already in 1:12, 2:1, and 2:6. The severity of this day emerges in the final clause, "You have slaughtered [טבחת] without pity [לא חמלת, lit. 'not shown pity']." The use of a new and harsh verb discloses Jerusalem's intensity in prayer. Her children and elders have died; what is more, they have been slaughtered. God's lack of pity has already been documented in 2:2 and 2:17, where God swallows up and tears down, respectively. Jerusalem understands what has happened as only an informed participant can. Her reuse of concepts demonstrates her full acceptance of what the narrator has said and what the prophetic speaker has explained to her.

22 Jerusalem continues her description of the results of God's wrath begun in 2:21c, though the governing metaphor shifts. Now she compares the day of the Lord to an "appointed feast" (כיום מועד) called for by God himself. Of course, the book has already referred to judgment as God's "day" in 1:12, 1:21, 2:1, and 2:21. Also, the book refers to Jerusalem's loss of מועד, "appointed festivals," in 1:4 and 2:6, and to the day of defeat as a מועד, "festival," in 1:15 and 2:7. Because God has invited Babylon to an appointed time for a trip to the temple, Jerusalem has no appointed time for worship. Priests and prophets have been killed (2:20c), so no functionaries are available for services anyway.

When God called for this day, the guests he invited were Jerusalem's "terrors on every side" (מגורי מסביב). God invited their worst nightmare by inviting their most powerful enemy. This fairly rare phrase is distinctly Jeremianic, for it appears in Jer 6:25, 20:3, 20:10, 46:5, and 49:29. In fact, Jeremiah gives his opponent Pashur this very name in Jer 20:3 and uses the phrase to describe his own persecution in Jer 20:10. The term also occurs in Ps 31:14 (ET 31:13) in a context in which the psalmist admits he is in trouble (Ps 31:1–9); he states that he sighs and weeps (Ps 31:10–11) and has become a reproach to his adversaries (Ps 31:12–14). The psalm concludes with expressions of trust and praise (Ps 31:15–23) and exhortations to wait on the Lord (Ps 31:24–25). Clearly, this psalm has many thematic connections with Lamentations as a whole. Thus, the phrase in 2:22a coincides with prophetic judgment imagery and psalmic lament, as does most of 2:1–22. In Jer 20 the prophet expresses trust in God, though only in the process of stating how serving God has caused him horrible pain (see Jer 20:7–18). Similarly, the psalmist calls on the Lord before deliverance occurs and, like Jeremiah, asks the Lord to defeat his enemies (Ps 31:18; Jer 20:12). It is more than possible that here Jerusalem follows these two examples. All three texts admit that terror has come; all three mention enemies, yet only the prophetic and psalmic texts mention God's good character. Even with this "omission," however, Jerusalem is indeed taking the advice given in 2:18–19 and has begun to pray in a fashion not unlike two similar biblical examples.

Jerusalem stresses the thoroughness of God's judgment in the next line. After the Lord's invitation to terror was accepted, "There was not on the day of the LORD's wrath [ולא היה ביום אף־יהוה] fugitive or survivor [פליט ושריד]." These last two nouns appear together in Josh 8:22 and Jer 42:17 and 44:14. The first instance occurs in the context of Israel's victory over Ai, while the final two are used to describe what will happen if the post-destruction Israelites flee to Egypt. The day of the Lord comes with great terror, great loss, and great sorrow.

Finally, Jerusalem returns to the theme of lost children (see 1:5; 2:4, 11–12, 18, 20–21). Those she "tenderly cared for and raised" (אשר טפחתי ורביתי) have fallen to the "enemy" (איבי) mentioned so often in the book. The word translated "tenderly cared for" also appears in 2:20b, where it also refers to Jerusalem's precious children.

Jerusalem has prayed for her children, just as instructed. So she has asked God to "see" her problems (1:9c, 11c, 20a; 2:20a), has described her predicament (1:12–16), has confessed her sin (1:18–19), has asked God to punish her enemies (1:20–22), and has asked God to "see" and by implication to stop the terrors her children, prophets, and priests face. In other words she has worked through the "set" parts of an individual or corporate lament. She has at best left a statement of faith in God implicit at this point, and at worst refuses to make one. She has taken the counsel of the first-person speaker in 2:11–19, so she has hardly simply gone her own way. At the same time, it may not be possible for this sort of pain to stop all at once. After all, crops take time to grow, cities time to rebuild, and lives time to heal. Living in between judgment and renewal cannot be easy either.

Explanation

This chapter must be read against the background of the day of the Lord's anger (1:12, 21; 2:1, 22). In biblical theology this day comes on Israel only after the people have repeatedly broken their covenant with the Lord, refused to heed the prophets the Lord sent to warn them, and maintained their rebellion in the face of a clear foreign threat (see 2 Kgs 17). Perhaps no prophetic book better expresses this sad, lengthy process than Jeremiah, though Hosea, Amos, and Zephaniah certainly come close in a more compact way. When the day of the

Lord comes, it brings the covenant curses found in Deut 27–28. Thus, these two theological streams need brief elaboration.

Deut 27–28 sets forth specific consequences for sin, many of which are found in Lamentations, especially in Lam 2. For instance, Deut 28:25–35 warns that Israel's enemies will defeat them and that this defeat will be so devastating that Israel "shall be a horror to all the kingdoms of the earth" (28:25 ESV). Their bodies will be food for the birds (28:26) and their sons and daughters "given to another people" (28:32 ESV). They and their king will go into exile (28:36–44) before a hard and ruthless nation (28:45–51). This nation will lay such a horrible siege on them that they will eat their own children rather than starve (28:52–57). Their children will suffer and die from horrible diseases (28:58–63), and the nation will live in constant dread (28:64–68). The parallel text Lev 26:14–39 offers similar warnings. It is important to recall that in the OT the Lord sends these consequences centuries after disobedience has begun to unfold.

In the prophetic books the Lord's servants, the prophets, warn the people to return to the Lord before such things happen to them. Isaiah (e.g., 2:15), Hosea (e.g., 1:5), Joel (e.g., 2:1), Amos (e.g., 1:2–4:13), and many of the rest of the prophets declare God's day of judgment. This day will punish Israel's sins and those of other nations, often by means of foreign armies. Jer 21–39 repeatedly states that Babylon will overwhelm Jerusalem if the people do not repent or, failing such repentance, surrender to Babylon.

Lam 1–2 depicts and mourns woes associated with this invasion. In doing so these chapters bring to bear a third theological stream, which is found in the type of poems found in Pss 73–89, where the kingdom's fall is a major theme. For example, Pss 74 and 89 mourn the loss of temple and Davidic monarchy. Besides expressing shock, sorrow, and confusion, these texts have a "What now?" flavor to them. In Lamentations chaps. 3–5 take up the "What now?" theme, while in Psalms chaps. 90–106 serve the same function. Both Lamentations and Psalms use lament forms to express the many types and levels of pain and outrage Israel felt. Yet neither rests there; each goes on to press for a renewed relationship with the covenant God who is the only source of the hope they recognize (see "Theological Purposes in Lamentations" in the Introduction). Lamentations is not simply about placing blame; it is also about finding ways to express pain *and* rebuild community and worship.

Perhaps it is at this point that a word about Zion theology is in order. There can be no question that Isa 25, 65–66, Ezek 40–48, and several of the psalms assert a glorious future for Zion. Ultimately Zion is the place where God lives with his people in the absence of death and sin. Thus, no simple "Jerusalem equals Zion" formula works. Still, these texts and companion texts like Hag 2:1–9 promise much about a new temple and restored city. It must be remembered, though, that these passages about future glory follow texts about the day of the Lord and massive destruction. So it is appropriate to consider the glory of Zion to be a theme subsequent, but not secondary, to, the covenantal curses and day-of-the-Lord passages. If so, then passages like Lam 1–2 and Pss 73–89 grow in importance since they create a bridge from the day of the Lord to the glory of Zion.

This passage unfolds in three major parts: vv 1–10, vv 11–19, and vv 20–22. The first section describes in third-person speech how the day of the Lord's wrath has come, thereby causing the nation's defeat and loss of inhabitants and worship (see Deut 28:25–51; Ps 74). Apparently the same narrator found in 1:1–9b, 10–11b, and 17 speaks here. The second section mourns the terrors Jerusalem's children have endured (2:11–12) and then urges Jerusalem to cry out to the Lord who has brought the disaster (2:13–19). Here a first-person voice speaks, expressing prophetic viewpoints much like Jeremiah's. Finally, the third section depicts Jerusalem's cries to the Lord to once again "see" what has happened and act on her behalf (see 1:9c, 11c, 20–22). She prays for her children as the previous speaker counseled. She has endured the day of God's wrath and questions whether it should be so severe.

Chap. 2 advances the book's thematic movement in certain specific ways. It builds on the description in chap. 1 of the lonely, sinful, devastated, yet praying city by addressing the specific elements of the day of the Lord introduced in 1:12 and 1:21. In particular, 2:1–10 carefully chronicles God's activity as warrior, as Israel's enemy, and as the one who planned Jerusalem's downfall. All these images have parallels in prophetic and psalmic literature. It introduces a first-person speaker who agrees with the narrator and Jerusalem's perspective on why the punishment came, but who takes the step of advising Jerusalem to pray on behalf of the innocent, a prayer he evidently believes the Lord will answer. This speaker also uses images from the prophets and psalms. Chap. 2 depicts Jerusalem accepting this advice. She laments by describing the people's suffering and asking if such things should occur. In particular she prays for her little ones, the group most vulnerable and most harmed in days of punishment. Other instructions and responses unfold in chaps. 3–5.

This poem raises the important matters of divine severity, human responsibility, and innocent suffering because of the actions of the wicked. Judgment can be violent, and Lamentations never attempts to hide this fact. It also claims that this particular brand of violence is associated with justice, not with abuse. At the same time, Lamentations states that the innocent at times suffer because of the sins of others, and Jerusalem's children experience this reality. God's warnings had not been enough to change the hearts and deeds of a nation bent on ignoring the danger to their children and equally bent on raising those children to act in a similarly rebellious manner. Judgment in this case stops the generational vicious cycle of self-defeating activity. Even so, the recipients of this punishment, all of whom admit their sin, may well wonder at the severity of the day of the Lord. They must view the severity of their punishment as evidence of the seriousness of their sins. This chapter and this book as a whole relate a message hard to hear, read, or accept: when the day of the Lord comes, one can only cry out to God in a way that confesses sin, asks questions about suffering, and intercedes on behalf of the innocent.

I Am the Man (3:1–66)

Bibliography

Berges, U. "'Ich bin der Mann, der Elend sah' (Klgl 3.1): Zionstheologie als Weg aus der Krise." *BZ* 44 (2000) 1–20. **Brandscheidt, R.** *Gotteszorn und Menschenleid.* **Buchanan, A.** "The Role of Protest in Lamentations." Th.M. thesis, Australian College of Theology, Kensington, 2001. **Dennison, J. T., Jr.** "The Lament and the Lamenter: Lamentations 3:1–23." *Kerux* 12 (1997) 30–34. **Driver, G. R.** "Hebrew Notes on 'Song of Songs' and 'Lamentations.'" In *Festschrift Alfred Bertholet.* Ed. W. Baumgartner et al. Tübingen: Mohr (Siebeck), 1950. 134–46. **Ferris, P. W., Jr.** *Genre of Communal Lament.* **Gottlieb, H.** "Das kultische Leiden des Konigs: zu den Klageliedern 3:1." *SJOT* 2 (1987) 121–26. ———. *Study on the Text of Lamentations.* **Gous, I.** "Psychological Survival Strategies in Lamentations 3 in the Light of Neuro-Linguistic Programming." In *Old Testament Science and Reality.* Ed. W. Wessels and E. Scheffler. Pretoria: Verba Vitae, 1992. 317–41. ———. "Sosiologiese eksegese van die Oude Testament (Lam 3)." *SK* 14 (1993) 67–83. **Gurewisz, S. B.** "The Problem of Lamentations 3." *ABR* 8 (1960) 19–23. **Heim, K. M.** "The Personification of Jerusalem and the Drama of Her Bereavement in Lamentations." In *Zion, City of Our God.* Ed. R. S. Hess and G. J. Wenham. Grand Rapids, MI: Eerdmans, 1999. 129–69. **Jahnow, H.** *Hebräische Leichenlied.* **Kaiser, W. C., Jr.** *Biblical Approach to Suffering.* **Lee, N. C.** *Singers of Lamentations.* **Linafeldt, T.** *Surviving Lamentations.* **Löhr, M.** "Der Sprachgebrauch des Bucher der Klagelieder." *ZAW* 14 (1894) 31–50. ———. "Threni III. und die jeremianische Autorschaft des Buches der Klagelieder." *ZAW* 24 (1904) 1–16. **McCarthy, C.** *The Tiqqune Sopherim and Other Theological Corrections in the Masoretic Text of the Old Testament.* OBO 36. Göttingen: Vandenhoeck & Ruprecht, 1981. **McDaniel, T. F.** "Philological Studies in Lamentations, I-II." *Bib* 49 (1968) 27–53, 199–220. **Miller, C. W.** "Poetry and Personae: The Use and Function of the Changing Speaking Voices in the Book of Lamentations." Ph.D. diss. Iliff School of Theology and University of Denver, 1996. **O'Connor, K. M.** *Lamentations and the Tears of the World.* **Owens, P. J.** "Personification and Suffering in Lamentations 3." *Austin Seminary Bulletin: Faculty Edition* 105 (1990) 75–90. **Porteous, N.** "Jerusalem-Zion: The Growth of a Symbol." In *Verbannung und Geimkehr.* FS W. Randolph, ed. A. Kuschke. Tübingen: Mohr (Siebeck), 1961. 235–52. **Praetorius, F.** "Threni III, 5, 16." *ZAW* 15 (1895) 326. **Provan, I.** "Past, Present and Future in Lamentations 3:52–66: The Case for a Precative Perfect Re-examined." *VT* 41 (1991) 164–75. **Rudolph, W.** "Der text der Klagelieder." *ZAW* 56 (1938) 101–22. **Saebø, M.** "Who Is 'the Man' in Lamentations 3? A Fresh Approach to the Interpretation of the Book of Lamentations." In *Understanding Poets and Prophets.* FS G. W. Anderson, ed. A. G. Auld. Sheffield: JSOT Press, 1993. 294–306. **Weissblueth, S.** "*Mipî ʿelyôn lōʿ tēṣēʾ hārāʿôt wehaṭṭôb.*" *Beth Miqra* 32 (1986–87) 64–67.

Translation

א	1	I am the man who has seen[a] affliction by (the) rod of his anger.	(4+2)
א	2	Me he has driven away and made walk (in) darkness and not light.	(3+3)
א	3	Surely against me he turns again and again his hand all the day.	(4+3)

ב	4	*He has swallowed up my flesh and my skin;*	(3+2)
		he has shattered my bones.	
ב	5	*He has besieged and surrounded me*	(3+2)
		*(with) bitterness*ᵃ *and weariness.*	
ב	6	*He has made me dwell in a dark place,*	(2+2)
		like the ones long dead.	
ג	7	*He has walled me in and I cannot escape;*	(4+2)
		he has made my chains heavy.	
ג	8	*Even when I cry out and call for help,*	(4+2)
		*he rejects*ᵃ *my prayer.*	
ג	9	*He has walled in my ways with cut stones;*	(3+2)
		he has made my paths crooked.	
ד	10	*He is a bear lying in wait for me,*	(4+2)
		a lion in hiding.	
ד	11	*He turned me aside from my path and tore me to pieces;*	(3+2)
		he made me desolate.	
ד	12	*He bent his bow and set me up*	(3+2)
		like the target of an arrow.	
ה	13	*He brought into my kidneys*	(2+2)
		the sons of his quiver.	
ה	14	*I have become a laughingstock to all my people,*ᵃ	(4+3)
		the object of their mocking song all the day.	
ה	15	*He has fed me full of bitter herbs;*	(2+2)
		he has made me drink wormwood.	
ו	16	*He has broken*ᵃ *my teeth in the gravel;*	(3+2)
		he has pressed me down in the ashes.	
ו	17	*My soul rejects*ᵃ *peace;*	(3+2)
		I have forgotten goodness.	
ו	18	*Indeed I said, "My endurance has perished,*	(3+2)
		and my hope from the LORD."	
ז	19	*Remember my affliction and my wandering,*	(3+2)
		the wormwood and the bitterness.	
ז	20	*You will indeed remember,*	(2+3)
		*and your soul*ᵃ *will meditate*ᵇ *about me.*	
ז	21	*This I cause to return*ᵃ *to my heart;*	(4+3)
		therefore I have hope.	
ח	22 ᵃ	*Indeed the* LORD's *(acts of) covenant mercy never cease;* ᵇ	(5+4)
		indeed his (acts of) compassion never end.	
ח	23	*(They are) new every morning;*	(2+2)
		great is your faithfulness.	
ח	24	*"The* LORD *is my portion," says my soul;*	(4+4)
		therefore I will hope in him.	
ט	25	*The* LORD *is good to those who wait for him,*	(3+2)
		to (the) soul who seeks him.	
ט	26	*It is good that he wait silently*ᵃ	(3+2)
		for the salvation of the LORD.	
ט	27	*It is good for the man that he bear*	(4+2)
		the yoke in his youth.	

׳	28	*Let him sit alone and keep silent,* *for he laid it upon him.*	(3+3)
׳	29 a	*Let him place his mouth in the dust;* *there may yet be hope.*	(3+3)
׳	30	*Let him give his cheek to the one striking;* *let him be filled with disgrace.*	(3+2)
כ	31	*For he will not reject forever—* *the Lord.*	(4+1)
כ	32	*For though he causes grief he will have compassion,* *according to the abundance of his covenant mercies.*[a]	(4+2)
כ	33	*For he does not afflict from his heart,* *nor grieve the sons of man.*	(4+3)
ל	34	*To crush under his foot* *all the prisoners of the earth,*	(3+3)
ל	35	*to turn aside a man's justice* *in the presence of the most high,*	(3+3)
ל	36	*to subvert a man in his case,* *the Lord does not countenance.*	(3+3)
מ	37	*Who spoke this and it came to pass* *if the Lord did not command (it)?*	(4+3)
מ	38	*From the mouth of the most high, does not come forth* *the bad and the good?*	(4+2)
מ	39	*Why should a living man complain,* *a man about his sins?*	(4+3)
נ	40	*Let us search our ways and let us examine thoroughly,* *and let us return unto the* LORD.	(3+2)
נ	41	*Let us lift up our hearts*[a] *and hands*[b] *to God in the heavens.*	(4+3)
נ	42	*We have indeed transgressed and rebelled;* *indeed you have not forgiven.*	(3+3)
ס	43	*You have covered (yourself) with wrath and pursued us;* *you have killed and not shown pity.*	(3+3)
ס	44	*You have covered yourself with a cloud;* *no prayer can pass through.*[a]	(3+2)
ס	45	*Offscouring and refuse you have made us* *in the midst of the peoples.*	(3+2)
פ	46 a	*They have opened their mouths against us,* *all our enemies.*	(3+2)
פ	47	*Terror and pitfall come upon us,* *devastation and shattering.*	(4+2)
פ	48	*Streams of tears descend (from) my eyes* *because of (the) shattering of (the) daughter of my people.*	(4+3)
ע	49	*My eyes flow* *and do not cease;* *there is no respite.*	(2+2+2)
ע	50	*Until he looks out and sees,* *the* LORD *from heaven.*	(3+2)

ע	51	*My eyes afflict my soul*	(3+3)
		*because of*ᵃ *all the daughters of my city.*	
צ	52	*They have indeed hunted me like a bird,*	(3+2)
		my enemies—for no reason.	
צ	53	*They threw me alive into the pit*	(3+3)
		and cast stones on me.	
צ	54	*The waters closed over my head;*	(4+2)
		I said, "I am cut off!"	
ק	55	*I called on your name, O LORD,*	(3+2)
		from the depths of the pit.	
ק	56	*You heard my voice;*	(2+3+2)
		you did not close your ears	
		(to my cry) ᵃ*for relief, for help.*ᵃ	
ק	57	*You came near on the day I called out to you;*	(3+3)
		you said, "Do not fear."	
ר	58	*You have taken up, O Lord,*	(2+2+2)
		my soul's case;	
		you have redeemed my life.	
ר	59	*You have seen, O LORD, the wrong done to me;*	(3+2)
		please judge ᵃ *my cause.*	
ר	60	*You have seen all their vengeance,*	(3+3)
		all their plots against ᵃ *me.*	
ש	61	*You have heard their taunts, O LORD,*	(3+3)
		all their plots against me.	
ש	62	*The lips of those who rise up against me*	(2+2+2)
		and their murmuring	
		(are) against me all the day.	
ש	63	*Behold, (in) their sitting and their standing,*	(3+2)
		I am (the subject of) their mocking song.	
ת	64	*Requite them fully, O LORD,*	(4+2)
		according to the work of their hands.	
ת	65	*Give to them dullness of heart,*	(4+2)
		(as) your curse upon them.	
ת	66	*Pursue*ᵃ *in wrath and destroy them*	(3+3)
		*from under the heavens,*ᵇ *O LORD.*	

Notes

1.a. MT ראה, "who has seen," acts like a relative clause without a particle. LXX reads ὁ βλέπων, "the one seeing," which is a ptc.

5.a. LXX reads κεφαλήν μου, "my head," for ראש, "bitterness." Gottlieb notes that the problem is that "the word pair ראש ותלאה, in which the specialized term for a poisonous plant (ראש is traditionally rendered 'gall') is combined with the more general concept 'trouble'" (*Study on the Text*, 39). He correctly argues that "the unusual character of the combination" makes it likely that MT is original. Albrektson thinks the LXX translator "did not understand the meaning" (131). Rudolph (*ZAW* 56 [1938] 110), following Praetorius (*ZAW* 15 [1895] 326), concludes that if LXX is correct, then MT should read ראשי תלאה, "my head sorrow," which is the most minimal change. Given the evidence, MT is followed.

8.a. שחם is a *hapax legomenon* that some Heb. texts take to be the same as שחם, "blocks, shuts out" (Gottlieb, *Study on the Text*, 39–40). Driver ("Hebrew Notes," 139) concludes that Arabic parallels indicate that "rejects" or "frustrates" is the best meaning, and this reading is followed here.

14.a. The Masoretes preferred עמים, "people," to עמי, "my people," and the pl. form appears in Syr. and about fifty Heb. MSS. Albrektson argues that one's view of whether the poem is collective or individual in nature is definitive here (*Studies in the Text and Theology*, 137). Gottlieb notes that "the great majority of manuscripts" read עמי, and correctly argues that overall the textual evidence supports that reading (*Study on the Text*, 41).

16.a. LXX reads καὶ ἐξέβαλεν, "and he drove out," which means the translator read ויגרש, thus mistaking the word's final letter.

17.a. This reading follows McDaniel (*Bib* 49 [1968] 201) and Hillers ([1992] 114), both of whom treat the מ as enclitic.

20.a. This translation takes שׂיח, "consider, meditate, talk about," as the root for ותשׁיח instead of שׁחה, "bow down," or שׁוח, "sink down," and thus coincides with LXX's καταδολεσχέω, "chatter," and supports the Kethib over the Qere. See Albrektson, *Studies in the Text and Theology*, 142–43, and Gottlieb, *Study on the Text*, 42–43, for arguments in favor and against this reading.

20.b. This word is a *tiqqune sopherim*. Though Hillers ([1992] 114–15) disputes this conclusion, it is probable that the text originally read נפשך. See McCarthy (*Tiqqune Sopherim*, 120–23) for a fuller discussion.

21.a. LXX reads τάξω = אשׁים, "I will set."

22.a. Vv 22–24 do not appear in LXX.

22.b. This translation reads תמו with the Syr. and Aram. versions. See Gottlieb for a defense of this decision (*Study on the Text*, 45–46), and see Albrektson (*Studies in the Text and Theology*, 145–46) for a defense of MT.

26.a. The construction ויחיל ודומם, "and strength and silence," is very rare. Several emendations have been offered. See Albrektson, *Studies in the Text and Theology*, 146–48, for a thorough discussion.

29.a. This verse is missing in several LXX MSS.

32.a. This translation agrees with the Qere. In both MT and LXX the word is sg.

41.a. MT reads sg., while LXX, Syr., and Vg. render the word as a pl.

41.b. LXX reads ἐπί (על), "upon," for אל, "to." If correct, the literal reading of the phrase is: "Let us raise our hearts on hands, to God in the heavens."

44.a. MT מעבור, "from prayer," may have a negative connotation or indicate the direction of the prayer. LXX reads εἵνεκεν (בעבור), "on account of a prayer."

46.a. Some Gk. and Syr. MSS transpose the פ (vv 46–48) and ע (vv 49–51) lines for alphabetic consistency.

51.a. For this usage of מן see GKC §119z.

56.a-a. LXX's εἰς τὴν δέησίν μου εἰς τὴν βοήθειάν μου, "to my prayer, to my help," is probably an effort to translate a rare and difficult Heb. phrase rather than evidence of a textual variant. See Albrektson (*Studies in the Text and Theology*, 163–65), Gottlieb (*Study on the Text*, 53–54), Rudolph (*ZAW* 56 [1938] 115), and Renkema (453–54) for a survey of opinions on this phrase.

59.a. LXX reads ἔκρινας, "you have judged," which implies שפטת (impf.) instead of שפטה (impv.). Syr. agrees. Rudolph (*ZAW* 56 [1938] 115) and other critical scholars accept this reading. Gottlieb (*Study on the Text*, 54) attributes this reading to these experts' desire to place the verse's action in the past, which he correctly notes is unnecessary. The similar endings of the two possibilities may also have led to confusion.

60.a. Many Heb. MSS, Syr., Tg., and Vg. read עלי, "upon me," or "against me," for לי, "to me," or "for me." Thus, they make the final line of 3:60 match its counterpart in 3:61. No real change in meaning is at stake.

66.a. LXX supplies a pronominal suff., αὐτούς, "them," here.

66.b. LXX reads τοῦ οὐρανοῦ (שׁמים), "the heavens," a reading followed by the majority of translations.

Form/Structure/Setting

Lam 3 is the most discussed chapter in the book. Scholars have offered an array of opinions on its authorship, date, form, structure, and setting. These discussions derive from many factors, including this chapter's distinctive acrostic pattern, thematic differences from chaps. 1, 2, 4, and 5, and its placement at the center of the book. Each of these issues affects the interpretation of the poem in isolation and in the book as a whole.

Lam 3 follows an acrostic pattern quite different from that of any other chapter in the book. No two chapters are exactly alike. Chaps. 1 and 2 are the closest, since each one has twenty-two sections of three lines each, with the first word of each section beginning with a succeeding letter of the alphabet. Even these two poems are distinguished by reversing the ע-פ sequence in the second one. The fourth poem has twenty-two sections of two lines each, with the acrostic pattern following the same alphabetic sequence as that in chap. 2. Chap. 5 is not technically an acrostic. Though it has twenty-two one-line sections, these sections are not alphabetically arranged. Chap. 3, on the other hand, has twenty-two three-line sections, and each line in the section begins with the same letter. Despite being the same length as chaps. 1 and 2, this poem is the most acrostic of the four acrostic poems (Saebø, "Who Is 'the Man' in Lamentations 3?" 295). This and its central location lead many commentators to conclude that it has special significance in the structure of Lamentations and in its theology.

Like the previous two poems, Lam 3 mixes more than one genre on the way to achieving the thoroughness of an acrostic. Westermann (168–69) locates a personal psalm of lamentation in vv 1–25, to which vv 64–66 was added as a tentative conclusion; a communal psalm of lamentation in vv 42–51; a personal psalm of praise in vv 52–58; and an expansion that follows no particular psalm form in vv 26–41. He concludes that its acrostic form holds the poem together. Brandscheidt (*Gotteszorn und Menschenleid*, 213, 222–23) argues that the chapter exhibits a strong instructional tone that includes wisdom elements. This is especially true for vv 34–39. Gerstenberger ([2001] 496) likewise stresses the poem's generic diversity and concludes that "the text utilizes various elements from older complaint and lament rituals to form a new genre of mourning song, adequate for the ongoing commemorative services in Judean congregations in and near Jerusalem, but also in the diaspora." Like other scholars, Gerstenberger ([2001] 492–96) notes that no elements of dirges for cities or sanctuaries appear here. Rather, the overall effect is to set an agenda for communal lament.

These experts are correct in their assertions about which types of traditional literary genres appear in Lam 3. Aspects of communal lament, individual lament, wisdom-based psalmic observations, and instructions like those found in Pss 37 and 73 are all in evidence. Likewise, as Lee argues (*Singers of Lamentations*, 166–68), the sorts of prophetic exhortation, reflection, and interaction found in Lam 2 and Jer 4–10 also occur. The poem is an eclectic acrostic. It uses multiple genres, associated themes, and shifts in speaker to make its point. The acrostic format provides the formal structural cohesion that the poem requires and should be viewed as evidence of careful thought and artistry.

As was true in Lam 1 and 2, changes in point of view determine this poem's structure. There are at least four of these shifts since 3:1–24 uses first-person singular speech, 3:25–39 exhibits third-person masculine singular speech, 3:40–47 uses first-person plural speech, and 3:48–66 uses first-person singular speech. The problem with dividing 3:1–24 from 3:25–39 is that the "I" in 3:1 may offer comments at least through 3:39, when a clearer alteration occurs. Another problem with positing a new speaker every time the point of view seems to change is that the chapter's first speaker could be part of the "we" and "us" portions of the chapter. Regardless, these changes in perspective match shifts in subject matter, so they are as valuable for delineating structure as similar changes are in Lam 1 and 2.

Within these four broad sections, chap. 3 begins with testimony about what one person has learned through suffering (vv 1–24). It continues with a description about what it is good for a person to do in such circumstances (vv 25–39) and then moves to exhortations for community prayer (vv 40–47). Finally, the chapter ends with a prayer of confidence in the Lord (vv 48–66). Each major section has subsections, and these are often based on changes in governing metaphors. For example, 3:1–24 begins with "I am the man who has seen affliction" and ends with "I will hope in him." In between these assertions the text uses darkness (vv 1–6), walk (vv 7–9), various traps and dangers (vv 10–18), and confessions concerning God's goodness (vv 19–24) as structuring images. In 3:25–39, the poet states what is good for a suffering person to do (vv 25–30) and then emphasizes God's justice (vv 31–36) and sovereignty (vv 37–39). Next, 3:40–47 calls the people to prayer (vv 40–41), confesses their sins (vv 42–45), and notes what their enemies have done to them (vv 46–47). Finally, 3:48–51 expresses the speaker's grief, 3:52–54 states what the enemies have done, 3:55–63 reveals how God helped the speaker in the past, and 3:64–66 professes confidence in what God will do to the people's enemies.

Though it is indeed possible to posit multiple speakers in this chapter, as Buchanan ("Role of Protest," 16–19) and Miller (see "Poetry and Personae," 141–55) do very competently, this commentary takes the position that the same person speaks throughout. This decision is based on the similarity of message in all sections of the text, as well as on connections between chap. 2 and chap. 3 (see below). It is therefore all the more important to chart the many options scholars have offered for determining the identity of the "I" in chap. 3. To summarize a complicated discussion in what may well be an overly simple manner, experts have posited at least six basic opinions on the matter.

1. Scholars who hold to the traditional view of Jeremianic authorship of Lamentations conclude that the prophet himself is the speaker. Calvin, Keil, Streane, Cannon (*BSac* 81 [1924] 42–58), Wiesmann, W. C. Kaiser, Jr. (*Biblical Approach to Suffering*), Huey, and others conclude that the prophet shares what he has learned about God and Israel's situation through his own experiences. Lee (*Singers of Lamentations*) at least strongly implies that the linguistic connections between Jeremiah and Lamentations lead her to agree. Though some of these scholars use tradition as one reason for their conclusion, they primarily base their assertion on linguistic evidence. Thus, this view correctly notes the connections between Jeremiah and Lamentations yet does not explain why Lamentations itself never names Jeremiah when his prophecy does so fairly often.

2. Some scholars claim that the speaker is not literally Jeremiah but one who speaks like Jeremiah. Rudolph championed this view, arguing that the speaker is an idealized Jeremiah who stands as a paradigm for suffering (227–45). As Saebø ("Who Is 'the Man' in Lamentations 3?" 299) points out, Löhr (*ZAW* 24 [1904] 31–50) had reached a similar conclusion much earlier, as had Budde (91–93). More recently Brandscheidt (*Gotteszorn und Menschenleid*, 350) has agreed with this possibility. The strengths of this position are that it acknowledges the linguistic connections between Jeremiah and Lamentations and emphasizes the

prophet's role as sufferer and mediator for the people. Its chief weakness is that it attempts to enjoy the benefits of Jeremianic authorship without accepting the accompanying historical responsibilities. Further, the book itself offers only "I" for "a name"—nothing else.

3. A few scholars have tried to identify the "I" with a specific biblical character other than Jeremiah. For example, Porteous ("Jerusalem-Zion," 244–45) suggests that King Jehoiachin, who was deported in 597 B.C.E., may be "the man" (3:1) who has suffered yet found that God still has mercy based on the kind treatment extended him after thirty-seven years in exile (see 2 Kgs 25:27–30; Jer 52:31–34). If he is the speaker, then God's faithfulness (see Lam 3:22–23) may have the Davidic promise as its specific focus. In this scheme the king serves as a representative of the people's suffering and may therefore serve the same function as the servant of the Lord in Isaiah (Porteous, "Jerusalem-Zion," 245). Saebø ("Who Is 'the Man' in Lamentations 3?" 302–4) agrees that "the man" is a royal figure but suggests that Zedekiah, the nation's last king, not only suffered greatly but also fits the time frame in question. These two possibilities have the advantage of keeping the Davidic covenant in view, a matter that the linguistic ties between Lam 2 and Ps 89 (see *Comment* on chap. 2) indicate was of concern to the poet. They also demonstrate that Jeremiah is not the only plausible candidate. At the same time, the linguistic and thematic connections are fairly nebulous, since "darkness" (3:2, 6) does not necessarily translate into Zedekiah's blindness; nor does Zedekiah's rise in the ranks of exiled leaders meet the conditions of the praise in 3:48–66.

4. Some experts have argued that Zion, representing the whole nation, speaks here and in chaps. 1 and 2. Eissfeldt affirms this opinion (*Old Testament*, 502–3) and is followed by Albrektson (*Studies in the Text and Theology*, 127–29). The advantage of this viewpoint is that Jerusalem can either be personified as "I" or include the whole of the populace ("we"). Therefore, the switch from individual to plural forms can be subsumed under one character. Of course, the fact that Jerusalem is nowhere else in Lamentations identified as a man makes this identification very hard to maintain. Also, this opinion seems to treat the whole book as it if has but one speaker, a view that this commentary believes cannot be sustained.

5. Some writers have concluded that the speaker is an individual who represents others, yet they argue that no one particular historical figure fits the portrait. They do not think Jerusalem is intended since she plays such a different role in the book. Rather, they conclude that the sufferer is "everyman" (Hillers, [1992] 122), one who suffers as all the people have (Renkema, 348–52) yet suffers anonymously (Kraus, 53–59). This opinion keeps the anonymous "man" anonymous, which certainly seems to be the book's intention. It also takes seriously how this individual suffers with the people. But it does not note sufficiently the connections with chap. 2 or with the book of Jeremiah.

6. Some scholars prefer to consider the "I" as somehow representing the whole of the people without naming any particular character. Gerstenberger writes that behind the "I" there "may be hidden the whole community" ([2001] 493). Gordis (172–74) considers the "I" a case of "fluid personality," or one in which a first-person character may move easily between being alone or being part of a group. This possibility shares the strengths of the "everyman" and collectivist viewpoint. It also shares the weaknesses related to lack of specific connection to earlier parts of Lamentations and to Jeremiah.

Form/Structure/Setting

Though one should be cautious on this point, perhaps an option based on these opinions' strengths and (hopefully) avoiding their weaknesses can be found. Provan (81) starts in the right direction when he notes the similarities between 2:11 and 3:48, then writes, "It seems much more likely, then, that it is this narrator, whose voice has already dominated chapters 1 and 2, who is himself the speaker for most of chapter 3. It cannot be denied, of course, that, as in chapters 1 and 2, he feels himself to be closely identified with Zion and her people. . . . Their suffering is his suffering, and he can exhort them to join him in repentance (cf. vv. 40–42)." Lee (*Singers of Lamentations*, 167) adds that the one offering first-person mourning speech in 2:11 and urging prayer in 2:18–19 is probably the one speaking in 3:1–24. The point here is that Provan and Lee argue correctly that chaps. 1 and 2 provide an important clue to the identity of the speaker in 3:1.

So far in the book there have been one third-person speaker and two first-person speakers. None of these speakers really disagrees with the other, so content alone cannot solve the problem of sorting them out. The first-person speaker in 2:11–19 addresses the readers (2:11–12) and Jerusalem (2:13–19). Jerusalem addresses others in 1:12–16 and 1:18–19 and the Lord in 1:20–22 and 2:20–22. The identification of "the man" in 3:1 hardly coincides with the lonely widow-mother-vassal Jerusalem. It is possible, then, that the first-person speaker in 2:11–19 is the speaker in 3:1–24, especially since 2:11–12 and 3:48–49 are so similar. If the dividing of this speaker from the narrator is correct, then this interpretation is correct. If not, then Provan's identification is appropriate.

Besides an ability to weep for Jerusalem (2:11–12; 3:48–49), what characteristics do 2:11–19 and 3:1–66 share? First, both have been part of Jerusalem's woes (2:11–12; 3:1–9). Second, both stress opponents' mocking (2:15–16; 3:14, 61–62). Third, both call others to prayer (2:18–19; 3:40–47). Fourth, both credit God with causing pain (2:17; 3:1–18). Fifth, both offer counsel to Jerusalem. These likenesses make the connection between 2:11–19 and 3:1–66 all the more probable.

This speaker takes a prophetic viewpoint similar to Jeremiah's in both texts. Like Jeremiah, he attributes the devastation to the Lord. Like Jeremiah, he calls on the people to seek the Lord in prayer. Like Jeremiah, he believes future hope does exist. Like Jeremiah, he describes personal suffering alongside national woe. Clearly, this "I" has similar views to and has endured pain like Jeremiah's. Why not just call the "I" Jeremiah? Because the book does not do so, and because people like Baruch, Ebed-melech, and possibly others agreed with and learned from Jeremiah. For whatever reason, the poet makes all three connections without offering a name.

The speaker also offers a strong wisdom-oriented viewpoint. He speaks of his suffering, how he has endured it, and what he has learned about God through it. He tells others what is good to do and leads them in prayer. All of these activities have clear wisdom parallels in Psalms and Job. Thus, the speaker is versatile enough to embrace prophetic and wisdom beliefs.

This speaker is not collective Israel nor everyman, at least not if those terms are meant to be general depictions of suffering as a whole. This speaker works with people who have sinned and prayed and are now waiting to see what God will do to their tormentors. He counsels them as a fellow sufferer and sinner, he portrays God as good even within the most desperate of circumstances, and he joins their prayers for relief from enemies. Therefore, he works within a specific situation, not within all suffering at all times. He is a leader within a specific context.

To summarize, this speaker, who is the same as the one in 2:11–19, moves from personal observation, to collective prayer, to concluding praise and petition. This movement allows the book to progress theologically beyond a sin-punishment scheme to factors that include God's character and the fate of Zion's opponents. The speaker's set pieces reflect the multiplicity of forms in the chapter and by doing so highlight the thoroughness inherent in acrostics.

As might be expected, a chapter that elicits so many opinions on speakers and structures also engenders a number of possible settings. Since these options really relate to the introductory matters of authorship and date (see above), they will only be dealt with briefly here. Basically there are three standard opinions on the setting.

First, most scholars conclude that this chapter, like the others, was written soon after the fall of Jerusalem, or at least between 587 and 538 B.C.E. They reach this conclusion even though this chapter's contents differ from that of chaps. 1, 2, 4, and 5 since the description of suffering and statements about God are similar to those in the rest of the book. Most scholars who hold to Jeremianic authorship or to the unity of the book take this approach, and as the Introduction to this commentary indicates (see "Authorship and Date" and "Poetic Form and Meter"), this work does so too.

Second, some experts date chap. 3 well after 587 B.C.E. These writers may be divided into two basic groups, the first of which believes that all the poems are later regardless of who wrote them and the second of which thinks that chap. 3 is later than two or more of the other poems. This second group treats chap. 3 as if it is a commentary on or corrective to the earlier chapters. Group one includes Budde (91–93), Löhr (xiv–xvi), Haller (91–92), Boecker (13–15), and others. Group two includes Meek (4), Westermann (72–73), and others. Of course, this interpretation of chap. 3 requires the poem to be read in isolation from the others, either because of hermeneutical presuppositions or because of the conviction that chap. 3 does not describe the same setting as the rest of the book. It may also require, as in the case of Westermann, a determination to treat as earlier the laments that offer less interpretation of 587 B.C.E.

Third, some commentators simply believe that the poems are too general to be dated with any degree of accuracy. Provan (7–19) and K. M. O'Connor ([2001] 1013–16) represent this position, and it is likely that many writers will adopt this view in the future. While their caution has merit, the arguments offered for a general dating after 587 B.C.E. but before the rebuilding of the temple, mourned as lost in Lamentations, make sense.

Therefore, this commentary treats Lam 3 as a composition written between 587 and 520 B.C.E., with a preference for the earlier part of that era. It has a unique purpose in the book (see *Comment* below). Yet its verbal and thematic connections to chap. 2 mark it as part of an ongoing discussion, liturgy, or exhortation in the book as a whole. Its speaker reflects and expands the theology and needs already expressed in the book. Lament continues, but lament is not simply expressing pain. It is also a means of probing and restoring relationships with God and healing personal and national lives and circumstances. While it is wrong to treat laments as merely "a way to fix things," it is also wrong to treat them as a way to shout about pain with no further intentions. Lam 3 helps bridge the gap between God and the people, and this bridging was certainly needed in the years immediately following 587 B.C.E. as desperately as at any other point in Israel's history.

Comment

Chap. 3 unfolds in four broad sections: vv 1–24, vv 25–39, vv 40–47, and vv 48–66. The first section emphasizes what a first-person speaker has learned about suffering and about God's faithfulness. The second section highlights the speaker's response to God's sovereignty and goodness. The third section calls for prayer in light of what Israel's enemies have done, and the fourth section expresses confidence in God's positive actions on Israel's behalf. This structure moves readers, or attempts to move readers at least, from reflective advice to confidence in God's ultimate goodness.

1–6 This first section uses darkness as a unifying metaphor that describes the results of the day of the Lord in the speaker's life. This opening section ties chap. 3 to the preceding chapters. These verses also personalize the judgment, allowing this person to identify with Jerusalem and paving the way for a fellow sufferer to offer advice to the bereft city.

1 The speaker announces, "I am the man" (אני הגבר), which signals a shift in speakers from 2:20, and adds "who has seen affliction" (ראה עני). This phrase connects this speaker to 1:3 and 1:7, where the narrator describes Jerusalem's affliction, and 1:9c, where Jerusalem asks Yahweh to see her affliction. This speaker has endured the pain God sent for the city's sins, though he offers no confession of sin at this point.

His affliction occurs because of the "rod of his [the Lord's] anger." The word for "his anger" (עברתו) also appears in 2:2, where the narrator reports that "in his anger" on the day of his wrath (2:1) the Lord has broken down Jerusalem's strongholds and brought down the kingdom and its officials. It also occurs in Jer 7:29, a text that relates a "lamentation" (קינה) for "the generation of his anger" (את דור עברתו). This word usually depicts fierce anger and harsh results of this anger, so the speaker shares in the judged ones' sorrow. He is able to speak from experience.

2 Metaphors invoking the day of the Lord continue. God has made the man walk (וילך; a *hipʿil* imperfect third-person masculine singular) in "darkness and not light" (חשך ולא אור). Joel 2:1–2 and Zeph 1:14–16 portray the day of the Lord as a time of deep darkness. More specifically, Amos 5:18 uses this exact phrase to describe the day's severity. Given this background, Renkema asserts that this expression "suggests an implicit recognition of the fulfillment of a former announcement of judgment" (354). The speaker understands, then, that he and his hearers have experienced what the Lord threatened. Warnings were ignored and consequences have come.

3 God's punishment afflicts the speaker constantly. The root שוב followed by another verb describes repeated action (Renkema, 354), so the phrase ישב יהפך, "he turns again and again," or "he returns—he strikes over and over," denotes God's repeated striking of the speaker. "His hand" (ידו) moves back and forth against the speaker "all the day" (כל היום), so no relief comes. This same "hand" bound Jerusalem's transgressions into a yoke of foreign domination in 1:14 and destroyed the city in 2:8.

4 The speaker uses two familiar governing verbs as he continues to describe his plight. First, he states, "He has swallowed up [בלה] my flesh and my skin [בשרי ועורי]." Some form of בלה, "swallow up," appears in 2:2, 5, 8, and 16 to describe the various levels of destruction God causes. Second, the speaker adds that "he has shattered my bones" (שבר עצמותי). Different forms of שבר, "shatter," occur in 1:15, 2:9, and 2:11 to describe the shattering of Jerusalem's young men, defenses, and the city itself, respectively. This repetition underscores the speaker's sharing in Jerusalem's agony. He has suffered personally the way the populace has suffered collectively.

5 Obviously, Jerusalem's destruction has been a pervasive theme in Lamentations so far. Just as obviously, Babylon laid siege to the city as a prelude to entering her streets, harming her people, and sacking her temple. In this verse the speaker states that God "built against me" (בנה עלי), and that God "surrounded" (ויקף) him. Taken together, these metaphors may be translated "besieged" (see Hillers, [1992] 113). "Bitterness and weariness" (ראש ותלאה; see *Note* 5.a.) lurk outside, ready to conquer the speaker. His fate has been the same as the city's.

6 The darkness of the day of the Lord mentioned in 3:2 is as dark as the darkness of the grave here. Three psalms may serve as background material for the speaker at this point. Ps 143:3 mirrors this verse exactly, except that the first two words are transposed. It seems likely that Lamentations cites Ps 143:3 and reverses the words for the acrostic's sake, rather than the opposite (contra Renkema, 358). The psalm relates the psalmist's great dilemma and counts on God's character as his main means of hope. Both Lam 3:6 and Ps 143:3 use "those long dead" (כמתי עולם) as a metaphor for those whom God seems to have put in a dark place (במחשכים הושיבני) and forgotten. Thus, both passages eventually call on God to remember and act on their behalf.

Ps 88:4–8 (ET 88:3–7) likewise depicts an individual in dire straits who has been placed by God in the grave, which is described as a dark place (במחשכים). Once again this situation makes the psalmist feel as if God has forgotten him. Therefore, the psalmist cries out to God in Ps 88:14–19 (ET 89:13–18) even as enemies surround him, a setting very much like Lam 3:1–6.

Ps 74:18–20 asks God to remember the afflicted in a time when the secret places, the dark places of earth (מחשכי ארץ), are filled with violence. As the comments on Lam 2 indicate, the author of Lamentations almost certainly knew this psalm or vice versa. At the very least the two writers shared stock phrases. Though this last connection is less obvious and thus less likely than the previous two possibilities, it does offer one more text where trouble, a felt separation from God, and prayers for help stand together.

This verse indicates that, like Jerusalem, the speaker has all but died. God has sent the darkness of the day of the Lord, the darkness of the grave itself, and the terrors of siege warfare against him. Yet he has not died, nor has Jerusalem. So both he and the city must decide how to live now, in these very horrible circumstances. Death might have been or seemed preferable, but it is not an option now.

7–9 The governing metaphor now shifts from darkness to ways God constricts the speaker's movements. Walls, chains, stones, and crooked paths hem in the speaker until he prays for help. Even then he receives no relief. He lives in darkness; worse yet, he is trapped and chained there.

7 God turns the man's darkness into "a hermetically sealed prison from which there is no possibility of escape" (Renkema, 361). According to the speaker, "He has walled me in [גדר בעדי] and I cannot escape/go out [ולא אצא]." The root גדר occurs in Hos 2:8 and Job 19:8 in the same sense as here, for each text stresses how God walls in someone specifically or apparently as a punishment. Ps 88:9 (ET 88:8) includes the phrase "and I cannot escape" (ולא אצא), so the author may continue to use that psalm as a touchstone, or vice versa (Reyburn, *Handbook*, 79). As if the wall were not enough, the Lord has placed heavy chains on the man, so the prisoner has no way to escape.

8 Beseeching his jailer is the only avenue of relief open to the speaker. Lam 2:11–19 has already placed Jerusalem in a similar situation. When God has judged, only God can heal or give relief. Yet "even when" (גם כי) he cries out (אזעק), the very thing the prophetic speaker counsels in 2:18, God rejects his prayer. Things seem to be at an impasse. Though his cry for help is rejected here (ואשוע), by 3:56 the Lord listens to a cry for help (לשועתי). This poem as a whole may indicate movement in a positive direction.

9 Once again the speaker turns to גדר, "walled in," imagery. He claims God "walled in my path/road with cut stones" (גדר דרכי בגזית). His "road" was his calling out to God. This road has been blocked by "stones that have been cut to a proper shape before being used to build a wall" (Reyburn, *Handbook*, 80). These stones may well be the materials for his prison. At the very least they are solid, prepared, fixed, and intentional building materials. God has purposefully shut him in. No cry for help, no prayer, or way of escape, exists.

10–18 Now the speaker expands his list of depressing metaphors still further. God is a ravenous bear or lion (vv 10–11), a deadly archer (vv 12–13), and a person who feeds the speaker bad food and treats him harshly (vv 15–16). The result is that the speaker has become a laughingstock (v 14) and has lost peace and hope (vv 17–18). This section concludes the speaker's descent into despair. Only death or renewed hope can follow.

10 At first it appears that death may be the speaker's fate. God is "a bear lying in wait" (דב ארב), an image used in judgment passages such as Isa 59:9–11, Hos 13:8, and Amos 5:19. Just as ominously, the Lord is a "lion in hiding" (אריה במסתרים), a metaphor used to describe enemies in Ps 17:12. Also, Jeremiah often calls enemies "lions" (Jer 4:7; 5:6; 49:19; 50:44; see Keil, 407). If the speaker ever did get out of prison, a terrible beast would attack him (see Amos 5:18–20, where a similar idea unfolds in a judgment passage).

11 The speaker proceeds as if such a thing did happen. He says, "He turned me aside from my path [דרכי סורר] and tore me to pieces [ויפשחני]." The reference to "my path" is identical to the one in 3:9, so the passage takes on a nightmarish tone. Walled in (3:9) or led off (3:11), the result is dire either way. In this instance, he claims, "He [God] made me desolate" (שמני שמם). Some form of the word translated "desolate" here, which can also mean "laid waste" (BDB, 1030–31), appears in 1:4, 1:13, and 1:16 to describe Jerusalem's gates, Jerusalem herself, and Jerusalem's children. Once again the speaker identifies with the city by claiming to have experienced what she experienced.

12 To further identify with the devastated city, the speaker claims, "He bent his bow" (דרך קשתו), a phrase equivalent to the first two words in 2:4. Here the Lord makes the speaker his target, whereas in the earlier passage the Lord leads an army against his people. God hunts him (see Berlin, 91).

13 The archer image concludes in this verse. Thus, the author allows the governing metaphor to cross over alphabetic lines, since the ד segment ends in 3:12.

This example of enjambment further testifies to the poet's skill. Having drawn his bow (3:12), the Lord finds his target, for "the sons of his quiver" (בני אשפתו), his arrows, find their mark in "my [the speaker's] kidneys" (בכליותי). God's arrows sink into the inner recesses of his being, which may well be what kidneys signify here.

14 As the textual note on this verse indicates (see *Note* 14.a.), the phrase לכל עמי, "to all my people," is the source of a good bit of scholarly debate. Some scholars find it hard to believe that the man could be speaking about his own people. For example, Provan (88) writes, "This simply does not fit with the tone of other sections of the poem, in which the speaker identifies himself with his people (cf. vv. 40–48), but seeks vengeance on his persecutors (cf. vv. 61–66, particularly v. 63, where he repeats that he is the subject of 'their songs')." Given this opinion, Provan argues for the plural "peoples," which refers to non-Israelites.

On the other hand, Hillers ([1992] 127) thinks such cruelty from his own people "is part of what he had to endure." Berlin (82) agrees with Hillers, as does Renkema (369–71), who concludes that the speaker is ridiculed for continuing to trust in God despite all that has happened to Jerusalem and to himself. Though either reading is possible, the singular reading has the most ancient textual support, adds the greatest amount of pain in context, and calls for the greatest eventual trust in the Lord. Certainly Jeremiah discovered that fellow sufferers could mock him (see Jer 39–44), so this is hardly a foreign concept.

Therefore, the speaker has not just endured the taunting of foreign enemies, an indignity he shares with Jerusalem (see 1:7). Rather, he has felt the sting of taunts hurled at him by his own people. God has been his enemy, foreigners have devastated his homeland, and some of his own people have mocked his faith. He has at least had Jeremiah-like experiences (see Jer 1:17–19).

15 At this point the speaker adds food imagery to the darkness, imprisonment, animal, and archery metaphors. God has fed him במרורים, "bitter herbs," such as those used in Passover meals (Renkema, 371–72), because nothing else is available. This word may have the symbolic meaning "bitter things" since Job 9:18 uses a very similar phrase (כי ישבעני ממרים), "but makes me drink deep of bitter things") in this manner. Having fed him bitter herbs, the Lord gives him a drink of לענה, "wormwood," juice to complete his meal. As Berlin (91) observes, "Wormwood, a plant with a bitter taste, is often used metaphorically for bitterness or sorrow (cf. Amos 5:7; 6:12; Prov. 5:4). This word and its synonyms occur frequently in this chapter (also in vv. 5, 19)." She considers this a metaphor for exile, but the speaker shares Jerusalem's suffering, which may indeed be worse than that experienced by the exiles (see Jer 29).

16 Continuing the feeding metaphor, the speaker states, "He has broken my teeth in the gravel" (ויגרס בחצץ שני), which probably refers to what he must eat, though it may also indicate both eating gravel and being placed in a lowly position. In current English usage "eating dirt" is a picturesque way of saying that someone is abased. Here the phrase provides a bridge from eating bitter items (3:15) to feeling humiliated and hopeless (3:17–18), as does the speaker's comment "He has pressed me down in the ashes" (הכפישני באפר).

17 Having expressed what God has done to him, the speaker now describes his despair over what has unfolded (Hillers, [1992] 128). He admits "My soul rejects peace/wholeness" (ותזנח משלום נפשי) and adds "I have forgotten goodness" (נשיתי טובה). These phrases are clearly parallel to one another, with "rejected" and "forgotten" complementing each other and "wholeness/peace" and "goodness" doing the same. With God acting like an enemy to him (3:1–16) as well as to Jerusalem (2:4–5), what sort of peace and wholeness could he feel? His physical home is demolished, and his God is against him. What can he do?

18 Clearly, he may either turn to Yahweh again, or he can abandon all attempts to find relief. Here he begins to choose the former option by mentioning God's name for the first time, albeit by stating that "my endurance" (נצחי) and "my hope" (ותוחלתי) have "perished" (אבד) "from the LORD" (מיהוה). God has stamped out this old hope (Renkema, 379), perhaps so that a new understanding of God can take its place. Whatever the speaker thought has been radically altered. What remains to be seen is whether any new grasp of divine character and activity will result in revitalized strength and hope.

19–24 These are the best-known verses in Lamentations. They have been used as the basis for hymns, choruses, and the bulk of sermons that have been preached from Lamentations. This section provides a transition from stating the extreme hardships of the past to confessing God's faithfulness as a beginning for a new season of faith for himself and for all who will agree with his conclusions. Having come to this understanding himself, he proceeds to offer his discoveries to others. Confession gives way to instruction and, eventually, to praise in the rest of the chapter.

19 Having demonstrated that he has endured divine opposition on the day of the Lord in 3:1–18, which establishes his solidarity with Jerusalem, the speaker now prays, the very thing the city is counseled to do in 2:11–19. Jerusalem asks God to ראה, "see," in 1:9, 11, 20 and 2:20, and now the speaker pleads with God, "Remember [זכר] my affliction [עניי] and my wandering [ומרודי], the wormwood [לענה] and the bitterness [וראש]."

This beginning to the prayer echoes several texts. For example, in Exod 2:23–25 God sees, hears, knows, and remembers Israel, which leads the Lord to send Moses to begin the series of events that lead to the exodus. In Lam 1:7, Jerusalem remembers "her affliction and her wanderings" (עניה ומרודיה), the very things that the speaker asks God to remember here. Thus, one more time the speaker joins his suffering with Jerusalem's. In effect, then, when he prays that God "remember" and thereby remove his affliction and wandering, he also prays for Jerusalem's affliction and wandering. As a co-sufferer, to pray for himself means to pray for the whole group. Further, in 1:9 Israel has not remembered "his footstool" (Jerusalem) on the day of his wrath. This prayer intends to help everyone involved remember what must be remembered for the shattered covenant relationship to be repaired. The reappearance of לענה, "wormwood," from 3:15 indicates that the speaker is concerned with his own personal circumstances, not just with Israel's.

20 Depending on one's translation of this verse (see *Notes* 20.a. and 20.b.; Provan, 91–92), "the expression of a hopeful attitude either follows at once, at v. 19, or . . . at v. 21, after an amplified description of the man's inner despondency" (Hillers, [1992] 128). Hillers ([1992] 128), Berlin (82–83), and Renkema (380–81) take the former position, while Westermann (161) and Albrektson (*Studies in the Text and Theology*, 141–45) appear to take the latter. Though there are certainly problems with accepting the latter viewpoint, this seems the best possibility. By using an infinitive absolute, the speaker strongly affirms his belief that God will indeed remember and give careful consideration to his request.

21 Having assured himself that God will definitely do as he has asked and remember him, the speaker moves to the next level of confidence, one that restores assurance. In 3:18 he states that he has lost his hope in Yahweh, while here the act of bringing to mind (אשיב אל לבי) God's covenant remembering (Exod 2:23–25; 3:19–20) and God's covenant mercies (see 3:22) restores that lost hope. The repetition of forms of אוחיל, "hope," clearly means a reversal in attitude about the situation. As the chapter progresses the author slowly dismantles the speaker's sense of defeat through a more positive use of words that first appear in 3:1–18.

22 The speaker bases this renewed hope on "the infinite compassion of the Lord" (Keil, 413). Two key terms define God's character. The speaker affirms that "the LORD's (acts of) covenant mercy" (חסדי יהוה) "indeed" (an asseverative כי; Gordis, 179) "have not/never cease" (לא תמנו; see *Note* 22.b.). God's חסד, "covenant mercy," "describes the disposition and beneficent actions of God toward the faithful, Israel his people, and humanity in general" (*NIDOTTE*, 2:211). Not even the coming of the day of the Lord against Jerusalem signals the end of God's covenant mercy. If this is true, then nothing can exhaust the divine impulse to act graciously. The speaker asserts that "indeed [a second asseverative כי] his (acts of) compassion never end." The term for "compassion" comes from רחם, a word that "signifies a warm compassion, a compassion which goes the second mile, which is ready to forgive sin, to replace judgment with grace" (*NIDOTTE*, 3:1094). God's willingness to start fresh after this horrible period of sin followed by judgment is not in doubt, at least in the speaker's mind.

This confession coincides with at least two significant covenantal passages. In Exod 34:6–7, Yahweh states that he will renew the covenant that Israel broke through the golden calf incident because he is "compassionate and gracious" (רחום וחנון) "and full of mercy and faithfulness" (ורב חסד ואמת). In Deut 30:1–11, Moses promises that even though all the covenant consequences found in Deut 27–28 might befall Israel, if they turn back to Yahweh and obey him the Lord will have compassion (ורחמך) and restore them to the covenantal relationship as well as to the land. Joel 2:13–14 and Jonah 4:2 combine the elements of God's character found in Exod 34:6–7 with the possibility of repentance found in Deut 30:1–10. Like Lamentations, these texts occur in a context of judgment, though of the two only Joel 2:13–14 seems to presuppose the actual experiencing of disaster.

Thus, Lam 3:22 agrees with one of the most extraordinary teachings in the OT. Though Israel sinned against God through idolatry, immorality, oppression, and other forms of long-term covenantal adultery to such an extent that he finally punishes severely, the Lord will still start over with penitent Israelites. In other words, God's determination to bless and heal is as thorough and unusual as his determination to punish, if not more so. The road back to covenantal relationship may well be long and difficult, especially given the level of sin and the depth of punishment. Nonetheless, it is possible to begin.

23 With this understanding of God's covenant mercy and compassion in mind, the speaker further confesses that "they" (either the plural חסדי, "[acts of] mercy," or the חסדי, "[acts of] mercy," and רחמיו, "[acts of] compassion," taken together) are "new every morning" (חדשים לבקרים). As Reyburn (*Handbook*, 86) explains, the word "new" does not mean "something that never existed before, but rather a fresh renewal of what has been experienced before." Each new day the proofs of God's grace flow from his compassionate nature (Keil, 414). Each new day dawns with the possibility of covenant renewal for a punished people. This opportunity lasts as long as God lasts since it is grounded in his personal character.

At this point the speaker praises God directly by declaring "great is your faithfulness" (רבה אמונתך). Renkema (389) states that "faithfulness" expresses "a characteristic of God in relationship with a human person made manifest in his deeds. Characteristics of such fidelity are consistency, stability, truth, and permanence." God's covenantal fidelity and integrity remain intact no matter how things may seem. Human beings may not wish it were so, but judgment for sin as promised proves this faithfulness. Gratefully, so does God's promise to start anew with a terribly compromised covenant partner, and it is this facet of Yahweh's faithfulness that the speaker affirms here.

24 This verse completes the speaker's change of attitude from despair to nascent hope. The same soul that in 3:17 claims to reject peace claims here "The LORD is my portion" (חלקי יהוה). This confession leads to a reversal of 3:18, where the speaker claims his hope has perished, for he now claims that because God is his portion, "therefore [על כן] I will hope in him [אוחיל לו]." This last phrase coincides with the "therefore I will hope/have hope" (על כן אוחיל) in 3:21, so the repetition underscores the renewal of the once-lost hope.

This renewal stems from the speaker's beliefs about God's character in covenantal context stated in 3:20–23. It also stems from the speaker's willingness to let God be his portion, or his reward. Two passages illustrate this attitude. In Num 18:20 God tells the Levites that they have no inheritance or portion in the land but states, "I am your portion" (אני חלקך). The Levites had to abandon all other plans for inheritance. Similarly, in Ps 73:26, a psalm in which the poet confesses God's goodness (73:1) yet also the poet's own questions about that goodness, the poet confesses that God is "my portion" (וחלקי). So the psalmist no longer cares how the wicked prosper; instead, he focuses on the goodness of having God for a refuge. Simply stated, God is enough to satisfy the writer, and the same is apparently true of the speaker in Lam 3:24.

25–39 The speaker extends his discussion to include instances of what it is good for a person to do in the present circumstances, given that God is good (vv 25–30). He then proceeds to emphasize God's justice (vv 31–36) and sovereignty (vv 37–39). As he does so, the speaker continues to rebuild the assurance and hope declared lost in 3:1–18. He instructs his readers so that they may discover and share the truth he has learned.

25 Vv 25–27 all begin with the word טוב, "good." This first verse offers the consistent biblical confession that "The LORD is good" (טוב יהוה), which is also found in such diverse texts as Pss 34:9 (ET 34:8) and 86:5, Hos 3:5, and Neh 9:25 (see Keil, 414; Renkema, 392, for a discussion of these texts and God's goodness). Yet God's goodness has a specific focus here. God is good "to those who wait for him" (לקוו); God is good "to the soul who seeks him" (תדרשנו).

This assertion agrees with both prophetic and psalmic texts. Ps 34:9–11 (ET 34:8–10) invites readers to "taste and see that the LORD is good" (34:9), asserts that "the man who takes refuge in him" is blessed (34:9), and concludes that "those who seek the LORD lack no good thing" (34:11). The usage of "the LORD is good" (טוב יהוה), "the man" (לגבר), and "those who seek the LORD" (ודרשי יהוה), all of which have near equivalents in Lam 3:25–27, indicates that, even if one of the passages does not quote the other, they certainly share a common theology and vocabulary. They are also both evidently wisdom oriented. Amos 5:4 and 5:6 exhort readers to "seek the LORD" (דרשו את יהוה), and Amos 5:14 tells them to "seek good and not evil" (דרשו טוב ואל רע), which indicates that seeking the Lord and seeking good are synonymous. Those who truly desire the Lord enough to seek him diligently will receive good from the Lord.

26 Though the phrase "it is good to wait silently" (טוב ויחיל ודומם) is a rare construction in the OT (see *Note* 26.a.), the concept of waiting silently for God's deliverance certainly is not (see Pss 37:9; 62:2, 6 [ET 62:1, 5]). Lam 2:10 describes the elders of Zion sitting in stupefied silence. This silence, however, seems to be one of expectation. Renkema (396) argues that this silence in 3:26 "ought to be understood as more than simply sitting in a sort of paralyzed amazement. The present text speaks rather of a tenacious intensification of 'being silent,' of a conscious option for remaining silent." In other words, this text transforms silence from a posture of the defeated to one of the soon-to-be delivered. Further, this silence does not preclude prayer, given 2:11–19 and 3:19–24. Thus, the silence heightens the waiting that will eventually be rewarded with "the salvation of the LORD" (לתשועת יהוה), though at this point the speaker does not specify what such salvation entails.

27 The speaker concludes the טוב, "good," section by stating that it is good "for the man [לגבר] that he bear [כי ישא] the yoke in his youth [על בנעוריו]." Of course, the repetition of גבר, "man," here reminds readers of the speaker's self-designation in 3:1 and also points forward to 3:35, where the term appears in the context of the sort of justice a man can expect from God. While "for the man" here may serve as an emblem for men in general, it certainly includes the speaker in this context.

Two other terms echo earlier texts. First, the speaker refers to a yoke he must bear. In 1:14 Jerusalem states that Yahweh fashioned her sins into a yoke so heavy that when it was placed on her neck her strength failed. Thus, the yoke mentioned here may well be the yoke of sin, yet it is at least likely that the speaker's suffering is the yoke. As Keil (415) explains, "In the present context the yoke is that of sufferings, and the time of youth is mentioned as the time of freshness and vigour, which render the bearing of burdens more easy. He who has learned in youth to bear sufferings, will not sink into despair should they come on him in old age." Of course, sin—whether the speaker's, the populace's, or both—caused these sufferings, so both sin and suffering should be kept in mind. Second, as the Keil quotation indicates, the term בנעוריו, "in his youth," expresses either the length of time (for a short while) or level of strength one has for bearing this yoke. A form of this term for "youth" appears in a comprehensive statement in 2:21 ("young man and elder," נער וזקן) and later as a parallel to "choice men" in 5:13 (בחורים . . . ונערים). In a time such as the text describes, a time when old and young alike are afflicted, it is best for the young man to bear this burden. The difficulty will eventually pass. He will not grow old bearing this yoke.

28 V 26 stated that it is good to wait silently for God's deliverance. Now the speaker adds, "Let him [the man] sit alone and keep silent [ישב בדד וידם], for he [God] laid it upon him [כי נטל עליו]." The first half of the verse echoes 1:1 and 3:26. Lam 1:1 declares, "How lonely sits the city" (איכה ישבה בדד העיר), a phrase that differs from 3:28 only in the latter verse's subject and exhortative tone. The determination to sit alone and silent because of an awareness of God's activity transforms the sitting from sheer loneliness to quiet, confident expectation. It is ironic for the speaker to counsel silence, but this silence amounts to dogged, determined expectation born out of an awareness of harsh reality and God's goodness. To wait silently here means to confess God's power in the situation ("he laid it upon him"), to trust in the Lord's faithfulness and covenant mercy (3:19–24), and to embrace humility in the face of what has happened. All these things define what it is good to do (3:25–27).

29 Humility and patience receive more attention in vv 29–30. In 2:10 the elders sit on the ground in silence and throw dust on their heads, a practice that reflects ancient mourning rituals. Now the speaker states that it is good to place one's mouth in the dust (יתן בעפר פיהו) as an act of voluntary obeisance. The reason for this action is that "there may yet be hope" (אולי יש תקוה). Fuerst (238) writes that "this is no sceptic's concession, but rather the open-hearted confession of one who is leaning towards the future, ready for what God will bring and willing to rest upon that. He has no guarantee and no tokens of anticipated victory except the conviction gained from experience that God is gracious (verses 22–24)." In other words, the speaker is able to humble himself to the dust because he believes God has laid this situation on him (3:28) and because he has determined that Yahweh is his portion in life (3:24).

30 As if loneliness, silence, and bowing down were not enough, the speaker now adds, "Let him ['the man'; see 3:27] give his cheek to the one striking [יתן למכהו לחי]; let him be filled/sated with disgrace [ישבע בחרפה]." Of course, the invaders inflicted all these indignities (and more) on Jerusalem's citizens, but the speaker counsels the reader to accept these humiliations as coming from the Lord for a purpose. What has happened has not been a case of fate, political failure, or loss of national nerve. It has been God's work, which changes the advice from stoic resignation to "positive and creative elements in faith" (Davidson, 196).

31 How can one possibly accept the speaker's assertions about what is good to do (3:25–30)? How can one possibly accept that it is better to submit to God's will if this suffering is indeed God's will? In v 30 the speaker begins a nine-verse response to these and related questions. As in 3:19–24, his convictions about God's character form the basis of his previously stated conclusions.

Vv 31–33 each begin with an explanatory conjunction (כי). The first of these joins with a negative particle (לא) to assert that God will not "reject forever" (יזנח לעולם). In 2:7 the narrator comments that God has rejected his altar, and in 3:17 the speaker states that his soul rejects peace. Now he begins to reject the rejection of peace because he believes God does not reject forever. As Renkema (405) observes, the speaker affirms that God does not stay angry forever (Ps 103:9), though he waits to say why this is so.

32 At this point the speaker explains why he believes that God's wrath will not be endless. In short, he continues to believe what he stated in 3:22–24. Based on Exod 34:6–7 and Deut 30:1–11, he concludes that God indeed does cause grief (הוגה), yet he also has compassion (ורחם), a concept found in 3:22, "according to the abundance of his covenant mercies/steadfast love" (כרב חסדו), a concept also found in 3:22. The speaker believes that after the Lord "has caused sorrow, He shows pity once more, according to the fulness of His grace. Compassion outweighs sorrow" (Keil, 416). God has forgiven so often in the past that it seems impossible that his kindness could ever be exhausted. Indeed, the enormity of the current situation testifies to the incredible love and patience God must possess (Renkema, 408).

33 Having asserted that it is good to submit humbly to God's punishment because God will not reject forever (v 31) and because God's compassion is extraordinary (v 32), the speaker adds a third reason. He asserts that though God does indeed afflict one if necessary (see 3:1 and 3:19), the Lord "does not afflict from his heart" (לא ענה מלבו). God's first instinct is not to judge but rather to bless. He does not wish to grieve the sons of man (ויגה בני איש). God's heart is not in this sort of activity, though he is well able to judge as needed, as Lamentations proves. If God prefers not to punish, then the hope remains that he will return to compassion, which 3:22 and 3:32 strongly imply is the substance of his heart. Afflicting and grieving must inevitably come to an end. According to Gottwald (*Studies*, 99), "The expression 'he does not afflict from the heart' is the high watermark in Lamentations' understanding of God. . . . The angry side of his nature, turned so unflinchingly against Jerusalem, is not the determinative factor in the divine purposes. Begrudgingly, regretfully, if there is no other way toward his higher purposes, he may unleash the forces of evil, but 'his heart' is not in it."

34 Not only is his heart not in afflicting and grieving the sons of men; neither is it in allowing injustice and oppression to flourish on earth. This fact emerges in vv 34–36 through a trio of infinitive clauses, each of which describes a form of injustice, whose "objects depend on ראה" ("countenance"; see Keil, 417). God does not "countenance" wrongdoing, so Israel's recent experiences must have some other purpose.

The first infinitive clause asserts that God does not desire "to crush under his foot [לדכא תחת רגליו] all the prisoners of the earth [כל אסירי ארץ]." Though it is possible that the text refers to persons crushed under the Babylonians' feet or crushed under oppression in general (see Keil, 417; Westermann, 178; Brandscheidt, *Gotteszorn und Menschenleid*, 64), the pronominal suffix "his" probably refers to God. After all, he sent Babylon against Jerusalem. The point here is a subtle one. God does not crush the prisoner, the exile, willingly ("from the heart"), nor does he sanction such activity on earth in general circumstances. Thus, the current crushing is a temporary judgment that will at some unspecified time in the future give way to the normal course of things.

35 The second infinitive clause adds that God does not countenance or approve of the turning aside of "a man's justice" (משפט גבר). This notion of turning aside justice occurs elsewhere (see Exod 23:2, 6; Deut 16:19; 24:17; 27:19) and "refers to the violation of fundamental rights, particularly of those who can barely, if at all, defend themselves, namely the poor and the foreigner, the widow and the orphan" (Renkema, 414). Only the wicked defraud the defenseless in this matter, and their brazenness is such that they do so "in the presence of the most high" (נגד פני עליון). Of course, the wicked may believe God does not care or will not act (see Zeph 1:12). They commit sins against the widow, resident alien, and fatherless thinking that God does not see (Ps 94:1–7).

But God does see? Whenever "a man's justice" is denied, God sees. The problem here is that the oppressor has triumphed with God's approval. Once again, such is not God's heart or God's vision for the world. Thus, change will occur sometime.

36 The third infinitive clause states that God does not approve when one decides to "subvert a man in his cause/dispute in court" (לעות אדם בריבו). The infinitive literally means to make something crooked (BDB, 736), so it refers to treating one's lawsuit or protest in a crooked or bent manner.

To summarize 3:34–36, God does not wish to crush the prisoners or see them crushed (v 34). God does not wish to turn aside justice or see it turned aside (v 35). God does not wish to pervert justice or see it perverted (v 36). Therefore, what has been happening constitutes an alien act of God, for, as Isa 28:21 points out, judgment is God's unusual act, not his normal one.

37 Several previous texts have established God's complete sovereignty over Israel's situation by stating unequivocally that the Lord has afflicted Jerusalem because of her sins (1:5, 12–16; 2:1–10). Likewise, 3:1–36 has indicated that God has turned his hand against the speaker despite God's merciful and faithful character. The Lord does not approve of injustice, so whatever has happened has been a temporary epoch in Israel's life, however long "temporary" may be. In vv 37–39 the speaker continues to affirm God's control over his situation and Jerusalem's future. By doing so he eliminates any misconception that may have arisen that because God does not countenance injustice he must not have been in control of the events surrounding Jerusalem's fall.

The speaker begins with an argument based on God's status as creator (Brandscheidt, *Gotteszorn und Menschenleid*, 65). He asks, "Who spoke and it came to pass" (מי זה אמר ותהי), a phrase very close to Ps 33:9, which asserts, "For he spoke and it came to pass [כי הוא אמר ויהי]; he commanded and it stood [הוא צוה ויעמד]." Ps 33 also includes other terms found in Lam 3, such as God's faithfulness (באמונה; Ps 33:4), justice (ומשפט; Ps 33:5), and covenant mercy (חסד; Ps 33:5), as well as the need to wait on and hope in the Lord (Ps 33:20–22). Thus, both Lam 3 and Ps 33 use creation imagery to stress God's sovereignty in an overall context of waiting on the Lord in perilous times. In Ps 33:9 the creation motif stresses how the inhabitants of earth should fear their creator, while in Lam 3:37 the motif is used to claim that the same Lord who spoke the words that moved creation has spoken the words that brought Jerusalem's devastation. No one else possesses the power to rule in this manner.

38 Further, the speaker asserts, "From the mouth of the most high, does not come forth the bad and the good [הרעות והטוב]?" This query has already been answered in Lamentations and in earlier texts such as Amos 3:6 and Isa 45:7, both of which state that good and bad, as experienced by human beings, come from the Lord. The same "most high" who knows when all injustice occurs (3:35) declares that pleasant and unpleasant experiences will take place. Since 3:31–36 has already revealed the essence of God's heart, the reader can expect hard times to end.

As Hillers ([1992] 130) explains, "God is, after all, the creator (v. 37), and though he brings about both good things and bad things (calamities, trouble, not moral evil; cf. Amos 3:6), this reference to his creative omnipotence is intended to be comforting, because the creator and what he has made cannot in the final analysis be evil." The speaker seems to realize that if God is not in control of the bad things (again, seen from a human perspective), then he may also not be in control of good things (seen here as relief from the current situation). In short, the fact that God sent judgment means he can restore their fortunes. That he does not judge from the heart means that hopes for relief are not baseless.

39 This verse contains some difficult concepts. First, the speaker asks, "Why should a living man complain?" The word translated "complain" (יתאונן) comes from a root that occurs only here and in Num 11:1 (BDB, 59). Renkema (423) notes that in Num 11:1 the term "points to a rebellious complaint resulting from problematic situations which were considered to be the fault of others (YHWH, Moses)." There Israel blamed God and Moses for hardships immediately after the nation left Sinai for Canaan. Here the speaker argues that such baseless, self-justifying, and blame-shifting complaints should not be made.

Second, the speaker wonders whether a "living man" (אדם חי) should complain. According to Berlin (95), the phrase "seems to suggest that it is better to be alive, even with suffering, than to be dead (if this is the sense, it is the antithesis of Job's view). God is showing mercy by keeping a person alive. Moreover, how can he complain about his punishments when they are justified because of his sins?" Berlin correctly claims that the passage indicates that those who have survived are ultimately better off than the dead, a belief eventually expressed by Job following his dogged attempts at vindication. This conviction also appears in Jer 45:1–5, where God tells Baruch that his life is his reward in the dark days of Babylonian domination. Thus, the living man, who corresponds to the man (אדם) seeking justice in 3:36, should accept life as a gift, not blame God for his dilemma.

Third, a man (גבר; see 3:1, 27, 35) should not complain about what his sins have caused. Hillers ([1992] 130) concludes that "about his sins" (על חטאיו) probably refers to punishment, or what the man's sins have brought upon him. Therefore, "this is the first time it is implied in the poem that the man's troubles have been due to his own sins—he is being punished—and that he should call into question not the goodness of God but his own goodness. Thus the line leads into the ensuing call for repentance." In other words, the speaker realizes that what he has endured has indeed come from God's hand (see 3:37–38), yet only because of how he himself has acted. What he has suffered did not come from God's heart (3:33). Ultimately it came from his own. Realizing this truth is similar in importance to grasping the nature of God for the speaker. His goal is not just to lament, but to instruct and to renew his (and others') relationship to God. In this way his experiences become meaningful, perhaps even redemptive.

40–47 So far the speaker has stated what he has learned about suffering and the nature of God (3:1–24) and has explained what he believes it is good to do in his and the people's current circumstances (3:25–39). Now he exhorts the people to pray even as he implicitly implores God to hear them if they do seek him. Thus, he moves the poem from the predominantly personal to a more communal scope. He will move back to a largely individualistic point of view in 3:48–66, yet he never loses the nation's concerns altogether. Rather, the effect of the rest of chap. 3 is to end the poem as it began—with the speaker and Jerusalem's fortunes inextricably linked.

40 This verse summons the speaker's people "to self-examination and repentance" (Provan, 100). The speaker expresses the need for self-examination through two cohortative terms. His exhortation, "Let us search our ways [נחפשה דרכינו] and let us examine (our ways) thoroughly [ונחקרה]," uses verbs that denote searching or testing and careful, thorough review of a matter (BDB, 344, 350). Perhaps the speaker intends for them to think matters over as he has done. If they do, they will come to the conclusion that they need to return to Yahweh (ונשובה עד יהוה), a phrase that admits sin and fleeing from God as well as repentance that leads to reconnecting with God.

This verse indicates clearly that the speaker agrees with the narrator (1:5) and Jerusalem (1:12–16) that sin has led to God's acting like an enemy (2:1–10) and to God's causing him and Jerusalem horrible pain (2:11–22; 3:1–18). He does not claim the mantle of innocent sufferer, though he will at least imply in 3:43–47 that the punishment is either too severe or sufficient by now to cover the transgressions in question. Honesty about personal and national failure eliminates any sense of self-serving outrage.

41 Returning to the Lord begins with the heart, the very place where sin and rebellion originate. If love for God starts in the heart (Deut 6:4–9), so does repentance (Deut 4:30–31; 30:1–10; Jer 4:3–4). Thus, the speaker exhorts the readers, "Let us lift up our hearts" (נשא לבבנו); then he adds either "on hands" or "and with respect to hands" (see *Note* 41.b.). He counsels the raising of hearts, not just hands; the raising of hearts and hands as one; or the use of the hands to raise the heart to God. Any of these possibilities yields the same message: the people must engage in supplication (Berlin, 95) "to God in the heavens" (אל־אל בשמים). They have sinned against God, and he has punished. Thus, they must return to him (3:40), the one they have offended, from their hearts.

42 Now the speaker expresses the shared sins of the nation. By using the first common plural pronoun with a first common plural verb, the speaker emphasizes the two verbs in the verse's first half-line. He confesses, "We have indeed transgressed and rebelled" (נחנו פשענו ומרינו), which is a bald, heartfelt statement. Noun forms of פשע, "transgress," occur in 1:5, 14, and 22, where the narrator (1:5) and Jerusalem (1:14, 22) claim that God has punished the city because of her "transgressions." Similarly, verbal forms of מרה, "rebel," appear in 1:18, where Jerusalem admits she rebelled against God's word, and in 1:20, where Jerusalem confesses that she has been very rebellious (כי מרו מריתי). Clearly, the speaker places himself within the group of rebellious transgressors, just as he placed himself among the punished in 3:1–18. He speaks as an individual who is part of a collective whole.

In the second half of the verse the speaker reports God's reaction to their rebellion and transgressions: "indeed you have not forgiven" (אתה לא סלחת). Like the first half-verse, a pronoun is used to heighten the subject of the verb. God has not let these sins go unnoticed, unchecked, or unpunished. Because his sense of justice requires punishment in this instance, God has not pardoned or let such actions pass (see Keil, 421).

Westermann and Berlin suggest that the withholding of forgiveness may introduce a theological problem. Westermann (182–83) writes that the phrase "presupposes that the people have admitted their guilt," so it amounts to an accusation against God such as those commonly found in the psalter. God has not forgiven when he would normally be expected to do so. Berlin (96) takes the matter further, commenting, "The old theology has proved to be false. Contrary to Jer 18:5–12, which teaches that if the people repent God will change his mind about punishing them, our poet concludes that there is no direct relationship between repentance and forgiveness. This may be the most disturbing idea in the chapter, and in the entire book." So far Berlin indicates that Lam 3:42 overturns the Bible's general rule that forgiveness automatically (and immediately) follows repentance. She then adds, "The poet does not, however, reject the power of repentance; rather, he implies in the next two verses that repentance would be effective if only it could reach God. That it does not reach him is God's fault. In a masterfully ironic allusion, the poet reinterprets a major religious principle about divine immanence." Thus, Berlin asserts that the poet deftly shifts attention from the matter of human sin to a divine unwillingness to hear penitent prayer—at least for some unspecified time.

There are several issues Berlin raises that deserve comment, but only a few will be noted here. First, repentance is a common theme in Jeremiah, and Jer 18:5–12 is but one of over one hundred references to this theme in the book. One of the most interesting texts is Jer 14:19–22, where the prophet wonders why God has struck the people when they have acknowledged their sin. Has God broken his covenant? God's response in Jer 15:1–9 indicates that Jeremiah may have confessed his sin and the people's sin, but the people remain rebellious. So the sheer mention of repentance by even a true penitent may not necessarily signal actual repentance of the whole group. In such a situation the Lord continues on the path of eventual judgment.

Second, repentance and forgiveness do not bring immediate relief. Relief may take some time (see Deut 30:1–10). Nor does fervency prove sincerity. Third, this statement may be a literary device, as Westermann indicates, perhaps one that attempts to play on God's distaste for punishment, as Renkema (432) concludes. If so, then the writer follows literary convention and does not necessarily make any new point about the relationship among confession, repentance, and forgiveness.

Fourth, the speaker has barely begun his prayer, which does not conclude until 3:66. If he has determined that God will not hear in this case, it is strange for him to recount past deliverances in 3:52–57 and conclude with such confidence in what God will do in 3:58–66. Rather, the speaker reports how things have been as he delivers the early part of his prayer. They have sinned, and God has not pardoned at this point; he has already stated that God would not punish without reason (3:25–39). God will hear eventually, though as Berlin points out (96) it will be according to his own sense of true repentance and an appropriate end to the punishment.

43 In this verse the speaker uses four words that have already been prominent in descriptions of God's judgment throughout Lamentations. First, after starting the verse with a form of the same word that begins 3:44, the speaker mentions God's wrath (סכתה באף), a concept that appears in 1:12 and 2:1 (2x), 3, 6, 11, and 22 (see also 3:66; 4:11, 20). In all of the earlier passages, "wrath" is part of the day of the Lord, which is likely the case here. The speaker connects this confession to what the book has already emphasized about God's day of reckoning.

Second, he states, "You have ... pursued us" (ותרדפנו). Some form of רדף, "pursue," is used in 1:3, 6, as well as in 4:19 and 5:5. Like אף, "anger," this term occurs in the narrator's description of God's punishing acts (see 2:1, 3, 6), though it does not appear in Jerusalem's speeches. Once again, this usage ties the confession to previous assertions about Israel's guilt and Yahweh's judgment.

Third, he adds, "you have killed" (הרגת), a concept found in 2:4 (ויהרג, "and he killed") and in 2:21 (הרגת). Both usages in chap. 2 occur in the context of general descriptions of God's judgment, with the first coming in a speech by the narrator and the second occurring in a speech by Jerusalem. Thus, the speaker in 3:43 joins his voice with that of the other major figures in the book.

Fourth, he concludes the verse by claiming, "you have ... not shown pity" (לא חמלת). Forms of חמל, "show pity," with the negative particle appear in 2:2, 17, and 22. In other words, each speaker in chap. 2 agrees that God has judged more than severely. This final connection to previous texts underscores this verse's role as a summary verse that also pushes the speaker's prayer forward.

44 While God has covered Jerusalem with his wrath (3:43), he has covered himself with a cloud (סכותה בענן לך). This covering makes it impossible for their prayers to pass through to him (מעבור תפלה). He has made himself unavailable to his people. The only closeness to God they feel at this moment is closeness to his anger and to his distance from them.

45 The description of woes continues. While God remains aloof behind his cloud of hiding (see Hillers, [1992] 132), the people suffer on earth. Yahweh does not respond to their prayers, but he does continue to act like an enemy. The speaker says, "Offscouring and refuse you have made us" (סחי ומאוס תשימנו). Both these nouns appear only here in the OT (see BDB, 695 and 549, respectively), which may testify to the unusual nature of what has happened.

If their suffering is unique, it is also humiliating, for it unfolds "in the midst of the peoples" (בקרב העמים). Provan (101) observes that "the thought is that people regard Israel with the same distaste as they would their bodily waste and rubbish, and treat her accordingly. There are several earlier references, of course, to the contemptuous attitude of those observing Israel's difficulties (cf. v. 14; 1:7–8; 2:15–16), and there can be little doubt, in view of v. 46, that it is to this that v. 45 also refers." The speaker links this prayer to earlier passages in the book. Israel's humiliation is an established fact.

46 Once again the speaker links his prayer to an earlier passage. This time he reports, "They have opened their mouths against us [פצו עלינו פיהם], all our enemies [כל איבינו]," which is nearly identical to 2:16. The difference is that the prior text was directed to Jerusalem (עליך, "against you") and the subsequent one is directed to Yahweh. As he has already made plain in 3:1–18, the speaker shares Jerusalem's woes, shame, and enemies. Therefore, he is an able instructor and prayer leader.

47 Now the speaker uses hunting imagery to describe the sudden, unexpected, and terrifying nature of the enemy's actions against Israel. He asserts, "Terror and pitfall [literally, a pit] come upon us" (פחד ופחת היה לנו). These nouns appear together in Isa 24:17, a judgment text against the whole earth, and in Jer 48:43, a judgment text directed against Moab. According to Renkema (439), ופחת, "pitfall," suggests a trap or pit dug for the purpose of catching and killing an animal, and פחד, "terror," usually describes human reaction to God's judgment (Exod 15:16; Isa 19:16; 33:14; Mic 7:17; Jer 49:5) or unexpected appearance (Isa 2:10, 19, 21). So the speaker uses imagery from judgment passages to describe how the people have been pursued and frightened by their enemies. These words' assonance and alliteration reinforce their connected activity and expected reaction.

Israel's terror and pitfalls include "devastation and shattering" (השאת והשבר). The first term typically depicts destruction, devastation, chaos, or death (BDB, 981). The second noun occurs in 2:11, 13; 3:48; and 4:10, all in the context of the effects of judgment (the verbal form of שבר, "shatter," appears in 1:15; 2:9; 3:4). Jerusalem's fate could hardly be worse. God has shut them out, harmed them, and turned them over to awful circumstances.

48–66 Having identified with their pain in 3:1–18, stated his confidence in God's character and advised the people on a course of action in 3:19–39, and expressed the nation's pain and dismay in 3:40–47, the speaker now prays earnestly for and with the people. While doing so he describes his personal grief at Jerusalem's predicament (vv 48–51), declares what the enemy has done (vv 52–54), confesses how Yahweh has helped him in the past (vv 55–58), and confidently asks God to see and punish the nation's foes (vv 59–66). This format thereby combines elements of individual and corporate lament and personal praise, just as the earlier portion of the chapter links individual and corporate lament elements and wisdom/instructional themes. By the end of this segment the speaker concludes that Yahweh will deal with the enemies that 3:45–47 features so prominently.

48 The speaker begins with a description of his own sorrow. Like Jerusalem in 1:16, his eyes fill with tears (see also 2:11, 18). He reports, "Streams of tears descend (from) my eyes" (פלגי מים תרד עיני) on account of the shattering (על־שבר) mentioned in the previous verse. Since Jerusalem is the one shattered here, the speaker feels a particularly personal loss, for she is the "daughter of my people" (בת עמי). This very intimate phrase also occurs in 2:11, thus providing a second strong link to that verse, as well as in 4:3, 6, and 10, connecting chap. 4 to the previous two chapters. Other daughter images include "daughter of Zion" (1:6; 2:1, 4, 8, 10, 13, 18; 4:22), "daughter of Judah" (1:15; 2:2, 5), "daughter Jerusalem" (2:13, 15), "daughters of my city" (3:51), and "daughter of Edom" (4:22 [2x]). While "daughter of Zion" and "daughter of Judah" both refer to Jerusalem, they focus on divine presence and national identity imagery, respectively. Similarly, "daughter Jerusalem" and "daughter of my people" express the speaker's close relationship to the city and its inhabitants. Thus, this familial metaphor includes personal, civic, and national aspects. While the repetition of eye imagery and the repetition of the phrase concerning the city's shattering do not prove that the same person speaks in 2:11 and 3:48, these similarities at least leave that possibility open.

49 In 3:48 the term עיני, "eyes," occurs in the exact center of a verse that begins with *pe*. Now the word begins the *ayin* section of the poem, and it will begin 3:51 as well. Once again the poet uses enjambment to connect the various parts of the poem (see 3:47–48). This time the poet's eyes and tears bring the two segments together.

Here the speaker claims, "My eyes flow and do not cease" (עיני נגרה ולא תדמה). He will accept or take no respite (מאין הפגות) until God acts (see 3:50). Taken together, 3:48–49 reads very much like Jer 14:17. The latter text includes "my eyes" (עיני) having tears without ceasing (ואל־תדמינה) over the virgin daughter Jerusalem's shattering (שבר). Both passages, then, portray an involved, interceding, determined individual praying persistently for divine help.

50 This grief will continue "until he looks out [as out of a window—BDB, 1054] and sees" (עד ישקיף וירא). Of course, the "he" is Yahweh, who dwells in heaven (יהוה משמים). The force of the verse is that the speaker will keep crying and interceding until God looks out of the windows of heaven, which are currently covered with clouds of anger (3:43–44), and sees what they are facing. Indeed, here "sees" means "acts." Given this verse, it is apparent that God has not yet answered Jerusalem's prayers in 1:9, 11, and 20.

51 This grief penetrates into the speaker's inner being. His tears are the outward expression of his inner pain. As in 3:49, the speaker opens the verse with עיני, "my eyes." This time he states that these eyes "afflict my soul" (עוללה לנפשי)

because of everything (מכל) that has happened to "the daughters of my city" (בנות עירי). The word בנות, "daughters," here "could either be a reference to the young women of Jerusalem, raped in all probability by the victorious enemy troops, and carried off into captivity, or it could be a reference to the fate that had befallen all the other towns throughout the land, towns thought of as the daughter towns of mother Jerusalem" (Davidson, 199–200). The former option would be in keeping with the deeply personal nature of this chapter and the speaker's speech in 2:11–19, while the latter option would allow for a broad national scope. Both possibilities unite concern and tragedy. While the former option seems most likely, it is important to keep the sum total of the nation's daughters in mind.

52 At this point the speaker moves in an explicitly personal direction. Westermann observes that 3:52–58 "has a structure which corresponds, line for line, to the descriptive psalms of praise or psalms of thanks" (184). He adds that "this is the psalm of an individual" (185). This personal reflection stands as evidence of what Yahweh will do for the people as a whole. If God answered him in this manner, then it is possible that the Lord will answer the nation in a similar manner. At the same time his comments allow the speaker to personify, to embody, the griefs of the whole nation (Harrison, 230).

As he does in 3:1–18, the speaker identifies with what the people have suffered. They have been hunted by their enemies (3:46–47), and likewise he reports, "They have indeed hunted me like a bird" (צוד צדוני כצפור). Who? His enemies, and that for no good reason (איבי חנם). This denunciation of enemies could easily be misunderstood. In 3:39, 42 he confuses his own sins and those of the people. Does he now recant his confession?

Provan (104) concludes that the text indicates that these enemies "were accountable for their actions, even when they were being used" by God to punish Israel and notes that this concept is applied to Assyria in Isa 10:5–19. Renkema (446) thinks the phrase "really points to the arbitrariness with which the enemy abuse both the people and the גבר [man]. The enemy makes no distinctions and is no respecter of persons." Westermann (186) adds that the reference aims at "bystanders who, without reason, are hostile to the one being persecuted." Thus, the speaker admits to being treated as badly by others as the nation itself has been and proclaims that this suffering has in some measure been excessive or added to by persons other than Babylon. If non-Babylonians are intended, then the reference to Edom in 4:20 makes more sense, as may also the prayers in 1:18–22, 2:20–22, and 3:64–66.

53 Having captured the speaker, the enemies threw him into a pit and cast stones on him. The verb translated "they threw" (צמתו) has an insidious aura. It can mean "put an end to" or "exterminate" (BDB, 856), though it also may refer "to enemies who either seek to silence the speaker or are being themselves silenced (2 Samuel 22:41; Psalms 18:42; 54:5[7]; 69:4[5]; 73:27; 88:17; 94:23[2x]; 101:5, 8; 143:12; Lamentations 3:53)" (*NIDOTTE*, 3:819). Therefore, this verse indicates that the speaker was placed in a pit for the purpose of silencing him. Of course this image reminds readers of how Joseph was treated in Gen 37 and how Jeremiah was treated in Jer 38:4–28, as well as in episodes found in Jer 11:18–12:6, 18:18, 20:1–6, 26:7–15, and 37:11–16 (see Rudolph, 243). Like Jeremiah, the speaker has suffered unjustly, perhaps even at the hands of his own people.

54 Berlin (97) points out that this cistern may be even worse than Jeremiah's or Joseph's. She writes, "But our poet's cistern is full of water and is closed at the top, making it a more dangerous place of confinement." She adds that Ps 88:6–7 shares a vocabulary similar to this verse, and Reyburn (*Handbook*, 100) notes the parallels between this passage and Jonah 2:3–5. Thus, the speaker endured what Jeremiah faced or more, and felt as lost (אמרתי נגזרתי) as Jonah in the belly of the whale. Clearly, the speaker was in dire need of help.

55 Like Jonah and Jeremiah, the speaker called out (קראתי) to the one who could deliver him. He confesses, "I called on your name, O LORD, from the depths of the pit." The phrase "depths of the pit" (מבור תחתיות) is used elsewhere to designate the lowest part of pavement (Ezek 40:18–19) or of a building (1 Kgs 6:6; BDB, 1066). Renkema (450–51) observes, "Such language is to be found in the songs of thanksgiving in the Psalms. It is precisely here that we find that YHWH drew his supplicants from the pit and thereby saved them from the power of the kingdom of death (Ps 30:2, 40:2–4; cf. Ps 18:4–20, 103:4)." In an extreme situation in the past the speaker called out to God. The fact that he does so again here testifies to his confidence in Yahweh, which he stated clearly in 3:19–39.

Scholars have offered several opinions on how to translate the perfect-tense verbs in 3:55–57. Keil (427) believes these verbs convey "the full assurance from which the request comes" and translates them as present perfect tense ("You have heard"). Provan (105–7; see also idem, *VT* 41 [1991] 164–75) argues that the verb expresses pleas in the present tense. These are not quite commands. Rather, they convey hope and earnest pleading ("Hear my plea; do not close your ear"). He thinks it is not impossible for the verses to refer back to past experiences but concludes that there is "no parallel to such a construction elsewhere in the OT" (105). Hillers ([1992] 112, 133) and Berlin (81, 97) agree with Provan's approach.

On the other hand, Renkema (451–53) disagrees with Provan. He grants the possibility that Provan suggests, but argues that 3:55–57 must be read in the context of the speaker's statements of trust earlier in the chapter. If one reads this way, Renkema argues, then one understands that in "the enormity of his [the speaker's] affliction he experiences God's fidelity" (452). Thus, he translates the verbs in the present tense ("you hear"), for this verse describes his ongoing, not desired, relationship with the Lord.

This commentary translates the verbs in the past tense, which Westermann (164, 186–87) also does. The section relates that the speaker faced horrible circumstances in the past. He was hunted, trapped, virtually entombed—in other words, all but killed during a time when many people were killed. But God delivered him, just as God delivered Jeremiah, Jonah, and many psalmists. This fact helps him hope that God will punish those who, though hardly pure themselves, punished him and his people (3:64–66). He is still "here," still alive, and that in itself proves that God's current kindness builds on God's past mercy, however severe that mercy may have been.

56 When the speaker called on the Lord, his God heard (שמעה) his voice (קולי). Indeed, the speaker confesses, "you did not close [אל תעלם] your ear [אזנך] to my relief, to my help [לרוחתי לשועתי]." Though there is no governing verb in 3:56b, the assumed verb is "call," which begins 3:55. God did not shut his ears at that time, so it is likely that he will look (3:50) through the veiling cloud (3:43–44) and respond now.

57 Furthermore, the speaker continues, "You came near on the day I called out to you" (קרבת ביום אקראך). As Harrison (230) writes, this "verse furnishes a characteristic response of a God who answers his faithful children while they are actually supplicating Him (cf. Is. 58:9; 65:24)." It is also a characteristic response when unfaithful people return to the Lord (see Deut 30:1–10; Jonah 2:1–10). God hears and forgives.

Not only did God hear; the Lord also declared, "Do not fear" (אמרת אל תירא). Kraus (67) notes that such divine declarations of comfort were a feature of both Israelite and Akkadian psalms. אל תירא, "do not fear," also appears in Jer 1:8, where God reassures Jeremiah in the prophet's "call experience." God comforts the fearful and the hurting, and he did so for the speaker.

58 But God did not "merely" speak heartening words to the one in danger. Rather, he took up the speaker's cause. Stated more literally, "You argued, O Lord, the (legal) arguments of my soul" (רבת אדני ריבי נפשי). In effect, God became the speaker's "lawyer" (see Davidson, 202), for the root of "argued" and "arguments" is ריב, a common word for contention, dispute, or legal action (see *NIDOTTE*, 3:1105–6). Renkema (456) observes that the Lord intervened when the speaker faced an unjust and dangerous enemy.

Having become the speaker's defender, however, the Lord did even more. He became the "redeemer" of the speaker's life (גאלת חיי), a concept also "found in Leviticus 25:25ff., 47–54; Ruth 4:1–12" (Ash, 359). This term refers here to God's intervention on the speaker's behalf, to his liberation from his enemies (see *TLOT*, 1:288–96). In this case the speaker was given his life, which according to Jer 45:1–5 was a precious reward in the dangerous days surrounding the Babylonian invasion.

59 Now the speaker begins (see Westermann, 187) his closing "argument" as a prelude to his request that God punish his enemies (3:64–66). He asserts, "You have seen, O LORD, the wrong done to me" (ראיתה יהוה עותתי). The speaker claims that the Lord has done for him what Jerusalem asked him to do for her in 1:9, 11, and 20: God has seen what the speaker endured.

Based on what God has seen, the speaker asks, "Please judge my cause/case" (שפטה משפטי). This imperative clause is the first indication that the speaker desires God to judge the oppressors. He wants God's justice to replace that of his foes (Renkema, 458). Only when God grants this request will relief truly come.

60 For the second verse in a row the speaker states, "You have seen" (ראיתה). This time God has seen "all their vengeance" (כל נקמתם) and "all their plots" (כל מחשבתם) against the speaker. Taken together, these terms do not mean "the outcome of revenge, but the thought of revenge cherished in the heart; it does not, however, mean desire of revenge, or revengeful disposition, but simply the thinking and meditating on revenge" (Keil, 427–28). God knows when the enemies plot and when they act out their plans. He has seen and must surely act.

61 Yahweh has also heard the enemy's taunts (שמעת חרפתם יהוה). The speaker mentions receiving taunts patiently in 3:30, and such taunting is a regular feature in psalms of lament (see Pss 69:10 [ET 69:9]; 79:4; see Provan, 108; Berlin, 97). Similar phraseology also occurs in Jer 11:18–20 and 20:11–12, two of the prophet's confessions. He had endured such taunts before, yet he calls on God to react to those mockings now. Thus, he is like Jeremiah, who prayed for the people yet discovered their animosity against him, and like the psalmists, who trust God—and ask God—to deal with enemies in due time. As in 3:60b, this verse ends with a reference to their plots. Vv 59 and 60 begin with the same word, while vv 60 and 61 conclude with a nearly identical phrase. This interlocking technique in 3:60–61 links the contents of lines that begin with different letters of the alphabet.

62 The secrecy motif begun in 3:60 continues. Enemies have plotted, according to 3:60–61. Here their lips שפתי, "mutter, whisper, or murmur." In other words they gossip or speak quietly, yet malevolently, about the speaker (see Reyburn, *Handbook,* 103), and they do so "all the day" (כל היום). Presumably God has heard these whispers as clearly as he heard the taunts in 3:61.

63 Finally, the speaker asks the Lord to observe closely (הביטה—see 1:11, 12; 2:20; 4:16; 5:1) that in his enemies' sitting and rising (שבתם וקימתם) he is the subject of their mocking songs (מנגינתם). This imperative begins the speaker's process of asking God to do specific things to his (and the people's) enemies. A form of "mocking song" occurs in 3:14, where the speaker states that he has been a mocking song to his own people. The enemies included in this prayer may well include foreign countries such as Edom and citizens of Judah, not just Babylonians. Regardless, the speaker wants God to deal with them.

64 According to the speaker, God has seen (3:59–60) and heard (3:61) what has transpired. He has used an imperative to ask God to observe that the enemies' taunts focus on the speaker (3:63). Now four imperfects conclude the prayer (3:64–66). Provan (108) writes, "The verbs of these final three verses of the chapter are all imperfects, either expressing confidence that God will eventually deal with the enemies (RSV) or, more probably, continuing the pattern of vv. 56–61, asking that he would do so (JB, NEB, NIV)." Gottwald (*Studies,* 15) follows the first option, Hillers ([1992] 112) and Berlin (81) follow the second, Westermann (164) mixes the two possibilities, and Rudolph (236–37) opts for the past tense. Either the future or imperatival option suits the context, for the speaker believes God will act because God has acted in the past. He urges God to do so now by using a clear imperative in 3:63 and confident implied imperatives in 3:64–66.

What the speaker wants is for God to "return to/requite them fully/in full measure [תשיב להם גמול] . . . according to the work of their hands [כמעשה ידיהם]." He wants God's justice for the enemies, having accepted God's justice for Israel already. As Hillers ([1992] 133) writes, "Even when Israel was conscious of her own rebellion against God, as in this poem (vv. 39–42), and acknowledged the justice of such punishment as was meted out to her, this guilt never meant to her that her enemies were justified in the atrocities they committed. On the contrary, belief in divine justice meant that Yahweh should deal just as strictly with the nations as he did with Israel." At this point the speaker agrees with Jerusalem's plea in 1:22 and the narrator's sentiments in 4:22. Israel's enemies must be judged not only because of divine justice but also because of the very practical fact that Israel can only gain relief when enemies from far (Babylon) and near (Edom) face severe troubles of their own.

65 Continuing his conclusion, the speaker asks, "Give to them dullness of heart" (תתן להם מגנת לב), which the speaker considers God's "curse, oath, or execration" (BDB, 46) "upon them" (תאלתך להם). Without question, God's "curse" on Israel was experiencing the covenant consequences for disobedience outlined in Lev 26 and Deut 27–28 and described in gruesome detail in Lam 1, 2, and 4. The "curse, oath, or execration" for the enemies is a covering of some sort (BDB, 171) over their hearts. Kraus (68) suggests that the text indicates the sort of blindness the Sodomites experienced in Gen 19:11 or the Syrians encountered in 2 Kgs 6:18, or the hardness of heart God tells Isaiah to expect in Isa 6:8–10. Though it is impossible to say for certain, these suggestions are certainly in keeping with the verse's tone. It may well be that "dullness of heart" itself is the "curse." After all, such dullness keeps them from responding positively to any divine overture.

66 This verse begins with two words whose roots echo several earlier texts. The first (תרדף, "pursue") occurs in some form in 1:3, 6; 3:43; 4:19; and 5:5. Each of those verses describes foes pursuing Israel, so this passage requests a reversal of those events. The second word (באף, "in wrath") or some variation of it appears in 1:12 and 2:1, 3, 6, 11, and 22 in contexts that refer to the day of the Lord. Of course, in 3:43 both words are used to describe how God pursued Israel. Now the speaker wants Yahweh to pursue in wrath as Israel was pursued in wrath and thus "destroy them" (ותשמידם) from the face of the earth, "from under the heavens, O LORD" (following the LXX—see *Note* 66.b.).

The speaker concludes with a strong statement against the foes that is based on a firm belief in God's justice (see Berlin, 97–98). O'Connor ([2001] 1057) considers this ending enigmatic, for the speaker moves toward hope yet does so in a way that is "inexplicable, unbidden, that arises without theological resolution. The status of this hope, therefore, will always be controversial." Renkema (473), on the other hand, concludes that the speaker's turn from despair lies in "praying with hope and trust to YHWH whose divine name is the final word." This turning emerges from the reflection on God's nature found in 3:19ff. The speaker's attitude changes as the chapter unfolds, as he reflects on what has happened and on the Lord's "mercy," "faithfulness," and "heart" (motives). His usage of praise within lament flows from confidence in God. His statements allow the poem to stand as personal and corporate lament yet also allow it to operate as a statement of hope for those who agree with the speaker's definition of what is "good" (see 3:25–27). In this book hope can only emerge from pain if it is to emerge at all. No other trajectory is possible.

Explanation

Several commentators consider Lam 3 the theological heart of the book (see Westermann, 66–76, for a survey of opinions). This decision is appropriate in many ways, for this chapter sets forth the book's clearest expression of God's character and attitude toward the suffering nation. This chapter also provides the nation its most extensive instruction on how to relate to the Lord at this point in its history. How the people respond to this information may well determine the speed with which they restore their covenantal bond with their God, which will in turn determine how quickly they receive relief from their foes. At the same time, this chapter continues to express the pain the nation feels. The speaker is a participant in the nation's woes. He has endured what they have endured, seen what they have seen, questioned what they have questioned. Therefore, his observations, exhortations, and prayers are authentic and relevant for the original reader and to each successive generation of readers.

As the preceding paragraph indicates, this commentary interprets the chapter as having one speaker. This speaker agrees substantially with the others in the book. Indeed, his agreement with the speaker in 2:11–19 is so significant that that he may be the same speaker or one heavily influenced by that prophetically oriented speaker's thought (see above). At the same time, the speaker includes wisdom themes not found in chap. 2. He stresses the nature of suffering, the character of God, the way to think through the implications of suffering in relation to God's character, and the way to pray after the suffering has been mentally, spiritually, physically, and emotionally "digested."

The chapter unfolds in four parts. First, in vv 1–24 the speaker describes the pain he has endured as one of the suffering people of God and asserts what he has learned about the Lord. This description and the commentary qualify him as someone who has the experience necessary to instruct the rest of the people about what he has learned. Second, in vv 25–39 the speaker states what it is "good" to do in the present circumstances. Third, in vv 40–47 the speaker leads the people in a prayer of confession of sin and description of what their enemies have done. This type of prayer appears several times in Psalms. Fourth, in vv 48–66 the speaker concludes the chapter with a personal prayer of confidence in the Lord. Such prayers are common in Psalms. What is unique about this chapter is the way the acrostic form gathers together various types of poems to forge them into a coherent whole that expresses pain, the nature of God, the way forward for the whole people, and personal confidence in Yahweh. This breadth of poetic expression offers a full-orbed approach to the problems the book addresses, for it allows readers who have sinned to state pain yet also to find a way to renew relationship with the Lord.

This chapter moves from personal pain to personal faith, then to instruction for many, and finally to a prayer for full deliverance. The speaker is not schizophrenic or inconsistent. He does suffer, as several verses make clear, but he thinks clearly at a resting point from that suffering. He trusts God's bedrock character and counsels others to do the same. Of course, some contemporary theologians may think it odd for him to trust the very person that punished him, but the speaker seems to place blame where it belongs—on the people, including himself, rather than on God. At the same time, he truly desires deliverance. To the extent that what he thinks about God is true he has real hope for the future. As he trusts the Lord he finds a renewed relationship with God, and his firm conviction is that the nation as a whole will find the same thing to be true. They can learn what he has learned and come back to the Lord.

How the Gold Has Tarnished! (4:1–22)

Bibliography

Buchanan, A. "The Role of Protest in Lamentations." Th.M. thesis, Australian College of Theology, Kensington, 2001. **Cohen, A.** "Lamentations 4:9." *AJSL* 27 (1910–11) 190–91. **Driver, G. R.** "Hebrew Notes on 'Song of Songs' and 'Lamentations.'" In *Festschrift Alfred Bertholet*. Ed. Walter Baumgartner et al. Tübingen: Mohr (Siebeck), 1950. 134–46. **Emerton, J. A.** "The Meaning of *'abnē qōdeš* in Lamentations 4:1." *ZAW* 79 (1967) 233–36. **Ferris, P. W., Jr.** *Genre of Communal Lament*. **Fries, S. A.** "Parallelen zwischen den Klageliedern Cap. IV, V und der Makkabaerzeit." *ZAW* 13 (1893) 110–24. **Gottlieb, H.** *Study on the Text of Lamentations*. **Gous, I.** "Mind over Matter: Lamentations 4 in the Light of the Cognitive Sciences." *SJOT* 10 (1996) 69–87. **Guillaume, A.** "A Note on Lamentations IV 9." *ALUOS* 4 (1962–63) 47–48. **Heim, K. M.** "The Personification of Jerusalem and the Drama of Her Bereavement in Lamentations." In *Zion, City of Our God*. Ed. R. S. Hess and G. J. Wenham. Grand Rapids, MI: Eerdmans, 1999. 129–69. **Jahnow, H.** *Hebräische Leichenlied*. **Kaiser, W. C., Jr.** *Biblical Approach to Suffering*. **Linafeldt, T.** *Surviving Lamentations*. **Löhr, M.** "Sind Thr. IV und V makkabäisch?" *ZAW* 14 (1894) 51–59. **Miller, C. W.** "Poetry and Personae: The Use and Function of the Changing Speaking Voices in the Book of Lamentations." Ph.D. diss. Iliff School of Theology and University of Denver, 1996. **O'Connor, K. M.** *Lamentations and the Tears of the World*. **Rudolph, W.** "Der Text der Klagelieder." *ZAW* 56 (1938) 101–22.

Translation

א	1	How the gold has tarnished!	(3+3)
		How changed ª the pure ᵇ gold!	
		The sacred stones are scattered	(3+3)
		at the head of every street.	
ב	2	The precious sons of Zion,	(3+2)
		worth their weight in fine gold,	
		how they are counted as earthen pots,	(4+3)
		the work of a potter's hands!	
ג	3	Even the jackals ª extend a breast;	(4+2)
		they nurse their young.	
		The daughter ᵇ of my people has become cruel,	(3+3)
		like the ostriches in the desert.	
ד	4	The nursing one's tongue cleaves	(3+3)
		to the roof of his mouth because of thirst.	
		The little ones ask for bread;	(3+3)
		there is no one breaking it for them.	
ה	5	Those feasting on delicacies	(2+2)
		are desolate in the streets.	
		Those brought up wearing crimson	(3+2)
		embrace ash heaps.	
ו	6	The iniquity of the daughter of my people has been greater	(4+2)
		than the sin of Sodom,	

		the one overthrown in an instant,	(3+4)
		without a hand laid on it.	
ז	7	Her Nazirites were purer than snow;	(3+2)
		they were whiter than milk.	
		Their bodies ᵃ were ruddier than coral,	(3+2)
		their form like sapphire.	
ח	8	Their appearance is blacker than soot;	(3+3)
		they are not recognized in the streets.	
		Their skin has shriveled on their bones;	(4+3)
		it has become as dry as wood.	
ט	9	It was better for those who were pierced (by) a sword	(4+2)
		than for those who were pierced (by) famine,	
		ᵃthose whose (life) flows away from being pierced through	(3+2)
		from lack of the fruit of the field.ᵃ	
י	10	The hands of compassionate women	(3+2)
		have boiled their own children.	
		They have become their food	(3+3)
		during the shattering of (the) daughter of my people.	
כ	11	The LORD completed his anger;	(3+3)
		he poured out his burning wrath.	
		He kindled a fire in Zion,	(3+2)
		and it has consumed her foundations.	
ל	12	The kings of the earth did not believe,	(4+3)
		nor all ᵃ the inhabitants of the world,	
		that foe or enemy could enter	(4+2)
		the gates of Jerusalem.	
מ	13	Because of (the) sins of her prophets,	(2+2)
		(the) iniquities of her priests,	
		the ones casting down in her midst,	(2+2)
		(the) blood of (the) righteous,	
נ	14	they wandered blind ᵃ in the streets;	(3+2)
		they were defiled by the blood	
		so no one could touch	(3+1)
		their garments.	
ס	15	"Turn aside! Unclean!" ᵃthey called to them.ᵃ	(4+4)
		"Turn aside! Turn aside! Do not touch!"	
		For they were ruined, so they wandered.	(4+2+3)
		Those among the nations said,	
		"They shall no longer sojourn (with us)."	
פ	16 ᵃ	The face of the LORD has scattered them;	(3+3)
		he no longer shows regard for them.	
		The face of the priests they did not honor;	(4+3)
		to the elders they did not show favor.	
ע	17	Our eyes were ever looking	(3+3)
		to our empty help.	
		In our watching we watched	(2+4)
		for a nation that did not save.	

Notes

צ	18	They hunted our steps	(2+2)
		so that we could not walk in our open places.	
		Our end drew near,	(2+2+3)
		our days were fulfilled;	
		thus our end came.	
ק	19	Swifter were our pursuers	(3+2)
		than (the) eagles (in the) heavens.	
		They chased us in the mountains;	(3+3)
		they lay in wait for us in the desert.	
ר	20	The breath of our nostrils, the anointed of the LORD,	(4+2)
		was captured in their pits—	
		the one of whom we said,	(2+3)
		"In his shade, we will rest among the nations."	
ש	21	Rejoice and be glad, O daughter of Edom,	(4+3)
		O dweller ᵃ in the land of Uz.ᵇ	
		Even to you (the) cup ᶜ shall pass;	(4+2)
		you shall become drunk and strip yourself naked.	
ת	22	The punishment for your iniquity is completed, O daughter of Zion;	(4+3)
		he will no longer keep you in exile.	
		He will visit your iniquity, O daughter of Edom;	(4+3)
		he will uncover your sins.	

Notes

1.a. ישנא comes from שנה, "change" (see GKC §77d; BDB, 1039). Hillers ([1992] 137) emends to שנא, "hated," because he believes that MT "does not yield satisfactory sense."

1.b. LXX reads τὸ ἀργύριον (= הכסף, "silver"). Albrektson (*Studies in the Text and Theology*, 173) argues that since Job 31:24 has the same parallel phrasing, it is likely that the translator stressed variety over strict accuracy here. See 4:6.

3.a. LXX "confused MT's תנין, which is of course plural of תן 'jackal,' with תנים 'dragon, sea-monster'"—a mistake it also makes in Mic 1:8 and Jer 9:10 (Albrektson, *Studies in the Text and Theology*, 174).

3.b. LXX reads θυγατέρες (= בנות, "daughters"). Gottlieb (*Study on the Text*, 61), Albrektson (*Studies in the Text and Theology*, 175–76), and Hillers ([1992] 139) consider this reading either a conscious or unconscious error based on the translator's view of the context.

7.a. LXX omits עצם, "bones." Syr. reads "bone," not "body," which Albrektson (*Studies in the Text and Theology*, 181) considers unwarranted. Driver ("Hebrew Notes," 140) suggests that the מ has been transposed. Thus, he offers the reading "they were more ruddy than the bone of (red) corals." This suggestion hardly improves the sense of the verse. The phrase is difficult in MT (see Gottlieb, *Study on the Text*, 62–64) yet understandable.

9.a-a. This half-verse is universally recognized as very difficult (see Driver, "Hebrew Notes," 140–41; Albrektson, *Studies in the Text and Theology*, 183–84; Renkema, 517–18). Gottlieb (*Study on the Text*, 64) correctly concludes that an extended "piercing" metaphor unfolds here, which partly explains the unusual language.

12.a. The Qere and LXX read כל, "all," instead of וכל, "and all." No significant change in meaning results.

14.a. LXX reads ἐγρήγοροι αὐτῆς (= עריה, "her watchmen"). Driver ("Hebrew Notes," 141) suggests עֲרֻמִּים or עָרֹם, "naked." Gottlieb (*Study on the Text*, 65) notes that the blind prophet is a common motif (Mic 3:6–7).

15.a-a. LXX reads קרא, "call," as an imperative. Several commentators delete the phrase as a gloss due to metrical considerations, but no MS evidence supports the phrase's deletion (see Gottlieb, *Study on the Text*, 66).

16.a. Some Heb. MSS and LXX transpose vv 16–17 to maintain the פ-ע alphabet sequence.

21.a. The Qere drops the final *yod* from this word.

21.b. LXX and Vg. omit עוץ, "Uz" (see Albrektson, *Studies in the Text and Theology*, 194).
21.c. LXX reads τὸ ποτήριον κυρίου, "the cup of the Lord." Syr. and other versions agree with MT.

Form/Structure/Setting

One might think Lam 4 an anticlimactic poem after the theological intensity of chap. 3. The text returns to statements about Jerusalem's losses, her children's agony, and how the Lord has punished a sinful people. K. M. O'Connor thinks that this chapter "conveys a sense of exhaustion and remoteness, as if the strong man [the speaker in chap. 3] had brought sorrow and fury as far as they could go" ([2001] 1059). Dobbs-Alsopp concludes that the text offers a very matter-of-fact description of suffering that uses this "normality" to highlight its horrible nature (129). These comments about tone and poetic strategy are accurate to a point, but one should note that this fourth poem continues the book's movement toward the renewal of the relationship between God and Israel. This movement began in chaps. 1 and 2, then intensified in chap. 3. Chap. 4 furthers this process by continuing to stress the causes of the suffering and the shared nature of that suffering, but also by announcing the end of the people's exile and judgment. This chapter builds on chap. 3 by indicating that the people's prayers have been heard, their punishment has ended, and their enemies will be punished. This statement of release from divine judgment hardly solves all of Jerusalem's problems. Great suffering still afflicts the populace. They do not know how long the current pain will last before the new situation causes it to ebb, then cease altogether.

Chap. 4 is similar in form and content to chaps. 1 and 2 (see the Introduction and also the *Form/Structure/Setting* sections on those chapters). All three chapters begin with the plaintive "How!" Each poem describes Jerusalem's woes in great detail, and each chapter utilizes first- and third-person points of view. But the three chapters differ in their acrostic form. Chaps. 1 and 2 consist of three-line verses in which the first word of each verse begins with the succeeding letter of the alphabet. Chap. 4, on the other hand, consists of two-line verses in which the first word of each verse begins with the succeeding letter of the alphabet. Like chap. 2, it follows the sequence of *pe* then *ayin*, which distinguishes chap. 2 and chap. 4 from chap. 1. Chap. 4 is shorter by one-third than chaps. 1 and 2, yet it is crafted in a way that reminds readers more of the first two chapters than of chap. 3.

Shea notes that the first three chapters consist of sixty-six lines, chap. 4 consists of forty-four lines, and chap. 5 consists of twenty-two lines. He then concludes that this pattern indicates that the book itself "dies away" just as the book's *qinah* meter does (*Bib* 60 [1979] 103–7). The number of lines does become fewer, but the book does not die out thematically. Chap. 4 offers an excellent summary of the book's theology, while chap. 5 offers a strong concluding prayer.

Like all the poems in Lamentations, chap. 4 mixes lament and dirge elements. It also mixes individual and community traits. Westermann argues that vv 1–10 represent a community's complaint, vv 11–13 constitute an accusation against God, vv 17–20 amount to a report of the king's capture, and vv 21–22 offer a prayer of retribution against Edom (197–99). Ferris (*Genre of Communal Lament*, 103) concludes that such mixing of forms makes it impossible to assign this text to any particular genre. As in earlier chapters, certain aspects of dirges appear, such as the cry of "How!" and detailed descriptions of suffering within the afflicted city. But as was true in the first three poems, the city does not die, though it is certainly devastated. Therefore, the mixing of related forms here under the umbrella of the acrostic format allows the poem to be thorough in its depictions of woe and thereby stunning in its concluding pronouncement of the end of divine punishment. It continues the book's emphasis on detailing the people's excruciating pain, while at the same time highlighting their sin and the path they are walking to a renewed relationship with God. In this chapter this thoroughness includes an absolute statement about the end of the city's punishment.

As a lament/prayer, then, this poem gives the people the chance to express hope. At the same time, this hope is embryonic. A fully restored relationship with God has hardly occurred at this point. Still, description, confession, intercession, and supplication have had an effect on the people. They move a small step closer to renewal.

As in the first two chapters, the fourth poem's structure unfolds as shifts in speakers occur. As Miller's excellent survey indicates, scholars have offered a variety of approaches to the voices in Lam 4 ("Poetry and Personae," 181–86). He correctly concludes that first-person singular references to "my people" occur in 4:3, 6, and 10 and that first-person plural references to various elements of "our" suffering appear in 4:17–20. Otherwise, third-person speech occurs, with the speaker commenting about Jerusalem in indirect speech ("she," "her") in every instance except 4:22, where he addresses Jerusalem directly ("your"), noting that her punishment is completed.

One must try to determine who is speaking in each instance. Miller argues that Jerusalem is the source of all the first-person speeches in 4:1–16. He further asserts that the same narrator as in chaps. 1 and 2 issues the third-person speeches in 4:1–16, and claims that the nation's leaders speak in 4:17–22 ("Poetry and Personae," 186). Heim concludes that a single member of the community speaks in 4:1–16, that the "citizens of Jerusalem as a group express their recognition that no one could save them from their doom" in 4:17–20, and that a person distinct from the community (probably the narrator) speaks in 4:21–22 ("Personification of Jerusalem," 164–65). The list of options could be extended, but the point is clear: there is no consensus on the identity and number of speakers in the chapter.

It is necessary to come to a decision in order to follow the poem's flow of thought. The following conclusions will be used in the commentary that follows. Virtually every scholar who addresses this problem writes that 4:1–10 is basically third-person narration with first-person comments (see above). It has the same basic characteristics of the first-person speech in chap. 3. The section has the same concern with Jerusalem's children as does 2:11–19 and includes the term "my people." A member of the community speaks in both passages. It is likely that the same person, whom the commentary identified in chap. 2 as a prophetic voice, speaks in both instances. Similarly, 4:11–16 shares the same viewpoint on Jerusalem's woes and the cause of them as do 1:1–11 and 2:1–10, both of which are texts that voice a third-person narrator's point of view. This voice does not necessarily come from the community, for it is more distant, more matter of fact than the others in the book. It makes sense to identify 4:11–16 with the narrator from earlier chapters. It is harder to determine the speaker in 4:17–20, but the tone, contents, and use of "our" links it to 3:40–47, where the "man" leads the people in prayer, or simply exhorts them to pray. As in 3:40–47, the speaker identifies fully with the inhabitants of Jerusalem. Therefore, 2:11–19, 3:1–66, and 4:1–10 share the same point of view and very similar terminology. It is a valid option, then, to assign these sections to the same first-person speaker. The speaker in 4:21–22 addresses Edom and Jerusalem directly in a manner similar to the way Jerusalem was addressed in 2:11–19. Yet the speech also exhibits some of the same detached characteristics of the narrator passages. It seems that the speaker from 2:11–19, 3:40–47, and 4:1–10 may also speak here. The prophetic voice is the one that delivers the news that God will punish Edom and that Jerusalem's punishment has ended. The next best option is to conclude that a new, authoritative voice offers this information. Perhaps the most interesting fact about the voices in this chapter is that Jerusalem herself never speaks.

Having offered tentative conclusions about the speakers' identities, how do their speeches dictate the chapter's structure? Overall, the chapter moves from comments that reflect the book's earliest statements about Jerusalem's plight to its more recent comments on Jerusalem's movement back to God. The chapter moves from descriptions of woe to an assertion of release from judgment. In the first speech (vv 1–10) a voice from the community details the horrors Jerusalem has faced and continues to face. In the second speech (vv 11–16) the narrator adds his depiction of the terrors Jerusalem has experienced because of her sin. In the third speech (vv 17–20) a speaker from the community describes the fall of the city, which included the capture of the monarch. In the fourth and final speech (vv 21–22) a prophetic voice pronounces woe on Edom and relief for Jerusalem. The most comforting aspect of this sequence is the final speech. Jerusalem has been waiting since the first verse in Lamentations for the news that God has finished punishing.

This poem's setting has already been discussed in the Introduction, as well as in the *Form/Structure/Setting* segments of the other chapters. That material will not be repeated in full here. Only selected comments will be made.

The setting in chap. 4 has usually been treated alongside that of chaps. 1 and 2. This tendency may be traced to the similarities between the three chapters (see the discussion of form above). Whatever decision scholars make about the setting of one of these poems normally determines what that expert thinks about all three. There are exceptions to this generality. Rudolph (209–11) treats chap. 1 as referring to the problems Judah experienced in 597 B.C.E. but considers chaps. 2 and 4 to be depictions of the 587 B.C.E. debacle (221; 250). Nonetheless, the general principle holds true.

Most scholars date the three poems within a reasonably short time after the beginning of the exile. At the very least, they consider the poems products of some time between 587 and 520 B.C.E., and that is the position taken in this commentary. There are exceptions to this generalization. Fries argues that chap. 4 should be dated in the Maccabean era because of linguistic parallels between Lamentations and Maccabees. Also, he draws this conclusion because the events described are so comprehensive that they appear to have been reflected upon for a long period of time (*ZAW* 13 [1893] 110–24). O. Kaiser (106–10, 174–80) claims that chap. 4 expresses assurance about the end of judgment in a way that links it with postexilic literature. He determines that the poem fits best with

Malachi's era (ca. 450 B.C.E.). The problem with Kaiser's hypothesis is that the poem continues the book's descriptions of the aftermath of Jerusalem's destruction. The knowledge that judgment has ceased is new. The city has not yet begun to recover. The temple is not rebuilt, and the woes depicted are not like those mentioned in Malachi. There is a lack of food in both books, but the situation is much worse in chap. 4 than in Malachi. Similar arguments can be made against Fries's conclusion.

Though a date relatively soon after the destruction is the best option, it is evident that some time has passed between the destruction and chap. 4. The suffering of Jerusalem's children is portrayed as an ongoing problem, and the chapter presents the people's plight as close enough in time to be quite fresh in their minds, yet long enough ago that they are told what they had hoped to hear in earlier chapters: God's punishment has ended. In other words, a date between 587 and 520 B.C.E. makes sense of the shorter and longer aspects of time found in the poem.

Like chaps. 1–3, then, chap. 4 describes a people plagued with the disasters associated with their capital city's devastation. The city is not dead, but it is horribly wounded, terribly disfigured. Its people must return to the Lord if they are to gain relief, and they know that Yahweh is their only source of hope. In the ashes of the city in the years after the ultimate Babylonian invasion, this poem helped the people express their pain, explore the source of their pain, and learn that the door to a new relationship with Yahweh may well have swung open, or at least cracked open a bit.

Comment

Lam 4 is composed of four speeches that move the text from description of woe to pronouncement of the end of divine punishment. This pronouncement comes at the end of the poem, so giving voice to pain remains the heart of the chapter. As in chaps. 1 and 2, every speaker in chap. 4 agrees that the pain has been and still is horrible, that Israel's sin caused the pain, that the pain is sufficient punishment for the sin, and that relief is needed. Every speaker agrees that the Lord has sent this woe and that only the Lord can end it. Thus, chap. 4 continues the book's movement toward reconciliation between Israel and God by stressing personal and corporate lament that proceeds slowly, yet purposefully, from confession to insistent petition to initial resolution.

1–10 This section returns to the theme that marked 1:12–16 and 3:1–18—the suffering of Jerusalem's inhabitants—and to the theme that was so prominent in 2:11–22—the suffering of Jerusalem's children. These children have been scattered like the very stones of the destroyed temple (4:1–2). They are starving because of their parents' sins (4:3–6). Their older counterparts have been so disfigured by lack of food that the speaker concludes that those who died by the sword fared better than those who survived the invasion (4:7–10). These images are set in the context of divine judgment. This time the text compares what has happened to Jerusalem unfavorably with what happened to Sodom (4:6). It is hard to imagine a more telling comparison than one that ties the elect people to the most sinful city in the book of Genesis, a place that harbored fewer than ten righteous people (Gen 18:22–33).

1–2 These verses contain two exclamations of "how!" (איכה) terrible things have become for the chosen nation. The book focuses on the inhabitants, with special reference to the children. These precious persons fall dying in the streets like the stones of the temple that tumbled under their own weight.

1 Chap. 1 begins with an exclamation of "how!" the city sits alone, and chap. 2 begins with an exclamation of "how!" the Lord has punished in his wrath. Chap. 4 uses the exclamation to begin a comparison between the destruction of the temple and the dying of Jerusalem's inhabitants. Here what amazes and moves the speaker is how "the gold has tarnished" (יועם זהב), or "has grown dim." Of course, technically speaking, gold does not tarnish, as Hillers points out ([1992] 137). Berlin may be right when she claims that the gold has grown dim in color because of being covered in dirt. The gold has not gone dark on its own; rather, it has dimmed because of how it has been treated (104). This ill treatment, which is described in the rest of the chapter, explains why the "pure/good gold has changed" (ישנא הכתם הטוב) in its appearance (see *Note* 1.b. for a defense of this translation).

Having used the image of precious gold, the speaker now states, "The sacred stones are scattered at the head of every street." The subject of the sentence, אבני־קדש, "sacred/holy stones," may derive from any one of several backgrounds. Emerton notes that experts have suggested that the term refers to temple treasures, jewels on the high priest's garments, amulets, or, as Emerton believes, "precious stones" (*ZAW* 79 [1967] 233–36). Renkema (494–95) disagrees because he believes that the "holy stones" refer to the temple itself. In other words, he thinks that the chapter begins with a description of the destruction of the temple, so subsequent images of human beings are to be compared to the temple's demolition.

While it may well be that the throwing down of the temple is the source of the comparison for the throwing down of the people, the people, not the temple, are the focal point here. As in 2:19, they suffer "at the head of every street" (בראש כל־חוצות). Also, 4:5, 8, and 14 contain references about the people's suffering "in the streets." So it seems likely that the precious stones are the people themselves, a conclusion that in no way diminishes the significance of the temple's destruction.

2 The comparison between the people and precious stones continues in 4:2. This time the speaker focuses clearly on "the precious sons of Zion" (בני ציון היקרים). They are so precious that they are "worth their weight in fine gold" (המסלאים בפז), or more literally "being weighed against gold" (BDB, 698). This phrase combines a *puʿal* participle with a noun for purest gold (BDB, 808), so it is linguistically rare itself. Despite their value, however, the speaker exclaims "how!" they are treated as if they are merely earthenware pots, the "work of a potter's hands" (מעשה ידי יוצר). Rather than receiving special treatment befitting their status as God's people, they endure rough and careless handling. No wonder the gold has grown darkened by filth.

3–6 Two very harsh comparisons frame this section. Jerusalem has become harder of heart than jackals (4:3) and punished more severely than Sodom (4:6). These images surround others that emphasize death and starvation. The first two instances of "my people" underscore the personal nature of the devastation (see 3:48–51).

3 Jerusalem's mothers have grown less maternal than a jackal. After all, "Even the jackals extend a breast" (גם־תנין חלצו שד), but the "daughter of my people has become cruel" (בת־עמי לאכזר). This cruelty is highlighted by the use of the emphatic *lamed* on the adjective (Hillers, [1992] 139). In fact, the daughter has become "like the ostriches in the desert" (כיענים במדבר), an animal Job 39:13–17 depicts as abandoning its eggs (see Berlin, 106). The word translated "jackals" could also possibly mean "sea monsters," but most commentators and the Qere take the former option (see *Note* 3.a.). Either reading brings to mind judgment passages, for jackals populate desolate punished cities (Provan, 112; see Jer 9:10 [ET 9:11]), and sea monsters figure in several metaphorically oriented judgment texts (Renkema, 499–501; see, e.g., Isa 13:22, 34:13). The daughters of Jerusalem share ruins with the jackals, and only the jackals have enough energy and nourishment to offer the breast to their young. Compassion ends when strength fails.

4 As a result of their mothers' lack of compassion brought on by lack of power, the "nursing one" (יונק), whom 2:11 depicts as crying out for food and fainting in the streets, has its tongue cleave to the roof of its mouth "because of thirst" (בצמא). Berlin observes that the image of the tongue cleaving to the mouth occurs in Ezek 3:26, Job 29:10, and Ps 137:6, all texts that portray individuals as unable to make a sound. These "infants are so weak from starvation that they no longer cry when hungry" (Berlin, 106). As in 2:12, the "little ones" (עוללים), those old enough to articulate words, beg for bread, but their mothers have nothing to give them. There is no one to break bread (פרש, literally "spread out"; see 1:10, 13) for them.

5 Prominent adults share the children's plight. These individuals were not dependent on their mothers' breasts for food. Rather, they once ate rare and royal foods (למעדנים; see BDB, 726; see Gen 49:20). Now they are "desolate in the streets" (שמו בחוצות), a phrase that combines the desolation metaphors found in 1:4, 13, 16; 3:11; and 5:18 with street metaphors found in 1:20 and 2:11, 19, 21, as well as in later passages in this chapter (4:8, 14). They die the same way that the infants do. Starvation claims victims of all ages and classes. It is truly no respecter of persons. These adults were once rich, for they were "brought up wearing crimson" (האמנים עלי תולע; see Gen 38:28; Josh 2:21; Isa 1:18). They wore expensive clothing fashioned by the best dyeing processes (see *NIDOTTE*, 5:300–301). Now they "embrace ash/dung heaps" (חבקו אשפתות), a phrase that encompasses all the ways that one can attempt to live among garbage. God raises the needy from such places (1 Sam 2:8; Ps 113:7), yet drives the wicked from places of prominence to places where they scavenge among the refuse of society. It is hard to conceive of a clearer statement of reversal of fortunes.

6 The book returns to the cause of the people's suffering. The speaker makes the astounding claim that "the iniquity of the daughter of my people has been greater [ויגדל עון בת־עמי] than the sin of Sodom [מחטאת סדם]" (for the use of a comparative *mem* see GKC §133a). Scholars have debated whether the words denote punishment or transgression here, especially in light of 4:22. Keil observes that commentators often take the former meaning but asserts that the words simply mean "iniquity" and "sin" (434–35). Gordis (189) disagrees, as does Berlin, though she also concludes that the concept of sin is not entirely absent (107). Renkema (508–9) thinks that the people's sin is the focal point in both 4:6 and 4:22, but he does state that the greater the sin the greater the divine response to that sin will be. Hillers offers a mediating position when he writes, "The Hebrew terms involved call to mind both moral deficiency and its consequences, in this case" ([1992] 139). The verse's context bears out this interpretation, for the next phrase describes how Sodom was overthrown. Jerusalem's sins have been great, so she has suffered a great and terrible destruction. This mentioning of עון, "iniquity," links this speech once again to 2:11–19, for 2:14 highlights the fact that Jerusalem's prophets failed to expose the people's iniquity. The city fell to invaders. It also links this passage to 4:21–22, where the text emphasizes the end of the people's punishment by mentioning the end of Jerusalem's "iniquity."

Her devastation has been slower and more agonizing than Sodom's. Sodom was "overthrown in an instant [ההפוכה כמו־רגע], without a hand laid on/whirled against it [ולא־חלו בה ידים]." This slow, horrible punishment in comparison to Sodom's swift judgment indicates the magnitude of Jerusalem's sins. Simple comparison of Sodom's specific sins to Jerusalem's is not necessarily the force of this passage. Rather, readers are led to a clearer understanding of the enormity of covenantal infidelity. Jerusalem was more sinful not because of extreme sexual sin but because of extreme covenant unfaithfulness, though at times the two concepts merge. The text focuses here on the fact that God's special people sinned greatly and have suffered greatly, not on the specific elements of that sin.

7–10 These verses conclude the first speaker's description of the community's plight. As before, this speaker mixes semidetached third-person narration and first-person statements about "my people" (see 3:48–51). In this way the one lamenting stands with the people yet apart from them. His comments relate to the city's Nazirites (4:7–8) and to the fact that those who died in the invasion suffered less than have those who remained alive (4:9–10). As in 4:3–6, the speaker's lamenting leads readers to understand that Jerusalem's suffering equals or surpasses that of any other subjected city.

7 Having spoken about the city's mothers, children, and adults—in other words the general populace—in 4:1–6, the speaker moves on to describe the fate of Jerusalem's Nazirites. As in 4:1–6 he does so by noting how their fortunes have changed dramatically. Scholars debate the identity of נזיריה, "her Nazirites." Haller (108) and Rudolph (248) conclude that the text should read נעריה, "her young men," because of the passage's interest in Jerusalem's offspring. Few experts follow this emendation since there is no strong textual support for it. Several commentators translate the word as "noble" or "prince," for Gen 49:26 and Deut 33:26 use the word to denote one who wears a crown (see Berlin, 101; Keil, 435; Renkema, 511–12). Fewer writers take the word to mean the religious group by the same name (see Num 6:1–21). Hillers thinks that the text could refer to the "men under a special vow to abstain from wine and from contact with the dead, and to let their hair grow long" ([1992] 140), yet he also notes the possibility that the term designates leaders. Calvin (464–65) concludes that the religious group is intended here and claims that the demise of such a special group of people highlights the city's fall and horrible destruction.

Though the majority interpretation may certainly be valid, it is just as possible to interpret the text as referring to the highly committed religious group. The other civic and religious leaders are designated in clear ways in the book (e.g., 1:5; 4:20). Amos 2:11–12 includes the Nazirites with the prophets when denouncing Israel's lack of attention to God's word. It is possible that the group appears here in a similar capacity to emphasize that even the persons devoted to Yahweh have suffered greatly in the destruction. Finally, 4:1–6 focuses on children who suffer through no fault of their own. Therefore, it may well be that a similar thing happened to the Nazirites. The most dedicated people suffered along with the wicked on the day of the Lord's wrath.

These Nazirites were once flawless in appearance, but now they have changed dramatically. They were at one time "purer than snow [זכו ... משלג] ... whiter than milk [צחו מחלב]." Their "bodies" (literally their "bone" [עצם], which stands for the whole body as in Prov 16:24 [see Provan, 114]) were once "ruddier than coral" (אדמו ... מפנינים), while "their form, or appearance, was like sapphire" (ספיר גזרתם). All these images point to classic descriptions of physical perfection and beauty such as those that appear in Song 5 (see Renkema, 513–14). This group of people had all the appearance of being well fed, well cared for, and well favored by God.

8 Like Jerusalem's children (see 2:11–12; 4:3–4), however, the Nazirites have suffered the ravages of starvation. Their once white faces are now "blacker than soot" (חשך משחור תארם). As a result, "they are not recognized in the street" (לא נכרו בחוצות). Of course, the streets are the place where all sorts of misery occurs (see 2:21; 4:5, 8, 14, 18). These sufferers are like Job, whose appearance was so marred that he was unrecognizable to his friends (Job 2:12). Their skin "has shriveled/contracted on their bones [צפד עורם על־עצמם]"; indeed, "it has become as dry as wood [יבש היה כעץ]." Not only has their skin changed color because of hunger; their skin sticks tightly on their bones. Whereas 4:7 uses עצם, "bone," as a symbol of wholeness and health, 4:8 uses the possessive form of the word (עצמם) to highlight the Nazirites' nearness to death.

This segment of the book (4:1–8) offers a clear and memorable description of the people's suffering. It includes images from earlier texts, repetition, and the use of rare words. Berlin (103–4) comments that the passage also uses color imagery effectively. She writes, "This chapter is one of the most graphic in the book in its description of the physical suffering of the people of Jerusalem, and what makes it especially vivid is the use of color. In fact, color is one of the striking features of the chapter: gold and scarlet (vv. 1, 2, 5), white, red, sapphire, black (vv. 7, 8). Bright colors represent the earlier conditions; as the famine progresses, the colors are erased from the picture and all that remains is dullness and blackness." So color imagery is one more way the book stresses the reversal of fortunes, for the people's health and hopes faded as surely as bright colors diminish over time.

9 This verse expresses sentiments similar to those found in 4:6. In the earlier verse the speaker states that Jerusalem's suffering has been greater than that experienced by Sodom, presumably because Sodom's punishment occurred all at once rather than over a long period of time. Here the speaker asserts that things went better for those who died in the invasion than for those who lived, probably for the same reason.

In 3:25–27 the "man" begins each of the lines with the word טוב, "good." There it is good to wait on God and to bear punishment meekly, for God is good. Here the speaker states that "good it was/it was better [טובים היו] for those who were pierced by the sword [חללי־חרב] than for those who were pierced by famine [רעב מחללי]." Either way the people are "pierced," and either way they die. But those who die of famine die more slowly and thereby in more agony. Piercing imagery has already appeared in 2:12, where Jerusalem's children are depicted as dying like a man pierced in battle.

Jeremiah contains a good bit of sword and famine imagery as well. In Jer 14:12 the Lord declares that he will consume the people "by the sword and by the famine and by the pestilence" (בחרב וברעב ובדבר). Yahweh also tells Jeremiah to send the people to their appointment with the sword and famine in Jer 15:2, and in Jer 16:1–4 he reveals that many sons and daughters of Jerusalem will perish by sword and famine. Babylon's sword is identified as the means of Jerusalem's destruction in Jer 21:1–10, while in Jer 43:11 Yahweh threatens the rebellious refugees in Egypt that the sword will overtake them there. Lam 4:9 indicates that Jeremiah's threats have materialized (see Lam 2:17). The situation has proven as terrible as he warned it would be. Hunger has pierced children and adults alike.

The speaker intensifies the piercing imagery in 4:9b. Not only have the people been pierced by hunger; they have been "pierced through, riddled" (מדקרים, "the ones pierced through") by the "lack of the fruit of the field" (מתנובת שדי; see *Note* 9.a-a.). *Puʿal* forms of this word for severe piercing appear only here and in Jer 37:10 and 51:4, texts that highlight terribly wounded soldiers. Hunger has completed the work begun by Babylon's soldiers. In fact, it has inflicted more agony on several individuals than they were able to inflict themselves.

10 The section ends with an image used previously in 2:20, where Jerusalem asks God if women should eat their offspring, no doubt as a consequence of a terrible siege. In this verse, which echoes the covenant consequences found in Lev 26:29 and Deut 28:52–57, "compassionate women" (נשים רחמניות), probably the kindest in the land, "have boiled their own children" (בשלו ילדיהן). This terrible image of boiling children not only echoes Deut 28:52–57, where Moses warns that delicate women will eat their children during the punishing siege; it also echoes 2 Kgs 6:29, where women boil and eat a child during a siege in Elisha's time. Such activities by normally kind women indicate the level of the reversal of their fortunes and underscore the severity of the situation caused by divine judgment of their covenantal infidelity. The abnormal has become normal during "the shattering of (the) daughter of my people" (בשבר בת-עמי), a phrase that closely parallels similar expressions in 2:11 (על שבר בת-עמי) and 3:48 (על שבר בת-עמי).

11–16 At this point the poem uses a more detached voice, one that seems to coincide with the narrator's in chaps. 1 and 2. No longer are the inhabitants of Jerusalem called "my people," as in 4:3, 6, and 10. Rather, this speaker mentions "her foundations" (4:11), "her prophets" (4:13), and "her priests" (4:13). Description takes the place of overt empathy, though sympathy is hardly absent. Vv 11–12 focus on Jerusalem's punishment as part of the day of the Lord, while vv 13–16 describe the sins and agonies of Jerusalem's priests and prophets. That those punished are guilty does little to lessen one's compassion in light of their plight.

11 Virtually every word in 4:11a appears earlier in the book in texts evoking the day of the Lord. The verse starts with the declaration that "the LORD completed his anger" (כלה יהוה את-חמתו). The idea is that God "gave full vent" (RSV) to his anger or gave it out until it was complete in its application and effects, until it "fulfilled the purpose for which it was stirred" (Renkema, 521). Forms of כלה appear in 2:11 and 2:22, in the former case to state the totality of the speaker's grief and in the latter instance to comment that Jerusalem's enemies have decimated the populace. The word חמתו, translated "his anger," is used in 2:4, where God's anger is compared to the pouring out of fire (שפך כאש חמתו). Finally, the fact that "he poured out his burning wrath" (שפך חרון אפו) reminds readers of the "pouring out" mentioned in 2:4, 19 and 4:11, 13, the fierceness noted in 1:12, and the "wrath" highlighted in 1:12; 2:1, 3, 6, 21, 22; and 3:43, 66. The narrator instructs readers to observe that Jerusalem has experienced the day of the Lord, not just a string of bad luck brought on by political failures. The text continues to link the covenant curses found in Lev 26 and Deut 27–28 with the prophets' emphasis on the day of the Lord.

If 4:11a reminds readers of day-of-the-Lord themes connected to Deuteronomistic theology, then 4:11b reminds them of Zion theology by stating that God "kindled a fire in Zion" (ויצת אש בציון). Prior to 4:11 the book refers to Zion eleven times. These instances include references to Zion's empty roads (1:4), ruined walls (2:8, 18), tent (2:4), sons (4:2), loss of majesty (1:6; 2:10), desperation (1:17), and need for comfort (2:1, 6, 13). Now the narrator emphasizes how the Lord's day has started a fire that has "consumed her foundations" (ותאכל יסדתיה). This phrase reminds readers of Amos 1:3–2:5, where the prophet reports that fire will consume several places under God's wrath, including Judah. Lam 4:11b reveals that the word of the Lord through Amos has come to pass. God has sent the fire that Amos promised would come. This passage also reminds readers of 1 Kgs 9:1–9, where Yahweh tells Solomon that ingrained, intractable sin may lead to the temple's destruction. God spares Jerusalem/Zion in 2 Kgs 19:35–37, while Pss 46, 48, and 76 celebrate God's choice and protection of the chosen city. But only Zion in its glorified eschatological state remains forever (Isa 65:17–25). Lamentations helps (see Jer 7:1–8:3) relieve any notion that the mere existence of Jerusalem, whatever its inhabitants' relationship to God, equals Zion. Any sinful sort of "Zion" will be judged.

12 Jerusalem's destruction must have been a result of the day of the Lord, for no other explanation makes sense to bystanders. This verse asserts that the "kings of the earth" (מלכי־ארץ) "and all the inhabitants of the inhabited world" (וכל ישבי תבל), in other words all persons great and small, "did not believe" (האמינו לא) that Jerusalem could be breached. Yet enemies have entered her gates, a fact that Lam 1 has already made very clear.

The kings of the earth probably did not spend tremendous amounts of time wondering about Jerusalem's defensive measures (Provan, 116–17). At the same time, that is no reason to conclude that many would have been surprised that the city fell, as Berlin believes (110). Certainly the text may be hyperbolic (see O. Kaiser, 182) or a way to emphasize Jerusalem's reversals, as Hillers concludes ([1992] 149). Still, it is true that Jerusalem stood for many years, and surely was known for withstanding Assyria's incursions and for rebelling against Babylon from time to time and somehow managing to survive (see Renkema, 525). It is not far-fetched to think that kings marveled that the long surviving city had now fallen. This wonderment on the part of foreigners adds texture to the general theme of the day of the Lord, for it indicates that the day of the Lord was not just something the Israelites noticed. It was an event of sufficient magnitude to cause their neighbors to consider what God had done.

Most scholars focus on the mindset of the people of Jerusalem more than on that of the kings and inhabitants of the earth. Kraus (78), Weiser (356), Berlin (110), Provan (117), Re'emi (122), and others argue that even if world leaders did not believe in Jerusalem's inviolability, many, many inhabitants of Jerusalem did. Therefore, they were shocked when the city fell. This point is well taken, as the comments on 4:11 indicate. Still, this verse highlights what non-Israelites thought. At the very least the verse includes foreigners, whatever their specific beliefs about Jerusalem, with people of Jerusalem as persons surprised at the city's fall. The day of the Lord draws attention. It changes attitudes and causes puzzlement when it does not inspire awe. God's wrath is left as the best explanation for what has happened.

13 The book remains steadfast in its opinion about why the day of the Lord has come. As in 1:5, 8, 14, 18; 2:14; and 3:39, the speaker lays the responsibility for what has occurred at the feet of a sinning people. Yahweh is in the right (1:18); Jerusalem has sinned greatly for a long period of time and has rejected God's word through the good prophets (2:17). Nowhere in the book is this belief contradicted. Here the text focuses on the prophets' and priests' sins, a theme that also appears in 2:14.

It is hardly strange for this speaker to assert that Jerusalem fell "because of (the) sins of her prophets" (מחטאת נביאיה) and because of the "iniquities of her priests" (עונות כהניה). Several OT passages cite false prophets as a primary reason for the people's self-delusion. Elijah battled prophets of Baal (1 Kgs 18), Jeremiah withstood Hananiah and other prophets with whom he disagreed (Jer 27–28), Jeremiah criticized other prophets he considered false (Jer 5:30–31; 23:9–40), and the list could be extended (see 1 Kgs 22). Likewise, priests who fail to teach God's people God's word are criticized severely in a number of passages (see Hos 4:1–9; Mal 2:1–9; and others). They also contribute to the nation's demise.

This passage attacks specific parts of their behavior that are particularly unbecoming in religious leaders. Indeed these prophets and priests are "the ones casting down in her midst, (the) blood of (the) righteous" (השפכים בקרבה דם צדיקים). Renkema (527–28) correctly links the concept of casting down the blood of the righteous to texts such as Jer 26, where Jeremiah preaches the word and then is denounced by the prophets and priests, who tell the officials and people that Jeremiah ought to die (Jer 26:1–11). At this point in the narrative Jeremiah explains that if they kill him they will "bring innocent blood on themselves" (Jer 26:11–15). The officials, people, priests, and prophets relent based on their opinion of Micah of Moresheth's ministry (Jer 26:16–19). The passage does not end at this point, however, for it then mentions a prophet named Uriah, who was killed because of what he preached (Jer 26:20–23). Thus, innocent blood was shed, even though it was not Jeremiah's. The use of the general term צדיקים, "the righteous," in this verse probably extends the type of persons killed beyond the prophets. The charge is that some persons who knew the Lord by faith and who thereby lived as he commanded (see Ps 1) were put to death, presumably for disagreeing with the priests and prophets who had the power to do so. God punished such activities through the fall of Jerusalem.

14 It is difficult to determine the identity of the subject of the clause נעו עורים בחוצות, "they wandered blind in the streets" (see *Note* 14.a.). Kraus (79–80) thinks the righteous are intended; Westermann (202), Berlin (110), and Renkema (530–31) deem the priests and prophets the subject; and Hillers ([1992] 149–50) and Provan (117–18) conclude that the people as a whole are meant. The first viewpoint takes the closest group (linguistically) as the subject. The problem is determining in what manner those sinned against are unclean. The second viewpoint interprets the blood of 4:14 as the innocent blood of the righteous spilled on their slayers' hands. Thus, the priests and prophets have become unclean because of what they have done. This reading best fits the immediate context. The third viewpoint endeavors to interpret 4:14 in light of 4:15–16, so the people rejected by the nations include all Israel, not just their religious leaders. Though this last idea grapples seriously with the context, the second reading makes the best sense of the passage. The priests and prophets shed innocent blood (4:13) and were appropriately considered unclean because of the blood on their hands (4:14). Having been rejected as unclean by their own people, they were unacceptable refugees as far as the nations were concerned (4:15). With no place to go, they were scattered still further by Yahweh (4:16). Whether at home or abroad, no honor or refuge was given to these leaders (4:16).

The priests' and prophets' blindness and uncleanness relate to being "defiled by the blood" (נגאלו בדם). Provan (117–18) writes, "Blindness could be a metaphor either for their distress (cf. Deut 28:29; Isa 59:10; Zeph 1:17) or their lack of moral sense in the absence of any guidance from above (cf. Isa 42:18–20)." Keil (439) adds that passages like Jer 23:12 and Isa 29:9 threaten the people with "blind and helpless staggering" if they continue in their sinful ways. Having shed the blood of the righteous, the blood on their hands and on their clothing can only make them ritually and morally unclean. No wonder, then, that "no one could touch their garments" (בלא יוכלו יגעו בלבשיהם), a phrase that addresses the totality of their uncleanness more than it does any specific significance of the priestly garments.

15 Though they have hardly followed the Lord's will for prophets and priests, at least they cry out "Turn aside—unclean" (סורו טמא) as Lev 13:45 directs lepers to do. These former leaders are not literally leprous, but their actions have had deadly consequences nonetheless. It is appropriate for them to warn people not to touch them (אל־תגעו). Indeed the threefold use of "turn aside" (סורו) makes the former leaders' warning quite urgent.

The second line is hard to translate, but its basic meaning is clear. The difficulty lies in the first phrase (כי נצו), where the verb is a *hapax legomenon* that may derive from the root נצה, "fly," or נוץ, "fall in ruins," or, if Rudolph (249) is correct, possibly נוד, "wander." Most scholars adopt one of the first two options. If the root נוץ is right, then the word means "ruined" or "destroyed" (*HAL*, 1:715), so the line would mean something like "because they were ruined/destroyed [like a city; see Jer 4:7], thus they wandered." If the root נצה is correct, then the word means "flee" (*HAL*, 1:682; BDB, 663), which would mean that the line reads "they flee, so (or indeed) they wander." Keil defends this rendering, claiming, "The idea is as follows: Not only were they shunned at home, like lepers, by their fellow-countrymen, but also, when they wished to find a place of refuge beyond their native land, they were compelled to wander about without finding rest" (440). Though either reading is feasible, the first option is probably best since it continues the destruction imagery by applying it to the religious leaders. They are as destroyed as the city itself, so they wander among the nations.

But the nations have no interest in their plight. In fact, "they said among the nations" (אמרו בגוים), in the places where "they wandered" (see 4:14a for the same verbal form), that they may no longer (לא יוסיפו) sojourn as resident aliens (לגור) in their countries. These blood-covered, blinded, unclean persons can find no place of refuge. Who wants them? They turned from their God, turned against their own people, and disgusted the nation that defeated them. Their plight portrays the sad results of the day of the Lord in their lives.

16 As in 4:11, the narrator makes it clear that Yahweh has caused the priests' and/or elders' punishment, a theme that has already appeared in 1:4, 19 and 4:13, and will occur again in 5:12. "The face/presence of the LORD has distributed/scattered them" (פני יהוה חלקם). God has driven them away from their homeland, to the nations, where they receive no welcome whatsoever. Yahweh "no longer shows regard for them" (לא יוסיף להביטם). Just as the nations "no longer" (4:15b) welcome the fugitives, so the Lord "no longer" shows particular care, respect, or personal interest in them. To drive home this point, the second half of the verse emphasizes that "the face of the priests" (פני כהנים), which parallels the mention of the Lord's face in 4:16a, "they [the nations] did not honor" (לא נשאו), which parallels God's similar attitude in 4:16ab. Further, the nations show no mercy to the elders (זקנים לא חננו), regardless of their age or their prominence. Because of what they have done, these individuals must bear the full force of the day of the Lord's wrath. They have sinned, suffered, fled, and been rebuffed. God has seen to it that they do not escape with the blood of their people on their hands. Wherever they flee, the divine punishment reaches them, so thorough in nature is the day of Yahweh.

17–20 As he does in chap. 3, this speaker identifies fully with the suffering nation. Indeed, he uses נו, "us," to indicate who suffers under God's wrath. In this segment he recounts the siege and fall of Jerusalem in sequential detail, beginning with the siege and the city's hope for reprieve. The unique aspect of this section is the description of the king's capture. Priests, elders, mothers, and soldiers appear previously in the book, but there has been no explicit mention of the king. This reference brings the Davidic covenant into closer contact with the book's depiction of the nation's woes and thereby links royal theology to the already prevalent covenantal and Zion imagery.

17 Jerusalem's populace never ceased looking for a political solution to their problem, even though their lack of covenant commitment caused the city's siege (see Berlin, 112). Their eyes were completely devoted (תכלינה עינינו) to the task of looking. They never ceased trying to see a delivering nation appearing on the horizon. Provan (121) suggests that Edom is the nation that does not come to Jerusalem's aid since that country is denounced in 4:22. It is more likely, however, that Berlin (112), Renkema (546–47), Kraus (81), Hillers ([1992] 150–51), and others are correct to identify Egypt as the nation in question. Hillers writes, "In vain, he [the speaker] says, speaking of the days just before the city fell, they had worn out their eyes looking for help from Egypt (Jer 37: 5–10), who once again proved herself a 'broken reed' (Isa 36:6). As we know from Jeremiah (34:21–22; 37:5–11), the Babylonian army at one point was drawn away from Jerusalem temporarily by the advance of an Egyptian army; as Jeremiah predicted, the relief to the city was ephemeral" ([1992] 150). Looking for such "help" (אל עזרתנו) simply proved to be "vanity/emptiness" (הבל). God was their only hope, and they rejected that hope; the future they chose for themselves was thereby secured.

In one of the relatively rare examples of strict synonymous parallelism found in Lam 1–4, the speaker reemphasizes the carefulness of their watching and its futility in 4:17b. The statement "in our watching we watched" (בצפיתנו צפינו) refers to persons watching as if in a watchtower or other place for a sentinel (BDB, 859). This watching was intense, as is evidenced by the context and by the use of the *pi'el* stem. Such watching grew out of desperation as much as out of vigilance. Sadly, the awaited nation "did not save/deliver" (לא יושע). The passage seems to describe a city under siege, holding out yet in grave trouble, hoping for an ally to come and drive the invading army from their gates. Careful watching and desperate hoping, however, resulted only in disappointment.

18 Because no ally came to stop the siege, the enemy had the luxury of waiting for Jerusalem's inhabitants to come outside the gates, at which point they could attack the unfortunate city dwellers. The speaker describes this situation by claiming that the enemy "hunted our steps" (צדו צעדינו). As Renkema (551) observes, this reading parallels 3:52, the צ section of that poem, where the text states, "They have indeed hunted me" (צוד צדוני). Keil notes that the verb means to "search out, pursue; and the figure is taken from the chase" (442). Given this parallel with chap. 3, there is insufficient reason to emend the text to read the root as צרר, which makes the phrase "they drove me into a corner," or "hemmed me in," as Rudolph (249), Gordis (194), and others do. Nor is it likely that the best reading is from the root צדה: "They lay in wait" (see *HAL*, 2:1010).

These enemies hunted the people's very footsteps as they tried to walk in open places. This phrase may refer to attempts to escape, to fear of walking anywhere near the city gates, or even to nightmarish fears that the invaders know their every move (see Renkema, 551–52; Keil, 442). ברחבתינו, the term for "open places," which also occurs in 2:11–12, can refer to a market place, a plaza, or uninhabited land near a city gate (see *HAL*, 2:1212–13; O. Kaiser, 184). There was no place that they did not feel the watching eyes of their enemies. The Babylonians encircled the city, watching as carefully for a chance to complete their task as the people within watched for a delivering army. As time passed, the inhabitants of Jerusalem understood that time was nearly gone. The speaker states, "Our end drew near [קרב קצינו]; our days were fulfilled [מלאו ימינו]." To emphasize the point further, and to add to the reader's sense of dread, the speaker concludes, "thus our end came" (כי־בא קצינו). The twofold usage of "end" (קצינו) leaves the reader with no doubt about the account's outcome.

19 Once the people attempted to flee, the Babylonians proved "swifter . . . than (the) eagles (in the) heavens" (קלים היו . . . מנשרי שמים). These "pursuers" (lit. "our pursuers" [רדפינו]), who are mentioned previously in 1:3 and 1:6, were not only swift; they were also relentless. They chased the people on the mountains (על־ההרים דלקנו) and lay in wait for them in the desert (במדבר ארבו לנו). As was true while the inhabitants of Jerusalem waited in the city, the people had nowhere to flee where the Babylonians would not find them. As K. M. O'Connor writes, "Their pursuers were swift as eagles, aggressive, cunning, and exhausting" ([2001] 1065).

These pursuers were so effective because Yahweh aided them. After all, Lam 3:43 states that Yahweh pursued Jerusalem, and in 3:66 the speaker asks God to pursue Israel's foes. God has fought against the city; he has become their enemy, according to 2:1–10. In 3:10 the speaker portrays God as a bear lying in wait (דב ארב הוא לי) for him, which is language close to that employed in 3:19b. The Babylonians are the human instrument of Jerusalem's defeat, but it is Yahweh who wields that instrument.

20 According to 2 Kgs 25:4–7 and Jer 39:1–10 and 52:1–11, when Jerusalem was about to fall, the king and some of his officials attempted to escape by fleeing through a gate between two walls. They fled toward the desert but were overtaken by the Babylonians, who forced the king to watch them kill his sons and then blinded him. This description corresponds to the contents of Lam 4:17–19. No help came, the Babylonians were extremely watchful, and when the king fled the enemy caught him. If the king with all his helpers could not escape, then what hope did typical citizens have against such a foe?

The capture of the king affects the speaker quite deeply. He calls the king "the breath of our nostrils" (רוח אפינו), a term used to describe Canaanite and Egyptian leaders in the literature of those countries (see Hillers, [1992] 151–52; Kraus, 82). In this passage the metaphor at least means that the people felt their lives depended on their monarch (Berlin, 113). Without him they felt they had no protection or security (K. M. O'Connor, [2001] 1065). In other words, they had counted on him to do what kings were traditionally supposed to do.

But they believed more than this about their king. They believed that he was "the anointed of the LORD" (משיח יהוה), the one chosen by God to lead their people, the chosen son of David (see 2 Sam 7; Ps 2; and so on). Gerstenberger ([2001] 499) suggests that the text most likely refers to a future messiah, but Zedekiah was the current embodiment of that promise. If he was in exile, the lineage of and promise to David were imperiled. As Renkema writes, "Although many a Davidic king had been rather disappointing in this regard, the people's expectations of him continued undiminished. Each new Davidic king had the potential to fulfill those expectations" (557). With the monarch in Babylon, such hopes could have been viewed as dashed forever. When the king "was captured in their pits" (בשחיתותם) the way the speaker in 3:53–55 was thrown in a pit, the people's hopes in Zedekiah and in the future of the Davidic lineage were severely damaged. With the city of David and the lineage of David fallen, the country was indeed bereft.

The people had hoped that "in his shade" (בצלו) they could "rest among the nations" (נחיה בגוים). This concept of shade is another metaphor for protection. Often, as in Pss 17:8 and 91:1, the Lord is called Israel's shade, so the connection between the Lord and the Lord's anointed may be made (see Weiser, 359). Indeed, Isa 32:1–2 portrays the coming righteous king and his officials as shelters, hiding places, and shade from the heat. The mention of rest among the nations evokes Israel's hopes for a homeland where they could live in peace. This is a major theme in Joshua (1:13, 15; 21:44; 22:4; 23:1) when Israel was promised rest from all her enemies in the new land. According to 2 Sam 7:10–11, God promised David that he would give Israel a place where they would be disturbed no more and in which he would give David rest from enemies. At the temple dedication Solomon thanked God for giving Israel rest in the land, a blessing that the temple's existence symbolized (1 Kgs 8:56). Now, instead of living "among the nations" as a special people (see 1:1) the people have been scattered "among the nations" (see 1:3) like their leaders have been (see 2:9; 4:15). Their "rest" has come to an end, and they can only cling to promises of the possibility of national and individual renewal such as those found in Deut 30:1–10.

21–22 This concluding speech has two significant elements. It emphasizes the joy that Edom has felt over Jerusalem's demise while at the same time stressing Edom's certain destruction. The Edomites should enjoy Jerusalem's pain while they can, for they will soon suffer in a similar manner. And it highlights the end of Jerusalem's punishment, or at least strongly hints that the end has begun. Given the contents of this speech, it is probable that a prophetic voice speaks here. If so, it is possible that the same speaker who begins the section concludes it (see *Form/Structure/Setting* for this chapter).

21 For the first and only time the book identifies a specific enemy. Edom was descended from Esau, and Edom and Israel were traditional rivals. Located southeast of Judah, Edom was known for slave trading (see Amos 1:6, 9) and for wisdom (1 Kgs 4:29–34), as well as for its citizens' hatred of Israel (see Jer 49:7; Obadiah). According to Ps 137:7, Ezek 25:12–14, Joel 4:19 (ET 3:19), and Obad 10–14, they demonstrated their hatred by killing refugees and other acts of treachery. The Edomites were a historical enemy, not only a symbolic one (Renkema, 561).

Given this background, it is easy to see that 4:21a is ironic in tone. When the speaker tells Edom "rejoice and be glad" (שׂישׂי ושׂמחי), he means "be glad while you can" (Westermann, 205). The reference to Edom's location as "in the land of Uz" (בארץ עוץ) reflects the ancient nature of the Edom-Israel conflict (see Gen 36:28; 1 Chr 1:42–43). Edom's rejoicing will be short lived because, the speaker says, "even to you (the) cup shall pass" (גם־עליך תעבר־כוס). Re'emi explains, "In Old Testament times a man did not drink to another, but handed him over a cup of wine, thus symbolizing his 'future portion' or destiny. So, in metaphor, God could hand over a cup to man. It could be a cup of happiness to come (cf. Ps. 23:5), but it could also be a cup of woe, of the wrath of God (Pss. 60:3; 75:8; Isa. 51:17; Jer. 25:15–17; Ezek. 23:32–34)" (125). Without question, the cup is the cup of judgment, for once Edom drinks of the cup she becomes drunk and strips herself naked (תשׁכרי ותתערי). She suffers the sort of shame, confusion, and degradation that Jerusalem has felt and endured (see 1:7, 21; 3:61–63). Jer 49:7–22 states: Edom will fall. She will drink the cup of judgment (49:12), and having drunk she will become the sort of byword among the nations that she has made Jerusalem (49:14–22). Her nakedness will be seen, just as Jerusalem's has been (see 1:8).

22 The speaker interrupts his comments about Edom to make an important assertion about Jerusalem. Though Edom's woes are about to begin in earnest, Jerusalem's fortunes have reached their lowest point and must by implication begin to improve. After all that has been said in the book, the speaker now assures Jerusalem, "The punishment for your iniquity is completed, O daughter of Zion" (תם־עונך בת ציון). As in 4:6, the word translated "punishment for your iniquity" (עונך) may refer to iniquity, guilt due to iniquity, or punishment for iniquity, depending on the context (see BDB, 730–31; *HAL*, 1:800–801). Since a contrast between the current situation and the end of exile appears in this verse, it is most likely that either of the latter two meanings is accurate. Renkema disagrees, noting that the situation hardly got better quickly, if at all, in the book (564–66). Renkema is correct that pain continues, but renewal and rebuilding can hardly take place overnight. Some time of slow, hard reconstruction of life and society would likely follow the devastation the book describes. Thus, Hillers, who represents the majority of scholars in this instance, is correct when he writes, "Although this line, even if read as a declarative sentence and not as a wish, is not yet a clear announcement of salvation for Zion (cf., e.g., Isa. 40:2, 'Her iniquity is pardoned'), yet it comes closer to being an expression of hope than almost anything else in the book is. It recognizes that with the fall of the city and the beginning of the exile the flood tide of Yahweh's wrath had passed. Not so for Edom; her judgment day was yet to come" ([1992] 152–53). Chap. 5 will build on this incipient hope to petition God for full recovery of the nation's lost status and standing with Yahweh.

Because their punishment is complete, the Lord will "no longer keep you in exile" (לא יוסיף להגלותך). The presence of two *hipʿil* verbs in this phrase underscores that God has caused this exile. In 4:15b the speaker states that the nations no longer wish to have Jerusalem's leaders in their midst. Now the same term indicates that Yahweh no longer drives them into such places. God causes the punishment to end as surely as he caused it to begin. Now hope can begin to take specific historical shape.

In contrast to Jerusalem's fresh start, Edom will now begin to endure the sort of pain her old foe has experienced. Now, "He [Yahweh] will visit your iniquity, O daughter of Edom" (פקד עונך בת־אדום). פקד is a root often associated with judgment passages (see BDB, 823–24), so the metaphor indicates that God will punish iniquity, as it does in Jer 5:9, 29; 6:15; and so on, as well as in Zeph 1:8–9, 12; 2:7; and 3:7. As a result, "he will uncover your sins" (גלה על־חטאתיך), a phrase that means he will send Edom into exile, the same way that the uncovering of Jerusalem meant her introduction to exile in 1:3. Edom's sins lead to judgment just as certainly as Jerusalem's leaders' unwillingness to uncover the people's sins led to Jerusalem's woes according to 2:14. This ending mirrors Joel 4:19–20 (ET 4:19–21), Amos 9:11–12, and Obad 19–21 in the sense that all these texts stress Israel's renewal and Edom's downfall in the context of the day of the Lord.

The contrast between the current status of Jerusalem and Edom is now complete. Edom should rejoice while she can since her guilt caused by iniquity will soon result in uncovering, or exile that will bring her great trouble and humiliation. On the other hand, Jerusalem's considerable suffering will now begin to recede even though her pain will hardly cease all at once. Having the worst over is small consolation, though it is at least the beginning of hope. This embryonic hope is similar in form to that expressed in 3:19–39. There the speaker based the inception of new hope on the character of God, while here the same sort of hope must emerge out of the belief that Yahweh's punishment of guilt has ceased.

Explanation

This chapter includes the various speakers from chaps. 1–4 save one: Jerusalem. These speakers forge an acrostic lament that incorporates elements of individual and corporate lament, as well as aspects of the dirge. As in chaps. 1 and 2, the alternation of speakers helps structure the chapter. Chap. 3 features only one speaker, but that speaker participates in this chapter alongside all the other voices. These speeches take the reader toward the inception of renewal—first through description, then through promise.

In 4:1–10 the speaker first heard in 2:11–19 and again in chap. 3 stresses the terrible deprivations experienced by "my people," especially the children in that group. These deprivations include food, beauty, and dignity. Next, in 4:11–16 the narrator from 1:1–11, 17 and 2:1–10 offers a description of what sin has brought into Jerusalem's life. As before, this speaker stresses that what has occurred is part of the day of the Lord. Then, in 4:17–20 the first-person speaker from 2:11 and chap. 3, whose speech is marked by his association of himself with Jerusalem's woes, states how the city was besieged and how the king was taken captive. Finally, in 4:21–22 a prophetic speaker reveals that the Lord has ended the people's punishment and begun Edom's. This revelation hardly means happy times immediately follow, only that the worst is over. Still, this embryonic hope offers the people some sense that they have a future. It allows them to pray together in chap. 5 that God will respond positively to their situation. Until 4:21–22 the speakers pray for the pain to stop. In chap. 5 the nation asks for restoration to their prior relationship with Yahweh.

Theologically, this chapter brings together several of the main themes in the OT. First, in 4:1–10 the speaker uses terminology for the people's suffering that coincides with covenantal consequences passages like Lev 26 and Deut 28. This language is similar to that found in 2:11–19, where the speaker appears previously. Second, in 4:11–16 the speaker uses day-of-the-Lord terminology like that found in the prophetic literature. Of course, the same speaker, the narrator, employs similar themes in 1:1–11 and 2:1–10. Third, the speaker in 4:17–20 stresses the fall of the city and the concomitant fall of the Davidic lineage. In this way the speaker deftly links Zion and Davidic imagery to discuss the most devastating news Israel could hear, that Zion is not inviolable nor the Davidic lineage untouchable. Of course, 2 Sam 7 and 1 Kgs 8 had already made these points, but some of the people did not recall this vital theological information. Fourth, in 4:21–22 the speaker uses anti-Edom prophetic imagery as part of a declaration that Jerusalem's punishment has ended. The speaker agrees with texts such as Deut 30:1–10 that state that God will eventually restore a repentant Israel. It also connects with passages that denounce Edom and other nations for their treachery against Israel. Through these emphases, the chapter acts as a theological summary of Lamentations that keeps faith with the rest of the OT canon. While doing so, the speakers in no way minimize the pain the nation experiences. The book manages to combine technical skill, a lamenting style of acrostic, and theological continuity.

Since the judgment has ended, the Lord "will no longer keep" the people "in exile." Renewal will begin with the cessation of the exile and then will move into a stage in which the people return. All this activity cannot happen overnight. It would not be unusual for restoration to take nearly as long as the covenant breaking. In fact, if the Babylonian invasion of ca. 552 B.C.E. is the fulfillment of the prophecy concerning Edom, then many years may pass before discernible progress becomes evident. Still, the end of exile should come as a tremendous relief for Jerusalem. Perhaps she can expect that the promises associated with return from exile found in Deut 30:1–10 may come true.

As the chapter ends, the people have the promise of a better future than when it started. The involved prophetic speaker has described Jerusalem's woes, particularly those of her children (vv 1–10), and has announced the completion of divine judgment (vv 21–22). Between these speeches the narrator has reemphasized that what has occurred has been an example of the day of the Lord (vv 11–16). Whatever relief there is must stem from God's decision to cease his hostility against them. The chapter's conclusion agrees with this point. The speaker from chap. 3 once again describes what it was like to endure the devastation surrounding the invasion (vv 17–20). Since he has already confessed God's faithfulness and merciful nature in 3:19–39, the end of judgment would not catch him totally by surprise. Jerusalem and all these speakers must join with one voice in seeking the Lord and asking the Lord to respond favorably. At that point in time the relationship will be restored and the people can move beyond the mere cessation of divine punishment to a new walk with Yahweh.

Remember, O LORD *(5:1–22)*

Bibliography

Bergler, S. "Threni V—Nur ein alphabetisierendes Lied: Versuch einer Deutung." *VT* 27 (1977) 304–20. **Brunet, G.** "La cinquieme Lamentation." *VT* 33 (1983) 149–70. **Dobbs-Allsopp, F. W.** "Linguistic Evidence for the Date of Lamentations." *JANESCU* 26 (1998) 1–36. **Driver, G. R.** "Hebrew Notes on 'Song of Songs' and 'Lamentations.'" In *Festschrift Alfred Bertholet.* Ed. W. Baumgartner et al. Tübingen: Mohr (Siebeck), 1950. 134–46. ———. "Notes on the Text of Lamentations." *ZAW* 52 (1934) 308–9. **Ferris, P. W., Jr.** *Genre of Communal Lament.* **Fries, S. A.** "Parallele zwischen den Klageliedern Cap. IV, V und der Maccabäerzeit." *ZAW* 13 (1893) 110–24. **Gordis, R.** "The Conclusion of the Book of Lamentations (5:22)." *JBL* 93 (1974) 289–93. **Gottlieb, H.** *Study on the Text of Lamentations.* **Gous, I.** "Lamentations 5 and the Translation of Verse 22." *OTE* 3 (1990) 287–302. **Jahnow, H.** *Hebräische Leichenlied.* **Johnson, B.** "Form and Message in Lamentations." *ZAW* 97 (1985) 58–73. **Lachs, S. T.** "The Date of Lamentations V." *JQR* 57 (1966–67) 46–56. **Linafeldt, T.** *Surviving Lamentations.* **O'Connor, K. M.** *Lamentations and the Tears of the World.* **Renkema, J.** "Does Hebrew *ytwm* Really Mean 'Fatherless'?" *VT* 45 (1995) 119–22. **Rosenfeld, A.** "Aqrostikhon be-'ekhah pereq 5." *Sinai* 110 (5752) 96. **Rudolph, W.** "Der Text der Klagelieder." *ZAW* 56 (1938) 101–22. **Shea, W.** "The *qinah* Structure of the Book of Lamentations." *Bib* 60 (1979) 103–7. **Wiesmann, H.** "Die Textgestalt des 5. Kapitels der Klagelieder." *Bib* 8 (1927) 339–47. **Zenner, P. J. K.** "Thr 5." *BZ* o.s. 2 (1904) 370–72.

Translation

1	*Remember, O* LORD, *what has happened to us;*	(5+3)
	have regard for and see our disgrace.	
2	*Our inheritance has been thrown down to strangers,*	(3+2)
	our homes to foreigners.	
3	*We have become orphans, fatherless;*	(4+2)
	our mothers are like widows.	
4	*Our water for silver we drink;*	(3+3)
	our wood for a price they bring.	
5	*By*[a] *our necks we are driven hard;*[b]	(3+4)
	we are weary, and[c] *we have no rest.*	
6	*We have given (the) hand to Egypt,*	(3+3)
	(to) Assyria to have enough bread.	
7	*Our fathers sinned; they are no more;*	(3+3)
	we have carried their iniquities.	
8	*Servants rule over us;*	(3+3)
	there is no one tearing (us) from their hand.	
9	*At peril of our lives we get our bread*	(3+3)
	because of the sword of the desert.	
10	[a]*Our skin is wrinkled as by a furnace*[a]	(3+3)
	from the burning heat of famine.	
11	*Women are raped in Zion,*	(3+3)
	virgins in the cities of Judah.	

12	*Officials are hung up by their hands;*	(3+3)
	the faces of (the) elders are not respected.	
13	*Choice young men bear (burdens) at the grinding mill,*	(3+3)
	and boys stagger under (loads) of wood.	
14	*The elders have ceased from (the) gate,*	(3+2)
	the choice young men from their music.	
15	*The joy of our hearts has ceased;*	(3+3)
	our dancing has been cast down into mourning.	
16	*The crown has fallen from our head;*	(3+5)
	woe to us, for we have sinned.	
17	*Because of this our heart has become faint;*	(5+4)
	because of these things our eyes grow dim.	
18	*Because Mount Zion is desolate,*	(4+3)
	jackals prowl in it.	
19	*You,*[a] *O LORD, reign forever;*	(4+3)
	your throne (endures from) generation to generation.	
20	*Why do you continually forget us?*	(3+3)
	Why do you forsake us for so many days?	
21	*Restore us, O LORD, to yourself, and we shall be restored.*[a]	(4+3)
	Renew our days as in times past	
22	*even* [a] *though you have indeed rejected us*	(4+4)
	and have been exceedingly angry at us.	

Notes

5.a. Gottlieb (*Study on the Text*, 69) and others suggest reading the noun על, "yoke," for the prep. על, "on, upon, by." Albrektson (*Studies in the Text and Theology*, 197–98) correctly notes that this change is unnecessary in this context.

5.b. Gottlieb (*Study on the Text*, 69), Driver ("Hebrew Notes," 142), and Albrektson (*Studies in the Text and Theology*, 198) all suggest that Syr.'s "driven hard" may well be a better rendering for נרדפנו than the normal "pursued."

5.c. LXX, Tg., and Vg. all read ולא, "and not," here. They may simplify a difficult form, but the reading does make sense.

10.a-a. Several Heb. MSS read the pl. עורינו, "our skins," for the sg. עורנו, "our skin," so that the subject and verb match in number (see Albrektson, *Studies in the Text and Theology*, 199–200). Driver (*ZAW* 52 [1934] 308) defines נכמרו as "wrinkled" based on linguistic and medical evidence. See also Rudolph, *ZAW* 56 (1938) 121–22.

19.a. LXX and Syr. read ואתה, "and you," but Tg. agree with MT. No significant change in meaning is at stake.

21.a. The Qere reads ונשובה, simply using ה to indicate the vowel.

22.a. See the *Comment* on v 22 for the options for translating כי אם as "even though."

Form/Structure/Setting

There are several ways that this poem diverges from its predecessors. First, it is the shortest and least acrostic of the five poems in Lamentations. It consists of twenty-two one-line verses, so the chapter is one-third the length of chaps. 1–3 and one-half the length of chap. 4. Though it has twenty-two lines, the same number as the number of letters in the alphabet, there is no alphabetic sequence. Concerning this number of verses, Berlin (116–17) writes, "Most commentators, when making this observation, seem to imply that the chapter was fashioned to conform in length to the other chapters of the book. This may be so, but on the other hand, there are among the psalms chapters that contain twenty-two verses (Pss 33 and 103) and many that contain twenty-one or twenty-three verses (e.g., Pss 34, 38, 49). So the number of verses in Lam 5 may be incidental." Some uncertainty exists, then, about the purpose of the chapter's length. Second, the chapter consists mostly of balanced lines of three words to each half-line instead of the unbalanced (three words then two words) line of the *qinah* meter (see Introduction). As in the earlier chapters, there is no absolutely set pattern to the number of words in the lines. Still, this general pattern produces more clear parallel phrasing, less enjambment, and fewer synthetic parallels than the earlier chapters (see Provan, 124; Hillers, [1992] 161; Renkema, 576–80). Third, there is only one speaking voice in the chapter rather than alternating voices. Fourth, and related to the third point, the poem is the most consistent literary piece in the book, for it sticks very closely to the communal lament form.

The poem is not altogether different from the first four chapters. Though Berlin's observations are correct, the chapter does use the same number of verses as the other poems. It also continues to lament and press for a restored relationship with God and a resultant easing of pressure and pain. It builds on the previous chapter to make its points, and it includes themes found in the earlier portions of the book. Thus, the chapter fits into Lamentations as a whole even though it does so in a unique way, and it is appropriate to examine its form, structure, and setting to determine why this is so and what the chapter contributes to the book's message.

Chap. 5 consists of twenty-two, usually balanced, lines that unfold in a way that "closely resembles a traditional community lament" (Westermann, 211). Gunkel includes Lam 5 in his list of communal complaint songs (*Introduction to Psalms*, 82) and observes that the poem contains such elements as complaint over misfortune, a petition to God to change the situation, and self-reproach for how the situation came about in the first place (88). He suggests that "Lam 5 may have been sung during one of the festivals at the ruins of Jerusalem, like the ones mentioned in Zech 7" (88). Westermann (211–13) basically agrees with Gunkel, asserting that the text includes an opening address and plea for God to remember the people (v 1), a community complaint (vv 2–18), a sentence of praise (v 19), an accusation against God (v 20), a second, framing plea (v 21), and a concluding question (v 22). He concludes that aspects of the dirge have influenced the poem, especially in its description of woe, but he believes that the absence of an opening mournful cry indicates that the poem is not formally a dirge. Gerstenberger ([2001] 501–2) agrees with Gunkel's and Westermann's decisions on form, structure, and the role of the dirge, as does Dobbs-Allsopp (140–42). These representative form critics reach what amounts to astounding agreement in the context of Lamentations studies. Writing before the advent of form criticism, Keil divides the chapter into three parts: a request that God consider Jerusalem's disgrace (v 1), a description of the disgrace (vv 2–18), and a request that God restore the people to his favor (vv 19–22). He concludes that the chapter's speaker places the congregation's "distress and supplication before the Lord" (446). Thus, he comes to virtually the same conclusions about the poem's forms as later form-critical scholars do.

But not every Lamentations scholar shares these experts' opinions. For instance, Renkema argues that the poem is a collective prayer that corresponds in some ways to the collective lament, yet he claims that there are differences between chap. 5 and typical collective laments. These differences include the unusually lengthy complaint segment, the lack of any mention of the sanctuary or liturgy, the concrete connection to a specific historical situation (the fall of Jerusalem), and the presence of elements of retrospection and trust in Yahweh (586). Renkema concludes that the text combines aspects from various types of poetry to offer worshipers a new and unique form. Berlin seems to agree with Renkema at least in part, for she writes that chap. 5 is a prayer that "resembles in part the communal laments in the book of Psalms and shares some traits with penitential prayers of the Second Temple period" (116). This emphasis on Lam 5 as a prayer follows an ancient tradition since some Greek and Latin manuscripts designate the poem as a "prayer."

Though Renkema is correct that this chapter does not follow the communal lament form exactly (if such an exact form really exists), the poem unfolds very much like communal laments such as Pss 44, 60, 74, 79, 80, and 83 (see Dobbs-Allsopp, 140). It is striking that the speakers only refer to themselves and the people in first-person plural or second-person plural forms, that there is a detailed complaint, and that the concluding plea for help is so evident (see Kraus, 86). At this point the people pray together. There are no complementary or competing voices. Everyone wants the same thing. Though this poem does have its own unique approach to the communal lament, it is nonetheless very close to this type of lament. The twenty-two lines give enough of an acrostic flavor to remind readers that thoroughness is still the major artistic goal.

Given the preceding conclusion, it is fairly simple to delineate the chapter's structure. However, because of controversy about how to interpret its final verses, it is not simple to determine the flow of the chapter's argument. The first two segments are fairly straightforward. V 1 urges God to "remember," "pay close attention," and "see" what has happened to the people. Thus, it certainly serves as a very strong opening plea. Next, vv 2–18 express the woes that the people have endured and continue to endure, with vv 2–10 stressing economic impoverishment; vv 11–14 emphasizing social humiliation, even abuse; and vv 15–18 highlighting social and political disintegration (Berlin, 116).

Vv 19–22, on the other hand, present interpreters with several options, which are noted in the comments below. At the risk of seeming to decide the matter ahead of time, v 19 confesses that Yahweh reigns forever and is followed by v 20 asking why the Lord has forsaken them for so long. V 21 urges Yahweh to cause the people's restoration so that the relationship can be restored to its ancient standing. Finally, v 22, the most controversial part of the text, follows the positive statement about God's sovereignty in v 20 and the urgent plea for restored relationship in v 21 with the hope that such will be the case even though God has been extraordinarily angry with the people, his people. This section, which amounts to a plea for a specific sort of help, concludes the book on a cautiously hopeful note, though without a word from the Lord. Still, it is important to note that it is not unreasonable for many commentators to disagree with this assessment. The linguistic data are not simple to assess, and not everyone agrees that punishment could possibly have ceased if the conditions are as bad as chap. 5 reports.

Unlike the previous chapters, there are no alternating speakers in chap. 5. K. M. O'Connor suggests that the community replaces all the speakers from chaps.

1–4 ([2001] 1067). This may be true, but it is equally likely that all the speakers from the earlier chapters join with one voice here. If so, then they represent the community, or may join with the community as a whole. Regardless of a final decision on this matter, the united voice agrees with the previous speakers. This voice concludes that only God can bring relief from the pain he has caused, and this voice is not content only to express pain, for it moves to the necessary ultimate goal of reconciliation between God and the nation. In this way the united voice shares the general viewpoint of all the previous speakers and also includes their particular emphases, such as the city's awful pain, significant sin, and relationship with a severe, yet compassionate God. The united voice does not simply ask for the ceasing of pain, as important as that need is; it asks for the restoration of relationship with God, which is the means of the cessation of pain.

As was stated in the *Form/Structure/Setting* section of chap. 4, William Shea argues that just as the *qinah* meter has a 3:2 stress in its lines, so the book of Lamentations reflects a 3:2 structure (see *Bib* 60 [1979] 103–7). That is, the book's structure "dies out" the way the book's chief rhythm does. The first three chapters each have sixty-six lines, while the last two chapters have forty-four and twenty-two, respectively. Instead of the message dying out or exhausting itself, however, the book moves toward a summary of themes in chap. 4 and agreement in voice and point of view in chap. 5. One can perhaps as justifiably argue that the book moves to a firm conclusion. The people's united plea is vigorous and laced with as much hope as the situation probably warrants. Though Shea works creatively with the whole of the book and correctly treats the book as a whole piece, his emphasis on the book fading out is not the approach this commentary takes. Rather, it emphasizes the ways in which chaps. 4 and 5 conclude the book's drive toward lament, penitence, renewal, and relief.

As is true of all five chapters, the geographical setting is surely Jerusalem (see 5:18) and Judah (see 5:11) after the city fell to Babylon (see Kraus, 86–87). The chapter describes circumstances in which Jerusalem suffers greatly. Judah has no political or economic freedom. Jerusalem has no status among the world's cities. The temple lies in ruins, so worship is greatly hampered. Hunger and death are everywhere. Clearly, life is a combination of oppression, deprivation, and disgrace.

It is impossible to fix an exact date for this poem. Estimates vary widely. Johnson suggests that the chapter "is the oldest part" of Lamentations, concluding that chaps. 1–4 "were added as an alphabetical composition" based on the twenty-two verses of chap. 5 (*ZAW* 97 [1985] 72). Gordis (127) writes, "Chapter 5, being a liturgy, is typological rather than specific, yet it seems to reflect an extended period of national subjection and Zion's desolation. It is therefore best dated circa 530 B.C.E." Dobbs-Allsopp thinks that the linguistic evidence indicates that Lamentations was written between 586 and 520 B.C.E., and that a date between 540 and 520 B.C.E. is likely (see *JANESCU* 26 [1998] 1–36). Westermann posits that chap. 5 is an expansion of a psalm of communal lament carried over from pre-exilic patterns of worship. After the fall of Jerusalem it was expanded and adapted to the new realities of Judah, and stood with chaps. 1, 2, and 4 in the original collection of the book. He dates the chapter fairly soon after Jerusalem was destroyed (Westermann, 219–20). Brunet argues that chap. 5 is a composite of two poems, 5:1–14 and 5:15–22, with the first poem dating from ca. 580 B.C.E. and the second from ca. 570–540 B.C.E. (see *VT* 33 [1983] 149–70). Provan (7–19), Hillers ([1992] 9–10), and Berlin

(33–36) do not think it is possible to set specific dates, though Berlin (35) states that the building of the second temple sets a final date for the book's composition.

Like chaps. 1–4, this chapter fits in the time between the fall of Jerusalem in 587 B.C.E. and the rebuilding of the temple in 520–515 B.C.E. Though enough time has passed for the conditions to be described as ongoing—however long people have to suffer to offer such descriptions—not enough time has passed for the temple construction to occur. Enough time has passed to memorialize the agony and use the prayer/lament in worship—however long it takes for creative hurting people to write prayers that cry out to God—but not enough time has passed for the prayer to assume or record a response. As Hillers writes, the chapter's style, like that of the whole book, "is deliberately universalizing, using conventional and traditional descriptions of the fall of a city that, by their very nature and intent, resist efforts to treat them as documentary films of what happened" ([1992] 10).

Comment

1 V 1 offers a strong plea that Yahweh understand the people's situation and act on their behalf. This plea stands on its own as an introduction to the poem. It sounds much like earlier calls to the Lord, such as those found in 1:9c, 11c, and 20 and 2:20. But the verse as a whole is even more intense than those pleas since the opening imperative "remember, O LORD" (זכר יהוה) is followed in the second half of the verse by two subsequent imperatives: "have regard for" (הביט) and "see" (וראה). Renkema observes that these imperatives "combine to make Lam 5:1 perhaps the most insistent prayer found in the Old Testament" (589). What the people want the Lord to remember, have regard for, and see is "our disgrace" (את חרפתנו), a word that serves as a summary of all that they have endured.

The first imperative evokes images from earlier parts of Lamentations and from psalms that have already been accessed in the book. Forms of זכר, "remember," occur in 1:7, 9; 2:1; and 3:19, 20. In the first instance the people remember in their time of affliction how things used to be, the very thing they want God to recall now. In 1:9 and 2:1 the people failed to remember to plan for the future, and Yahweh refused to remember the covenant people, respectively. This current prayer indicates that the people wish for such forgetting to be in the past. Perhaps more significantly for the understanding of 5:1, in 3:19 the speaker asks Yahweh to remember his affliction and wandering, and reports in 3:20 that his soul certainly recalls what he has suffered and what he continues to suffer. In effect 5:1 asks the same thing, though it describes the affliction and wandering as humiliation/disgrace. All these texts indicate that the remembering called for here basically means "take note of and make changes in the current situation," not "stop forgetting." Since God caused the situation, it is hardly possible that he does not recall what is happening.

The next two imperatives are used not only in Lamentations but also in Pss 74 and 89. In both these psalms the words appear in conjunction with חרף, "scoff/disgrace," which makes it probable either that Lamentations cites those texts or that all these passages work from some shared stock phrases. In 1:11 the two imperatives appear together where Jerusalem asks God to "see . . . and consider, for I am despised," while in 1:12 Jerusalem asks those passing by to "consider/understand, and see" if there has ever been suffering like hers. Jerusalem asks the same thing of Yahweh in 2:20. These imperatives appear together in texts where Jerusalem calls out to God or others and when the whole group calls out to the Lord with one voice. The imperative ראה, "see," occurs by itself in 1:9c, which is where Jerusalem first voices her desires to Yahweh. Such seeing and considering amounts to having a clear understanding of the situation and changing it.

In Ps 74, a passage also echoed in chap. 2 (see *Comment* there), the speaker asks Yahweh to "remember . . . how the enemy scoffs" (Ps 74:18; זכר זאת אויב חרף יהוה) and to "remember how the foolish scoff at you all the day" (Ps 74:22 ESV; זכר חרפתך מני נבל כל היום). These imperatives follow a description of how the enemy has defiled and vandalized the temple (Ps 74:4–8). This, plus the appearance of forms of זכר, "remember," and חרף, "scoff," in close proximity, make some connection between Ps 74 and Lam 5 likely. The same is true of Ps 89, another psalm echoed in chap. 2 (see *Comment* there), for forms of זכר, "remember," and חרף, "scoff," also occur in close proximity there. In Ps 89:51–52 (ET 89:50–51) the speaker uses the words to ask Yahweh to deal with the enemies' scorning of Israel, a context similar to 5:1.

In Lam 5:1 the people use multiple standard imperatives alongside a stock way of describing disgrace to emphasize the seriousness of their situation and their plea. It is hard to imagine what they can do to sound more urgent and earnest. What they mean by חרפתנו, "our disgrace," becomes apparent in the poem's next section as they offer a lengthy description of what they have endured. The people have enjoyed the Lord in a manner very recognizable as pleas/statements of confidence or incipient hope in texts that deal with similar circumstances.

2–18 This long descriptive segment may be divided into several parts. Berlin (116) divides the section into three basic parts: descriptions of economic impoverishment (vv 2–10), descriptions of social humiliation and degradation (vv 11–14), and descriptions of social and political disintegration (vv 15–18). Renkema breaks 5:1–10 into two parts: loss of inheritance (vv 1–4) and oppression and hunger (vv 5–10). He believes 5:11–14 stresses defilement, affliction, death, and grief and posits that 5:15–18 highlights grief at Zion's devastation (Renkema, 587–621). These designations fit well with Berlin's larger structural divisions, though Renkema does not treat 5:1 as a separate part of the poem. These descriptions offer a last look at what the city suffers and thereby stand as final evidence that her people have experienced the day of the Lord in full measure and may now be treated more gently.

2 Economic loss begins with the loss of land and houses. The people state that "our inheritance [נחלתנו] has been thrown down/turned over to strangers [נהפכה לזרים]." In general terms this first half-verse means that Judah has lost the land to an invading army and to unscrupulous persons preying on their weakness. In theological terms the first word evokes memories of the fact that Israel is God's inheritance. Moses prays that the Lord will receive Israel as such in Exod 34:9, and God's positive response is assumed in context. In Deut 4:20 Moses tells the people that they are God's inheritance and then explains in Deut 4:21, 38 that the land is their inheritance. The land is the tangible evidence of this close relationship with their covenant Lord. Losing the land means losing the hard evidence that the people are God's inheritance and that he offers them blessing commensurate with that inheritance. It is not surprising for this loss to be described as a throwing down or turning over. Jerusalem states in Lam 1:20 that her heart is thrown down within her, the speaker in Lam 3:3 claims that God throws down his hand on the man, the speaker in Lam 4:6 notes that Jerusalem's throwing down was worse than Sodom's, and the people claim in Lam 5:15 that their dancing has been thrown down/turned aside. Forms of הפך thereby provide the means to describe all sorts of downcast feelings and physical attacks.

The second half-verse underscores the hostile nature of those doing the destroying. The word for "foreigners" (לנכרים) is not a neutral or benevolent term. It often stands for "an enemy aggressor or alien occupier," for "foreigners with a completely different background and without the slightest sensitivity for the way things are done in the land of Israel" (Renkema, 592). These are not friendly strangers but the sort of harsh opponents promised in Lev 26 and Deut 28.

3 Having described Jerusalem's loss of inheritance and exposure to threatening foreigners, the people move on to depict their lack of familial resources. Once again the text has theological meaning that grows out of historical circumstances. Given the loss of fathers in battle and to exile, however large or small the number may have been, the people are accurate to state, "We have become orphans, fatherless" (יתומים היינו אין אב). The word for "orphans" (יתומים) is flexible. It does not necessarily mean "a person who has lost both parents," though such can be the case. It can mean "one whose father has died," which is the meaning here, as the explanatory "fatherless" (אין אב) makes plain. The same sense probably applies in Exod 22:21 and Deut 10:18 (BDB, 450). Those without a father or without a father and a mother were persons who had no advocate unless the community stood up for them. It was possible that such dependent persons were sold into slavery in some instances in Israelite history (see 2 Kgs 4:1). They were certainly at risk (see Hillers, [1992] 163).

Many Israelites fit this description. War, starvation, and deportation surely took fathers from their children. The issue is not whether all Israelite children were in this position. Rather, it is simply to state the obvious situation—orphans, those without strong advocates—existed after the fall (see O. Kaiser, 193). It is also true that Israel had no "father" in the sense that their king no longer ruled over and protected the people (see 4:20). All Israel was without a political father to lead them (see Budde, 105). Worse yet, as Renkema (593–98) observes, this singular "father" may indicate that Israel's ultimate father, Yahweh (see Hos 11:1–4), has also turned them over to foreigners. Their covenant father has revoked their inheritance and has refused to consider them his inheritance (see 5:2). Clearly, stripped of their biological, political, and spiritual father(s) the people are as "fatherless" as one can be.

Their mothers remain, yet they too feel the loss of the children's father, so they "are like widows" (כאלמנות). As with the orphans, the issue here is not in exactly what ways these women are widows. Their husbands may have been killed, captured, or missing, or the women may simply have been abandoned in hard times. All these possibilities make women "like a widow" or even actual widows. Thus, such "widows" existed historically, and they figure in this description.

This designation of widowhood parallels what 1:1 says about Jerusalem herself. Therefore, it is appropriate to note the possibility that Judah's cities are referenced here (see Renkema, 596). Like Jerusalem, then, the nation's cities have suffered losses of men, women, and children just as Jerusalem has. Again, such was the case. These cities could be compared to mothers who have lost family members through any of the means possible in warfare. Rudolph suggests that Jerusalem herself may be the mother meant here (260). Though not as likely as the Lord's potential designation as father, the possibility would mean that the people have lost their reference point for worship. Again, such was definitely the case historically.

Using pliable terms like "orphan" and "like a widow" allows the poem to evoke multiple ideas and emotions in the reader. It also allows the persons praying to take the entirety of this dire situation to Yahweh. The God who left them to foreigners, who left them without advocate, can return and help them. As the poem unfolds, this is exactly what the people eventually ask (see 5:19–22). If Yahweh accepts them as his inheritance and returns to his children, then they can in turn receive their inheritance back from the hostile persons who have wrenched it from their grasp. These "orphans" need such protection from their "father" (see Provan, 126).

4 Without home, inheritance, or parental support, the people suffer understandable hardship. Unlike normal children, who can expect parents to provide basic resources like water and food, these children must purchase their own. Nothing is free when others take over one's inheritance. Indeed, the word translated "price" (במחיר) in 4b may indicate exorbitant or oppressive rates, for it intensifies the "silver" in 4a, and often in the OT relates the price of wicked activity (see BDB, 564). As 4:1–10 has already indicated, Jerusalem's children can expect little aid. Their earthly parents are powerless to help them; their heavenly father has turned their earthly parents over to the results of their sin. Thus, as a nation, these "children" cry out together for Yahweh to see what they endure and remember the past relationship with him. Indeed, if he is their father, they are asking him to recall a relationship that cannot ever be past in the strictest sense of the word.

5 Economic woes are fueled here by oppression and lead to hunger and abject poverty. Others have taken Israel's inheritance, her land, so those who remain are slaves (or nearly so) in their own homeland. The first half of the verse is difficult to translate (see *Notes* 5.a. and 5.b.). Still, it clearly yields the sense that the people are driven hard by their necks (על צוארנו), perhaps by means of a yoke, though the phrase may well simply be a colloquial way of describing harsh punishment (see Provan, 127; Hillers, [1992] 163; Keil, 448). The second half of the verse underscores the fact that individuals who have no sympathy press the people to work beyond their physical limits. Though the people report growing very weary while striving to do what they are commanded to do (יגענו; see *HAL*, 1:386), they must work on anyway. Despite their effort and obvious exhaustion, they are not allowed to rest (לא הונח לנו). Since the word for rest is from the *hopʻal* stem, the phrase indicates that their master does not give the passive group (the worker) a break from labor. Lack of inheritance and lack of familial support have left these "children" at the mercy of the harshest sort of taskmasters.

6 This verse presents interpreters with several challenges. First, one must determine whether the text refers to the past, to the present, or to both. Second, it is necessary to determine what the phrase "we have given (the) hand" (נתנו יד) references. Third, it is important to decide if the mentioning of Egypt (מצרים) and Assyria (אשור) is literal or figurative, and whether the names mean the nations themselves or exiles in those lands. Fourth, it is necessary to determine if the phrase "to satisfy ourselves with bread" (לשבע לחם) is a literal or figurative statement. Each of these matters relates to the nature of the people's complaint/plea and thus what they want Yahweh to do for them. Each of these matters divides Lamentations experts.

As for the first matter, the people address what they feel and experience now by stating how they came to suffer this way. Therefore, they claim that current suffering stems in part from poor alliances made in the past with other nations. It is not necessary, then, to decide between past and present emphasis. This interpretation is in keeping with earlier texts, such as 1:2, 12, 19 and 4:17–20, that emphasize Judah's alliances with and dependence upon allies who could not or would not save them in their hour of crisis. Having chosen poor allies to begin with, the people have no good ally to aid them now. Past choices made by predecessors have led to a miserable present. At the same time the current generation's own acknowledged sinfulness indicates that they would not have acted differently had they been in their parents' place.

The next two issues may be examined in tandem. There are two ways that the phrase "we have given (the) hand to Egypt (and to) Assyria" may be understood. One way to understand the phrase is to consider it a statement of past foreign policy, as was implied above. That is, Judah spread out their hands in alliance with nations like Egypt and Assyria (Kraus, 88; Rudolph, 261; Hillers, [1992] 163). Of course, such foreign-policy decisions did occur in Israelite history, and ultimately these nations did not help Jerusalem.

Another option is to interpret it as an indication that people fled Jerusalem and went to other lands in a desperate attempt to get bread. Renkema argues that "certain Judeans chose voluntary exile and subjected themselves to a foreign authority in the hope that they might get enough food to satisfy their hunger" (603–4). He adds, "Spurred on by Babylon's threatening actions, many people had already fled from Judah to the bordering lands of Moab, Ammon and Edom (cf. Jer 40:11f). The desire for security and food is also mentioned in Jer 42:14f where Egypt is spoken of as the 'land of bread.' Jeremiah 44:1 also notes that many Judeans fled to Egypt" (604). Renkema admits that the difficulty with this interpretation is the presence of "Assyria" and decides that the linking of Egypt and Assyria is a traditional way of describing foreign territory (604). Keil also concludes that the verse refers to present distress and asserts that the reference to Assyria is a way of mentioning Babylon (449). Provan suggests that the text may indicate that the people had to seek help from outsiders, whether Jews living abroad or foreigners (128).

Though she is basically in agreement with Provan, Berlin offers a suggestion that may point the way forward. She writes, "The combination of Egypt and Assyria is a conventional word association (word pair) dating from the realpolitik of an earlier era but used symbolically in the postexilic period. . . . I would take seriously the notion that the Jews in exile could help those remaining in Judah; but building on Provan's observation, I sense that Egypt and Assyria became the symbol of both false alliances and places of exile" (119). This solution makes the best sense in context, for it offers the best account of all the data. Jerusalem continues to suffer from alliances made in the past, a fact her people recognize. Presently her children must go abroad for food, where they ask help from the same people who either defeated them or failed to help them in the past. The verse's language once again leaves open all relevant historical possibilities since it includes hardships past and present.

The fourth matter may be resolved in a manner similar to the second and third issues. Obviously, the phrase "to have enough/satisfy ourselves with bread" refers to the hunger that stems from scarcity and high prices (see 5:4). At the same time, it is a good metaphor for the nation's search for help in time of political trouble (see Hos 2:9–10 [ET 2:7–8]). The choice of words allows the people to state that the problems they face have very old roots. They do not place all the blame on their predecessors, but they include prior generations' sins with their own.

7 This understanding of v 6 as linking the past and the present aids an appropriate interpretation of v 7 and its sister passage v 16. Experts have disagreed over how to understand these passages. Dobbs-Allsopp interprets 5:7 as a statement of fact/protest against Yahweh for making the current generation suffer for what prior generations did (145–46). K. M. O'Connor agrees, and writes, "The previous generation surely sinned collectively, but for the speakers, 'fatherless orphans' (v. 3), the punishment is truly excessive, for it continues into their own generation. Quietly they resist the theology of the narrator, Daughter Zion, and of the strong man that sin explains the frightful conditions of their lives. In this poem they express no repentance" ([2001] 1069). On the other hand, Provan (128) notes that the OT teaches that one generation can suffer for the sins of another (see Exod 20:5), yet at the same time the OT contains confessions of individuals in which they consider themselves part of earlier generations' sins (see Dan 9:16). Hillers ([1992] 164) takes a similar approach, noting that the tone of 5:7 and 16 differs from Jer 31:29 and Ezek 18:2, which quote Israelites who blame their parents' sins for their own hard times, despite evidence for their own sins. Berlin believes that 5:7 and 16 stress that punishment for recent and past sins continues more than they emphasize whether the sins of the fathers or children have caused the problem (120–21).

Lam 5:7 states historical reality, as does 5:16, and the two statements appear in the same major section of chap. 5. The people are historically correct when they state, "Our fathers sinned; they are no more" (אבתינו חטאו אינם). Passage after passage in the OT testifies that Israel's sin, practiced over decades and centuries, led to national disaster (see 2 Kgs 17; Jer 39, 52). It is just as true that the fathers are אינם, "no more," a word that means "have died" (see Gen 42:13), for they have died, have been exiled, and have fled (see 2:1–10; 4:1–16; 5:2–3). It is likewise true that what the people now endure may be traced to the fathers' iniquities (אנחנו עונתיהם סבלנו). The word for "carried" here (סבלנו) refers to vicarious suffering, as it does in Isa 53:4, 11. They are suffering for decisions made by others. It is also historically true to state that the current generation has committed noteworthy sins and made colossal political missteps (see Jeremiah). They confess as much in 5:16, a passage that agrees with 1:18–22, 2:20–22, and 3:40–42. In the book as a whole the people admit guilt for and express pain over punishment that covers long-term and short-term iniquity. Whatever pardon comes from Yahweh, then, must be as thorough as centuries-old iniquity.

8 So far the people have reported loss of inheritance (v 2); loss of familial, political, and spiritual parents (v 3); scarcity of food and water (v 4); and oppression by their captors (v 6). They have admitted that earlier alliances have led to present woe (vv 6–7). Now they lament the fact that "servants rule over us"

(עבדים משלו בנו) and the corresponding fact that "there is no one tearing (us) from their hand" (פרק אין מידם). The grip of the oppressor has led to hardship, and this situation is not likely to change unless God intervenes.

Who are these "servants"? Various options have been proposed. Surveying past opinions, Keil notes that the term has been interpreted as referring to Babylon in general (Keil's opinion), Babylon's soldiers, Babylon's chosen governors (Hillers, [1992] 164, and Rudolph, 261, agree with this position), and slaves placed in charge of Israel (Keil, 450). Renkema adds possibilities such as nations Judah once ruled, Edom, and a ruler of another nation approved by Babylon (606–7). Provan writes that it is impossible to determine with absolute accuracy the group meant. He concludes, "It is likely in any case that the language is partly influenced by the desire, evident in other verses of the chapter, to emphasize what a great reversal of fortunes has taken place, and consequently that it should not be pressed" (129). The language employed is general enough to include the multiple historical realities Judah faced. Babylon certainly ruled them. Babylon's chosen governors (see Jer 40) also ruled them, and nations Babylon lets afflict Jerusalem ruled them as well. Rebels also ruled Judah in the sense that their actions affected others (see Jer 42). No doubt servants rose to power and abused that power (see 2 Kgs 25:12 for this potential). The language used allows every possibility to remain in play. Therefore, it allows every outrage to be included in this prayer.

These ruthless servants of Babylon and of self-interest are well established. Judah has no way to get rid of them. Unlike Esau, whose father promises him that eventually he will tear himself loose from his brother's yoke (Gen 27:40; ופרקת עלו מעל צוארך), Jerusalem remains without specific hope. Unlike the worshipers in Ps 136:24, who profess that God has torn them loose from their foes (ויפרקנו מצרינו), Judah has no deliverer in sight. In other words, the people are currently less hopeful than was Esau, less favored than previous generations have been.

9 V 4 has already stated that water and wood are terribly expensive when they are available at all, and v 6 has noted the lengths people must to go to obtain bread. Now the people heighten the description of their plight. They claim that it is "at peril of our lives we get our bread" (בנפשנו נביא לחמנו), which is hardly an unexpected assertion given the precarious nature of their existence. But the next half-verse is less clear. It gives the reason for the risk of life as "the sword of the desert" (מפני חרב המדבר).

As is the case in previous verses, this phrase allows variations on the basic interpretation, which is that Jerusalem's inhabitants are in such desperate shape that they must risk their lives to secure life's basic necessities. Hillers thinks that the "sword" is a lack of law and order in the land ([1992] 164). Kraus concludes that "sword" refers to marauding bandits such as those in 2 Kgs 13:20–21 (89). Berlin believes that "sword" stands for famine, as in Deut 28:22 (121). Renkema asserts that the half-verse reminds readers that the city was watched constantly (see 4:19), so when people went out to get hidden stores of food (see Jer 41:8), they were cut down by enemies (607). The phrase covers each of these possibilities, which underscores the truth of the statement. They face death from a variety of sources. Perhaps even the "servants" noted in the preceding verse provide some sort of "sword."

10 With limited bread and water, it is understandable for the people to suffer hunger-related physical deterioration. Sadly, they state that "our skin is wrinkled as by a furnace" (עורנו כתנור נכמרו). The "furnace" receives its heat from famine (מפני זלעפות רעב). Just as the Nazirites were disfigured by hunger in 4:7–8, so the people have been marred by the effects of slowly starving to death. The wrinkled skin (see *Note* 10.a-a.) comes from loss of weight, and the discoloration of skin comes from malnutrition.

11 As terrible as economic woe is, it is not the most devastating type of pain Jerusalem endures. Abuse of all kinds exceeds woe associated with monetary deprivation. Young women, young men, elders, and officials all suffer the most humiliating of attacks on their persons. Though it is possible to treat these verses as descriptions of things that occurred during the city's fall, it is more likely here that the people describe current general lawlessness (see Hillers, [1992] 164; Berlin, 122; Renkema 609–10). Lack of law enforcement leads to danger. Oppression rules.

With sober realism, the people report that "they [the enemies] raped women in Zion, virgins in the cities of Judah." The word translated "raped" (ענו) "has the general sense of doing violence, humiliating, oppressing, and in this context it refers to a man forcing a woman to have sex" (Reyburn, *Handbook,* 137). Forms of the word have this meaning in Gen 34:2 and 2 Sam 13:14, texts in which Dinah and Tamar, respectively, are raped. This situation is widespread, for it pertains "in Zion" (בציון) and "in the cities of Judah" (בערי יהודה). Women are not truly safe anywhere, a situation that the book noted as early as 1:4 and 1:18.

12 Nor are the traditional ruling groups safe. Jerusalem's "officials are hung up by their hands" (שרים בידם נתלו). Concerning the meaning of this hanging by the hands, Dobbs-Allsopp (146) writes, "The image of princes being hung in 5:12 signifies either execution (e.g., Gen 40:19; Esth 2:23) by hanging or being impaled on a stake (as, for example, in the Assyrian reliefs depicting the siege of Lachish, *ANEP,* 372, 373) or exposure of the corpses (after execution) as a means of degradation and for instilling fear in the survivors (e.g., Josh 8:29; 1 Sam 31:10)." This latest degradation of the princes/officials follows earlier ones. In 1:6 this group has become like deer fainting without pasture, and in 2:9 they are scattered among the nations. Now they are judged harshly for whatever reason the oppressor wishes. Thus, the officials who stay in the land fare worse than those scattered abroad.

Likewise, "the faces of (the) elders are not respected" (פני זקנים לא נהדרו). This verbal form comes from the root הדר, "honor." The noun הדרה, "adornment," appears in 1:6, so loss of honor ties the officials' and elders' woes here. In 1:19 Jerusalem states that elders have perished, in 2:10 the narrator reports that some of them sit on the ground in stunned silence, and in 4:16 the narrator states that they receive no mercy in the land where they have been scattered. Now they are not offered the respect due their age and status. Shame remains a major theme in the book.

13 The report on the various groups mentioned earlier in the book continues. Here "choice young men" (בחורים) and "boys/young men" (ונערים) are burdened beyond their capacity. Already 1:18 has stated that, along with some of the young women, some of the choice young men, who are probably soldiers or at least potentially soldiers, have gone into captivity. Jerusalem expected these men to protect her (1:15), but instead most of them lie in the dust of the street (2:21). Those who remain "grind" (טחון), most likely at a corn mill (see Provan,

131), a task usually reserved for slaves or animals (see Reyburn, *Handbook*, 139). Their younger counterparts gather wood until they collapse under the load (בעץ כשלו). Of course, many of their number have already perished (see 2:21), and, like the choice young men, those that remain do arduous manual labor. As with shame, reversal of fortunes continues its role as unifying theme.

14 This verse both concludes a section (vv 11–14) and provides a transition to the next segment (vv 15–18). It finishes the current section by revisiting two groups, the "elders" (זקנים) and the "choice young men" (בחורים), that appear in v 12 and v 13, respectively. The former group has "ceased from (the) gate" (משער שבתו), while the latter group has ceased "their music" (מנגינתם). Thus, the people complete their report of what has happened to the young women, the choice young men, the elders, the young men, and the officials. At this juncture of the book's closing poem, the people report that things have not gotten better for these children of Zion. It is therefore appropriate to continue to bring their plight before the Lord and hope for renewal.

The verse provides a transition to the next segment by emphasizing how normal daily life has degenerated to the point of virtually ceasing altogether. The gate was the place where decisions were made, business was conducted, people greeted one another, and some entertainment took place (see Keil, 452). It was natural for older men to sit there and perform their social function, and it was natural for younger men to enjoy music there. That all this natural activity has ceased indicates that the city has no more civic activity, no more celebrations, no more freedom to conduct normal community life (see Berlin, 123–24).

15 A clear progression marks the chapter so far. Jerusalem was given over to outsiders (vv 2–3), physical sustenance became tenuous when it was not totally impossible (vv 4–10), oppressors ruled the people ruthlessly (vv 11–13), and community life ceased (v 14). Now the people stress both the loss of normal community life and the grief that this loss has incurred. Reversal of fortune and collective shame mark vv 15–18. Joy is no more, mourning has replaced dancing, and Zion lies as desolate as her people's emotional state. As before, Yahweh remains their only hope for changed circumstances, so they pray to the one who punished them in the first place.

V 15 begins with the declaration, "The joy of our hearts has ceased" (שבת משוש לבנו). The usage of שבת, "has ceased," here clearly connects this phrase to v 14, where שבתו, "they have ceased," is the governing verb. In v 14b music stopped, and here joy or rejoicing has ceased. The reason for the "joy" (משוש) in this verse is not identical to the occasion for music in the previous verse, however, for there the music probably refers to music made on various occasions, while the joy in this verse is probably liturgical in nature (Gerstenberger, [2001] 503). Renkema (615) observes that the loss of rejoicing here is like the loss of rejoicing at festival and worship threatened in Hos 2:13 (ET 2:11). Indeed the same word is used (with the third-person feminine possessive pronoun) in both texts, though the Hosea passage refers to pagan rituals. Fuerst makes a similar comment about the loss of joy predicted in Jer 25:10 (259). It is likely, then, that this verse once again reminds readers that what has happened to Jerusalem has occurred in spite of prophetic warnings. Joy over appropriate worship need never have ceased.

Liturgical imagery continues in the second half of the verse: "our dancing has been cast down into mourning" (נהפך לאבל מחלנו). Berlin believes that the rejoicing mentioned in the first half of the verse "refers to the festive celebrations at the temple, which have now been transformed into lamentations for its loss. Joy is not a state of mind but a ritual experience performed in the presence of God, while mourning signals the absence of God" (124). Rituals associated with joy such as dancing have given way to rituals associated with sorrow and mourning. Jerusalem's situation has not improved as the book has proceeded, for 1:4 states that the roads to Zion mourn (דרכי ציון אבלות) because no one comes to the regular festivals, and 2:6 notes that Zion has been made to forget both Sabbath and festival. All these passages relate the loss of festival to the loss of the temple, so religious life remains as barren as community life.

16 With liturgical loss stated plainly one more time in v 15, the people move toward a clear statement about the desolation of Zion in v 18. Now they say, "The crown has fallen from our head" (נפלה עטרת ראשנו). Berlin believes that the crown is the Davidic kingship. Thus she thinks the verse laments the loss of kingship and temple worship (124). Renkema, on the other hand, suggests that the crown may be Jerusalem itself, the city's walls, or the temple on Zion; he then concludes that the temple is the best option given this verse's similarity of content with chaps. 1 and 2 (616–17). Lamentations certainly mourns the loss of Zion more often than it does the loss of the Davidic kingship, though the latter concern emerges directly in 4:20. Kraus (90) notes that Jer 13:18 links the loss of kingship and the loss of the nation's cities, so both images may be intended here, for Jerusalem's devastation includes city, people, cult, and king.

The people confess the sins that have caused all this pain. As in 1:18–22, admission of guilt appears: "woe to us, for we have sinned" (אוי נא לנו כי חטאנו). This phrase includes the dual understanding that sin has occurred and that punishment has followed the sin, an understanding that marks 1:5, 8, 14, 18, 22; 2:14; 3:42; and 4:6, 13, 22 (Wiesmann, 259). It upholds God's righteousness in the matter of Jerusalem's demise (Weiser, 366). Renkema observes that אוי נא, "woe to us," occurs only here and in Jer 4:31 and 45:3 (617–18). In the former text the daughter of Zion cries out before murderers, while in the latter text Jeremiah quotes Baruch's self-pitying, though understandable, complaint about personal deprivation. The text reminds readers of prophetic warnings; Jerusalem has fallen according to the word of the Lord (see 1:21).

The book never wavers in its conviction that God has punished because of what the covenant people have done. It never moves away from the conviction that the long-announced day of the Lord has come upon Israel. At the same time, it never flags in prayer. It maintains a dogged determination to confess sin adequately enough to restore the people's relationship with their covenant partner, who is also their judge.

17–18 Vv 17 and 18 tie together the various elements of vv 15–18. Three consecutive half-lines begin with an explanatory על, "because." The first of these is joined to a masculine singular demonstrative adjective (זה). Apparently זה, "this," refers to the fact that they have sinned and brought woe upon themselves (see Hillers, [1992] 159). This realization leads them to state that "our heart has become faint" (היה דוה לבנו), a comment very close in content to 1:13, where Jerusalem states that God's judgment has left her "faint all day" (כל היום דוה).

The second of these is joined to a plural demonstrative adjective (אלה). Though it is impossible to know with absolute certainty, אלה, "these things," most likely refers to all that has been listed in 5:2–16. These disasters are summarized by 5:18, which comments that Zion is desolate and patrolled by wild animals. All "these things" make the people's "eyes grow dim" (חשכו עינינו), perhaps with tears, since 1:16a contains a similar construction (על אלה אני בוכיה; see Renkema, 619). If so, then they weep here as Jerusalem did in chap. 1 and as "the man" did in chap. 3. They are discouraged but not unable to see any hope, as K. M. O'Connor asserts ([2001] 1070).

The third introduces a summary clause. Faintness of heart and darkness of eyes result "because Mount Zion is desolate" (על הר ציון ששמם), a fact established already in 1:4, 13, 16; 3:11; and 4:5. Zion's desolation includes loss of people, palace, and temple. To underscore this utter lack of human activity, the line section concludes with the notation that "jackals walk/prowl in it" (שועלים הלכו בו). These animals were known to haunt ruins (see Ezek 13:4). With such terrible circumstances a daily experience, no wonder the nation expresses sorrow.

19–22 This final section closes the book on a hopeful, yet uncertain, note. It is hopeful in that the people confess God's enduring power and authority (v 19), as well as his ability to restore and renew (v 21). It is uncertain in that the people state bluntly that God has cast them off for a very long time (v 20), which makes them wonder aloud if God ever intends to restore them (v 22). As has been true throughout the book, Israel realizes that all they can do is confess sin, confess God's authority, express their pain, and urgently ask God to deliver them. Though the book's message has taken many forms and presented readers with many new angles, this unified message has remained intact throughout every successive segment.

19 Despite all that the people have endured, they have not lost their fundamental faith in Yahweh's absolute sovereignty. They may question his decision about the scale of his anger and the longevity of their punishment, but they still assert, "You, O LORD, reign forever [אתה יהוה לעולם תשב]; your throne (endures from) generation to generation [כסאך לדר ודור]." As Keil observes, "The glory of Zion, the earthly habitation of the Lord, is at an end, but the throne of the Lord endures eternally" (453–54). He adds that the eternal nature of God's throne is "expressed as the ground of hope, in nearly the same words as Ps. cii. 13" (454). In Ps 102:13–14 (ET 102:12–13), the psalmist confesses that God is enthroned and thus remembered throughout all generations (ואתה יהוה לעולם תשב וזכרך לדר ודר); asks the Lord to have pity on Zion; and, finally, argues that it is time to have pity on her. Renkema (623–24) notes that Pss 45:7–8 (ET 45:6–7) and 93:2 indicate that God's throne remains forever and observes that the former passage stresses God's righteousness. Ps 90 also claims that God has existed from generation to generation (90:1) and that God has been God from everlasting to everlasting (90:2). Based in part on these confessions, the psalmist asks God how long his people must suffer and implores God to restore them to favor (90:13–17).

If such parallel passages are in the background here, then the verse underscores determined prayer based on faith in a sovereign God. The prayer reminds God, who is not circumscribed by time, that it is time to act on Zion's behalf, while the faith in divine sovereignty, longevity, and righteousness keeps the people focused on taking their pain to their covenant God. Thus, they emulate not only the authors of Pss 90 and 102 but the speaker in 2:11–19 and "the man" from chap. 3 as well. Expressions of pain do not mean that belief in divine uprightness has dissipated. Indeed, that the people still pray may well indicate that if anything their faith remains evident in the face of overwhelming pressure to discard it.

20 The people are as aware of their own finitude as they are of Yahweh's infinitude. They wonder why God continually forgets them (למה לנצח תשכחנו); they wonder why he has forsaken them for so many days (תעזבנו לארך ימים). This intensive parallelism highlights two factors: the lengthy nature of their experience and the loss of covenantal fellowship with Yahweh.

The first reference to duration (לנצח) is similar to Ps 74:1, where the writer asks, "Why, O God, do you cast us off continually" (למה אלהים זנחת לנצח). The recurrence of למה, "why?" and לנצח, "continually," is particularly striking, as is the emphasis on the devastation of Zion in both passages. As was noted in the *Comments* on chaps. 2 and 4, Lamentations refers to Ps 74 on more than one occasion, or at least shares a common stock of terms. Further, Ps 89, another passage that Lamentations seems to know or at least share elements with, likewise uses לנצח, "continually," in a question about the duration of Israel's suffering (see Ps 89:47 [ET 89:46]). As for the second reference to duration, לארך ימים, "for so many days," Renkema notes that this combination only occurs here and in Pss 23:6 and 93:5; he then claims that the phrase indicates "the incessant sequence of days which the people experience one by one as days of unremitting affliction" (626). The first reference focuses on continual action, while the second focuses on the affliction associated with that action. The first phrase references similar questions in like-minded psalms, while the second phrase intensifies the first expression.

The verse's two verbs underscore the covenantal nature of the people's loss. These same two forms appear in Isa 49:14, where Zion states that Yahweh has forsaken and forgotten her (ותאמר ציון עזבני יהוה ואדני שכחני). In Isa 49:15 Yahweh reassures Zion of his love. Therefore, such statements are probably intended to gain a positive response from the Lord, and the parallel passage in Isaiah indicates that such response can in fact result. Though the word for "forgotten" does not appear often in Jeremiah, the word for "forsaken" does, for Jer 2–6 states repeatedly that Israel has forsaken Yahweh. God's people have broken their covenant with Yahweh by being unfaithful through idolatry, so they will suffer the consequences of those actions. At this point in Lamentations, however, the people implore Yahweh to see that they are no longer in this rebellious state. They have come to understand their faults, their culpability, and their dependence on Yahweh. Given these realizations, they wonder how much longer the already lengthy punishment must continue. They are not as they were before, so why cannot Yahweh return to what he was before punishment began?

21 As Westermann (217) and Gerstenberger ([2001] 503–4) indicate, this verse constitutes a clear plea for restoration. But the people do not simply ask that their fortunes be restored. They request that they be restored to Yahweh, their covenant partner. They desire a restored relationship (Berlin, 125). They have endured the day of the Lord and the sustained punishment that followed it. They realize that God has forsaken them in response to their forsaking of him. They have used language found in covenantal texts like Pss 74 and 89, Isa 49:14–15, and Jer 2–6. All these factors testify to their need and desire for covenant renewal.

They begin with a command and a confession of faith. They urge Yahweh, "Restore us, O LORD, to yourself, and we shall be restored" (השיבנו יהוה אליך ונשוב). This phrase parallels Jer 31:18, where Ephraim asks, "Restore me and I will be restored, for you are Yahweh my God" (השיבני ואשובה כי אתה יהוה אלהי). Both texts confess that Yahweh must effect renewal, for Yahweh has been the wronged party in the covenant. It is up to him, then, to decide whether to continue in the relationship. Both texts also assert that, if Yahweh is so inclined, the people will indeed be restored. God's sovereignty is not in question in this chapter, as 5:19 has already proven. The passage does not ask the Lord to restore them so that they may then repent. Confession and repentance have occurred. What remains to be seen is when or if renewed relationship will result in changed circumstances.

If Yahweh is so inclined, the people desire to have things as they were in the past. They wish God to "renew our days as in times past" (חדש ימינו כקדם). This renewal of days gone by stands in sharp contrast to the forsaking for many days mentioned in the previous verse. These people have encountered many reversals in this book, and they want one more. This time they want a reversal of fortunes back to the times when they enjoyed precious things (see 1:7—כל מחמדיה אשר היו מימי קדם, "all her precious things that / were from days of old") rather than to continue to encounter the judgments announced long ago (see 2:17—אשר צוה מימי־קדם, "which he commanded from days of old"). Renewal would mean the end of forgetting and forsaking.

22 This final verse has sparked a great deal of discussion because of its opening clause and how it affects the book's conclusion. In v 21 the people asked the Lord to restore them along lines also found in Jer 31:18, a passage that leads to the promise of a new covenant and other long-term blessings in Jer 31:31–40. In v 22 they begin with an enigmatic כי אם, "even though," and then conclude with easily understood terminology: "you have indeed rejected us and have been exceedingly angry with us" (מאס מאסתנו קצפת עלינו עד מאד).

Albrektson (*Studies in the Text and Theology*, 205–7) and Gordis (196–98) have offered excellent summaries of the options for translating and interpreting כי אם. Though other possibilities can be elaborated, perhaps the following survey will describe the problem. First, since the LXX and Syriac do not translate אם, "if," it is possible that the word should be deleted. On the other hand, these two translations may well be trying to make the best sense they can of a difficult clause, a task with which virtually every Lamentations commentator would sympathize. Second, the phrase could mean "unless," since texts that include the clause (for example, Gen 32:27; Lev 22:6) have that meaning. The problem with this conclusion is that these texts all include a negative particle prior to the clause, so 5:22 does not fit this pattern (see Gordis, 197; Hillers, [1992] 160). This fact does not deter Westermann (217–19) and Albrektson (*Studies in the Text and Theology*, 206–7) from deciding that this meaning is still the most natural option. Keil offers a variation on this approach, for he believes that the clause is negative but that it introduces a hypothetical situation, "the actual occurrence of which is out of the question" (454). Third, some translations (e.g., RSV) have turned the clause into a question, "Or have you . . . ?" This rendering seems to be an attempt to make sense of the clause, for there is no syntactical reason whatsoever to conclude that the clause introduces a question. Fourth, Hillers concludes that the clause should be read as an adversative ("but, rather"; see Hillers, [1992] 160–61). In this reading the phrase means that the people have prayed for renewal (v 21), but what they receive currently is continued rejection and divine anger (v 22). Thus, the verse does not contradict 5:21. Instead, it states the obvious: Israel desires a restored covenant relationship with Yahweh and all that relationship's benefits, but such has not yet occurred. Fifth, Gordis (198) argues that כי אם should be translated "even if, although." He bases his decision on the clause's usage in Jer 51:14, Isa 10:22, Amos 5:22, and Lam 3:32–33, as well as on the structure of 5:21–22 and parallel texts like Ps 89:51–52. He then concludes that the verse's verbs should be translated as pluperfects. Thus, he translates 5:21–22 as, "Turn us to Yourself, O Lord, and we shall be restored; renew our days as of old, even though You had despised us greatly and had been very angry with us." Sixth, Linafelt (*Surviving Lamentations*, 60) claims that the clause means "unless," which means that the book trails off with no word from God. Thus, the book is left with an open ended "conclusion." Berlin rightly observes, "This interpretation may resonate with the modern reader, but it is likely too modern for the ancient author" (126). Seventh, Berlin herself concludes that the clause should be read "in a restrictive sense, in opposition to what went before" (125). This reading leaves the people in a quandary, for they state that Yahweh has done the opposite of what they desire. Such an interpretation probably lies behind the Jewish practice of repeating v 21 after v 22, or of transposing the two verses (see Wiesmann, 264–67).

Sorting out these possibilities and deciding on the best option is by no means a simple task. Several of these possibilities reflect grammatical options listed in GKC §163, and several of them have some level of contextual support. Nonetheless, it is necessary to come to a conclusion on the matter. First, the options that have no syntactical backing, such as treating the verse as a question or as an open-ended statement should be eliminated, though these suggestions are by no means totally baseless. Second, syntactical options that require elements that this passage lacks should also be eliminated. The most significant erasure would be the "unless" possibility, but the lack of a preceding negative particle surely must carry some weight. Third, though the Greek and Syriac omission is significant, this passage is probably a prime example of considering the more difficult reading the original one. Also, the clause appears in 3:32, so the book itself offers a precedent for the term's usage. Fourth, though it is possible that 5:21–22 sets up a hypothetical situation that cannot possibly come to pass, it seems unlikely that the text employs this strategy. The book is so anchored to reality that one wonders if such a switch in strategy would occur. Fifth, for similar reasons it seems unlikely that the book ends with the people at odds with God's decision to punish. The problem is not that the people resent the lack of relief because they believe their confession has been enough to move God to sympathy. The problem is that they wonder what more must be done to restore the covenant relationship. They have never professed innocence.

Hillers and Gordis offer the best possibilities. Hillers observes, correctly, that the verse may simply read "but (at this point in time) you have rejected us; you have been very angry with us" ([1992] 160–61). Therefore, the people call for a change in the current situation. Gordis's suggestion that כי אם means "even, although" is an even better solution for three reasons. First, it maintains Hillers's view of what the people pray, for it allows the people to state their current situation while showing faith in God's eventual favor. Second, it coincides with the probable meaning of the same phrase in 3:32. There the speaker sets up a contrast between what the people experience now and what they will eventually experience. He observes that God will not punish forever (3:31), then states that "even though he afflicts, indeed he shows compassion, according to his great covenant mercy" (3:32). So 5:22 would read, "even though you have indeed rejected us, and have been exceedingly angry with us." The people would be stating that they ask the Lord to restore them even though he has been justifiably angry with them. Third, this option is in keeping with the term's usage in passages Gordis cites (see Jer 51:14; Isa 10:22; Amos 5:22). All these texts express reversals of some type. Thus, though other possibilities are certainly viable, the rendering "even though" is the best option. This decision does not mean, however, that Gordis's argument for the pluperfect rendering of the verbs is convincing.

By using an infinitive absolute followed by a perfect-tense verb, the people state emphatically that Yahweh has rejected them (מאס מאסתנו). This verb has covenantal implications. In Lev 26:15 Yahweh warns that rejection of the law will lead to the infliction of the covenant curses outlined in Lev 26:16–39, most of which are paralleled in Lam 1, 2, and 4. Jer 6:19 states that Israel has rejected God's law, which in turn leads God to reject Israel in Jer 6:30. Similarly, in Jer 7:29 Yahweh announces that he has rejected "the generation of his wrath." In Jer 14:19 the prophet asks if God has rejected Israel forever. Lev 26:44–45 has already answered this question, for it states that, even after the covenant curses have fallen, the Lord will not reject the people once and for all. Rather, he will remember the covenant and be their God. Likewise, Jer 31:37, 33:24, and 33:26 indicate that Yahweh will not reject Israel completely, though he has rejected them for a time. The people are able to expect the Lord to reverse this rejection at a future time of his choosing.

Much the same can be said of the divine anger the people currently endure. Though the process of exile has ended (4:22), much suffering remains, and this suffering is explained as a result of God's ongoing, extreme, justifiable anger. This description of Yahweh's anger and the plea for renewal parallels Isa 57:14–21. There the Lord states that he desires to revive the lowly (Isa 57:15) and asserts that he will not remain angry indefinitely (Isa 57:16; ולא לנצח אקצוף). Rather, he will heal those he has struck, though he will not give peace to the wicked (Isa 57:17–21). The people count on this sort of description of Yahweh's character. In this way 5:22 parallels 3:19–38, where Yahweh's severity is not taken as primary to his character or as the final stage in his relationship with Israel. However long the process, the people's plea indicates that they believe that the covenant relationship can and will be restored. But Yahweh must determine to restore them to himself. Israel's many confessions in the book point out their belief—never altered—that they caused the breach in covenant that led to their long punishment. They hope now that just as judgment came, so now renewal will come as well. Passages like Lev 26:44–45, Isa 57:14–21, and Jer 31–32 indicate that the wicked will not be restored, so the people place themselves in Yahweh's hands, having done all they know to do to turn from the sins that they believe caused their punishment.

Explanation

In many ways this chapter is the simplest to explain, especially if one considers the passage's form. The passage unfolds as a fairly straightforward community lament, for it includes an opening address (v 1), a lament/description of woes (vv 2–18), and a plea for renewal of the covenant relationship (vv 19–22). At the same time, the final four verses have sparked considerable discussion, as the commentary above has already indicated. Taken as a part of the book as a whole, this chapter summarizes the purpose and message of Lamentations.

The opening plea (v 1) addresses Yahweh directly, the very thing 2:11–19 and 3:48–66 encourage the people to do. Israel's disgrace stands at the heart of the verse, just as it does in 1:12–16. As the whole book confesses, only God can remove this disgrace. Israel's future remains totally in Yahweh's hands.

The description of Israel's woes also evokes earlier images. Israel suffers economic deprivation brought on by the invasion and loss of their land (vv 2–10). Such images of desolation and oppression mark 1:1–11, 2:1–10, and 4:1–10. The people confess their fathers' sinfulness in v 7 and admit that their punishment has something to do with the nation's historic attitude toward their covenant obligations. Israel has also suffered terrible social oppression, including the rape of women, mistreatment of elders, and abuse of choice young people (vv 11–14). Again, passages such as 1:1–11, 2:20–22, 3:1–18, and 4:1–10 also highlight these outrages. The mistreatment and suffering of children are a special concern in all these passages as well. Finally, Israel has suffered disruption of political and social fabric (vv 15–18). Loss of king, temple, and cult receive particular attention, as they do in 1:1–11, 2:1–10, and 4:17–20. In 5:16 the people confess their sins, not just those of their elders. It has taken many years and many sins to arrive at this situation. No matter how frustrated the people become in the book, they never waver from the conviction that their sins have caused the breach in their relationship with Yahweh.

Despite their admission of guilt, however, the people believe it is possible to be restored to their position in the covenant. Thus, they offer a final plea for renewal (vv 19–22). This plea is based on God's sovereign character (v 19), as it is in 2:11 and 3:19–38. Given this character, the people press Yahweh to consider the time of punishment over (v 20). They ask that God renew them even though he has rightly been angry with them for some time (vv 21–22). God has not answered yet, but texts such as Lev 26:44–45 and Deut 30:1–10 offer hope that confession and divine compassion will lead to the end of the period of rejection, as do the convictions stated in 2:11–19 and 3:19–38.

When the book ends, Israel has not yet heard directly from Yahweh. The matter now rests with him. But the people have done what they must to return to the one who can restore them. Pain has been expressed. The people have recognized their culpability for what has happened. They press Yahweh for relief, but they do not claim that this relief is owed them. They confess God's power and righteousness, and lay claim to the hope for renewal found in similar covenant passages. God's promises are in their favor, so restoration of covenant relationship is on the horizon. The timing of that restoration remains up to God alone. Still, being in this position is, ironically, a better place than the people occupied for some time. Their situation will improve because of the covenant with Yahweh, and their careful and heartfelt lamenting is the means by which that improvement will come. Their lament has been for the purpose of renewal, and the whole of biblical theology indicates that this purpose will be served.

Index of Authors Cited

Song of Songs

Abraham ben Isaac ha-Levi Tamakh 62, 63
Adeney, W. F. 77
Albrektson, B. 156, 157
Albright, W. F. 81, 82, 251, 253
Alden, R. L. 31, 203, 213, 258, 259
Alexander, P. S. 59, 61
Allison, D. C. 175, 182
Alshich, M. 59, 63, 64
Alter, R. 40
Anderson, A. A. 164
Arbel, D. V. 84, 85, 258
Astell, A. W. 59, 70
Ayo, N. 97, 98

Barthes, R. 91, 96
Beare, F. W. 175, 183
Bekkenkamp, J. 85
Benjamin, D. 164
Bergant, D. 164, 166, 209
Berlin, A. 40, 43
Bernard of Clairvaux 69
Black, F. C. 35, 38, 39, 84, 86, 203, 211, 235
Black, J. A. 47, 48, 90
Bloch, A. A. 125, 126, 128, 141, 231, 232
Bloch, C. 125, 126, 128, 141, 231, 232
Blumenthal, D. R. 97, 98
Boer, R. 97, 103
Brenner, A. 14, 18, 35, 38, 84, 85, 86, 140, 235, 240
Brettler, M. Z. 84
Bright, J. 203, 212
Brooke, G. 135
Brooks, C. 91
Brown, J. P. 184
Brown, P. 59, 67, 68, 97, 100, 101
Broyde, M. J. 14, 15
Bullock, C. H. 76, 81
Burrowes, G. 73
Burrows, M. S. 59, 69
Butting, K. 84, 85, 86, 87, 156

Cahill, J. B. 59, 66
Callow, J. 125
Campbell, J. 97, 107, 111
Carr, G. L. 81, 177, 178, 208
Chaucer, G. 59, 68, 75, 118, 120
Chave, P. 84, 86
Christensen, D. L. 40, 45
Collins, T. 40
Cooper, J. S. 47, 48
Corney, R. W. 92
Cotterell, P. 123
Cotton, J. 72
Craigie, P. C. 166
Crim, K. R. 184
Cross, F. M., Jr. 40, 45
Cureton, R. D. 92

Dahood, M. 125, 128
Dale, A. M. 164
Davidson, R. M. 97, 98
Davies, W. B. 175, 182
Davis, E. F. 35, 39

Deckers, M. 231
De Hoop, R. 41
Delitzsch, F. 79, 80, 83
Dessel, J. P. 235, 245
Dever, W. 14, 20, 23
Dijk, F. van 85
Dillow, J. C. 97, 99
Dirksen, P. B. 175, 177
Dorsey, D. A. 25, 31
Dove, M. 59, 69
Driver, G. R. 17, 175, 180
Driver, S. R. 164
Durham, J. 72

Edmée, Sister 169, 170
Eichrodt, W. 184, 191
Elder, D. 59, 74
Elliot, M. T. 25, 28, 29
Elliot, M. W. 97, 99
Emerton, J. A. 135, 137, 138
Emmerson, G. I. 76, 79
Epstein, I. 175, 181
Exum, J. C. 25, 30, 31, 84, 85, 86, 136, 203, 206, 212
Ezra ben Solomon of Gerona 62

Falk, M. 35, 39, 84, 85, 161
Feuillet, A. 61, 71, 87, 88
Flavel, J. 72
Fohrer, G. 13, 83
Fontaine, C. R. 84, 86
Foster, J. L. 47, 49
Fox, M. V. 14, 16, 21, 22, 25, 27, 29, 30, 47, 49, 50, 51, 52, 54, 55, 56, 81, 83, 129, 135, 137, 149, 152, 170, 176, 178, 180, 186, 190, 191, 193, 206, 208, 209, 210, 211, 216
Fredericks, D. C. 14, 16, 17, 18
Freedman, D. N. 40, 45
Fuerst, W. J. 138

Garrett, D. A. 19, 31, 86, 88, 175, 177, 184, 196
Geraty, L. T. 241, 242
Gerleman, G. 128, 178, 188, 190, 220, 222
Gersonides, *see* Levi ben Gershom
Gibson, J. C. L. 156, 159
Giles of Rome 68
Gill, J. 73
Gledhill, T. 27, 97, 99, 174, 215
Glickman, S. C. 97, 99
Goitein, S. D. 84, 85
Good, E. M. 35, 40
Goppelt, L. 60, 74
Gordis, R. 14, 27, 141, 161, 221
Goulder, M. D. 25, 76, 79, 80
Gray, G. B. 40
Grober, S. F. 25, 28, 140, 148
Grossfeld, B. 60, 61
Guillaume de Saint-Thierry 71
Gundry, R. H. 175, 183
Guyon, Madame 71

Haïk-Vantoura, S. 40
Hall, D. 92, 95

Hallote, R. 235, 245
Hamilton, V. 140, 152
Harrison, R. K. 60, 77
Hein, R. 97, 106
Hermann, A. 47, 49
Hess, R. 203, 207
Hill, A. E. 218
Holladay, W. L. 41, 46, 135, 138, 203, 212
Honeyman, A. M. 184
Hrushovski, B. 41, 45
Hunt, P. N. 140

Israelit-Groll, S. 203

Jacob, I. 244, 247
Jacob, W. 244, 247
Jacobsen, T. 47, 48
Jakobson, R. 41, 97, 111
Jeremias, J. 175, 183
Joffe, A. 235, 245
John of Ford 60
Joüon, P. 71

Kallas, E. 72
Keel, O. 25, 27, 29, 53, 99, 140, 144, 147, 148, 149, 152, 159, 160, 162, 177, 186, 190, 191, 192, 196, 197, 208, 214, 221, 225, 228, 234, 237, 239, 244, 245, 247, 248, 249, 254
Kellner, M. M. 60, 62
Kimelman, R. 60, 66
King, P. 203, 209, 210, 235, 240
Kinlaw, D. F. 97, 107
Kitchen, K. A. 227
Knight, G. A. F. 98
Konkel, A. 140, 145
Korpel, M. C. A. 41
Kramer, S. N. 81, 82
Kugel, J. L. 41, 42, 43, 45

LaCocque, A. 14, 20, 86, 87, 88, 89, 90
Landy, F. 21, 161
LaSor, W. S., et al. 18
Lee, G. M. 218
Lemaire, A. 156, 157, 159
Levi ben Gershom (Gersonides) 62, 64
Lévi-Strauss, C. 97, 107, 108, 109, 110, 112, 115
Lewis, C. S. 60, 74, 75, 97, 102, 106, 107, 110, 111, 117
Lichtheim, M. 47, 49, 184, 195
Littledale, R. F. 73
Loder, J. 97, 107
Loewe, R. 60, 61
Longman, T. III 18, 24, 25, 27, 30, 59, 98, 124, 214, 215, 224, 239, 240
Lowth, R. 41, 42
Lundbom, J. R. 169
Lyke, L. L. 184, 196

Maranda, E. K. 97, 109
Maranda, P. 97, 109
Martínez, F. G. 218, 222
Matter, E. A. 60, 67, 70
Matthews, V. 164

Index of Authors Cited

Mazar, A. 20, 23
McCambley, C. 60, 66
Meek, T. 81, 82
Merkin, D. 84, 86
Meyers, C. 35, 39, 84, 85
Miller, P. C. 60, 66
Moor, J. C. de 41
Munro, J. 210
Murphy, R. E. 16, 18, 21, 24, 25, 27, 35, 38, 64, 82, 97, 98, 136, 156, 161, 163, 170, 176, 179, 180, 181, 186, 192, 205, 210, 213, 221, 223, 232, 237, 239, 243, 246, 251, 254, 255, 264

Neighbor, R. E. 73, 74
Newberry, T. 60, 73
Newton, A. L. 60, 73
Norris, R. A., Jr. 60, 66

O'Connor, D. 47, 53
O'Connor, M. 41, 45, 46, 47
Ogden, G. S. 131
Origen 64, 65, 66, 67, 87, 89, 98, 117
Ostriker, A. 84, 85

Page, D. 164
Pardee, D. 41
Paul, S. M. 231, 232
Payne, R. 97, 99
Phipps, W. E. 60, 64, 203, 215
Polaski, D. C. 84, 86
Pope, M. 17, 18, 25, 26, 53, 51, 62, 63, 71, 77, 79, 82, 83, 84, 99, 132, 140, 141, 144, 161, 174, 179, 181, 188, 193, 206, 208, 213, 223, 225, 232, 233, 237, 239, 249, 254, 261
Price, J. D. 41
Provan, I. 78, 79, 80, 99

Rabin, C. 14, 19
Rainey, A. F. 227
Renan, E. 81
Robert, A. 61, 71, 87, 88
Roth, M. 164
Rowley, H. H. 82
Rudolph, W. 174, 191, 197, 219

Saebø, M. 14, 140
Sasson, J. M. 47, 48
Sasson, V. 14, 25
Schmidt, N. 82
Schökel, L. A. 41
Schweizer, E. 175, 182
Segal, M. H. 14, 19
Sendrey, A. 41
Shea, W. H. 25, 30, 31
Shippey, T. 97
Shults, F. L. 97, 107, 109, 115
Simon, M. 60, 61
Snaith, J. G. 97, 99
Soden, W. von 149
Soulen, R. N. 36, 39
Stadelmann, L. I. J. 71, 72
Stager, L. 203, 209, 210, 235, 240
Stanford, W. B. 221
Stern, E. 20, 225, 227, 235, 241, 242
Stuart, D. K. 41, 45
Sviri, S. 118

Thomas, D. W. 203, 207
Thompson, H. O. 242
Thomson, R. W. 60, 70
Tolkien, J. R. R. 14, 74, 97
Tournay, J. R. 60, 61, 71, 87, 88, 264
Tov, E. 14, 16
Treat, J. C. 14, 16
Trible, P. 84, 85, 97, 99, 235, 245
Tromp, N. J. 251, 255
Turner, D. 60, 71

Vance, D. R. 41
Vendler, H. 36, 92, 94, 95, 96

Waldman, N. M. 184, 193
Walker, L. L. 140, 149
Walsh, C. E. 84, 86, 97, 100, 203, 211, 215
Walton, J. 164
Warren, R. P. 91
Waterman, L. 76, 78
Watson, W. G. E. 36, 37, 41, 45, 47, 251, 255
Webster, E. C. 25, 30
Weems, R. J. 84, 85, 133, 156, 161
Wenham, G. 164, 165, 166
Westenholz, J. G. 47
Whedbee, J. W. 36, 38
White, J. B. 21, 27, 47, 49, 52, 56
Williams, J. M. 41
Woods, T. E. P. 77

Young, I. 14, 16, 17, 18, 25

Zlotowitz, M. 64

Index of Principal Topics

Song of Songs

Allegorizing
  Christian, Catholic 64–72
  Christian, Protestant 72–74
  critique of 74–76
  Jewish 60–64
Aramaic 17

Beauty and aesthetics 133–34, 153

Cultic interpretations 81–83, 174

Dramatic interpretations
  critique of 80–81, 174
  three-character 77–79
  two-character 79–80

Feminist interpretations 84–86
Funerary interpretations 83–84

Heroic quest, concept of 112–14, 138–39, 171–74

Love poetry
  Egyptian 21–22, 49–57
  interpretations 90–91
  Mesopotamian 47–48

Metaphor 37–39, 149–50, 160–61
Myth, significance of 110–14, 192–93

Poetry
  Hebrew 40–47
  lyric 91–97

Solomon 18–19, 22–25
Song of Songs
  authorship of 22–25, 123–24
  canonicity of 13–15
  date of composition 15–22
  Hebrew text of 15–16
  motifs of 36–37, 153–55, 205–6, 221–22
  structure of 25–35, 126–28, 135–36, 142–44, 169–70, 176, 186–88, 200–201, 204–6, 219–20, 226–27, 231–32, 237–38, 252, 259, 264
  unity of 25–35, 57–59
Subversive interpretations 86–90

Theology in Song of Songs 97–121, 256–57
Tirzah 20, 227–28

Virginity 111–14, 164–68, 172–74, 205–17, 259–63

Waṣf 186–89, 220–30, 237–50
Wedding ceremony, Israelite 177–84
Wedding interpretations 83

Index of Authors Cited

Lamentations

Aalders, G. C. 271
Adeney, W. F. 271
Ahuvyah, A. 274, 331
Albrektson, B. 274, 281, 282, 283, 296, 317, 318–19, 316, 320, 323, 325, 334, 335, 336, 370, 371, 384, 402, 403, 406, 413, 433, 434, 454, 470
Albright, W. F. 367, 370
Alexander, P. S. 274, 281, 285
Allegro, J. M. 281, 282
Alshekh, M. 271
Alter, R. 274, 278, 279
Anderson, A. A. 281, 282
Anderson, G. A. 274
Ash, A. L. 271, 361, 427

Barth, K. 278
Barthélemy, D. 274
Baumgartner, W. 274
Begrich, J. 274
Benjamin ben Aaron of Zalozce 274
Berges, U. 399
Bergler, S. 453
Berlin, A. 271, 274, 278, 279, 283, 299–300, 411, 412, 413, 420, 421–22, 426, 427, 428, 429, 438, 439, 440, 441, 443, 444, 446, 448, 454–55, 456, 457–58, 459, 462, 463, 465, 466, 467, 469, 471
Bettan, I. 271
Biddle, M. 331
Boecker, H. J. 271, 408
Bonaventure 271
Bosman, H. J. 274
Bouzard, W. C., Jr. 274
Bracke, J. M. 274
Brandscheidt, R. 271, 274, 399, 404, 405, 418, 419
Brooks, R. 274
Brug, J. F. 274
Brunet, G. 274, 453, 457
Buccellati, G. 367
Buchanan, A. 367, 399, 405, 431
Budde, K. 271, 274, 292, 293, 294, 305, 308, 309, 310, 348, 405, 408
Bugenhagen, J. 271
Bullinger, H. 271
Bush, F. W. 285

Calvin, J. 271, 288, 290, 292, 387, 388, 392, 405, 440
Cannon, W. W. 274, 283, 290, 292, 293, 294, 405
Caro, H. I. 274
Castro, C. de 271
Cheney, T. K. 271
Childs, B. S. 283, 285, 305, 316
Coffman, J. B. 271
Cohen, A. 274, 431
Cohen, C. 274, 331
Cohen, M. E. 274
Cohen, S. 274
Condamin, A. 340
Cowles, H. 274
Craigie, P. L. 283, 285

Cross, F. M. 331
Crowley, E. J. 271

Dahood, M. 274, 281, 282, 331, 367, 370
Daiches, S. 367
Dalglish, E. R. 271
Davidson, R. 271, 392, 417, 425, 427
De Hoop, R. 274
Del Rio, M. A. 271
Dennison, J. T., Jr. 274, 399
Deursen, F. van 271
Dillard, R. B. 284
Dobbs-Allsopp, F. W. 271, 274, 284, 299, 321, 323, 331, 434, 453, 455, 456, 457, 463, 465
Dori, Z. 274
Dorsey, D. A. 274
Driver, G. R. 281, 331, 335, 399, 403, 431, 433, 453, 454
Driver, S. R. 284, 285, 286–87, 290, 292
Droin, J. M. 271
Durlesser, J. A. 274

Eichler, U. 275
Eissfeldt, O. 275, 284, 285, 406
Ellicott, C. J. 271
Ellison, H. L. 271, 297
Emerton, J. A. 431, 438
Everson, A. J. 275
Ewald, H. 271, 289, 292, 331, 335
Exell, J. S. 271

Ferris, P. W., Jr. 275, 310, 312, 313–14, 315, 316, 328, 331, 367, 399, 431, 434–35, 453
Figueiro, P. A. 271
Fitzgerald, A. 275
Follis, E. 275, 331, 352
Freedman, D. N. 275, 305, 309
Fries, S. A. 431, 436, 437, 453
Fuerst, W. J. 271, 417, 466

Gaab, J. F. von 271
Gadd, C. J. 275, 284, 294
Garr, W. R. 275, 305, 309
Gelin, A. 271
Gerstenberger, E. 271, 298, 373, 374, 389, 404, 406, 448, 455, 466, 469
Ghislerius, M. 271
Gordis, R. 271, 275, 283, 296–97, 335, 336, 344, 367, 370, 391, 406, 414, 439, 447, 453, 457, 470–71, 472
Gosdeck, D. M. 271
Gottlieb, H. 275, 281, 283, 331, 336, 353, 367, 370, 371, 399, 402, 403, 431, 433, 453, 454
Gottwald, N. K. 272, 275, 283, 295–96, 316, 317, 318, 319, 320, 323, 331, 338, 391, 418, 428
Gous, I. 275, 367, 399, 431, 453
Graetz, N. 275
Gray, G. B. 275
Green, M. W. 275, 310, 313
Gross, H. 272
Grossberg, D. 275, 305

Grossfeld, B. 275, 367
Guest, D. 275
Guest, J. 272
Guillaume, A. 431
Guinan, M. D. 272
Gunkel, H. 275, 280, 293–94, 314–15, 331, 336, 455
Gurewisz, S. B. 399
Gwaltney, W. C., Jr. 275, 284, 295, 310, 312–13

Ha'adni, M. 275
Habel, N. C. 272
Hallbäck, G. 275
Haller, M. 272, 292, 353, 375, 408, 440
Hallo, W. W. 275
Hamon, M. 272
Hardt, H. von der 272, 289
Harrison, R. K. 272, 284, 285, 358, 363, 364, 425, 427
Heater, H. 305
Heim, K. M. 367, 399, 431, 435
Helberg, J. L. 275
Henderson, E. 272
Hillers, D. R. 272, 275, 282, 283, 296, 297, 305, 306, 309, 312, 315, 331, 334, 335, 336, 344, 345, 346, 347, 352, 353, 354, 356, 358, 362, 363, 370, 371, 373, 375, 377, 378, 379, 391, 403, 406, 410, 412, 413, 419, 420, 423, 426, 428, 433, 438, 439, 440, 443, 444, 446, 448, 455, 457, 458, 460, 461, 463, 464, 465, 467, 470, 471
Hinton, L. B. 272
Hitzig, J. 272
Horgan, M. 275, 281, 282
House, P. R. 305, 316, 328
Hubbard, D. A. 285
Huelsemann, J. 272
Huey, F. B. 272, 291, 292, 405
Hunger, J. 275
Hurowitz, V. 331

Jacob ben Hayyim Feivush, ha-Kohen 275
Jahnow, H. 275, 284, 293, 294, 305, 315, 331, 336, 367, 399, 431, 453
Jensen, I. L. 272
Johnson, B. 275, 306, 307, 310, 373, 453, 457
Joseph Hayyim ben Elijah al Hakam 275
Joyce, P. 275

Kaiser, B. B. 276, 331
Kaiser, O. 272, 284, 285, 297, 355, 360, 385, 436–37, 443, 447, 460
Kaiser, W. C., Jr. 276, 399, 405, 431
Kartveit, M. 276
Kasser, R. 276
Keil, C. F. 272, 288, 289, 290, 292, 294, 335, 336, 348, 353, 354, 362, 363, 371, 384, 385, 389, 391, 405, 414, 415, 416, 417, 418, 421, 426, 427, 439, 440, 445, 447, 455, 461, 462, 464, 466, 468, 470

Kent, D. G. 272
Klein, J. 276
Knabenbauer, J. 272
Knight, G. A. F. 272, 295
Kodell, J. 272
Kohen Stedek, B. 276
Kramer, S. N. 276, 284, 294, 295, 310, 311
Krašovec, J. 276
Kraus, H. J. 272, 295, 334, 335, 336, 345, 353, 355, 357, 362, 371, 375, 406, 427, 429, 443, 444, 446, 448, 456, 457, 464, 467
Kugel, J. L. 278, 279
Kuist, H. T. 272

Lachs, S. T. 453
Lamparter, H. 272
Lanahan, W. F. 276
Landa, N. H. S. 276
Landy, F. 276
Langedult, P. 276
LaSor, W. S. 284, 285
Lee, N. C. 276, 284, 299, 373, 374, 377, 378, 384, 385, 391, 394, 404, 405, 407
Levenson, J. 322
Levine, E. 276, 281, 282-83, 304
Linafeldt, T. 276, 316, 321, 322, 331, 367, 372, 399, 431, 453, 471
Löhr, M. 272, 276, 292, 358, 389, 399, 405, 408, 431
Longman, T. III 284
Lowth, R. 272, 278, 279
Lundmark, J. 272

Marcus, D. 276
Mayer, F. 272
McCarthy, C. 399, 403
McDaniel, T. F. 276, 284, 294, 295, 310, 311-12, 331, 345, 367, 371, 399, 403
McGee, J. V. 272
Meek, T. J. 272, 295, 360, 362, 408
Meinhold, J. 367
Michalowski, P. 276, 310, 311, 312, 313
Miller, C. W. 367, 373, 385, 399, 405, 431, 435
Mintz, A. 276
Moore, M. S. 276
Moskowitz, Y. Z. 272
Müller, H. P. 272

Nägelsbach, C. W. H. 272
Nathansohn, J. 276
Neusner, J. 276

O'Connor, J. M. 277, 278, 279, 335
O'Connor, K. M. 272, 276, 298-99, 316, 322, 323, 331, 367, 373, 374, 387, 399, 408, 429, 431, 434, 447, 448, 453, 456, 463, 468
Oecolampadius, J. 272
Oettli, S. 272
Origen 272
Owens, P. J. 399

Paffrath, T. 272
Paschasius Radbertus 272
Peake, A. S. 272, 292, 362, 376
Pham, X. H. T. 276
Pick, S. 276
Piscator, J. 273
Plöger, O. 273, 296, 297, 361
Porteous, N. 276, 399, 406
Praetorius, F. 331, 367, 399, 402
Preuss, H. D. 316, 325, 326
Provan, I. 273, 297, 319, 321, 323, 331, 343, 347, 350, 352, 354, 355, 358, 359, 367, 371, 375, 376, 378, 379, 382, 385, 389, 390, 391, 392, 399, 407, 408, 412, 413, 420, 423, 425, 426, 427, 428, 439, 441, 443, 444, 445, 446, 449-50, 455, 457, 461, 462, 463, 464, 465-66

Raabe, A. 276
Re'emi, S. P. 273, 297, 336-37, 346, 443, 449
Rendtorff, R. 284, 285
Renkema, J. 273, 276, 280, 283, 298, 306, 307, 308, 310, 316, 319, 321, 323, 331, 335, 336, 337, 340, 341, 342, 345, 349, 350, 352, 353, 354, 356, 357, 359, 360, 361, 362, 363, 367, 374, 376, 378, 381, 382, 384, 385, 386, 391, 394, 403, 406, 409, 410, 412, 413, 415, 416, 417, 418, 420, 422, 423, 425, 426, 427, 429, 438, 439, 440, 441, 442, 443, 444, 446, 447, 448, 449, 453, 455, 456, 458, 459, 460, 462, 464, 465, 466, 467, 468, 469
Reyburn, W. D. 276, 411, 414, 426, 428, 465, 466
Ricciotti, G. 273
Ringgren, H. 273
Robinson, T. H. 276, 281, 331, 334
Rosenfeld, A. 453
Rudolph, W. 273, 276, 281, 283, 291, 292, 331, 335, 348, 367, 371, 399, 402, 403, 405, 425, 428, 431, 436, 440, 445, 447, 453, 454, 461, 464
Ruppert, L. 276
Ryken, P. 277

Sæbø, M. 399, 404, 405, 406
Salters, R. B. 273, 277, 331
Schneider, H. 273

Selms, A. van 277
Seow, C. L. 331
Shea, W. H. 277, 306, 309-10, 434, 453, 457
Shelomoh, D. 277
Slavitt, D. R. 277
Smart, J. 278
Smit, G. 273
Smith, J. 273
Sorotzkin, Y. 277
Stoll, C. D. 273
Streane, A. W. 273, 288, 289-90, 292, 376, 392, 405
Strobel, A. 273

Tanhum ben Joseph of Jerusalem 277
Tarnow, J. 273
Taylor, R. R. 277
Thenius, O. 289, 292
Thomas, W. 277
Thompson, J. A. 277
Tigay, J. 277
Tobiah ben Elieser 273
Tossanus, D. 277

Udall, J. 273

Vaihinger, J. G. 273
Van der Heide, A. 277
Vermegli, P. M. 273
Vital, B. ha-Cohen 277

Waltke, B. 277, 335
Walton, J. H. 310, 311
Weintraub, N. 277
Weiser, A. 273, 295, 375, 443, 448
Weissblueth, S. 277, 399
Westermann, C. 273, 277, 278, 279, 280, 283, 297, 298, 299, 301, 307, 314, 315, 316, 317, 319, 320, 321, 323, 336, 337, 340, 343, 347, 352, 354, 355, 357, 361, 363, 364, 371, 373, 375, 386, 392, 393, 404, 408, 413, 418, 421, 422, 425, 426, 427, 428, 429, 434, 444, 449, 455, 457, 469, 470
Wiesmann, H. 273, 277, 290-91, 292, 345, 353, 375, 405, 453, 467, 471
Wright, J. S. 273

Yamamuro, G. 273
Young, E. J. 284, 285

Zenner, P. J. K. 453
Ziegler, J. 273
Zlotowitz, A. 384

Index of Principal Topics

Lamentations

Acrostic 278, 302 306–8, 316, 337, 340, 342, 343, 344, 347, 349, 352, 364, 365, 371 372, 375, 403, 404, 408, 410, 411, 424, 428, 430, 434, 450, 451, 454, 455, 456
Ai 396
Ammon 346, 355
Aramaic version of Lamentations 282–83, 288, 371, 403
Ark of the Covenant 325, 377
Assyria 295, 345, 346, 443, 461, 462, 465

Baal 362, 444
Babylon 343, 346, 347, 355, 357, 358, 359, 377, 383, 390, 391, 393, 395, 410, 418, 425, 428, 437, 442, 446, 447, 448, 451, 463
Baruch 407, 420, 467

Children, suffering of 375, 386, 387, 391, 392, 393, 394, 398, 434, 437, 438, 439, 442, 450, 466, 473
Confession 375, 378, 380, 421, 422, 425, 430, 435, 451, 467, 468, 470, 473
Covenant
  Abrahamic 382
  Davidic 326, 379, 406, 446, 448, 451, 467
  Mosaic 379, 382, 383, 386
  New 326

Damascus 358
David 325, 348, 349, 353
Davidic dynasty 281, 382, 397
Day of the Lord 357, 358, 364, 365, 374, 375, 376, 377, 379, 380 381, 383, 384, 386, 395, 396, 397, 398, 409, 410, 414, 427, 429, 443, 444, 446, 451, 459, 467, 469
Dead Sea Scrolls 282
Deuteronomistic theology 296, 317, 318, 323, 325, 326
Dinah 465
Dirge 315, 336, 337, 338, 339, 340, 372, 376, 404, 434–35, 450, 455

Ebed-melech 407
Edom 327, 347, 383, 424, 428, 434, 436, 446, 448–49, 450, 451, 464
Egypt 345, 347, 355, 446, 461, 462
Ephraim 469
Esau 464
Exile 305, 347, 349, 351, 352, 384, 385, 386, 388, 397, 412, 434, 448, 449, 450, 451, 459, 460, 463, 465
Exodus, the 379, 412, 413

Form criticism of Lamentations 292, 293, 314–16, 404, 434–35, 455

Gaza 358
God
  as abusive 322, 398
  as creator 419
  as enemy 380, 381, 395, 413

compassion of 324, 327, 328, 329, 414, 417, 418, 471, 472
faithfulness of 303, 317, 320, 324, 328, 329, 378, 409, 415, 417, 419, 429
forgiveness of 324, 422, 427
goodness of 322, 372, 405, 408, 415, 416
judgment of 324, 326, 327, 328, 329, 339, 358, 359, 360, 364, 365, 366, 375, 378, 379, 383, 384, 390, 394, 395, 396, 409, 411, 414, 415, 419, 434, 435, 436, 437, 450, 451, 452, 468, 469
lovingkindness of 324, 379
righteousness of 317, 320, 324, 327, 328, 329, 342, 360, 365, 366, 427, 444, 468
severity of 329, 394, 398, 409, 428, 472
sovereignty of 320, 322, 329, 359, 389, 390, 405, 408, 415, 419, 468, 470, 473
truthfulness of 324, 327
wrath of 376, 379, 380, 385, 393, 395, 409, 423, 443, 444, 446, 449, 472
Gomorrah 358

Hagar 346
Hananiah 358, 444

Jacob 360, 377, 379
Jeremiah 278, 284–93, 299, 300, 302, 303, 305, 319, 338, 347, 385, 386, 388, 395, 396, 398, 405, 406, 407, 412, 422, 425, 426, 427, 442, 444, 463
Jerusalem, inviolability of 318, 325–26, 443
Job 441
Jonah 426
Joseph 425
Joshua 348, 353

Lachish 465
Lamentations
  ancient Near Eastern Literature and 310–14
  authorship and date of 283–303, 408
  place in canon 305
  poetic form and meter 305–10
  text of 281–83
  theology of 316–29
  use in liturgy 278, 303–4, 305, 413
Laments 279, 280, 282, 285, 293, 300, 301, 303, 315–16, 321, 323, 324, 325, 328, 329, 336, 337, 338, 339, 340, 346, 347, 365, 372, 393, 395, 404, 408–9, 424, 429, 434–35, 437, 455, 456, 463, 472
Sumerian 294–95, 309, 310–14

Masoretic text 281–83, 305, 334, 335, 336, 370, 371, 384, 391, 402, 403, 433, 434, 454
Micah 444
Micaiah 362
Moab 338, 355

Monotheism 314, 328
Moses 348, 351, 353, 390, 413, 420, 459

Naomi 345, 350
Nazirites 440, 441, 465

Persia 295
Philistia 346
Polytheism 314
Praise 315, 377, 404, 455, 464, 466
Prayer 324, 327–29, 358, 375, 393, 394, 405, 407, 408, 411, 413, 423, 429, 430, 434, 451, 456, 458, 470, 471
Priests 384, 385, 388, 394, 444, 445, 446
Prophets, false 381, 384, 388, 394, 440, 444, 445

Qere 335, 336, 370, 371, 389, 403, 433, 434, 439, 454
Qinah 281, 290, 292, 299, 308–10, 316, 338, 434, 455

Repentance 358, 362, 383, 388, 389, 391, 392, 397, 414, 421, 422, 427, 470
Reversal 317, 324, 338, 339, 344, 345, 346, 348, 365, 377, 378, 415, 442, 466, 470

Sarai 346
Septuagint version of Lamentations 281–82, 288, 305, 334, 335, 336, 353, 370, 371, 402, 403, 433, 434, 454, 470, 471
Shiloh 325, 326, 350
Sidon 346
Sodom 358, 437, 438, 439, 440, 441, 460
Solomon 346, 348, 349, 353, 443
Syriac version of Lamentations 281–82, 284, 288, 334, 335, 336, 353, 370, 371, 403, 454, 470, 471

Tamar 465
Temple
  Second 304, 456
  Solomonic 281, 300, 304, 311, 318, 319, 325, 350, 356, 375, 376, 381, 382, 383, 384, 395, 437, 438, 448, 467, 473
Tyre 338, 339, 346, 389

Uncleanness 354, 355, 356, 361, 365, 444, 445
Uriah 444

Vulgate version of Lamentations 284, 288, 334, 335, 336, 370, 371, 403, 434, 454

Zedekiah 406, 448
Zion 296, 301, 303, 318, 319, 321, 323, 325–26, 327, 328, 349, 350, 351, 352, 353, 354, 360, 365, 372, 376, 377, 380, 381, 382, 385, 386, 389, 392, 397, 406, 407, 416, 424, 438, 443, 449, 451, 463, 466, 467, 468, 469